REA's Test Prep Books Are The Best!

(a sample of the <u>hundreds of letters</u> REA receives each year)

" In preparing for the LSAT, I purchased a number of books... This was by far the most helpful... *The Best Test Preparation for the LSAT* was excellent for learning how to take the LSAT and do well, which I *did*. "

Student, Minneapolis, MN

" My students report your chapters of review as the most valuable single resource they used for review and preparation. "

Teacher, American Fork, UT

" Your book was such a better value and was so much more complete than anything your competition has produced — and I have them all! "

Teacher, Virginia Beach, VA

" Compared to the other books that my fellow students had, your book was the most useful in helping me get a great score. "

Student, North Hollywood, CA

" Your book was responsible for my success on the exam, which helped me get into the college of my choice... I will look for REA the next time I need help. "

Student, Chesterfield, MO

" Just a short note to say thanks for the great support your book gave me in helping me pass the test... I'm on my way to a B.S. degree because of you! "

Student, Orlando, FL

(more on next page)

(continued from front page)

" I just wanted to thank you for helping me get a great score
on the AP U.S. History exam... Thank you for making great test preps! "
Student, Los Angeles, CA

" Your *Fundamentals of Engineering Exam* book was the absolute best
preparation I could have had for the exam, and it is one of the major
reasons I did so well and passed the FE on my first try. "
Student, Sweetwater, TN

" I used your book to prepare for the test and found that the advice and the
sample tests were highly relevant... Without using any other material, I earned
very high scores and will be going to the graduate school of my choice. "
Student, New Orleans, LA

" What I found in your book was a wealth of information sufficient to shore up
my basic skills in math and verbal... The practice tests were challenging and the
answer explanations most helpful. It certainly is the *Best Test Prep for the GRE*! "
Student, Pullman, WA

" I really appreciate the help from your excellent book. Please keep up
the great work. "
Student, Albuquerque, NM

" I am writing to thank you for your test preparation... your book helped me
immeasurably and I have nothing but praise for your *GRE* preparation."
Student, Benton Harbor, MI

(more on back page)

The Best Test Preparation for the

LSAT

Law School Admission Test

Richard Dikh

7th Edition

Robert K. Burdette, Ph.D., J.D.
Former Instructor of English
University of Michigan, Ann Arbor, MI

Anita Price Davis, Ph.D.
Professor Emerita of Education
Converse College, Spartanburg, SC

Christopher Dreisbach, Ph.D.
Associate Professor of Philosophy
Villa Julie College, Stevenson, MD

Theodora Glitsky, M.A.
Instructor of Philosophy
Harris-Stowe State University, St. Louis, MO

Timothy M. Hagle, J.D., Ph.D.
Assistant Professor of Political Science
University of Iowa, Iowa City, IA

H. Hamner Hill, Ph.D.
Chair, Department of Philosophy
Southeast Missouri State U., Cape Girardeau, MO

Clayton Holland, J.D.
Doctoral Student
University of Texas, Austin, TX

Connie Mauney, Ph.D.
Associate Professor of Political Science
Emporia State University, Emporia, KS

John E. Parks-Clifford, Ph.D.
Chair, Department of Philosophy
University of Missouri – St. Louis, MO

Wesley G. Phelan, Ph.D.
Assistant Professor of Political Science
Eureka College, Eureka, IL

John G. Robison, Ph.D.
Chair, Department of Philosophy
University of Massachusetts – Amherst, MA

Garrett Ward Sheldon, Ph.D.
Associate Professor of Political Science
University of Virginia – Clinch Valley College, Wise, VA

Paul C. L. Tang, Ph.D.
Chair, Department of Philosophy
California State University – Long Beach, CA

Research & Education Association
Visit our website at
www.rea.com

Research & Education Association
61 Ethel Road West
Piscataway, New Jersey 08854
E-mail: info@rea.com

The Best Test Preparation for the
LAW SCHOOL ADMISSION TEST (LSAT)

Printed in the United States of America

Library of Congress Control Number 2006934177

International Standard Book Number 0-87891-854-X

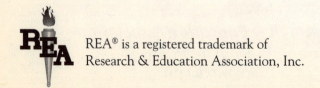

REA® is a registered trademark of
Research & Education Association, Inc.

CONTENTS

About Research & Education Association

Founded in 1959, Research & Education Association (REA) is dedicated to publishing the finest and most effective educational materials—including software, study guides, and test preps—for students in middle school, high school, college, graduate school, and beyond.

REA's Test Preparation series includes books and software for all academic levels in almost all disciplines. Research & Education Association publishes test preps for students who have not yet entered high school, as well as high school students preparing to enter college. Students from countries around the world seeking to attend college in the United States will find the assistance they need in REA's publications. For college students seeking advanced degrees, REA publishes test preps for many major graduate school admission examinations in a wide variety of disciplines, including engineering, law, and medicine. Students at every level, in every field, with every ambition can find what they are looking for among REA's publications.

REA presents tests that accurately depict the official exams in both degree of difficulty and types of questions. REA's practice tests are always based upon the most recently administered exams, and include every type of question that can be expected on the actual exams.

REA's publications and educational materials are highly regarded and continually receive an unprecedented amount of praise from professionals, instructors, librarians, parents, and students. Our authors are as diverse as the fields represented in the books we publish. They are well known in their respective disciplines and serve on the faculties of prestigious high schools, colleges, and universities throughout the United States and Canada.

Today REA's wide-ranging catalog is a leading resource for teachers, students, and professionals.

We invite you to visit us at *www.rea.com* to find out how "REA is making the world smarter."

Acknowledgments

In addition to our authors, we would like to thank Larry B. Kling, Vice President, Editorial, for his editorial guidance; Pam Weston, Vice President, Publishing, for ensuring press readiness; Anne Winthrop Esposito, Senior Editor, for coordinating revisions; Wesley G. Phelan, Ph.D., for his editorial contributions and expert insight into the LSAT; Robert Erle Barham, M.Phil., for his editorial contributions; Jeff LoBalbo, Senior Graphic Designer, and Rachel DiMatteo, Graphic Designer, for typesetting revisions.

LSAT

Law School Admission Test

STUDY
COURSE
SCHEDULE

LSAT Study Course Schedule

The following study course schedule will help you thoroughly prepare for the LSAT. Although the schedule is designed for 12 weeks of preparatory work, it can be condensed into a six-week program by combining two weeks of preparation into one. Be sure to set aside enough time each day for study purposes. If you choose the 12-week program, you should plan on studying for one hour per day. If you choose the six-week program, you should plan on studying for at least two hours per day. In addition, depending on your time schedule, you may find it easier to study during the weekend. No matter what your schedule, however, keep in mind that the more time you devote to studying for the LSAT, the more prepared and confident you will feel on the day of the exam.

Week	Activity
1–2	Read and study the introduction and review sections for the LSAT on the following pages. Then, take and score Practice Test 1 to determine your strengths and weaknesses. You should have someone with good writing skills critique your essay. Any area(s) in which you perform poorly will require more time and attention. For example, if you obtain a low number of correct answers on the Reading Comprehension section, we suggest you study the Reading Comprehension review more thoroughly. You should treat your performance on the other sections in the same manner, going over the appropriate topical material in this book.
3	Study the Reading Comprehension review. Be sure to complete all the drills.
4	Study the Logical Reasoning review. Complete all the drills.
5	Study the Analytical Reasoning review. Complete all the drills.
6	Study the Writing Sample review. Make sure to write the sample essay. It should be read and graded by someone with strong writing skills who can offer constructive criticism.

Week	Activity
7	Take Practice Test 2 and, after scoring your exam, review thoroughly all of the explanations to the questions you answered incorrectly. This will help to strengthen your weaknesses.
8	Take Practice Test 3. Note any improvement in comparison with Practice Test 2.
9	Take Practice Test 4 and review all of the explanations to the questions you answered incorrectly.
10	Take Practice Test 5 and review all of the explanations to the questions you answered incorrectly.
11	Take Practice Test 6 and review all of the explanations to the questions you answered incorrectly.
12	Retake one or more of the practice tests using the extra answer sheets provided. Then, continue to study the reviews of the areas in which you are still weak.
	Good Luck!

LSAT
Law School Admission Test

INTRODUCTION

You Can Achieve a Top LSAT Score

By reviewing and studying this book, you can achieve a top score on the Law School Admission Test. The LSAT is probably unlike any exam that you have taken in college. Rather than testing prior knowledge of facts specific to a subject area, the LSAT measures reasoning and verbal skills. Perhaps the tests closest to the LSAT in look and feel are general college entrance exams, which also test verbal and reasoning skills.

The purpose of our book is to prepare you thoroughly for the LSAT by providing six full-length practice exams that accurately reflect the LSAT in degree of difficulty, question type, and format. Our exams are based on the format of the most recently administered LSATs and include every type of question that you can expect to see come test day. Following each practice exam is an answer key complete with detailed explanations and solutions designed to clarify the material for you. Our objective is not only to provide the answers, but also to explain why the answer to a particular question is more acceptable than the other possible choices. This approach helps intensify your review and thus sharpens your grasp of the material you're most likely to encounter on the real LSAT. By completing all six exams and studying the explanations that follow, you will discover your strengths and weaknesses and thereby concentrate on the sections of the exam that are more challenging or difficult.

About the Test Experts

REA's exams have been carefully prepared by test experts in the various LSAT subject fields. Our authors have taken the time to examine and research the mechanics of the real LSAT to create the types of practice questions that will accurately depict the exam and appropriately challenge you. Our experts are highly regarded in the educational community, having studied at the master's and doctoral levels and taught in their respective fields at competitive colleges and universities throughout the United States. This book brings the benefit of their in-depth knowledge directly to you, providing targeted, carefully calibrated material in strict alignment with the LSAT. Each question is clearly and extensively explained in order to help you achieve a top score on the Law School Admission Test.

About the LSAT

The LSAT is required by all U.S. and Canadian law schools that are members of the Law School Admission Council and is a central criterion for admission. Every year, tens of thousands of applicants submit LSAT results, along with other undergraduate records, as part of the highly competitive law school admissions process.

Every law school has its own formula for evaluating applicants, and every school weights LSAT scores differently. As a general rule, however, it is crucial to achieve a high LSAT score to have a good chance at admission. This is especially important if you are applying to a prestigious law school. At some schools, your LSAT score can receive as much as twice as much emphasis as your undergraduate grades.

The LSAT is administered by the Law School Admission Council, a non-profit corporation based in Newtown, Pa. Some 137,000 LSATs were given in 2005–2006. The LSAT is offered four times a year—in September, December, February, and June. Many law schools require applicants to take the LSAT by December for admission the following fall. Even so, taking the test earlier—in June or September—would be well advised.

Format of the LSAT

The Law School Admission Test assesses verbal skills, logical and analytical reasoning skills, and writing skills, all of which are abilities that have been found to contribute to the successful completion of law school studies. It does not test prior knowledge of data or facts specific to any field of study.

Six distinct sections comprise the LSAT. The sections are made up of multiple-choice questions designed to test various skills. The number of questions per section varies yearly.

The order in which the sections of the LSAT appear varies from one test administration to the next. Only the Writing Sample is consistent, always appearing last. In other words, you can take the test one day and the sections may appear in this order:

Logical Reasoning, Analytical Reasoning, Variable Section, Logical Reasoning, Reading Comprehension, and the Writing Sample.

You could take the test again, only to find the sections ordered this way:

Analytical Reasoning, Reading Comprehension, Logical Reasoning, Logical Reasoning, Variable Section, and the Writing Sample.

Section	Number of Questions	Scored†/ Unscored	Minutes
1 Reading Comprehension	26 to 28	Scored	35
2 Logical Reasoning	24 to 26	Scored	35
3 Logical Reasoning	24 to 26	Scored	35
4 Analytical Reasoning	22 to 24	Scored	35
5 Variable Section	varies*	Unscored	35
6 Writing Sample	1 essay	Unscored	35

*Total Scored Questions — **varies** but ranges up to 101*

Total Testing Time — 210 minutes (3¹/₂ hours)

* The number of Variable Section questions depends on which of the multiple-choice sections is being repeated.

† "Scored" means counted toward your LSAT score.

1. **Reading Comprehension** — a 35-minute section of 26 to 28 comprehension questions based on brief reading passages

2. **Logical Reasoning** — a 35-minute section of 24 to 26 inferential questions based on mini-reading passages

3. **Logical Reasoning** — a 35-minute section of 24 to 26 inferential questions based on mini-reading passages

4. **Analytical Reasoning** — a 35-minute section of 22 to 24 mind teaser-type questions

5. **Variable Section** — an unscored section used to pretest new questions or preequate new test forms. The Variable Section is not identified and is not counted toward your score. **Since this book is**

**for the purpose of practicing, we have eliminated the Variable
Section from each practice exam.**

6. **Writing Sample** — a 35-minute essay on an assigned topic

About the Review Sections

Our reviews cover all the sections tested on the LSAT: Reading Comprehension, Logical Reasoning, Analytical Reasoning, and the Writing Sample. They are written to help you learn and understand the basic concepts needed to pass the LSAT. Each review is complete with strategies, tips, and drills to help reinforce your test-taking abilities. To ensure your chances of performing well, be sure to thoroughly study these reviews.

Scoring the Exam

Your LSAT score is based upon the number of questions you answer correctly (your raw score), which is then converted into a scaled score. The range of LSAT scaled scores runs from 120 to 180. Since the Writing Sample is graded by the law schools to which you apply and the Variable Section is experimental, they will not count toward your score.

In addition to your scaled LSAT score, you will receive a percentile ranking. This ranking compares your performance on the LSAT to that of other students who have taken the test. The average person obtains a raw score of approximately 65 and a percentile ranking of roughly 51 on the LSAT. This indicates that the student has scored equal to or better than 50 percent of other students who have taken the exam.

**(See the Scoring Worksheet, Conversion Chart, and LSAT Score
Distribution Table on the following pages.)**

COMPUTING YOUR SCORE

1. Use the Answer Key at the end of each exam to check your answers.

2. Use the Scoring Worksheet below to compute your raw score.

3. Use the score Conversion Chart to convert your raw score into the 120 to 180 LSAT scale.

4. Use the LSAT Score Distribution Table to determine your performance among other students who have taken the LSAT.

SCORING WORKSHEET

1. Enter the number of questions you answered correctly in each section.

	Number Correct
Section I	_____
Section II	_____
Section III	_____
Section IV	_____

2. Enter the sum here: _____
This sum is your raw score.

For Example:
17 correct answers on Section I
21 correct answers on Section II
19 correct answers on Section III
25 correct answers on Section IV
Equals 82 correct answers total

Looking at the Conversion Chart (on the next page), you see that your raw score of 82 corresponds to an expected Scaled Score range from 162-171, which is higher than the average of 151.

Looking at the low end of the Scaled Score which is 162 and comparing it to the LSAT Score Distribution Table, you see that you would have scored equal to or better than 87.7% of other students who have taken the LSAT.

Looking at the high end of the Scaled Score which is 171, you see that your score may have been high enough to fall into the top 98th percentile, which means that your score would have been equal to or better than 98% of other students who have taken the LSAT.

Conversion Chart

For Converting Raw Scores to the 120-180 LSAT Scale

Raw Score	Expected Scaled Score Range	Raw Score	Expected Scaled Score Range	Raw Score	Expected Scaled Score Range
0	120–120	34	131–140	68	153–162
1	120–120	35	132–141	69	153–163
2	120–120	36	132–141	70	154–163
3	120–120	37	133–142	71	155–164
4	120–121	38	133–143	72	155–164
5	120–121	39	134–143	73	156–165
6	120–122	40	135–144	74	157–166
7	120–123	41	135–144	75	157–166
8	120–123	42	136–145	76	158–167
9	120–124	43	137–146	77	159–168
10	120–124	44	137–146	78	159–168
11	120–125	45	138–147	79	160–169
12	120–126	46	139–148	80	161–170
13	120–126	47	139–148	81	161–170
14	120–127	48	140–149	82	162–171
15	120–128	49	141–150	83	162–172
16	120–128	50	141–150	84	163–172
17	120–129	51	142–151	85	164–173
18	121–130	52	142–152	86	164–173
19	121–130	53	143–152	87	165–174
20	122–131	54	144–153	88	166–175
21	122–132	55	144–153	89	166–175
22	123–132	56	145–154	90	167–176
23	124–133	57	146–155	91	168–177
24	124–133	58	146–155	92	168–177
25	125–134	59	147–156	93	169–178
26	126–135	60	148–157	94	170–179
27	126–135	61	148–157	95	170–179
28	127–136	62	149–158	96	171–180
29	128–137	63	150–159	97	172–180
30	128–137	64	150–159	98	172–180
31	129–138	65	151–160	99	172–180
32	130–139	66	152–161	100	173–180
33	130–139	67	152–161	101	174–180

This chart approximates how your raw score translates into an actual final LSAT score. Your actual LSAT score may not fall into the range you obtain from the practice tests.

LSAT Score Distribution Table

(Percentile Ranking)

Scaled Score	Est. % Below for LSAT*	Scaled Score	Est. % Below for LSAT*
180	99.9	149	43.9
179	99.9	148	41.0
178	99.8	147	36.6
177	99.6	146	32.3
176	99.5	145	29.6
175	99.4	144	26.2
174	99.1	143	22.4
173	98.9	142	20.0
172	98.4	141	17.2
171	98.0	140	15.1
170	97.6	139	12.2
169	96.8	138	10.9
168	96.0	137	8.5
167	95.1	136	7.5
166	93.9	135	6.2
165	92.8	134	4.7
164	90.9	133	4.0
163	89.6	132	3.3
162	87.7	131	2.7
161	85.6	130	2.1
160	82.9	129	1.5
159	80.4	128	1.2
158	77.8	127	0.9
157	74.4	126	0.7
156	70.7	125	0.5
155	67.6	124	0.4
154	64.2	123	0.3
153	60.0	122	0.2
152	55.7	121	0.1
151	52.1	120	0.0
150	47.7		

*The entries in this column reflect the estimated percentages of candidates scoring below the score given. Score distribution may vary from administration to administration.

LSAT Test-Taking Strategies

HOW TO BEAT THE CLOCK

Every second counts, so you want to use the available test time for each section in the most efficient way. Here's how:

1. Memorize the test directions for each section of the test. On the day of the exam, this will keep you from wasting valuable time reading directions instead of answering the test questions.

2. The LSAT is composed of items that will challenge you at three separate levels: relatively easy, medium, and difficult. Answer the easier ones first; save the tough ones for later. It's not worth entangling yourself in a difficult question when you can be answering questions you can breeze through.

3. Pace yourself. Work steadily and prepensely. Most of all, don't get bogged down.

GUESSING STRATEGY

1. If you are uncertain of a question, you should guess at the answer rather than not answer at all. You will not be penalized for answering incorrectly, since wrong answers are not counted. This means that you should never leave a space on your answer sheet blank. Even if you do not have time to guess at an answer, be sure to fill in every space on the answer sheet. Since you will not be assessed a penalty for a wrong answer, you will receive credit for any questions you answer correctly by luck.

2. If time is short and you cannot make educated guesses, do not simply guess at random. Use one letter and fill in all your guesses with that letter. Guess choice "E," however, on all multiple true/false type questions. These suggestions are statistically proven to be one and a half times as effective as blind guessing.

OTHER MUST-DO STRATEGIES

1. As you work on the test, make sure your answers correspond with the numbers and letters on the answer sheet.

2. Feel free to write in this book, as you are allowed to write in the test

booklet of the actual exam. Do not try to solve difficult problems or questions in your head. Work the problem out in your test booklet. Get in the habit of drawing a small sketch or diagram as this is a proven technique for correctly solving problems.

3. If you are completely uncertain of a question, skip it at first. You will have also saved time to go on to questions about which you are certain. If time allows, go back and try to make educated guesses for the questions you missed.

Contacting the LSAT Administrator

To obtain an LSAT registration information book or to learn more about the Law School Admission Test, contact:

Law School Admission Council
Box 2000
Newtown, PA 18940-0998
Phone: (215) 968-1001
Website: www.lsac.org

LSAT
Law School Admission Test

REVIEWS

PREPARING FOR THE LSAT

As previously mentioned the LSAT contains five scored sections: a Reading Comprehension section, two Logical Reasoning sections, an Analytical Reasoning section, and a Writing Sample. The following reviews explain these sections in detail and provide strategies and tips to help you select the correct answers. Also presented are examples with detailed explanations. By using the reviews in conjunction with the Study Course Schedule and practice tests, you will be able to sharpen your skills and score well on the LSAT.

READING COMPREHENSION REVIEW

The Reading Comprehension Section of the LSAT is designed to measure your ability to read complex, lengthy passages similar to the readings in law school assignments. The questions which follow each passage indicate to some degree your ability to understand and comprehend the passage, and to reason. You can expect the Reading Comprehension Section to be one of the most difficult sections on the LSAT. The passages are to the point, without titles to guide you, and are based on a variety of subjects. Since the structure of the Reading Comprehension Section usually does not vary, however, you can begin to prepare for this test and have a head start on other students!

THE DIRECTIONS

You should study the directions now, as this will prevent your having to take precious seconds to study them on the day of the test. Instead, you should quickly skim the directions during the exam to refresh your memory.

Take a few minutes NOW to study the directions below:

DIRECTIONS: Each passage in this section is followed by a group of questions to be answered on the basis of what is **stated** or **implied** in the passage. For some questions, more than one of the choices could conceivably answer the question. However, you are to choose the **best** answer; that is, the response that most accurately and completely answers the question, and blacken the corresponding space on your answer sheet.

Below are tips on following directions:

➤ Tip 1 | Notice that you are instructed to choose the <u>best</u> answer, based only on what is <u>stated</u> or <u>implied</u> in the passage. This means that all test takers will start out on equal footing in regard to knowledge of the topics since no one will have previously read the passages. Knowing this should increase your confidence. You are not to base your answer choice on information you already know <u>if it is not in the passage!</u>

➤ Tip 2 | **Be sure that the response you choose answers the question.** For instance, you should not select an answer

simply because it is a true statement; the answer must be the one which **best** answers the question.

READING PRACTICE

Reading many types of materials in the weeks before you take the LSAT can help you "shape up" for this important test. As you read a newspaper, magazine, or book, you can also prepare for the LSAT. After you read a passage, practice answering these questions:

➤ What was the main idea of the article?

➤ Why did the author write the article? What was the purpose?

➤ What was the structure of the passage?

➤ How did the author make the main points?

➤ Were there specific details? If so, what were they?

➤ Were there implied ideas? If so, what were they?

➤ Can the information be applied?

➤ What was the tone of the passage or the attitude of the author?

The reading comprehension questions on the LSAT will require you to find these items.

CONTENT OF THE PASSAGES

The Reading Comprehension Section of the LSAT usually contains four passages for you to read. Each passage is about 450 words in length. The subjects of the passages include law, the humanities, the natural sciences, the social sciences, and ethics.

The category of humanities can include theater, literature, architecture, art, music, and philosophy. Passages may cover topics like the film making of Alfred Hitchcock, the writing of Sherwood Anderson, the design of Gothic architecture, the use of collage as an art medium, jazz as a means of musical expression, and the comparisons and contrasts of deductive and inductive thinking.

The category of natural sciences can include chemistry, geology, physics, and astronomy. A natural science reading passage on the LSAT, then, might include information on consumer chemistry, photosynthesis, sedimentary rocks, friction, and galaxies.

The social sciences typically include anthropology, psychology, history, sociology, and archaeology. Reading passages may cover such topics as Cro-Magnon man, behaviorism, the causes of the American Revolutionary War, the caste system, and Pompeii.

Since so many disciplines may be represented on the LSAT, it is likely that at least some of the material will be unfamiliar to you. Remind yourself again that the questions which follow the passage will not require prior or additional knowledge of the material; the passages alone will be adequate for answering the comprehension questions. No one will have an advantage because of prior knowledge or experience with all the material, but you will have an advantage because of your preparation with this book.

ORDER OF READING THE PASSAGES

Many students find it helpful to read first the passages which appear easier, more familiar, and more interesting to them; these students save the longer, more difficult passages for last. Other students consider the searching for the easier passages to be a waste of valuable time and they simply plow ahead. When you begin to work through the sample tests, you might wish to try both methods to see which works better for you.

READING SPEED

There is no best rate of reading. "Good" readers adjust their rate to the purpose for which they are reading. Successful readers, however, are aware of the strategies they use in reading. You can improve your reading skills and your performance on the reading comprehension sections of tests like the LSAT by becoming aware of these successful strategies and practicing them.

The average person reads at the rate of about 250 words per minute. Since the average reading passage on the LSAT is about 400 words, this means that it takes less than two minutes to read one of the passages.

Since there are four passages, this means that only about 10 of the assigned 35 minutes should be spent actually reading the passages.

What speed should you use? Reading very slowly is not the best approach to use. Reading too slowly may give your mind time to wander and reduce your comprehension. Reading as fast as you can comfortably read will help you to comprehend better. YOU DO NOT HAVE TO BE A SPEED READER TO DO WELL ON THE LSAT. In fact, reading too fast may cause reduced comprehension. Most of the LSAT passages are short passages which do not require a speed reader to complete successfully.

As you prepare for the LSAT, however, you should determine your reading speed. To do this, use the following passage. Get out your watch and prepare to time yourself! Read this passage now.

PASSAGE

"From *Fort Apache* on," writes Andrew Sarris, "Ford's films seemed to have abandoned the Tradition of Quality for a Cult of Personality." As the critical mainstream veered increasingly toward astringent social relevance, the ex-poet laureate looked increasingly irrelevant, as he holed up in Monument Valley
(5) churning out matinee Westerns. In fact, the bitterness of social comment in Ford's movies was more acerbic than before. The '30s revolutionary had not embraced the establishment. But what Ford had to say, Americans did not wish to hear. To his credit, he no longer sought prestige by couching his thought within trendy styles. Instead his pictures became intensely private, formulated
(10) within well-worn commercial genres, fraught with myth, irony, and double-leveled narratives. Still today, many a casual critic, underestimating Ford, not only misses the subtlety, but also misconstrues denunciations as celebrations.

This period is distinguished by the vitality of its invention, at every level of cinema, but with particular intensity in montage, motion, and music. Ford at his
(15) most energetic intellectually is also Ford at his most optimistic. The defeatism of the preceding period has been largely rejected—or at least recontextualized. Although virtually all the pictures take place in the past (or in Africa or Korea), it is evident that Ford felt some hope in America.

In this period the community theme in Ford is in ascendance, a period of
(20) social analysis, akin to the early '30s pictures. Military or military-like societies are chosen because they provide clear sets of the customs, ideologies, and structures relevant to America. Although 10 prior pictures dealt with such groups, only two had attempted quasi-documentary approaches to such communities. But of the 33 films made after 1948, 18 are directly concerned with
(25) studying the problems of military communities, while nine others treat, in much

the same terms, quasi-military communities (wagon trains, missionaries, political parties, police), while two others have military life as a background. In all 33 films the specific question is, "What makes people tick? Why do they do what they do?" or, 29 times, "What makes people fight?"

(30)   There is less determinism and more free will than elsewhere in Ford in this period. Duty, previously regarded by the hero as divinely appointed, henceforth resides in the group and is socially assigned.

But the films grow progressively darker. A few old men sustain the viability of society, only faith can find an ontological distinction between man and ape,
(35) the parade is a substitute for the insufficiency of reason. The films dwell on the coercive tendencies of society, of instruments becoming malevolent institutions. The period concludes with *The Searchers*, a farewell to youth and the entry of Ford's work of acute ambivalence, of a dialectic equivalent to pessimism and uncertainty about Good and Evil. Yet even so, these eight years constitute a
(40) period of glory, of stability and sureness, more blessed with masterpieces than any other period.

The number of words in the passage above is 480; divide this number by the number of minutes it took you to read the passage. Compare your reading rate with the average of 250 words per minute.

If you need to improve your reading speed, you can do this easily. For practice purposes choose an article from a magazine or newspaper; you may even use one of the many passages from the tests. (Remember, however, that reading a passage ahead of time may make your using it later in a timed test less valid.) Time yourself as you read and try to read faster on each paragraph until you read about 250 words per minute.

Some people read slowly because of a habit called regression, or reading the same section more than once. If you have this habit of regression, you can break yourself from rereading by a simple device. Simply take a piece of paper and place it above the line you are reading. Move the paper down the page line by line as you read. If you try to reread above the line you are now reading, the piece of paper will prevent you from doing so. You will be encouraged to read carefully since regressing will be difficult for you; your comprehension should be improved.

To practice improving your reading speed, you might find it helpful to move your finger or the tip of a pencil down the center of the page. The pencil tip should move slightly faster than your normal reading speed; move the finger or pencil down the page at a slow, steady pace. Do your best to keep up with the pencil or finger tip. The moving object will

encourage you to read smoothly and help prevent you from starting or stopping frequently. This will help you to read more quickly and to make steady progress as you read. MOST IMPORTANTLY increasing your reading speed (up to a point) will increase comprehension and result in fewer regressions which harm comprehension. Improved comprehension is the reason for trying to increase reading speed. One does not have to be a speed reader to perform well on the Reading Comprehension Section of the LSAT.

Now test your reading speed on the passage below. Try using 1) the finger/pencil tip device to speed up your reading or 2) the piece of paper placed just above the line you are now reading.

PASSAGE

The First Amendment to the Constitution of the United States guarantees that Congress shall not make a law prohibiting the free exercise of religion or respecting an establishment of religion. Many voices in the country offer conflicting ideas. A Chief Justice of the Supreme Court of the United States described the
(5) separation of church and state as a wall based on bad history, a guide which is useless to judging, and a metaphor which should be discarded. A contemporary, prominent church pastor viewed this enforced separation of civil and religious authority as the result of the work of an infidel. A religious leader of the colonial period reaffirmed this amendment by asking that government continue to let
(10) people speak as they please and worship freely whether it be none, one, or 20 gods. In the modern context, then, it seems that threats to religious freedom still exist. Separation of church and state is not universally accepted.

The number of words in the passage above is 157; divide this number by the number of minutes it took you to read the passage. Compare your rate with your reading rate on the longer passage. Did you improve? Now compare your reading rate with the average of 250 words per minute. Do you need to practice even more? Since the LSAT passages are short and succinct, it is unlikely that you will not be able to finish most of the Reading Comprehension Section(s).

TIPS ON READING SPEED

> ➤ **Tip 1** — Try to compete with **yourself** as you prepare for the LSAT. For example, if the national average reading speed is 250 words per minute but you are only reading at 120 words per minute, try to improve on the 120 words per minute (**without** decreasing your understanding).

> ➤ **Tip 2** — Set possible goals for yourself. The earlier you begin to study, the more time you will have to sharpen your skills. By allowing ample time to prepare, you will be able to answer more questions than the person who began studying only the week before the LSAT administration.

> ➤ **Tip 3** — Remember that improving reading speed is not a means in itself. Improved comprehension with fewer regressions **must** accompany this speed increase.

THE QUESTIONS

Following each of the four passages on the LSAT are five to eight questions based on the information in the passage. These questions might be taken from several categories (or types) of comprehension, which can be identified or tested.

The Reading Comprehension Section presents four types of questions:

1. Knowledge-based questions,

2. Comprehension questions,

3. Application-type questions, and

4. Analysis questions.

QUESTION TYPE 1: Knowledge-Based Questions

Knowledge-based questions are formed at the literal level and come directly from the reading material. Only a passive reading is required for knowledge-based questions. You are expected to know only what the author presents; you are to receive the literal message of the writer. You

must not only look for a direct statement from the passage, but you must also make sure the statement has the specific details to answer the question.

You must **read the lines** to answer the questions. Consider the following passage:

PASSAGE

The First Amendment to the Constitution of the United States guarantees that Congress shall not make a law prohibiting the free exercise of religion or respecting an establishment of religion. Many voices in the country offer conflicting ideas. A Chief Justice of the Supreme Court of the United States described the
(5) separation of church and state as a wall based on bad history, a guide which is useless to judging, and a metaphor which should be discarded. A contemporary, prominent church pastor viewed this enforced separation of civil and religious authority as the result of the work of an infidel. A religious leader of the colonial period reaffirmed this amendment by asking that government continue to let
(10) people speak as they please and worship freely whether it be none, one, or 20 gods. In the modern context, then, it seems that threats to religious freedom still exist. Separation of church and state is not universally accepted.

QUESTION

1.   Colonial religious leaders

    (A)   were unanimously opposed to the First Amendment because it was the result of the work of an infidel.

    (B)   were not faced with the threat to religious freedom as their modern counterparts are.

    (C)   sometimes reaffirmed this amendment and asked government to continue to allow people to speak and worship freely as they volunteered to do.

    (D)   and Supreme Court justices consistently opposed the separation of church and state.

    (E)   ensured that never again would there be opposition to religious freedom in American society.

A question which is on the literal level, or knowledge-based, comes directly from the reading passage. This particular question requires you to complete the sentence. Line 9 states that a colonial religious leader reaffirmed the first amendment by asking that government continue to let

people speak as they please and worship freely whether it is none, one, or twenty gods that they worship. Answer (C) reiterates this thought and is the correct answer.

By looking at the remaining answer choices, each can be determined wrong based on the information in the passage. It was a contemporary pastor, not a colonial leader, who stated that the amendment was the work of an infidel; answer (A) should not be selected. All generations have been threatened by a loss of religious freedom as is evidenced by the quotations given; answer (B), therefore, is not the correct answer. Supreme Court Justices have not consistently opposed the separation of church and state; many have upheld this separation. (D) could not be the correct answer. Colonial religious leaders could not (and did not) ensure that the nation would not be threatened by a loss of religious freedom. In fact, there is still a threat to religious freedom in the United States today. (E) is, therefore, incorrect.

QUESTION TYPE 2: Comprehension Questions

You must sometimes use a variety of skills to answer comprehension questions. You might be required, for example, to order events, to define words, to compare, or to contrast. The comprehension-type question might require you to derive the meaning of a word or phrase from the context of the passage. Unlike the literal-type question, the answer will not be explicitly stated in the lines; rather you must read **between the lines**, or at the inferential level. Questions which require you to determine the meaning or purpose of words or phrases used in the passage are inferential or comprehension questions. Another example of a comprehension question is one in which you must infer the information or ideas from the passage. **Be sure you can justify your choice**! Consider the following question based upon the paragraph below.

PASSAGE

The First Amendment to the Constitution of the United States guarantees that Congress shall not make a law prohibiting the free exercise of religion or respecting an establishment of religion. Many voices in the country offer conflicting ideas. A Chief Justice of the Supreme Court of the United States described the
(5) separation of church and state as a wall based on bad history, a guide which is

useless to judging, and a metaphor which should be discarded. A contemporary, prominent church pastor viewed this enforced separation of civil and religious authority as the result of the work of an infidel. A religious leader of the colonial period reaffirmed this amendment by asking that government continue to let
(10)   people speak as they please and worship freely whether it be none, one, or 20 gods. In the modern context, then, it seems that threats to religious freedom still exist. Separation of church and state is not universally accepted.

QUESTION

2.   The order of events in the passage

    (A)   begins in the present and concludes in the present.

    (B)   is chronological.

    (C)   deals entirely with history.

    (D)   is all important.

    (E)   begins in the present and moves to the past, at which point the passage ends.

(A) is the best answer since the passage does indeed begin in the present and conclude in the present. The passage is not chronological since it moves back and forth between the past and the present; (B), therefore, is not the best answer. The passage is not all historical (C) since there are items from the present. The order of events is **not** all important; it does not really matter which event really comes first or second. (D) is not all important. Since the passage does not conclude in the past, (E) is not the best answer to this **comprehension question concerned with the order of events in the passage**.

QUESTION TYPE 3: Application-Type Questions

The application question requires you to use or apply the information given in the passage to a new or different situation. Be sure you can justify your reasoning! Consider the following passage and the application question which follows.

PASSAGE

The First Amendment to the Constitution of the United States guarantees that Congress shall not make a law prohibiting the free exercise of religion or respect-

ing an establishment of religion. Many voices in the country offer conflicting ideas. A Chief Justice of the Supreme Court of the United States described the
(5) separation of church and state as a wall based on bad history, a guide which is useless to judging, and a metaphor which should be discarded. A contemporary, prominent church pastor viewed this enforced separation of civil and religious authority as the result of the work of an infidel. A religious leader of the colonial period reaffirmed this amendment by asking that government continue to let
(10) people speak as they please and worship freely whether it be none, one, or 20 gods. In the modern context, then, it seems that threats to religious freedom still exist. Separation of church and state is not universally accepted.

QUESTION

3.   The colonial religious leader quoted above would, if given the following choices, probably advocate

(A) an opening prayer in the school each day.

(B) a period of silent prayer which all the students in a school would observe.

(C) a prayer time conducted by a different religious group during each school day.

(D) for the schools a structured devotional period with a formal program which does not recognize any particular group yet gives attention to religion.

(E) no structured devotional time during the school day.

(E) is the best answer since it permits students freedom; they can worship no god if they please. It also prescribes no set way of worshipping so that students who do worship a god can worship as they please. Answer (A) suggests an opening prayer in the school each day. Such a prayer time would be a problem to the child who worshipped no god; (A) would be an inappropriate answer. (B) would be incorrect since it suggests that all children—even the ones who worship no god—must observe this time. Conducting a prayer time each day (C) and conducting a formal devotional period (D) would not be acceptable to one who worshipped no gods. No structured devotional time (E) is the most appropriate.

QUESTION TYPE 4: Analysis Questions

An analysis question may require you to break the passage into parts, to determine the main idea or the primary purpose of the passage, to describe how the author makes his or her points, to identify the tone of the passage or to describe the attitude of the author as revealed by the language of the passage. Be sure any answer you choose for the main idea question

1.   covers the main points of the article and

2.   is material that is contained only in the passage.

An example of such a question is given after the passage below.

PASSAGE

The First Amendment to the Constitution of the United States guarantees that Congress shall not make a law prohibiting the free exercise of religion or respecting an establishment of religion. Many voices in the country offer conflicting ideas. A Chief Justice of the Supreme Court of the United States described the
(5)   separation of church and state as a wall based on bad history, a guide which is useless to judging, and a metaphor which should be discarded. A contemporary, prominent church pastor viewed this enforced separation of civil and religious authority as the result of the work of an infidel. A religious leader of the colonial period reaffirmed this amendment by asking that government continue to let
(10)   people speak as they please and worship freely whether it be none, one, or 20 gods. In the modern context, then, it seems that threats to religious freedom still exist. Separation of church and state is not universally accepted.

QUESTION

4.   The main idea of the author is that

   (A)   separation of church and state is a decision which is not likely to change.

   (B)   separation of church and state is inevitable.

   (C)   separation of church and state is desirable.

   (D)   separation of church and state has never existed.

   (E)   separation of church and state was prohibited by the First Amendment to the Constitution.

The writer hints at his/her views when she/he mentions "threats to religious freedom"; one knows that he/she values—not opposes—religious freedom. The author also states that separation of church and state is not always accepted. From these statements one can deduce that the author believes that there are still threats to the separation of church and state; (A) is incorrect. The author also states that the separation of church and state is still threatened; (B) is incorrect. The author states that the First Amendment guarantees this right; the separation of church and state must have existed at some time. (D), then, cannot be correct. The separation of church and state was **guaranteed**, not prohibited by the First Amendment to the Constitution. (E) is not the correct answer. The reader should have chosen (C).

A FOUR-STEP APPROACH

When you take the Reading Comprehension Section of the LSAT, you will have two tasks:

1. to read the passage and

2. to answer the questions.

Of the two, carefully reading the passage is the most important; answering the questions is based on an understanding of the passage. Here is a four-step approach to reading:

Step 1: preview,

Step 2: read actively,

Step 3: review the passage, and

Step 4: answer the questions.

You should study the following exercises and use these four steps when you complete the Reading Comprehension Section of the LSAT.

STEP 1: Preview

A preview of the reading passage will give you a purpose and reason for reading; previewing is a good strategy to use in test-taking. Before beginning to read the passage (usually a four-minute activity if you pre-

view and review), you should take about 30 seconds to look over the passage and questions. An effective way to preview the passage is to read quickly the first sentence of each paragraph, the concluding sentence of the passage, and the questions—not all the answers—following the passage. A passage is given below. Practice previewing the passage by reading the first sentence of each paragraph and the last line of the passage.

PASSAGE

That the area of obscenity and pornography is a difficult one for the Supreme Court is well-documented. The Court's numerous attempts to define obscenity have proven unworkable and left the decision to the subjective preferences of the justices. Perhaps Justice Stewart put it best when, after refusing to define obscen-
(5) ity, he declared, "But I know it when I see it." Does the Court literally have to see it to know it? Specifically, what role does the fact-pattern, including the materials' medium, play in the Court's decision?

Several recent studies employ fact-pattern analysis in modeling the Court's decision making. These studies examine the fact pattern or case characteristics,
(10) often with ideological and attitudinal factors, as a determinant of the decision reached by the Court. In broad terms, these studies owe their theoretical under-pinnings to attitude theory. As the name suggests, attitude theory views the Court's attitudes as an explanation of its decisions.

These attitudes, however, do not operate in a vacuum. As Spaeth explains,
(15) "the activation of an attitude involves both an <u>object</u> and the <u>situation</u> in which that object is encountered." The objects to which the court directs its attitudes are the litigants. The situation—the subject matter of the case—can be defined in broad or narrow terms..One may define the situation as an entire area of the law (e.g., civil liberties issues). On an even broader scale the situation may be defined
(20) as the decision to grant certiorari or whether to defect from a minimum-winning coalition.

Defining the situation with such broad strokes, however, does not allow one to control for case content. In many specific issue areas, the cases present strik-ingly similar patterns. In examining the Court's search and seizure decisions,
(25) Segal found a relatively small number of situational and case characteristic variables explain a high proportion of the Court's decisions.

Despite Segal's success, efforts to verify the applicability of fact-pattern analysis in other issue areas and using broad-based factors have been slow in forthcoming. Renewed interest in obscenity and pornography by federal and state
(30) governments, the academic community, and numerous antipornography interest groups indicates the Court's decisions in this area deserve closer examination.

The Court's obscenity and pornography decisions also present an opportunity to study the Court's behavior in an area where the Court has granted significant decision-making authority to the states. In *Miller v. California* (1973) the Court

(35) announced the importance of local community standards in obscenity determinations. The Court's subsequent behavior may suggest how the Court will react in other areas whether it has chosen to defer to the states (e.g., abortion).

QUESTIONS

1. The author wrote this article to

   (A) explain the Court's decision in *Miller v. California.*

   (B) discuss fact-pattern analysis.

   (C) define obscenity.

   (D) criticize current research.

   (E) argue for studying the Court's obscenity decisions.

2. According to the author, the Court's obscenity decisions have relied on

   (A) personal judgments.   (D) established definitions.

   (B) objective legal analysis.   (E) Justice Stewart.

   (C) fact-pattern analysis.

3. The tone of the author is

   (A) ironic.   (D) concerned.

   (B) hostile.   (E) negative.

   (C) sarcastic.

4. Based on the passage, in Line 17 the *situation*

   (A) describes the type of litigants.

   (B) is all important to Spaeth.

   (C) concerns what the case is about.

   (D) only involves civil liberties issues.

   (E) is the medium.

5. From the passage, *judicial attitudes* can probably be defined as

   (A) attitude objects.   (D) fact patterns.

   (B) subjective preferences.   (E) judicial definitions.

   (C) case characteristics.

6.   The author makes the main points

    (A)   by the use of persuasive words.

    (B)   by referring to other studies.

    (C)   by using an historical approach.

    (D)   by using statistical findings.

    (E)   by referring to the church and moral education.

7.   The author's attitude toward the study of the Court's decisions is that such a study

    (A)   is unnecessary.

    (B)   has been successful.

    (C)   should avoid attitude theory.

    (D)   may shed light on the Court's behavior.

    (E)   will not involve the medium.

8.   To develop this passage the author

    (A)   presents the evidence supported by a theory.

    (B)   weighs the pros and cons of a plan.

    (C)   describes causes and effects of events.

    (D)   presents past consequences of a decision.

    (E)   debates both sides of a moral issue.

You should have read the following:

That the area of obscenity and pornography is a difficult one for the Supreme Court is well-documented.

Several recent studies employ fact-pattern analysis in modeling the Court's decision making.

These attitudes, however, do not operate in a vacuum.

Defining the situation with such broad strokes, however, does not allow one to control for case content.

Despite Segal's success, efforts to verify the applicability of fact-

pattern analysis in other issue areas and using broad-based factors have been slow in forthcoming.

The Court's obscenity and pornography decisions also present an opportunity to study the Court's behavior in an area where the Court has granted significant decision-making authority to the states.

The Court's subsequent behavior may suggest how the Court will react in other areas where it has chosen to defer to the states (e.g., abortion).

These few sentences tell you much about the entire passage. You know the topic of your passage: The difficulty that the Supreme Court has in making obscenity and pornography decisions. You know that recent studies have used fact-pattern analysis in modeling the Court's decision. You have learned also that attitudes do not operate independently and that case content is important. The feasibility of using fact-pattern analysis in other areas and broad-based factors have not been quickly verified. To study the behavior of the Court in an area in which they have granted significant decision-making authority to the states, one has only to consider the obscenity and pornography decisions. In summary, the author suggests that the Court's subsequent behavior may suggest how the Court will react in those other areas in which decision-making authority has previously been granted to the states. As you can see, having this information will make the reading of the passage much easier.

You should have also looked at the stem of the question in your preview. You do not necessarily need to spend time reading the answers to each question in your preview. The stem alone can help to guide you as you read.

The stems in this case are:

1. The author wrote this article to . . .

2. According to the author, the Court's obscenity decisions have relied on . . .

3. The tone of the author is . . .

4. Based on the passage, in Line 17 the *situation*...

5. From the passage, *judicial attitudes* can probably be defined as ...

6. The author makes the main points ...

7. The author's attitude toward the study of the Court's decisions is that such a study ...

8. To develop this passage the author ...

STEP 2: Active Reading

After your preview, you are now ready for your active reading. This means that as you read, you will be engaged in such things as underlining important words, topic sentences, main ideas, and words denoting tone of the passage. If you think underlining can help you save time and help you remember the main ideas, feel free to use your pencil!

Read carefully the first sentence of each paragraph since this often contains the topic of the paragraph. You may wish to underline the topic sentence.

As you read, you should note the structure of the passage. There are several common structures for the passages. Some of these structures are described below.

MAIN TYPES OF PARAGRAPH STRUCTURES

1. The structure is a main idea plus supporting arguments.

2. The structure is a main idea plus examples.

3. The structure includes comparisons or contrasts.

4. There is a pro and con structure.

5. The structure is chronological.

6. The structure has several different aspects of one idea. For example, a passage on education in the United States in the 1600s and 1700s might first define education, then de-

scribe colonial education, then give information about separation of church and state, and then outline the tax opposition and support arguments. Being able to recognize these structures will help you recognize how the authors have organized the passage.

STEP 3: Review the Passage

After you finish reading actively, take 10 or 20 seconds to look over the topic sentences you have underlined and the key words and phrases you have marked. Now you are ready to enter step 4 and answer the questions.

STEP 4: Answer the Questions

Now go back and answer the eight questions. As you answer the questions, be careful to mark your answer choices on the correct line of the answer sheet. Some students prefer to put a large check mark beside the correct answer and then to record all the answers for a passage at the same time. Whether you prefer to mark the answers one at a time or to record them a group at a time, **always check the question number and the number on the answer sheet as you mark your answers.**

FOUR-STEP APPROACH – DETAILED EXPLANATIONS OF ANSWERS

1. **(E)** The author begins the passage by discussing the Court's obscenity and pornography decisions. The next few paragraphs explain considerations relevant to the examination of the Court's decisions in general. In the fifth and sixth paragraphs the author presents his case for additional study of the Court's obscenity decisions in the theoretical context outlined in the preceding paragraphs. (A) is incorrect because we are only told in the briefest terms what the court decided in *Miller v. California*. In addition, *Miller* is not mentioned until the last paragraph, and only as an additional reason to study the Court's obscenity decisions. (B) is incorrect because the discussion of fact-pattern analysis is used to set the theoretical context in which the author believes the Court's obscenity decisions should be based. (C) is incorrect because no definition of obscenity is given in the passage. We are only told that previous attempts by the Court to define obscenity have proven unworkable, and Justice Stewart refused to define it. (D) is incorrect because the author is not criticizing current research. The author is arguing not enough research has been done in a particular area, not that too much

has been done in others. The only mention of other research (and we do not know if this research is current) is that of Segal, which the author characterizes as "successful." This question requires one to give the purpose of the passage or the reason why the author wrote it; question 1 is an example of an **analysis question**.

2.   **(A)**   In the passage the author argues that the Court's obscenity decisions should be studied using fact-pattern analysis. In the second and third paragraphs we are told that the theoretical underpinnings of fact-pattern analysis lie in attitude theory. Attitude theory, we are told in the last sentence of the second paragraph, "views the Court's attitudes as an explanation of its decisions." As used in the passage, "the Court" is clearly intended to mean the justices who collectively cast their votes to render a decision. This position is emphasized by the quote by Justice Stewart. Because the decisions rely on personal judgments, they cannot also rely on objective legal analysis, making (B) incorrect. (C) is incorrect because fact-pattern analysis is described in the passage as a method of **analyzing** the Court's decisions, not **making** them. (D) is incorrect because we are told in the first paragraph that the Court's definitions have proven unworkable, and no other definitions are mentioned in the passage. (E) is incorrect because there is no indication in the passage that Justice Stewart speaks for the Court (i.e., the other justices). Those familiar with Court history may know that at one time Justice Stewart did wield the crucial fifth vote in obscenity cases, but this fact is not mentioned in the passage and still does not imply Stewart spoke for the other justices.

This question is an example of a **comprehension question**. The passage states the court has "left the decision to the subjective preferences of the justices." This term **subjective** is best interpreted as "personal decisions."

3.   **(D)**   If you used the tips given earlier, you know that **concerned** is a good word choice for tone. It is a good choice and the correct choice. The other choices—(A) ironic, (B) hostile, (C) sarcastic, and (E) negative—are poor and incorrect in view of the tips and in view of the passage itself.

Asking for the "tone of the author" makes question 3 an example of an **analysis question**; the tone is not stated.

4.   **(C)**   We are told in the fourth sentence of the third paragraph that the situation is "the subject matter of the case," i.e., what the case is about. (A) is incorrect because in the third sentence of the third paragraph we are told the litigants are the attitude objects, and there is no other mention of *types* of litigants. (B) is incorrect because there is no indication *anything* is all important to Spaeth. In addition, Spaeth emphasizes (in his quotation) the words *objects* and *situation* indicating that both are important to him. In the third paragraph we are told that the situation may be broadly defined. Parenthetically, we are then given the example of civil liberties issues. The *e.g.* means "for example." Thus, civil liberties issues are not necessarily the *only* type of situation. (E) is incorrect because the mention of a medium in the first paragraph refers to the form which the obscene or pornographic materials take.

Question 4 is a *knowledge question* since Line 17 states, "The situation—the subject matter of the case—can be defined in broad or narrow terms."

5.   **(B)**   The conclusion is reached from the definition of the attitudes in attitude theory and the example provided by Justice Stewart's comment on how he determines whether materials are obscene. (A) is incorrect because attitude *objects* are described as part of what judicial attitudes are directed toward. The other part being the attitude situation. Thus, (A) is incomplete. (C) and (D) are essentially the same things (at least within the context of this passage). As explained by the Spaeth quotation the *activation* of an attitude requires both an object and a situation. From the definitions of these terms and the plain meaning of "case characteristics" and "fact patterns" it should be clear these characteristics and patterns are the objects and situations which activate the judicial attitudes, but they are not the attitudes themselves. Thus, both (C) and (D) are incorrect. (E) is incorrect because the only mention of definitions occurs in the first paragraph where the author tells us the Court's definitions of obscenity proved unworkable. Judicial *attitudes* are discussed in positive terms, leaving one to conclude they are not *definitions*.

This question is a **comprehension question** since the reader must define a term.

6.   **(B)**   To give credibility to the writing, the writer refers to other studies and experts. (B) is the best answer. Persuasive words (A) do not give credibility to the writing; frequent references to history (C) or to statistical findings (D) are not made. The writer does not try to gain credibility by references to the church and morals (transfer); (E) is not the best answer. (B) is the best answer and should be chosen.

Question 6 is an **analysis question** which requires the reader to determine how the author makes the main points.

7.   **(D)**   The author makes this suggestion in the final paragraph by indicating an analysis of the Court's post-*Miller v. California* behavior may yield insight into how the Court will behave in other areas "whether it has chosen to defer to the states." (A) is clearly incorrect because the author's entire argument is that the Court's obscenity decisions should be studied. As support for this argument, the author notes in the fifth paragraph that there has been renewed interest in obscenity and pornography by "federal and state governments, the academic community, and numerous antipornography interest groups." (B) is incorrect because the author's argument, that the Court's obscenity decisions need to be studied, *assumes* that they have not been previously studied according to the author's standards, or at least not successfully (but the passage contains no information on any unsuccessful studies). (C) is also incorrect based on the author's primary argument. The author *wants* the Court's obscenity decisions to be studied using fact-pattern analysis, which is related to attitude theory. Thus, it is impossible, given the author's position *and* avoid attitude theory. (E) is incorrect because at the end of

the first paragraph the author specifically asks what role the materials' medium plays in the Court's decision.

Question 7 (in which one must determine the author's attitude) is an **analysis question**.

8.   **(A)**   (A) seems to be the best answer. The author states in paragraph one, "That the area of obscenity and pornography is a difficult one for the Supreme Court is well-documented." The author continues in the passage to present this documentation. Answer (A) suggests that evidence to support a theory is presented; this seems to be most correct. The pros and cons of a plan (B) are not presented. The causes and effects of events (C) are not given, so (C) is not the best answer. Past consequences of a decision (D) are not included; (D) is not the best answer. Both sides of a moral issue (E) are not presented; (E) is not the best answer. You should have selected (A).

Question 8 is an **analysis question**; the reader must break the passage into parts to determine how the author develops the passage.

ADDITIONAL TIPS FOR ANSWERING QUESTIONS

Consider these tips:

> ➤ **Tip 1**   You will find that quite frequently some answers are predictable.

> a)   Strong emotions are often avoided on the LSAT. You might find an author being "admiring" or "disapproving," but not usually "irrational" or "highly enthusiastic."

> b)   The answer to "a main idea question" is usually found in the first sentence or the last sentence of the first paragraph or the last paragraph.

> ➤ **Tip 2**   Try not to spend too much time deciphering the meaning of words and statements upon first reading the passage. It will be helpful to go back over specific parts of the passage for in-depth understanding after reading each question.

> ➤ **Tip 3**   Watch out for questions with line numbers! The answer might not be found on the line which is indicated.

> ➤ **Tip 4**   While reading the passages, look particularly for the tone, the main idea, the topic sentences, the theme, and the purpose—especially if the stem of the questions seems to be asking for these.

> **➤ Tip 5** | Use caution with direct quotations from the passage.

> **➤ Tip 6** | Paraphrasing is more likely to be the best answer—not direct quotations. Choices which are word for word repeats of materials from a passage are usually trap answers.

> **➤ Tip 7** | The Reading Comprehension Section of the LSAT usually contains some opinion passages. Very often the authors will distinguish their beliefs from "conventional wisdom."

> **➤ Tip 8** | Enter the Reading Comprehension Section with a positive attitude. Say to yourself, "I knew how to prepare for the test. I know the types of questions I will encounter. I know what the directions will be like. There will be no surprises for me. We will all enter the Reading Comprehension Section on an equal footing since answers will be based on information in the passage and not on prior knowledge." A positive attitude will help your score since you will feel more self-confident and will not become easily rattled.

Drill: Reading Comprehension

Passion! What better word is there to describe opera? The vital core of opera is passion—sometimes violent, or joyful, loving, hateful, ecstatic, melancholic, vengeful; the gamut of emotions are exposed on the operatic stage and are transformed through the beauty of the music and the human voice. These emo-
(5) tions enter into an exalted state and, like everything else about opera, they are bigger than life. In opera, the ordinary becomes extraordinary.

Not only does passion reign on the operatic stage, but it also elicits as intense a response on the other side of the curtain. Opera audiences are known to erupt into wild outbursts—either giving performers wildly enthusiastic ovations and
(10) showering the stage with bouquets of flowers, or loudly hissing and booing and, even worse, throwing tomatoes and other "symbols of displeasure" onto the stage. Passion is returned with passion; indeed, the ardent devotion of some opera fans has stimulated the formation of cult-like groups around certain charismatic performers. It isn't difficult to understand how listeners can be awed by opera's
(15) grandeur and transported by the passions unfolding onstage.

Opera stands as one of the great cultural achievements of Western civilization. It represents a glorious fusion of the arts, combining drama, music, dance, and the visual arts. No one art form can be discounted, opera requires each of its

components to fulfill its essential role—anything less, and the opera suffers.
(20) Perhaps no one understood this better than Richard Wagner, who insisted that he did not compose opera as such but, rather, created *Gesamtkunstwerk* ("Total-artwork"). He meant by this a synthesis of poetry, music, drama, and spectacle, in which each element cooperatively subordinates itself to the total purpose. That total purpose—the music-drama (opera)—is not a mere "entertainment" but a
(25) profound and compelling work of art that elevates the listeners and resonates with our humanity.

Yet opera is pure artifice. If in the ordinary theater our disbelief must be willingly suspended in order to make the illusion of the play work, in opera that is no longer the question. We simply accept a world in which, among other
(30) things, people sing—beautifully—whether of love, of death, or of murder, or whatever. Thus, Samuel Johnson had a valid point in defining opera as "an irrational entertainment." The late Kenneth Clark, the eminent British art historian, once asked, "What on earth has given opera its prestige in Western civilization—a prestige that has outlasted so many different fashions and ways of
(35) thought?" He finds the answer in Dr. Johnson's definition: ". . . because it **is** irrational. 'What is too silly to be said may be sung'—well, yes; but what is too subtle to be said, or too deeply felt, or too revealing or too mysterious—these things can also be sung and only be sung."

Unusual for a rarefied pleasure (which it is oftentimes considered), opera
(40) today enjoys a flourishing and growing popularity. With the advent of modern technology, opera is able to reach millions of people around the world who would otherwise not be exposed to its splendor. The phonograph enabled opera to be brought into people's homes and, later, radio provided opera with a powerful and pervasive forum from which it attracted new listeners. More recently, the
(45) cinema and, especially, television have been instrumental in introducing opera to uninitiated audiences and converting many into fans.

1. The primary purpose of the passage is to

    (A) compare the works of Wagner.

    (B) describe the joy of opera.

    (C) report on the resurgence of opera.

    (D) critique the artificiality of opera.

    (E) compare the works of *Gesamtkunstwerk*.

2. By calling opera *pure artifice*, the author in Line 27

    (A) is attacking its value.

    (B) recognizes the importance of *Gesamtkunstwerk*.

    (C) agrees with the comment of Samuel Johnson.

    (D)   acknowledges its unrealistic character.

    (E)   is criticizing Wagner's operas.

3.   From the passage, Clark's explanation for the longevity of opera

    (A)   relies precisely on its artificial nature.

    (B)   is based on the mutual passion created by audience and artists.

    (C)   is that it has adapted to technological change.

    (D)   is derived from Gesamtkunstwerk.

    (E)   denies its irrationality.

4.   The author argues wild outbursts of approval or symbols of displeasure by opera fans show

    (A)   the inconsistent quality of modern opera.

    (B)   the lack of sophistication of most audiences.

    (C)   audience indifference.

    (D)   the artificial nature of opera.

    (E)   the depth and breadth of emotional reactions.

5.   Based on the information in the passage, one can conclude

    (A)   that a booming video market may put an end to opera attendance.

    (B)   that videos may bring opera to many homes.

    (C)   that opera is an art form of the past.

    (D)   that opera has never been popular but may become so in the future.

    (E)   that opera was popular at the time it was first performed but was never popular after that time.

      The promise of finding long-term technological solutions to the problem of world food shortages seems difficult to fulfill. Many innovations that were once heavily supported and publicized, such as fish-protein concentrate and protein from algae grown on petroleum substrates, have since fallen by the wayside. The
(5) proposals themselves were technically feasible, but they proved to be economically unviable and to yield food products culturally unacceptable to their consumers. Recent innovations, such as opaque-2 maize, Antarctic krill, and the wheat-rye hybrid triticale, seem more promising, but it is too early to predict their ultimate fate.
(10)   One characteristic common to unsuccessful food innovations has been that, even with extensive government support, they often have not been technologi-

cally adapted or culturally acceptable to the people for whom they had been
developed. A successful new technology, therefore, must fit the entire sociocultural system in which it is to find a place. Security of crop yield, practicality of
(15) storage, palatability, and costs are much more significant than had previously
been realized by the advocates of new technologies. For example, the better
protein quality in tortillas made from opaque-2 maize will be of only limited
benefit to a family on the margin of subsistence if the new maize is not culturally
acceptable or is more vulnerable to insects.
(20)   The adoption of new food technologies depends on more than these technical
and cultural considerations; economic factors and governmental policies also
strongly influence the ultimate success of any innovation. Economists in the
Anglo-American tradition have taken the lead in investigating the economics of
technological innovation. Although they exaggerate in claiming that profitability
(25) is the key factor guiding technical change—they completely disregard the
substantial effects of culture—they are correct in stressing the importance of
profits. Most technological innovations in agriculture can be fully used only by
large landowners and are only adopted if these profit-oriented business people
believe that the innovation will increase their incomes. Thus, innovations that
(30) carry high rewards for big agribusiness groups will be adopted even if they harm
segments of the population and reduce the availability of food in a country.
Further, should a new technology promise to alter substantially the profits and
losses associated with any production system, those with economic power will
strive to maintain and improve their own positions. Since large segments of the
(35) populations of many developing countries are close to the subsistence margin and
essentially powerless, they tend to be the losers in this system unless they are
aided by a government policy that takes into account the needs of all sectors of
the economy. Therefore, although technical advances in food production and
processing will perhaps be needed to ensure food availability, meeting food
(40) needs will depend much more on equalizing economic power among the various
segments of the populations within the developing countries themselves.

6.   With which of the following statements would the author most likely agree?

      (A)   Agribusiness groups have consistently opposed technological inno-
            vations.

      (B)   Agribusiness groups act chiefly out of economic self-interest.

      (C)   Agribusiness groups have been misunderstood by Anglo-American
            economists.

      (D)   Agribusiness groups nearly always welcome technological innova-
            tions.

      (E)   The economic success of agribusiness groups in developing coun-
            tries will automatically improve living conditions for all people in
            those countries.

7. Which of the following statements best summarizes the author's evaluation of the importance of technological advances in solving the problem of world food shortages?

   (A) They will succeed only if all people are given adequate technological educations.

   (B) They remain the single greatest hope in solving the problem of world food shortages.

   (C) They are ultimately less important than economic reforms in developing nations.

   (D) They will succeed only if the governments of developing countries support them.

   (E) They will succeed only if they receive widespread acceptance among powerful agribusiness groups.

8. According to the passage, some past technological food innovations, such as protein from algae grown on petroleum substrates, have failed because

   (A) they were not technologically feasible.

   (B) they did not receive adequate governmental support.

   (C) local producers did not understand the new technology.

   (D) they did not produce culturally acceptable food products.

   (E) producers were unwilling to alter their production systems.

9. Which of the following constitutes the author's primary criticism of Anglo-American economists' studies of technological innovations?

   (A) They do not understand that profit motives have a major influence on technology.

   (B) They are biased in favor of technological innovations.

   (C) Their focus has been almost exclusively on Western societies and cultures.

   (D) They do not understand the role of Third World governments in shaping economic developments.

   (E) They underestimate the importance of sociocultural factors in analyzing technological changes.

10. According to the passage one can assume that *triticale* is

   (A)   a nonliving form.

   (B)   an animal.

   (C)   a rock produced by grains of sand subjected to pressure.

   (D)   a low form of animal life.

   (E)   a plant.

READING COMPREHENSION REVIEW

ANSWER KEY

Drill: Reading Comprehension

1.	(B)	6.	(B)
2.	(D)	7.	(C)
3.	(A)	8.	(D)
4.	(E)	9.	(E)
5.	(B)	10.	(E)

DETAILED EXPLANATIONS
OF ANSWERS

Drill: Reading Comprehension

1.   **(B)**   This should be clear from the first paragraph. The remainder of the passage describes some of the specifics of why people find such joy and pleasure in opera. As part of this description the author mentions Wagner's creative philosophy, but he does not mention any of Wagner's specific works. Thus (A) is incorrect. Similarly, in the last paragraph the author notes the increased popularity of opera due to increased exposure via the mass media. Here again, however, the author is merely making one point in his overall theme of why opera is so popular. Thus, (C) is also incorrect. (D) is incorrect because in the fourth paragraph the author reports with enthusiasm the comments of Kenneth Clark who suggested that the artificiality of opera is what made it so popular and enduring. The author makes no plea for the support of opera, especially financially. In the last paragraph the author suggests opera is growing in popularity. Thus, (E) is incorrect.

2.   **(D)**   In the fourth paragraph the author favorably reports the comments of Kenneth Clark. Clark notes that it is the irrationality or silliness of opera which allows revelation of one's innermost thoughts and feelings. Thus, the author favorably concurs that opera is artificial, making (A) incorrect. Undoubtedly the author recognizes the importance of Gesamtkunstwerk (otherwise he would not have mentioned it in such a positive manner), but by the time the author mentions the artificiality of opera he has moved on to another point in his discussion unrelated to Gesamtkunstwerk. Thus, (B) is incorrect. (C) is incorrect because the author does not conclude opera is irrational entertainment—a negative conclusion, but rather, that it is opera's irrationality which makes it entertaining. (E) is incorrect because the author mentions the artificiality of opera in favorable terms, and he also does not criticize Wagner's operas.

3.   **(A)**   This is made clear in the quoted material attributed to Clark in the fourth paragraph. (B) is probably true as an explanation for the longevity of opera, but it is the author's explanation not Clark's, and is thus incorrect. Similarly, (D) is also probably true, but, again, not part of Clark's explanation, and, again, incorrect. The author seems to be making the general point raised by (C), which undoubtedly has contributed to opera's increased popularity. Here again, however, this is not part of Clark's explanation and is incorrect. (E) is incorrect because Clark does not deny opera's irrationality; rather he accepts it as a reason for its longevity.

4.   **(E)**   In the second paragraph the author describes the manifestations of the passion between opera and its audiences. The conclusion to be reached is that opera triggers a wide range of deeply felt emotions (approval to displeasure).

Such outbursts, positive or negative, cannot be said to be the result of audience indifference, making (C) incorrect. The author does not specifically indicate that there is inconsistency in the quality of operatic productions. The symbols of displeasure might be directed toward the action occurring onstage or toward a particularly heinous character. In addition, we can probably assume that if the quality of the production was inconsistent, opera would not be growing in popularity. Thus, (A) is incorrect. (B) is also incorrect because the author also does not suggest that outbursts with approval as a return of audience passion for the passion found on the stage. (D) is incorrect because the author's comments on audience outbursts and the artificiality of opera are part of two different points: the return of passion for passion and the entertaining nature of opera's irrationality.

5. **(B)** is the correct answer. Opera has adapted to many technological changes; the video screen may be another medium for the opera. The booming video market will probably be another medium for the opera; (A) is incorrect because it states that the video market may put an end to opera attendance. (C) should not be selected; the opera is not an art form of the past. (D) is incorrect; the opera has been very popular in the past and continues to be popular. (D) states that opera has never been popular so it is an incorrect statement. (E) is incorrect because it states that opera was popular at the time it was first performed but it was never popular thereafter. (B) is the best answer.

6. **(B)** The author believes that "profit-oriented business people" are motivated by a desire to "increase their incomes." Technological innovations per se are neither welcomed nor opposed by agribusiness groups but are considered only in terms of profitability. (A) and (D) are incorrect. Anglo-American economists have recognized the influence of profit motives on technological change; (C) is incorrect. The author believes that agribusiness groups will adopt innovations that increase profits even when these innovations harm the poor and reduce food availability; (E) is incorrect.

7. **(C)** The author believes that technological advances may be needed to solve the problem of world food shortages, but that equalizing economic power among various segments of the population in developing countries will ultimately be more important in addressing this problem (hence (B) is incorrect). (A), (D), and (E) may be true, but they are less important than economic reform.

8. **(D)** The author believes that technological advances in food production must not only be economically viable and technologically feasible but must also produce food that is culturally acceptable to consumers; cultural acceptability is a problem with protein from algae and fish-protein concentrate. He says producing protein from algae was technologically feasible; (A) is incorrect. The author does not mention whether this technology received governmental support or was understood by local producers; (B) and (C) are incorrect. He believes that profit-

motivated producers will alter production systems if doing so results in economic gain; (E) is incorrect.

9. **(E)** The author believes that Anglo-American economists have mistakenly disregarded the "substantial effects of culture" on technical change. They have correctly stressed the importance of profit motives in shaping technological innovations. (A) is incorrect. (B), (C), and (D) may or may not be true; the author offers no evidence to support any of these assertions.

10. **(E)** is the correct answer. Context clues can be used to help the reader. The passage states ". . . Antarctic krill, and the wheat-rye hybrid triticale seem more promising . . ." The reader knows that wheat and rye are plants and that the word *hybrid* refers to plants. (E) is the best answer to this comprehension question. Plants are living; (A) refers to a nonliving form. (A) is wrong. Triticale is neither an animal (B) nor a rock (C); neither (B) nor (C) should be chosen. Triticale is not a low form of animal life; (D) is incorrect. (E) is the right answer to the comprehension question.

LOGICAL REASONING REVIEW

The Logical Reasoning Section evaluates your ability to understand, analyze, and criticize the arguments in the passages. To do well on this section you must be able to reason critically and logically. This section has approximately 23 mini-passages, each of which is followed by one or two questions. Each section has a total of 24–26 questions, with a 35 minute time limit. The mini-passages are usually 20 to 100 words long and are drawn from a variety of sources. The sources include articles in the humanities, the social and natural sciences, editorials, advertisements, and speeches. Some of the passages may also be fictional conversations or arguments created especially for the test.

There are nine basic types of Logical Reasoning questions. Each of the questions requires you to perform one of the following logical operations:

1. Questions that ask you to determine the main point or conclusion of an argument;

2. Questions that ask you to detect the underlying assumption of an argument;

3. Questions that ask you to form a conclusion based on the premises or evidence provided;

4. Questions that ask you to identify the principles being applied in the passage and apply those principles to a different case;

5. Questions that ask you to determine the method of argument or persuasion being used;

6. Questions that ask you to find errors and misinterpretations in the argument;

7. Questions that ask you to evaluate the strength of the argument;

8. Questions that ask you to determine how additional information would affect the argument given;

9. Questions that ask you to assess whether the conclusion is consistent with the argument which is made to support it.

THE DIRECTIONS

You should study the directions now, as this will prevent your having to take precious seconds to study them on the day of the test. Instead, you should just quickly skim them during the exam to refresh your memory.

Take a few moments NOW to study the directions.

DIRECTIONS: The questions in this section are based on the reasoning contained in brief statements or passages. For some questions, more than one of the choices could conceivably answer the question. However, you are to choose the **best** answer; that is, the response that most accurately and completely answers the question. You should not make assumptions that are by commonsense standards implausible, superfluous, or incompatible with the passage. After you have chosen the best answer, blacken the corresponding space on your answer sheet.

Below are tips on following directions.

| ➤ Tip 1 | Notice that you are instructed to choose the best answer, that most accurately and completely answers the questions. In addition, you should not make assumptions that are implausible, superfluous, or incompatible with the passage based on common knowledge. |

| ➤ Tip 2 | Be sure that the answer you choose answers the question. |

THE QUESTIONS

LSAT questions do not require you to have any knowledge of the terminology of formal logic. For example, you will not have to identify 'ad hominem' arguments (statements which attack a speaker's character or reputation, instead of showing weaknesses in his argument). Nor will you have to understand terms such as 'syllogism' or 'inductive reasoning.' However, knowing these terms and being able to identify different types of arguments will definitely help you answer the questions within the time limits.

Although no formal knowledge of logic is required, you will need to understand terms such as 'premise,' 'argument,' 'assumption,' 'inference,' and 'conclusion.' Let's take a brief look at these terms.

LOGICAL REASONING TERMS

An ARGUMENT, in the most precise sense of the word, consists of a premise or premises and a conclusion which is inferred from the premises. A PREMISE is a proposition which is assumed as already proven. For this reason a premise is also an ASSUMPTION. It is the logical starting point of the argument. An INFERENCE is a process of reasoning whereby, starting from one or more premises, you move to a conclusion which follows from the premises. An inference can involve a necessary logical consequence of the premise(s) or a probability derived from the premise(s). The CONCLUSION is the point or idea which is inferred from the argument and which the argument is meant to support. All arguments, then, will consist of premise(s), inference(s), and conclusion. An example of a simple argument is:

Premise: No dogs are amphibians.

Conclusion: No amphibians are dogs.

Most arguments are more complex than this example. Some fill entire books and constitute complete systems of philosophy. Regardless of the length of logical arguments, they may be classified under two general headings: deductive and inductive.

DEDUCTIVE ARGUMENTS

Deductive arguments are those whose premises are intended to provide absolute proof of the conclusion.

EXAMPLE

Major premise: All whales are mammals.

Minor premise: Orca is a whale.

Conclusion: Orca is a mammal.

In this example, the conclusion follows of necessity from the premises. If all whales are mammals, then any given whale will be a mammal. The example above is also called a SYLLOGISM. A syllogism is a deductive argument with a major premise, a minor premise, and a conclusion.

A deductive argument is considered VALID when the inference from the premises is a necessary one. If whales are mammals and Orca is a whale, then Orca must be a mammal.

A deductive argument may be valid, but not true. Such a deductive argument is referred to as an 'unsound' argument. An unsound argument occurs when one of the premises is false, but the conclusion follows necessarily form the argument.

EXAMPLE

Major premise: All whales are cold-blooded.

Minor premise: Orca is a whale.

Conclusion: Orca is cold-blooded.

This is a valid argument. If all whales are cold-blooded, and Orca is a whale, then of necessity Orca must be cold-blooded. However, the major premise is false, so the conclusion is not necessarily true (in fact, it is false in this example).

When taking the LSAT it will be important for you to remember the difference between valid and invalid deductive arguments, and sound and unsound deductive arguments. Sometimes you will be given a passage which contains a valid but unsound deductive argument. You will then be asked to choose the answer which contains the same type of argument. Don't waste time forming objections to the arguments. Simply identify the mistake and look for the answer which makes the same type of mistake.

INDUCTIVE ARGUMENTS

Inductive arguments differ from deductive arguments in that the inference involved in getting from the premises to the conclusion is a probable, not a necessary, one. Inductive arguments involve an interpretation of some experience or experiences.

EXAMPLE

Premise: The sun came up today, yesterday, and every previous day of my life.

not necessary

Conclusion: The sun will come up every succeeding day of my life.

As you can see, the argument is based on experience. The conclusion does not follow with absolute certainty. There may be a time in which the sun will not come up anymore. It may be tomorrow. However, it is very probable that the sun will come up tomorrow and every other day of our lives.

Inductive arguments deal with probabilities. Their conclusions are more or less probable based on the supporting evidence. Inductive arguments are termed stronger or weaker depending on the probability of the conclusion.

EXAMPLE

Premise: Jill Black has used her electric can opener thousands of times, and it has never malfunctioned.

Conclusion: Therefore, it won't give her any problem with the can she's now opening.

This argument is invalid, since the conclusion does not follow, even if we assume the premise to be true. But notice that, even though the conclusion may be false, it is UNLIKELY that it is false. This is a strong argument because, given that the premise is true, it is unlikely that the conclusion is false.

We could rewrite the passage about Jill Black to produce a weak argument.

EXAMPLE

Jill Black's new can opener didn't give her any problem on the first can, so it will open thousands of cans without malfunctioning.

This argument is weak, because it is dangerous to make such a generalization on the basis of such scant experience.

SUMMARY

1.   A valid argument is one in which, given that the premises are true, it is impossible that the conclusion is false.

2. A valid argument in which the premises are true is called a sound argument.

3. A strong argument is one in which, given that the premises are true, the conclusion is unlikely to be false.

4. A weak argument is one in which the premises offer little support for the conclusion.

Look back at the list of operations the logical reasoning test will require you to do. Number 7 is "evaluate the strength of the argument." It should be clear to you now that this will apply to inductive but not to deductive arguments.

FROM GENERAL TO SPECIFIC AND FROM SPECIFIC TO GENERAL

We can make one other observation now about the difference between deductive and inductive arguments. Deductive arguments move from general premises to specific conclusions. In our example of deductive reasoning, we moved from the general premise that all whales are mammals to the specific conclusion that Orca is a mammal.

Inductive arguments move from specific premises to general observations. In our example of inductive reasoning, we moved from the specific observation that the sun had come up that day, to the inference that it will come up every succeeding day. In answering some of the questions, you will save time by knowing whether the sample argument moves from general premises to a specific conclusion, or from specific experiences to general conclusions.

EXAMPLE

All bird dogs instinctively hunt pheasants. English setters are bird dogs. Therefore, Rover, an English setter, will hunt pheasants.

Which of the following has a logical structure most like the logical structure of the argument above?

(A) I have had three pairs of Wilcot shoes, all of which have been comfortable. Therefore, all Wilcot shoes are comfortable.

(B)   The tree you just transplanted will not live, because I have transplanted many trees this time of year, and they all died.

(C)   Studies show that great athletes generally do cross-training. If you
want to be a good basketball player, you should play baseball this
spring.

(D)   All Tiaras have air-cooled engines. Your new car is a Tiara, therefore, it has an air-cooled engine.

(E)   A majority of people surveyed preferred brand Y over brand X.
Therefore, brand Y is a better buy.

The passage uses a deductive argument to reach its conclusion. It
reasons from the general premise that all bird dogs hunt pheasants, to
the specific conclusion that a particular bird dog will hunt pheasants. You
must look for the answer choice which also uses a deductive approach.
(A) is an inductive argument. It reaches the general conclusion that all
Wilcot shoes share a characteristic (comfort) from the particular experience of three pairs of those shoes. Answer (B) uses the same type of
argument, that since something has happened several times it will happen again. Answer (C) is the same type of argument in a slightly different
form. Any time a study is cited, an inductive argument is being used.
Studies examine individual members of a group and try to generalize from
the findings about those individuals. All of the great athletes studied do
cross-training, so the generalization is that cross-training is a key to being
a great athlete. Answer (D) is a deductive argument. It starts from the
major premise that all members of a class have characteristic A, so any
member of the class must have that characteristic. This is the form of
argument used in the main passage, so (D) is the answer. Answer (E) is
very similar to answer (C). Since a majority of people surveyed prefer
brand Y, we generalize that it must be the better buy.

LOCATING PREMISES AND CONCLUSIONS

To do well on the logical reasoning section of the LSAT, you must be
able to locate the premises and conclusions in the arguments. In our
sample arguments above, this is easy because the premises are given
first and are followed by the conclusion. This is not always true of arguments. Sometimes the conclusion comes first and is followed by the
premises.

EXAMPLE

Bill will not be able to change the oil in his car. To change the oil, he needs a wrench for removing the drain plug, and he does not have one.

In this example the conclusion comes first, followed by the premises. We could make this argument conform to the standard pattern:

Major premise: To change the oil in a car, one must have a wrench to remove the drain plug.

Minor premise: Bill does not have a wrench.

Conclusion: Bill will not be able to change the oil in his car.

Now the premises appear first and the conclusion appears last. The logic of the argument remains the same.

WHAT IS THE AUTHOR TRYING TO PROVE?

One way to determine which statements are premises and which is the conclusion is to ask yourself what the author is trying to prove. Remember, the conclusion is what the author wants to prove, and the premises are the assumptions which support the conclusion. Ask yourself what the author is trying to prove in the following argument.

Ann got bonus points on her assignment because she turned it in early, and all assignments turned in early received bonus points.

What is the author trying to prove? That Ann turned her assignment in early? No. If that was the author's purpose, we would expect to see something like this: "The assignments were due on Thursday, but Ann turned hers in on Wednesday. Therefore, she turned it in early." If the author wanted to show that early assignments got bonus points, we would expect to see something like: "Mr. Simms said that all early assignments would receive bonus points." However, we do not see either of these statements supported by argument or evidence. They are the assumptions or premises of the argument. What we do see are statements that support the idea that Ann got bonus points. We know, then, that Ann got bonus points is the conclusion.

LINGUISTIC INDICATORS

Many times the premises and conclusion may be determined by what may be termed 'linguistic indicators.' Linguistic indicators are words which indicate the function of a phrase or sentence within an argument. Premise indicators include:

… proves	… implies
… shows	… means
… establishes	

The three dots before each word represent the premise. With the words above, the premise will precede the linguistic indicator. Sometimes, however, the premise will follow an indicator:

since …	inasmuch as …
because …	seeing that …
for …	insofar as …

Conclusion indicators include:

accordingly …	which means that …
as a result …	which proves that …
so …	it can be inferred that …
it follows that …	therefore …
consequently …	hence …
which shows that …	thus …

Here are some examples of arguments which use linguistic indicators:

Since you have to have an invitation to go to the party, Sam can't go because he didn't get one.

Most people don't doubt their own reasoning ability. Therefore, few want to study logic.

Jo did well on the LSAT, which proves that she is smart.

UNCOVERING HIDDEN (UNSTATED) PREMISES

Some of the logical reasoning questions on the LSAT will ask you to find the underlying assumption of an argument. The underlying assumption is a hidden or unstated premise of an argument. An unstated premise, in turn, is one that must be true for the argument to be valid.

EXAMPLE

This is purple passion perfume, so it must be expensive.

This little argument has an explicit premise, that this is purple passion perfume. It also has an explicit conclusion, that this perfume must be expensive. The conclusion does not follow logically from the given premise. For the argument to be valid, we must make the assumption that purple passion perfume is expense. What is left out, then, is the premise that purple passion perfume is expensive. The complete argument is:

Major premise (unstated): Purple passion perfume is expensive.

Minor premise (stated): This is purple passion perfume.

Conclusion: This perfume is expensive.

Whenever a logical reasoning question asks you to identify an unstated premise, you should read the passage carefully, asking yourself 'What is necessary for the argument to be valid?'

EXAMPLE

Karen checked the costume and found no sewing mistakes. Therefore, the costume had no sewing mistakes.

Which of the following is an unspoken assumption of the argument?

(A) The costume is a good replica of the clothes of the time period covered in the play.

(B) The seamstress who sewed the costume has sewed many such costumes without making any sewing mistakes.

(C) Karen sewed the costume herself.

(D) Karen is a professional seamstress.

(E) Karen never fails to find sewing mistakes in costumes.

The answer to the question is (E). If we are to conclude that the costume has no sewing mistakes because Karen failed to find any, then we must assume that Karen never misses any mistakes that might exist. Answer (A) is beside the point, since the passage says nothing about the costume being a replica of the clothes of any time period. Answer (B) might support the conclusion that the costume has no sewing mistakes, but it doesn't help us to understand how the author of the passage concludes there are no mistakes based on Karen's examination of the costume. Answer (C) fails to explain how Karen's examination of the costume is authoritative with regard to there being no mistakes. Answer (D) is the strongest alternative to (E). It fails, however, because it is not necessary to assume that Karen is a professional seamstress in order to reach the conclusion. What is necessary is the simple assumption that had there been a mistake, she would have found it.

Look at the following passage and identify all of the hidden premises:

The reason we have a huge federal budget deficit is because congressmen are so interested in getting re-elected that they vote for any federal spending project in their home districts. Therefore, if we want to get the federal budget under control, we must pass term limitations on congressmen.

There are a number of hidden premises in this passage. First, it is clear the speaker assumes that Congressional spending (not declining revenues or some other factor) is responsible for the budget deficit. Second, the speaker assumes that congressmen vote for spending in their home districts in order to get re-elected. Third, the speaker assumes that term limitations will remove congressmen's motives for voting for spending projects in their home districts. Fourth, the speaker assumes that removing that motive will result in spending decreases by Congress.

There is another type of question which appears often in the logical reasoning section of the LSAT and is closely related to finding hidden premises. This type of question asks you to identify the statement which either strengthens or weakens the conclusion drawn in the passage. When the question calls for the answer choice that weakens the argument, the answer will be one which undermines a hidden premise. When the question calls for the answer choice that strengthens the conclusion, the answer will be one which supports a hidden premise.

EXAMPLE

Contrary to popular perceptions, rock climbing is a very safe sport. The number of people who die each year rock climbing is about the same as the number of people who die each year bicycling. And the number of people who die each year bicycling is nearly the same as the number of people who die each year jogging. So the fact is, rock climbing is no more dangerous than bicycling or jogging.

Which of the following, if true, would most seriously weaken the author's conclusion?

(A) Statistics show that many more people jog and bicycle than rock climb.

(B) The number of bicyclists killed each year is very small only because there are laws governing the use of the roads.

(C) Jogging is among the safest forms of physical exercise. Were the author to compare fatalities from skydiving, the number would be much higher.

(D) Most people would much rather take their chances jogging and bicycling than they would rock climbing.

(E) All forms of mountaineering, taken together, kill many more people than are killed by cars while bicycling or jogging.

The author argues that rock climbing is no more dangerous than bicycling or jogging. His proof is that no more people are killed rock climbing than doing either of the other two. (For his argument to be strong, it must be true that just as many people rock climb as jog or bicycle.) If a thousand times as many people jog and bicycle as rock climb, but the same number are killed in each of the three activities, it would follow that rock climbing is a thousand times more dangerous. Therefore, the correct answer is (A). Answer (B), even if true, would have no effect on the argument. It makes no difference WHY the number of bicyclists killed each year is small, so long as the numbers killed in each activity are about the same. Answer (C) might actually strengthen the author's argument. If jogging is a safe sport, and the same number are killed jogging and rock climbing, then rock climbing may also be relatively safe. The author is not dealing with people's preferences, but is, rather, trying to establish that rock climbing is as safe as jogging or bicycling. Therefore, what people prefer to do, (D), is beside the point. Answer (E)

has no effect on the argument. It may be true that other forms of mountaineering are much more dangerous than rock climbing. However, the author is not arguing that all forms of mountaineering are safe. He is interested only in proving that rock climbing is safe.

COMMON FORMS OF INDUCTIVE ARGUMENTS

Some questions on the LSAT ask you to identify the type of argument used in the passage. Normally, this involves one of the common forms of inductive reasoning. Let's look at various forms of inductive reasoning which you might encounter.

1. Generalization

In an inductive generalization, something is said to be characteristic of an entire class of things based on the fact that it is characteristic of certain individuals of that class.

EXAMPLE

Every tennis player I've played at club X is a serve and volleyer. Therefore, most of the tennis players at club X are probably serve and volleyers.

This is an invalid argument, and probably not a very strong one. The determining factor here is how many players the author has played relative to the total number of players at club X. If the author has played 45% of the players, the conclusion is strengthened. If he has played only 5%, the conclusion is weakened.

For a generalization from members of a class to the whole class to be warranted, the sample must be REPRESENTATIVE of the class. This means that, ideally, the sample must possess all of the relevant features of the class, and in the same proportion. No generalization based on an unrepresentative sample is trustworthy. For that reason, the questions on the test are likely to focus on the representativeness of the sample.

EXAMPLE

A survey done last month at Central Mall showed that 89% of the shoppers surveyed said they do most of their shopping on the east side of town. Therefore,

it is safe to say that if the mall had been placed on the east side of town, rather than in the center of town, merchants in the mall would receive more business.

The argument above depends on which of the following assumptions?

(A) Business is likely to pick up at Central Mall as the town grows to the west.

(B) The shoppers sampled were representative of all shoppers at Central Mall.

(C) Each of the shoppers surveyed visited several stores in the mall.

(D) Each of the shoppers surveyed visited only one store in the mall.

(E) Stores in the mall cater to those from the east side of town.

The answer is (B). For the author to draw a valid conclusion from the sample population, that population must be representative of all shoppers at the mall. On the other hand, the survey might have been taken only at the east exit to the mall, in which case most of those surveyed might well be residents of the east part of town who parked on that side of the mall. In that case, it would be logical to expect them to do most of their shopping near their homes on the east side of town. If the author had done the survey at the west exit, many shoppers might have said they do their shopping on the west side of town.

The conclusion of the argument is that business would be better in the mall if it had been placed on the east side of town. This conclusion is based on two assumptions: (a) that the preference of those surveyed to shop on the east side of town represents a general preference of shoppers in the town; (b) that since most people prefer to shop on the east side of town, businesses located there receive more business than those located in the center or on the west side of town. To reach the conclusion it is not necessary to assume that business will pick up as the town grows to the west (assumption possibility (A)), although that might in fact happen. Nor is it necessary to assume that each shopper surveyed visited several stores in the mall (assumption possibility (C)). Whether the shoppers surveyed visited one or several stores while in the mall has little or no effect on the conclusion. Therefore, we may eliminate answer choices (A), (C), and (D). Choice (E) is not an assumption on which the argument is based. It would harm the survey's credibility if the stores catered to east siders, but the argument does not depend on this.

Will the Conditions Continue into the Future?

A generalization may be strengthened or weakened based on whether the time period on which the generalization is made is representative of the future. If the conditions observed in the sample are unlikely to continue into the future, the conclusion will be weakened.

EXAMPLE

Sam was 30 pounds overweight when he started his diet. He lost 10 pounds in the first three months. Therefore, he will be down to the appropriate weight in six more months.

The conclusion in this argument is valid only if Sam continues to lose weight at the same rate. However, it may prove more difficult for him to lose weight at the same rate as he approaches his target weight. Therefore, the conclusion may prove to be incorrect.

2. Causal Arguments

A causal argument is one which states that something, Y, caused something else, Z. Causal arguments establish a cause and effect relationship between two phenomena. Let's say you ate a green apple. Before you ate it, your stomach felt fine. After you ate it, you had a stomach ache. You reason that eating the apple caused your stomach ache, thus you have made a causal argument.

Many passages on the LSAT involve causal arguments. In causal argument questions you are usually asked to: (a) identify a causal argument, (b) recognize an alternative explanation, or (c) recognize that the argument makes the logical fallacy *post hoc, ergo propter hoc* (in other words, because X follows Y, Y must cause X). Let's look at examples of each of these.

EXAMPLE OF A (Identify a Causal Argument)

The price of cotton clothes shot through the roof in June of this year. This year's cotton harvest will likely be one of the worst on record, and this no doubt accounts for the rise in prices.

The argument in the passage above does which of the following?

(A)   cites expert opinion to prove a point

(B)   relies on statistical data to prove a point

(C)   offers an explanation of a phenomenon

(D)   criticizes a commonly held opinion

(E)   argues by analogy

The answer is (C), since the author of the passage is making a causal argument to explain the rise in prices. The author does not, (A), cite any expert opinion. Nor are any statistical data offered, (B). Answer (D) is not correct because the author does not refer to any commonly held opinion which he criticizes. Answer (E) is incorrect because there is no attempt by the author to use a similar situation to prove a point in the present case.

EXAMPLE OF B (Recognize an Alternative Explanation)

The price of cotton clothes shot through the roof in June of this year. Government projections say this year's cotton harvest will likely be one of the worst on record, and this no doubt accounts for the rise in prices.

Which of the following, if true, would most seriously weaken the conclusion of the argument above?

(A)   Demand for cotton clothes has fallen rapidly since the price increase.

(B)   There was an industry-wide strike in the cotton clothes manufacturing industry in May.

(C)   Most cotton for the clothes industry comes from domestic production.

(D)   Government projections of crop harvests are correct about 70% of the time.

(E)   Consumers don't pay as much attention to government projections as manufacturers and retailers do.

The answer to the question is (B), because it provides an alternative explanation for the rise in prices. If there was a strike in the manufacturing industry in May, production would have gone down. This would be more likely to drive up the price of cotton clothes in June of this year than would projections of a poor harvest in the fall. Answer (A) is incorrect because (a) demand decreased AFTER the price increase, so it could not be a

cause of the price increase; and (b) decreased demand would be more likely to cause a fall rather than a rise in prices. Answer (C) would strengthen the conclusion, not weaken it. If most cotton for clothing comes from domestic production, then projections of a poor harvest would likely have a greater impact on prices than if most cotton for clothes came from foreign production. Answer (D) might weaken the argument somewhat, since government projections are incorrect about 30% of the time. Still, a record of being correct 70% of the time is pretty good, so the government projection would tend to make manufacturers anticipate a shortage of cotton in the near future. Answer (E) does not weaken the argument, since hiking prices would most likely be a response of manufacturers and retailers to the government projections. If (E) is true, consumers would be more likely to react to the price hikes themselves (perhaps by buying fewer cotton clothes), than to the government projections.

EXAMPLE OF C (Recognize that the argument makes the logical fallacy "post hoc, ergo propter hoc")

Jack: The night before the chemistry final I went out and got drunk. I made an A on the test.

Pete: My physics final is tomorrow. Let's go out and get drunk tonight so I can make an A on my final.

Pete makes which of the following mistakes in the passage above?

(A) He cites an example to prove a point

(B) He assumes that event A caused event B simply because A preceded B.

(C) He identifies a contradiction in Jack's statement.

(D) He reiterates his conclusion rather than supplying evidence to support it.

(E) He misinterprets the meaning of the words 'got drunk.'

The answer is (B). Pete assumes that the reason Jack made an A was because he got drunk, and he makes that assumption on the grounds that getting drunk preceded getting an A. He does not (A) cite any examples to prove a point. He does not (C) identify any contradiction in Jack's statement. He does not (D) reiterate a conclusion. He does not (E) misinterpret the meaning of the words "got drunk."

3. Circular Reasoning

Circular reasoning refers to a type of argument in which the speaker assumes as a premise that which the argument is supposed to prove.

EXAMPLE

God must exist because the Bible says so, and the Bible is the authoritative word of God.

What we have here is an argument which supposedly proves that God exists based on the authority of the Bible. But the authority of the Bible depends on God's existence. Some proof! An LSAT question based on such reasoning might look like this:

EXAMPLE

God must exist because the Bible says so, and the Bible is the authoritative word of God.

The argument in the passage above makes which of the following errors?

(A) It confuses two different meanings of a word.

(B) It treats a dissimilar event as analogous to the present one.

(C) It assumes what it tries to prove.

(D) It makes a claim by overgeneralizing from specific evidence.

(E) It contains a logical contradiction.

The answer is (C), for the reasons explained above. Answer (A) is incorrect because there is no ambiguity about the meaning of the words in the argument. Since no events per se are discussed, answer (B) is incorrect. Answer (D) may appear plausible at first glance, but does not apply to this case. Overgeneralization occurs when an author asserts that A will follow B repeatedly because A followed B once, or asserts that because one member of a class possesses a certain trait all members of the class possess that trait. Answer (E) is incorrect because there is no logical contradiction in the argument. A logical contradiction occurs when both parts of an argument cannot be true. In the present case, it may be true both that God exists and that the Bible is the authoritative word of God.

4. Ad Hominem Arguments

We have already briefly discussed ad hominem arguments. They are arguments which attack the speaker instead of trying to refute his argument. The identity or character of the speaker usually has no influence on the quality of the argument. Saying "Mrs. Brown is ignorant, so her argument that high school students shouldn't be allowed to eat lunch off campus is preposterous" does not refute the argument, it only makes Mrs. Brown mad. Passages on the LSAT which contain ad hominem arguments will usually ask you "The passage above does which of the following?" The answer will be something like "Attacks the person making the argument."

5. Ambiguity

Some questions on the test will turn on ambiguous use of words or phrases. A word or phrase is ambiguous if it can be assigned more than one meaning and it is not clear from the context which meaning is appropriate.

EXAMPLE

She did nothing well.

This might mean that nothing she did was done well. Or it could mean that she was good at doing nothing. Other examples are:

He was hot.

I know a little German.

I broke his glasses.

Many items on the test which employ ambiguity will offer a verbal exchange between two speakers and then ask you something like: "The disagreement between (person 1) and (person 2) cannot be resolved until _____ ." The answer will be something like: "Agree on a definition of the word _____ (whichever word is ambiguous).

CATEGORICAL ARGUMENTS

There is one type of deductive reasoning which deserves special

treatment. It is called categorical reasoning. Passages on the LSAT which use categorical arguments will require you to reach conclusions based on descriptions of classes or categories. There are four standard forms of categorical statements:

a. all x are y;

b. no x are y;

c. some x are y;

d. some x are not y.

Statement a. means that one class is completely contained in the other. Statement b. means that the classes have no members in common. Statements c. and d. mean that the classes have some, but not all, members in common.

Now let's look at a common form of LSAT question which uses a categorical argument.

EXAMPLE

No firefighters are on the planning commission.
Some politicians are on the planning commission.
Some politicians on the commission are lawyers.
All members of the commission serve two years except lawyers, who serve one-year terms. All politicians on the planning commission who are not lawyers are female.

If all of the above statements are true, which of the following must also be true?

(A) All politicians on the commission are also lawyers.

(B) Some of the lawyers on the commission are also firefighters.

(C) Some of the firefighters are politicians.

(D) The politicians on the planning commission all serve one-year terms.

(E) All female politicians on the planning commission who are not lawyers serve two-year terms.

Notice that the passage asks you "which of the following MUST be true?" To answer this question you must go through a process of elimina-

tion. Answer (A) cannot be true because sentence three of the passage says that SOME of the politicians on the commission are lawyers. This means that not all are lawyers. Answer (B) cannot be true, since sentence one of the passage says that no firefighters are on the commission. Some of the firefighters may be politicians, (C), but they may not be politicians on the commission. However, there is nothing in the passage that requires any politicians to be firefighters, so answer (C) fails. Sentence four of the passage says that all non-lawyers serve two years on the commission. Sentence three says that only some of the politicians on the commission are lawyers, which means that some politicians on the commission are non-lawyers. Therefore, some politicians serve two-year terms, and answer (D) fails. Answer (E) must be true. Since all politicians on the commission who are not lawyers are female, and all non-lawyers on the commission serve two-year terms, all female politicians who are not lawyers must serve two-year terms.

☞SHORTCUT

The same question can be answered much more easily through the use of a Venn diagram. A Venn diagram is a graphic illustration of claims made in a categorical argument. A Venn diagram consists of circles which represent the classes mentioned in the argument. The examinee can find the answer much more easily by using a Venn diagram than by using the logical process of elimination described above.

Let's look back at the four standard forms of categorical statements. Each can be represented by the use of Venn diagrams.

a. all x are y

For this kind of statement, draw two circles, one inside the other.

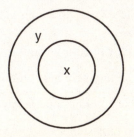

The diagram indicates that all x are contained in y.

b. no x are y

For this kind of statement, draw two circles that do not overlap one another.

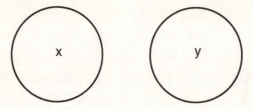

The diagram indicates that the classes x and y are completely separate.

c. some x are y

For this type of statement, draw two circles that partly overlap one another.

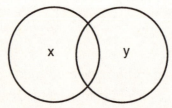

The diagram indicates that the two classes have some members in common.

d. some x are not y

Draw the same type of diagram as for c. above. The diagram indicates that the two classes have some members in common.

Now, let's solve again the example presented earlier, this time using a Venn diagram.

EXAMPLE

No firefighters are on the planning commission.

Some politicians are on the planning commission.

Some politicians on the commission are lawyers.

All members of the commission serve two years except lawyers, who serve one-year terms. All politicians on the planning commission who are not lawyers are female.

If all of the above statements are true, which of the following must also be true?

(A)   All politicians on the commission are also lawyers.

(B)   Some of the lawyers on the commission are also firemen.

(C)   Some of the firefighters are politicians.

(D)   The politicians on the planning commission all serve one-year terms.

(E)   All female politicians on the planning commission serve two-year terms.

To solve the question, first draw two circles, one each to represent firemen and the planning commission. The two circles do not overlap, since the classes have no members in common. Label one circle F for firemen and the other PC to indicate planning commission.

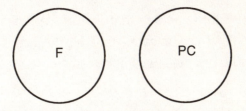

Next, draw a circle which partly overlaps PC. Label it Pol to indicate politicians.

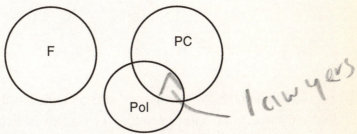

Now, draw a circle which partly overlaps PC and Pol. Label it L for lawyer. This circle will overlap Pol in two places. First, it will overlap only some of that part of Pol which is inside PC. It does not completely overlap that part of Pol which is in PC, because only some of the politicians on the commission are lawyers. Second, it will overlap part of Pol which is outside PC. It does not completely overlap that part of Pol which is outside PC, because we cannot be sure that all politicians who are not on the commission are lawyers. In addition, circle L should overlap part of PC which is not overlapped by Pol. This is so because we tell from the

passage whether or not some lawyers are on the commission who are not politicians.

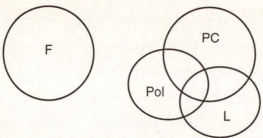

Next, place a 1 (one) in those parts of L which overlap PC. This indicates that all lawyers on the commission serve one-year terms. Place a 2 (two) in that part of Pol which overlaps PC but does not overlap L. Also place a 2 (two) in the rest of PC which does not overlap L. This indicates that all non-lawyers serve two-year terms.

Last, place an F for female in that part of Pol which overlaps PC but does not overlap L. This indicates that all politicians who are on the commission and who are not lawyers are female.

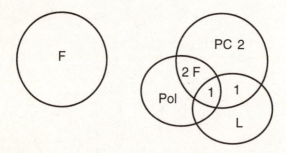

Now, using the Venn diagram, you can answer the question. We see that (A) need not be true, since all of Pol which intersects PC does not also intersect L. (B) need not be true, although it may be true. (C) need not be true, although it may be true. (D) cannot be true, since part of Pol which intersects PC has 2 in it. (E) must be true, since that part of Pol which intersects PC but not L has both F and 2 in it.

Using Venn diagrams may seem time consuming, and perhaps even counterproductive. However, when you take the test you will be under considerable pressure, and it may be difficult to keep all the relationships straight in your mind. If you draw the Venn diagrams correctly, they will yield the correct answer every time.

ADDITIONAL TIPS FOR ANSWERING QUESTIONS

Consider these tips:

➤ **Tip 1** Remember, whenever a study is used to support a claim, an inductive argument is being employed.

➤ **Tip 2** Look for themes in the first and last sentences of passages. That's where they can usually be found.

➤ **Tip 3** Use diagramming where it is helpful in understanding the argument and the type of reasoning used.

➤ **Tip 4** Use the process of elimination to weed out choices.

➤ **Tip 5** Read the passage carefully for ideas.

➤ **Tip 6** If the questions following a passage are short, you may want to read them first, so that you know what to look for when reading the passage.

Drill: Logical Reasoning

1. The latest study indicates that women who exercise daily have a higher rate of metabolism than women who do not exercise, lending support to the view that lack of exercise contributes to slow metabolism.

    The argument would be weakened most by pointing out which of the following?

    (A) Statistics can be deceiving.

    (B) Many genetic backgrounds were represented in both the exercising and non-exercising groups.

    (C) Participants in the study were chosen at random from a larger population.

    (D) Some women who did not exercise had higher rates of metabolism than some women who did.

    (E) Many variables, such as the ages and diets of participants were not accounted for in the study.

2. An advertisement I just heard says that more dentists recommend Doubledent gum for their patients who chew gum. If that is true, Doubledent is preferred by a majority of dentists for their patients who chew gum.

    Which of the following is the strongest objection to the conclusion in the passage?

    (A) Not all dental patients chew gum.

    (B) Dentists should not recommend any brand of gum, since chewing gum may damage expensive dental work.

    (C) Some dentists do not recommend Doubledent for their patients who chew gum.

    (D) The phrase "more dentists recommend Doubledent for their patients who chew gum" is too ambiguous to provide support for the author's conclusion.

    (E) Dentists are not the best qualified persons to judge which gum their patients should chew.

3. No one under age 35 is a Vietnam veteran. Some Vietnam veterans are on the school board. All members of the school board are under age 50.

    Assuming the above statements to be true, which of the following is/are necessarily true?

    I.   Every member of the school board is between the ages of 35 and 50.

    II.   Vietnam veterans on the school board are between the ages of 35 and 50.

    III. Some members of the school board are over age 34.

    (A) I only   (D) I and II only

    (B) II only   (E) II and III only

    (C) III only

4. Who is responsible for crime? It is not the criminal. He is just a sick person in need of professional counseling. It is not the victim, who just happens to be in the wrong place at the wrong time. It is not the police, who have been hampered in law enforcement by citizens who refuse to get personally involved in stopping crime. No, you and I are the responsible parties.

    The reasoning of the author of the above passage is most like that of the person who would argue that

    (A) physicians are to blame for illness.

see p. n. 78

(B)   public apathy is responsible for deaths caused by drunken drivers.

(C)   criminals are responsible for murder.

(D)   foremen are responsible for poor performance by workers.

(E)   companies are responsible for toxic waste.

5.   South Korea, a developing country, has a high rate of economic growth. Brazil, a developing country, has a low rate of economic growth. Japan, a developed country, has a high rate of economic growth. The United States, a developed country, has a low rate of economic growth.

Which of the following most closely expresses the main point of the passage above?

(A)   High economic growth rates can be expected in some developing countries.

(B)   High economic growth rates can be expected in some developed countries.

(C)   High or low economic growth rates cannot be predicted on the basis of whether a country is developing or developed.

(D)   High or low economic growth rates can be predicted by a variety of factors.

(E)   There is no way to predict which countries will have high or low economic growth rates.

6.   Barry: My company started out with a 51% share of the whitchit market in 1982. My company's sales of whitchits has increased by an average of 4% per year since then. Since there is, and has been, only one other company which sells whitchits, my company is currently the major competitor in the whitchit market.

Sue: Your company is no longer the major competitor in the whitchit market. Your company currently has only 48% of the market, compared to my company's 52%.

Assuming all statistics quoted in the passage to be true, which of the following must necessarily be true?

(A)   Overall sales of whitchits has increased since 1982.

(B)   Sue's company has increased its sales by an average of 4% per year since 1982.

(C)   If overall sales by Sue's company declines, overall sales by Barry's company will increase.

(D)   A third company has started selling witchits.

(E)   Sue is twisting the statistics to make her company look better.

7.   Nobody complains that it is morally wrong for time and weather to cause houses and cars to deteriorate. However, let someone put a dent in another's car or cause damage to another's house, and everyone says that the perpetrator has done an injustice. This shows just how arbitrary we all are in making moral judgments.

Someone criticizing the conclusion in the passage above would most likely point out that

(A)   morality is always arbitrary, since it depends on arbitrary societal standards.

(B)   the discrepancy is a result of ambiguity in the term 'damage.'

(C)   weather does not dent cars.

(D)   many people make arbitrary decisions.

(E)   nature is unable to make choices about its actions, while people can.

8.   Regardless of what Jim says, baseball is a more refined sport than ice hockey. This is so because more refined people watch baseball rather than ice hockey. You can tell which people are more refined simply by the fact that they prefer the more refined sport to the less refined one.

A logical criticism of the argument above would emphasize that it

(A)   establishes a general rule on the basis of one experience.

(B)   appeals to questionable authority.

(C)   engages in circular reasoning.

(D)   attacks a speaker's reputation, rather than addressing his argument.

(E)   fails to give exceptions to a general rule.

9.   At a district managers' meeting the speaker said: We have instituted a no-smoking policy at our plant to discourage workers from taking breaks. Before the policy went into effect, workers took an average of 1.9 breaks per day. Now that average is down to 1.3.

Which of the following may be inferred from the passage about the way that a worker's wages are determined?

(A)   Workers are paid a fixed hourly rate.

(B)   Workers are paid according to seniority.

(C)   Workers are paid for each unit produced.

(D)   Workers are paid on the basis of overall plant production.

(E)   Workers are paid for time spent in actual production.

10.   Coach: Angie, you are failing to improve at volleyball because you are not practicing your spiking technique.

Angie: Coach, I spend more hours per day at practice than anyone on the team. Last night I was still at practice while everyone else showered.

The major flaw in Angie's response is that she

(A)   misunderstands the word 'practice.'

(B)   avoids the problem by referring to practicing in general, rather than practicing the specific technique.

(C)   disputes the coach's claim by stressing that her spiking technique is fine.

(D)   avoids the problem by stressing what she does best.

(E)   assumes that the coach is overly critical of her.

LOGICAL REASONING REVIEW

ANSWER KEY

Drill: Logical Reasoning

1.	(E)		6.	(A)
2.	(D)		7.	(E)
3.	(E)		8.	(C)
4.	(B)		9.	(A)
5.	(C)		10.	(B)

DETAILED EXPLANATIONS
OF ANSWERS

Drill: Logical Reasoning

1. **(E)**   Answer (A) is a generalized statement that tells us nothing about any misuse of statistics in this particular study. Answer (B) would strengthen the study, since it would control for one variable, genetic background. In other words, if all members of one group were from the same genetic background and all members of the other group were from another background, it could be true that differences in genetic background account for the differences in metabolic rate, and exercise had little or no effect on metabolic rate. Answer (C) would strengthen the results of the study. By choosing participants at random, we help ensure that they are representative of the general population. Answer (D) is the most attractive alternative to (E). However, some variation would not affect the value of the study. No generalization from a study such as this need be true in every case to be valid. Answer (E) is the best. Failure to control variables is one of the major problems in studies such as this. By not controlling for variables such as diet and age the study might have overlooked alternative explanations for differences in metabolic rates.

2. **(D)**   Answer (A) fails because the passage itself implies that some patients do not chew gum. The conclusion is that Doubledent is preferred by dentists for patients who DO chew gum. Answer (B) is certainly an objection to the conclusion in the passage, but not the strongest one. The dentists are not said to recommend that everyone chew gum, only that those who already chew gum should use a certain brand. The implication is that if the patient must chew gum, he or she should chew the brand least likely to do damage. By saying that "more dentists recommend Doubledent," the passage implies that not all do. Answer (C), then, tells us nothing that is not apparent in the passage. Answer (D) is the best answer. By saying "more dentists recommend Doubledent gum . . ." the ad tells us very little. The statement could mean that more recommend it now than before, although the number may have only gone from a single dentist recommending it to two. The statement could mean that more recommend it than another brand, although it is still next to the last in number of recommendations. Since ascertaining the exact meaning is impossible, the phrase is too ambiguous to be useful in forming conclusions. Answer (E) is probably not a true statement. If dentists are not qualified to make judgments about which gum is best for their patients, who is?

3. **(E)**   This is an example of categorical reasoning, for which you can use a Venn diagram. Draw one circle for Vietnam veterans. Label it VV and put in it 35+. Draw another circle which partially overlaps VV. Label it SB and put in it

50-. In the section of the two circles which overlaps, put 35+ and 50-. Now test statements I–III against the diagram. I. cannot be true, since the only thing we know about all members of SB is that they are under 50 (50-). Some may be under 35. II. is true, since the overlapping part of VV and SB are 35 or older (35+) and under 50 (50-). III. is true, since some Vietnam veterans are on the school board (the overlapping part of the circles), and they are 35 or older. The answer, then, is (E).

4. **(B)** The author does not blame the perpetrator (the criminal), the victim (the one who suffers from the act), or the police (those responsible for stopping the perpetrator). Instead, he blames the public for apathetically refusing to get involved. Answer (A) is incorrect because the physician is analogous to the police. Answer (B) is the best because it blames public apathy, not the one immediately responsible for the act. Answer (C) is incorrect because it blames those immediately responsible, whereas the author of the passage does not. Answer (D) is incorrect because the foremen, who are analogous to the police in the passage, are blamed. Answer (E) is incorrect because companies would be analogous to the criminals in the passage.

5. **(C)** While the passage gives some support for both (A) and (B), neither is the main point. If the author wished to make either point, there would be no need for a discussion of countries with low growth rates. Answer (C) is the best. It takes into account the discussion of countries with high and low growth rates and countries which are developed and developing. The main point of the passage is that both developed and developing countries may have either high or low growth rates. There is no way, based on the variables 'developing or developed,' to predict which countries will have high and which will have low growth rates. Answer (D) fails because the passage says nothing about which factors might be helpful in making such a prediction. Answer (E) fails because the passage does not consider and dismiss other factors which might aid such a prediction.

6. **(A)** Statement (A) must be true. The only companies selling whitchits are Barry's and Sue's. If Barry's company has sold more whitchits each year since 1982, but has lost market share, the total amount of whitchits sold must have increased since 1982. Statement (B) must not be true. If Barry's company had the largest market share in 1982, and has increased its sales by 4% per year since then, it follows that Sue's company would have had to increase its sales by more than an average of 4% per year since 1982. If Sue's company had not increased its sales by more than an average of 4% per year, her company could not have overtaken and passed Barry's company as the leader in whitchit sales. An average of 4% is not enough. Statement (C) need not be true. A 10% decline in sales by Sue's company might correspond to a 10% decline in total sales of whitchits. Sales by Barry's company might remain exactly the same even if sales by Sue's company decline. Statement (D) is false because it is

stated that only two companies are in this market. Sue is not necessarily twisting statistics, so (E) is not necessarily true.

7. **(E)** The clear difference between weather and human action is (E), that humans can make choices about what they do, whereas nature cannot. For that reason, we hold humans but not nature responsible for actions. Answer (A) does not get to the root of the problem, which is that where there is no choice, no moral judgment can be made. Answer (B) is incorrect because the meaning of 'damage' is clear enough for the purposes of the passage. Answer (C) is incorrect, since denting a car is only one type of damage the author could have mentioned as an example. Answer (D) fails for the same reason as (A), that weather cannot be measured by moral standards.

8. **(C)** The problem with the passage is that it presupposes what it is trying to prove, namely that baseball is more refined than ice hockey. We know baseball is more refined based on the premise that people who watch it are more refined. But we know they are more refined because they watch it. So we have this problem: our premise, that more refined people watch baseball, depends on our conclusion, that baseball is more refined. The truth of our premise depends on the truth of our conclusion. Answer (A) is out, since no particular experience is cited from which a general rule is drawn. There is no appeal to authority, (B). Answer (D) receives some scant support from the reference to Jim, but Jim's reputation is not attacked. (E) is incorrect.

9. **(A)** The speaker says that the ban on smoking was meant to discourage breaks. Therefore, breaks must cost the plant money. The most obvious way for this to be true is if the worker is paid by the hour, (A). Then, if a worker was on a break, he or she would still be getting paid, even though not producing. This would cost the plant money. Seniority, (B), is incorrect. If the workers were paid for each unit produced, (C), they would not be getting paid for time spent on breaks. If they were paid on overall plant production, (D), breaks would not necessarily cost the plant money. If they were paid only for time spent in production, (E), breaks would not necessarily cost the plant money.

10. **(B)** There is no reason to believe that (A) Angie does not understand the word 'practice.' She does (B) avoid the problem by referring to practice in general, rather than practicing the specific technique. She does not (C) dispute the coach's claim about her technique, only that she does not practice enough in general. She does not (D) stress what she does best. Nor does she necessarily assume that the coach is overly critical of her, only that he is mistaken this time.

ANALYTICAL REASONING REVIEW

The Analytical Reasoning Section of the LSAT is designed to test your Deductive Reasoning Skills. Such skills, briefly put, enable you to examine evidence provided by an author and arrive at conclusions that follow from such evidence. Deductive reasoning, if it is done correctly and if the evidence given is true, leads you to conclusions that are true and follow with certainty from the evidence. What significance does this have in how you approach this section of the LSAT? You will be given evidence, often in the form of statements of conditions, that you are to take as true, and you will have to determine what conclusions follow with certainty from that evidence or what conclusions are possible. You can think of the evidence or statements of conditions as **clues**, and you must determine the necessary or possible conclusions from those clues.

Below is a very simple example of a deductive reasoning problem:

Betty, Eva, and Maria were planning on going to a party together. However, the day before the party, two of the women had an argument, such that the following conditions resulted:

CLUE #1: If Betty went, then Maria did not go.

CLUE #2: Eva went only if Betty went.

CLUE #3: If Maria went, then either Betty or Eva did not go.

CLUE #4: Maria went to the party.

QUESTION

How many of these young women went to the party?

(A) All three of them

(B) Two of them

(C) One of them

Note what occurs in this example. You are given a set of conditions (clues) that you are to take as true, and from those conditions (clues) you are to identify the conclusion that follows from them. The question that you must ask yourself is "Which of the three choices follows with necessity from the conditions (clues) given?" And that is the question that you

will have to ask yourself throughout this section of the LSAT. But now for the solution to this example.

SOLUTION

Clue #4 told us that Maria went to the party. Since Clue #1 told us that if Betty went to the party, then Maria would *not* go, we know immediately that Betty did not go since Maria went. So Betty did not go to the party. And since Betty did not go to the party, we also know that Eva did not go, since Clue #2 told us that Eva would go only if Betty went. As you can see, these conclusions follow with certainty from the conditions given. And so you can conclude that only one of the women went to the party, and that was Maria. The correct answer is (C).

Note that in solving this problem it was not necessary to use Clue #3. Also note that to solve this problem you had to read the conditions/clues carefully in order to determine what conclusions followed from the conditions.

DEDUCTIVE REASONING SKILLS

In solving any problem it is important that you examine evidence carefully and then be able to see what conclusions follow from that evidence. This is especially important in the legal field, where evidence is the basis of legal cases. As was stated earlier, when you examine evidence and determine what conclusions follow with certainty, then you are reasoning deductively.

Deductive reasoning skills are not something foreign to you. Everyone has them, although they are not developed in all to the same degree. Even infants and toddlers have such skills. For example, the infant who knows when his parents are home, and knows that by crying he will get one of them to hold him, is using deductive reasoning skills. And the toddler who touches a hot stove, pulls back immediately, and does not touch the stove again is also using such skills. You use them as well every day of your life. Just think of the last time it was raining as you were getting dressed to go to school. Did you take an umbrella? Did you wear a raincoat or other type of protective clothing? If so, you were probably reasoning in the following way:

It's raining, and I will get wet if I don't take an umbrella or wear a raincoat. I don't want to get wet, so I'll take an umbrella or wear a raincoat.

Such reasoning, as with the infant and toddler examples, is deductive reasoning. You then, already have such skills. What is being tested on the LSAT, then, is not whether or not you have such skills, but the degree to which they are developed in you.

THE DIRECTIONS

You should study and learn the directions to the Analytical Reasoning Section before taking the actual LSAT. Doing so will help you to save valuable testing time, since you will need only to skim the directions on the day of the exam. The official directions for the LSAT Analytical Reasoning Section are provided here for you to review.

DIRECTIONS: Each group of questions in this section is based on a set of conditions. In answering some of the questions, it may be useful to draw a rough diagram. Choose the response that most accurately and completely answers each question and blacken the corresponding space on your answer sheet.

Below are tips on following directions.

➤ Tip 1 | As you can see, you are asked to choose the response **that most accurately and completely answers each question.** Although other answers may seem to be correct, only one is the best answer so make sure to work through the problem carefully.

➤ Tip 2 | You are also instructed that drawing diagrams may be useful, so use them whenever possible.

THE QUESTIONS

To really understand what is expected of you in the Analytical Reasoning Section of the LSAT, it is important that you go over complete examples of each type of problem and see the Model of Reasoning used to solve that problem. In what follows you will find:

1. an example of each type of problem.

2. a step-by-step explanation/method of how to approach and

solve each type of problem. We can also call this the Model of Reasoning used to solve the problem.

3. strategies you can use to solve each type of problem.

4. the solution.

Note that on the actual LSAT, you will be given between four and six questions based on the same passage and conditions; however, in the examples that follow, only one question will be presented and discussed per passage.

There are six basic types of deductive reasoning questions that often appear on the LSAT. Each type is distinguished by the type of relationship expressed in the evidence or the conditions given to you:

1. Attribute Assignment Questions

2. Conditional Relationship Questions

3. Familial Relationship Questions

4. Ordering Relationship Questions

5. Spatial Relationship Questions

6. Time Assignment Relationship Questions

QUESTION TYPE 1: Attribute Assignment Questions

Again, in this type of question you will be given a group of people or objects, a list of attributes and a set of conditions, and you will have to determine who or what has what attribute. The following is an example of such a question. Read through the passage and conditions below and think about what method you could use to approach this problem, and then try to answer the question that follows using that method.

PASSAGE

Albert, Bob, Charlie, Dirk, Edgar, and Frank are going to a play-off game in a distant city and have rented an eight-passenger van (two seats in the first row and three seats each in the second and third rows) for the trip. One of the men always wears a red hat, another is nearsighted, one dislikes Frank, one wears a toupee, one is Charlie's son, and one is diabetic.

Let us call the men A, B, C, D, E, and F, and let us call the attributes r, n, f, t, c, and d, in order to make it quicker and easier to solve the problems.

CONDITIONS/CLUES

1.   The man who is wearing the toupee is the driver, and he is sitting next to Frank, who is sitting directly in front of Charlie's son.

2.   Edgar is sitting next to the man who always wears a red hat.

3.   Albert is sitting in the center seat of the second row.

4.   The man who dislikes Frank is the only person sitting in the last row of the seats in the van.

5.   The man who is nearsighted is seated directly behind Dirk. Edgar is seated to Albert's right.

QUESTION

1.   The person who always wears a red hat is

(A)   Albert.   (D)   Dirk.

(B)   Bob.   (E)   Edgar.

(C)   Charlie.   (F)   Frank.

The first step you should take in answering any question on the LSAT is to **read the question carefully** and **determine what type of relationship(s) is/are expressed in both the passage and the list of conditions**. In this passage you are given a list of names, in this case men who are going to a play-off game, and a list of characteristics. In the conditions, you are given clues as to who has what characteristic. And the question asks you to determine who it is that has a specific characteristic, in this case, who always wears the red hat. This, then, is an Attribute Assignment Question.

When you come across such a question, the next step you can take is to use a chart, diagram, or both to keep track of the conditions, and

although you don't have to do this, the chart/diagram method has saved time for many students. Because some of the conditions in this problem refer to the seating arrangement in the van, this question could also be considered a spatial relationship problem. It is often the case with Analytical Reasoning Questions that you will find the different types of questions mixed in one problem. We will use both a chart to keep track of the attributes and a diagram to record their seating arrangement. You know that there are six men and six characteristics. One possible chart is the following:

	r	n	f	t	c	d
A						
B						
C						
D						
E						
F						

Remember:

A = Albert	r = red hat
B = Bob	n = nearsighted
C = Charlie	f = dislikes Frank
D = Dirk	t = toupee
E = Edgar	c = Charlie's son
F = Frank	d = diabetic

You should fill in the spaces with "X"s or "O"s, based on the information given in the condition statements—X means "is not," and O means "is." You know that they are going in an eight–passenger van. Reading through each condition/clue, we can construct a diagram of the seating arrangement in the van in the following way:

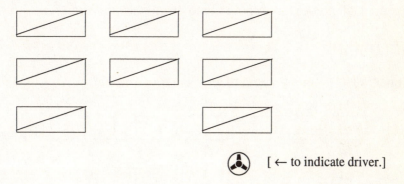

[← to indicate driver.]

Since you will be inserting two pieces of information—the person's name and his attribute—the squares are split in half to make it easier to see what information you still need.

CONDITION/CLUE #1

The man who is wearing the toupee is the driver, and he is sitting next to Frank, who is sitting directly in front of Charlie's son.

Now you should ask yourself what conclusions follow from this condition/clue, and you can use the chart and diagram to keep track of these conclusions.

CONCLUSIONS

1. Frank is NOT the man wearing the toupee, since he is sitting next to the man who is wearing it (the driver).

2. Frank is NOT Charlie's son, since Frank is sitting directly in front of Charlie's son.

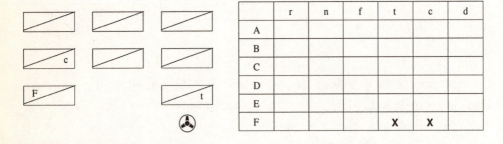

	r	n	f	t	c	d
A						
B						
C						
D						
E						
F				X	X	

CONDITION/CLUE #2

Edgar is sitting next to the man who always wears a red hat.

CONCLUSION

Edgar is NOT the man who always wears a red hat.

	r	n	f	t	c	d
A						
B						
C						
D						
E	X					
F				X	X	

CONDITION/CLUE #3

Albert is sitting in the center seat of the second row.

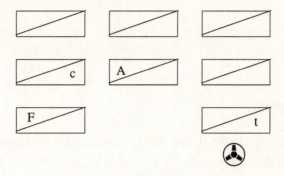

By looking at the above diagram, we can draw the following conclusions:

1. Albert is NOT Charlie's son, since he is not sitting directly behind Frank.

2. Albert is NOT wearing the toupee, since he is not in the driver's seat.

We now show this on the chart:

	r	n	f	t	c	d
A				**X**	**X**	
B						
C						
D						
E	**X**					
F				**X**	**X**	

CONDITION/CLUE #4

The person who dislikes Frank is the only person sitting in the last row of seats in the van.

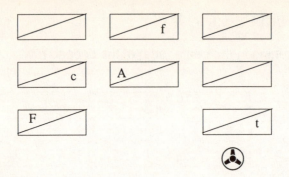

CONCLUSIONS

1. Frank is NOT the person who dislikes Frank, since he is sitting up front.

2. Albert does NOT dislike Frank since he is not in the last row of seats in the van.

	r	n	f	t	c	d
A			X	X	X	
B						
C						
D						
E	X					
F			X	X	X	

CONDITION/CLUE #5

The man who is nearsighted is seated directly behind Dirk.

CONCLUSIONS

1. Dirk is NOT nearsighted.

2. The person who is nearsighted is NOT sitting in the last row of seats in the van, since Clue #4 told us that the only person seated there was the one who dislikes Frank. From this, and from our diagram:

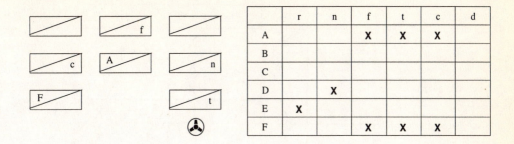

	r	n	f	t	c	d
A			X	X	X	
B						
C						
D		X				
E	X					
F			X	X	X	

it follows that

3. the person who is nearsighted is seated directly behind the driver, and therefore

4. the driver is Dirk, and therefore,

5. Dirk is wearing the toupee.

We can also conclude that neither Albert nor Frank are nearsighted, because of the seating arrangement determined thus far.

	r	n	f	t	c	d
A		X	X	X	X	
B				X		
C				X		
D	X	X	X	O	X	X
E	X			X		
F		X	X	X	X	

CONDITION/CLUE #6

Edgar is seated to Albert's right.

CONCLUSIONS

1. Edgar is Charlie's son.

2. Edgar is NOT nearsighted.

3. Edgar does NOT dislike Frank.

	r	n	f	t	c	d
A		X	X	X	X	
B				X	X	
C				X	X	
D	X	X	X	O	X	X
E	X	X	X	X	O	X
F		X	X	X	X	

Looking at the above chart, we now know that:

1. Albert is NOT Charlie's son.

2. Albert does NOT dislike Frank.

3. Albert is NOT wearing the toupee.

4. Albert is NOT nearsighted.

5. And since Edgar, who is Charlie's son, is seated to Albert's right and next to the man who always wears a red hat, then we can also conclude that Albert is the man who always wears the red hat.

The correct answer, then is (A) Albert. Looking at the finished diagram and chart we can see that:

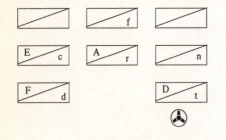

	r	n	f	t	c	d
A	O	X	X	X	X	X
B	X			X	X	X
C	X			X	X	X
D	X	X	X	O	X	X
E	X	X	X	X	O	X
F	X	X	X	X	X	O

1. Frank is the diabetic.

2. Dirk wears the toupee.

3. Edgar is Charlie's son.

4. Either Bob or Charlie (but not both) is nearsighted.

5. Either Bob or Charlie (but not both) dislikes Frank.

Again, this example demonstrates how you will be given conditions/ clues, and from those conditions/clues you will have to determine what conclusions follow from them.

In summary, the method you should follow in approaching Attribute Assignment Questions is the following:

1. Read the passage carefully and determine what relationship is expressed in the passage and conditions. If you have been given an attribute assignment problem,

2. Read through each clue and determine what conclusions follow.

3. You can keep track of the conclusions via either a diagram or a chart or both.

4. Do not impose your own assumptions/beliefs on the conditions/clues, but rather take them as they are given to you. The importance of this will be made clearer when we get to Familial Relationship Questions.

QUESTION TYPE 2: Conditional Relationship Questions

A second type of question that you may find on the LSAT is the Conditional Relationship Question. These require that you are able to identify how certain actions are related to or affect other actions, many times how certain people's actions affect others' actions. The deductive reasoning problem presented earlier about Betty, Eva, and Maria is an example of a Conditional Relationship Question. Another example is the following:

PASSAGE

Curly is a ringmaster of a one-ring circus, and he must decide what acts will perform during this Saturday's matinee. The matinee runs for only one hour, and acts must be scheduled according to how long they take to set up, perform, and take down. He is considering six acts for the matinee: the knife-thrower, the trapeze artists, the clowns, Dynamo the Human Cannonball, the elephants, and finally, Pogo the Dancing Dog.

CONDITIONS/CLUES

1. Either Dynamo the Human Cannonball or the clowns must perform, as both acts draw big crowds and hence big profits.

2. If the knife-thrower performs, then there won't be time for the trapeze artists to perform.

3. If the elephants perform, then the trapeze artists will not be able to perform because of set-up problems.

4. Either the elephants or Pogo the Dancing Dog must perform, since there must be at least one animal act for the children in the audience.

5. If the trapeze artists do not perform, then the clowns will not be able to perform, since the clown act is tied into the trapeze act.

6. As it turns out, Dynamo the Human Cannonball will not perform, as he broke both arms in an automobile accident.

QUESTION

2. Which one of the following statements is true?

    (A) The clowns, the elephants, and the trapeze artists will perform in the Saturday matinee.

    (B) Only the clowns and the trapeze artists will perform in the Saturday matinee.

    (C) Only the elephants and the clowns will perform in Saturday's matinee.

    (D) Only the clowns, the trapeze artists, and Pogo the Dancing Dog will perform in Saturday's matinee.

    (E) Only Pogo the Dancing Dog and the knife-thrower will perform in Saturday's matinee.

After you have read through the passage and the conditions/clues and have determined that you are being presented with a Conditional Relationship Question, that is, a question where you are asked to determine

how certain actions will affect other actions, the next step is to determine if any of the conditions/clues or conclusions that follow from the conditions/clues have any terms in common. What are terms? They are words or groups of words that express a meaning. For example, in the above set of conditions, condition #1 has a term in common with condition #6, and that term is 'Dynamo the Human Cannonball.' Grouping these two conditions together we get:

1.   Either Dynamo the Human Cannonball or the clowns must perform.

6.   As it turns out, Dynamo the Human Cannonball can't perform . . .

Now ask yourself what conclusion follows from these two conditions/clues. Note that in this type of question we do not go through each condition separately and determine what conclusions follow, as we do with some other types of questions; rather we ask what conclusions follow from pairs or groups of conditions. In this case the conclusion that follows is:

CONCLUSION #1

The clowns must perform.

How do we know this? Well, if either Dynamo or the clowns MUST perform, and since Dynamo will not perform, we know that the clowns must perform. Next we can pair conclusion #1 with condition #5, as they have the term 'clowns' in common:

5.   If the trapeze artists do not perform, then the clowns will not be able to perform, since the clown act is tied into the trapeze act.

Conclusion: The clowns must perform.

What follows from this pair?

CONCLUSION #2

It follows that the trapeze artists will perform.

Note that if one of these acts performs, the other must perform as well, since the acts are tied together. Now we can group conclusion #2 with conditions #2 and #3, which all have the term 'trapeze artists' in common:

2. If the knife-thrower performs, then there won't be time for the trapeze artists to perform.

3. If the elephants perform, then the trapeze artists will not be able to perform because of set-up problems.

Conclusion: The trapeze artists will perform.

Since we know that the trapeze artists WILL perform, and because of time limitations in condition #2 and set-up problems in condition #3, we can conclude:

CONCLUSION #3

The knife-thrower will not perform.

CONCLUSION #4

The elephants will not perform.

The only condition that has not been examined is condition #4. Note that both it and conclusion #4 have the term 'elephants' in common:

4. Either the elephants or Pogo the Dancing Dog must perform . . .

Conclusion: The elephants will not perform.

From this pair we can conclude that:

CONCLUSION #5

Pogo the Dancing Dog must perform, since at least one animal act is needed to satisfy the children in the audience.

From the above, then, we know that the clowns, the trapeze artists, and Pogo the Dancing Dog will perform, and that the knife-thrower, the elephants, and Dynamo the Human Cannonball will not. The correct an-

swer to the question is (D): Only the clowns, the trapeze artists, and Pogo the Dancing Dog will perform in Saturday's matinee.

In sum, in approaching Conditional Relationship Questions:

1. Carefully read through the passage and the conditions/clues.

2. Note what conditions/clues have terms in common, and group those that have terms in common together.

3. Ask yourself what conclusions follow from those pairs/ groups?

4. Note if any conclusions you arrive at have any terms in common with any of the conditions/clues. If so, group those together as well and determine what further conclusions follow.

5. Be sure to work with what you are given. Do not impose your own assumptions or beliefs on any of the conditions/ clues.

6. Note that in this type of problem, it is not necessary to draw a diagram or a chart.

☞ SHORTCUT

Once you have become proficient at using the methods of solving the Conditional Relationship type of Analytical Reasoning Problems, you may find using symbolic notation is helpful as a way to speed up your work.

Symbolic Notation is simply putting the words of the problem into shorthand which is easier and quicker to understand. Also, the actual process of "translating" problems into symbolic notation will help you comprehend more clearly the methods you are using to solve the problems.

This is an alternative means to solving the problem—if you find symbolic notation too difficult and confusing, it will probably hinder you more than help you, so don't even worry about it. It is not necessary to use symbolic notation to solve Analytical Reasoning Problems; however, it may help you solve them faster, if you already have a good grasp on the methods described in the Review Section.

The symbols you will use are as follows:

& (ampersand) = "AND"

V = "OR"

~ (tilde) = "NOT"

→ = "IMPLIES," or "IF, THEN"

You will also use the letters of the alphabet to stand for anything you want. For instance:

LET

A   = Alan brings the flowers to Margo's wedding.

B   = Bernice brings the flowers.

A & B   = Alan AND Bernice bring flowers.

A V B   = Alan OR Bernice bring flowers.

A → ~B = IF Alan brings flowers, THEN Bernice will NOT bring flowers.

Let's take one of the sample problems from the review:

Betty, Eva, and Maria were planning on going to a party together. However, the day before the party, two of the women had an argument, such that the following conditions resulted:
1.   If Betty went, then Maria did not go.
2.   Eva went only if Betty went.
3.   If Maria went, then either Betty or Eva did not go.
4.   Maria went to the party.

First, we need to figure out our key:

LET

B = Betty went to the party.

E = Eva went to the party.

M = Maria went to the party.

Now, let's translate the conditions using our symbols:

1. B ➜ ~ M

2. B ➜ E

3. M ➜ (~B V ~E)

4. M

Condition/Clue #4 gives us the information we need to uncover who actually went to the party. Since we know that M is true (Maria went to the party), we use this information to change Condition/Clue #1,

B ➜ ~M

which also means

M ➜ ~B

since saying "If Betty went to the party, then Maria did not go" is the same as saying "If Maria went to the party, then Betty did not go." Therefore, since we know that M is true, we also know that B is NOT true, that Betty did NOT go to the party.

What about Eva? Well, condition #2,

B ➜ E

can also be said as

~B ➜ ~E

since Eva would not go without Betty. Since we know that ~B is true, we now know that ~E is also true, so Eva did not go either.

To solve the circus problem, you may use symbolic notation as well. Here are the conditions translated into symbols:

K	= Knife-thrower performs.	T	= Trapeze artists perform.
C	= Clowns perform.	D	= Dynamo performs.
E	= Elephants perform.	P	= Pogo performs.

1. DVC

2. K → ~T

3. E → ~T

4. E V P

5. ~T → ~C

6. ~D

Again, we begin with the last statement and apply it to the others. Because condition #1 states

D V C,

and we know that ~D is true, then C must be true. Next, we have to skip to a condition that includes C or D, which brings us to condition #5, which we will restate to fit the conclusions we have already drawn:

C → T

Therefore, T must be true. We return to condition #2, which can be stated as

T → ~K.

This tells us that K is NOT true, since T is true. From condition #3, we learn that E is NOT true, using the same reasoning. Finally, since condition #4 states that either E or P must be true, and we already know that E is NOT true, P is true.

So C (the clowns), T (the trapeze artists) and P (Pogo) are all performing in the show.

Try using symbolic notation to help you solve your Conditional Relationship Questions faster. If it does not help you, or if you have trouble understanding it, don't worry, it is not necessary to use symbolic notation to solve these problems, rather it is a shortcut for those who already understand the reasoning behind the solution methods.

QUESTION TYPE 3: Familial Relationship Questions

In Familial Relationship Questions you will be given certain conditions concerning family members, and based on those conditions you will have to determine the relationships between those family members. The simplest way to approach such questions is to construct a chart or family tree that accurately reflects the relationships expressed in the conditions. Following is a Familial Relationship Question. Carefully read through the passage, the conditions/clues, and the question.

PASSAGE

Mary and John Smith, following an old Sicilian tradition, named their six children in the following way:

CONDITIONS/CLUES

1. Their first child, a son, was named after the child's paternal grandfather. If their first child had been a daughter, she would have been named after her paternal grandmother.

2. Their second child, another son, was named after the child's maternal grandfather. If their second child had been a daughter, she would have been named after her maternal grandmother.

3. Their third child, a daughter, was named after one of the child's paternal aunts. If the child had been a son, he would have been named after one of his paternal uncles.

4. Their fourth child, a son, was named after one of the child's maternal uncles. Had this child been a daughter, she would have been named after one of her maternal aunts.

5. Their fifth child, another daughter, was named after one of the child's paternal aunts.

6. Their final child, a son, was named after one of the child's maternal uncles.

Mary and John Smith's children, from oldest to youngest, are Vincenzio, Vito, Michelle, Joseph, Catharine, and Anthony.

Note: Children of siblings may have the same first name.

The tradition results in many people in the extended family having the same first names.

Mary Smith has only two siblings.

John Smith has five siblings: two sisters and three brothers.

Their third child, Michelle, is married to a man who has two sisters.

QUESTION

3.   If Mary and John Smith's daughter Michelle has four children, all daughters, what will her youngest daughter's name be if she follows this old Sicilian tradition?

(A)   Michelle   (D)   Mary Jo

(B)   Mary   (E)   Antonia

(C)   Catharine

As stated earlier, the easiest way to approach this type of problem is to construct a diagram or family tree which accurately depicts the relationships expressed in the conditions. Reading through the passage and conditions, we can conclude:

1.   John's father was named Vincenzio, since John and Mary's first son was named Vincenzio. This is in accord with condition #1.

2.   Mary's father was named Vito, since Mary and John's second child, a son, was named Vito. This is in accord with the second condition.

3.   John's two sisters are named Catharine and Michelle, since John and Mary's third and fifth children, daughters, were named Michelle and Catharine, respectively. This is in accord with conditions #3 and #5.

Finally, we can conclude

4.   Mary has two brothers, her only two siblings, and their names are Joseph and Anthony, respectively. This follows from conditions #4 and #6.

From these conclusions and what we have been given about John and Mary's children, we can construct the following diagram:

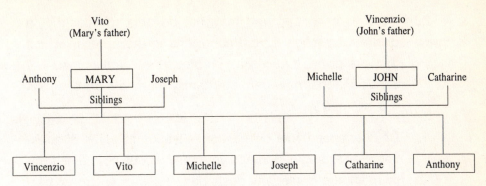

Looking at the diagram and the conditions, we can now answer the question. If Mary and John's daughter Michelle has four children we can conclude:

1. It is not possible to determine the name of her first daughter, as the child must be named after the child's paternal grandmother (condition #1), and we have not been given this piece of information about Michelle's husband's family.

2. Michelle's second daughter, following condition #2, will be named Mary, after the child's maternal grandmother.

3. It is not possible to determine her third daughter's name, because again, we have not been given the names of Michelle's husband's sisters.

However, we can determine Michelle's fourth daughter's name. The fourth condition tells us that the fourth child is to be named after one of the child's maternal aunts, that is, after one of the child's mother's sisters. Since Michelle has only one sister, Catharine, her fourth daughter will be named Catharine. The correct answer to the question, then, is (C) Catharine.

In sum, in answering Familial Relationship Questions:

1. Carefully read through the passage and conditions. After you have determined that you have been given a Familial Relationship Question,

2. Construct a diagram or family tree. Do this by first reading through a condition, and then doing that part of the diagram.

3. Keep in mind that you may not be able to construct a diagram by following the conditions in the order in which they are given. If necessary, regroup the conditions so that conditions that have terms or family members in common are grouped together.

4. Do not impose your own assumptions on this type of question. For example, perhaps your family does not name family members in the way described in this problem. Or perhaps you do not define 'second cousins' in the way that it may be defined in a question you may encounter on the LSAT. Do not argue with the conditions given to you. Rather take them as true and determine what conclusions follow from them.

QUESTION TYPE 4: Ordering Relationship Questions

Ordering Relationship Questions require that you determine the temporal order of events. Below is an example of such a question. Read through the passage, the conditions/clues, and the question. Then think about how you might go about solving this problem — that is, what method would you use? Next, think about why you chose that method. Try to solve this problem using your method, and then look at the solution below, which suggests two methods that can be used in approaching this type of problem.

PASSAGE

It's Herbert's birthday, and six of his closest friends have been invited to his surprise birthday party: Adam, Ben, Carol, Dora, Edwin, and Fred.

Note: No one arrives at the same time, and "before" and "after" do not imply "immediately before" and "immediately after."

CONDITIONS/CLUES

1. Edwin arrives before Fred.
2. Dora arrives before Ben, but not before Carol.
3. Edwin arrives after Ben and after Carol.
4. Adam arrives before Ben.

QUESTION

4.   Which of the following is one possible order of their arrival?

   I.   Carol, Adam, Dora, Ben, Edwin, and Fred

   II.   Carol, Dora, Adam, Ben, Edwin, and Fred

   III. Adam, Carol, Dora, Ben, Edwin, and Fred

   (A) I only   (D) II and III only

   (B) II only   (E) I, II, and III

   (C) I and II only

   As you should do with all of the Analytical Reasoning Questions on the LSAT, first read through the passage and conditions and determine what type of relationship is being expressed. In this case you are asked to consider how Adam, Ben, Carol, Dora, Edwin, and Fred are related to each other regarding the order of their arrival at Herbert's birthday party. After you determine that the relationship being expressed is one of temporal ordering, then go on to the first question and determine if a chart or diagram is necessary to answer the question. In this case, a chart/diagram is not necessary. Note that the question asks you to determine possible orders of their arrival, and you are given three choices. The simplest way to approach this question, and the first method that we will use to solve this problem, is to read through each of the choices and see if it satisfies each of the conditions. If so, then it is a possible order of their arrival.

   The three possible orders you are given are:

   I.   Carol, Adam, Dora, Ben, Edwin, and Fred

   II.   Carol, Dora, Adam, Ben, Edwin, and Fred

   III. Adam, Carol, Dora, Ben, Edwin, and Fred

   Which of these orders satisfies the required conditions?

   The first condition states that Edwin arrives before Fred. As you can see, all three orders satisfy this condition.

   The second condition states that Dora arrives before Ben, but not before Carol. Again, all three choices satisfy this condition.

The third condition states that Edwin arrives after Ben and after Carol. All three choices also satisfy this condition.

Finally, the fourth condition states that Adam arrives before Ben. This condition is also satisfied in each of the three orders given.

Since all four conditions are satisfied in each of the three choices, the correct answer is (E) I, II, and III.

This Ordering Relationship Question was fairly simple. In this case, you did not have to go through each condition and determine what conclusions follow. However, you could have solved the problem by doing just that, and you may have to determine what conclusions follow on the actual LSAT if you are given an Ordering Relationship Question. Therefore, for practice and again to see this model of reasoning in action, we will solve this problem using a second method, and that is to read through each condition/clue carefully and determine what conclusions follow, and to keep track of those conclusions on a chart.

CONDITION/CLUE #1

Edwin arrives before Fred.

CONCLUSIONS

1. Fred does not arrive first.

2. Edwin does not arrive last.

These conclusions can be indicated on the chart, with 'X' meaning 'no' and 'O' meaning 'yes.'

	First	Second	Third	Fourth	Fifth	Sixth
Adam						
Ben						
Carol						
Dora						
Edwin						X
Fred	X					

CONDITION/CLUE #2

Dora arrives before Ben, but not before Carol.

CONCLUSIONS

1. Ben does not arrive first.

2. Dora does not arrive first.

3. Dora does not arrive last.

4. Carol does not arrive last.

As indicated on the chart:

	First	Second	Third	Fourth	Fifth	Sixth
Adam						
Ben	X					
Carol						X
Dora	X					X
Edwin						X
Fred	X					

CONDITION/CLUE #3

Edwin arrives after Ben and after Carol.

CONCLUSIONS

1. Edwin does not arrive first.

2. Edwin does not arrive second, since he must arrive after Ben, and from condition #2, we know that Ben does not arrive first.

3. Ben does not arrive last.

4. Carol does not arrive last.

As indicated on the chart:

	First	Second	Third	Fourth	Fifth	Sixth
Adam						
Ben	X					X
Carol						X
Dora	X					X
Edwin	X	X				X
Fred	X					

CONDITION/CLUE #4

Adam arrives before Ben.

CONCLUSIONS

1. Ben does not arrive first (this is also derived from condition #2)

2. Adam does not arrive last.

	First	Second	Third	Fourth	Fifth	Sixth
Adam						X
Ben	X					X
Carol						X
Dora	X					X
Edwin	X	X				X
Fred	X					

Looking at the above chart, we can immediately see that:

1. Fred arrives last, and

2. Either Adam or Carol must arrive first.

Going back over the conditions and conclusions, and grouping those that concern Edwin together, we know that Edwin arrives before Fred, after Ben, and after Carol (conditions 1 and 3), and since both Dora and Adam arrive before Ben (conditions 2 and 4), we also know that Edwin arrives after Dora and after Adam.

Since Edwin arrives after Ben, after Dora, after Carol, and after Adam, we know that Edwin must be the fifth person to arrive at the party. This can be indicated on the chart:

	First	Second	Third	Fourth	Fifth	Sixth
Adam				X	X	X
Ben	X					X
Carol			X	X	X	X
Dora	X					X
Edwin	X	X	X	X	O	X
Fred	X	X	X	X	X	O

And since both Adam and Dora arrive before Ben, and since Dora arrives after Carol, we can also conclude that Carol arrives before Ben, that is, Ben arrives after Adam, Carol, and Dora. Thus, Ben must be the fourth person to arrive.

	First	Second	Third	Fourth	Fifth	Sixth
Adam				X	X	X
Ben	X	X	X	O	X	X
Carol			X	X	X	X
Dora	X			X	X	X
Edwin	X	X	X	X	O	X
Fred	X	X	X	X	X	O

Combining these conclusions with the fact that either Adam or Carol must arrive first, we arrive at the three possible orders given to us in the question. However, by following this model of reasoning, we also know why Ben, Edwin, and Fred must arrive fourth, fifth, and sixth respectively, and why Carol or Adam must arrive first.

Ordering Relationship Questions that appear on the LSAT may require that you employ this more complex method. Note that this method required deductive reasoning. But again, depending on the question, the first and simpler method presented may suffice.

In sum, in approaching Ordering Relationship Questions:

1. Read the passage and conditions carefully and determine what relationship is expressed. If you have been given an Ordering Relationship Question,

2. Look at the questions and determine if it is necessary to go through each condition and determine what conclusions follow. If it is necessary

3. Keep track of those conclusions via a chart or diagram. If it is not necessary,

4. Read through the choices that you are given in the questions, and determine which of the choices satisfies all of the given conditions.

5. Again, do not impose your own assumptions/beliefs on the conditions/clues, but rather take them as they are given to you.

QUESTION TYPE 5: Spatial Relationship Questions

In Spatial Relationship Questions, you will have to determine how objects are spatially related. The following is an example of such a question. Carefully read through the passage, the conditions/clues, and the questions.

PASSAGE

Irving Park, a midsized city, has recently celebrated the opening of its new subway system. The system has the four following lines or routes:

CONDITIONS/CLUES

1. The Addams Line, which begins at point A, proceeds directly east passing through stops B and C, and ending at stop D.
2. The Green Line, which begins at point G, stops at points E and C, and ends at stop H.
3. The Red Line, which begins at point R, proceeds east and then due north where it stops at points B and E respectively, and ends at stop F.

4. The Irving Line, which begins at point I, proceeds due north with a stop at C, and ends at stop J.

QUESTIONS

5a. Stop D is in what directional location to stop E?

(A) Northeast   (D) Southeast

(B) Southwest   (E) Directly north

(C) West

5b. What stop is closest to stop H?

(A) D

(B) J

(C) A

(D) R

(E) You can't tell based on the information given.

After you have read through the passage and conditions/clues and have determined that you are dealing with a Spatial Relationship Question, the next step you should take is to visualize, on paper, the relationships expressed in the conditions/clues. That is, draw a diagram that expresses the spatial relationship expressed in the conditions/clues.

The first condition concerns the Addams Line. We know that it begins at point A, proceeds directly east passing through stops B and C, and ends at stop D. Visually, this can be depicted as follows:

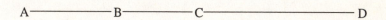

A————————B————————C————————————————D

The second condition tells us that the Green Line begins at point G, stops at points E and C, and ends at point H. We need to skip this condition for now and come back to it, because we don't know where stop E is located. NOTE: **With this type of question, it may not be possible to go through the conditions in the order in which they are given.**

Going to the third condition, we know that the Red Line begins at point R, goes east and then north where it stops at points B and E respectively, and then ends at point F:

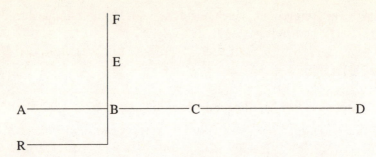

Now that we know that stop E is directly due north of B, we can go back to the second condition. Adding the Green Line to our diagram:

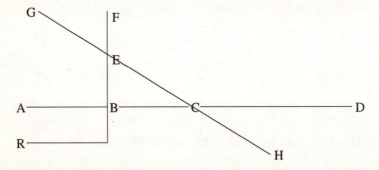

Finally, we go to the fourth condition, which tells us that the Irving Line begins at point I, proceeds due north with a stop at C, and ends at stop J. This results in the finished diagram:

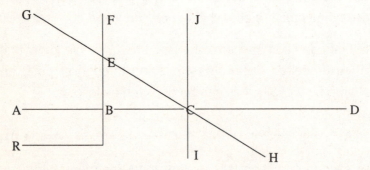

Looking at the diagram, we can easily see that stop D is southeast of stop E. The correct answer, then, is (D) Southeast. Also note that since we were given no measurements regarding distances in this problem, it is not possible to determine which stop is closest to stop H. The correct answer to the second question is (E) You can't tell based on the information given.

In sum, in approaching Spatial Relationship Questions:

1. Read through each condition and do one part of the diagram at a time.

2. Keep in mind that it might not be possible to draw the diagram by going through the conditions in the order in which they are given. It may not be possible, for example, to diagram the relationship expressed in the second condition until you have diagrammed the relationships expressed in a later condition.

3. Again, do not impose your own assumptions or beliefs on the conditions/clues.

QUESTION TYPE 6: Time Assignment Questions

Time Assignment Questions require that you are able to identify relationships regarding date and time blocks. That is, given certain date and/or time blocks, events/people, and conditions linking the two, you must determine who or what goes in each time block. Following is an example of a Time Assignment Question. Carefully read through the passage, the conditions/clues, and the questions.

PASSAGE

A television executive in charge of programming is considering two possible lineups of five new shows for the new season. When the lineups are completed, he will present both to the Vice-President of Programming for approval. However, at present only one lineup is completed; the other is only partially completed. The five new shows that will go into the lineups are the following: a news show, a situation comedy, a detective drama, a musical/variety show, and a nighttime soap.

Each show is an hour long, and the time slots are 6:00, 7:00, 8:00, 9:00, and 10:00.

CONDITIONS/CLUES

1. In both of the lineups, the drama will be shown in the 7:00 time slot.
2. The news show will be on at 10:00 in only one of the lineups.
3. In both of the lineups, the nighttime soap will immediately follow the musical variety show.

Again, one lineup is complete; the other lineup is only partially complete.

QUESTIONS

6a. Which of the following statements about the completed lineup is false?

(A) The situation comedy will be in the 6:00 time block.

(B) The musical variety show will be in the 8:00 time block.

(C) The nighttime soap will be in the 9:00 time block.

(D) The situation comedy will be in the 8:00 time block.

(E) The news show will be in the 10:00 time block.

6b. Which of the following statements about the incomplete lineup is false?

(A) Either the news show or the situation comedy can appear in the 6:00 time block.

(B) Either the musical variety show, the news show or the situation comedy can appear in the 8:00 time block.

(C) Neither the situation comedy nor the news show can appear in the 9:00 time block.

(D) Either the situation comedy or the news show can appear in the 9:00 time block.

(E) The nighttime soap cannot appear in the 8:00 time block.

After reading through the passage and determining that you are being presented with a Time Assignment Question, the next step is to go through each condition and construct a chart—in this case two charts, one for the completed lineup and one for the incomplete lineup—to reflect the relationship expressed in each condition:

	6:00	7:00	8:00	9:00	10:00
Lineup #1					
Lineup #2					

CONDITION/CLUE #1

In both the completed and the incomplete lineups, the drama show will be shown at 7:00:

	6:00	7:00	8:00	9:00	10:00
Lineup #1		drama			
Lineup #2		drama			

CONDITION/CLUE #2

The news show will be on at 10:00 in only one of the lineups:

	6:00	7:00	8:00	9:00	10:00
Lineup #1		drama			news
Lineup #2		drama			

CONDITION/CLUE #3

In both lineups, the nighttime soap will immediately follow the musical variety show. From this condition and from looking at the above chart, we can deduce that since the drama show immediately follows the 6:00 time slot, then

1. Neither the musical variety show nor the nighttime soap can appear in the 6:00 time block in either lineup, and so in the first lineup

2. The musical variety show must appear in the 8:00 time block and the nighttime soap must appear in the 9:00 time block.

	6:00	7:00	8:00	9:00	10:00
Lineup #1	not m.v. not soap	drama	mus. var.	soap	news
Lineup #2	not m.v. not soap	drama			

We can also deduce that:

3. The situation comedy must appear in the 6:00 time block in the first lineup:

	6:00	7:00	8:00	9:00	10:00
Lineup #1	Sit. Com.	drama	mus. var.	soap	news

As you can see from the above chart, the first lineup is the completed lineup. The correct answer to the first question, then, is (D) The situation comedy will be in the 8:00 time block.

However, determining the second lineup (the incomplete lineup) is not as easy. We know from the above that:

1. Neither the musical variety show nor the nighttime soap can appear in the 6:00 time block:

Lineup #2	not m.v. not soap	drama			

We also know from condition #3 that the nighttime soap immediately follows the musical variety show. From this we can conclude:

4. The nighttime soap cannot follow the drama, and therefore cannot appear in the 8:00 time block:

	6:00	7:00	8:00	9:00	10:00
Lineup #2	not m.v. not soap	drama	not soap		

We can also conclude that

5. The musical variety show cannot appear in the 10:00 time block, since the soap must follow it, and the 10:00 time block is the last block.

	6:00	7:00	8:00	9:00	10:00
Lineup #2	not m.v. not soap	drama	not soap		not m.v.

By the process of elimination, or deduction, we can see that:

6. Either the news show or the situation comedy can appear in the 6:00 time block.

7. Either the musical variety show, the news show, or the situation comedy can appear in the 8:00 time block.

8. Neither the situation comedy nor the news show can appear in the 9:00 time block, since if they did it would not be possible for the nighttime soap to immediately follow the musical variety show (condition #3).

From conclusion #8 and the fact that the drama is in the 7:00 time block, it follows that:

9. Either the musical variety show or the nighttime soap is in the 9:00 time block,

	6:00	7:00	8:00	9:00	10:00
Lineup #2	news or sit. com.	drama	m.v. or news or sit. com.	m.v. or soap	

and finally,

10. Either the situation comedy or the soap can appear in the 10:00 time block, but not the news show (condition #2).

From the above, you can see that the correct answer to the second question concerning the incomplete lineup is (D) Either the situation comedy or the news show can appear in the 9:00 time block. That is, it is false that either the situation comedy or the news show can appear in the 9:00 time block.

In sum, in answering Time Assignment Questions:

1. Carefully read through the passage and the conditions/clues.

2. Construct a chart, and go through each condition/clue, accurately filling in the chart.

3. As you go through each condition and fill in the chart, ask yourself what conclusions follow from each condition/clue, and make note of these on the chart as well.

4.   Again, do not impose your own assumptions/beliefs on the conditions or the questions, but take what is given to you as true.

ADDITIONAL TIPS FOR ANSWERING QUESTIONS

Consider these tips:

➤ **Tip 1**   Do not spend too much time on any one question; pace yourself.

➤ **Tip 2**   Do not rush to finish every problem in the section.

➤ **Tip 3**   Read the problems carefully; make no assumptions.

➤ **Tip 4**   Family tree and ordering relationships are often the basis for the questions which appear in this section.

➤ **Tip 5**   When using charts, do not make them complicated.

➤ **Tip 6**   Since you are not required to have knowledge of the subject presented in a passage, all of the information you will need to answer a question correctly will be provided in the passage. Occasionally, a question will include additional information not found in the passage, but this information can only be used to answer that particular question. For example, question 3 may add information such as, "Assuming that X attends the conference. . . ." Such information should not then be applied to any other Analytical Reasoning Question.

DRILL: Analytical Reasoning

QUESTIONS 1–5

The Bocce family has just hosted a 50th wedding anniversary party for Guido and Maria at their favorite Italian restaurant, Salducci's. Among the family members attending were the following:

Jim Jr., who is Maria's only greatgrandson, Kathy's grandson, and the only child of Jim, who is Kathy's only child

Maria's only two siblings: Dora and Tony

Jack, the oldest of Dora's two grandsons, and the only son of her daughter Jane

Carol, Jane's only sibling

Tony's only daughter, Louise, who has one daughter, named Mitzi

Guido and Maria's six daughters. Guido and Maria have no sons

Tony's grandnephew, Joe

Keep in mind that in this family

- children of first cousins are considered second cousins
- children of second cousins are considered third cousins
- a grandnephew is the grandson of one's brother or sister
- a greatgrandnephew is the greatgrandson of one's brother or sister
- neither Maria nor Guido has been married before
- five of Guido and Maria's daughters are childless

1. Joe's closest blood relative is

    (A) Kathy.

    (B) Jane.

    (C) Carol.

    (D) Tony.

    (E) Maria.

2. What relation is Jim Jr. to Tony?

    (A) Nephew

    (B) Grandnephew

    (C) Greatgrandnephew

    (D) No blood relation

    (E) Cousin

3. Which of the following statements about Joe and Jack is false?

    (A) Joe and Jack are first cousins.

    (B) Joe and Jack are second cousins.

   (C)   Joe and Jack are Dora's grandsons.

   (D)   Joe and Jack are Maria's grandnephews.

   (E)   Joe and Jack are Jim's second cousins.

4.   Louise's daughter, Mitzi, is what relation to Jim?

   (A)   First cousin   (D)   Aunt

   (B)   Second cousin   (E)   No blood relation

   (C)   Niece

5.   Which of the following statements about Joe is false?

   (A)   Joe is Jim's first cousin.

   (B)   Joe is Jim's second cousin.

   (C)   Joe is Jane's nephew.

   (D)   Joe is Dora's grandson.

   (E)   Joe is Maria's grandnephew.

QUESTIONS 6–10

Alvin, Frank, George, Henry, Sam, and Irving planned a week-long fishing trip to Lake Carlisle. However, two days before they were to depart, they argued over what type of bait was best for catching trout. The argument became quite heated, and some of the men were so angry with the others that they decided they would not go if the others went.

If both Sam and Alvin went, then Irving went.

If Irving went, then George went.

If Frank went, then Sam also went.

Either Sam or Henry will go.

Alvin went.

George did not go.

6.   How many of these men went on the fishing trip?

   (A)   1   (D)   4

   (B)   2   (E)   5

   (C)   3

7.   Which of the following statements is true?

   (A)   Either Sam didn't go or Alvin did go.

(B)   Sam went, but Alvin did not.

(C)   Frank went, and Sam did not.

(D)   Both Irving and Sam went.

(E)   Sam went, and Frank did not.

8.   If George had changed his mind and had gone on the fishing trip, but all other conditions remained the same, which of the below statements would follow with certainty?

(A)   Alvin did not go.

(B)   Irving did not go.

(C)   Henry did not go.

(D)   Frank did not go.

(E)   None of the above.

9.   Which of the following does NOT follow from George not going?

(A)   Irving did not go.

(B)   Alvin went.

(C)   Sam did not go.

(D)   Irving went.

(E)   Henry went.

10.   If Alvin had changed his mind and had decided not to go, but all of the other conditions remained the same, which of the following statements would follow with certainty?

(A)   Irving went.

(B)   Sam went.

(C)   Irving did not go.

(D)   Sam did not go.

(E)   None went.

ANALYTICAL REASONING REVIEW

ANSWER KEY

Drill: Analytical Reasoning

1.	(C)		6.	(B)
2.	(C)		7.	(A)
3.	(B)		8.	(E)
4.	(B)		9.	(D)
5.	(A)		10.	(C)

DETAILED EXPLANATIONS
OF ANSWERS

Drill: Analytical Reasoning

Questions 1–5

Since each of the questions for this passage requires us to identify relationships between family members, we will first construct a family tree by going through the conditions and then we will turn to the questions.

We know that Guido and Maria have six daughters and no sons. We also know that five of their six daughters are childless, and that Jim, Jr. is Maria's only greatgrandson, Kathy's grandson, and the only child of Jim, who is Kathy's only child.

From these conditions we can conclude that Kathy is Maria's daughter. The relationships expressed in these conditions may now be visually represented as follows:

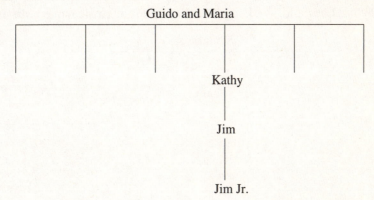

Since the remainder of the conditions focus on Maria and her two siblings Tony and Dora, the diagram below will focus on these three individuals.

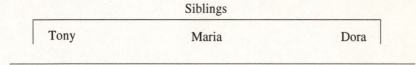

We also know from the conditions given that Dora (Maria's sister) has two children: Carol and Jane. It is also stated in the conditions that Jane has one son: Jack.

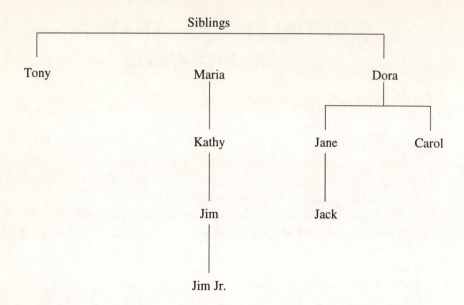

Going to Maria's brother Tony, we know that Louise is his only daughter and that she has one child. We know that the child is a female named Mitzi:

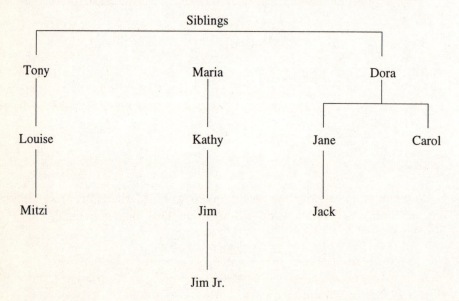

Finally, we know that Tony's grandnephew Joe is at the anniversary party. We know that a grandnephew is the grandson of one's brother or sister. Going back to the conditions, we know that Maria has only one child who has children, and that is Kathy. We also know that Kathy has only one child, Jim. So Joe is not Maria's grandson. Joe must, then, be Dora's grandson, and since Jane only has one son, Joe must be Carol's son:

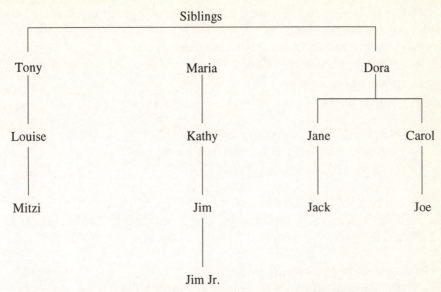

Siblings

Tony   Maria   Dora

Louise   Kathy   Jane   Carol

Mitzi   Jim   Jack   Joe

Jim Jr.

The diagram is now complete, and we can answer the questions.

1. **(C)**   Question 1 asks us who Joe's closest blood relative is. Of the choices given, we can easily see that the correct answer is (C) Carol, who is his mother.

2. **(C)**   Question 2 asks us what relation Jim Jr. is to Tony. Looking at the diagram, we see that Kathy is Tony's niece, her son Jim is Tony's grandnephew, and so Jim's son Jim Jr. is Tony's greatgrandnephew. Note that this corresponds to how 'greatgrandnephew' is defined in the conditions. The correct answer, then, is (C) Greatgrandnephew.

3. **(B)**   Question 3 asks which of the statements given about Joe and Jack is false. Looking at the diagram, we can see that Joe and Jack ARE first cousins. It follows, then, that they are not second cousins. It is not necessary to go through the remaining choices. The correct answer is (B) Joe and Jack are second cousins. This is the statement that is false.

4. **(B)**   Question 4 asks us what relation Louise's daughter Mitzi is to Jim. Looking at the chart and at the definition of 'second cousin,' you can see that Mitzi and Jim are second cousins, i.e., they are children of first cousins (Louise and Kathy are first cousins). The correct answer is (B) Second cousin.

5. **(A)**   Finally, Question 5 asks us which of the given statements about Joe is false. Looking at the diagram, we know that Joe is Maria's grandnephew, that is, the grandson of Maria's sister Dora. We also know that Joe is Dora's grandson and Jane's nephew. And again, by the definition of 'second cousin,' Joe is Jim's second cousin (that is, they are the children of first cousins Carol and Kathy). However, Joe is NOT Jim's first cousin. The correct answer to Question 5, then, is (A) Joe is Jim's first cousin, that is, it is false that Joe is Jim's second cousin.

6. **(B)** Following the suggested method, we will group together conditions that have terms in common.

First, conditions 2 and 6 are grouped together:
>   (2) If Irving went, then George went.
>   (6) George did not go.

We can conclude that (conclusion 1) Irving did not go.

Now we pair this conclusion with condition 1:
>   (1) If both Sam and Alvin went, then Irving went.
>   (Conclusion 1) Irving did not go.

We can conclude that (conclusion 2):
>   Both Sam and Alvin did not go, that is, either Sam did not go or Alvin did not go.

Pairing this conclusion with condition 5:
>   (Conclusion 2) Either Sam did not go or Alvin did not go.
>   (5) Alvin went.

We can conclude that (conclusion 3) Sam did not go.

Now we pair up condition 3 with conclusion 3:
>   (3) If Frank went, then Sam also went.
>   (Conclusion 3) Sam did not go.

We can conclude that (conclusion 4) Frank did not go.

Finally, we pair condition 4 with conclusion 3:
>   (4) Either Sam or Henry will go.
>   (Conclusion 3) Sam did not go.

We can conclude that (conclusion 5) Henry went.

In sum, we know that Alvin and Henry went, but that George, Irving, Sam, and Frank did not go. The correct answer to Question 6, then, is (B) 2.

7. **(A)** Question 7 gives us five statements, and we have to determine which of the five statements is true. Having already deduced conclusions from the conditions, this question is easily answered. We know that Sam did not go on the fishing trip, so (B), (D), and (E) are false. We also know that Frank did not go, so (C) is false. The only option left is (A). It is true that Sam did not go and it is also true that Alvin did go. The correct answer, then, is (A) Either Sam didn't go or Alvin did go.

8. **(E)** Question 8 changes one of the original conditions, and you have to determine what follows from the new condition 'George did go on the fishing trip' and the remaining original conditions.

None of the conditions states that George will go only if Irving goes, so we can't conclude anything about Irving. Also, since the conditions don't tell us that Irving will go only if both Sam and Alvin go, we can't conclude anything about Sam and Alvin. Finally, as Frank and Sam are linked together in one condition, and Sam and Henry in another, and since we can't conclude anything about Sam, we can't conclude anything about Frank or Henry. The correct answer, then, is (E) None of the above.

9. **(D)** Question 9 asks us which of the options does NOT follow from George not going. Again, we can refer to the conclusions that we have already deduced in Question 7. We know Irving definitely did not go, Henry and Alvin did, and Sam did not. The correct answer, then, is (D) Irving went. That is, it does not follow that Irving went.

10. **(C)** This question also changes a condition. Here, the condition 'Alvin went' is changed to 'Alvin did not go.' However, all of the other conditions remain the same, and you are asked to determine which of the statements presented follow with certainty from this changed condition in conjunction with the remaining original conditions. In answering this question, we must again group the conditions together.

First, we will group conditions 2 and 6 together:
>   (2) If Irving went, then George went.
>   (6) George did not go.
We can conclude that (conclusion 1) Irving did not go.

Now we can group condition 1 with conclusion 1:
>   (1) If both Sam and Alvin went, then Irving went.
>   (Conclusion 1) Irving did not go.

We can conclude that it is not true that both Sam and Alvin went, that is, either Sam did not go or Alvin did not go. We know from the changed condition that Alvin did not go. However, it could be true that Sam did not go either. In other words, even though we know that Alvin did not go, it does not follow with certainty that Sam did go or that he did not. So we cannot conclude anything about Sam. However, looking at our options, we see that one corresponds to a conclusion we have already deductively drawn, and that is 'Irving did not go.' The correct answer, then, is (C) Irving did not go.

WRITING SAMPLE REVIEW

The Writing Sample is a 35-minute essay on an assigned topic. The Writing Sample will always appear at the end of the LSAT and, therefore, will always be completed last. It's important to note that this is not a scored section, and thus it will not impact your LSAT score. Nonetheless, copies of your answer will be sent to the law schools to which you apply. Each law school will decide how your writing sample will be weighted, if at all.

You will be presented with one of two types of writing sample prompts, a "decision" prompt or an "argument" prompt. The decision prompt requires you to make an argument favoring one position over another, given certain criteria. The argument prompt requires you to evaluate an argument. Regardless of the type of prompt you receive, be assured that there is no "right" or "wrong" answer. In addition, both prompts are designed to do the same thing: provide law schools with a way to assess how skillfully and clearly you can make or analyze an argument. Law schools may look at the reasoning, mechanics, organization, and vocabulary used in the essay.

THE DECISION PROMPT

The decision prompt asks you to make an argument for choosing one position over another, given certain criteria and certain facts. You must then write a logical, concise, and persuasive essay supporting the position you have taken. During the 35 minutes allowed for the writing sample, you will be expected to review the given facts, pick a clear position to defend, support your position eloquently and effectively, write within the framework of the given facts, and deal with opposing arguments and facts.

HOW TO WRITE THE DECISION ESSAY

Analyzing the Decision Topic

Before you begin your essay, you will need to understand the essay writing topic. The topic will be presented in three steps:

1. You will read an opening statement that will tell you what you will have to argue when you write your essay.

2. You will be given a set of guidelines that must guide your decision.

3. You will be provided with two factual situations, from which you must choose one based on the given guidelines. The two situations presented in the prompt will be balanced enough so that either of them can be argued reasonably. There will be no obviously right answer; it is therefore all the more important that your writing be effective and persuasive.

Your main objective should be to write a logical and concise essay that supports your position as convincingly as possible. Your essay should be organized into roughly four or five paragraphs. You should state the theme in the first paragraph and use the last paragraph to restate and summarize your position. The middle paragraphs should contain an argument for one of the two situations, based on the given criteria and the given facts.

Before you begin writing, take a few minutes (and only a few) to organize your thoughts. Scratch paper will be provided, so you may wish to jot down the points you intend to cover in each part of the essay.

Your Introduction

The introduction should state your position simply and directly. It should include brief references to the situation you have chosen, but it should also clarify your understanding of the given guidelines on which you base the premises of your argument. Essentially, the introduction says: "Position X will fulfill guidelines A and B because . . . ." If you are concerned that your introduction might omit important arguments that may develop during your writing of the essay, keep the introduction focused solely on the guidelines as you state your position. The argument that follows will then amplify and support the introduction.

Your Argument

You should present and justify your argument in the middle paragraphs. When choosing a position, you will probably be better off choosing the one with more "pro" arguments, because generally you will have more to write. However, as you write you should not ignore opposing arguments or ignore facts contrary to your position. An effective essay demonstrates that opposing arguments have been considered and dealt with. An easy way to do this is to use "Even though" sentences that acknowledge a contrary fact or argument but that immediately rebut them with a counterargument or consideration.

In every argument paragraph, you should apply one of the guidelines to the situation you have chosen to support. Open each paragraph with a sentence that lets the reader know what you will be discussing in that paragraph. For example, you may first wish to state the guideline being discussed. Then you should proceed to apply the guideline to your chosen situation, indicating how and why your position is more effective than the other position. No matter how you choose to attack the essay, be sure to address each of the guidelines.

Your Conclusion

The conclusion should tie together your argument and make a final statement about your position. It may represent a small model of the preceding essay, beginning with a brief restatement of your position. You

should relate how your position fulfills the guidelines within the given situation, and then summarize your argument. End with a subdued flourish, but do not be cute or trite. In addition, do not bring up points that were not discussed in the essay. Finally, make sure to read the essay so you can catch misspellings and clarify punctuation.

Remember—the writing sample is meant primarily to measure your ability both to express your thoughts in standard English and to organize those thoughts in a rational structure. Your thoughts need not be "correct," original, or profound, and there is no "right" or "wrong" position. However, you are expected to understand the assignment: Explain how this position will fulfill the guidelines in the stated situation. Even though you may have chosen your position almost arbitrarily, concentrate on structuring your argument and on expressing it simply and calmly while restricting yourself to the given situation and guidelines.

A SAMPLE DECISION WRITING TOPIC

You should make sure to study and learn the directions to this section of the LSAT so that you do not waste valuable time reading them during the test. The directions will appear as follows:

GENERAL DIRECTIONS

<u>Directions:</u> You will have 35 minutes in which to plan and write an essay on the topic inside. Read the topic and the accompanying directions carefully. You will probably find it best to spend a few minutes considering the topic and organizing your thoughts before you begin writing. In your essay, be sure to develop your ideas fully, leaving time, if possible, to review what you have written. Do not write on a topic other than the one specified. Writing on a topic of your own choice is not acceptable.

No special knowledge is required or expected for this writing exercise. Law schools are interested in the reasoning, clarity, organization, language usage, and writing mechanics displayed in your essay. How well you write is more important than how much you write.

Confine your essay to the blocked, lined areas on the front and back of the separate writing sample response sheet. Only that area will be reproduced for law schools. Be sure that your writing is legible.

DECISION PROMPT DIRECTIONS

The scenario presented below describes two choices, either one of which can be supported on the basis of the information given. Your essay should consider both choices and argue for one and against the other, based on the two specified criteria and the facts provided. There is no "right" or "wrong" choice: a reasonable argument can be made for either.

SAMPLE DECISION TOPIC

The following is an example of the decision type of writing sample topic that will appear on the LSAT. It has been labeled so that you can easily recognize and analyze each of the different parts of the topic.

(Opening Statement)

A university is considering adopting one of two financial plans. Present an argument in favor of adopting one of the following financial plans over the other. Both policies will result in a roughly equal loss of students. As the cost to the university of both policies is about the same, two other considerations should shape your decision:

(Guidelines)

• The university wants to retain its current mix of ethnic and socioeconomic diversity.

• The university wants to maintain its reputation for academic excellence.

(Situations)

Option A calls for providing funding to the very best of the financially needy students. Currently, the university provides some degree of aid to half its students. Under this option, the university would provide full financial support to half of all student aid recipients: those with the best grades. The remaining half of student aid recipients who are not supported would almost certainly have to leave the university. Most of those who left would be minorities and other traditionally disadvantaged people. About 25 percent of the student body would be forced to leave.

Option B calls for providing partial funding to all current student aid recipients. The university would not provide full funding to any student, and roughly half of those currently receiving financial aid would not be able to continue their schooling. It should be noted, however, that the misery would be equally shared and that the diversity of the student body would be maintained. Again, the university would lose about 25 percent of its current students.

A WRITING SAMPLE

(Introduction)

The university faces a difficult situation, one that affects the future of the school and the students enrolled there. The university prides itself on the diversity of its student body and its educational excellence. The two proposed financial aid policies force the university to choose between these twin goals. Because the fundamental mission of the university is academics, the university should adopt Option A.

(Argument)

Option A allows the university to maintain its reputation for academic excellence by retaining the top academic achievers. As long as the university is noted for the quality of its education and students, it will always be able to attract a diverse student body. Should the university lose its reputation for educational excellence, however, the quality of applicants would soon begin to deteriorate. Once tarnished, a reputation is virtually impossible to restore. The university should, therefore, adopt Option A, as it best suits the university's long-term interests. To meet its concerns about socioeconomic and ethnic diversity, the university should consider other recruitment or admissions activities that could help create and retain that diversity.

While Option B—which calls for spreading the burden equally—appears at first glance to be the correct choice, it is not. Though Option B seems to be "fair" and "democratic," it is also biased, as it inherently favors wealthier students. By giving no preference to better students, the university would effectively be forcing students to drop out on the basis of their finances rather than their academic record. As an institution of higher learning, the university should make some effort to emphasize academics instead of money. Most would probably agree that a poor but gifted student has more to offer the university community than a wealthy mediocre student.

Despite the apparent unfairness of Option A, it is also unfair to fail to recognize and reward the hard work and achievements of the university's best students. Above all else, it is the quality of the university's graduates, not their number, that is the source of the university's prized reputation. The university must not dilute that reputation over the long term to ensure short-term diversity of the student body.

(Conclusion)

In summary, Option A is the financial aid plan that would best reward those students who have struggled to achieve academic excellence and that would best maintain the university's reputation as a quality school. It is for these reasons that the university should choose Option A.

THE ARGUMENT PROMPT

The argument prompt presents you with a one-paragraph argument, that is, a conclusion based on supporting evidence, and asks you to evaluate that argument. The argument will always be flawed in some way, so your job is to point out the errors. To determine what those errors are, you must rely on the very same skills tested in the Logical Reasoning section of the exam. Pay close attention to the conclusion the argument attempts to draw and the evidence used to support that conclusion. Look for assumptions, flaws and invalid reasoning, ways to strengthen or weaken the argument, and counterexamples. You must then write an organized essay that describes the problems you found.

HOW TO WRITE THE ARGUMENT ESSAY

Analyzing the Argument Topic

The argument topic is fairly straightforward. First, a lead-in statement indicates the author or the source of the argument. Then a short paragraph states the (flawed) argument. Last, the question asks you to discuss how well reasoned you find the argument. Notice that you are NOT asked to present your opinion on the subject matter of the argument. Instead, you must analyze the structure and soundness of the given argument.

When brainstorming for potential flaws, you can use the directions for the argument essay as a guide, because it indicates the types of errors you should be searching for:

For example, you may want to discuss how the logic of the argument is flawed or could be improved, or what counterexamples or alternative explanations would undermine the argument. You may also want to consider what, if any, questionable assumptions underlie the reasoning and what additional information or evidence may have been overlooked that would strengthen or weaken the argument.

After you have determined the flaws in the argument, you should write an organized essay that contains roughly five paragraphs: an introduction that clearly indicates your thesis, a body consisting of a few paragraphs that contain your argument, and a conclusion.

Your Introduction

While there is no mandatory format for the introduction, a successful strategy is to begin the essay with a summary of the argument and then to briefly touch on each flaw you will discuss. For instance, you could first provide a synopsis of the conclusion and the evidence used to support that conclusion. Then you could proceed to list the flaws you found in the argument. Your introduction might say, in essence, "Conclusion C does not follow from evidence A and B, because of flaws X, Y, and Z" or "X argues for conclusion C based on evidence A and B. This argument is flawed because . . . ." No matter how you begin, keep your introduction short and to the point.

Your Argument

The middle paragraphs of your essay should discuss the flaws and weaknesses in the argument point by point. Each paragraph should begin with a topic sentence that lets the reader know what you will be discussing. Do not simply point out assumptions and flaws; explain how the assumptions and flaws weaken the argument. Develop counterexamples, and point out alternative explanations.

Your Conclusion

As with the decision essay, the conclusion of an essay based on an argument prompt should tie everything together and make a final statement. An effective way to close is to briefly restate your analysis and indicate ways in which the argument could be strengthened.

A SAMPLE ARGUMENT WRITING TOPIC

ARGUMENT PROMPT DIRECTIONS

<u>Directions:</u> For this essay you are presented with an argument that offers reasons for drawing a particular conclusion. Your essay should analyze and evaluate the line of reasoning and use of evidence in the argument. For example, you may want to discuss how the logic of the argument is flawed or could be improved, or what counterexamples or alternative explanations would undermine the argument. You may also want to consider what, if any, questionable assumptions underlie the reasoning and what additional information or evidence may have been overlooked that would strengthen or weaken the argument. Note: You are NOT being asked to present your personal opinion on the subject with which the argument is concerned.

SAMPLE ARGUMENT TOPIC

Editorial:

"Centerville should make the highway that most commuters use to get into the city a toll road. Because a majority of those who work in Centerville commute from surrounding areas, a toll road would easily raise much-needed revenue for maintenance of the badly worn highway. A toll would also be a fair solution, because it only impacts those who will use the highway. If they are going to use it, why shouldn't they pay for it? Finally, a toll would help alleviate overall traffic congestion coming into and out of the city by filtering out those who do not need to use the highway during rush hour."

Discuss how well reasoned you find this argument.

A WRITING SAMPLE

(Introduction)

The author of the editorial argues that a popular commuter highway should be converted into a toll road as a fair method of raising revenue and alleviating traffic congestion. These claims about money, fairness, and traffic are questionable, because the author ignores the potential consequences of instituting the toll—namely, diverting traffic into other areas of the city. If traffic is diverted, then the author's claims will be undermined.

(Argument)

By claiming that the toll will easily raise revenue, the author assumes that many commuters will continue to use this highway to get into the city after the toll is instituted. However, this ignores the likely effect of the toll. Requiring commuters to pay for access to the highway will cause at least some commuters to cease using this particular highway. Depending on the amount of the toll and the availability of alternative routes, the toll could cause many to seek out substitute roads that will not cost any money. In fact, in her claim about reducing overall traffic, the author assumes precisely that the toll will not only divert traffic but also prevent a critical mass from driving at all. These anticipated effects may make the toll an ineffective revenue-raising measure.

The potential consequences of the toll road also call into question the author's claim that the toll road would only affect users of the road. The road does not exist in a vacuum; those who stop using it will seek different routes. Thus, the toll road may increase traffic on other highways and byways, impacting drivers throughout the area. Depending on the location of alternate routes, the toll could increase traffic in areas inappropriate for or unaccustomed to heavier traffic, such as residential areas. The increased traffic could, in turn, create safety problems in those areas. Hence, the toll not only affects the users of the road but also the surrounding areas. The author fails to consider these externalities.

In addition, the author suggests that it is a matter of fairness to charge those who will use the road to pay for maintenance of the badly worn road. But using the toll in this manner raises questions about fairness. Is it fair to exclusively charge future users for damage caused by past users of the highway? Furthermore, is it fair to potentially price some residents out of access to what may be the quickest route to work or home? To make her argument stronger, the author of the editorial needs to wrestle with these sorts of questions instead of simply assuming that her definition of fairness is uncontroversial.

Lastly, the author's claim that the toll would alleviate traffic overall is questionable. Here the author makes a faulty generalization. Although a toll may decrease traffic on this particular highway, the toll will not necessarily decrease overall traffic. As indicated earlier, the toll may simply divert traffic to other areas, and may actually create more traffic problems if those areas are unequipped for the increase in traffic flow.

(Conclusion)

The editorial's arguments in favor of a toll road are incomplete at best. The author ignores potential consequences of the toll, over-generalizes, and fails to support her claims adequately. She should discuss the impact of the toll on other roads and on the people unable to afford to pay the toll. Without consideration of these factors, the editorial's argument is weak.

ADDITIONAL TIPS FOR WRITING THE ESSAY

Consider these suggestions:

1	Read the assignment with deliberate speed.
2	If you have a decision prompt, choose a position immediately, without regard to your personal biases. If you have an argument prompt, do not write your personal opinion on the topic; instead, look for assumptions and flaws in the argument.
3	Outline your essay ideas on scratch paper. Make sure your ideas are well organized.
4	Plan your essay within the parameters of the allotted 35 minutes.
5	Bear in mind that this is a writing-reasoning exercise, so do not waste time expounding personal morals, ethics, or political convictions.
6	Keep your sentences relatively short and in control.
7	For each sentence, think about sentence structure—then write.
8	Use terms and phrases from the writing sample prompt.
9	Strive for precise expression and economy of language. The most effective writing is clear and concise.
10	Avoid slang, "intellectual" jargon, and "in" words or phrases. Keep it simple.
11	Avoid contractions and clichés, which do not work well in formal writing.
12	Avoid "set-up" phrases like *It would seem that...* *It is my opinion that...* *In today's complex world, it is often true that...*
13	To clarify the expression of your reasoning, introduce statements with words such as *since, because, although, therefore, thus,* and *however.*
14	Avoid *I* and *we* throughout your essay. The third person approach will focus your thoughts on the assignment.

LSAT
Law School Admission Test

TEST I

TEST I

Section I

Time—35 minutes
26 Questions

(Answer sheets appear in the back of this book.)

DIRECTIONS: The questions in this section are based on the reasoning contained in brief statements or passages. For some questions, more than one of the choices could conceivably answer the question. However, you are to choose the **best** answer; that is, the response that most accurately and completely answers the question. You should not make assumptions that are by commonsense standards implausible, superfluous, or incompatible with the passage. After you have chosen the best answer, blacken the corresponding space on your answer sheet.

1. No one can be on the baseball team who does not buy his own glove. If Nathan is not on the baseball team, Peggy will not date him.

    Which of the following can be deduced from the statements above?

    (A) If Nathan buys a glove, he will be on the baseball team.

    (B) If Nathan buys a glove, Peggy will date him.

    (C) If Nathan makes the team, Peggy will date him.

    (D) If Peggy dates Nathan, he bought a glove.

    (E) If Nathan buys a glove, he will date Peggy.

QUESTIONS 2–3

On February 1, 1985, President Reagan stated to Congress:

"In order for arms control to have meaning and credibly contribute to national security and to global or regional stability, it is essential that all parties to agreements fully comply with them. Strict compliance with all provisions of arms control agreements is fundamental, and this administration will not accept anything less. To do so would undermine the arms control process and damage the chances for establishing a more constructive U.S.-Soviet relationship."

2. Which of the following statements is a reasonable inference which can be drawn from the above passage?

(A) President Reagan had evidence that the Soviets were cheating on past arms control agreements.

(B) Arms control agreements are necessary for national security.

(C) Reagan considered Soviet compliance with past treaties a prerequisite for future negotiations.

(D) Reagan was skeptical of the merits of arms control agreements.

(E) Since the Soviet Union wants good relations with the U.S., it can be expected to comply with past treaties.

3. Which of the following is a premise of the president's statement?

(A) The arms control process is the responsibility of Congress, as well as the president.

(B) Arms control treaties with which each side complies can contribute to global stability.

(C) The U.S. must adopt the most advanced technology for verifying Soviet compliance with arms control treaties.

(D) The superpowers can never trust each other enough to have faith in arms control negotiations.

(E) Arms control negotiations should be abandoned in favor of increased expenditures on defense.

4. The phrase "public interest" or "national interest" is often used by government officials to justify their actions. Presidents refer to the national interest when they take military action abroad or call upon U.S. citizens to make sacrifices in accepting reductions in favored domestic programs. Interest groups, too, claim that their goals are in accord with the public interest. Such a claim is often heard when a business group asks for high tariffs to reduce "unfair" competition from foreign countries, or when an environmental organization asks for greater government regulation to prevent air and water pollution, or when a teachers' organization asks for increased expenditures on educational programs.

Which of the following may be inferred from the above argument?

(A) We should ignore the claims of officials and interest groups that say they are acting in the public interest.

(B) Public officials and interest groups are very likely to act in the public interest.

(C) There is very little doubt about what constitutes the public interest.

(D)   The "public interest" is the commonly accepted standard by which to judge the actions of participants in the political process.

(E)   Self-interested behavior by individuals and groups is a natural part of the political process.

5.   Becker and Edberg, tennis players who are of equal ability, are playing a five-set match. They have played two sets and Edberg has won both. Smith reasons that it is highly unlikely for one of two players of equal ability to win three sets in a row. He decides to bet $100 on Becker in set three.

Which of the following is the best formulation of the principle presupposed in Smith's reasoning?

(A)   If X, Y, and Z are each improbable, then the joint occurrence of them all is improbable.

(B)   If X and Y are each improbable, then the occurrence of X, Y, and Z together is equally improbable.

(C)   If the joint occurrence of X, Y, and Z is improbable, then each of X, Y, and Z is improbable.

(D)   If the joint occurrence of X, Y, and Z is improbable, then Z is improbable, given that X and Y have occurred.

(E)   If the joint occurrence of X and Y is improbable, then the occurrence of an analogous event, Z, is also improbable.

6.   In a dissent to the Supreme Court's 1989 decision concerning First Amendment protection for flag burning, Chief Justice Rehnquist wrote the following:

"Uncritical extension of constitutional protection to the burning of the flag risks the frustration of the very purpose for which organized governments are instituted. The Court decides that the American flag is just another symbol, about which not only must opinions pro and con be tolerated, but for which the most minimal public respect may not be enjoined. The government may conscript men to fight and die for the flag, but the government may not _____."

Based on the information in the passage, which of the following statements best completes the last sentence?

(A)   prohibit the burning of the banner under which they fight.

(B)   give them the support necessary to win.

(C)   place any limits on speech.

(D)   protect them in fighting for the flag.

(E)   tell civilians back home not to disrespect them.

7.   A man notable for the intensity of his religious convictions, Augustine
     cannot be said to have cared much about politics for its own sake — or
     even politics for the sake of the good life. Politics for the sake of God?
     Yes, but Augustine would have thought the emphasis strange. He was not a
     primary political theorist, but rather a theologian so powerful that his view
     of man touched almost every subsequent Western political theorist. He was
     a spokesman for the Church in the moment when it irreversibly came to
     terms with the political.

The passage as a whole supports which of the following conclusions?

(A)   If Augustine had not been a theologian, he would not have influ-
      enced the development of political theory.

(B)   Since Augustine's writing was mainly theological, his influence on
      political theory was minimal.

(C)   If Augustine had been a political theorist, his influence on theology
      would have been substantial.

(D)   A discussion of Augustine's writings should not be included in a
      book on political theory.

(E)   Augustine's view of man influenced the development of political
      theory.

QUESTIONS 8–9

The English constitution developed slowly over several hundred years and
has never been formalized into one document. French constitutions — and there
have been 17 of them since the Revolution — are always spelled out with logic
and clarity. Whereas the Americans regard their constitution with an almost
religious awe, not to be touched in its basic provisions, the French, and most
European countries other than Britain, have seen constitutions come and go and
are not averse to rewriting the basic rules of their political game every few
decades.

8.   Which of the following can be validly inferred from the facts or premises
     expressed in the passage above?

(A)   The American constitution is outdated because of citizens' attitude
      toward it.

(B)   The French value logic and clarity in their political institutions, while
      Americans value continuity.

(C)   The Americans are more like the French than they are to the English
      in their attitudes toward constitutional change.

    (D)   Americans see their politics as a religion.

    (E)   Most countries stick to one constitution and do not amend it.

9.   Which of the following is the primary purpose of the passage?

    (A)   To contrast the French attitude toward constitutional change with that of the Americans and English.

    (B)   To show that constitutions may be changed often in developed countries.

    (C)   To show that comparative studies of the constitutions of other nations can be fruitful.

    (D)   To prove that the French constitution is better than the English or American constitutions.

    (E)   To introduce the reader to a discussion of the English constitution.

QUESTIONS 10–11

It is clear that families, in some form, have always been found in human societies. Even in modern societies, with many opportunities for alternative lifestyles, the family remains strong. Much has been written about the high divorce rate in the United States, and some writers suggest the American family is on the verge of extinction. Nothing can be further from the truth. The high American divorce rate is accompanied by the highest rate of remarriage in the world.

10.   Which of the following conclusions can be reasonably inferred from the above passage?

    (A)   The high divorce rate in the U.S. is a sign of the strength of the family.

    (B)   The American family is not becoming extinct, it is only changing.

    (C)   The high rate of remarriage in the U.S. is to be expected, given the high divorce rate.

    (D)   Modern views on the family are similar to ancient ones.

    (E)   Americans' views on family life are representative of the views of peoples in other nations.

11.   According to the passage, which of the following is true?

    (A)   There are many benefits for a society served by a healthy family system.

(B)   The family has actually become stronger with the development of modern society.

(C)   At one point in social evolution the family was the master institution.

(D)   The family is a basic institution of human society.

(E)   Throughout history the family has been an important economic unit.

12.   In the earliest human societies social control was the exclusive task of the kinship system. The dominant family member, often a dominant male, would enforce social control within the family. Or in more democratic kinship systems, social control was enforced collectively against deviant members. The kinship system also had the task of enforcing social control externally. If a family member was injured by someone from outside, other members of the family were responsible for avenging the wrong.

Which of the following objections, if true, would be logically relevant to the argument above?

(A)   Studies have shown that in some ancient societies' families, females were dominant.

(B)   Ancient Sumerian tablets which have just been translated indicate that families put members to death for violating rules against incest.

(C)   Social scientists are, by and large, not interested in ancient methods of social control.

(D)   Deviant members are dealt with on a one-to-one basis.

(E)   Families let a jury decide the punishment for harming one of their own.

13.   There are students, as well as faculty, who are active in campus politics. All who are active in campus politics are encouraged to join the University Governing Board.

If the statements above are true, which of the following must also be true?

(A)   All who are encouraged to join the University Governing Board are active in campus politics.

(B)   All who are encouraged to join the University Governing Board are faculty or students.

(C)   Some who are encouraged to join the University Governing Board are not students or faculty.

(D)   Some students are encouraged to join the University Governing Board.

(E)   Some students are not encouraged to join the University Governing Board.

14.   I love you. Therefore I am a lover. All the world loves a lover. Therefore you love me.

In terms of its logical structure, the argument above most closely resembles which of the following?

(A)   Adam is a man. Men are homo sapiens. Therefore, Adam is a homo sapien. Homo sapiens are rational. Therefore, Adam is rational.

(B)   Sam got to work on time yesterday, the day before, and for the last 50 working days. Therefore, Sam is dependable. Dependable people get raises. Therefore, Sam will get a raise.

(C)   I like to talk to Pete. Therefore, I am a patient person. Everyone likes to talk to patient people. Therefore, Pete likes to talk to me.

(D)   An orderly universe had to be created by a rational God. The universe is orderly. Therefore, God is rational. A rational God would not allow sin to go unpunished. You sinned. Therefore you will be punished.

(E)   Lifting weights strengthens the body. You lift weights, therefore you are strong. Strong people are happy. Therefore you are happy.

15.   If the college does not increase tuition, it must cut back expenditures for athletics. Cutting athletics will anger the alumni. If the alumni get angry, they may reduce donations. Reduced donations will result in decreased building maintenance. However, if the college raises tuition, the students will protest.

If all of the statements in the above are true, which one of the following statements must also be true?

(A)   Failure to increase tuition will result in decreased building maintenance.

(B)   Either the students will protest, or the alumni will be angry.

(C)   Reductions in donations will cause higher tuition.

(D)   Increasing tuition will result in greater funding for athletics.

(E)   If expenditures for athletics are cut, there is no way for the college to continue the present levels of donations and building maintenance.

16. Voter registration drives have increased the percentage of the voting age population which is registered by 10% since 1950. However, the percentage of the voting age population which votes in presidential elections has declined by 15% since 1950. Therefore, the cause of the low turnout is not registration requirements, but the public's declining interest in national politics.

Which of the following statements, if true, would necessarily strengthen the conclusion above?

(A) Voter turnout for state and local elections has also declined since 1950.

(B) Candidates for the presidency now campaign three weeks longer than they did in 1950.

(C) More people than ever view the government in Washington as too distant to help them solve their problems.

(D) People find it too difficult to register to vote.

(E) The voting age should be reduced.

17. Women's age at first marriage is directly related to their formal educational attainment. Moreover, early marriage influences later decisions by women on whether or not to further their formal education. Unfortunately, we cannot draw any conclusions from these observations, because we know so little about the variables involved.

Which of the following is most probably the point to which the author's statements lead?

(A) Knowledge of the average age of first marriage for women is critical to understanding the educational needs of society.

(B) The relationship between marriage and educational attainment for women is worth studying.

(C) Early marriage discourages women from gaining further education.

(D) The relationship between marriage and education for women has been ignored by social scientists.

(E) Age at first marriage is the most important factor in predicting a woman's educational attainment.

QUESTIONS 18–19

Truth is best discovered through dialogue. The lone individual, when presented with a problem, may reason his way to an answer. But the best test of that answer is its ability to overcome any plausible objections. It is for this reason that Plato presented his philosophy in the form of dialogues between Socrates and his fellow Athenians.

18. Following the logic in the above passage, if we believe that we have the correct answer to a question, but do not know what plausible objections to it may exist, we could believe it to be true for any of the following reasons EXCEPT

   (A) we are inclined to think it is the best answer.

   (B) we know that it is better than alternative answers.

   (C) a majority of people think it is true.

   (D) it fits our preconceptions of what is true.

   (E) it appears to explain the facts as we know them.

19. If a scientist presented a paper describing a new theory of cold fusion at a conference, but refused to accept comments and criticism from the audience, the author of the above passage would most likely

   (A) disagree, because cold fusion is not a very controversial subject.

   (B) disagree, because raising objections will make the audience more interested in the paper.

   (C) disagree, because the comments might raise objections to the theory which the scientist has overlooked.

   (D) agree, because the paper describes a theory, not an explanation which has been widely accepted.

   (E) agree, because a conference is not the appropriate setting for a dialogue.

20. The assertions that government should pass minimum wage laws to assure everyone a tolerable standard of living have been bolstered recently by the argument that many employers would take advantage of unskilled laborers if they could. Yet, even if that were true, it would not follow that government should pass minimum wage laws. Many unskilled workers are not worth the minimum wage, and are thus effectively shut out of the job market by such laws.

   The argument which the author makes in the above passage is based on the assumption that

(A) government has no business interfering in employer-employee relations.

(B) employers will not hire employees who are not worth the minimum wage.

(C) employers, if left alone, would not take advantage of unskilled workers.

(D) government cannot effectively enforce minimum wage laws.

(E) unskilled workers should not look to government for economic aid.

21. The school newspaper's article yesterday concerning the health risks associated with eating foods cooked in animal fats had a positive impact. The cafeteria normally serves french fries cooked in animal fat, but today's menu had baked potatoes instead. One would assume the change was made because of yesterday's article.

A valid criticism of the above argument might emphasize that it

(A) draws an analogy between unrelated events.

(B) generalizes from one event to another event of the same kind.

(C) wrongly assumes that the cafeteria manager reads the school newspaper.

(D) questions the reasons for the cafeteria's switch from fried to baked potatoes.

(E) assumes that because one event occurs before another, the first event is the cause of the second.

22. The director of corporation R has been effective in streamlining the business, even though he has little previous experience with business management. Similarly, the director of corporation S has managed to increase profits, despite his lack of management training. Therefore, the fact that director of corporation T is new to business management will not necessarily have an adverse affect on his performance.

Which of the following assumptions underlies the above argument?

(A) Previous training and experience is undesirable for managers of corporations.

(B) What is true for the directors of some corporations may be true for directors of other corporations.

(C) Business management training is a prerequisite for a corporate director's success.

(D)   Few corporate managers have previous business management training.

(E)   Corporations do not seek to hire directors with previous training.

23.   Despite the environmental damage caused by strip mining of coal, we must allow the project at Grand Bank to go ahead as scheduled. The National Energy Commission has estimated that demands for electrical power will increase by 12% in the tri-state region in the next 10 years. Besides, citizens of the three states have overwhelmingly expressed their opposition to building more nuclear power plants. Any surpluses of electrical power brought about by the Grand Bank Project can always be sold to other states in the region.

Which of the following, if true, would most seriously weaken the above argument?

(A)   Past estimates of the National Energy Commission have underestimated future energy demands.

(B)   Even with the Grand Bank project going full tilt, energy shortages might develop in the future.

(C)   The state has reserves of natural gas which could fire electrical generators, and which have not been developed.

(D)   Citizens have expressed no opinion on strip mining for coal.

(E)   Coal-generated electricity is no cheaper than nuclear-generated electricity.

QUESTIONS 24–25

Intelligent people always vacation in the Bahamas rather than in Hawaii. One can identify intelligent people by the fact that they have gone to the Bahamas rather than Hawaii.

24.   A logical criticism of the above argument would likely point out that the author

(A)   uses the term "intelligent" in too broad a sense for it to have any meaning.

(B)   generalizes from one example to prove a point about a whole class of people.

(C)   presupposes the very point he is trying to establish.

(D)   assumes that the Bahamas are a better vacation spot than Hawaii.

(E)   fails to prove that the Bahamas are a better vacation spot than Hawaii.

25. The reasoning in which of the following passages is most like that in the passage above?

   (A) Homemakers prefer Vizz to Cleansit for their household cleaning chores. Since homemakers are the best judges of home cleaning products, Vizz must be better.

   (B) Homemakers prefer Vizz to Cleansit for their household cleaning chores. Vizz may be used on a variety of surfaces, therefore, it is the best choice.

   (C) Advanced tennis players prefer the new oversized rackets to the standard sized ones. The oversize rackets have more power, which is why advanced players prefer them.

   (D) People with class drive Porsches rather than Volkswagens. Porsches usually last longer than Volkswagens.

   (E) People with class drive Porsches rather than Volkswagens. You can identify people with class by the fact that they drive Porsches.

26. Which of the following draws a conclusion about a group that is based upon a fact about its individual members?

   (A) The office staff all go to Al's Grill for lunch. Therefore, we can find Lynn, the secretary, there at 12:00.

   (B) I didn't like the looks of the red Camaro. When I buy one it will be blue.

   (C) That chili tastes good. Therefore, the beans, peppers, and tomato sauce from which it is made also taste good.

   (D) Each of the threads in the blouse is monochrome. Therefore, the blouse is monochrome.

   (E) You can't trust Ed's advice on the stock market. He is a broker, and all brokers want to do is make a sale to get their commission.

STOP

If time still remains, you may review work only in this section.
When the time allotted is up, you may go on to the next section.

Section II

Time—35 minutes
23 Questions

(Answer sheets appear in the back of this book.)

DIRECTIONS: Each group of questions in this section is based on a set of conditions. In answering some of the questions, it may be useful to draw a rough diagram. Choose the response that most accurately and completely answers the question and blacken the corresponding space on your answer sheet.

QUESTIONS 1–5

The class is going to perform the fairy scenes from *A Midsummer Night's Dream*. The roles to be performed are Oberon, Titania, Bottom, Puck, Peaseblossom and Cowslip.

From oldest to youngest, the performers are Allie, Bobby, Cary, Donny, Eddy, and Fergie, respectively.

The person playing Oberon is not Eddy, but is younger than the person playing Bottom.

The person playing Titania is younger than those playing Peaseblossom and Cowslip, but older than the one playing Puck.

The person playing Bottom is younger than the one playing Cowslip.

1. If the person playing Bottom is older than the one playing Peaseblossom, who must be playing Cowslip?

    (A)   Allie   (D)   Donny

    (B)   Bobby   (E)   Eddy

    (C)   Cary

2. Which of the following is a possible arrangement of the players by role, from oldest to youngest?

    (A)   Cowslip, Bottom, Oberon, Peaseblossom, Titania, Puck

    (B)   Cowslip, Bottom, Oberon, Titania, Peaseblossom, Puck

    (C)   Cowslip, Bottom, Peaseblossom, Titania, Oberon, Puck

    (D)   Cowslip, Peaseblossom, Bottom, Puck, Titania, Oberon

    (E)   Peaseblossom, Bottom, Cowslip, Oberon, Titania, Puck

3. If Cary plays Oberon, who must play Bottom?

    (A) Allie
    (B) Bobby
    (C) Donny
    (D) Eddy
    (E) Fergie

4. Which of the following CANNOT be a possible arrangement of players by role from oldest to youngest?

    (A) Cowslip, Peaseblossom, Bottom, Oberon, Titania, Puck

    (B) Peaseblossom, Cowslip, Bottom, Titania, Puck, Oberon

    (C) Cowslip, Peaseblossom, Puck, Bottom, Titania, Oberon

    (D) Peaseblossom, Cowslip, Bottom, Oberon, Titania, Puck

    (E) Cowslip, Peaseblossom, Titania, Puck, Bottom, Oberon

5. If Eddy plays Puck, which of the following might play Titania?

    (A) Bobby
    (B) Fergie
    (C) Donny
    (D) Allie
    (E) Bottom

QUESTIONS 6–11

George, Henry, Irene, Janet and Kay are members who would run for office if asked by the nominating committee, though none of them would run without such a request.

If George were asked to run, he would run.

If Henry were asked to run, he would run to prevent Kay from winning.

If Irene were invited to run, she would run just in case Janet did as well.

If Janet were asked, she would run just in case George did not.

If Kay is asked to run, she would run just in case Irene did not.

6. If all five were asked to run, how many candidates will run?

    (A) 1
    (B) 2
    (C) 3
    (D) 4
    (E) 5

7.   If all but George were asked to run, how many candidates will run?

   (A) 0   (D) 3

   (B) 1   (E) 4

   (C) 2

8.   If only Henry, Irene, and Kay are asked to run, which of them will?

   (A) Henry

   (B) Irene

   (C) Kay

   (D) All of them will run

   (E) Henry and Kay will run

9.   If only George, Henry, and Irene are asked to run, which of them will?

   (A) George

   (B) Henry

   (C) Irene

   (D) All of them will run

   (E) None of them will run

10. Which of the following pairs of people could not run on the same slate?

   (A) George and Henry   (D) Henry and Kay

   (B) George and Irene   (E) Irene and Janet

   (C) George and Kay

11. If the committee wanted both Henry and Janet to run, which of the following would they ask to run?

   (A) George, Henry, and Janet only

   (B) Henry, Irene, and Janet only

   (C) Henry, Irene, and Kay only

   (D) Henry, Janet, and Kay only

   (E) Henry and Janet only

QUESTIONS 12–16

The Weymouth Ferry was fully loaded except for space for six tons of deck cargo. The purser had ten crates that had not yet been brought aboard.

One crate weighed 1,000 pounds.

Two crates weighed a ton each.

Three crates each weighed a ton and a half.

The last four crates each weighed two tons.

12. What is the maximum number of these crates that can be stowed in the space available for deck cargo?

    (A) 3   (D) 6

    (B) 4   (E) 7

    (C) 5

13. What is the minimum number of crates that can be taken aboard and exactly fill the available deck cargo space?

    (A) 2   (D) 5

    (B) 3   (E) 6

    (C) 4

14. If the three ton-and-a-half crates are taken aboard, what is the maximum number of additional crates that can be stowed in the available space?

    (A) 5   (D) 2

    (B) 4   (E) 1

    (C) 3

15. If the 1,000-pound crate costs $10 to ship, each one-ton crate costs $20, each ton-and-a-half crate costs $30 and each two-ton crate $25, what is the maximum shipping charge the purser can collect from the available tonnage?

    (A) $75   (D) $120

    (B) $90   (E) $150

    (C) $110

16. If the 1,000-pound crate cost $10 to ship, each one-ton crate costs $20, each ton-and-a-half crate $30 and each two-ton crate $25, how much shipping charge is the purser guaranteed if he uses at least half the available tonnage?

(A) $40   (D) $55

(B) $45   (E) $60

(C) $50

QUESTIONS 17–21

There are seven pieces left on the chessboard: the White King, White Queen, White Knight, White Rook, Black King, Black Bishop, and Black Pawn. From the point of view of the white player,

> The White Rook, White King and Black Pawn are nearer than the White Queen, while the Black Bishop, Black King, and White Knight are farther away than the White Queen.
>
> The White Rook is in the same column as the White Knight, but nearer.
>
> The Black King is in the same column as the Black Pawn, but farther away.
>
> Twice as many pieces are to the right of the White Queen as are left of the White Queen.
>
> The diagonal from the Black Pawn, going left and away from the White player, passes through the White Rook, White Queen, and Black Bishop, in order from near to far.

17. White King lies in what direction from White Queen?

  (A) Toward the Black Player in the same column.

  (B) Away from the White Player in the same column.

  (C) Toward the White Player and to the left.

  (D) Toward the White Player and to the right.

  (E) Away from the White Player and to the right.

18. What is the maximum number of pieces that might lie to the right of the Black King in the same row?

  (A) 0   (D) 3

  (B) 1   (E) 4

  (C) 2

19. Which of the following statement must be true?

  (A) The White Rook is nearer to the White Player than the Black Pawn.

  (B) The Black Pawn is nearer to the White Player than the White King.

(C) The White King is to the right of the Black Bishop, from the White Player's point of view.

(D) The White Queen is to the right of the Black King, from the White Player's point of view.

(E) The White Knight is to the left of the Black King, from the White Player's point of view.

20. How many of the pieces may be nearer to the Black Player than the Black Bishop?

(A) 4   (D) 1

(B) 3   (E) 0

(C) 2

21. What is the maximum number of pieces that can be left of the White Rook, from the White Player's point of view?

(A) 0   (D) 3

(B) 1   (E) 4

(C) 2

QUESTIONS 22–23

Breeders have discovered the following things about Connoisseur Cavies.

They come in three colors: Coal, Smoke, and Ash.

It is impossible to breed a pair of different colors successfully.

It is impossible to breed an offspring successfully with its parent.

Male offspring of a pair of Coals are Ash; female offspring of a pair of Coals are Smoke.

Female offspring of a pair of Smokes are Coal; male offspring of a pair of Smokes are Smoke.

Male offspring of a pair of Ashes are Coal; female offspring of a pair of Ashes are Ash.

22. If a male cavy and his father are the same color, that color could

(A) only be Smoke.

(B) only be Coal.

(C) only be Ash.

(D) be any of the three except Coal.

(E) be any of the three colors.

23. If a female cavy is the same color as her granddaughter, which of the following must always be true?

(A) They are both Coal.

(B) They are both Ash.

(C) The grandmother is her granddaughter's father's mother.

(D) The granddaughter is her grandmother's daughter's daughter.

(E) The granddaughter's mother is also the same color.

STOP

If time still remains, you may review work only in this section.
When the time allotted is up, you may go on to the next section.

Section III

Time—35 minutes
28 Questions

(Answer sheets appear in the back of this book.)

DIRECTIONS: Each passage in this section is followed by a group of questions to be answered on the basis of what is **stated** or **implied** in the passage. For some questions, more than one of the choices could conceivably answer the question. However, you are to choose the **best** answer; that is, the response that most accurately and completely answers the question, and blacken the corresponding space on your answer sheet.

The judicial branch is a coequal part of the United States government, and yet it has escaped the degree of scientific scrutiny given to the executive and legislative branches. This is not to say the judicial branch has lacked all scrutiny, only that it has traditionally been viewed from a perspective different from the
(5) other two branches of government. The executive and legislative branches have traditionally been viewed as political entities. Judges and the judicial branch have fostered the idea that they are nonpolitical arbiters of the law. In *Marbury v. Madison*, the landmark United States Supreme Court case which established judicial review under the United States Constitution, Chief Justice John Marshall
(10) rhetorically asked who should determine the meaning of the Constitution. He answered himself by pointing to the fact that members of the other two branches were politically motivated, and only judges were qualified to be truly nonpolitical arbiters of the law. These statements by Chief Justice Marshall were certainly not the beginning of what is generally known as the "cult of the robe," but they are a
(15) classic example in American jurisprudence.
Following Marshall's reasoning, the study of the judiciary has traditionally used the case analysis method, which concentrates on individual cases. Each case must be decided on the basis of cases which have preceded it. Although it may be acknowledged that each case differs from any other case in many ways, past
(20) cases must still be examined to find the general principles which are then applied to the present dispute.
This reliance on precedent, known in legal terms as *stare decisis*, and its accompanying detailed examination of each case has caused legal scholars, to paraphrase Wieland, to not be able to see the forest for the trees. To get a more
(25) accurate picture of the workings of the judiciary it is necessary to step back from the cases. One must remain cognizant of the details, but not to such a degree that they inhibit the ability to see the greater whole. This is not to say analysis of individual cases has no place in the scientific study of the judiciary. Indeed, as was pointed out by Joyce Kilmer, there is always a place to appreciate the beauty
(30) of a tree, but there are also times when we must consider the tree as a part of the greater forest.

Although judicial scholars by and large do not subscribe to the myth that judges are nonpolitical arbiters of the law, there is substantial interest in judicial biographies, and case studies. Judicial biographies and case studies are certainly (35) useful in interpreting particular judicial decisions, examining the opinions of a particular judge, or discussing specific points of law, but to optimize the results of such efforts, in terms of scientific study, such research must be viewed within the framework of a more comprehensive theory of judicial decision making.

1. The primary purpose of the passage is to

    (A) suggest that judges are political decision makers

    (B) complain that no one studies the judiciary

    (C) advocate another way of studying the judiciary

    (D) describe the case analysis method

    (E) attack the doctrine of judicial review

2. Chief Justice Marshall's argument assumes

    (A) judges are better educated than executives or legislators.

    (B) politically motivated individuals are biased

    (C) only judges understand the Constitution

    (D) it is better to study individual cases

    (E) reliance on precedent is unnecessary

3. According to the passage, the "cult of the robe" (line 14) can be best described as

    (A) the interpretation of the Constitution

    (B) the study of prior cases

    (C) a method of studying the courts

    (D) the use of individual cases in decision making

    (E) the belief judges are neutral decision makers

4. According to the author, the "cult of the robe"

    (A) should be studied more closely

    (B) should be used instead of *stare decisis*

    (C) has misled researchers

    (D) has led to a lack of scientific study of courts

    (E) has inhibited the study of individual cases

5.   The reference to Wieland in line 24 is intended to

      (A)   advocate broader studies of the courts

      (B)   suggest that courts are organic entities

      (C)   argue that judges are political

      (D)   decry the use of precedent

      (E)   support the case analysis method

6.   The reference to Kilmer in lines 28–31 is intended to

      (A)   point out the beauty of studying court.

      (B)   argue that individual courts are unimportant

      (C)   support reliance on precedent

      (D)   suggest case analysis has some benefits

      (E)   discourage belief in the "cult of the robe"

7.   According to the author, the problem with detailed examination of each case is that

      (A)   every case is different

      (B)   it does not recognize the political aspects of courts

      (C)   too many details obscure a broader understanding of how courts work

      (D)   it relies on the "cult of the robe"

      (E)   one should ignore the details of cases

8.   The author's attitude toward case studies and judicial biographies can be summarized as being

      (A)   skeptical   (D)   disdainful

      (B)   supportive   (E)   indifferent

      (C)   neutral

     Duke William the Conqueror's victory at Hastings guaranteed to him and his army a permanent stay in England. Harold, the one Anglo-Saxon leader of great ability, had perished and no man or group of men left behind was equal to organizing successful resistance to the Normans. Thus, despite the fine opportu-
(5) nity that yet remained to inspire the mass of the Anglo-Saxons to heroic and stubborn resistance, there was no leadership to call it forth. It was now but a question of how long it would take the Normans to march around the island

suppressing local and ill-organized defenses. Rightfully, some Anglo-Saxon lords and prelates regarded London as the key to defense and rallied the surviving
(10) forces there. They immediately elected as king Edgar the Etheling, the last male descendant of the West Saxon dynasty, to provide a symbol of resistance and unity. But he was a mere youth with no flair for leadership. Within five days of Hastings, William had his army on the march towards London. Dover and Canterbury fell without resistance, but he failed to take London Bridge by
(15) assault. Not having the equipment necessary to storm London, William fell to devastating a band of land encircling London, blocking all approaches. Deprived of reinforcements and obviously impressed by the terrible and methodical thoroughness with which William laid waste the approaches, some of Edgar's followers soon lost heart; the first to offer submission to William was Stigand,
(20) the Archbishop of Canterbury. The rest were soon to follow. A meeting was then held between William and the leading Anglo-Saxon lords and Londoners; the latter, realizing the futility of further fighting and the desirability of a strong ruler, agreed to cease resistance and surrender London. On Christmas Day William was crowned king of England in Westminster Abbey and was acknowl-
(25) edged lawful sovereign by the verbal assent of the assembled Anglo-Saxons and Normans. Meanwhile William strengthened his hold upon the new land, starting construction of castles such as the Tower of London, levying taxes to pay for his army, receiving the homage of lords, and confiscating the lands of those who had resisted his invasion. By March of 1067 he was so completely in control that he
(30) felt able to return to Normandy, leaving England under the direction of trusted Norman lieutenants.

However much William's presence was required in his duchy, he had to neglect it for England within nine months. His lieutenants ruled a seething land too harshly and caused more discontent than order by their undiplomatic policies.
(35) The suppression of an abortive attempt by Kentishmen to make the Norman Eustace of Boulogne king signaled to William the urgency for return. During the next eight years he was to be sporadically occupied in stamping out the last embers of Anglo-Saxon resistance to foreign rule.

9. The primary purpose of the passage is to

   (A) chronicle the exploits of William the Conqueror

   (B) describe the importance of London in the fall of England

   (C) show the importance of strong leadership

   (D) attack William's decision to return to Normandy

   (E) downplay the importance of Harold's death at Hastings

10. According to the author, London was the key to England's defense but

   (A) it could not withstand William's assault

   (B) it could not stand after being cut off

    (C)   it fell due to the treachery of Anglo-Saxon lords

    (D)   William conquered England without it

    (E)   it did not resist William's advance

11.   Given the importance of a lack of leadership in England's fall, the author probably feels William's decision to return to Normandy to be

    (A)   unnecessary   (D)   ironic

    (B)   important   (E)   administrative

    (C)   of no consequence

12.   If William's lieutenants had ruled less harshly and more diplomatically William would not have been forced to return to England. According to the passage, this statement is

    (A)   unlikely, given the length of time William needed to stamp out resistance efforts

    (B)   quite likely, given the necessity of administrative delegation

    (C)   false since William did not leave England

    (D)   irrelevant since William was from England originally and would have returned anyway

    (E)   unimportant since William would have returned to England in any event

13.   According to the author, the election of Edgar as king (lines 10–12) was to

    (A)   return a Saxon to the throne after Harold's defeat

    (B)   serve as a rallying point for the remaining forces

    (C)   prevent William from becoming king

    (D)   follow the line of succession from Harold

    (E)   abide by the English constitution

14.   According to the author, after Harold's death the fate of England was

    (A)   in serious doubt

    (B)   dependent on the rise of another strong leader

    (C)   in the hands of the archbishop of Canterbury

    (D)   dependent on a counterattack from Normandy

    (E)   clear as to the final result

15.   After his assault on London, William

   (A)   returned to Normandy

   (B)   went to Hastings where he defeated Harold

   (C)   marched to Kent to put down a rebellion

   (D)   increased his power over England

   (E)   defeated Edgar at Saxony

The idea that moral rules are absolute, allowing no exceptions, is implausible in light of such cases as The Case of the Inquiring Murderer, and Kant's arguments for it are unsatisfactory. But are there any convincing arguments against the idea, apart from its being implausible?

(5)   The principal argument against absolute moral rules has to do with the possibility of conflict cases. Suppose it is held to be absolutely wrong to do A in any circumstances and also wrong to do B in any circumstances. Then what about the case in which a person is faced with the choice between doing A and doing B — when he must do something and there are no other alternatives

(10) available? This kind of conflict case seems to show that it is *logically* untenable to hold that moral rules are absolute.

Is there any way that this objection can be met? One way would be for the absolutist to deny that such cases ever actually occur. The British philosopher P. T. Geach takes just this view. Like Kant, Geach argues that moral rules are

(15) absolute; but his reasons are very different from Kant's. Geach holds that moral rules must be understood as absolute divine commands, and so he says simply that God will not allow conflict situations to arise. We can describe fictitious cases in which there is no way to avoid violating one of the absolute rules, but, he says, God will not permit such circumstances to exist in the real world.

(20) Do such circumstances ever actually arise? The Case of the Inquiring Murderer is, of course, a fictitious example; but it is not difficult to find real-life examples that make the same point. During the Second World War, Dutch fishermen regularly smuggled Jewish refugees to England in their boats, and the following sort of thing sometimes happened. A Dutch boat, with refugees in the

(25) hold, would be stopped by a Nazi patrol boat. The Nazi captain would call out and ask the Dutch captain where he was bound, who was on board, and so forth. The fishermen would lie and be allowed to pass. Now it is clear that the fishermen had only two alternatives, to lie or to allow their passengers (and themselves) to be taken and shot.

(30) Now suppose the two rules "It is wrong to lie" and "It is wrong to permit the murder of innocent people" are both taken to be absolute. The Dutch fishermen would have to do one of these things; therefore a moral view that absolutely prohibits both is incoherent. Of course this difficulty could be avoided if one held that only one of these rules is absolute; that would apparently be Kant's way out.

(35) But this dodge cannot work in every such case; so long as there are at least two "absolute rules," whatever they might be, the possibility will always exist that

they might come into conflict. And that makes the view of those rules as absolute impossible to maintain.

16. The primary purpose of this passage is to

    (A) discuss the role of Dutch fishermen during the Second World War

    (B) argue against absolute moral rules

    (C) show the difference between Kant and Geach

    (D) point out the inconsistency of moral rules

    (E) consider hypothetical philosophical problems

17. According to the author, Geach's position (lines 13–19) is

    (A) the Dutch fishermen were breaking the law so no conflict exists

    (B) absolute moral rules are an impossibility

    (C) the same as Kant's position

    (D) illustrated by The Case of the Inquiring Murderer

    (E) divine intervention prevents conflicts between absolute moral rules

18. From the context of the passage, The Case of the Inquiring Murderer is most likely

    (A) a hypothetical one, illustrating potential conflict

    (B) the name for the situation in which the Dutch fishermen found themselves

    (C) an example Geach used to illustrate his position

    (D) an argument in support of absolute moral rules

    (E) a real example of conflicting moral rules

19. The author's attitude toward Kant's position is

    (A) agreement   (D) reluctant acceptance

    (B) disbelief   (E) disdain

    (C) indifference

20. According to the author, Geach finds cases of hypothetical conflict to be

    (A) irrelevant to the real world

    (B) impossible to find

(C)   unlikely to occur

(D)   proof that absolute moral rules do not exist

(E)   an important support for Kant's position

21.   If there are at least two absolute moral rules the author argues

    (A)   they might not come into conflict

    (B)   only hypothetical cases will show potential conflict

    (C)   the possibility of conflict detracts from the possibility of both being absolute

    (D)   Geach's position is untenable

    (E)   then one of them must not be absolute

22.   The author's basic argument is

    (A)   the impossibility of absolute moral rules

    (B)   a denunciation of the writings of Kant

    (C)   an illustration of the difference between free will and determinism

    (D)   an example of the moral dilemma faced by the Dutch fishermen

    (E)   a listing of important moral rules

      The horseshoe crab (*Limulus*) was once thought to possess a primitive, simple eye that had been largely bypassed by evolution. In fact, evolution has served the crab well. Anatomical and physiological studies are showing that the 350-million-year-old animal has developed a complex, sophisticated visual
(5) system that incorporates elegant mechanisms for adapting its sensitivity to daily cycles of light and darkness.

      Humans see only dimly at night, but the world of horseshoe crabs may be nearly as bright at night as during the day. Inquiry into the mechanisms by which *Limulus* performs this feat has added to knowledge of a most intriguing phenom-
(10) enon. The brain and its sensory organs are not merely passive recipients of information from the outside world. Instead the brain actively controls those organs to optimize the information it receives.

      Over the past decade my colleagues and I have explored in considerable detail how horseshoe crabs adapt their visual systems. Our most important
(15) finding is the discovery of a 24-hour biological clock in the crab's brain that transmits nerve signals to its eyes at night. These signals work to increase the eyes' sensitivity to light by a factor of up to one million. Oddly enough, this extraordinary nighttime increase in sensitivity went undetected until the late 1970s even though the horseshoe crab's visual system is among the most thor-
(20) oughly studied in the animal kingdom.

The complex interaction between the brain and the eye of *Limulus* is only one example of the intricate relations between the brain and the sensory organs of almost all animals. The pioneering neuroanatomist Santiago Ramon y Cajal first uncovered two-way communication between the brain and the eye of a bird in (25) 1889; he found connections between neurons in the upper brain stem and neurons in the retina. In 1971 Frederick A. Miles of the National Institutes of Health showed these connections carry signals that change the way the retina codes spatial information and so should alter the way a bird sees its world.

Similar efferent connections have been found in many other animals, from (30) the nerves that heighten overall sensory response in some fish to those that transmit signals from the brain to the ear in humans and other primates. Efferent neural connections from other parts of the brain outnumber the afferent connections from the optic nerve in the human lateral geniculate nucleus, where the initial stages of visual processing are performed. It appears that the brain, as (35) much as the eye, determines how people see.

People and birds are complicated, however; no one knows exactly how they see, much less how their brains modulate that vision. The work done on simpler neural systems such as *Limulus* may help elucidate such questions in more complicated species. Ultimately a series of ever more complex studies, founded (40) on work on the horseshoe crab, may explain how the incomplete and unstable picture that sensory organs provide, modulated both by the brain and the environment, gives rise to such direct and incontrovertible impressions as the image of a sunset, the smell of a rose or the sound of a Bach fugue.

23. The primary purpose of the passage is to

   (A) complain not enough research has been done on the horseshoe crab

   (B) suggest that the brain has some control over what the eye sees

   (C) point out the similarities between the visual systems of humans and crabs

   (D) describe the types of neural connections

   (E) argue that the visual systems of crabs are too simple to study

24. The author has studied

   (A) the nocturnal activities of horseshoe crabs

   (B) the reasons for human inability to see at night

   (C) two-way communication between the eye and the brain

   (D) the primitive visual system of *Limulus*

   (E) adaptation in the visual system of *Limulus*

25. The mention of the crab's "24-hour biological clock" in line 15 refers to

    (A) the great age of this creature

    (B) the fact that the crab never sleeps

    (C) how nerve signals are attuned to regular changes in light levels

    (D) the reproductive cycle of *Limulus*

    (E) the activity cycle of horseshoe crabs compared to birds and humans

26. According to the author, his most important finding involves

    (A) the discovery that the crab's brain is an active part of its visual system

    (B) the discovery of the similarities between visual systems of birds and crabs

    (C) realization of how people see

    (D) the discovery that the human visual system is derived from that of the crab

    (E) a determination of the age of *Limulus*

27. From the passage, efferent connections are most likely

    (A) the stems which attach the crab's eye to its body

    (B) a neural connection found exclusively in birds

    (C) a kind of timer for the crab's biological clock

    (D) connections which carry two-way communications

    (E) what causes humans to see dimly at night

28. According to the author, the study of the visual system of horseshoe crabs

    (A) may lead to greater understanding of more complex systems

    (B) is of little importance

    (C) explains why crabs have survived so long

    (D) will show why the system has not evolved

    (E) shows that the connection between the brain and the eye is simpler than originally thought

STOP

If time still remains, you may review work only in this section.
When the time allotted is up, you may go on to the next section.

Section IV

Time—35 minutes
24 Questions

(Answer sheets appear in the back of this book.)

DIRECTIONS: The questions in this section are based on the reasoning contained in brief statements or passages. For some questions, more than one of the choices could conceivably answer the question. However, you are to choose the **best** answer; that is, the response that most accurately and completely answers the question. You should not make assumptions that are by commonsense standards implausible, superfluous, or incompatible with the passage. After you have chosen the best answer, blacken the corresponding space on your answer sheet.

1. I had stuck to my resolution of not eating animal food. I considered the taking of every fish as unprovoked murder, since none of them could ever do us any injury that might justify the slaughter. But, I had formerly been a great lover of fish, and when one came out of the frying pan, it smelled appetizing. I balanced between principle and inclination, till I recollected that, when the fish were opened, I saw smaller fish taken out of their stomachs; then I thought, "If you eat one another, I don't see why we can't eat you."

    Which sentence below best characterizes the writer's conclusion?

    (A)   Fish eat other fish.

    (B)   It is murder to eat fish.

    (C)   There is nothing wrong with eating fish.

    (D)   Fish smell appetizing in a frying pan.

    (E)   We shouldn't eat animal food.

2. John, I know you're soft on this and I forgive you, but the fact is we own everything. They don't own their own backsides. We own them. We own them because we're better. There isn't anything that we can't own in any corner of the world wherever we might want it. (Name your tastes, John. These people are our servants....) Why shouldn't we enjoy ourselves?

    From this passage which of the following may the reader conclude?

    (A)   The speaker thinks he owns John.

    (B)   The speaker regards John as an equal.

    (C)   John is a servant of the speaker.

(D)   The speaker really does own everything.

(E)   John doesn't enjoy anything.

3.   The spectacle of the dead whose bones were always being brought up to the surface of the cemeteries, as was the skull in *Hamlet*, made no more impression upon the living than did the idea of their own death. They were as familiar with the dead as they were familiar with the idea of their own deaths.

Which of the following is NOT support for the writer's conclusion?

(A)   The cemeteries' surfaces displayed bones.

(B)   The people discussed in the passage were impressed by death.

(C)   The death of others was familiar.

(D)   The death of oneself was expected.

(E)   There is a skull in *Hamlet*.

4.   I want to discuss the view that the respect and tolerance due from one system to another forbids us to ever criticize any other culture. This "moral isolationism" is not forced upon us, and it makes no sense at all. People take it up because they think it is respectful. Nobody can respect what is entirely unintelligible to them. To respect someone, we have to know enough about him to make a *favorable* judgment, however general and tentative.

Which of the following is NOT a premise for the writer's conclusion?

(A)   We cannot respect what we do not find intelligible.

(B)   Respect implies a favorable judgment.

(C)   A favorable judgment implies some knowledge of the object of the judgment.

(D)   We should never criticize any other culture.

(E)   Moral isolationism is not respectful.

5.   Never before had Boris Yeltsin gone so far as to demand that Mikhail Gorbachev relinquish his power. In the power struggle in the Soviet Union, Yeltsin had consummated the divorce between Gorbachev and the "reform camp" — of which Yeltsin had become the nearly uncontested leader, thanks to Soviet leaders who have turned to the right. It would appear that the U.S.S.R. had entered a phase in which even the lowest of blows is permitted. By publicly demanding the resignation of the Soviet President, Yeltsin had crossed the line beyond any possible reconciliation with Gorbachev.

If the assertions in this passage are true, which of these assertions must also be true within the time frame to which the passage refers?

(A)   Yeltsin is the Soviet President.

(B)   Yeltsin and Gorbachev may reconcile.

(C)   Yeltsin has not taken a turn to the right.

(D)   Gorbachev is a member of the reform camp.

(E)   Gorbachev is the uncontested leader of the U.S.S.R.

6.   The exact risk of a patient contracting HIV from an infected surgeon is not known, but hospital officials say the risk is low. "No one has ever found a case in the medical field," says John Bartlett, director of the Hopkins AIDS program. Last year, a patient reported contracting AIDS from a dental surgeon, but the allegation has not been proven. As of December 1st, the Federal Centers for Disease Control reported 24 documented cases and 16 possible cases of health care workers contracting HIV through their jobs.

Which proposition below, if true, would strengthen the hospital officials' conclusion?

(A)   The allegation of the dentist's patient is false.

(B)   There were only 20 documented cases of health care workers contracting HIV.

(C)   There really were 16 possible cases of health care workers contracting HIV, in addition to the 24 documented cases.

(D)   The dentist mentioned had never been tested for HIV.

(E)   John Bartlett was a surgeon at Hopkins.

7.   Scientific and technologic innovations produce changes in our traditional way of perceiving the world around us. We have only to think of the telescope, the microscope, and space travel to recall that heretofore unimagined perceptions of the macrocosm and the microcosm have become commonplace. Yet, it is not only perceptions, but also conceptions of the familiar, that have become altered by advances in science and technology. If the mind is nothing but electrical processes occurring in the brain, how can we explain Einstein's ability to create the theory of relativity or Bach's ability to compose the Brandenburg Concertos?

Which of the following is most likely the writer's conclusion?

(A)   The microcosm and macrocosm have become commonplace.

(B)   There are heretofore unimagined perceptions.

(C)   The mind is nothing but electrical processes.

(D)   Advances in science and technology suggest that the mind is more than electrical processes.

(E)   The telescope, the microscope, and space travel are advances in science and technology.

8.   [This was written in 1995] *Today*'s biggest problem has been the defection of young female viewers. The show has made a number of major moves which have had two things in common: the problem with the young female audience has been made worse, and Gumbel has masterminded these moves. Not only has Gumbel helped exacerbate the alienation of female viewers, but he is also a problem himself. Although he is surely one of the most able broadcasters on television, Gumbel's Q score (the crucial measure of name-recognition and popularity with the American public) is now in the single digits.

Which of the following best summarizes the writer's argument?

(A)   Gumbel is in trouble because female viewers have alienated him.

(B)   Gumbel is one of the most able broadcasters on television, because his Q score is in the single digits.

(C)   Young female audiences are worse because the *Today* show is suffering.

(D)   Gumbel is a problem, because the *Today* show has made major moves.

(E)   *Today* is suffering because Gumbel has alienated female viewers and his Q score is low.

9.   Only the Eternal is always appropriate and present, and is always true. Only the Eternal applies to each human being, whatever his age. The changeable exists, and when its time has passed it is changed. Therefore, any statement about it is subject to change. That which may be wisdom when spoken by an old man about past events, may be folly in the mouth of a youth or of a grown man when spoken of the present. The youth would not be able to understand it and the grown man would not want to understand it.

If the propositions in this passage are true, which of the following must also be true?

(A)   Any statement about the Eternal is subject to change.

(B)   Wisdom about past events is not Eternal.

(C)   The Eternal does not apply to youth or old men.

(D)   Youth cannot understand wisdom.

(E)   Grown men do not want to understand wisdom.

10.   We assume that only by legal restraints are men to be kept from aggressing on their neighbors; and yet there are facts which should lead us to qualify our assumption. So-called debts of honor, for the nonpayment of which there is no legal penalty, are held more sacred than debts that can be legally enforced; and on the Stock Exchange, where only pencil memoranda in the notebooks of two brokers guarantee the sale and purchases of many thousands, contracts are safer than those which, in the outside world, are formally registered in signed and sealed parchments.

Which of the following propositions is NOT supported by this passage?

(A)   Debts of honor cannot be enforced legally.

(B)   We should qualify our assumptions that only by legal restraints are men to be kept from aggressing on their neighbors.

(C)   Formally registered contracts are not necessarily safer than contracts made between two Stock Exchange brokers who note the contracts in their notebooks.

(D)   Only by legal restraints are men to be kept from aggressing on their neighbors.

(E)   Some nonlegally enforceable debts are more sacred than those that can be legally enforced.

11.   It should be borne in mind that the knowledge which the men of 3000 C.E. will possess, if all goes well, may make all our aesthetics, all our psychology, all our modern theory of value, look pitiful. Poor indeed would be the prospect if this were not so. The thought, "What shall we do with the powers which we are so rapidly developing, and what will happen to us if we cannot learn to guide them in time?" already marks for many people the chief interest of existence.

Which of the following is NOT a premise of this passage's argument?

(A)   Our aesthetics, psychology, and modern theory of value look pitiful.

(B)   It would be bad if knowledge did not improve.

(C)   Our powers are rapidly developing.

(D)   We should be able to guide our rapidly developing powers in time.

(E)   For many people rapid development of our powers is their chief interest of existence.

12. Analysis shows that magic rests everywhere on two fundamental principles: first, that like produces like, effect resembles cause; second, that things which have once been in contact continue ever afterwards to act on each other. The former principle may be called the Law of Similarity; the latter, that of Contact of Contagion. From the one, the magician infers that he can produce any effect he desires merely by imitating it in advance; from the other, it is inferred that whatever he does to a material object will automatically affect the person with whom it was once in contact.

Which of the following are premises of the magician's argument?

(A) Like produces like.

(B) He can produce any effect he desires.

(C) Whatever he does to a material object will automatically affect the person with whom it was once in contact.

(D) Things which have been in contact continue ever afterwards to act on each other.

(E) Both A and D are premises.

13. The saddest thing about the editor's rant against multiculturalism in the special issue "Race on Campus" is how little of this "new orthodoxy" actually exists. Believe me, Aristotle, Augustine, Milton, Shakespeare, Cervantes, and Hegel are alive and well in the academy. In fact, the juicy attacks by the multiculturalists have probably gotten more students to read these books than any dry appeal to the "best that has been said or thought." There's nothing like a charge of intellectual obscenity to pack the house.

Based on this passage, which of the following is a position of the editor who ranted against multiculturalism?

(A) Little of the new orthodoxy of multiculturalism exists.

(B) Aristotle, Augustine, and Milton are alive and well in the academy.

(C) A charge of intellectual obscenity will pack the house.

(D) Juicy attacks by the multiculturalists have gotten students to read books.

(E) There is a new orthodoxy of multiculturalism.

14. Few writers have inspired more criticism, and more of it theoretically polarized and mutually hostile, than Ezra Pound. The critic who would engage Pound's work finds himself or herself framed from the outset by a kind of critical Cold War, one which forces him into something resembling the role of Marc Antony at the funeral in *Julius Caesar*. Pound critics come time and time again either to bury or to praise this strange and disturbing individual, who is seen by turns either as a fascist and anti-Semite in his very composition and genesis or as a literary genius.

Which of the following is NOT a premise of this passage?

(A) Pound was an anti-Semite.

(B) Pound is often seen as a literary genius.

(C) Pound is often seen as a fascist.

(D) Critics of Pound find themselves framed by a kind of critical Cold War.

(E) The critic often resembles the role of Marc Antony at the funeral in *Julius Caesar*.

15. Internships are historically common. References to apprenticeships are found as early as 2100 B.C.E. in the Code of Hammurabi. Greek and Roman sources also allude to this phenomenon. The concept was further developed in the English guilds of the Middle Ages, flourished through the 16th century in Europe, and even found its way to colonial America. Physicians' training includes a formal one-year internship after graduation. Similarly, the role an internship experience should play in legal assistant training programs and the value of an internship in meeting the needs of the student and the internship sponsor are extremely important today.

What is the main conclusion of this passage?

(A) Physicians' training includes a formal one-year internship after graduation.

(B) Internship programs are historically common.

(C) References to apprenticeships are found as early as 2100 B.C.E. in the Code of Hammurabi.

(D) Legal assistant trainees should have internships.

(E) Apprenticeships are similar to internships.

16. Textbooks have become the object of considerable attention in recent years and for good reason. Clearly, these packaged curricula are the essential source of information for students and teachers alike in public elementary

schools. They outweigh all other sources in determining the day-to-day teaching and learning activities in classrooms. Their influence on the nature and consequences of elementary education is considerable, although not very well understood.

Which of the following is NOT one of the premises of this argument?

(A) Textbooks are packed curricula.

(B) Textbooks are the essential source of information for students in elementary schools.

(C) Textbooks are the essential source of information for teachers in elementary school.

(D) Textbooks outweigh all other sources in determining the day-to-day teaching in classrooms.

(E) Textbooks deserve the considerable attention they have been receiving.

17. Previous analyses of verbal content have shown that the three network television newscasts are much more alike than different in their story selection, story order, and portrayal of events on the evening news. Yet, there is no evidence to suggest that there is a corresponding similarity in visual form, or the state, structure, or character in which visual information or content appears. The visual form is important in conveying the meaning, significance, or aesthetic value of the visual content.

Which of the following, if true, would weaken this passage's argument?

(A) Visual form is less important than verbal content.

(B) Visual form conveys aesthetic value of visual content.

(C) Network news stories and their verbal forms have remained static over the past 30 years.

(D) The three networks tend to select similar stories.

(E) There has been as much analysis of visual form as of verbal content.

18. The production of new translations of the Bible is an awesome task. One cannot even begin to calculate the thousands of hours of individual and committee work involved, without standing back in amazed appreciation for those who have committed themselves to such an undertaking. When we multiply the amount of labor expended on one such translation by the number of new translations that have exploded around us in recent years, it is clear that the modern world's hunger for the Word is no less than that of less media-saturated generations of long ago.

What is the conclusion of this argument?

(A)   There has been an explosion of translations of the Bible in recent years.

(B)   The production of new translations of the Bible is an awesome task.

(C)   The less media-saturated generations of long ago had a greater hunger for the Word than the modern world has.

(D)   We should multiply the amount of labor over one translation by the number of new translations.

(E)   People are as interested in the Bible today as they were before.

19.   It looks as though I'll have to put new siding on the house this year. Dave next door just had to have his house done, and his place was built the same time as mine and by the same contractor.

Which of the following, if true, would most weaken the above argument?

(A)   The contractor guaranteed that the present siding would last for two more years.

(B)   The neighbor's siding is composition while the speaker's siding is redwood.

(C)   The speaker cannot afford new siding this year.

(D)   Dave, the neighbor, is an expert carpenter, but the speaker is not.

(E)   Dave and the speaker both wash their sidings annually.

20.   The whole universe must have had a beginning, since each thing in it had a beginning.

Which is the principal fault in the above reasoning?

(A)   The speaker argues from the fact that each thing began at some time, to the claim that there was some one time at which all things began.

(B)   The speaker fails to take into account the question of what could have caused the universe to begin.

(C)   The speaker argues that the whole has some property simply because all of its parts do.

(D)   The speaker argues that one thing is similar to another in one property just because they are both similar in another property.

(E)   The speaker fails to deal with the fact that things last for longer or shorter times and that the universe may, thus, be the longest-lasting thing.

21. When a mother says "Wise drivers buckle up" to her 16-year-old daughter who is about to take her first solo drive, she means "Buckle your seat belt." If she did not mean this, her remark would not be relevant to the daughter's situation. At that moment, the daughter seemed to have no interest in the apparent information her mother's remark conveyed.

    The speaker obviously assumes that

    (A)   teenagers are never interested in what wise drivers do.

    (B)   what is relevant to a person's situation rarely interests that person.

    (C)   the mother is worried about her daughter's safety.

    (D)   the meaning of a remark will be relevant to the hearer's situation.

    (E)   teenagers tend not to use seat belts when driving.

22. A recent study found that body builders who took steroids had significantly lower levels of high-density lipoproteins in their blood than did otherwise similar men who did not take steroids. The average was 50% lower for the steroid users, and the drop varied directly with the size of the steroid dose. Low levels of high-density lipoproteins in the blood are known to be correlated to high risk of heart attack.

    Which of the following is the most accurate conclusion of the study discussed?

    (A)   Body building is hazardous to the builder's health.

    (B)   Taking steroids causes heart attacks.

    (C)   Taking steroids significantly increases the likelihood of a heart attack.

    (D)   Taking steroids lowers the level of high-density lipoproteins in the blood.

    (E)   Body building lowers the level of high-density lipoproteins in the blood.

23. The fact that a person is an expert in one field does not give his statements about other areas any special force. So, when Dr. Spock, the famous baby doctor, talks about problems in the world economy, we should

    (A)   reject what he says, since this is not his field.

    (B)   accept his views, since he is an expert.

    (C)   subject his views to the same scrutiny we would give anyone else's.

    (D)   ignore his views, since he is only a baby doctor.

(E) accept his view if he is found to be an expert on the world economy as well.

24. If Einstein's theory is correct, then light from certain stars, which are actually behind the sun, can be seen during a total solar eclipse. The standard theory holds that this light cannot be seen, since the sun is in the way. But, at every eclipse since Einstein's theory was published, such stars have been seen and photographed. Thus, Einstein's theory is clearly true.

This case is most like which of the following in its logical features?

(A) Copernicus explained the known phenomena with an explanation that contradicted the standard theory.

(B) Kepler explained some recently discovered, and not yet explained phenomena, with an explanation that contradicted the standard theory.

(C) Galileo observed moons around Jupiter, where the standard theory said moons could not exist.

(D) Halley correctly predicted the appearance of a comet, which the standard theory said could not be done, on the basis of a new theory.

(E) Herschel discovered Uranus by looking exactly where the standard theory said a new planet should be.

STOP

If time still remains, you may review work only in this section.
When the time allotted is up, you may go on to the next section.

LSAT Writing Sample

(Answer sheets appear in the back of this book.)

General Directions

You will have 35 minutes in which to plan and write an essay on the topic below. Read the topic and the accompanying directions carefully. You will probably find it best to spend a few minutes considering the topic and organizing your thoughts before you begin writing. In your essay, be sure to develop your ideas fully, leaving time, if possible, to review what you have written. **Do not write on a topic other than the one specified. Writing on a topic of your own choice is not acceptable.**

No special knowledge is required or expected for this writing exercise. Law schools are interested in the reasoning, clarity, organization, language usage, and writing mechanics displayed in your essay. How well you write is more important than how much you write.

Confine your essay to the blocked, lined areas on the front and back of the separate writing sample response sheet. Only that area will be reproduced for law schools. Be sure that your writing is legible.

Sample Topic

Directions: The scenario presented below describes two choices, either one of which can be supported on the basis of the information given. Your essay should consider both choices and argue for one and against the other, based on the two specified criteria and the facts provided. There is no "right" or "wrong" choice: a reasonable argument can be made for either.

Baldwin State University, located in Los Angeles, California, is required to accept California high school students who graduate in the top 20 percent of their class. The university is striving to enhance its image as a progressive, high-quality school. It is also trying to recruit top-notch faculty members. Two candidates are finalists for a tenure-track position in the mathematics department of Baldwin State with a specialization in statistics. Write a recommendation supporting the appointment of one of the finalists over the other, keeping in mind the following criteria:

- Baldwin State is looking for an assistant professor who is both a teacher and a scholar.

- Baldwin State considers teaching, research, and university service (in that order) the criteria for promotion and tenure.

The first finalist is Margaret Jones, 26, who has just completed her doctorate in statistics from Yale University and graduated with highest honors. Jones received

her B.A. degree from Oberlin College and her M.A. degree from the University of Pennsylvania; both degrees are in mathematics. She already has one year of full-time teaching experience in addition to three years as a teaching assistant. Her reviews from students are mixed and on a scale of 1 to 5 (with 5 being the highest), she averages a 2.85 on the question "Rate the effectiveness of this instructor." Although she is friendly, Jones has a nervous personality, talks rapidly, and, when questioned, tends to give answers that are longer than necessary. She holds regular office hours but is generally unwilling to meet with students beyond those hours. Jones has cowritten three textbooks on mathematics and is currently working on her own book about statistics. She has assured the mathematics department of Baldwin State that she is eager to pursue her research agenda at the university.

John Smith is the other finalist. Smith is 30 years old and holds a doctorate in statistics from Oregon State University and a B.A. degree from Iowa State University, where he majored in philosophy and economics. His M.A. degree is from the University of Washington–Seattle, where he majored in mathematics and took a minor in economics. Smith has three years of full-time teaching experience at the University of West Virginia and several years experience as a part-time lecturer and teaching assistant. His evaluations from students are exceptionally positive, and they especially note his patience and willingness to spend extra time with them. His relaxed personality also encourages student participation in the classroom. Smith has thus far published two papers in respected journals and is cowriting a textbook on statistics with applications to various fields.

STOP
If time still remains, you may review work only in this section.

TEST I

ANSWER KEY

Section I — Logical Reasoning

1.	(D)	8.	(B)	15.	(B)	22.	(B)
2.	(C)	9.	(A)	16.	(C)	23.	(C)
3.	(B)	10.	(B)	17.	(B)	24.	(C)
4.	(D)	11.	(D)	18.	(B)	25.	(E)
5.	(D)	12.	(B)	19.	(C)	26.	(D)
6.	(A)	13.	(D)	20.	(B)		
7.	(E)	14.	(C)	21.	(E)		

Section II — Analytical Reasoning

1.	(A)	8.	(E)	15.	(D)	22.	(A)
2.	(A)	9.	(A)	16.	(B)	23.	(D)
3.	(B)	10.	(B)	17.	(C)		
4.	(C)	11.	(D)	18.	(A)		
5.	(C)	12.	(C)	19.	(E)		
6.	(C)	13.	(B)	20.	(C)		
7.	(C)	14.	(D)	21.	(D)		

Section III — Reading Comprehension

1.	(C)	8.	(A)	15.	(D)	22.	(A)
2.	(B)	9.	(C)	16.	(B)	23.	(B)
3.	(E)	10.	(B)	17.	(E)	24.	(E)
4.	(D)	11.	(D)	18.	(A)	25.	(C)
5.	(A)	12.	(A)	19.	(B)	26.	(A)
6.	(D)	13.	(B)	20.	(A)	27.	(D)
7.	(C)	14.	(E)	21.	(C)	28.	(A)

Section IV — Logical Reasoning

1.	(C)	8.	(E)	15.	(D)	22.	(D)
2.	(B)	9.	(B)	16.	(E)	23.	(C)
3.	(B)	10.	(D)	17.	(A)	24.	(D)
4.	(D)	11.	(A)	18.	(E)		
5.	(C)	12.	(E)	19.	(B)		
6.	(A)	13.	(E)	20.	(C)		
7.	(D)	14.	(A)	21.	(D)		

DETAILED EXPLANATIONS OF ANSWERS

Section I – Logical Reasoning

1. **(D)** Answer (A) assumes that buying a glove is the only requirement for being on the team. There may be other, unstated, requirements, such as a tryout, or age restrictions. A premise may state "if not A, then not B." A reader may not assume on that basis "if A, then B." That is an invalid assumption. Answer (B) makes the same error as Answer (A), but makes it twice. Just because he buys a glove does not mean he will make the team. In addition, that he makes the team does not mean Peggy will date him. We know that if he does not make the team, she will not date him. This does not mean that if he does, she will. Answer (C) repeats the second mistake of Answer (A). In Answer (D) Peggy dates Nathan. We know that making the team was necessary for that. We also know that buying the glove was necessary for making the team. Therefore, he bought the glove. Answer (E) assumes that if he buys the glove he will make the team. (See explanation for (A).) It also assumes that if he makes the team, he will want to date Peggy, and that she will date him. None of this is established.

2. **(C)** Answer (A) need not be true. Reagan might have merely suspected Soviet non-compliance. Or he may have made the statement to ward off anticipated non-compliance. This answer asks you to assign a motive for the President's statement, when many different motives are possible. Answer (B) is not supported by the statement. Reagan says that compliance is necessary in order for arms control agreements to contribute to security. This implies that arms control negotiations with which one side does not comply might actually damage the other side's security. Answer (C) is supported by the following: Reagan says that his administration would not accept anything but full compliance with (present) treaties. Acceptance of non-compliance would undermine the arms control process and damage the U.S.-Soviet relationship. An undermined negotiation process and a damaged relationship suggest no more negotiations. Answer (D) cannot be right, since Reagan implies in the first sentence that arms control treaties with which each side complies can contribute to security. Answer (E) is not correct, because the passage gives no information about Soviet desires or intentions. Even if the Soviets want good relations, one could not rule out the possibility that they might cheat if they thought no one would find out.

3. **(B)** Answer (A) gains little support from the passage. The president's statement is made to Congress, but Congress is not asked to cooperate with the president, or to do anything else. Answer (B) is supported by sentence one. The

sentence states that in order for arms control to have meaning and credibility both sides must comply. This, of course, implies that arms control agreements with which both sides comply can increase global stability. Answer (C) is a possible conclusion which one could draw from the statement. It is not a premise of it. Nor is it supported by the statement. Reagan has identified a desired outcome, compliance with treaties, but has not hinted at how that outcome might be achieved. Answer (D) assumes that the two sides' faith in the treaty depends only on trust. It might depend on other factors, such as the technology available — or the methods adopted in a treaty — for verifying compliance. Answer (E) is without support for two reasons: 1. Reagan does not imply that arms control should be abandoned, only that compliance should be required; 2. he says nothing about preferring measures other than arms control for promoting national security.

4.   **(D)**   Answer (A): While officials and groups often make this claim, they are not always being truthful. However, they may sometimes be. Instead of merely ignoring the claim, we must judge its truthfulness. Answer (B): Even though they often claim to be, there is no reason, based on the passage, that they are making truthful claims. Answer (C): If there was little doubt, then specious claims would present no problem. We would know immediately if a claim was false, and the group or official could easily be held responsible by the public for lying. Answer (D): Since officials and groups attempt to justify their behavior by saying it furthers the public interest, they must be assuming that that is the standard by which the public will judge them. Answer (E): While this may be true, it is not substantiated by the passage. The passage says nothing about whether self-interested or public interested behavior is more common or natural to the political process.

5.   **(D)**   The answer cannot be (A). X equals Edberg winning set 1; Y equals Edberg winning set 2; and Z equals Edberg winning set 3. Any of these, taken alone, is equally probable or improbable, given that the players are of equal ability. Answer (A) assumes that each, taken alone, is improbable. Answer (B) is not correct, for the same reason. The answer assumes that X and Y are improbable, when they are, taken alone, equally probable or improbable. Answer (C) assumes that because it is improbable that Edberg will win three sets in a row, it is improbable that he win any of the first three sets. That is not what Smith assumes. What Smith does assume is that since Becker has a 50/50 chance of winning a given set, it is not likely that Becker will lose three in a row. Answer (D) is correct. Smith assumes that since Becker has a 50/50 chance of winning any given set, it is not likely that he will lose three in a row. Since he has lost two in a row, he is likely to win set three. Answer (E) is wrong because the statement says Smith assumes that it is unlikely one of two players of equal ability will win three sets in a row. It did not say he assumes that the player will not win two sets in a row. That is the assumption upon which the answer is based.

6.   **(A)**   This answer best completes the thought of the sentence. The passage states that the government may not prevent burning of the flag, which is the

banner under which conscripted Americans fight. (B) Preventing flag burning is not the only way in which the government may support American soldiers. Nothing prevents the government from giving them support in the form of training and equipment, for example. (C) One cannot assume on the basis of the passage that government can place no limits on speech; only that it cannot prevent flag burning. (D) The passage does not say that the government cannot protect the men, either by supplying the best equipment or leaders. It only states that the government cannot stop flag burning. (E) Flag burnings might not be meant to show disrespect for fighting men. It might be a statement against an act of government which was unrelated to the draft or war.

7.   **(E)**   (A) While this may be true, it also may not. If Augustine had not become a theologian, he might have become a political theorist. In that capacity he might have influenced the development of political theory as much or more than he did. (B) The passage clearly states that Augustine's influence on political theory was great, since his view of man touched nearly almost every subsequent Western political theorist. (C) Just because he, being a theologian, influenced political theory, does not mean that had he been a political theorist he would have influenced theology. The passage does not establish that the influence of theology on political theory is reciprocal. (D) Since Augustine's influence on theory was substantial, one must understand his thought to know how it affected the subsequent development of political theory. Therefore, it is appropriate that a discussion of his work be included in a book on political theory. (E) This is clearly established by the passage, which states that his views touched almost every subsequent Western political theorist.

8.   **(B)**   (A) This may not be inferred from the passage. Americans do not think that the basic provisions of their constitution should be changed. However, it is entirely possible that those basic provisions are as timely now as when the constitution was written. The passage does not indicate otherwise. (B) This is clearly inferred from the passage. French constitutions are always spelled out with logic; therefore, the French must value logic in their constitutions. Americans are unwilling to change the basic features of their constitution; therefore, they must value continuity in their political institutions. (C) In the third sentence, the Americans and the British are portrayed as unlike the French and other Europeans. The way in which they are unlike the others is that they do not change their constitutions very often. Therefore, the Americans are more like the English than the French in their attitudes toward constitutional change. (D) The paragraph states Americans regard their constitution with religious awe, not that they see it as a religion. (E) In the last sentence, it is stated that many countries rewrite the basic rules of their political game.

9.   **(A)**   This is the best answer, because the passage shows that the English and Americans are averse to constitutional change, while the French are not. (B) The example cites examples of countries with as well as without constitutional change as well as the opposite. It never mentions the term "developed countries," as it should if the purpose was Answer (B). (C) While this answer is plausible, it

is not the best. The passage never refers to the advantages to be gained from such a study. Rather, it assumes as a given that such studies are fruitful. (D) The author never passes judgment on whether logic or continuity is preferable in a constitution. Therefore, this answer is not the best. (E). The primary emphasis in the passage is on the French, not the English constitution. First the French is compared to the English; next it is compared to the American.

10. **(B)** (A) The author says that the high divorce rate is interpreted by some as a sign of the weakness of the American family. He argues, however, that the high rate of remarriage offsets the high divorce rate. He is certainly not arguing that the high divorce rate, in itself, is a sign of strength of the family. (B) This is the best answer. The high divorce rate and the high rate of remarriage are both changes which the family is currently experiencing in America. It is not, however, on the verge of extinction. As he says, nothing could be further from the truth than that the American family is becoming extinct. (C) If the high rate of remarriage could be expected, given the high divorce rate, the author would not need to supply this bit of information. As it is, he is compelled to supply the information in order to counter the argument that the high divorce rate shows a decline in the strength of the American family. (D) Nothing in the passage leads to such an inference. On the contrary, high divorce rates are said by the author to be cited by some as evidence of a decline in the family. Therefore, high divorce rates must mark a change in attitude toward the family. (E) The passage does not support such an inference. Rather, Americans' attitudes toward divorce seem to be different from those of other modern peoples, as evidenced by Americans higher divorce rates.

11. **(D)** (A) The passage says nothing about the value of a healthy family system to society. (B) The passage is arguing that the family has not become weaker, not that it has gotten stronger. (C) One cannot deduce this on the basis of the passage. Perhaps it always was, and still is, the master institution. Perhaps it never was. One cannot tell, because of insufficient evidence. (D) This is the best answer. Since the family has always existed in human society, one may say that it is a basic institution of that society. (E) The passage says nothing about the economic aspect or function of the family.

12. **(B)** (B) is relevant. It substantiates the point of the passage, which is that kinship units practiced social control. (A) is not relevant. The passage states that the dominant member was often a male, which is the same as admitting that males were not always dominant. (C) is not relevant. The passage is concerned with making a point, not with what groups might be interested in the topic. (D) is not relevant to the argument because the passage states that deviant members were often dealt with collectively. (E) is also not relevant because it is stated in the last sentence that family members were responsible for avenging the wrong.

13. **(D)** (A) need not be true. That all who are active in campus politics are encouraged to join does not mean that everyone who is encouraged to join is active in campus politics. Some may not be active, yet be encouraged to join.

Answer (B) need not be true. The passage states that all faculty and students who are active in campus politics are encouraged to join. This does not necessarily mean that others, who are not students or faculty, are not encouraged to join. Perhaps administrators or community leaders are also encouraged to join. Answer (C) need not be true. It is possible that only faculty and students are encouraged to join, and no one else. The passage does not specify. Answer (D) must be true. The passage states that there are students active in campus politics, and that all those in that category are encouraged to join. Answer (E) need not be true. It is possible that all students are active in campus politics. Therefore, all students would be encouraged to join.

14. **(C)** The argument is structured to show that certain feelings which one person has for another must be reciprocated. In other words, the feelings in the first person must produce like feelings in the second person. Answer (C) best parallels that type of reasoning. Only one difference occurs between the passage and Answer (C). In the passage, the object of the feelings is being addressed. In answering the object of the feeling was being spoken of in the third person. Answers (A), (D), and (E) employ standard syllogistic reasoning. The syllogism is the method used in deductive reasoning. The syllogism takes the form:

If $A = B$
And $B = C$
Then $A = C$

In Answer (A) the argument is:

Adam = Man;
Man = Rational;
therefore Adam = Rational.

Answer (D) uses a slightly different formulation:

If A then B;
A, so B.
If B, then C cannot be present without D.
B with C, therefore D follows. In the passage,
A = orderly universe;
B = rational God;
C = sin.

15. **(B)** (A) This cannot be the answer. The alumni may or may not reduce donations if they get angry. If they do not reduce donations, maintenance may well stay the same. (B) The students will protest if tuition is raised. If tuition is not raised, athletics will be cut. This will anger alumni. So, either the students will protest, or alumni will be angry. (C) The statements do not establish a causal relationship between reductions in donations and higher tuition. The statements establish that reduced donations will cause less maintenance, and nothing else. The alumni may get angry about something other than cuts in athletics. Then they may reduce donations even though tuition is not increased. (D) Funding for athletics may remain constant even though tuition is increased. (E) The state-

ments do not establish that alumni will get angry if athletics is cut, only that they may. Therefore, it is possible for tuition to be increased, for alumni not to get angry, and for donations and maintenance to remain the same.

16. **(C)** (C) If more people view the government in Washington as remote and of little help, this would strengthen the conclusion that their interest would be directed away from national politics. (A) The fact that turnout for state and local elections has declined might mean that interest in state and local politics has declined. This does not necessarily mean that interest in national politics has also declined. (B) Candidates may campaign longer for any number of reasons which are unrelated to declining interest in national politics. Perhaps there are more candidates, and the public needs longer to weigh their qualifications against each other. Perhaps the laws governing campaign financing have changed, and candidates now have more money to spend campaigning. (D) If this were true, it would not strengthen the conclusion but take away from it. (E) would not strengthen the conclusion nor take away from it.

17. **(B)** (A) This answer draws a conclusion from the statements, when the author says plainly that not enough is known about the variables to draw any conclusion. (B) The author establishes a relationship between age at first marriage and formal educational attainment; and between early marriage and later decisions about getting more education. However, the variables are not understood. The author obviously thinks the relationship between marriage and educational attainment is worth studying, or he would not discuss the topic. Therefore, we may assume that he would like to see more work done in order to bring further information about the topic to light. (C) The author says that early marriage influences women's decisions about furthering their formal education. He does not say whether that influence is positive or negative. Answer (C) assumes the influence is negative. (D) We cannot assume that simply because all the variables are not understood, social scientists have ignored the topic. This cannot be true, according to the information given, because enough is known to establish the relationships which are discussed. This means that the topic has received some attention. (E) This is a conclusion. However, the author says that no conclusions can be drawn, since not enough is known about the variables. Perhaps the most important factor for predicting educational attainment is socio-economic background prior to marriage. We simply cannot tell, based on the passage.

18. **(B)** Choices (A), (C), (D), and (E) are possible choices. The only choice which is not possible is (B). According to the passage, the best test of an answer is its ability to overcome objections. If we do not know what objections to an answer exist, we have not seen the answer put to the test. If we have not seen it put to the test, we do not know how strong it is. Therefore, we cannot judge its strength relative to other possible answers.

19. **(C)** (A) One cannot judge, based on the passage, whether cold fusion is controversial or not. Even if it is not controversial, the author of the passage would argue that since the theory the scientist is presenting is new, he should

accept criticism in an attempt to discover how well it meets plausible objections. (B) While this might be true, it would be of much less importance to the author of the passage than discovering the strength of the new theory. That could be done only by the scientist's accepting criticism and objections to the paper. (C) This is the best answer. By accepting comments, the scientist might discover objections to his new theory which he had previously overlooked. This would give him the opportunity to see if the theory could overcome the objections, or have to be modified in some way to accommodate those objections. (D) A theory is a tentative explanation of some phenomenon, which is deserving of consideration until it is proven wrong. For the scientist not to accept objections would mean that he was unwilling to have the theory tested to see if it was valid. Therefore, the author could not agree with the scientist's decision for the reason which Answer (D) proposes. (E) A conference of scientists would be the perfect place for a dialogue about the merits of a scientific theory. Since both those presenting papers and those listening to presentations are likely to be well trained in the field, a very good dialogue could be expected.

20. **(B)** (A) The argument does not assume this. It does not argue, for example, that government should not pass laws to regulate overtime pay, or to maintain minimum working conditions. (B) This is the correct answer. The last sentence says that minimum wage laws shut out of the job market employees who are not worth that pay. To be shut out of the job market means not to be hired. The clear assumption is that employers do not hire such people. (C) The author leaves this question to the side in the sentence which reads, "Yet, even if that were true...." Thus, the author is willing to grant the assumption that employers would sometimes take advantage of unskilled workers. (D) This cannot be the answer. If government could not enforce minimum wage laws, the laws would have no effect on the job market. The laws would not shut anyone out of the job market. (E) Again, the argument does not establish that government has no role to play in helping unskilled workers. Perhaps it should be responsible for unemployment benefits, national health care, or countless other such programs.

21. **(E)** (A) First, the statements do not draw an analogy. An analogy shows how one thing resembles another. The article and the menu change are not necessarily analogous. We do not know the reason for the menu change. If it was not motivated by concern about animal fat, it is not like the article in any way. Second, since we do not know the reason for the change, we do not know if the events are related or not. (B) The argument is not generalizing, but attempting to establish causation. It is trying to establish that the article brought about the menu change. In addition, we do not know if the events share any of the same characteristics. The first event is the publishing of an article showing concern about animal fats in the diet. The second is a menu change that might have been a response to shortages of animal fat to fry potatoes in. Therefore, instead of being of the same type, the events may be totally dissimilar. (C) Even if the menu change was a response to the article, the manager might have been told of it,

instead of having read it himself. (D) This answer assumes that some reason has been given by the cafeteria for the switch. None was mentioned in the passage. The passage is not questioning the reason, but postulating a reason where none has been given. (E) This is the answer. Just because the article appeared yesterday and the menu change today, does not mean that the one caused the other. Any of a number of other factors could have caused the change.

22.   **(B)**   (A) The statements do not substantiate this. Just because the author can point to two untrained managers who have succeeded does not mean that training is always undesirable for managers. (B) The author is showing that, in some cases, lack of previous training was not a hindrance to on-the-job performance of managers. One may assume, then, that there are cases where such training is not necessary for success. It is possible that the director of corporation T is one of those who will succeed despite lack of training. He may be like the directors of corporations R and S in that respect. (C) This cannot be true, according to the information given in the passage. The passage cites two cases where managers succeeded despite lack of previous training. (D) Just because the passage cites three examples of corporate managers without training does not mean that the author assumes that few managers have such training. In fact, the author assumes the opposite. If few have such training it would not be necessary to argue that the director of corporation T may succeed despite lack of such training. (E) One would infer the opposite from the argument. If it is necessary to cite examples of some who have succeeded despite lack of training, it would appear that training is normally a prerequisite for success. Therefore, corporations would seek to hire those with previous training.

23.   **(C)**   (A) If past estimates have been low, present estimates may also be low. This means that the demand will probably be as great or greater than predicted. This is a good argument for going ahead with the project, not the opposite. (B) If energy shortages are still likely, they will be even more likely without the project. This is an argument in favor of the project. (C) This is the best answer. If alternate energy sources are available, perhaps they are less polluting and environmentally damaging than strip mining. They would then be preferable to strip mining. (D) If citizens have expressed no opinions, they may favor strip mining. This could, then, be in strip mining's favor. (E) While this may not be a good argument in favor of strip mining, it is also not an argument against it.

24.   **(C)**   This is an example of circular reasoning. The author argues that intelligent people choose one thing over another, and that act of choosing, by itself, makes them more intelligent. Look for the answer which duplicates this type of argument. (A) The word "intelligent" has at least this meaning in the passage: intelligence is something that enables one to make better choices. Therefore, (A) cannot be the answer, because it states that the term does not have any meaning. (B) The only thing that could be construed as an example is the choosing of one vacation spot over another. However, the passage cites no evidence to

show that that choice is an intelligent one. Therefore, this example cannot establish the point that they are more intelligent for having made it. (C) This is exactly what the passage does. (D) and (E) are both plausible answers. However, they do not get the major flaw of the argument, which is circular reasoning.

25. **(E)** You are seeking an argument which asserts something as a fact, then attempts to prove it by asserting it again in a slightly altered form. (A) This is a valid form of the syllogism. It takes the following form: Homemakers prefer Vizz; homemakers are the best judges of home products; therefore, Vizz must be better. (B) This offers two reasons why Vizz is better: Homemakers prefer it; and it is useful in more than one type of chore. (C) This offers two reasons to show why oversized rackets are preferable: advanced players — who should be good judges of rackets — prefer them; and they have more power. (D) This tells you two things about Porsches: people with class like them; and they last longer. (E) This attempts to establish that Porsches are better by arguing that people with class drive them. But the only way you know that those people have class is that they drive Porsches. This is identical to the reasoning in the passages.

26. **(D)** This question asks you to look for the answer which: (1) states a fact about the members of some group; (2) concludes that, because the fact is true of the individual members, it is true of the group which the members comprise. Answer (A) uses the opposite approach to what the question asks for. It concludes that a member of a group, Lynn, will be somewhere at a certain time, because the group as a whole is there at that time. Instead of extrapolating from a fact known about the members to a conclusion about the group, it extrapolates from the group to a particular member. (B) This answer draws no conclusions about Camaros as a whole, based on particular Camaros. It speaks only of a red Camaro and a blue one. (C) This answer states a fact about the group, chili, and draws a conclusion about the members based on that fact. This is just the opposite of what you are to look for. (D) This answer states a fact about the members of group, and draws a conclusion about the group based on that fact. Of course, the argument is flawed. But you were not asked to identify a flaw in the argument, but to identify a certain type of argument. (E) This answer draws a conclusion about Ed, a member of a group, based on a statement about the group as a whole.

Section II — Analytical Reasoning

QUESTIONS 1-5

Sample Diagrams

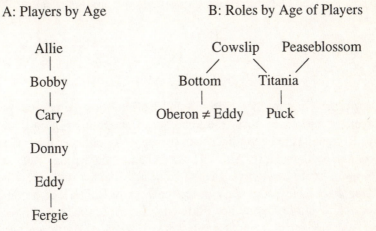

A: Players by Age

Allie
|
Bobby
|
Cary
|
Donny
|
Eddy
|
Fergie

B: Roles by Age of Players

Cowslip   Peaseblossom
/   \   /
Bottom   Titania
| |
Oberon ≠ Eddy   Puck

In the second diagram, those on different tracks (\ | /) are not ordered with respect to one another. Note: Only Peaseblossom and Cowslip can be played by Allie, the oldest, since everyone else is marked as younger than someone. Similarly, Fergie can play only Oberon or Puck.

1.　**(A)**　Revised Diagram B with information from this question.
　　Cowslip
　　Bottom
　Oberon　　Peaseblossom
　　　　　Titania
　　　　　Puck

Once Peaseblossom is said to be played by someone younger than someone else, only Cowslip is left to be played by the oldest, Allie. So, (A), that Allie plays Cowslip, must be right. Since Cowslip's player must be the oldest, it cannot be the second or third oldest (B) or (C) or any younger place (D). (E) is directly ruled out from the beginning, since whoever plays Cowslip must be older than the two who play Puck and Titania at least, and Eddy is older than only one person.

2.　**(A)**　This uses the original Diagram B.

(B) cannot be right because Titania has to be played by someone younger than the person playing Peaseblossom, so places four and five, at least, are reversed. Further, Peaseblossom cannot be played by Eddy, since whoever plays Peaseblossom has to be older than two other players and Eddy is older than only one. Eddy is also the reason (C) is wrong, for Eddy is explicitly said not to play Oberon, but that role is assigned Eddy in list (C). In list (D), Donny plays Puck,

but Donny is older than Eddy, who plays Titania. Since Titania's player has to be older than Puck's, list (D) is ruled out. (E) fails because the person playing Bottom has to be younger than the one playing Cowslip — places 2 and 3, at least, are reversed in this list. This leaves (A) as the right answer and indeed (A) is possible. The order runs down the left side of diagram B and then down the right.

3.   **(B)**   Revised Diagram B using information from this question:
Cowslip
Bottom
Oberon
Peaseblossom
Puck

If Cary plays Oberon, then Cowslip and Bottom must be played by the two older players, in order, to satisfy the left side of Diagram B. In particular, whoever plays Bottom has to be younger than someone — whoever plays Cowslip — and so cannot be the oldest, Allie. Thus, (A) must be wrong. But the person playing Bottom has to be younger than the oldest, Allie, but older than the person playing Oberon. Since that is Cary in this case, only Bobby can possibly fit in. So, (B) is right. Neither Donny nor Eddy can play Bottom since neither is older than Cary, the person playing Oberon. Thus, (C) and (D) are wrong. Finally, Fergie cannot play Bottom since there is someone younger than the Bottom player, namely, the Oberon player, but no one is younger than Fergie. Thus, (E) is wrong as well.

4.   **(C)**   This uses the original Diagram B.

The list (C) is not a possible ordering, since the person playing Puck has to be younger than the one playing Titania. Positions 3 and 5 in (C) are, thus, wrong. All of the other cases are possible. Nothing prevents Cowslip from being older than Peaseblossom or Titania from being younger than Oberon, so (A) satisfies the conditions. (D) is just (A) with a different, permitted choice of which of the top two is to be first. In (B) and (E) pieces from one path in Diagram B are inserted into other paths at places where relative positions are not determined, so the results continue to satisfy the rules.

5.   **(C)**   Revised Diagram B, using information from this question

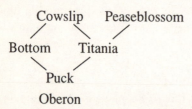

If Puck is played by the next to youngest, the youngest must play Oberon, since one of these two had to be played by the youngest. Thus, the person playing Puck must be younger than whoever plays Titania and the person playing Oberon is sure to be younger than whoever plays Bottom. Bobby cannot play Titania,

however, since Bobby is next to the oldest and the person playing Titania is younger than the players of both Cowslip and Peaseblossom. Thus, (A) is not possible. On the other hand, if Fergie is Titania, then the youngest would be playing Titania, and it is stated that this person is older than Puck. This conflicts with the conditions, so (B) is not possible. If Donny is Titania, Allie, Bobby and Cary can divvy up Cowslip, Peaseblossom, and Bottom in a number of ways within the conditions laid down. Thus, (C) is the right answer. (D) and (E) fail because they are the oldest and the conditions state that the person playing Titania must be younger than two other people.

QUESTION 6-11
Initial Summary

Assuming each asked,
G: G i.e., G will be in the list
H: H <=> K i.e., H runs just in case K does
I: I<=>J
J: J <=> -G i.e., Janet's running implies G does not and conversely
K: K <=> -I
Anyone not asked does not run

6.   **(C)**   Since he was asked, George will run. Since George will run, Janet will not, since she and George cannot appear on the same slate. Thus, not all five will run, so (E) is incorrect. Since Janet will not run, neither will Irene, who will run only when Janet does. Thus, at least two of the five will not run, so it is not true that at least four will run. (D) is false. Since Irene will not run, Kay will run. Thus, at least 2 will run — George and Kay, so (A), that only one will run, is false. Since Kay will run, so will Henry, who runs (when asked) whenever Kay does. Thus, George, Kay and Henry will all run. This makes 3, so (C) is correct. It is more than 2, so (B) is wrong.

7.   **(C)**   Since George was not asked, he will not run. Janet was asked, though, and, so, she will run because George does not. That means at least one person will run and, so, (A) is wrong. Irene, in turn, will run because Janet will and that means at least two people will run, not just one. So, (B) is wrong as well. But Irene's running means that Kay will not run, since she will not run with Irene. Thus, at least two of the five will not run, and so (E) which says four will run, is wrong. Finally, Kay's not running prevents Henry from running. Thus, only Janet and Irene will run, exactly two people. So, (C) is the correct answer. (D) fails, of course, because Harry does not run and thus three of the five do not, meaning that fewer than three do.

8.   **(E)**   Janet was not asked and so will not run. But then, Irene will not run, even though asked, for she will not run without Janet. Thus, (B) and (E), which includes Irene among the candidates, is wrong. Since Irene will not run,

Kay will. And, since Kay will run, so will Henry. Thus, just Kay and Henry will run. The fact that Kay runs means that (A), "only Henry," is wrong and similarly, the fact that Henry will run means that (C) is wrong. Thus, (E) is the right answer.

9.   **(A)**   George will run, because he was asked to. Janet was not asked to run, so she will not. But then, Irene will not run, for Janet will not. Thus, (C) and (D), which include Irene as a candidate, must be wrong. Kay will not run because she was not asked to. Consequently, Henry, though asked, will not run. (B) and (D), which have Henry as a candidate, are wrong. So, only George will run and only (A) is correct.

10.   **(B)**   If George were asked to run, he would. Consequently, Janet would not run even if she were asked to, for she never runs with George. But then, Irene, who will only run with Janet, would not run either. So, George and Irene cannot run together. (B) is correct. Continuing the same line of reasoning, starting with George running, since Irene does not run, Kay does, if asked, so George and Kay can serve together, needing only that they both are asked. So (C) is not a pair who cannot run together. And, if Kay runs and Henry is asked, he will run as well. Thus, neither (A) nor (D) is an impossible pair. Finally, if George is not asked, and so does not run, but Janet and Irene are asked, they will run together, Janet because George is not running and Irene because Janet is running. So (E) is also not an impossible pair.

11.   **(D)**   If George is asked to run, be will run. But if George runs, Janet will not. Since the committee wants Janet to run, the committee must not ask George. So, (A), which contains George, will not achieve the desired result. Janet will also not run if she is not asked, so (C), which does not ask Janet to run, will not work. Henry will not run if Kay does not and Kay will not run if not asked, so, since the committee wants Henry to run, it must ask Kay. Thus, Plans (A), (B), and (E), which do not ask Kay, will not work. This leaves plan (D), which will work: Janet will run because Irene will not (for the same reason). But then Henry will run as well, since Kay does.

12.   **(C)**   To get the largest number in, begin with the smallest and build up until capacity is reached. The total capacity is six tons or 12,000 pounds. So, one crate weighing 1000 pounds can go in, giving a total of 1000 pounds. Look at totals after various additions (in 1000 pound units)

total crates	#/weight	weight	total weight
1	1 @ 1	1	1
3	2 @ 2	4	5
6	3 @ 3	9	14

This is too much, but not putting all of the last group in gives

5	2 @ 3	6	11

So, a total of five crates can be stowed, making answer (C) correct. Clearly, using any of the heavier crates will allow no more crates to be stowed. Using only one of the 3000 pound crates and I of the 4000 pounders would still permit only five crates, though it would bring the total weigh up to 12,000 pounds.

As for the other answers, the chart above shows a way to have only three crates aboard and still have room for more (1 @1 and 2 @2 leaves room for 2 @3), so (A) is wrong. Similarly, (B) is shown wrong by the possibility of having four crates consisting of 1 @1, 2 @2, 1 @3 and still having room for 1 @3 or even 1 @4. (D) fails because the lightest possible using 6 crates is the combination listed first above and that weighs more than is available. Finally, (E) fails since it must inevitably weigh even more than a combination of six crates and that is already more than allowed.

13. **(B)**   To find the minimum number, start with the heaviest, in this case, the 4,000-pound crates. Three of them will exactly fill the 12,000 pound limit, so answer (B) is correct. Using lighter crates will require more crates to come up to the required weight. (A) has to be wrong, for the most that two crates could weigh is 8,000 pounds (2 @4,000) which is less than the amount allowed. The remaining cases fail because five is the maximum number of crates that can be stowed.

14. **(D)**   Given that 3 @3,000, i.e., 9,000 pounds, are stowed, only 3,000 pounds remain. With the crates available, the maximum number to fill that space would be

1	@1	1	1
1	@2	2	3

So, two more crates could be gotten on. The fact that this is possible, means that (E) only one more crate, does not represent the maximum. On the other hand, any combination involving more crates will weigh more than the permitted amount. (A), (B), and (C) must, then, all be wrong. In addition, each of these would involve more than five crates being stowed (the 3 @3 plus the addition number > 2) and five is the maximum number of crates which could be stowed.

15. **(D)**   Except for the two-ton crates, all the crates cost $10 per 1,000 pounds to ship. The two-ton crates cost less per 1,000 pounds. So, the maximum shipping charge would come from shipping 12,000 pounds at the higher rate, i.e., $120 total, answer (D). The purser could reach full capacity at this rate in several ways, for example one 1,000-pound crate, one 2,000-pound crate, and three 3,000-pound crates. (A) gives the rate for full capacity at the lower rate, three 2 ton crates @$25. But the higher rate is available and gives a larger total charge.

(B) could be reached by using two two-ton crates and two one-ton ones, but still uses part of the lower rate and so does not maximize the total charge. (C) is probably the result of not putting on a full six tons of cargo, using perhaps one 1,000-pound crate, two one-ton crates, and two one-and-a-half-ton crates — the maximum number but not the maximum tonnage allowable, and so not as high a charge as possible. (E) is not a possible charge at all, since even at the higher rate, it would require 15,000 pounds of cargo and there is only 12,000 available.

16.   **(B)**   The guaranteed total would be the minimum obtainable under the condition, that he use at least 6,000 pounds. Since, except for the cheaper two-ton crates, crates go for $10 per 1,000 pounds, this total must be at most $60, i.e., all 6,000 pounds at the highest rate. But it is possible to take some of this tonnage in two-ton crates at the lower rate, so $60 is not the minimum under the conditions and (E) is wrong. In particular, the purser could lead one two-ton crate at $25 and one one-ton crate at $20 for a total of $45 dollars in charges for three tons. So, (C) and (D) are also not minimum charges. On the other hand, there is no way to get down to $40 without taking on less than three tons, for, at the higher rate, $40 would only pay for two tons of freight, while the lower rate only applies to units of two tons each, one of which would be $25 but too light and two of which would be $50 and also too heavy. The nearest combinations of rates would be a two-ton crate and a 1,000-pound crate, which would be only $35 and would be too light or the two-ton and the one-ton which give the actual minimum noted. So, (A) does not give a minimum for the given conditions.

QUESTIONS 17-21

Original set up of the schematic

Black Player

White Player

Only items connected by lines are placed correctly relative to one another, except that position relative to the White Queen — left or right, nearer to or farther from the White Player is also set.

17.   **(C)**   The White King is given as nearer the White Player than the White Queen, so the cases which place it farther away, (B) and (E), must be wrong. The diagram above shows that four pieces are to the right of the White Queen and it is given that twice as many pieces are to the right as to the left of the White Queen. So, there must be at least two pieces to the left of the White Queen. Only the Black

Bishop is shown on the left and only the White King remains to be placed, so it must be on the left as well. So, the White King lies toward the White Player from the White Queen and to the left, (C). The fact that there are only six pieces besides the White Queen on the board and that are divided into those left and those right of the White Queen, with all accounted for, means that none are in the same column as the White Queen. Thus, neither (A) nor (B) can be correct. The fact that the White King must be to the left of the White Queen, as argued above, means that (D) and (E), which have it to the right of the White Queen, are not correct.

The final chart must be:

Black Player

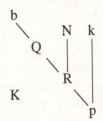

White Player

18.   **(A)**   Only the Black Bishop, White Knight, and Black King are beyond the White Queen, so only the Black Bishop and White Knight could be on the same row as the Black King, since all on the row must be the same distance from the White edge. Thus, (D) and (E), which say that there are three or four items on that row, must be wrong. Black King is in the same column as the Black Pawn and the Black Bishop is diagonally to the left and away from the Black Pawn, so the Black Bishop must also be to the left, not right, of the Black King. So, only the White Knight could be to the right of the Black King and (C), which says that two items might be, is wrong. But the White Knight is in the same column as the White Rook, which is to the left and away from the Black Pawn. The White Knight is thus to the left of the Black Pawn and so also of the Black King. So even the White Knight is not to the right of the Black King. Thus, (B) is wrong, for not even one piece is to the right of the Black King. So, (A), that no pieces are to the right of the Black King, is correct.

19.   **(E)**   The White Knight is in the same column as the White Rook and the White Rook is to the left of (and away from) the black Pawn, so the White Knight is to the left of the Black Pawn. But the Black King is in the same column as the Black Pawn, so the White Knight is also to the left of the Black King. Thus, the claim in (E) has to be true. On the other hand, the White Rook is farther from the White Player than the Black Pawn (and to the left), so (A) is false. The White Queen is on the left and away diagonally from the Black Pawn, so it is to the left of the Black Pawn. But the Black King is in the same column as the Black Pawn, so the White Queen is to the left, not right, of the Black King and (D) is false. (B) and (C) may be true, but do not have to be. The White King is

nearer to the White Player than the Black Bishop, but is not located left to right relative to the Black Bishop, so it is false that (C) must be true. Similarly, the Black Pawn is clearly to the right of the White King but is not located relative to it in distance from the White Player, so (B) does not have to be true.

20. **(C)** Nearer to the Black Player means farther from the White Player. So, the White Queen, which is nearer to the White Player than the Black Bishop, cannot be also nearer to the Black Player. This goes also for the pieces nearer to the White Player than the White Queen: the White King, the White Rook and the Black Pawn. Thus — including the Black Bishop itself, five pieces CANNOT be nearer the Black Player than the Black Bishop. This means that at most 2 can be, so, (A) and (B) are wrong. The two possibilities are the White Knight and the Black King, both of which are, like the Black Bishop, are farther from the White Player — so they are nearer to the Black Player — than the White Queen. But all that can be inferred for sure about these in relation to the Black Bishop is that they are right of it, from the White Player's point of view, not which is nearer to or farther from the White Player. Thus, both might be nearer the Black Player than the Bishop. So, (C) is the correct answer. Either (D) or (E) might be the number that actually is closer in a given case, for either or both of the White Knight and Black King could be as far or father from the Black Player as the Bishop, but none of these has to be true, so (C) might be, which is what is asked for.

21. **(D)** Because they are farther along the leftward diagonal from the Black Pawn than the White Rook, both the White Queen and the Black Bishop must be left of the White Rook. Thus, at least two pieces must be left of the White Rook and (A) and (B), which say that fewer than two are wrong. Further, since the White King is to the left of the White Queen, which is to the left of the White Rook, the White King is to the left of the White Rook as well. Thus, three pieces must be left of the White Rook and (C), which says that at most two are, is wrong. On the other hand, the Black Pawn is before the White Rook on the leftward diagonal and, so, is not left of the White Rook. The Black King is in the same column as the Black Pawn and so no farther left than the Black Pawn and thus also not left of the White Rook. Finally, the White Knight is in the same column as the White Rook and thus exactly as far left as the White Rook, so not left of the White Rook. Thus, so there cannot be four left of the White Rook and (E) is false. But three definitely are left of the White Rook, so (D) is correct.

QUESTIONS 22-26

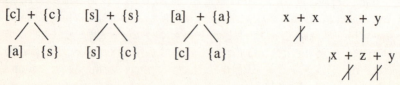

22. **(A)** Only Smoke cavies produce male offspring of the same color as the parents, so (A) must be right. Coal cavies produce neither offspring the same color as the parents, so (B) and (E) must be wrong. And (C) is wrong, because male offspring of an Ash pair is Coal, not Ash. (D) fails for the same reason as (C).

23. **(D)** The possible sequences of generations are {c}-{s}-{c}, {s}-{c}-{s}, and {a}-{a}-{a}. The other three patterns at the second generation result in a granddaughter of a different color from the grandmother: {c}-[a]-{a}, {s}-[s]-{c}, and {a}-[c]-{s}. What all the successful ones have in common is that the middle member is also female, i.e., that the granddaughter is the grandmother's daughter's daughter (D). The second (and third) patterns above show that (A) is false and the first and third show that (B) is also false. The three failing patterns all show that the middle link cannot be male, i.e., that (C) is false. And the first and second patterns – the no-Ash pairs – show that (E) is false.

Section III — Reading Comprehension

1. **(C)** This question requires the test-taker to pick the primary purpose of the passage. The passage begins by suggesting the courts have not received sufficient scientific scrutiny because they have not been viewed as political bodies. The passage continues by noting the traditional use of case analysis. The author argues that this method has too narrow a focus and does not allow one to see the broader aspects of the workings of courts. The author admits that case studies have some merit, but advocates broader, more scientific, studies. (C) is correct because the first two sentences of the passage suggest that the judiciary is not studied properly. Next the author describes why the judiciary is studied, using the case analysis method, then continues by pointing out the problems of this method. The author concludes the passage by suggesting greater benefits would occur if the judiciary were studied differently. (A) is incorrect because by stating it is a "myth that judges are nonpolitical arbiters of the law" (fourth paragraph), the author shows a belief that judges are political, and notes most judicial scholars are also aware that judges are political actors. The assertion by the author that judges are political actors is only one piece of evidence in support of his more general thesis. (B) is incorrect because the author clearly states, "[t]his is not to say the judicial branch has lacked all scrutiny, only that it has traditionally been viewed from a perspective different from the other two branches of government" (first paragraph). (D) is incorrect because very little information on the case analysis method is given. It is mentioned only as supporting evidence for the broader proposition that study of the judiciary must be more scientific. (E) is also incorrect. As with response (D), the passage only mentions judicial review in passing. The mention of judicial review is used only to give an example of how the cult of the robe has led people to view judges as being nonpolitical.

2. **(B)** Marshall's conclusion is that judges should interpret the Constitution because they are nonpolitical. This suggests whether decision makers are political makes a difference in how they interpret the Constitution. Marshall's assumption in choosing the courts for this task is that political actors such as executives and legislatures cannot be impartial. (A) is incorrect because there is no mention in the passage of education levels. The reference to qualifications in the passage concerns whether the decision makers are politically motivated, not how well educated they are. (C) is incorrect because there is no mention that Marshall believed judges to have a greater understanding of the Constitution. Again, Marshall emphasized the *political* differences between judges and other members of government. (D) is incorrect because Marshall's statements do not relate to the study of the judiciary. Marshall was concerned with interpretation of the Constitution. It is the author of the passage who is concerned with the study of the judiciary. The author only uses Marshall's comments as an example of the kind of thinking which led to the emphasis on studying individual cases. (E) is incorrect. As with (D), Marshall's comments do not pertain to the use of precedent. His comments are concerned with the *who* of interpreting the Constitution, not the *how*.

3. **(E)** The phrase *cult of the robe* is introduced immediately after Marshall's comments on the inability of the politically motivated branches of government to be nonpolitical arbiters of the Constitution (first paragraph). The author directly links Marshall's comments to the cult of the robe by saying his comments are "a classic example" of these beliefs. (A) is incorrect because the cult of the robe is shown to be a belief in the neutrality of judges, not a particular method of interpreting the Constitution. (B) is incorrect for the same reason as (A). In addition, it is *stare decisis* which is the *use* of past cases, not the cult of the robe. (C) is incorrect. The author argues that the cult of the robe has *influenced* the study of the courts, but it is not itself a method of study. (D) is incorrect. The author makes clear that the use of individual cases in decision making, or the use of precedent, is "known in legal terms as *stare decisis*" (third paragraph).

4. **(D)** In the third and fourth paragraphs the author argues belief in the cult of the robe has led to a reliance on the case analysis method. In the fourth and fifth paragraphs the author argues this method is inadequate. (A) is incorrect because the author argues that the cult of the robe is a myth. The author also indicates "judicial scholars by and large do not subscribe to the myth" (fourth paragraph). (B) is incorrect because the author is not contrasting the advantages of *stare decisis* and the cult of the robe. In addition, as mentioned in the explanation to question three, the cult is not a method, but the belief that judges are nonpolitical. (C) is incorrect because the author notes that most judicial scholars do not subscribe to the myth of the cult of the robe (fourth paragraph). The author continues by arguing that even though researchers do not believe the myth, they still focus on judicial biographies and case studies. Thus, according to the author, researchers are not being misled, but are also not properly studying the courts.

(E) is incorrect because just the opposite has occurred. The author is suggesting there is too much study of individual cases, which follows from the belief that judges are nonpolitical arbiters of the law (second paragraph).

5.   **(A)**   The paraphrase of Wieland suggests that by concentrating on the details of individual cases, researchers lose sight of the broader workings of courts. This fits the author's overall theme that broader studies of the courts must be undertaken. (B) is incorrect. The author is not suggesting courts are organic entities, or that they are trees. The reference to Wieland's statement about trees is intended as a metaphor for the consequences of examining something in minute detail. (C) is incorrect. Other parts of the passage do argue that judges are political, but the reference to Wieland does not. At this stage in the passage the author has already provided evidence of the cult of the robe, and how it has led to the traditional study of individual cases. In referring to Wieland, the author is suggesting that one loses sight of the greater whole when concentrating on individual cases. (D) is incorrect. Precedent, *per se*, is not a problem. The author says so in the reference to Joyce Kilmer by saying, metaphorically, that there is value in examining individual cases. According to the author, the problem is the *exclusive* reliance on precedent. It is for this reason the author advocates broader studies of courts (A). (E) is incorrect. The case analysis method relies on the study of individual cases. In referring to Wieland, the author is suggesting that something is lost or missing by only concentrating on the details (individual cases).

6.   **(D)**   In the preceding reference to Wieland, the author suggests something is lost or missing by concentrating only on individual cases. Nevertheless, in referring to Kilmer, the author suggests that the study of individual cases does have some merit. (A) is incorrect because the passage does not address the question of the beauty of studying courts. It can be assumed that the author feels the study of courts has merit. The reference to beauty, however, metaphorically suggests that there is value in studying individual cases. (B) is incorrect. The author is concerned about too much emphasis on individual *cases*, but the author does not mention individual *courts*. (C) is incorrect. As noted above, the reference to Kilmer is intended to recognize there is some merit in studying individual cases, but this does not mean researchers should *rely* on them. Attaching such a meaning to the Kilmer reference would make the author's arguments contradictory. (E) is incorrect. The author recognizes "judicial scholars by and large do not subscribe to the myth that judges are nonpolitical arbiters of the law" (fourth paragraph), so it is unnecessary to discourage belief in the cult. In addition, as with (C), if (E) were true it would lead to a contradictory argument by the author.

7.   **(C)**   This is the point of the Wieland reference. The author is arguing for broader studies of courts rather than narrowly focused biographies and case studies. (A) is incorrect. Although it may be true that every case is different in some regard, this is not the problem the author is addressing. The author is concerned with the method of studying cases, not the cases themselves. (B) is incorrect. The

author's concern is not with recognition of the political aspects of courts. The author recognizes that most judicial scholars do not believe judges are nonpolitical actors (fourth paragraph). Nevertheless, the author believes there to be undue reliance on case studies in judicial research, so the problem is not with recognition of the political aspects of courts. (D) is incorrect for the same reasons as (B). The cult of the robe is mentioned merely to show what led to the current reliance on case studies and judicial biographies. The author does not believe the cult of the robe to be a current problem (fourth paragraph). (E) is incorrect. The author specifically rejects any suggestion that the details should be ignored by stating: "One must remain cognizant of the details" (third paragraph).

8.   **(A)**   The author recognizes some value in the study of individual cases (fourth paragraph), but argues that such studies cannot grasp the broader aspects of how courts work. Thus, the author is skeptical as to the value of relying solely on individual case studies. (B) is incorrect. Although the author does recognize there is some value in case studies (fourth paragraph), the author's argument centers on the belief they are used too often. The author is unsupportive of continued *reliance* on case studies for judicial analysis. (C) is incorrect. The point of the passage is to argue for more broad-based studies and less reliance on case studies. It cannot, therefore, be said the author's attitude toward case studies is neutral. (D) is incorrect. The author recognizes there is some value in case studies and judicial biographies (fourth paragraph). The author is not disdainful of such studies, only concerned that they dominate judicial research and fail to capture the broader aspects of courts. (E) is incorrect. Indifference suggests not caring about case studies and judicial biographies. The author does care about them. The value of such studies is specifically noted (fourth paragraph). In addition, the author's argument centers on the belief that such studies are used too much in judicial research. Thus, it cannot be said the author is indifferent to case studies and judicial biographies.

9.   **(C)**   The author specifically mentions strong leadership four times in the passage: 1) the death of Harold left no one able to successfully organize a resistance, 2) the election of Edgar to provide a symbol of unity, 3) the submission of the English lords to William because he was a strong leader, and 4) England's increased resistance to foreign rule when William left the country. The passage certainly describes some of William's exploits, but not in sufficient quantity or depth to be considered a chronicle. Thus, (A) is incorrect. (B) is also incorrect. Although the passage does suggest the importance of London, it does so only as one point in a broader theme. The author uses the fall of London to show how English lords were impressed with strong leadership. (D) is incorrect because the author seems to recognize William's presence was needed there as well (perhaps a fifth reference to strong leadership). The author merely notes William's absence from England caused additional resistance without making a judgment about the decision to leave. (E) is incorrect because the author *emphasizes* the importance of Harold's death. Without Harold, there was no one of sufficient ability left to organize and lead England's defense.

10.   **(B)**   The author specifically notes the English lords rallied their surviving forces in London to resist William's advance. Thus, (E) is incorrect. We are told that William's assault on London bridge failed and he realized he did not have the equipment to storm London. This shows (A) to be incorrect. William did not give up on London and turn to other parts of England, as (D) suggests. Instead he laid waste to the area surrounding London, cutting it off from supplies and reinforcements (B). Although the Anglo-Saxon lords did meet with William and surrendered to him, these were peace talks and cannot be considered treachery, making (C) incorrect.

11.   **(D)**   The author emphasizes the importance of strong leadership throughout the passage. The implication is that William should have realized this as well. By killing England's only strong leader and being a strong leader himself, he was able to conquer England and become its king. It is thus ironic that William's strong leadership gained him two kingdoms, *both* of which required his presence. The author does not suggest William's return to Normandy was based on a whim or otherwise unnecessary (A), nor does he suggest it was for administrative purposes (E). The fact a resistance was organized in William's absence means it *was* of consequence (C). The author certainly feels the decision to return to Normandy was not unimportant (B). Nevertheless, it was not a key element in England's resistance effort. The length of time William spent putting down resistance efforts (eight years) does not suggest if he had stayed there would have been no attempt to resist foreign rule.

12.   **(A)**   The last sentence of the passage makes (A) the clear answer by suggesting resistance to foreign rule was more important than the poor leadership skills of William's lieutenants. It is true that William needed to delegate administrative duties (B), but the more important consideration is English resistance to foreign rule. The degree of resistance William faced suggests even benevolent and diplomatic lieutenants would have met resistance eventually. (C) and (D) are both clearly wrong. In the last paragraph we are told that William did leave England to return to his duchy. In addition, there would be no point in noting English resistance to foreign rule if William was from England. The harsh rule of William's lieutenants probably forced him to return to England much sooner than he expected or preferred, so it was important. The remaining portion of (E) is pure speculation not supported by the passage.

13.   **(B)**   As (B) suggests, the author says, "They immediately elected as king Edgar ... to provide a symbol of resistance and unity." Although Edgar was a Saxon, as was Harold, there is no suggestion in the passage that Edgar was a descendant of Harold's (D), nor that Edgar's heritage was of significance apart from serving as a rallying point. Thus, (A) is also incorrect. The purpose of electing Edgar king was to rally English forces to defeat William. There is no suggestion in the passage electing Edgar king would in any way prevent William's ascension to the throne other than his possible military defeat — which did not

occur (C). There is also no mention of constitutional requirements, which makes (E) irrelevant.

14.   **(E)**   The author notes that after the death of Harold there was a willingness to resist, but "no leadership to call it forth." Recognizing this lack of leadership and the strong leadership of William makes it clear the death of Harold signals the fall of England. This makes (A) wrong, and (B) is wrong simply because there was no strong English leader. There is no suggestion in the passage that the English planned to mount a counteroffensive in Normandy or had allies there who would. The entire passage is concerned with events in England, thus making (D) incorrect. Although the author notes Stigand, the Archbishop of Canterbury, was the first to submit to William, the implication seems to be that this was merely the first of what would eventually be many. There is no indication the archbishop was a determining factor in the fate of England (C).

15.   **(D)**   The author notes after his victory in London and ascension to the throne, "William strengthened his hold upon the new land." (A) is incorrect because William returned to Normandy three months after being crowned, and only after he felt he was in sufficient control. The passage begins with the battle of Hastings where Harold was defeated, and then William advanced on London. Thus, (B) is incorrect. (C) is wrong because we are told it was the resistance of Kentishmen which forced William to return to England from Normandy. (E) is wrong because Edgar was defeated at London, and also because Saxony is not part of England.

16.   **(B)**   The author begins the passage by suggesting absolute moral rules are implausible. He then provides evidence and examples leading to the conclusion that they are also impossible to maintain. (A) is incorrect because the discussion of Dutch fishermen is only mentioned as an example of how two absolute moral rules can come into conflict, forcing the actors (the Dutch fishermen in the example) to violate at least one of two absolute rules. The author does point out a difference in between Kant and Geach, but this difference is not central to the passage (C). The author mentions the difference to show how each philosopher deals with the possibility of conflicting absolute moral rules and then refutes each position. The author is not arguing against moral rules in general, nor is their inconsistency of paramount concern (D). The problem, according to the author, is the *absoluteness* of the rules. This is emphasized in the last sentence of the passage. The consideration of hypothetical philosophical problems (E) is used to show how absolute moral rules can come into conflict. The hypotheticals are used as examples only, and are not the central focus of the passage.

17.   **(E)**   The author notes Geach's position at the end of the second paragraph: "God will not permit such circumstances to exist in the real world." One may invent fictitious conflicts, but, according to Geach, since absolute moral rules are divine commands, God would not allow a conflict to arise in the real world. The

passage makes no mention of how Geach would explain the case of the Dutch fishermen (A), or the Inquiring Murderer (D). (B) is clearly the opposite of Geach's position. The author makes it clear in the second paragraph that although both Kant and Geach believe in absolute moral rules, their reasons are very different (C).

18. **(A)** The passage mentions The Case of the Inquiring Murderer, but does not tell us what it is about. Nevertheless, the author does indicate in the first sentence that it serves as an argument against absolute moral rules. In the third paragraph the author indicates the example of the Dutch fishermen provides a real example which makes the same point as that of the Inquiring Murderer; more than one absolute moral rule raises the possibility of conflict. We can deduce that The Case of the Inquiring Murderer also illustrates the possibility of conflict. Given the author's description of the two cases in the third paragraph (B) cannot be correct. The Case of the Inquiring Murderer is used to argue *against* absolute moral rules. Thus, (D) is incorrect, as is (C), since Geach supports the existence of absolute moral rules. (E) is incorrect because the author specifically states The Case of the Inquiring Murderer is fictitious.

19. **(B)** The author's purpose is to argue against absolute moral rules. He cannot, therefore, believe Kant's position which supports their existence. This makes (A) incorrect, as well as (D). Given the effort the author spends refuting Kant's position, it cannot be said that he is indifferent to it (C). Nevertheless, the author gives no indication that he thinks Kant's position is stupid, trivial, or otherwise deserving of disdain (E). He merely disagrees with Kant's position and attempts to prove it wrong.

20. **(A)** As noted in the explanation to question 17, Geach believes absolute moral rules to be of divine origin, and God will not permit conflict to actually arise. Geach may find hypotheticals interesting, but nevertheless irrelevant to the real world. By arguing God will not permit conflict to occur in the real world, Geach must recognize that examples of hypothetical conflict do exist, making (B) incorrect. Geach's position is not that examples of hypothetical conflict are un- likely to occur (C). It is that God will not allow them to occur. (D) is incorrect because it is clear from the passage that although Geach recognizes the existence of examples of hypothetical conflict between absolute moral rules, he still be- lieves they exist. (E) is incorrect because Kant's position supports absolute moral rules and the hypotheticals argue against them, and because there is no mention in the passage of Geach commenting on Kant's position.

21. **(C)** The author states this directly in the last paragraph to explain why Kant's defense is untenable. It is also in this last paragraph where the author rejects the possibility that if two absolute moral rules exist they will not come into conflict (A). The author feels Kant's defense, which is (E), is weak and cannot explain every possibility. (B) is more in line with Geach's position. The

author provides a real world example of conflict by discussing the Dutch fisher-men. (D) is incorrect because Geach's position raises a different defense, that of divine intervention.

22. **(A)** The passage begins by indicating the implausibility of absolute moral rules. It continues by presenting arguments, and eventually concluding, that they are also impossible to maintain. (B) is incorrect because the author is not denouncing Kant, merely trying to show why he is wrong with regard to absolute moral rules. Other writings by Kant are neither mentioned nor relevant. Geach's position may raise questions of free will versus determinism (C), but the author does not raise the issue in his arguments. The author's example of the Dutch fishermen (D) is just that, an example. It is used in support of the basic argument, but it is not the argument itself, i.e., the author is not trying to prove something about Dutch fishermen. The author's position against absolute moral rules makes (E) clearly wrong.

23. **(B)** The author describes the biological clock of the horseshoe crab with the conclusion that its brain transmits signals to its eye to allow it to see at night. The author then suggests that this finding may help to explain how humans see. (A) is incorrect because the author recognizes much work has been done on the horseshoe crab by showing surprise that the crab's biological clock has not been discovered before. (C) is wrong because the author begins the passage by noting the simplicity of the crab's visual system, and concludes by noting how complex the human visual system is. The author does briefly mention two types of neural connections associated with visual systems, but the point of the reference is how they are part of a visual system (D). The author finds it interesting that this discovery was only recently made with regard to a visual system which is one of the most thoroughly studied. From the importance the author places on the study we can assume the author would not argue the visual system of the crab is too simple to warrant further study (E).

24. **(E)** This is stated in the first sentence of the third paragraph. (A) is incorrect because it is not the nocturnal activities of horseshoe crabs which inter-ests the author, but how the crabs can adapt to changes in light levels. Human inability to see at night is only briefly mentioned in counterpoint to the ability of crabs. There is no indication in the passage that the author has also studied human visual systems (B). (C) is incorrect because it is what the author *discov-ered* while studying the horseshoe crab. In the first sentence of the passage the author seems to imply that the crab's visual system is no longer thought to be primitive. In addition, according to the author's statement in paragraph three, the point of his study was not the crab's visual system *per se*, but how the system adapted to different light levels. Thus, (D) is incorrect.

25. **(C)** The passage is describing how the horseshoe crab's visual system adapts to changing light levels. The author does not make any reference to

artificial lighting, so we can assume the changes are natural and follow the normal 24-hour day. The author does note the great age of *Limulus* (the horse-shoe crab), but this has nothing to do with its biological clock (except, perhaps, that it took that long to develop) (A). (B) is incorrect because there is no mention in the passage as to whether the crab sleeps. Mention of biological clocks in humans often refer to the fact women stop producing eggs later in life. In this passage, however, the reference concerns how the crab's visual system has adapted to daily changes from light to dark, not its reproductive system (D). The passage does not compare the cycles of humans and birds to that of the crab. The noted difference in the ability to see at night is a difference in what occurs during the cycle, not the cycle itself. Thus, (E) is also incorrect.

26. **(A)**   In the third paragraph the author specifically notes the importance of discovering the 24-hour biological clock in the crab. There is no indication in the passage that the author had any hand in determining the age of the species (E). In the first sentence of the last paragraph the author admits no one knows how people see, thus making (C) incorrect. Similarly, it is the author's *hope* that his discovery of the crab's adaptive system will aid in the study of the visual system of birds, but this has not yet occurred (B). (D) is incorrect because there is no indication in the passage that the human visual system is in any way related to that of the crab.

27. **(D)**   In the fourth and fifth paragraphs the author describes efferent and afferent connections. The fourth paragraph discusses two-way connections, then the fifth begins with the phrase "Similar efferent connections" from which we can deduce that efferent connections are two-way connections. (A) is wrong because there is no mention of the crab's anatomy or physical appearance. (B) is incorrect because the first sentence of the fifth paragraph specifically indicates these connections have been found in animals other than birds. If any such timer exists, it does so in the crab's brain, as we are told in the third paragraph. The discussion of efferent connections concerns how the information from the brain and timer reaches the eyes. Thus, (C) is incorrect. The passage is concerned with why crabs can see at night, not why humans cannot. From the passage we can gather it is the brain which controls whether humans or crabs can see at night. The efferent connections only carry the information. Thus (E) is incorrect.

28. **(A)**   This is the point of the author's last paragraph. Given the time the author has devoted to the study of the visual system of the crab and his hope that his discovery will help to explain more complex visual systems it would be wrong to conclude the author's study is of little importance (B). (C) is incorrect because the author does not attempt to explain *why* horseshoe crabs have survived so long, only that they have. There is no mention in the passage of why or how evolution takes place, and there is no indication that further study will do so (D). (E) is incorrect because just the opposite has occurred with respect to the crab. The crab's visual system was considered very simple, but the author discovered it to be more complex than originally thought.

Section IV — Logical Reasoning

1.   **(C)**   The writer *concludes* that it is all right to eat fish (C), on the *premise* that fish eat other fish (A). This is contrary to his previous views that it is murder to eat fish (B) and that we should not eat animal food (E). He apparently thought about changing his mind because the fish smelled appetizing in the frying pan (D).

2.   **(B)**   The speaker refers to John and himself as "we," as though they were both equal (B). It is not John, but the others that the speaker regards as servants (C) and that he claims to own (A). Since the passage simply states the speaker's opinion, we cannot decide whether the speaker really owns everything (D) or whether John does not enjoy anything (E).

3.   **(B)**   The writer's conclusion is that the subjects of the passage were not impressed with death. Hence, it would be inconsistent to suggest that these people were impressed by death (B). As support for his conclusion, the writer cites the cemeteries' surfaces' displaying bones (A), the familiarity of these people with the dead (C) and with the idea of their own death (D), and the analogy of the skull in *Hamlet* (E).

4.   **(D)**   The writer rejects the view that we should never take a critical position toward another culture. Hence, this view's assertion is contrary to, not a premise for, the writer's conclusion (D). As premises for rejection of this view, the writer asserts that we cannot respect what we do not find intelligible (A); respect implies a favorable judgment (B), and a favorable judgment implies knowledge of the object of judgment (C). And the writer implies that moral isolationism is not respectful (E), since it fails to meet the requirements of the premises.

5.   **(C)**   The passage claims that Yeltsin had taken the lead thanks to Gorbachev's turn to the right, not Yeltsin's own turn (C). The passage identifies Gorbachev, not Yeltsin, as the Soviet President (A), denies that Yeltsin and Gorbachev may reconcile (B), claims that Gorbachev is divorced from the reform camp (D), and names Gorbachev, not Yeltsin, as the uncontested leader of the U.S.S.R. (E).

6.   **(A)**   The hospital officials' conclusion is that the risk of a patient contracting HIV from an infected surgeon is low. This conclusion would be strengthened if the only reported case of a patient being infected by a surgeon turns out to be false, (A). It is impossible to judge the relevance of the information on health care workers becoming infected, since we are not told if any of them are surgeons, or how they became infected. Perhaps all of them are lab technicians, who became infected by handling blood and tissue samples, and who never came into

direct contact with patients. Therefore, (B) and (C) can be eliminated. That the dentist was never tested for HIV is irrelevant, since the passage admits that the report of his infecting a patient is unconfirmed (D). It is irrelevant whether or not Bartlett is a surgeon at Hopkins (E), since his authority for the statement in the passage rests on his being the director of the Hopkins AIDS program.

7.   **(D)**   The writer implies that Einstein's and Bach's mental abilities go beyond mere electrical processes and that advances in science and technology may help us to understand this (D). This contradicts the assertion that a mind is nothing but electrical processes (C). The premises are that there are heretofore unimagined perceptions (B) of the microcosm and macrocosm; that these perceptions, not the microcosm and macrocosm themselves, have become commonplace (A); and that these perceptions are due to the scientific and technological advances of the telescope, the microscope, and space travel (E).

8.   **(E)**   The writer's conclusion is about the *Today* show's problem — based on the premises that Gumbel has alienated female viewers and that Gumbel's Q score is low (E). The writer states (but not as a conclusion) that Gumbel is in trouble and is a problem because his Q score is low, not because female viewers have alienated him (A) or because the *Today* show has made major moves (D). He also asserts that the *Today* show is suffering because young female audiences are worse, not that the audience is worse because the show is suffering (C). And the writer claims that Gumbel is an able broadcaster *in spite of* his low Q score, not because of it (B).

9.   **(B)**   If the Eternal is unchangeable, but wisdom about past events may change from young man to grown man to old man, then such wisdom must not be eternal (B). The passage claims that statements about the changeable, not about the Eternal (A) are subject to change. The passage claims that the Eternal applies to every human being, contrary to answer (C). The passage also states that youth cannot, and grown men do not, wish to understand wisdom about the past, but it says nothing about understanding wisdom in general (D) and (E).

10.   **(D)**   The writer *denies* the proposition that only by legal restraints are men to be kept from aggressing on their neighbors (D). Thus, he attempts to support the claim that we should qualify the assumption of that proposition (B). As support he asserts that (1) debts of honor cannot be enforced legally (A), but are nevertheless more sacred than debts that can be legally enforced (E); and (2) formally registered contracts are not necessarily safer than contracts made between two Stock Exchange brokers who note the contracts in their notebooks (C).

11.   **(A)**   The passage concludes that knowledge in 3000 C.E. should surpass current understanding of aesthetics, psychology, and value. He does not claim that current understanding is pitiful now (A), so this is not a premise. He does claim or imply as premises that it would be bad if knowledge did not improve

(B), that our powers are rapidly developing (C), that we should be able to guide these powers (D), and that for many people rapid development of our own powers is their chief interest of existence (E).

12.   **(E)**   The magician's *premises* are that like produces like (The Law of Similarity) (A) and things which have been in contact continue ever afterwards to act on each other (The Contact of Contagion) (D). From these the magician infers the *conclusions* that he can produce any effect he desires (B) and whatever he does to a material object will automatically affect the person with whom it was once in contact (C). Thus, both (A) and (D) are premises (E), while neither (B) nor (C) is a premise.

13.   **(E)**   The passage disagrees with the editor's claim that there is a new orthodoxy of multiculturalism (E) and declares that little of the new orthodoxy of multiculturalism exists (A). Against the editor's position, the passage declares that Aristotle, Augustine, and Milton are alive and well in the academy (B); that a charge of intellectual obscenity will pack the house (C); and that juicy attacks by the multiculturalists have gotten students to read books (D).

14.   **(A)**   The passage notes that Pound is often seen as an anti-Semite. It does not assert, however, that Pound *was* an anti-Semite (A). The passage also notes that Pound is often seen as a fascist (C), or a literary genius (B), and that critics often find themselves framed by a kind of critical Cold War (D), and often resemble the role of Marc Antony at the funeral in *Julius Caesar* (E).

15.   **(D)**   The passage concludes that legal assistant trainees should have internships (D). One premise is that internships are historically common (B), with apprenticeships (which are treated as kinds of internships (E)) dating back to 2100 B.C.E. in the Code of Hammurabi (C). Another premise is that physicians' training includes a formal one-year internship after graduation (A).

16.   **(E)**   This argument's *conclusion* is that textbooks deserve the considerable attention they have been getting (E). The premises are that textbooks are packed curricula (A) which are the essential source of information for students (B) and teachers (C) in elementary school, and that they outweigh all other sources in determining the day-to-day teaching in classrooms (D).

17.   **(A)**   This passage argues that visual form is important to network television newscasts just as the verbal content of the story. If visual form were not as important (A), this would weaken the argument. The passage claims that the visual form's importance is due in part to the fact that it conveys the aesthetic value of visual content (B). If this is true, it would strengthen the argument. It is irrelevant to the importance of visual form whether or not network news stories have remained static over the past 30 years (C), whether the three networks tend

to select similar stories (D), and whether there has been as much analysis of visual form as of verbal content (E).

18.   **(E)**   This argument concludes that people are as interested in the Bible today as they were before (E). This contradicts the assertion that the less media-saturated generations of long ago had a greater hunger for the "Word" than the modern world (C). As one premise, the argument states that there has been an explosion of translations of the Bible in recent years (A). The argument does not claim that we *should* multiply the amount of labor over one translation by the number of new translations (D), although it does claim that if we do, we will understand the premise that the production of new translations of the Bible is an awesome task (B).

19.   **(B)**   The original argument moves from the fact that the two neighboring houses are similar in some characteristics (age and builder) to the claim that one further characteristic which one of them has (needing new siding) will be shared by the other. Clearly the builder and the siding's age are relevant to the state of the siding, so this argument has some initial plausibility. However, if the two houses differ in the highly relevant area of the material of the siding, as (B) proposes, much of that plausibility would disappear. Answers (A) and (C) do not address the similarities between the two houses and so have little to do with this argument. Nor with its conclusion — the siding may need replacing regardless of what the guarantee says or whether the owner can afford the repair. (D) does compare the two houses and notes a difference between them, but the skills of the owner are not obviously relevant to the issue of whether the siding will wear out at the same time. (E), on the other hand, finds a relevant similarity between the two houses, so would strengthen the argument rather than weaken it.

20.   **(C)**   The basic argument moves from the claim that each member (thing) of the whole (universe) has a certain property (began in time) to the claim that the whole has that property, the pattern described in (C). This is an inherently unreliable argument pattern, as knows anyone who has ever made a terrible-tasting mess by mixing together good-tasting things. This is not quite the same argument as that objected to in (A), for the original argument does not claim that everything began at the same time, though it does start by claiming that each thing began at some time. The objection in (B) also does not apply, since questions of causation are beyond the scope of the argument. Nor is (D) relevant, since the original argument does not compare the things in the universe and the universe as a whole for any other property than having a beginning. So it does not move from one such comparison to another. Finally, (E) does not apply, since it would not be illogical for the universe both to be the longest-lasting thing *and* to have had a beginning.

21.   **(D)**   There are two unspoken assumptions in the passage. The first occurs when the author interprets the mother's remark to mean "Buckle your seat belt."

As the next sentence in the passage indicates, if the remark did not mean "Buckle your seat belt," it would be irrelevant to the daughter's situation. Obviously, the author assumes that the mother's remark is relevant, which corresponds to answer (D). The second assumption is that the daughter will be uninterested in irrelevant comments. The answer cannot be (B), since it contradicts the second assumption. (A) is out since the passage says that the daughter is uninterested only for the moment in what wise drivers do. It may be reasonable to think that the mother wants her daughter to fasten her seat belt, but this does not clearly assume that teenagers generally do not use seat belts or even that this girl does not. So (E) is not necessarily assumed. Nor is (C), since the reason that the mother wants her daughter to fasten her seat belt is not given. It may be out of concern for the law or insurance rates, as much as for safety.

22. **(D)** This study only examines the relationship between using steroids and having a certain level of high-density lipoproteins in the blood. It found a regular pattern of lower levels with steroid users than with similar non-users and also a pattern of lower levels with higher steroid use. Both of these offer good support for the claim that steroid use causes the lower levels of lipoproteins, answer (D). The study did not look directly at the relationship between steroid use and heart attacks; this connection can only be made by bringing in the additional information — from some other source — about the connection between lipoprotein levels and heart attacks. Thus, both (B) and (C) go beyond this study. (A) goes against the study, for all of the subjects of the study were body-builders, yet only steroid users seem to have been affected. The same comment applies to (E), though it is more precise about the effect involved.

23. **(C)** Dr. Spock is presented as an expert in the care of small children ("famous baby doctor") and, by context, at least, not an expert in the world economy. However, the fact that he is not an expert does not mean that his views are wrong and, so, to be rejected. He may very well be right and even have good evidence for his views, even though he is not an expert. So, (A) and (D) are not the proper responses. Nor is (B), for he is not an expert on world economy but on child-rearing, so — as the first sentence says — his views on the former subject carry no special weight. That leaves him in the position of everyone else; his views must be evaluated on their own merit, without reference to his expertise in this or some other area. Finally, even if Dr. Spock were an expert in the world economy (E), it does not follow that his view is to be accepted, for experts can disagree and are sometimes demonstrably wrong. The usual procedures for evaluation are just somewhat different for experts, but the advice in (C) still applies.

24. **(D)** The logically crucial features of Einstein's case is that he predicted a phenomenon before it was observed and that the standard theory of the time said the prediction was wrong. Both of these features recur in Halley's case, though in slightly different form (the standard theory did not say that the comet would not appear on Halley's schedule, but only that it was impossible to predict the

appearance of the comets). Neither Copernicus (A) nor Kepler (B) predicted phenomena before they were observed, they merely accounted for the observed phenomena by theories different from the standard theory (and, in Kepler's case, more simply than the standard theory). Galileo (C) observed a phenomenon that the standard theory denied, but did not predict it before he observed it (nor did it follow from the theory he was using). Herschel (E) observed a phenomenon predicted by the standard theory, not one contrary to it.

LSAT Writing Sample — Demonstration Essay

Baldwin State University is seeking a teacher-scholar who will help enhance the image of the university and help prove that it is more than just a state college accepting local high school graduates. A major part of realizing this goal will be recruiting skilled teaching and student-oriented faculty. While the university has made it clear that it expects its faculty to make research contributions, it is also clear that the university views teaching as its highest academic priority, as indicated in the priority given to teaching in promotion and tenure decisions. The university should therefore appoint Mr. Smith to the tenure-track position of assistant professor.

Smith is clearly better suited to making teaching his first priority. He has three years of full-time experience at the University of West Virginia, and his student-teaching evaluations are excellent. Moreover, his friendly, relaxed style will be an asset in retaining students, as will his desire to spend as much time as necessary with students.

Certainly, another of the strong points of his candidacy is the fact that Smith has academic preparation in fields besides mathematics. His economics background is especially useful in allowing him to demonstrate practical applications of classroom lessons.

Though Smith's research background is perhaps less impressive than Jones's, he is nevertheless a scholar of high caliber in his own right. He has published two papers in respected journals, and is cowriting a statistics textbook. In addition, it should be kept in mind that his principal responsibility as a member of the faculty will be teaching, a task at which he clearly excels.

Ms. Jones's academic credentials are indisputably outstanding, and her research background is rather strong, especially for her age. She is coauthor of three textbooks and is working on a book of her own. In this position, however, the emphasis would be on teaching rather than research. The bulk of her time would be spent interacting with students, which is decidedly not her strength.

While Ms. Jones has excellent research potential, her teaching skills are weak. Her student evaluations have consistently been poor (a 2.85 is less than the mediocre midpoint of a 1-to-5 scale) and suggest that there is a problem with her teaching rather than the attitude of her students. Her unwillingness to spend extra time with students is a critical flaw in the character of any university faculty

member and cannot be remedied by a teaching skills improvement seminar.

While she may be a talented researcher, Ms. Jones is clearly a mediocre teacher at best. This shortcoming disqualifies her from further consideration for the position, as teaching would be a major portion of the responsibilities of this position.

The university should hire John Smith for the position. He has an excellent rapport with students and is a dedicated teacher. Furthermore, he is a knowledgeable scholar and has published serious works in noteworthy journals. His diverse educational background is also a major asset, as it gives the university some flexibility in terms of his teaching assignments. It should also be kept in mind that his attendance at state universities would most likely give him a better understanding of the average student we normally enroll at Baldwin State University.

Demonstration Essay Explanation

This essay is well written, because it follows the basic guidelines of good writing. The situation is clearly presented in the opening paragraphs, along with the author's position. Both the problem and the author's position are clearly and effectively stated; there is no ambiguity.

The writer uses varying sentence lengths and varying sentence structures to avoid the impression that the essay "drones" monotonously. This is more important than you might think. Style definitely counts in the grading of LSAT writing samples by individual law schools.

The essay systematically discusses the strengths and weaknesses of both candidates in relation to the two criteria for appointment to the position. In supporting a position, one must present relevant information regarding both candidates.

Opposing points are brought up and dealt with. In order for an essay to be credible, it must show that opposing viewpoints have been considered and outweighed. A one-sided essay is not effective.

Grammar, vocabulary, and punctuation are all very important. The reader's impression of even the most well-written essay can be destroyed by sloppy grammar, poor punctuation, and spelling errors.

LSAT

Law School Admission Test

TEST II

TEST II

Section I

Time—35 minutes
23 Questions

(Answer sheets appear in the back of this book.)

<u>DIRECTIONS</u>: Each group of questions in this section is based on a set of conditions. In answering some of the questions, it may be useful to draw a rough diagram. Choose the response that most accurately and completely answers the question and blacken the corresponding space on your answer sheet.

<u>QUESTIONS 1–5</u>

The Basic College Council is made up of representatives from the departments in the various divisions. From the Science Division is one representative from each of the departments of Chemistry, Mathematics, and Biology. The Social Science Division provides a representative each from History, Linguistics and Economics. A representative from Philosophy and one from Rhetoric serve for the Humanities Division.

All Council Committees are made up entirely of Council members.

Each committee has exactly four members.

Each committee has at least one member from each Division.

The representative from Chemistry will not serve on a committee with the representative from Biology.

The representatives from Mathematics and Economics always serve on the same committees.

The representative from Rhetoric will only serve on a committee on which the representative from Biology or the one from Economics, or both, serve.

1.   The representatives of which of the following groups of departments can serve together on a committee?

   (A)   Chemistry, Mathematics, History, Economics

   (B)   Chemistry, Mathematics, History, Philosophy

   (C)   Mathematics, Biology, Linguistics, Economics

   (D)   Mathematics, Biology, Economics, Rhetoric

   (E)   Biology, History, Economics, Rhetoric

2.   If both the representatives from the Humanities Division are on a committee, then the other two members of the committee can be representatives of

   (A)   Biology and History

   (B)   Biology and Economics

   (C)   Mathematics and History

   (D)   Chemistry and Mathematics

   (E)   Chemistry and Biology

3.   If the representative of Economics is on a committee, which groups of three might round out that committee?

   (A)   representatives of Chemistry, Mathematics, and Biology

   (B)   representatives of Chemistry, Biology, and Rhetoric

   (C)   representatives of Chemistry, Philosophy, and Rhetoric

   (D)   representatives of History, Economics, and Philosophy

   (E)   representatives of Mathematics, Philosophy, and Rhetoric

4.   If the representatives of Biology and Philosophy do not serve on a committee, representatives of both of which of the following pairs of departments must serve on that committee?

   (A)   Chemistry and Linguistics

   (B)   Chemistry and Economics

   (C)   Mathematics and History

   (D)   Mathematics and Economics

   (E)   History and Economics

5.   Which of the following is true?

   (A)   If the representatives of Chemistry and Mathematics are on a committee, the representative of Philosophy must also be on it.

   (B)   If the representative of Rhetoric is not on a committee, then the representatives of Mathematics and Biology must both be on it.

   (C)   If both Humanities representatives are on a committee, then the representative of Chemistry cannot be on it.

   (D)   If the representative of neither Mathematics nor Philosophy is on a committee, then the representative of Economics must be on it.

(E)   If the representative of neither Biology nor Economics is on a committee, then the representative of Linguistics cannot be on it.

QUESTIONS 6-10

Seated at the head of the Fraternal Frolic were, from left to right, Al, Bill, Charlie, Dave and Ed. Each of them belonged to exactly two fraternal organizations — Lords, Elm, Magic, Kobra, and Old Forest. The following conditions held for the five men.

The organizations fall into three groups: A, composed of Lords and Elms, B, composed of Kobra and Old Forest, and C, Magic alone.

The two organizations each person belongs to come from two different groups.

No person belonged to any organization to which a man sitting next to him belonged.

Bill belonged to the Magic and the Old Forest.

Ed belonged to the Lords.

6.   Which of the following must be true?

(A)   Al is an Elm.

(B)   Charlie is a Lord.

(C)   Charlie belongs to the Kobra.

(D)   Dave is an Old Forest.

(E)   Ed is an Old Forest.

7.   If only one of the men is both a Magic and in a Group B organization, which of the following must be true?

(A)   No more than two of the men are Lords.

(B)   No more than two of the men are Elms.

(C)   No more than two of the men are in Kobra.

(D)   No less than two of the men are both Magic and in Group A organizations.

(E)   No less than two of the men are Old Forest.

8.   Which of the following is a possible combination of memberships for Dave?

(A)   Elms and Magic

(B)   Magic and Kobra

      (C)   Lords and Old Forest

      (D)   Kobras and Lords

      (E)   Elms and Kobra

9.   If Charlie is an Elm, which of the following must be true?

      (A)   Charlie is an Old Forest.

      (B)   Dave is an Old Forest.

      (C)   Dave is a Magic and neither an Old Forest nor in Kobra.

      (D)   Ed is a Magic and neither an Old Forest nor in Kobra.

      (E)   Ed is an Old Forest.

10.   Frank sat down just to the right of Ed. Frank is in the Magic and Kobra, but the same conditions continue to apply to men at the table. Which of the following must be true?

      (A)   Charlie is a Lord and a Magic.

      (B)   Charlie is an Elm and in Kobra.

      (C)   Dave is an Elm and a Magic.

      (D)   Dave is an Elm and an Old Forest.

      (E)   Ed is a Lord and in Kobra.

QUESTIONS 11–13

    At the Four Plus Two talks, the representatives of the United States, Great Britain, France, Spain, Egypt, and Holland are seated around a round table. Each seat is next to two others and directly opposite one across the table. The seating is subject to the following conditions.

    The representatives of Egypt and Holland sit next to one another.

    The representative of France will not sit next to the representative of Egypt.

    The representative of the United States will not sit next to the representative of Spain.

11.   If the representative of France sits next to that of Holland and the representative of the United States sits next to that of Egypt, representatives of what countries must sit on either side of the representative of Great Britain?

      (A)   France and the United States

(B)   France and Egypt

(C)   France and Spain

(D)   The United States and Holland

(E)   The United States and Spain

12.   If the representative of the United States is directly across the table from the representative of Great Britain, representatives of which two countries must sit on either side of the representative of Spain?

(A)   France and Great Britain

(B)   France and Egypt

(C)   The United States and Holland

(D)   Holland and Great Britain

(E)   Great Britain and Egypt

13.   If the representative of France sits directly across the table from that of Egypt, any of the following could be true EXCEPT

(A)   the representative of the United States sits directly across from that of Great Britain.

(B)   the representative of Holland sits directly across from that of Spain.

(C)   the representative of the United States sits next to that of Great Britain.

(D)   the representative of Holland sits next to that of Great Britain.

(E)   the representative of Spain sits next to that of Great Britain.

QUESTIONS 14–18

The planning committee for a series of road rallies had seven checkpoints, T, U, V, W, X, Y, and Z to use. Each rally would start from a checkpoint and each lap would end by checking in at a checkpoint. No lap passes any checkpoint other than the one which ends it. Each rally would end by checking in at the last checkpoint, not necessarily the same as the one from which the rally started. The checkpoints were connected directly — that is, without passing any other checkpoints between — by roads as follows:

U is connected directly to V and W.

V is connected directly to T and Y.

W is connected directly to V, X, Y, and Z.

X is connected directly to Z.

14. Which of the following is a possible sequence of checkpoints to visit in a four-lap rally beginning at checkpoint U?

(A)   V, T, Y, W   (D)   W, V, T, X

(B)   V, W, Z, U   (E)   W, X, Z, W

(C)   V, Y, X, W

15. On a two-lap rally starting from checkpoint Z, which checkpoint CANNOT be visited?

(A)   T   (D)   W

(B)   U   (E)   Y

(C)   V

16. Which of the following is a complete and accurate list of possible second checkpoints in a rally beginning from checkpoint Y?

(A)   T, X, Z   (D)   T, U, V, W, X, Z

(B)   T, W, X, Z   (E)   T, U, V, W, X, Y, Z

(C)   T, V, W, X, Z

17. If a four-lap rally begins and ends at checkpoint U, and no checkpoint is passed twice, what checkpoint must end the second lap?

(A)   V   (D)   Y

(B)   W   (E)   Z

(C)   X

18. What is the greatest possible number of laps in a rally in which no checkpoint is checked into twice?

(A)   4   (D)   7

(B)   5   (E)   8

(C)   6

QUESTIONS 19–23

There were five students in the Professional Ethics seminar.

Two of them were female, the others male.

Two of the men were undergraduates.

One of the females was in graduate school.

One of the remaining students was in a professional school and the other was an undergraduate.

Two of the students were going into the ministry, two into medicine and the fifth into law.

The two students going into the ministry are the same sex.

19. If the two students going into the ministry have the same academic status, which of the following statements must be true?

(A) The ministry students are both male.

(B) The law student is female.

(C) The ministry students are both female.

(D) Both females are going into law

(E) One of the undergraduates is going into ministry.

20. If the law student is female, which of the following must be true?

(A) The ministry students are both male.

(B) All the male students are undergraduates.

(C) One of the female students has the same status as do two of the male students.

(D) The law student is in graduate school.

(E) One of the medical students is in a professional school.

21. If one of the female students is a medical student and in a professional school, which of the following statements must be true?

(A) The male students have different academic statuses.

(B) The medical students have the same academic status.

(C) The law student is either in graduate school or in a professional school.

(D) The law student is either in a professional school or is an undergraduate.

(E) The law student is either an undergraduate or in a graduate school.

22. If the medical students are of different sexes and the ministry students have the same status, then the student in graduate school must be

(A) a medical student.

(B) a ministry student.

(C) either a medical student or the law student.

(D) either a medical student or a ministry student.

(E) either a ministry student or the law student.

23. If the student in the professional school is a female ministry student, which of the following statements must be true?

(A) The student in graduate school is a ministry student.

(B) The medical students are both graduate students.

(C) The law student is female.

(D) The medical students are female.

(E) The other ministry student is male.

STOP

If time still remains, you may review work only in this section.
When the time allotted is up, you may go on to the next section.

Section II

Time—35 minutes
24 Questions

(Answer sheets appear in the back of this book.)

DIRECTIONS: The questions in this section are based on the reasoning contained in brief statements or passages. For some questions, more than one of the choices could conceivably answer the question. However, you are to choose the **best** answer; that is, the response that most accurately and completely answers the question. You should not make assumptions that are by commonsense standards implausible, superfluous, or incompatible with the passage. After you have chosen the best answer, blacken the corresponding space on your answer sheet.

1. Since 1806, when Lewis and Clark returned from their journey to the Oregon country, Americans had not taken much interest in the Far West. Major Long's expedition of 1819 reported the Great Plains "almost wholly unfit for cultivation," and laid down on the map of that region, which now supports a thriving population of several millions, the legend _____

    Which of the following best completes the sentence?

    (A) "The Great American Desert."

    (B) "The Far Western territory."

    (C) "The Indian Territory."

    (D) "The American Garden of Eden."

    (E) "The Next Promised Land."

2. If the legislature does not increase appropriations for education, the teachers will strike. However, the legislature can increase education appropriations only if it cuts back on highway repair, and that may anger motorists. It seems that the legislature must either refuse to increase education appropriations, or risk the wrath of motorists.

    If all of the above statements are true, which of the following statements must also be true?

    (A) Increasing education appropriations will lead to motorists' being angry.

    (B) Highway repair will be cut back only if the legislature increases appropriations for education.

(C) If the legislature cuts back on highway repair, the teachers will be angry.

(D) If the legislature considers increasing appropriations for education, motorists may be angry.

(E) The teachers will strike unless highway repair is cut back.

3. Amy and I were standing out in front of the mall today waiting for George to come by. After a few minutes Amy got impatient and walked away. I think the fact that she is impatient is the reason so many things go badly for her.

The argument above uses which of the following questionable techniques?

(A) treating a dissimilar event as analogous to the present one

(B) reiterating its conclusion, rather than supplying evidence to support it

(C) basing the argument on unreliable evidence

(D) making a claim by overgeneralizing from specific evidence

(E) confusing two different meanings of a word

4. A top expert on Native Americans lectured on the topic of early American mythology on the Yeti. During his lecture he said "Native Americans had a deep reverence for the Yeti, which we know as Bigfoot. Drawings have been discovered on cave walls which depict encounters with the creature. Also, stories were passed down from one generation to the next, describing the creature as shy and intelligent." A student at the lecture concluded that the expert's findings prove Bigfoot exists.

In contrast to the student's conclusion, a conclusion that can correctly be drawn from the expert's findings is

(A) there is no effective way of determining whether or not Bigfoot exists.

(B) Bigfoot must exist at the present time, since it existed in early America.

(C) the expert believed Bigfoot existed in early America.

(D) Native Americans believed in the existence of Bigfoot.

(E) Bigfoot may have existed in early America, but does not now exist.

5. Assault rifles should not be outlawed. After all, they are just another type of gun, and if one type of gun should be outlawed, why not all of them? But Americans have a long tradition of ownership of guns. Admittedly, assault rifles have few uses other than killing people; but what's at stake here is the American tradition of private ownership of guns.

Assuming each of the following statements is true, which could best be used to counter the author's argument?

(A) Assault rifles can be used for target practice.

(B) The American tradition of gun ownership included the ownership of hunting guns only.

(C) Assault rifles are used in many crimes.

(D) Assault rifles have only recently been developed.

(E) Police forces all around the country are in favor of a ban on the ownership of assault rifles.

6. Henry: Capitalism and environmentalism are mutually exclusive. Therefore a corporation cannot both make profits and protect the environment simultaneously.

Alice: But aren't many corporations doing precisely that? The REO corporation has made a nifty profit for the last several years, and at the same time it has spent millions of dollars on reforestation and reclamation of dead lakes in its vicinity. So, even though it puts primary emphasis on profits, it simultaneously helps protect the environment.

In order to refute Henry's conclusion, Alice

(A) demonstrates that corporate profits make protection of the environment possible.

(B) uses the word "environmentalism" in a different sense than Henry does.

(C) uses Henry's own premise to prove the opposite conclusion.

(D) shows that making a profit and protecting the environment are not mutually exclusive.

(E) changes an argument based on a definition into one based on an ethical consideration.

QUESTIONS 7–8

In July 1984, Richard Leakey and colleague Kamoya Kimeu found in Nairobi an almost complete *homo erectus* skeleton, the first recovered that was 1.6 million years old. The skeleton was that of a boy about 12 years of age. He was about five feet four inches tall and probably would have reached a height of six feet. His bones had been scattered and trampled in a swamp. In parts and portion, they were much like the human form today. Under him was volcanic material dating from 1.65 million years ago.

7. Which of the following hypotheses is best supported by the evidence above?

   (A) This find confirms that the human form, as we know it today, only recently developed.

   (B) This find confirms the antiquity of the human form.

   (C) The body may not be as old as believed because it could have fallen through a large burrow dug by a gerbil.

   (D) The body could have been imported to the area by a religious group that practiced human sacrifice.

   (E) The remains may have confused two different time periods.

8. The evidence from the find most seriously supports which of the following?

   (A) The belief that humans reached their present size more than a million and a half years ago, with some populations in poor areas becoming smaller recently.

   (B) The belief that people did not look like humans until 100 B.C.E.

   (C) The belief that humans did not exist 1.6 million years ago.

   (D) The belief that humans have grown larger through time.

   (E) The belief that human life really began on the continent of Europe.

QUESTIONS 9–10

Polls indicate that more citizens of Metropolis are Catholic than Protestant, and that those Catholics prefer to vote for other Catholics for public office. However, Smith should not assume that, because he is a Catholic, he is a shoo-in for mayor. As a sociologist at Metropolis College has pointed out, Smith has taken a strong stand against the use of contraceptives by married couples, and most Catholics in Metropolis do not agree with that position, even though it is the official teaching of the Catholic Church.

9. Which one of the following conclusions can be reasonably inferred from the passage above?

   (A) Polling methods are inadequate tools for predicting the winners of political races.

   (B) Belief in Catholicism is on the upswing in Metropolis.

   (C) Smith will lose the mayoral race.

   (D) Smith's views on the use of contraceptives may have an outcome on the mayoral race.

(E)   Many people in Metropolis like to think of themselves as Catholics, even though they are not.

10.   According to the passage, a non-Catholic candidate for mayor of Metropolis could best compete with Smith by

(A)   attacking the Catholic Church's stand on the use of contraceptives.

(B)   appealing to the voters' personal beliefs about the use of contraceptives.

(C)   appealing to the Protestant voters.

(D)   pointing out the contradiction between the Catholic Church's teaching and the beliefs of the Catholics in Metropolis.

(E)   pointing out that Smith is faithful to the Catholic Church's position on the use of contraceptives.

QUESTIONS 11–12

I think that it is improper for a nation to put up monuments to its famous men and women. Even though a citizen spends a lifetime in service to the country, he or she does not deserve to be deified. We scientists should imitate Prometheus, whom the ancient Greeks said brought fire down from Heaven to give to the superstitious and ignorant men of his time. We should teach that reason must displace myth, and that worthless idolatry must be abandoned.

11.   Which of the following is the main point of the passage above?

(A)   Reverence for the nation's heroes is to be expected from the citizens.

(B)   One is more likely to find idolatry among the ignorant and superstitious than among scientists.

(C)   Scientists should help educate the public not to deify national heroes.

(D)   Those who idolize national heroes are to be pitied.

(E)   The ancient Greeks worshipped fire.

12.   Which of the following is the point of the author's analogy about Prometheus?

(A)   Prometheus worshipped national heroes.

(B)   Scientists should imitate Prometheus by bringing something of benefit to superstitious people of the present.

(C)   Prometheus tried to persuade the ancient Greeks not to worship national heroes.

(D)   If Prometheus was alive today he would be a scientist.

(E)   Citizens should be ready to accept gifts from their benefactors.

13. Every time my leg aches it rains in 30 minutes. My leg aches now, so it will rain in 30 minutes.

Which of the following passages uses reasoning most similar to that in the above passage?

(A) I have seen 10 of Mr. Finster's movies, and each was horrible. Therefore, his last movie will be horrible also.

(B) The sun came up yesterday, the day before, and every other day of my life. Therefore, it will come up tomorrow.

(C) Charlie is constable of the parish. It is the constable's job to serve warrants. Therefore, I will get Charlie to serve this warrant.

(D) The engine coughs every time before it dies. It just coughed, so it will die.

(E) My leg's aching causes it to rain.

14. Some people say that they hate talking to answering machines; but those very people are likely to want answering machines themselves. That is like being against pranks unless you are the one playing them.

The analogy above would be most strengthened if it were true that

(A) most people have answering machines.

(B) pranks served some practical use for the person playing them.

(C) the person playing the pranks enjoyed them.

(D) the people on whom the pranks were played enjoyed them.

(E) using the answering machine was fun for the owner.

QUESTIONS 15–16

In some areas of the South landowners practice "clear-cutting" of large areas of forest. Clear-cutting produces quicker profits in the short run, because more board feet of wood can be harvested with it than with more selective harvesting procedures. However, this practice should be carefully regulated by the state governments, since it can be destructive to the environment. The erosion that is often caused by clear-cutting lessens the land's capability to produce similar resources for future generations.

15. In the passage above, the author makes which of the following arguments?

(A) If unregulated, landowners will sometimes harvest trees too rapidly, at the expense of future production.

(B) If government imposes regulations, landowners will make less money.

(C) If government does not impose regulations, there will be no forests in the future.

(D) It is easy for landowners to make a profit, regardless of what regulations are passed.

(E) Landowners will harvest forests regardless of what regulations are made.

16. Which of the following is an unspoken assumption of the passage above?

(A) It is immoral to let natural resources go to waste.

(B) Sometimes it is necessary for government to regulate private property in order to increase private profits.

(C) The individual's right to own property must sometimes give way to government's responsibility to protect the environment for future generations.

(D) The state governments should regulate the harvesting of forests.

(E) Landowners in the South have become irresponsible in their use of the land.

QUESTIONS 17–18

All golfers who are not club members are invited. All doctors are golfers, but there are doctors who are not invited.

17. Which of the following conclusions may be derived from the statements above?

(A) No doctors are invited.

(B) Some golfers are club members.

(C) Some doctors are invited.

(D) No golfers are invited.

(E) All golfers are doctors.

18. If the statements in the passage are all true, which of the following statements must be FALSE?

(A) Some who are not golfers are doctors.

(B) Some doctors are invited.

(C) If Drew is a doctor, he is not invited.

(D) Some doctors are club members.

(E) If Alice is invited, she is not a club member.

19. Either Sharon will fix lunch or Wes will go to a restaurant. If Sharon fixes lunch she will be late for work. Sharon's boss gets mad whenever she is late for work. However, Wes hates to go to restaurants, because when he does he usually gets indigestion.

    If all of the statements above are true, which of the following must be true?

    (A) If Sharon gets to work on time, Wes will get indigestion.

    (B) If Wes gets indigestion, Sharon got to work on time.

    (C) If Sharon is late for work, she fixed lunch for Wes.

    (D) If Sharon got to work on time, Wes went to a restaurant.

    (E) If Sharon's boss gets mad, she fixed lunch for Wes.

QUESTIONS 20–21

Family members have a responsibility to each other. In a crisis each member should be prepared to endure some self-sacrifice to preserve the well-being of every other member. A corporation is like a giant family. Thus, each employee of a corporation should be willing to endure some hardship for the sake of fellow employees.

20. Which of the following assertions, if true, will most seriously weaken the argument above?

    (A) Membership in the corporation is based on self-interest, whereas membership in the family is based on love.

    (B) Corporations experience few crises which require self-sacrifice on the part of employees.

    (C) One is always a member of a family before being an employee of a corporation.

    (D) One can be a good employee without being a member of a family.

    (E) Corporations are not "persons" in any real sense of the word.

21. Which of the following assertions, if true, would strengthen the argument above?

    (A) A corporation is like a family, in that the well-being of each employee has a direct effect on every other employee's well-being.

    (B) Corporations in which employees are well provided for usually make large profits.

    (C) Sometimes corporations expect self-sacrifice from an employee equal to the self-sacrifice one family member expects from another.

(D)   No employee should have to endure hardship.

(E)   A corporation can not be compared to a family.

22.   Dan tosses a coin 10 times and each time it lands heads up. Marie says the odds are very high that the coin will land tails up on the 11th toss. Dan reasons that the coin has no memory, and that the odds are 50/50 that it will land either heads up or tails up on any given toss. Therefore, he disagrees with Marie.

Which of the following is the best formulation of the reasoning used by Dan?

(A)   If events 1-11 are equally probable or improbable and are completely independent of each other, the occurrence of events 1-10 cannot be used to predict the likelihood of the occurrence of event 11.

(B)   In a series of events, if one of two possible outcomes occurs repeatedly, it is not unwise to assume that that same outcome will continue to occur.

(C)   While the coin has no memory, the fact that it lands heads up 10 times in a row indicates that it must be slightly weighted to that side.

(D)   Marie is mistaken because it is impossible to know what the odds are that the coin will land tails up on the 11th toss.

(E)   The likelihood of the coin landing tails up on the 11th toss should be computed only on the basis of the outcome of the previous toss.

23.   A record store employed a statistician to determine what percentage of the city's 30,000 residents shopped in the store at least once a week. The statistician decided to conduct a random survey of people in the mall in which the record store was located. Of 1000 surveyed, 500 said they shopped in the store at least once a week. The statistician concluded from this that 15,000 of the city's residents shopped in the store at least once a week.

The results of this survey were unreliable for which of the following reasons?

(A)   The number of people surveyed was too small.

(B)   The survey probably included a disproportionate number of people who shopped in the store once a week.

(C)   The statistician should have surveyed all 30,000 residents of the city.

(D)   The survey should have been conducted within the record store itself.

(E)   Random surveys are unreliable.

24. If the team does not have a winning season, fan interest will decline, the franchise will be in financial difficulty, and Coach May will be asked to resign. Therefore, it is imperative that the team have a winning season.

Which of the following beliefs can reasonably be attributed to the author of the above argument?

(A) It is desirable that Coach May be asked to resign.

(B) It is desirable for fan interest to decline.

(C) It is desirable for the franchise to be in financial difficulty.

(D) It is undesirable for the team to have a winning season.

(E) It is undesirable that Coach May be asked to resign.

STOP

If time still remains, you may review work only in this section.
When the time allotted is up, you may go on to the next section.

Section III

Time—35 minutes
27 Questions

(Answer sheets appear in the back of this book.)

DIRECTIONS: Each passage in this section is followed by a group of questions to be answered on the basis of what is **stated** or **implied** in the passage. For some questions, more than one of the choices could conceivably answer the question. However, you are to choose the **best** answer; that is, the response that most accurately and completely answers the question, and blacken the corresponding space on your answer sheet.

In earlier years during the Industrial Revolution, personnel practices of business and industry were mostly confined to hiring enough people to do the work, close supervision of employees to see that they did the work, and firing people if they did not abide by management guidelines. Labor had little influence
(5) on the system in the private sector. The management system was simple. In contrast, today personnel practices of business and industry have become complex and subject to influence of labor and government. Changes have occurred because society expects leaders in the private and public sectors to be sensitive to a number of social issues and to resolve difficulties that arise in the workplace.
(10)   Toward the end of the nineteenth century and early in the twentieth century, social issues were rarely considered part of the decision making process of employers. On occasion, constituents would press state or federal legislators to pass laws which would protect the health and/or morals of employees. Immediately the laws would be challenged in court. For example, a 1923 case dealt with
(15) a law that established a board authorized among other things, to determine minimum wages of female and child workers. In that case, the Supreme Court majority stated that "adult women … are legally as capable of contracting for themselves as men." The law was struck, and employer personnel practices continued to discriminate against women and children. If in the late 1880s and
(20) early 1900s the Supreme Court felt that the legislature had overstepped constitutional boundaries, those laws were made void, and management continued its harsh management policies, not only toward women and children, but also toward men.
Among the first of several court cases during the hectic years of the Indus-
(25) trial Revolution in America, comparison of policies showed that legislative and judicial branches were rarely unified in legal philosophy, setting national goals, and what could or could not be regulated. In a major case in 1918, the Supreme Court struck a federal law that penalized industry when it failed to abide regulations that specified ages and working hours of child employees. The children
(30) continued to work long hours. In 1923, a reporter interviewed the young man

who was a child plaintiff in the landmark case. At the time of interview, the respondent was a young man who was married. The toll of working in a cotton mill long hours for many years had affected Reuben Dagenhart's growth and denied him the opportunity to be educated. His mood was somber when he told
(35) the reporter: "It would have been a good thing for all the kids in the state if that law they passed had been kept." Had Reuben read the dissenting opinion when his case was reported by the Supreme Court in 1918, he would have found that four justices also felt that the child labor law should not have been struck. They concurred that Congress does indeed have a role in protecting the national
(40) welfare and in enforcing policy designed to "benefit ... the nation as a whole." In contrast, the majority of the court prevailed with a different interpretation of the Constitution and decried Congress's ulterior motive "to standardize the ages at which children may be employed...."

1. Which statement best illustrates personnel management in American history?

   (A) Since the beginning of the twentieth century, Congress and state legislatures have had wide latitude in correcting social ills in the private sector of business and industry.

   (B) Personnel practices have been fairly stable with little change after 1901.

   (C) During the years of the Industrial Revolution "big business" was highly respected by sociologists for its grave concern for the welfare of children and women employees — especially standardization of working hours.

   (D) Personnel management of business and industry has become increasingly complex as ideas change about social welfare.

   (E) If you read between the lines carefully, you will find that the executive branch played a key role in crumbling resistance to changes in working conditions.

2. Which statement describes some of the problems that have occurred in personnel management?

   (A) The author proposes that health of employees is a private matter and that government should keep out of personal lives of employees.

   (B) The author *applauds* the early twentieth century Supreme Court because it was a staunch advocate of equal rights of children and females by striking laws that provided special protections in the workplace.

   (C) Mood and attitude of ordinary workers toward personnel practices have not changed very much since 1900.

   (D) The Supreme Court's legal and social philosophy in two cases cited

above were aligned with industry's management theories and social philosophy.

(E) Male workers were exempt from unfair personnel rules in the workplace.

3. What values are reflected in the narrative provided by the author?

(A) The author is apparently a religious person because of his emphasis on moral issues.

(B) The author unfairly criticizes capitalism in the United States and is therefore a socialist.

(C) The author unfairly criticizes justices who write dissenting opinions and therefore leaves law unsettled.

(D) The author's choice of historical facts might lead the reader to consider motives of business and industry — such as profits — that led to hiring small children.

(E) One of the most important underlying premises in this article is a method of keeping children off the streets and out of mischief.

4. How would students of history describe the plight of women in the workplace toward the end of the nineteenth century?

(A) opportunity to get away from the children

(B) happy to have freedom to make contracts with their bosses

(C) competitive for higher positions usually held by men

(D) repressive

(E) employment mostly restricted to single women

5. In the early twentieth century, what was the role of government in determining wages of women who worked in factories, hospitals, and other businesses?

(A) The Supreme Court majority ruled that government should set minimum wages for private employees.

(B) The legislature was filled with men whose wives did not work; thus, they were insensitive to needs of working women.

(C) Presidents finally bargained with industrial owners who caved in and established a business board that established minimum wages.

(D) Some legislators tried to protect economic welfare and morals of women by establishing an agency with authority to set minimum wages, but courts abolished the law and the agency.

(E)   The judicial branch was more active in protecting women, children, and men than the legislative branch.

6.   How would one evaluate the judicial process and its influence on the economic and/or social realm of society?

(A)   The Supreme Court became a cohesive group of judges when considering the plight of child labor and the attempt to regulate personnel practices in the private sector.

(B)   Within a few years after his case was decided, the child plaintiff realized that his case proved detrimental to the welfare of large numbers of children in his state.

(C)   The majority opinion vividly portrayed a conscientious group of judges who were dedicated to the improvement of working conditions in factories and mills.

(D)   In the choice of a respondent for interview purposes, the reporter was obviously trying to cast governmental regulation in a poor light.

(E)   The judges who disagreed with the majority court opinion felt that legislatures must be restricted from too broad interpretation of the constitution.

7.   Which observation is the most appropriate conclusion that can be drawn from the author's text?

(A)   Some of the justices on the Supreme Court had difficulty in persuading most of the justices that legislation should be upheld when social welfare of the nation is at stake.

(B)   Congressional leaders failed to persuade most of the members of the House and the Senate that legislation should be passed in order to protect the social welfare of the nation.

(C)   The passage above is an excellent illustration of how the legislative branch and the judicial branch can lose their identities in the face of strong voter appeal in working class neighborhoods.

(D)   Young Reuben's case was first filed in the trial court in 1918 and was not decided until 1923, too late to help the child laborer.

(E)   The Supreme Court majority proposed that for the law to stand, Congress must standardize ages of employment.

Today the role of business and government in solving social problems remains a controversial topic. Children no longer work in factories. Working hours for both men and women are regulated by government. Some observers feel that New Deal legislation sponsored by President Franklin D. Roosevelt

(5) provided the major thrust for governmental regulation of private sector personnel practices that were too long within the exclusive jurisdiction of industry and business management. At first the Supreme Court struck Roosevelt-initiated statutes. But the sentiment of the country and appointment of men politically sensitive to the political goals of the President led to judicial support of laws

(10) designed to deal with social ills in the country. In the 1930s and early 1940s, Congress followed the leadership of the top executive who proposed such legislation as Social Security, workers' compensation, and mandatory minimum wages. At that time a desire for change was ripe due to economic chaos caused by the Great Depression. Business and industry managers were suddenly cast into

(15) a different role when Congress and the Supreme Court became allies in authorizing governmental intrusion into the private sector's arena. Swift changes led to new professional expertise required for interpretation of law, additional paperwork, and implementation of personnel policies.

By the 1950s, long-standing racial discrimination was challenged. Congress

(20) had remained too long aloof and generally ignored problems associated with inequality. The NAACP bypassed the legislative branch and took its case to the judicial branch. By the 1960s, President Lyndon Johnson influenced Congress to take bold steps that eventually called for changes in the workplace. Title VII was passed, and a reduction of inequities was expected. However, NAACP director of labor, Joann Aiggs, said in 1987 that racial discrimination remains, but federal

(25) legislation "does provide an avenue people can use to seek redress."

America has often been called a "melting pot" because of the varied ethnic, cultural, and racial heritages of its citizens. With the exception of a great flow of people from Africa before the early 1800s and the Chinese in the late 1880s, the majority of immigrants came from western Europe. The government set a

(30) national quota system. By the 1960s, laws changed and so did the national origin of immigrants, with the majority entering the country from Asia and Latin America. The number of immigrants has grown to around nine million people coming into the country during a 10 year span. When employers hire immigrants while jobs are scarce, citizens who have been in this country for more than one

(35) generation feel threatened. Competition for jobs is a major issue. Congressional response placed a large paperwork burden on the personnel departments of business and industry. The Immigration Reform and Control Act of 1986 penalizes employers who hire illegal aliens. Today, personnel offices must be accountable to government with regard to the legal status of their employees. Documents

(40) must show that non-citizens have acquired authorization to work in this country. Some observers feel that governmental rules may drive illegal aliens from the workplace and that no one else will want to perform the low-level tasks required in some of the jobs.

8. Which answer choice best summarizes the author's statements about the legislative change in the 1930s?

(A) It is evident that the author felt that President Roosevelt as chief executive should have stayed out of the legislative process and relied more on the judicial process.

(B) The author explained how President Roosevelt changed direction of government by showing a stronger social orientation than national leaders of judicial and executive branches in earlier years.

(C) Although new legislation was passed, the laws more or less left business and industry personnel policies intact by the 1940s.

(D) At first, President Roosevelt had to rely more on the courts than on stubborn legislators in order to pass laws designed to deal with social problems.

(E) The above paragraphs show that personnel practices of business and industry have little impact on social problems in the country.

9. What kinds of changes occurred due to strong leadership from the Oval Office?

(A) One can gather that bills sponsored by Roosevelt were successful in Congress because they were supported by the effective lobbying influence of business and industry.

(B) The reader can assume that when the Roosevelt administration enforced new laws described above, the manufacturing and business labor expenditures increased accordingly.

(C) Organizations representing the interests of business most likely welcomed changes in Supreme Court personnel appointed by Roosevelt.

(D) Roosevelt's keen interest lay in ending racial discrimination through passage of the Special Security Act.

(E) President Roosevelt was elected. He immediately appointed new justices to the Supreme Court. Then he submitted to Congress proposed legislation. The Supreme Court approved the bills, and then Congress passed the laws.

10. Although observers may argue about what really happened during Roosevelt's term of office, interpret the factual information presented by the author by selecting the best description below.

(A) New Deal legislation received its name from the deals the President made with business and industry for the purpose of pulling the rug out from under Congress, so to speak.

(B) Evolution and transformation of labor policies increased at a rapid pace during the Roosevelt administration.

(C) The author has inferred that historically the name "Great Depression" was a phrase that caught on after the press disclosed Roosevelt's mood when the Supreme Court struck down the first three social welfare bills passed by Congress.

(D)   Strange alliances are often formed in the political arena. Unorganized labor and their representatives in the legislature were seldom impressed with promises of reforms which would lead to a welfare state.

(E)   During Roosevelt's term of office, racial discrimination was addressed vigorously, ending with the passage of the Civil Rights Act of 1964.

11.   Below are several statements that deal with discrimination in the workplace. Choose the sentence that conforms to the author's analysis.

(A)   The recent immigration act is possibly the best example of affirmative action in recent years.

(B)   Illegal aliens are part of the establishment.

(C)   When business and industry employers ignored social problems associated with hiring illegal aliens, government eventually stepped into the vacuum created by private sector negligence and mandated constructive activities.

(D)   Private sector and public sector policy makers by and large have the same goals when trying to solve social problems of employees.

(E)   The author implies that the statement made by Joann Riggs shows how the ruling elite often fails to be responsive to public opinion through institutional mechanisms.

12.   What is the major problem that stems from the way problems of non-Caucasians are handled by government?

(A)   Conflict among job applicants competing for scarce jobs has heightened friction among citizens whose differences are based on cultural, racial, or ethnic factors.

(B)   The term "melting pot" reflects the resolution of problems through direct representation.

(C)   The author maintains that political socialization, in the long run, must be the major responsibility of each ethnic and racial group living in the United States.

(D)   The author refused to deal with the problem of income distribution for illegal aliens.

(E)   One of the most interesting disclosures is the under-the-table wheeling and dealing of President Johnson who sought to undermine the NAACP's goals when he proposed separate-but-equal policies in schools and the factories.

13. How did the federal government respond to evidence of widely practiced discrimination during other presidential administrations that followed the Roosevelt years?

    (A) Legislative leadership in eradicating racial discrimination was apparent, especially after special interests effectively pressured individual members of Congress immediately after World War II.

    (B) At first the judicial branch was the pathfinder in approving policies for eliminating racial discriminatory practices, but the administrative chief of the federal executive branch eventually prodded the legislative branch to pass major civil rights laws.

    (C) During the 10 to 15 years following President Roosevelt's death, the legislative branch moved speedily in the policymaking arena and protected black citizens more than the judicial and executive branches combined.

    (D) President Roosevelt, had he lived another 30 years, would have been ashamed of the executive and judicial branches when they overturned strong civil rights laws that he managed to push through Congress.

    (E) President Johnson was too busy with domestic and foreign policies to provide leadership in the civil rights movement.

Universal health coverage for all citizens is a political question staunchly supported by proponents and vigorously opposed by detractors. Both groups are emotionally committed to their idea of what is best for the nation. Today, health care coverage varies from business to business. Employees may or may not be
(5) covered by health insurance and/or retirement pension plans provided by employers. Congress has made small steps toward a national health plan through several laws. For instance, the Health Maintenance Organization Act was passed in 1973. Lobbyists have pressed for leaves of absence without fear of job loss when babies are born, children or parents are ill, or a parent experiences serious illness.
(10) The central issue for business and industry is a personnel management problem and labor costs. Who will perform work duties for up to 26 weeks while the employee is on leave without pay?

Not surprisingly, many female employees support leaves of absence for child-rearing purposes. The National Organization for Women has worked
(15) actively to support passage of the federal law. Senator Christopher Dodd feels that the bill will address problems of working mothers. He cited statistics to prove his point: "half of all mothers with infants less than a year old work outside home" and "85% of all women working outside the home are likely to become pregnant at some point during their career." Dodd maintained that "we must no
(20) longer force parents to choose between their job and caring for a new or sick child." The bill has its critics. The president of the California Merchants and Manufacturers Association projects discrimination against women in hiring

practices if the bill is padded. Roberta Cook of the California Chamber of Commerce said, "We're compassionate. We just don't think the issue should be
(25) the employer's responsibility. *That's* the issue."

Another social issue yet unresolved is drug use and management/labor relations. Employers must consider the problem from several vantage points. Accidents, absenteeism, and reduction of productive labor are expensive and wasteful. The constitutional right of privacy is often argued when personnel
(30) policies for testing and/or searches are proposed. Courts have given qualified approval to some methods that employers may implement. Employers in the private sector may require drug testing as a precondition for employment. Government personnel directors must be cautious in devising new policies. Based on nothing more than the goal of a drug-free work place in the public
(35) sector, large-scale drug testing of employees violates their right of privacy.

When comparing social issues in the late nineteenth and the early twentieth centuries with current social issues that affect personnel policies, the increasing number of complexities of labor/management relations are apparent. Yet the question can be asked: Were the emotional, physical, and economic damages
(40) experienced by workers in the early years less important than the emotional, physical, and economic damages experienced today? Reuben Dagenhart, plaintiff in the child labor case, was in his 20s an uneducated man who weighed only about 105 pounds. Today, the "Reubens" do not quit school at a tender age and work long hours at factories, but modern-day mothers are distraught when in
(45) some workplaces they face job loss if they take leave to attend to a sick child or parent. In the late twentieth century the legislative branch continues its struggles with competing pressures from labor and management while the judicial branch intercedes from time to time and makes hard decisions based on what the Constitution requires. Again national leaders must structure social policies when legal
(50) and social philosophies collide and when economic theories clash in the market place of ideas.

14. Why should people disagree about the health insurance issue described by the author?

   (A) In a truly representative democracy, voters naturally feel that the ultimate decision on health care should be made by members of Congress, who are wise and know best.

   (B) Many voters embrace the capitalist system where many decisions should be confined to the private sector without governmental policies which assure all people health care protection.

   (C) In the interest of promoting socialism, leaders of welfare groups fear expanded coverage.

   (D) Resistance to significant health care coverage at taxpayers' expense may be due to other factors, such as fear that government will refuse to pay for abortions and AIDS care.

(E)   The controversy about health care among groups can be explained in one word — entropy. The term means degradation followed by inert uniformity.

15.   Given the difficulty of legislating a universal health care plan, what appears to be the relationship between the business community and Congress?

(A)   With Congress under pressure to expand health coverage and yet not wanting to lose the support of business, it has passed a few laws allocating enough programs and funds to meet the immediate need of pleasing constituents who want to increase public health care.

(B)   The business world has already developed a universal health plan in which if a man or woman works, he/she has nothing to worry about.

(C)   Participative management in factories where workers help choose insurance plans has been sufficient to argue against Congress moving forward on health care issues.

(D)   Business has taken advantage of proponents of universal health care who follow the philosophy of Boren's testimony: "When in charge ponder; … When in doubt mumble."

(E)   The business community lacks concern for employees and their families.

16.   What is the current status of leaves of absence without pay?

(A)   Most employees are appalled at the new idea because they do not want to be away from their jobs which would mean loss of income and lowering of the standard of living.

(B)   Business's cry that it cannot afford to let people have a month or more off from work because it would drive up the price of products is ridiculous and is nothing more than the little boy crying "wolf."

(C)   Business opposes unpaid leaves of absence on the grounds that it will be burdened with training and paying replacement workers.

(D)   The policy on leaves seems to place an emotional hardship on families.

(E)   Congressmen who listen to supporters of the policy in which laws would protect people from being fired after the leave probably hear these lobbyists repeat time and again: "Caveat emptor" or "Let the buyer beware."

17.   What is the social significance of the leaves of absence policy?

(A)   Under the proposed policy, bonding of family members will be promoted.

(B)   With the prediction of an 85% growth in family units, our nation will naturally face a population explosion if the policy is ratified.

(C) A subsystem will develop in society composed of "working mothers" who only work occasionally between births and between child sickness.

(D) Business is solidifying its opposition against the bill through such spokespersons as Dodd and Cook.

(E) The Chamber of Commerce is compassionate toward working mothers, and therefore is pro-labor.

18. What are the constitutional issues of drug use in the workplace?

(A) The author infers that the right of privacy protects an employee against Murphy's Law: "If anything can go wrong, it will."

(B) For the public good, government has greater freedom in drug testing then managers in the private sector.

(C) Under the right of privacy, employees may refuse drug testing without fear of losing their jobs.

(D) Under the constitutional right of privacy, we can assume that applicants for a job may withdraw the application if the potential employer requires drug testing as a condition for the job.

(E) Bias rather than economics will figure most prominently when employers reject applicants whose tests are positive.

19. How can nineteenth and twentieth century social issues be compared?

(A) The author called for a return to policy making made on a value-free basis where economics was of prime importance.

(B) The author implies that the leaves of absence policy is based on Parkinson's Law: "Work expands so as to fill the time for its completion."

(C) The author concludes that although specific issues have changed, problems remain for employees and employers which have both social and economic significance.

(D) Reuben Dagenhart, if he is alive today and still working in a mill, absolutely would not support leaves of absence without pay.

(E) The author implies that legal and social philosophies should have more weight in policy making than economic theories.

20. How does the author feel about some of the recent personnel management issues?

(A) The author senses that unpaid leaves for birth of a child or sickness of a relative is not a simple issue.

    (B)   The author heavily criticizes married women employees for taking jobs away from males and then for complaining because they cannot take long leaves for personal reasons.

    (C)   When drug testing is discussed in the passage, the author feels that productivity outweighs the right to privacy.

    (D)   Reading between the lines, it soon becomes evident that the author is pro-labor and anti-management.

    (E)   Choice of how management deals with requests for leaves of absence is strictly a business decision, and government should stay out.

21.   Why does the author bring up the subject of Dagenhart again? (lines 41-43)

    (A)   Developing a central theme in his analysis, the author compares the health of workers before government-sponsored health-care facilities with the more affluent society today.

    (B)   The author feels that child workers and women are nothing but a group of whiners who do not recognize the valuable role that they play in our economy.

    (C)   The author attempts to make the point that emotional damage in earlier years was more devastating than today when the workforce is composed of adults.

    (D)   In a comparative analysis, the author cited examples of conditions when few legal protections were available for laborers and then cited more recent examples of more recent conditions which may be as crucial today as in earlier years.

    (E)   The author showed how problems of blue collar workers will never be solved because there are too many economists, philosophers, and lawyers in Congress.

Apprehension over the development and implementation of nuclear plants was confirmed in the minds of critics when the media announced the fuel melt-down at Three Mile Island in Harrisburg, Pennsylvania, in 1979 and again confirmed with the accident at the nuclear plant at Chernobyl in 1986. Environ-

(5) mentalists who had raised serious questions preceding and after the two catastro-phes continue to press for research and development of solar energy and other non-fossil sources, such as wind and geothermal.

The federal courts entered the process in the 1970s when an interest group charged the Atomic Regulatory Commission with unfair and inadequate proce-

(10) dures during a licensing process. Although the interest group convinced the United States Circuit Court of Appeals that closer judicial monitoring of the licensing process was within constitutional protections, it lost its case in the United States Supreme Court in *Vermont Yankee Nuclear Power Corporation v.*

Natural Resources Defense Council, Inc. in 1978. The Supreme Court held that
(15) the agency's informal rule making was based upon technical data, and the courts
should not become "Monday morning quarterbacks." Other activities of interest
groups, such as Public Concern, National Audubon Society, and Worldwatch
Institute, led to the demise of construction of nuclear plants with no new orders
by 1978. More recent concerns of interest groups and many citizens are radioac-
(20) tive waste disposal.

For many years nuclear scientists have had great influence on industrial and
political leaders, university administrator policymakers, and major professional
groups. As early as the 1950s, the slogan "atomic energy for peace" led to full-
scale plans for research and development which was supposed to provide safe,
(25) cheap, and unlimited sources of electricity. The bandwagon gained momentum,
and the nuclear reactor program became the buzzword of the 1950s and 1960s.
Enthusiasts promised that atomic energy would provide the solution for combat-
ting the greenhouse effect and for promoting industrial growth.

Problems developed when industry failed to meet its promises. Construction
(30) costs were higher than predicted. Construction was complex and plagued by
errors. The amount of time between initiation of construction and authorization
by government to begin electrical generation far exceeded all expectations.
Adding to the cost of construction and maintenance was the fact that plant
constructions were unique, with variation from plant to plant. Cancellations of
(35) nuclear reactors by utility companies became prevalent during this period of
time. Today, three large plants have not begun operation, and only 103 commercial nuclear plants generate electricity.

Pro-nuclear activists have gone back to the drawing board in search of new
ideas which will again generate enthusiasm for nuclear energy and funds for
(40) industrial and university research projects. The high cost of nuclear energy
remains the major factor in the decision making process of managers of utilities.
Over the years, stockholders have become disillusioned with investment in
utilities with nuclear powered plants, and management has responded accordingly.
(45)

22.   Which phrase best describes the main idea that the above paragraphs por-
tray?

(A)   The pluralistic nature of the American society

(B)   Stockholders' desire to invest in a single utility operated by the national government

(C)   A need for Congressional investigation of interest group infiltration
into industrial research laboratories and construction sites

(D)   Nuclear power is at best hopeless and should be abandoned

(E)   Nuclear power is dangerous and should be abandoned

23. Which statement summarizes the implication that can be drawn from the author's narrative?

   (A) Industrial giants place philosophical and humanitarian priorities over profits.

   (B) Nuclear energy is a dead issue in the United States.

   (C) In our capitalist system of government, pressure exerted by ordinary citizens may eventually have impact on major industrial development.

   (D) Utility companies have abandoned General Electric and Westinghouse production goals and have become active proponents of interest groups support of solar energy.

   (E) Few people can figure out the politics of decision making when technologies are complex.

24. Which statement puts into perspective current conditions in our country?

   (A) The safest, most economical, least controversial policy for development of energy alternatives to coal and oil is yet to be resolved by leaders in industry, universities, and interest groups due to the complexity of the issue.

   (B) The uncertainty of decision making by utility companies is rectified by the fact that these companies have safety and public service as the number one priority.

   (C) Historically, interest groups are composed of an odd assortment of people who manufacture issues in order to bond members to the organizations.

   (D) Technically, conditions for a bandwagon in support of nuclear energy that prevailed in the 1950s and 1960s are the same for today with the exception of the accidents at Chernobyl and Three Mile Island.

   (E) Even high school graduates know that companies dealing with fission and the like should be given a free hand in developing energy.

25. What is the major thrust of the above passages?

   (A) The author illustrates how federal judges' interpretations of the Fifth Amendment's due process guarantees that limits be placed on regulatory powers of the federal government at the expense of industrial freedom to operate nuclear power plants.

   (B) The author proposes that ultimate power of deciding controversies should be lodged in the courts when critical issues are highly scientific and technical.

(C) The paragraphs imply that the author feels unions and collective bargaining have destroyed the nuclear energy industry.

(D) The author raises questions about the role of the judicial branch in monitoring highly scientific and technical developments when federal agencies seem to ignore due process protections.

(E) The author appears to be a dogmatic social scientist with a narrow focus on humanitarianism.

26. What is the author's opinion about free enterprise and nuclear power plant construction?

(A) Only large factories and plants require nuclear energy for adequate electrical power; so let them pay for plants.

(B) Actually, small businesses must rely more on nuclear energy than large factories, according to the author. Let taxpayers pay for the plants.

(C) Business and industry have had to deal with high financial risks when investing in nuclear plants.

(D) Government always comes to the rescue of stockholders who face losses in the stockmarket.

(E) The author is disillusioned with the *laissez faire* system that prevails in this country.

27. What is the role of the federal agency and the courts when nuclear power plants are constructed?

(A) Under law, courts get first shot at the controversy with later appeal to the Nuclear Regulatory Commission.

(B) The courts have no authority with regard to nuclear power because technical terms are not legal terms.

(C) Under law, people or agencies unhappy or fearful that the regulatory commission has acted unfairly or unwisely may, after exhausting all agency processes so that fewer cases will be appealed to the court.

(D) The head of the agency and the chief judge work together in the rule making process so that fewer cases will be appealed to the court.

(E) The author infers that if the court continues to interfere, government staff should lobby Congress to remove judicial jursidiction.

STOP
If time still remains, you may review work only in this section.
When the time allotted is up, you may go on to the next section.

Section IV

Time—35 minutes
25 Questions

(Answer sheets appear in the back of this book.)

DIRECTIONS: The questions in this section are based on the reasoning contained in brief statements or passages. For some questions, more than one of the choices could conceivably answer the question. However, you are to choose the **best** answer; that is, the response that most accurately and completely answers the question. You should not make assumptions that are by commonsense standards implausible, superfluous, or incompatible with the passage. After you have chosen the best answer, blacken the corresponding space on your answer sheet.

QUESTIONS 1–2

Latex paint often has a tendency to prematurely crack and peel when applied to wooden structures. Many homeowners who have applied a new coat of paint to their houses are shocked when, after the first summer storm followed by several hot sunny days, the paint begins to crack and peel. Professional painters cite three factors, some or all of which are to blame for the premature cracking and peeling: (1) the paint was not thoroughly stirred before application; (2) the surface was not clean and dry before application; (3) the paint was applied in one heavy coat rather than two or more light ones.

1. If the claims of the professional painters are true, and if the surface was clean and dry before being painted, but premature cracking and peeling still occurred, it must be because

    (A) the paint was not thoroughly stirred before application.

    (B) the paint was applied in one heavy coat.

    (C) either the paint was not thoroughly stirred, or was applied in one heavy coat, or both.

    (D) either the paint was not thoroughly stirred, or was applied in one heavy coat.

    (E) the paint was not thoroughly stirred and was applied in one heavy coat.

2. Which of the following is an inference that can be drawn from the information about the cracking and peeling paint?

    (A) latex paint cracks and peels on all types of surfaces.

(B)   premature cracking and peeling often occur after the first summer storm which is followed by hot, sunny days.

(C)   premature cracking and peeling occur only after the first summer storm which is followed by hot sunny days.

(D)   premature cracking and peeling cannot be prevented.

(E)   premature cracking and peeling never occur on jobs done by professional painters.

The Cardinals and the Angels are in different leagues, and teams in different leagues never play each other. A baseball analyst was asked if the Cardinals' trade of Tom Coleman to the Angels for Vince Smith was a good one for the Cardinals. He replied "Well it may depend on Smith's batting average remaining as high as it was before. Angel Stadium has short fences, and his home run total there was the main reason for his high batting average. Cardinal Stadium has very long fences, and he will hit few home runs there. So I guess the trade wasn't that good."

3.   Assuming all of the analyst's premises are true, the conclusion would be the most strengthened if it were also true that

(A)   Tom Coleman's average will benefit from the shorter fences in Angel Stadium.

(B)   the analyst works as a broadcaster for the Cardinals.

(C)   Smith was the league leading home run hitter in Angel Stadium for the previous two seasons.

(D)   batting average was not the most important factor in judging the two players' relative abilities.

(E)   Smith will remain healthy for the remainder of the season, while Coleman will not.

QUESTIONS 4–5

For the past 10 years medical orthodoxy has advised women not to engage in such exercises as aerobics and swimming in the final three months of pregnancy. It was thought that such exercises caused extra stress, which was harmful for both the fetus and the mother. Two recent studies suggest, however, that swimming and aerobics, taken in moderation during that period, actually increase the mother and infant's chances of surviving childbirth. Mothers and infants in the exercise group in each study showed stronger heartbeats and better respiration than mothers and infants in the non-exercise groups.

4.   A national medical board is deciding whether to recommend that doctors encourage their patients to exercise in the last three months of pregnancy.

In addition to the information in the passage above, it would be helpful for the board to know:

(A) Whether both groups of women in each of the studies were given the same diet and got the same amount of sleep.

(B) The odds of accidental prenatal damage to the fetus during exercise.

(C) The reason or reasons why medical orthodoxy advised the opposite for the last 10 years.

(D) None of the above.

(E) All of the above.

5. Which of the following is/are not implied by the above passage?

(A) A stronger heartbeat increases the chances of surviving childbirth for mother and infant.

(B) There was a correlation between the exercise and the stronger heart-beats.

(C) Swimming and aerobics in moderation cause extra stress to the mother and fetus.

(D) Moderate swimming and aerobics can have an affect on respiration.

(E) The non-exercise group showed weaker heartbeats and respiration.

QUESTIONS 6–7

Will the United States land a man on Mars by the year 2010? At this time it is not obvious that we will. There are three obstacles that must be overcome. They are:

(1) where to get the $50 billion the program will cost

(2) how to design the computer technology necessary for such long-distance space travel

(3) how to create an space module which can support life during long-distance space travel

6. Which of the following conclusions derives the MOST support from the above passage?

(A) It may be impossible to create the needed computer technology.

(B) The space module is the most important requirement for the project.

(C)   Money may or may not be found to fund the project.

(D)   The author thinks the project is a waste of time.

(E)   The U.S. may not land a man on Mars by 2010.

7.   The passage above makes which of the following presuppositions?

(A)   If the money is available, the project will succeed.

(B)   It is highly unlikely that the project can succeed, regardless of whether the three obstacles are overcome.

(C)   If all three obstacles are overcome, the project is likely to succeed.

(D)   The computer technology will not be available for years.

(E)   Life support in a space module is the least important obstacle.

8.   Suppose that a man went back in time and met and killed one of his ancestors. The question arises, would the time traveler immediately cease to exist? I believe that he would.

Which of the following, if true, would be logically relevant to the passage above?

(A)   No one can go back in time.

(B)   The topic is so speculative that no one could possibly care about the answer.

(C)   No person could exist if a single one of his/her ancestors had not existed.

(D)   The construction of a time machine is scientifically impossible.

(E)   The chances of a time traveler finding one of his ancestors are near impossible.

9.   Two different makes of automobile, types X and Y, were tested in different types of driving. Type X was shown to hold up for more miles than type Y when the driving involved fewer, longer trips. Type Y was shown to hold up for more miles than type X when the driving involved more but shorter trips. On the basis of this study, researchers recommended that drivers who take fewer but longer trips purchase type X, and drivers who take more but shorter trips purchase type Y.

Taken separately, which of the following, if true, would call into question the researchers' recommendation?

(A) Some people's driving consists primarily of trips which are both few and short.

(B) The automobiles were serviced every 2000 miles, regardless of the type of driving involved.

(C) The gas used in both automobiles in the study was known to affect the engine life of different makes of autos differently.

(D) The same type of oil was used in both cars.

(E) The automobiles were tested on the same road but at different times.

10. In the battle of Atlanta during the American Civil War, Sherman defeated the Confederates by turning the flank of their defenses. The Germans used the same strategy successfully in their initial attack on France in World War II.

Assuming that the statements above are all true, they would support which of the following conclusions?

(A) History can produce scientific knowledge.

(B) History can be an instructive guide to action.

(C) The lessons of history can be used for good as well as evil purposes.

(D) History repeats itself.

(E) The Germans must have studied several types of warfare.

11. All veterans of the war are bitter about the outcome of the war, and some of the staff members in the office are bitter about the outcome of the war. Therefore, some of the staff members in the office are veterans of the war.

Which one of the following most closely parallels the reasoning used in the argument above?

(A) All children play, and some adults play. Therefore, some adults are children.

(B) All lawyers are rich, and rich people have fun. Therefore, lawyers have fun.

(C) All bicycles have two wheels. No cars have two wheels. Therefore, no cars are bicycles.

(D) All birds have beaks, and some reptiles have beaks. Therefore, reptiles and birds are members of the same species.

(E)   All balls roll, and all logs roll. Therefore, some logs are balls.

QUESTIONS 12–13

Elected officials should use their own best judgment in meeting the problems which face society. Modern society is based on a division of labor, with each person specializing in a particular field. Public officials are the experts on matters which affect the public, whereas the average citizen knows and cares very little about public policy. Therefore, the official should not concern himself with public opinion on any given policy question.

12.   It can be demonstrated that the author's reasoning is flawed if it is true that

   (A)   professional politicians sometimes disagree among themselves on what the best policy is.

   (B)   some citizens are very well-informed about public policy issues.

   (C)   the average citizen understands what is in the public interest as well as any public official does.

   (D)   the public bases its opinion on official policies.

   (E)   only one citizen knows about public policy.

13.   If all of the statements in the passage are true, which of the following can be derived from only what the author explicitly states?

   I.   The average citizen is not an expert on public policy.

   II.   A public official is an expert on public policy.

   III.   The average citizen could never become a public official.

   (A)   I only   (D)   I and II

   (B)   II only   (E)   I, II, and III

   (C)   III only

QUESTIONS 14–15

An automobile is waxed with Brand O wax. After being run through a car wash 52 times the wax finish still shines. On the basis of this experiment the manufacturer claims that Brand O wax produces a shine which is good for one year's wear on the typical automobile.

14.   The manufacturer bases the claim on which of the following unspoken premises?

   (A)   The typical automobile gets washed an average of once a week.

(B)   Automobile owners like to wax their automobiles once each year.

(C)   The person hearing the claim will not critically evaluate it.

(D)   People do not feel the need to keep their cars looking good.

(E)   Most people do not own a typical car.

15.   The conclusion of the passage above is flawed for which of the following reasons?

(A)   The experiment mistakes an effect for a cause.

(B)   The passage assumes a proposition is true because it has not been proven false.

(C)   The experiment controls only one of several variables which might affect the result.

(D)   The experiment was done by the company selling the wax.

(E)   All the advertisements are exaggerations of the truth.

16.   1.   All management are salaried.

2.   All workers are experienced.

3.   Some workers are management.

If all of the statements above are true, which of the following must also be true?

(A)   All who are experienced are salaried.

(B)   Some who are experienced are management.

(C)   Some workers are salaried but not management.

(D)   All workers are management.

(E)   All management are workers.

17.   Many of us are willing to participate in medical research so valuable information can be gained and doctors can learn how to better treat various problems. What bothers me about all of this is that we are being sent bills for "services rendered." As a post-polio, I don't think I should have to pay money to a medical school to get evaluated, so medical students and/or

doctors can learn more about post-polio syndrome.

Against what is the writer arguing?

(A) The willingness to participate in medical research.

(B) That valuable information can be gained and doctors can learn how to better treat various problems.

(C) Medical bills.

(D) Doctors are using patients as "guinea pigs" and charging the patients for the testing.

(E) The belief that medical students can learn more about post-polio syndrome.

18. The Office of Technology Assessment's report highlights the need for creative and ongoing development of teachers' technology skills. The full utilization of technology as a tool to enhance learning will depend largely on how skilled our teachers are in its use. Many teachers have embraced the use of technology to enhance learning; however, it is increasingly clear that as powerful technologies and software proliferate, teachers will need to learn more about these new tools on a continuous basis.

If we regard this passage as the set of premises, which of the following is the most reasonable conclusion?

(A) Many teachers have embraced the use of technology to enhance learning.

(B) There is an ongoing development of teachers' technology skills.

(C) Powerful technologies and software are proliferating.

(D) Technology enhances learning.

(E) The classroom teacher is a central factor in the full development of technology's use in the schools.

19. How best to meet the need, we all agree, should be left up to individual companies, because they are the ones that best understand the requirements of their customers. This brings me to another strategic policy goal: flexibility. Forecasting future use admittedly contains an element of uncertainty. That is why our nation needs public policies that give electric companies the flexibility to meet future demand, whatever the demand should turn out to be.

Which of the following is a premise of this argument?

(A) The nation has public policies designed to meet future electric demand.

(B) Customers must decide their own requirements for electrical use.

(C) Public policy flexibility must be allowed by electric companies.

(D) Electric companies cannot forecast future use with certainty.

(E) Electric companies must allow for changes in public policy.

20. As a preparation technique, it is important to evaluate every victim and witness, not only for what they have told the police and others, but also for their physical and mental characteristics. Too often, defense attorneys treat victims or witnesses as untouchable. At trial, that may be necessary but during the investigation process find out as much information about these individuals as possible. Use the same type of background information form you use when interviewing your client.

Which of the following is the conclusion of this argument?

(A) Victims and witnesses should be interviewed in the same way a client is interviewed.

(B) Victims and witnesses have physical and mental characteristics.

(C) Too often, defense attorneys treat victims or witnesses as untouchable.

(D) At trial it may be necessary to treat victims or witnesses as untouchable.

(E) Trials are necessary during the investigation process.

21. Turning bands of heavily armed hunters loose on some pigs seems to be a rather extreme method of protecting a golf course and some flowers. But the zeal of the response reflects the seriousness of the problem these pigs were starting to pose for California's native ecosystem. With few predators, pigs in the wild have multiplied dramatically in the past several decades. The pigs compete with native animals for food and territory. They sully crucial wildland water supplies, destroy rare native plants, and transmit a variety of dangerous diseases to wildlife and domestic livestock.

Which of the following is a justification offered by the writer for hunting the wild pigs in California?

(A) Golf courses need protecting.

(B) Wild pigs carry diseases dangerous to animals.

(C) Wild pigs foul wildland food supplies.

(D) Pigs will soon out number humans.

(E) Native plants are more important than pigs.

22. If there are indeed educational programs in place that try to instill abstract thinking apart from knowledge, Hirsch may have a point. I have never encountered any of these and doubt that they are as common as Hirsch supposes. My guess is that the shocking ignorance that so many observers have reported in today's children derives more from the failure of traditional school settings to engage their interest than from the Deweyesque pedagogy, which is really the exception rather than the rule in American schools.

What appears to be Hirsch's point, as the writer is attacking it?

(A) Traditional school settings engage today's children.

(B) The Deweyesque pedagogy is the exception rather than the rule in American schools.

(C) There is shocking ignorance among today's children.

(D) Ignorance in today's children derives from education programs that instill abstract thinking apart from knowledge.

(E) Educational programs that instill abstract thinking apart from knowledge are not common.

23. Mistakes and shortcomings in the Frelimo government's policies contributed to Mozambique's economic decline. From 1975 to 1983, the newly independent government pursued a socialist strategy of development based on large-scale, centrally planned, capital-intensive and import-dependent development projects both in industry and agriculture. The state sector received the preponderant share of investment. Few resources were channeled to peasant families and the private sector of the economy. The government's policies proved inappropriate to the prevailing economic conditions and consequently failed to halt the economic decline that followed the collapse of the colonial economy after independence in 1975.

Which of the following, if true, would weaken the writer's argument that Frelimo's government contributed to Mozambique's decline?

(A) Socialist strategies of development are based on large-scale development projects.

(B) Prevailing economic conditions made a socialist strategy of development appropriate.

(C) Prevailing economic conditions were not favorable for government policies.

(D) Economic decline could not be halted by government policies.

(E) The colonial economy collapsed after independence in 1975.

24. The notion of childhood egocentricism, even in early infancy, has all but been abandoned in the light of research and theorizing. It now appears that Piaget's methods underestimated young children's communicative abilities. Evidence against egocentricism comes from several lines of research. The first of these was experimental studies. These suggest that Piaget's subjects did not understand what was required of them; that their performance was hampered by irrelevant difficulties such as excessive burdens upon memory; or that children are unable to put difficult concepts into words.

    Which of the following statements is consistent with this argument's conclusion?

    (A) There is childhood egocentricism, even in early infancy.

    (B) Excessive burdens upon memory were relevant to the children's performance.

    (C) Piaget supported a notion of childhood egocentricism.

    (D) Children have poor communication abilities.

    (E) Evidence from experimental studies supports egocentricism.

25. Those who use oral evidence should not be on the defensive when faced with the issue of the respective value of documentary and oral sources. It would be beyond the scope of this book to discuss the defects of a great deal of documentary evidence. It is sufficient to note here that the various parliamentary inquiries into industrial conditions and social problems are often among the most useful documentary sources for social history. The verbatim evidence given to these inquiries is frequently indistinguishable from the sort of testimony given in an oral history interview.

    Which of the following, if true, would strengthen the writer's argument that oral sources are not necessarily inferior to documentary sources?

    (A) Verbatim evidence in documentaries is no more reliable than testimony given in oral history interviews.

    (B) The book cited discusses oral and documentary evidence.

    (C) Parliamentary inquiries into industrial conditions are useful oral history sources.

    (D) Those who use oral evidence are often faced with the issue of the respective value of documentary and oral sources.

    (E) Verbatim evidence given in parliamentary inquiries is frequently indistinguishable from documentary evidence.

STOP
If time still remains, you may review work only in this section.
When the time allotted is up, you may go on to the next section.

LSAT Writing Sample

(Answer sheets appear in the back of this book.)

General Directions

You will have 35 minutes in which to plan and write an essay on the topic below. Read the topic and the accompanying directions carefully. You will probably find it best to spend a few minutes considering the topic and organizing your thoughts before you begin writing. In your essay, be sure to develop your ideas fully, leaving time, if possible, to review what you have written. **Do not write on a topic other than the one specified. Writing on a topic of your own choice is not acceptable.**

No special knowledge is required or expected for this writing exercise. Law schools are interested in the reasoning, clarity, organization, language usage, and writing mechanics displayed in your essay. How well you write is more important than how much you write.

Confine your essay to the blocked, lined areas on the front and back of the separate writing sample response sheet. Only that area will be reproduced for law schools. Be sure that your writing is legible.

Sample Topic

Directions: For this essay you are presented with an argument (see next page) that offers reasons for drawing a particular conclusion. Your essay should analyze and evaluate the line of reasoning and use of evidence in the argument. For example, you may want to discuss how the logic of the argument is flawed or could be improved, or what counterexamples or alternative explanations would undermine the argument. You may also want to consider what, if any, questionable assumptions underlie the reasoning and what additional information or evidence may have been overlooked that would strengthen or weaken the argument. Note: You are NOT being asked to present your personal opinion on the subject with which the argument is concerned.

The following appeared in a letter to the school board in the town of Jetson:

"A recent study reported that a neighboring school district has had higher standardized test scores after introducing personal laptops into their classrooms. Moreover, because computers are so prevalent in society, basic computer proficiency is essential to success in college and the working world. Although there are computer labs at Jetson High, the computers are out of date, and access to them is limited. I urge you, therefore, to invest funds in personal laptops for each student at Jetson High School."

Discuss how well reasoned you find this argument.

STOP

If time still remains, you may review work only in this section.

TEST II

ANSWER KEY

Section I — Analytical Reasoning

1.	(D)	8.	(A)	15.	(A)	22.	(C)
2.	(A)	9.	(B)	16.	(E)	23.	(A)
3.	(E)	10.	(C)	17.	(D)		
4.	(D)	11.	(E)	18.	(C)		
5.	(C)	12.	(A)	19.	(A)		
6.	(C)	13.	(D)	20.	(A)		
7.	(B)	14.	(E)	21.	(E)		

Section II — Logical Reasoning

1.	(A)	8.	(A)	15.	(A)	22.	(A)
2.	(E)	9.	(D)	16.	(C)	23.	(B)
3.	(D)	10.	(B)	17.	(B)	24.	(E)
4.	(D)	11.	(C)	18.	(A)		
5.	(B)	12.	(B)	19.	(D)		
6.	(D)	13.	(D)	20.	(A)		
7.	(B)	14.	(B)	21.	(A)		

Section III — Reading Comprehension

1.	(D)	8.	(B)	15.	(A)	22.	(A)
2.	(D)	9.	(B)	16.	(C)	23.	(C)
3.	(D)	10.	(B)	17.	(A)	24.	(A)
4.	(D)	11.	(C)	18.	(D)	25.	(D)
5.	(D)	12.	(A)	19.	(C)	26.	(C)
6.	(B)	13.	(B)	20.	(A)	27.	(C)
7.	(A)	14.	(B)	21.	(D)		

Section IV — Logical Reasoning

1.	(C)	8.	(C)	15.	(C)	22.	(D)
2.	(B)	9.	(C)	16.	(B)	23.	(B)
3.	(C)	10.	(B)	17.	(D)	24.	(C)
4.	(E)	11.	(A)	18.	(E)	25.	(A)
5.	(C)	12.	(C)	19.	(D)		
6.	(E)	13.	(D)	20.	(A)		
7.	(C)	14.	(A)	21.	(B)		

DETAILED EXPLANATIONS OF ANSWERS

Section I – Analytical Reasoning

QUESTIONS 1–5

Initial Information

("<X, Y, Z>" means "at least 1 of X, Y, Z")

$$\text{Committee} = <C, M, B> + <H, L, E> + <P, R> = 4$$
$$\neq CB \text{ (or } = \cancel{CB}\text{)}$$
$$M <=> E$$
$$R => <B, E>$$

1. **(D)** (D) Clearly works. Each division is represented: Science by both Mathematics and Biology, Social Science by Economics, and Humanities by Rhetoric. Mathematics and Economics are both present for mutual support and Rhetoric is supported by both Biology and Economics. Chemistry is not on the committee to conflict with Biology. On the other hand, (A) contains no representative from the Humanities Division, Philosophy or Rhetoric, and, so, cannot form a committee. (C) has also omitted any representative of the Humanities Division and, therefore, cannot be a committee. (B) also cannot be a committee, because the representative of Mathematics, who is on the (B) list, only serves on committees with the representative of Economics, who is not on the (B) list. Conversely, (E) fails because the representative of Economics is on this list but will only serve on a committee with the representative of Mathematics, who is missing from this list.

2. **(A)** All of the divisions are represented and no restriction is violated in (A). Humanities is represented by both members, Science by Biology, which is also sufficient to support Rhetoric, and Social Science by History. Chemistry is not in the list to conflict with Biology and neither Mathematics nor Economics is in to require the other. List (B) fails in just this last respect, for the Economics representative is on it but the Mathematics one is not although they only serve on committees together. (C) fails in the opposite direction, having Mathematics but lacking Economics, although both are needed (if either is on). (D) and (E) both fail because the Division of Social Science is not represented at all. (D) also lacks Economics to go with Mathematics. And (E) violates the given rule that Chemistry and Biology do not serve together.

3.   **(E)**   The Economics representative will only serve with the Mathematics representative, but he is listed in only choices (A) and (E). The Chemistry representative will not serve with the Biology representative, but they are listed together in choices (A) and (B). Any committee that has Rhetoric also has at least Economics to support it. In short, only the suggested committee in (E) is possible within the restrictions of the question. The remaining answers fail since each has at least one member in the suggested committee that is not acceptable.

4.   **(D)**   Since the representative from Philosophy is not on the committee but someone from the Humanities Division has to be, the Rhetoric representative must be on the committee. Consequently, either Economics or Biology has to be represented on the committee, to satisfy the Rhetoric representative's restriction. But the Biology representative is not on this committee, so the Economics representative must be. But then, the Mathematics representative also must be on the committee, since neither Economics nor Mathematics serves without the other. Thus, (D) gives the list of the representatives who have to be on the committee. The fourth member of this committee might be the representative from Chemistry, Linguistics, or History. Any of (B), (C), or (E) might be on the committee, along with the other of the Mathematics–Economics pairings, but no particular one of them has to be. (A) is not even a possible pair on the committee, since it would make a five-person committee when added to the necessary Rhetoric, Economics and Mathematics.

5.   **(C)**   If both Humanities representatives are on the committee, then either the Biology or the Economics representative, or both, is on the committee, since the Rhetoric representative is. Now, if the Economics representative is on the committee, so is the Mathematics representative, since these two always serve together. Consequently, the committee would have its four members and there would be no room for a fifth. Neither Chemistry nor Biology could serve, so Rhetoric's mates cannot both be on this committee. If the Biology representative is on the committee, then the Chemistry representative is not, both because he will not serve with Biology and because the committee needs a representative from the Social Science Division. So, in either case, Chemistry will not serve on a committee on which both Humanities representatives serve. So, choice (C) is true.

   If the representatives of Chemistry and Mathematics are on the committee, then so is the representative of Economics, for the Mathematics representative never serves without the one from Economics. But, since the Economics representative serves on the committee, nothing prevents the Rhetoric representative from being the Humanities representative instead of the person from Philosophy. So, choice (A) is false.

   If the Rhetoric representative is not on the committee, then the Philosophy representative must be. But that places no special restrictions on the other members. For example, Philosophy, Chemistry, Linguistics, and History would make a legitimate committee. So choice (B) is false.

If the representative of Mathematics is not on the committee, neither is the representative of Economics, since these two always serve together. So, choice (D) is false.

If neither Biology nor Economics is represented on the committee, then Rhetoric is not either, since it goes with one or the other of these two. Thus, Philosophy represents the Humanities on this committee. Mathematics cannot be on because Economics is not. Thus, Chemistry must be on to represent the Science Division. And then History and Linguistics must represent the Social Science Division. So, Linguistics can — indeed, must — be on this committee. So, choice (E) is false.

QUESTIONS 6–10

The initial information, and some inferences from it, looks like this

		A	B	C	D	E
A	L		n		n	Y
	E		n			n
B	K	y	n	y	n	
	O	n	y	n		
C	M	n	y	n		

Since Bill is a Magic and an Old Forest, Al and Charlie can be neither of these. Hence, both of them must be in Kobra, since otherwise both their memberships would be in Group A. Consequently, Dave is not in Kobra, since Charlie is. Dave is also not a Lord, since Ed is one.

6.   **(C)**   As noted generally, Bill is a Magic and an Old Forest, so Charlie, sitting next to him, can be neither. But Charlie must be either in Kobra or Old Forest, else his memberships would all be in Group A and they have to come from two groups. So, he is in Kobra. As for the other claims here, Al might be an Elm, but he might equally well be a Lord, since Bill is neither and so does not force one choice. So (A) does not have to be true. Similarly, (B) does not have to be true. Charlie might be a Lord but he might equally be an Elm. Bill is neither and, so, the choice is not forced. (D) is a rather similar case: Dave is not a Kobra but he need not be an Old Forest, for he might be a Magic and one of the members of Group A. (E) is even less necessitated, for Ed might be either or a Magic or in Kobra rather than an Old Forest.

7.   **(B)**   Taking the new conditions into account gives the following chart

		A	B	C	D	E
A	L		n	y	n	Y
	E		n	n	y	n
B	K	y	n	y	n	
	O	n	y	n		
C	M	n	y	n		

Bill already is a Magic and in a Group B organization (namely, an Old Forest).

The claim says, then, that Bill is the only one and so that Dave is not one also. Dave may, then, be either a Magic and an Elm or an Elm and an Old Forest, since he cannot be a Magic and an Old Forest. So, in any case, Dave is an Elm. But then, Charlie is not an Elm, because he is next to Dave. Bill and Ed are already given as not being Elms, so there can be at most one other Elm than Dave, Al. Thus, (B), that there are at most two Elms, is true. (A) is false, since Al could equally well be a Lord and, so, with the certified Lord, Ed, and Charlie, who must be a Lord because he cannot be an Elm, there might be three Lords. As for (C), Al and Charlie are already in Kobra and nothing prevents Ed from being one, too, though nothing forces it either. (D) must be wrong because only Dave or Ed could be a Magic at all and one of them, for they are next to each other. So, at most one man can be both a Magic and either a Lord (if Ed) or an Elm (Dave). Finally, (E) does not have to be true, for, while either Dave or Ed might be an Old Forest, both have other possibilities. For example, Dave might be a Magic and Ed in Kobra.

8. **(A)** Dave cannot be a Lord, since he is next to Ed, a Lord. Thus, combination (C) is excluded. Similarly, Dave cannot be in Kobra, since he is next to Charlie who is in Kobra. Thus, suggestion (B) which includes Kobra, is wrong and, with it, answers (D) and (E). This leaves only (A), that Dave could be an Elm and a Magic, and nothing else listed. The combination is clearly possible and the other two suggestions have been shown impossible, so (A) is correct.

9. **(B)** The new information gives the following chart

		A	B	C	D	E
A	L		n	n	n	Y
	E		n	Y	n	n
B	K	y	n	y	n	y
	O	n	Y	n	y	n
C	M	n	Y	n	y	n

If Charlie is an Elm, then Dave is not an Elm, being next to him. Since Dave is already not a Lord, since next to Ed, the Lord, Dave must be a member of some organization from Group B. Since he cannot be in Kobra, being next to Charlie, who is in Kobra, he must be an Old Forest. Thus, (B) must be correct. (A), on the other hand, is just plain false, since Charlie is next to Bill, given as an Old Forest. Dave has to be a Magic as well as an Old Forest since he is not in an organization in Group A and so must be in the only one in Group C. But he also has to be in an organization in Group B (indeed, the Old Forest), so (C) is false. Since Dave is a Magic, Ed, sitting next to him, cannot be, so (D) is false as well. Finally, since Dave is an Old Forest, Ed cannot be, and (E) is false.

10. **(C)** The new information in this question gives the following chart

		A	B	C	D	E	F
A	L		n	y	n	Y	n
	E		n	n	y	n	n
B	K	y	n	y	n	n	Y
	O	n	Y	n	n	y	n
C	M	n	Y	n	y	n	Y

Since Frank is a Magic and in Kobra, Ed is neither. So, (E) which has Ed in Kobra, is wrong. Since Ed is already not an Elm, he must be a Lord and an Old Forest. Dave, being next to Ed, must, thus be neither of these. So, (D), which has Dave an Old Forest, is wrong. Dave is already not in Kobra, since he is next to Charlie, who is one, so he must be an Elm and a Magic, the only remaining organizations. Thus, answer (C) must be correct. Since Dave is an Elm, Charlie, being next to him, cannot be and (B) has to be wrong. Similarly, (A) must be wrong since Charlie, being next to Dave, the Magic, cannot be a Magic.

QUESTIONS 11–13
Initial Diagram

F̕   E   H

\\ | /

*

/ | \

   -US- -S-

11. **(E)** Since Egypt and Holland sit together, France and the United States must sit on their side of the pair. There are thus two seats remaining between them on the opposite side of the table from Egypt and Holland. These seats must be occupied by Spain and Great Britain. Spain cannot occupy the seat next to the United States, so Great Britain must occupy that seat and Spain the next one. This means that Great Britain is between the United States and Spain, so (E) is the correct answer. Again, because the United States and France sit on either side

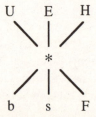

U   E   H
b   s   F

of Egypt and Holland, they cannot bracket a single seat, Great Britain. (A), then, is

incorrect. Similarly, since France is next to Holland which is next to Egypt, there is not a single seat containing Great Britain between them and (B) is incorrect. (D) is wrong for exactly parallel reasons, since only Egypt lies in a single seat between the United States and Holland, Great Britain does not. If France and Spain bracketed Great Britain, then Spain would be next to the United States, which is not permitted. Thus, (C) is wrong.

12.   **(A)**   Since the United States and Great Britain are opposite one another, there are two seats between them in each direction. Since Egypt and Holland sit next to one another, they must occupy one of these two two-seat blocs. The other is occupied, then, by France and Spain, one next to Great Britain and the other next to the United States. The one next to the United States cannot be Spain, so the bloc on that side must run U.S., France, Spain, Great Britain. Thus, Spain is flanked by Great Britain and France and answer (A) is correct. The fact that Egypt and Holland always are next to one another and so must go into the other two-seat bloc from the one containing Spain, separated by at least the United States and Great Britain, means that neither of them can be next to Spain. So, all the other answers must be wrong.

13.   **(D)**   If France is directly opposite Egypt, then, on one side there are two seats unassigned, while on the other, there is Holland next to Egypt, then an unassigned seat between Holland and France. The two-seat bloc cannot be filled by the United States and Spain, since they would then be next to each other. So, one of these seats must be filled by Great Britain. Great Britain is then separated from Holland by at least Egypt and, so, is not next to Holland. The situation in (D) cannot occur, so it is the required exception. The conditions in (A), (B) and (E) would be met by the arrangement (see figure on left) while (C) could be satisfied by interchanging the United States and Spain in that diagram.

```
   E  W                              B   E  W
   \ | /      - US -  - SU -         \ | /
    *                                 *
   / | \                            / | \
   F                               S  F  U
```

QUESTIONS 14–18
The map must look something like this:

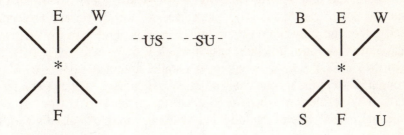

14.   **(E)**   Since T is connected only to V, any rally that goes on from T must return to V. Thus, neither (A) nor (D) is a possible course, since they move directly from T to some checkpoint other than V. (B) cannot be used, since it allows going directly from Z to U, whereas U can be reached from Z only by way of W. Similarly, (C) fails since it has a lap from Y to X, but Y can be reached from X only through W. This leaves only (E), which is possible, since W is connected directly to U, X to W, Z to X and W to Z.

15.   **(A)**   The shortest route from Z to T involves three laps, ending at W, V, and T, respectively. Thus, T cannot be reached in only two laps from Z, making (A) the correct answer. WU is a two lap course which runs from Z to U, so (B) does not give an impossible goal. Similarly, WV shows that (C) is not the correct answer. XW does this for (D) and WY for (E).

16.   **(E)**   Since the rally rules do not forbid coming back to the starting point, Y is a possible second checkpoint, after a first stop at V or W. Thus, only (E) can be complete. It is also accurate: the following courses will reach each indicated checkpoint at the end of the second lap: VT, VU (or WU), WV, WX, WY (or VY), WZ. All of the other answers are accurate but incomplete, since they omit checkpoints while all are reachable from Y in two steps.

17.   **(D)**   Since V and W are the only checkpoints directly connected to U, the first lap must end at one of them. The last (fourth) lap must begin at another of them, so that no checkpoint is passed through twice. The second checkpoint must then be directly connected with both of them, since it is the end of the second lap, which begins with one of them (whichever ends the first lap) and begins the third lap which ends with one of them (whichever begins the fourth lap). Only U and Y satisfy this condition. U is not listed, because it is the last checkpoint and so cannot also be the second without violating the "no repeat" rule. So, Y must be the second checkpoint visited and (D) is the correct answer. If V were the second checkpoint, either the rally would return to U in only three laps, WVU, or it would take more than four but would pass through V or W twice (WVTVU, for example, or WVYWU). So (A) is wrong. A parallel argument applies to W, so (B) is wrong. If Z were the second checkpoint, W would have to be used to get to it from U and W would have to be used again to get back to U from it. This violates the "no repeat" rule of the rally and so (C) is wrong. An exactly parallel argument rules out Z as the second checkpoint and (E) is the right answer.

18.   **(C)**   Since there are only seven checkpoints and each lap is to end with a different one, there can be at most seven laps. (E) has to be wrong in any case, then. On the other hand, the course beginning at W and going UVYWXZ runs six laps and so at least that many are possible. Thus, neither (A) nor (B) gives the maximum. It will be possible to get a rally of seven laps without repeats only if there is a lap that ends at T. That lap has to be the last one, since, in order to go

on from T the course would have to go back to V from which it came to T in the first place, violating the "no repeat" rule. So, there is a seven-lap rally of the sort wanted only if there is a six-lap rally ending with V, to which the trip to T could be added. Any such rally would have to start at W, since after at most four laps, W must be passed to get to further checkpoints and this passing cannot be a repetition. The first lap from W on this six-lap rally could not be to U, V, or Y, since that would either get to V before the end of the sixth lap or else would go back to W twice in order to get all six checkpoints in. So, the six-lap rally from W to V would have to start at either XZW or ZXW. But even then, the course has to come to V in at most two laps (UV or YV — or just directly to V) rather than the three needed for a six-lap rally to V. So, there is no six-lap rally to V, hence no seven-lap one to T and hence no seven-lap rally at all — under the "no repeat" condition. Thus, (D) is false also and (C), that the longest no-repeat rally is six laps, is correct.

19. **(A)** If the two ministry students have the same academic status, they must both be undergraduates, since that is the only status with more than one member in the class. Thus, claim (E) is false. Since they are of the same sex, then, they must both be male, for one of the two females is in graduate school. Thus, claim (A) is true and claim (C) is false. Claim (B) does not have to be true, though it might be, so answer (D) is not possible because only one female is in graduate school.

20. **(A)** If the law student is not one of the two females, then the two ministry students cannot both be females. So, since they are the same sex, both are males and answer (A) is correct. Each of the other answers might be true but need not be, as the fact that they contradict one another, as (B) and (C) do, shows. If the female law student is in professional school and the female medical student is in graduate school, with the male medical student an undergraduate, (C), (D), and (E) would all be false, though (B) would be true. On the other hand, if the male medical student is in professional school and the female law student is in graduate school, then the female medical student is an undergraduate, like the two ministry students, and (C) is true while (B) is false — and (D) and (E) happen to be true as well. So, none but (A) have to be true.

21. **(E)** If one of the female students is in a professional school, then, since the other female is in graduate school, the three undergraduates must all be male. Thus, (A), that the three males have different statuses must be wrong. Since one of the medical students is female and in a professional school, she must have a different status from the other medical student, who is either male and, so, an undergraduate, or the other female, and, so, in graduate school. Thus, (B) is false. The law student is either male, and so an undergraduate, or the other female, and so in graduate school. This is the situation described in (E), which is, thus, the correct answer. (C) and (D) both fail because they are tantamount, given that the only person in a professional school is a female medical student, to saying (C)

that the law student is female or (D) that the law student is male. Either could be true, but neither has to be.

22. **(C)** If the ministry students are of the same status, then they must both be undergraduates, since that is the only status for more than one person. Thus, it is not the case that one of them is in graduate school and (B) is not the right answer, nor are (D) and (E), since they allow a ministerial graduate student. Since one of the medical students is male, the two females must be the other medical student and the law student. One of these two is the graduate student, so that (C) is correct. (A) is wrong only because the information does not prevent the graduate student from being the law student.

23. **(A)** If one ministry student is female, so is the other. Thus, the graduate student, who is female, is also a ministry student, since there are only two females. That is, claim (A) is true. Further, the two females have exhausted all the non-undergraduate positions, so, all the males are undergraduates, as are all the students who are not preparing for the ministry. In particular, both the medical students must be undergraduates, so (B) is false. On the other hand, (C) and (D) are false, since all the females are ministry students. (E) is also false because it has been determined that the other ministry student is female.

Section II – Logical Reasoning

1. **(A)** The author's purpose is to show that early Americans were ignorant about the Far West. They (or many of them) thought of the Far West as unfit for cultivation. The legend must be one which expresses this misperception. Answer A does exactly that. A desert is a place where few plants will grow, meaning it is unfit for cultivation. Answer (B) would not have been a misperception or a product of ignorance, since it accurately described the area. Answer (C) again corresponded to the truth about the area. (D) is just the opposite of the Long expedition's perception of the area. He would not have described the region in terms that were the opposite of his perceptions of it. (E) is wrong for the same reason as (D).

2. **(E)** (A) The passage states that cutting back on highway repair MAY anger motorists, not that it WILL. Therefore, education appropriations could be raised without motorists getting angry. (B) Increasing education appropriations may not be the only factor involved. Perhaps highway repair will be cut back for other, unstated, reasons. (See also explanation for Question 1, Test 1). (C) The passage lends no support to this conclusion. If the legislature cuts back on highway repair, it may be because they have increased education appropriations. In that case, teachers would likely be happy. (D) The passage lends no support to this conclusion. Motorists may be angry if the legislature actually cuts highway repair. That is the extent of what we can learn or deduce from the passage about

what might make them angry. (E) The passage says that teachers will strike unless education appropriations are increased. Appropriations for education will be increased only if highway repair is cut. Therefore, if highway repair is not cut, education appropriations are not increased. This means the teachers will strike.

3. **(D)** The author is making a judgment about Amy, that she is impatient, on the basis of one event. This may be the only time in her life Amy has been impatient. If so, she could not correctly be characterized as impatient. To call someone impatient means that impatience is one of his or her regular traits. If this is the only time Amy has been impatient, and if things have gone badly for her before, something else was the reason. The author overgeneralizes, or, in other words, reaches a conclusion on the basis of too little evidence. Answer (A) is obviously not correct. The only event mentioned is Amy's behavior while waiting for George. Other things that have gone badly for her are mentioned, but we are not told enough about them to know if they are like or unlike the event described. Answer (B) is not correct, because the author does supply the set of facts about the event as evidence which (very weakly) supports the conclusion. Answer (C) could not be correct, because the author himself observed Amy's behavior, and he correctly assumed she left because she grew impatient. The problem with the evidence is not that it is unreliable, but rather that there is not enough of it to support the conclusion. (Note: generalization is a logical method of reasoning. It is used in a form of reasoning called induction. A person observes the same type of event occurring over and over many times. After extensive experience observing these events, the person is able to draw conclusions about what type of outcome to expect from another, similar event. The conclusion — the generalization — becomes more trustworthy the more experience it is based on.) Answer (E) is not plausible. The only word whose meaning could be confused is *impatient*. The author knows quite well what it means: not capable of waiting for events to unfold. He has observed this behavior once from Amy, and has correctly identified it. There is no other possible meaning for the word in this passage.

4. **(D)** The passage says nothing about methods of determining whether Bigfoot exists. For (A) to be the answer, some discussion of this topic in the passage would be necessary. (B) For this answer to be correct, the passage must establish that Bigfoot existed in earlier times. It does nothing of the sort. (C) The expert talks about beliefs of the Native Americans — beliefs which may or may not have had a foundation in fact. Again, the expert is only relating the beliefs of the Native Americans. He does not indicate whether he himself believed in Bigfoot. (D) This is the best answer. For the Native Americans to have revered the Bigfoot, they must have believed in it. One would not revere that which did not exist. Nor would they have described its characteristics if they had not believed in it. (E) Again, the existence of the Bigfoot is not proven by the passage.

5. **(B)** The best way to counter an argument is to show that one of the author's premises is untrue. This destroys the argument from within, without

having to prove the conclusion false. The answer which takes this approach is (B). The author of the passage states twice that ownership of assault rifles should be protected because ownership of guns is part of an American tradition. He admits that assault rifles have no use for hunting. But if the American tradition of gun ownership applies only to hunting weapons, it offers no support for the protection of assault rifles. The major premise of his argument is destroyed. (A) That assault rifles can be used for target practice neither adds nor detracts from the argument. The author of the passage said that they have few uses other than killing people. Target practice happens to be one of those other uses. Since it is unobjectionable in itself, it would not convince a proponent of assault rifles to be against them; nor would it convince an opponent to be in favor of them. (C) This is a plausible objection to the ownership of assault rifles. However, it does not, in and of itself, destroy the basis of the author's argument, which is that the American tradition supports gun ownership. (D) This is somewhat beside the point. They are still guns, and the author's argument is not weakened. One could argue that the tradition of gun ownership had not been meant to include such weapons, but that is the argument which is made more directly by (B). (E) This is a plausible objection to the argument. However, the author could probably point to groups around the country which favor his position. Logically speaking, an appeal to authority is not as effective for undermining an argument as disproving its premise.

6. **(D)** (A) Alice does not make this argument. She says that the REO Corporation both made profits and spent money on the environment. She does not argue that the profits made the environmental effort possible for the corporation. (B) Henry uses the word "environmentalism" to mean "protecting the environment." Alice uses the word to mean the same thing. Reforestation and reclamation of dead lakes are two examples of protecting the environment. (C) Alice does not use the premise "capitalism and evironmentalism are mutually exclusive." Rather, she disproves the premise. (D) This is what Alice does. She provides an example of a corporation which is engaged in both activities at once, thereby disproving Henry's premise that the two activities are mutually exclusive. (E) Ethical considerations are beyond the scope of the argument.

7. **(B)** Finding a 1.6 million year old skeleton that so closely resembles the human form confirms that the human form is *quite* old. Hence, (A) is incorrect. No evidence suggests that the body fell down a gerbil hole, so (C) is incorrect. The passage makes no mention of religious groups practicing human sacrifices; (D) is incorrect. There is no evidence that the remains may have confused two different time periods; (E) is incorrect. (B) is the correct choice; this body confirms the antiquity of the human form.

8. **(A)** (A) is the best choice. It was a surprise to most scientists that the skeletal remains of a child were the size and proportion that they were. The discovery seems to indicate that humans reached their present size more than a million and a half years ago; the smaller size seems to be a result of populations

in poor areas. (B) should not be selected; there was no magic date, like 100 B.C.E. (according to the passage), when humans looked like modern humans. (C) is not the best choice. Most scientists believed that humans existed 1.6 million years ago; they were not sure that these humans looked as much like modern humans as the skeletal remains indicated. (D) is not the best choice; the discovery *abolished* the belief that humans have grown larger through time. (E) should not be chosen since the passage does not support the belief that human life began on the continent of Europe.

9.   **(D)**   (A) The poll results which are cited deal not with who will win this particular mayoral race, but with: (1) the religious breakdown of the population of Metropolis; and (2) the fact that Catholics in Metropolis prefer to vote for other Catholics. The author does not assume, as we should not assume, that these are the only two factors which will determine the outcome of the mayoral race. It is very possible that if a poll had been done on the specific question of the mayoral race, it would correctly predict the winner. (B) The author cites no evidence which would support conclusions about the upswing or downswing of any religion in Metropolis. (C) The passage does not support this conclusion. We know that even though there are more Catholics than Protestants in Metropolis, they disagree with Smith on one issue. Whether or not that issue will determine the election is not made clear. (D) This is the best answer. The author tells us that there are more Catholic voters, that they prefer to vote for other Catholics, and that Smith is a Catholic. We would assume on the basis of this information that Smith will likely win the election. But then the author says that Smith may not be as likely to win as we might assume, because of his views on contraceptives which the Catholic voters do not share. The clear inference is that his views on contraceptives may swing many Catholic voters against him. Choice (E) expresses an opinion about adherence to Catholic doctrine that is beyond the scope of the passage. Nothing in the passage supports the inference that disagreement regarding official teaching precludes church membership.

10.   **(B)**   As we saw in item number 9 above, the inference from the passage is that the issue of contraceptive use may affect the race. The best way for another candidate to compete, then, would be to show how his views on that topic are closer to the voters' views than Smith's are. He would not want to raise the issue of religion, because that might reinforce the Catholics' tendency to vote for Smith, a Catholic. (A) This would likely anger the Catholic voters and reinforce their tendency to vote for Smith, a Catholic. Since Catholics are the majority, this is a losing strategy. (B) This is the best answer. By showing that his views on the issue are most like theirs, he attracts their votes while avoiding the issue of religion. (C) Since Protestants are in the minority, appealing to them without exploiting Smith's probable weakness among Catholics is not the best strategy. (D) This would stir up a big debate within the Catholic ranks over their religious beliefs, which likely would not help the opponent. (E) Again, this may cause Catholics to rethink their religious beliefs, and possibly vote for Smith as an orthodox Catholic.

11. **(C)**   The main point of the passage is (C), that scientists should educate the public not to deify national heroes. Two of the four sentences are devoted to this theme. Answers (D) and (E) gain no support from the passage. Answer (A) is somewhat plausible, but fails because the author does not mention reverence for national heroes. He speaks against their deification, that is, their being worshipped like gods; he does not say they should not be revered (i.e., treated with respect). Answer (B) may be a presumption of the passage, but not its main point.

12. **(B)**   (A) Nothing is said or implied about Prometheus worshipping anything or anyone. (B) is the best answer. As Prometheus brought fire to the ignorant and superstitious of his day, scientists of the present should bring truth to those who the author thinks are engaged in the worthless activity of hero worship. (C) Nothing is said or implied about Prometheus' teachings, if he had any. (D) We are not given enough information to establish this point as fact. (E) We are not told how the ancients accepted fire from Prometheus, or how men of the present will or should accept the scientists' teaching.

13. **(D)**   The passage states that when one thing happens, another follows shortly thereafter. It takes the form: if A then B. The only answer which takes this form is (D). Answer (A) is an inference that one member of a class will be horrible, because all the other members have been horrible. Answer (B) is an inference based on repeated past experience: X happened every other day of my life, so it is reasonable to assume it will happen tomorrow. Answer (C) is an example of deductive reasoning: if A = B; and B = C; then A = C. Answer (E) is a wrong interpretation of the events in the answer, that because the first thing happens before the second, it causes the second thing to happen.

14. **(B)**   The main difference between pranks and answering machines in the analogy is that answering machines have a practical use, while pranks are done simply for the pleasure of the prankster. If pranks had a practical use there might be some justification for them, even though they inconvenience those upon whom they are played. So the best answer is (B).

15. **(A)**   is clearly the answer. (B) is wrong, because: 1) it is possible that with regulations, landowners will make more money over the long term; and 2) the author is less concerned with landowners' profits than with preservation of the land. (C) is not true, because the passage says that clear-cutting is practiced in some areas of the South, not all over. Nor is it said to totally destroy the land's future productivity, only to lessen it. (D) and (E) may or may not be assumed by the author, but are neither the conclusion to which he argues.

16. **(C)**   Morality is beyond the scope of the passage, so eliminate (A). Eliminate (B) because the author is not concerned with profits, but with preserving the environment for future generations. (C) is clearly the best answer. The author feels that state governments need to regulate land use, regardless of the fact that

the land in question is owned by private individuals. (D) is not an unspoken, assumption, since it is stated in the passage. (E) brands all landowners in the South as irresponsible, when the passage says that clear-cutting is practiced in some areas.

17. **(B)** (A) The passage states that there are doctors who are not invited, not that no doctors are invited. There may be doctors who are not club members, and are invited. (B) The only golfers who are not invited are club members. All doctors are golfers, and there are doctors who are not invited. Therefore some of the doctor-golfers are club members. (C) To say that "there are doctors who are not invited" is not to say that some doctors are invited. Perhaps all of the doctors are not invited. (D) One cannot tell if any golfers are invited or not. Perhaps all golfers are club members, in which case none are invited. (E) That all doctors are golfers does not mean that only doctors are golfers.

18. **(A)** If this were true some doctors would not be golfers. The statement is necessarily false, since the second sentence states that all doctors are golfers. (B) We cannot tell from the passage if some doctors are invited or not, so this is not necessarily false. (C) Without knowing if Drew is a club member, we cannot say if he would be invited or not. (D) This statement must be true. Some doctors must be club members, since: all doctors are golfers; some doctors are not invited, and; the only golfers who are not invited are club members. (E) This need not be false. We cannot tell if anyone other than golfers is invited. If Alice is a golfer she is not a club member. If she is not a golfer, she may or may not be a club member.

19. **(D)** (A) The passage states that Wes usually gets indigestion from going to a restaurant, not that he always does. Nor can you assume that the only thing that will cause Wes to get indigestion is going to a restaurant. (B) This assumes that his getting indigestion will cause her to get to work on time. She may not fix him lunch, he may go to a restaurant and get indigestion, and she may still fail to get to work on time because traffic was heavy, or for X number of other reasons. (C) Fixing lunch for Wes is not established by the passage as the only thing that can possibly make her late for work. (D) This is the answer. Either she fixes lunch for him, or he goes to a restaurant. If she got to work on time, she didn't fix lunch for him. Therefore, he went to a restaurant. (E) Again, Sharon being late is not established by the passage as the only thing which can anger the boss.

20. **(A)** The passage attempts to draw an analogy between the family and a corporation, to show that employees in a corporation have obligations to each other similar to those of family members. To weaken the passage, one would show that the analogy breaks down at some point. The best way to do that is to show that the familial relationship is based on one motive or consideration, the corporate one or a very different motive. (A) This accomplishes the goal very well. If the corporation is based on self-interest, there is little motive for one

employee to sacrifice for the sake of another. Self-sacrifice is the opposite of self-interest. Therefore, if the corporate relationship is based on self-interest, little or no self-sacrifice could be expected from employees. (B) This would not overcome the argument that if and when such sacrifice was needed, it could be expected. (C) This is irrelevant, since the author is not arguing that the claims of the corporation take precedence over those of the family. (D) Again, this is irrelevant. The author is not arguing that it is necessary to be a member of a family in order to practice self-sacrifice. (E) Irrelevant again, because the self-sacrifice is being asked of one employee for the sake of another. The corporation is analogous to the family in the passage, not to the family members.

21. **(A)** (A) strengthens the argument because it adds to the analogy. It states another characteristic which the corporation and the family share. That characteristic shows that the reason one member should sacrifice for another is the same for the corporation and for the family. (B) is irrelevant. The answer does not state whether it is the corporation or fellow employees who are to do the providing. (C) The fact that the corporation expects it does not mean that the expectation is justified. The purpose of the passage is to justify, or support that conclusion. This answer fails to do so. (D) and (E) would both take away from the argument rather than strengthening it.

22. **(A)** Dan reasons that the coin has no memory. This means that the outcomes of previous tosses have no effect on the outcome of future tosses. That the coin landed heads up 10 times in a row is, then, irrelevant to the 11th toss. Since there are only two sides, there is an equal chance that it will land heads up or tails up on toss 11. Answer (A) is most like this reasoning. Eliminate (B) because it assumes that something caused the coin to land heads up 10 times in a row, and that same thing will probably cause it to land heads up on toss 11. Eliminate (C) for the same reason, although (C) goes on to state the assumed cause of the previous outcomes. Eliminate (D) because Dan says the odds are 50/50 on toss 11. Eliminate (E) because Dan does not believe that any previous toss can be used to predict the outcome of any later toss.

23. **(B)** The problem with the survey is that it is not representative of the population of the city as a whole. Surveying only those in the mall is very likely to give a biased result. The reason is that someone in the mall at any given time would be more likely to have shopped in a particular store in the mall than would the population of the city as a whole. It is very likely that there are people in the city who never come to the mall. They could not possibly be represented in the statistician's survey. In order to get a truly representative survey, the statistician would have to pick people at random from the whole population of the city. Answer (B) identifies the problem. Answer (A) is wrong because 1000 is plenty of people for a representative survey for a population of 30,000. Answer (C) is wrong because it is not necessary to survey the entire population to get a representative study. Answer (D) would produce even more biased results than the survey which was done, for obvious reasons. Answer (E) is just plain wrong.

Random surveys are very reliable, provided proper research techniques are used.

24. **(E)** Options (A), (B), and (C) would all take away from the author's argument. (D) totally undermines his conclusion, which leaves (E), and this is the only reasonable option.

Section III – Reading Comprehension

1. **(D)** Answer (D) nicely summarizes how management practices have had to change in order to take into consideration laws, agency rules, and court decisions. Answer (A) is incorrect. As the author explains, courts often struck laws designed to eradicate unhealthy and unfair practices. Answer (B) fails to take into account major changes, especially after the Supreme Court changed its interpretation of the Constitution. Answer (C) has missed the point of the author who pointed out that profit motives often led to harsh working conditions for children and women. Answer (E) is not totally correct. While the executive branch played a role, the judicial branch played the greatest role in protecting workers through upholding laws designed to protect health and safety.

2. **(D)** Answer (D) certainly reflects how management which did not want interference from government was most delighted with Supreme Court decisions that struck laws. Answer (A) has misinterpreted the author's intent as he provides information about the history and philosophy that lay behind court decisions. Answer (B) has confused the role of the court in the early 1900s and the fact that its decisions which protected contracts actually failed to protect women and children. Although there is room for improvement, Answer (C) did not take into consideration how poor working conditions in earlier years would depress workers much more than present-day work environments. Answer (E) cannot be supported by the description of management/labor conditions in the early years.

3. **(D)** Answer (D) is correct. The author has apparently chosen a topic that shows how profit motives can lead to poor personnel practices. Answer (A) is a narrow assessment of the author's values because morality is not confined to persons of the cloth. Answer (B) is wrong. One of the great freedoms in America is the ability to observe and express freely opinions about the way government operated over the years. Critics of capitalism are not necessarily socialists. Answer (C) offers the reader an opportunity to make a personal judgment on fairness. Actually, the author finds no problems when dissenting opinions are adopted by later courts in an effort to protect workers from poor working conditions. Answer (E) has gone far beyond the intent of the author. In fact in earlier years, children were indeed off the street, but suffering from terrible working conditions in factories, a system rejected by the author.

4. **(D)** Answer (D) correctly identifies how women were under repressive working conditions. While some mothers may have been happy to get away from

children and/or happy to agree to work long hours in unsanitary and unsafe conditions, most women were most likely miserable under the early policies of the private sector. Answers (A) and (B), therefore, are incorrect. With women caught in the lowest positions without power under court decisions and laws to change the poor conditions, it is reasonable to conclude that they offered no competition to male bosses (C). The marital status of female workers (E) is not discussed in the passage.

5.   **(D)**   Answer (D) discusses the 1923 case described in the passage. It should be recalled that the court justified its decision to strike the minimum wage law by stating: "adult women … are legally as capable of contracting for them-selves as men." Answer (A) incorrectly reports early court decisions that struck laws governing wages of workers. Answer (B) is only partially true. However, enough male legislators voted approval of laws protecting female workers to discount the conclusion that all males were insensitive to needs of female em-ployees. Answer (C) is wrong. The author offered no evidence that presidents played an active role in influencing private sector owners to increase wages through such agencies as an industrial board. Answer (E) contradicts the facts about the judicial role compared to the legislative role in protecting workers.

6.   **(B)**   Answer (B) is correct. After the young man married, Dagenhart expressed regret about the Supreme Court decision that "protected" him as a child laborer from governmental regulations. Answer (A), as the author shows, is incorrect in that Supreme Court decisions on laws governing working conditions were not unanimous opinions. Answer (C) may have correctly described the Supreme Court judges as being conscientious men, but most of the judges' dedi-cation was aimed at protecting free enterprise, not the workers. Answer (D) expresses a wrong opinion. Press exposure of Dagenhart's negative remarks about how his health made both industry and the court appear callous. Answer (E) has ignored the fact that dissenters voted to uphold laws that protected social welfare.

7.   **(A)**   Answer (A) reaches the correct conclusion about how disagreement among judges on the high bench indicated that the persuasive abilities of the minority judges were ineffective during those years. Answer (B) has incorrectly assessed the role of legislative leaders required to secure passage of controversial laws in years when industrial and business elite were economically and politi-cally powerful. Answer (C) has erroneously concluded without evidence in the paragraphs above that blue collar workers exercised political power at the polls. In Answer (D), the dates are incorrect. Answer (E) misinterprets the decision of the Supreme Court which staunchly opposed standardization of ages.

8.   **(B)**   Answer (B) is correct. Certain reforms such as child labor laws and regulated work hours were instituted before President Roosevelt took office. However, the major thrust of regulation occurred under his stewardship. Al-though he was powerless when the Supreme Court made void several new laws, he persisted, and appointed justices sympathetic to the goals of the president and

the public. Eventually, judicial and congressional support followed the leadership of the Chief Executive. It is the proper conclusion that Roosevelt's record showed that he was indeed more social welfare-oriented while in the Oval Office than earlier presidents. Answer (A) tries to figure out the author's preferences. His analysis of the judicial process does not indicate that he favored the judicial over the executive. Answer (C) is wrong. The pre-1950 laws initiated tremendous change in governmental regulation of management practices previously left to the private sector. Answer (D) deals with chronology. Reviewing the text above, the reader will find that the judicial branch resisted change wanted by both Congress and the President. Answer (E) deals with sociological inferences. Personnel practices of business and industry have an impact on social problems. During the 1930s and early 1940s, there was a widespread desire to change the personnel practices of the time. It was believed that this would reverse economic chaos caused by the Great Depression and thus lessen social problems. Today, personnel practices still play a role in the distribution of jobs. This has the potential to lead to problems within society.

9. **(B)** Answer (B) correctly assumes that such benefits as higher wages and fewer working hours would increase expenditures of manufacturing and business. Answer (A) requires review of how federal legislation attempted to change management/labor relations and improve the lot of the workers. Executive-sponsored bills described by the author were challenged in courts of law by business and industry. Answer (C) does not consider how new justices whose legal philosophy would radically increase the amount of government regulation, much to the detriment of freedom to make decisions in the private sector. Answer (D) is wrong. Check the paragraphs again, and note that the author correctly gave no credit to Roosevelt for aggressive leadership in civil rights. There is no such act. Answer (E) is chronologically and factually incorrect. Note that the author discusses how the Supreme Court voided social legislation supported by Roosevelt. Later, he nominated justices to the Supreme Court. Nowhere does the author suggest that the Supreme Court acted in an advisory capacity before Congress passed social legislation.

10. **(B)** Answer (B) correctly concludes that although Congress had tried in earlier years to make great differences in labor policies, it was not until the Supreme Court interpretation changed during Roosevelt's term of office that new labor laws were rapidly passed and enforced. Answer (A) is wrong. The author does not imply that the term New Deal originated from such bizarre circumstances. Answer (C) is wrong. The Great Depression dealt with the economic situation, the author did not suggest any other definition. Rather he writes of economic problems. Answer (D) has misinterpreted the author's analysis. Since the welfare state seeks to assure minimum standards of all people, both workers and their representatives agreed that labor conditions and wages should be improved. Answer (E) is incorrect. Note the dates cited by the author. Roosevelt was President during the 1930s and early 1940s. The Civil Rights Act was passed in 1964.

11. **(C)** Answer (C) correctly illustrates how governmental intrusion expands when leaders in the private sector fail to make fair policies. Answer (A) does not consider how the act works to the detriment of illegal aliens trying to find jobs rather than protecting them against discrimination. Answer (B) improperly assessed the status of illegal aliens. Their political weakness lies in the fact that they have very few links with those who are in power. Answer (D) is erroneous, as proved by the author as he traces tensions between the two sectors. Answer (E) misconstrues the statement, for she affirms that laws have provided ways to grieve unfair policies and behavior.

12. **(A)** Answer (A) is certainly well illustrated in the author's passage. As nine million people of foreign birth enter the United States when jobs are at a premium, friction will most likely develop. Answer (B) is incorrect in defining "melting pot" and introducing the term "direct representation," which was not suggested by the author. Answer (C) is wrong. In fact the author carefully outlines how government has addressed several issues that affect political socialization of immigrants. Answer (D) is in error. The author examined the problem of inequities that blacks experienced and how laws should help overcome inequality in the workplace — an important factor in income distribution. Answer (E) has misread the description of Johnson's role in fostering civil rights.

13. **(B)** (B) is the correct answer. Note how the NAACP successfully filed action in the federal court. Finally, President Johnson worked with Congress in fashioning civil rights laws. Answer (A) is incorrect. The record shows, as the author relates, that Congress was insensitive to the needs of black citizens during the years immediately following Roosevelt's administration. Answer (C) is wrong. Both the legislative and executive branches took little action in erasing inequality. Answer (D) wrongly assigns aggressive executive leadership in the civil rights movement to President Roosevelt. President Johnson's civil rights activities far exceeded Roosevelt's influence in passing laws, such as Title VII. Answer (E) is incorrect. Even though President Johnson was unable to completely erase racial discrimination, he took bold steps to reduce inequality. Title VII is one proof that President Johnson actively supported the civil rights movement.

14. **(B)** Answer (B) is correct. Many Americans are oriented toward a capitalistic system that promotes free enterprise, as opposed to health coverage for all people. Answer (A) is incorrect. Voters who leave choices in the hands of a few legislators do not reflect the meaning of representation of citizens in a democracy. Answer (C) is wrong. As government assumes more and more authority in areas where enterprise provides service to individuals, some observers feel that their country moves toward socialism. Answer (D) does not take into consideration the meaning of the term "universal" which would cover all medical expenses. Answer (E) cannot be justified according to the text above. Certainly, Congress has not degenerated to inert uniformity as the debate continues to polarize the legislators and their constituents.

15.   **(A)**   Answer (A) is correct. Congress has not mustered enough votes to pass a universal health care plan which, if it did, would alienate business. Yet Congress has on a piecemeal fashion passed such laws as the Health Maintenance Organization Act to satisfy supporters of increased government action. Answer (B) is wrong. Unfortunately, many employees in the private sector lack any kind of health coverage. Answer (C) overstates the situation. As the author portrays, rarely do workers, especially in non-union factories, have any bargaining power with regard the kind of insurance coverage. Answer (D) is not correct. As the author shows, pro-health care people certainly are not mumbling about what they want. Answer (E) is unfair for many industries. The author points out that employees in the private sector very well may be covered by virtue of business policies.

16.   **(C)**   Answer (C) is correct. Business's stance is to reject the leave of absence law because from where they sit, such leaves will have costs of hiring and training temporaries who as beginners will be less productive. Answer (A) is wrong. Job protection during times of stress or emergencies when employees must be away from work would be supported by most workers. Answer (B) is incorrect. Actually the policy on leaves would add to labor costs when production slows down due to absent employees or temporary employees. Training expenditures and expensive mistakes on the part of temporaries are examples of other costs. Answer (D) misunderstands the policy. The leaves are optional on the part of the employees. Answer (E) is wrong. The author would agree that people who support the leave policy would not use a slogan that raises suspicion.

17.   **(A)**   Answer (A) has made an assumption that is correct, based on the author's description of the policy. Under present circumstances, many mothers may not have an opportunity to stay home with the new baby or the sick child. Under the leaves policy, the family becomes a more cohesive unit. Answer (B) misquotes Senator Dodd's statistics. Answer (C) is a unfavorable judgment that is not based on the facts presented by the author. Women who must earn income will not become drop-in employees. Answer (D) has erroneously included Senator Dodd as politically allied with business. Answer (E) is wrong. The Chamber's compassion does not go so far as to work against the economic interests of business.

18.   **(D)**   Answer (D) is a correct assumption. Employees are under no obligation to undergo required drug tests when applying for a job, but employers, according to the author, may make the test one of the conditions during the hiring stage. Answer (A) is wrong. Unfortunately, no constitutional protection gives absolute protection against all misfortunes. Answer (B) has incorrectly interpreted the passage where the author warns public administrators to be very cautious in justifying why the tests are administered. Answer (C) may be incorrect at times. Personnel managers must know under what legal terms tests may be administered or a union employee may waste time and money grieving the tests. While prejudice may play a role, employers must think in terms of what a drug user will cost the company when he misses work, has accidents, etc. Answer (E) is not correct.

19.   **(C)**   Answer (C) is correct. The author compares the problems of earlier years with problems today and finds that emotional, physical, and economic needs have similar impact on employees, their families, and their employers for whom they work. Answer (A) is not correct. The author, especially in the last paragraph, implies that values should play a strong role making policies. Answer (B) is humorous but wrong. When employees are absent, the amount of work exceeds the usual amount of time required to perform the tasks, and therein lies the problem. Answer (D) is most likely the wrong conclusion. Reuben was denied a normal family relationship due to economic interests of the mill. He would probably welcome the advantage that leaves would offer his children. Answer (E) is wrong. The author recognizes that legal, social, and economic philosophies play an important role in determining policies that protect public and private interests.

20.   **(A)**   Answer (A) is correct. The author notes a few of the problems associated with unpaid leaves of absence. His question implies that management must find someone who is trained to perform the task and who is willing to work on a temporary, short-term basis. He also notes that implementing the policy will be expensive. Answer (B) is wrong. The author does not make a value judgment, but rather reports the large influx of female employees and the special needs that they have identified. Answer (C) is incorrect. The author restates the courts' opinion that the goal of a drug-free workplace based on large scale drug testing violates the right to privacy. Answer (D) is not the best choice. The tone of the passage suggests that the author is trying to analyze the situation by considering personnel problems from both labor and management's point of view. It does not become obvious that the author is pro-labor and anti-management. Answer (E) is incorrect. Although many people may share this opinion, the author does not imply that governmental regulation is inappropriate or unwarranted.

21.   **(D)**   (D) is the correct answer. For comparative purposes, the author cites (lines 41-43) the Dagenhart case to show that despite legal remedies that eliminated harsh child labor practices, legal remedies must be found to resolve more recent personnel problems. (A) is incorrect. While the author emphasizes the outcome of earlier practices and how they affected the health after a child laborer grew to become an adult blue collar worker, his conclusions are much broader than the economic state of society. (B) is wrong. "Whining" misrepresents the nature of the complaints which the author relates. Answer (C) is incorrect. Although the author recognizes that negative pressures on children in the workplace are quite different from negative pressures on adults today, he does not downplay current unresolved issues. Answer (E) is wrong. While elites base their arguments on conflicting theories and philosophies with regard to management policies in industry, business, and government, the author does not imply that these leaders are found only in the legislature.

22.   **(A)**   Answer (A) is correct. The author identifies several competing segments of our pluralistic society. Different groups of people vie for power in the policymaking arena. In this analysis, the author describes legislators, government

executives, interest groups, university faculty, and industry and business leaders with competing ideas and different operating centers of power. Answer (B) is incorrect. Stockholders are private citizens and groups who have independently chosen to invest in utilities that function in a capitalist system of government. The author does not imply that stockholders are interested in a socialist system of government. Answer (C) is incorrect. Although the author aptly describes a highly emotional environment created by conflicting views, the analysis does not lead the reader to conclude that members of interest groups have gained power in the atomic energy industry. Answer (D) is incorrect. The reader has misinterpreted the chronological analysis of events described by the author. Rather than propose that nuclear power is at best hopeless and should be abandoned, the author tends to be sympathetic toward the problems that have beset the development of atomic energy. Answer (E) has made the wrong inference. The author reports conflicting views about nuclear energy but does not recommend a non-nuclear policy.

23.   **(C)**   Answer (C) is correct. The essay vividly portrays how ordinary citizens in interest groups and as utility managers and stockholders can change the course of industrial development. Consider the facts that the author has presented, and it becomes clear that these people have been partly responsible for slowing the bandwagon of earlier years. Lack of orders and reduction in funds for research and development are the end product. Answer (A) is incorrect. The author does not imply that the bottom line of industry has changed from profits to higher ideals. However, he does imply that atomic energy, once major problems are eliminated, can improve the environment and provide a better quality of life. Answer (B) is incorrect. The fact that arguments are still prevalent and funds are still allocated for new research has kept nuclear energy a lively issue in the private and public sectors of our country and elsewhere. Answer (D) is wrong. While utility companies have quit ordering atomic reactors and constructing new plants, their major concern appears to be strictly a matter of business investment that will attract and keep investors. The author does not infer that solar energy has attracted serious attention of utility companies. Answer (E) in present-day politics is not correct. As the passage above implies, scientists, strong interest groups, and the media have kept those interested in the subject informed about controversial issues and how government plans to proceed.

24.   **(A)**   Answer (A) is correct. The overall theme of the author is the difficulty of finding a solution for supplying energy when alternatives are controversial and scientific developments are complex. The author in his short analysis makes a balanced presentation in that he considers the various views of leaders in industry, universities, and interest groups. Answer (B) is incorrect. Actually, the author has described the certainty of utility management as it responds to stockholders' concerns. Safety and good service, utility policy makers know, should be important factors that investors consider, but dividends paid to stockholders are of *major importance* in any business. Answer (C) is incorrect. The author does not let us know his personal feelings about interest groups, but he does carefully describe major concerns of interest groups who have organized to fight

the development of nuclear energy. The purpose of the essay is not to perform a psychological analysis of members of interest groups or any other group described in the study. Answer (D) is wrong. The author's comparison of the bandwagon effect in the 1950s and the 1960s does not support the thesis that conditions are the same with the exception of two unfortunate accidents. Rather the author has systematically described events that have dulled the enthusiasm for large public and private expenditures on research and construction of atomic plants. Although interest has revived somewhat, promoters of atomic energy today speak to an entirely different audience who have either experienced or witnessed failures and unexpected costs. Answer (E) states a deregulation preference that the author has not suggested.

25. **(D)** Answer (D) is correct. The author appropriately raises questions about whether judges who have little knowledge of scientific data have ability to monitor a specialized agency that appeared to ignore fair procedures during informal rulemaking. The author did not provide an answer for resolution of conflicts between scientific experts and aggrieved parties who feel the Constitution has been violated. The issue is one of importance since more than one hundred atomic plants are in operation and others may be built in the future. Answer (A) is wrong. The reader should carefully review the author's description of the case. Please note that the Supreme Court actually authorized wider discretion in informal rule making of the regulatory agency when it licenses nuclear plants. Answer (B) is incorrect. The author portrays some apprehension about the role of courts when judges are asked to decide controversies that are highly technical. Unfortunately, the author does not suggest where ultimate power of decision making should be lodged in these kinds of cases. Answer (C) is incorrect. It is possible that union contracts with high pay and many benefits have contributed to a rise in construction and maintenance costs of new nuclear power plants. However, budgets for construction of atomic plants include many more expensive line items. There is no evidence or implication in the text that shows the author is holding unions and collective bargaining responsible for the problems the nuclear energy industry is facing. Answer (E) expresses a bias against the author. The fairly objective passages do not prove his field of expertise or his personal views on the role of government in improving the welfare of mankind.

26. **(C)** Answer (C) is correct. The analysis provides an excellent example of a well-known theory that the regulated often co-opt the regulators. The author succinctly shows how the regulated (business and industry) have influenced the Department of Energy (the regulator) to allocate more money to the development of atomic energy than to solar energy. Leaders in the Department of Energy want the atomic energy research and development projects to succeed. Even the Atomic Regulatory Commission worries about the decline of construction of nuclear plants. Answers (A) and (B) are incorrect because the author makes no mention of funding for plants beyond the stockholders of energy companies. Arguments over safety, necessity, and functionality of plants are discussed, while dissention regarding funding is not. Answer (D) is incorrect. The author indicates that

stockholders have become disillusioned with investment in utilities with nuclear powered plants, but the fact that government comes to the rescue of stockholders who face losses in the stockmarket is not mentioned. Answer (E) is incorrect. The author has not stated or suggested that there is no governmental regulation of nuclear energy in this country.

27.   **(C)**   Answer (C) appropriately reflects what the author has written with regard to the way people who are dissatisfied with the administrative process may take their case to the courts. It should be noted that plaintiffs may not always win, as the *Vermont* case illustrates. Answer (A) has failed to understand the series of events described by the author where the judicial process was the final option. Answer (B) is wrong and the decision unfavorable to the interest group should not be interpreted to mean that the courts have taken themselves entirely out of the process although the author has shown how the courts have practiced self-limitation in these types of cases. Answer (D) has failed to reflect what the author chose to relate about the process. No place in the text does the author infer such an arrangement. Answer (E) is incorrect, although agency personnel may very well wish to eliminate the oversight of the judicial branch. The author does not promote the policy.

Section IV – Logical Reasoning

1.   (C)   The question asks you to identify the cause of a problem, when three possible causes have been listed. The key phrase in the passage for answering Question 1 is "some or all of which are to blame." This phrase means that the problem may be caused by all of the three factors acting together; by any two of them; or by any one of them alone. Since we are told that the surface was clean and dry, the problem was caused by: (a) both of the remaining factors, or; (b) either of the remaining factors acting alone. The only answer which covers the two possibilities is (C).

2.   **(B)**   (A) The passage says only that latex paint will prematurely crack and peel on wooden structures. You may not infer that it does likewise on other types of surfaces. There may be surfaces to which it permanently bonds. (Remember, on the LSAT, you must answer questions based upon information given in the passages, not on the basis of your own experiences.) (B) The passage says that *many* homeowners who have recently painted find premature cracking and peeling on their houses after this weather pattern has occurred. You can infer from this that, provided one of the three necessary conditions listed in the passage is present, this weather pattern often triggers the premature cracking and peeling. (C) You cannot infer that this weather always triggers the premature cracking and peeling. The passage does not establish this weather pattern as a necessary condition for the cracking and peeling. It may fail, at times, to trigger the cracking and peeling. Also, there may be other, unstated, factors which some-

times trigger it first. (D) The passage attributes the problem to three causes, all of which can be prevented. Presumably, if these three causes are eliminated, the problem will also be eliminated. (E) The passage does not establish that professional painters always observe the proper procedures to eliminate the problem. It establishes only that they know what causes the problem.

3.   **(C)**   This is a very difficult question. The reader is asked to interpret a lot of information in order to weigh the relative strength of the answers. (A) This would not necessarily strengthen the conclusion. One could reason either: (1) Coleman's average is now of little or no consequence to the Cardinals since teams from different leagues never play each other; or (2) the fact that Coleman's average improves because of Angel Stadium does not necessarily mean it would have improved if he had remained with the Cardinals. (B) We were already told that the premises are true. Knowing that the man is familiar with the Cardinals would not, then add any weight to the premises. The conclusion, then, gains no added strength. (C) This makes it very likely that he hit a lot of home runs there. Home runs hit there were the most important factor in his high batting average. Without them, his average will be much lower. A lower average would make him less likely to benefit the Cardinals. The conclusion is strengthened. (D) The analyst focuses on Smith's batting average, leaving out all other factors. He says the benefit of the trade to the Cardinals may depend on that factor. If he has not focused on the most important factor, the benefit of the trade may depend on other factors. The conclusion is weakened. (E) This weakens the conclusion, rather than strengthening it. The Cardinals have obtained a player who remains healthy, for one who gets injured. The Angels appear to have been bested in the trade, since Coleman will probably play less for the Angels than Smith will for the Cardinals.

4.   **(E)**   (A) This would definitely be important for the board to know. One of the most important aspects of scientific studies is controlling variables between control and experiment groups. If every conceivable variable could be controlled between two groups, any variance in outcome could be attributed to the single factor which is being tested for. In other words, if the only difference between the two groups of women was exercise in the last three months of pregnancy, the difference in heartbeat and respiration could, with much certainty, be attributed to that difference. (B) Of course the board would also like to take into account negative factors connected to exercise. If the chance of accidental damage was almost nil, the benefits of the exercise would outweigh it. If it was great the opposite would likely be true. (C) Again, the board would want to take into account all pertinent information. If there was some good reason for the opposite opinion prevailing 10 years ago, that would have to be investigated. Maybe that reason is now overcome by advances in medicine. But perhaps it has not. (E) is therefore correct because it includes all of the options and (D) must be incorrect.

5. **(C)** (A) This is clearly implied by the passage. The third sentence states that exercise increased the mother and infant's chances of surviving childbirth. The last sentence mentions stronger heartbeat as one of two ways in which the exercise group differed from the non-exercise group. The implication is that stronger heartbeat is one of two factors which increase the chances of survival. (B) This is clearly implied by the passage. The studies were done to test the effect of exercise on survival rates for childbirth. The two major differences in the exercise and non-exercise groups had to do with heartbeat and respiration. One would conclude, then, that if the studies were done properly (and the passage does not say otherwise) the difference in exercise caused the differences in heartrate and respiration. (C) Sentence 2 states that it was *thought* that exercise caused extra stress. In other words, it was never proven. Whether the recent studies agree with this earlier theory is not stated. Therefore, we cannot say that the passage assumes or implies this as true. (D) is definitely implied by the passage. (E) is implied in the passage if one considers that it is the opposite of the final sentence which states the exercise group had stronger heartbeats and better respiration.

6. **(E)** You are asked to choose the conclusion which derives the *most* support. This means that more than one of the choices may derive support from the passage. Let's take (E) first. It is supported by the fact that three obstacles must be overcome in order for the U.S. to land a man on Mars. If only one of the three is not overcome, the project will fail. (A) derives support from the passage, as does (C). However, (A) and (C), if true, strengthen (E). We are not told the likelihood of any of the three problems being overcome. However, we know that all three must be overcome for the project to succeed. It is less likely that all three will be overcome than it is that any one of the three will. Therefore, (E) derives more support than do (A) and (C). (B) and (D) derive no support from the passage.

7. **(C)** (A) This cannot be an answer. Even if the money is available, the other two obstacles might not be overcome. (B) The passage does not support this conclusion. The author says that three obstacles must be overcome for the project to succeed. The inference is that if they are overcome, the project will succeed. (C) This is the clear inference from the passage. Since only three obstacles are listed as having to be overcome, the author obviously assumes that they are the only things preventing success. (D) This is not the answer because it is not stated in the passage how long it would take to design the computer technology. (E) is incorrect because none of the three requirements is ranked by importance.

8. **(C)** (A) cannot be logically relevant, because the passage begins with the word "suppose." The author admits it is a hypothetical question; that is, he does not assume that the question has any foundation in reality. To prove something that he does not assume would not weaken the passage, logically speaking. (B) fails for the same reason. (C) is relevant, because it provides a premise which

can help answer the question. The syllogism would be as follows: No one can exist if a single one of their ancestors had not existed. Therefore, if a man went back in time and killed one of his ancestors, that man would cease to exist. (D) and (E), even if true, are not relevant because this is a hypothetical situation.

9.   **(C)**   (A) is not relevant, because the researchers made no recommendation for these people. The fact that these people exist does not weaken the recommendations made for those who are in the other two categories. Provided that the researchers conducted their experiments properly, their recommendations would still be good for the other two groups. (B) would not weaken the researchers' findings, but would strengthen them. It eliminates one variable, which makes the results more reliable. (D) and (E) also do this. (C) calls the results into question. Perhaps the gas affected the engine in one of the types of cars adversely, preventing it from winning one of the competitions. Therefore, the answer is (C).

10.   **(B)**   The passage cannot support (A). Scientific knowledge is knowledge which can be reproduced through controlled experiment. Researchers cannot control history in a laboratory experiment, nor does the passage establish any facts which argue the contrary. (B) is a conclusion which can be drawn from the passage. When presented with a problem, one can often look to the past to see how similar problems were solved. Sometimes, the very same solution to a problem can be successful again. (C) is not supported by the passage, because questions of good and evil are beyond its scope. (D) and (E) cannot be supported by the information given.

11.   **(A)**   This passage exhibits what is sometimes called "predicate logic." The author mistakenly infers that because "veterans" and "some of the staff members" share the same predicate, they must be identical categories. To put it differently, because "veterans of the war" and "some staff members" share a single characteristic, the author infers that some of the staff members are veterans of the war. Another example of this type of reasoning would be:

Jesus is a man;

I am a man;

Therefore, I am Jesus.

The answer which duplicates this type of reasoning is (A). Eliminate (B) and (C) because they are in the form of the standard syllogism, used correctly. (D) does not duplicate the passage in this respect: in the passage all veterans are bitter and some staff are bitter, therefore some staff are veterans. The sequence is All: Some: Some. The conclusion is made regarding SOME staff members. In (D) all birds have beaks and some reptiles have beaks, therefore, ALL birds and reptiles are of the same species. The sequence is All : Some : All. Eliminate (E) for a similar reason. The sequence is All : All : Some, instead of All : Some : Some.

12.   **(C)**   (A) This is plausible, but incorrect. The author argues that decision making should be left to the experts, with no input by the citizens. That the

experts might disagree from time to time does not invalidate the conclusion. As experts, they would still be in the best position to work out disagreements among themselves. Or, to put it another way, if the citizens know very little about public policy, they could not very well referee disputes between the experts. (B) The author says that the average citizen knows little, not that all citizens know little about public policy. He has as much as admitted that a few citizens may be very well informed about public policy. However, the influence of these few well informed citizens on public opinion may be miniscule. (C) The author claims that public officials are experts on public policy, while the average citizen knows little about it. On the basis of these premises, he concludes that public officials should ignore public opinion. Answer (C) undermines the premises, thereby seriously weakening the conclusion. The answer, then, is (C). (D) would not flaw the author's reasoning because the last statement says an official should not concern himself with public opinion on any given policy. Therefore, it does not matter how the public forms its opinion and what it is based on. (E) is also incorrect because it says the average citizen cares little about public policy and if only one person knows about public policy, the official has no need to worry.

13. **(D)** The author states that the average citizen knows little about public policy. Choice I. may be established on the basis of this claim. The author states that public officials are experts on public policy. Therefore, II. is explicitly established. Answer III. cannot be established on the basis of explicit statements. Public officials were not necessarily always experts on public policy. They specialized, and in the process became experts. Presumably, the average citizen, by doing likewise, could also become an expert on public policy.

14. **(A)** The manufacturer claims the shine will be good for one year on the typical car, based on the experiment in which a car is washed 52 times. The experiment is obviously meant to duplicate actual conditions that the typical car will experience in a year. The unspoken premise is, then, that the typical car will be washed an average of once per week for the year. Eliminate (B) because nothing is said or implied about what owners LIKE to do. Maybe they wax their cars once a year, but hate every second of it. Eliminate (C) because while the wax manufacturer may be hoping it is true, the claim or conclusion is not based on that as a premise. Remember, a premise is an assumption, stated or unstated, which supports or strengthens the conclusion. If (D) and (E) were correct, then the manufacturer could not make any of the claims in his advertisement, nor would there be a market for his product.

15. **(C)** The problem with the experiment is that it takes into account only one factor which may affect the life of the shine—washing. Sun, wind, dirt, and other factors may also affect the life of the shine, but they were not included in the experiment. The correct answer, then, is (C). With regard to (A) there is no effect in the passage which can be attributed to a cause. The passage assumes that the normal effect of 52 washings is a destroyed shine. That effect is not produced in this case, which is used as proof of the product's quality. Eliminate (B) be-

cause the passage does not assume without any evidence that the conclusion is true. It provides evidence for the truth of the conclusion in the form of the experiment. The only problem is that the experiment is flawed. Therefore (D) and (E) cannot be correct.

16. **(B)** For (A) to be true, all workers would have to be management. (B) is true, because all workers are experienced, and some are management. (C) may be true, but it cannot be proven or disproven by the passage. Therefore, it is not the best answer. (D) is not true, because the passage states that some, not all, workers are management. (E) is incorrect because some workers are management, which does not mean all management are workers. The answer is (B).

17. **(D)** As a post-polio victim, the writer expresses a willingness to participate in medical research (A), and acknowledges that medical students can learn more about post-polio syndrome (E) and that doctors can acquire valuable information and learn to better treat various problems (B). The writer neither supports nor attacks medical bills in general (C). However, the writer argues against being charged for participating in the medical research (D).

18. **(E)** The writer suggests, without trying to prove, that many teachers have embraced technology (A), that powerful technologies and software are proliferating (C), and that technology enhances learning (D). The writer suggests, contrary to answer (B), that there is not yet an ongoing development of teachers' technology skills, but there is need for such development. Based on these premises, we may conclude that the classroom teacher is a central factor in the full development of technology's use in the schools (E).

19. **(D)** The passage claims there is a need for public policy that gives electric companies flexibility to meet demand. This is contrary to the claim that the nation already has such a policy (A). And it is the converse of the assertion that electric companies should give public policy flexibility (C), (E). The passage claims that electric companies, not customers (B), should decide requirements for electrical use. But one explicit premise of the argument is that electric companies cannot forecast future use with certainty (D).

20. **(A)** The argument acknowledges, but not as a premise or conclusion, that defense attorneys treat victims and witnesses as untouchable (C), and that such treatment may be necessary at a trial (D). It also acknowledges the importance of victims' and witnesses' physical and mental characteristics (B). It is because of the importance of victims and witnesses that the argument concludes they should be interviewed in the same way a client is interviewed (A). The argument does not claim that trials are necessary during the investigation process (E).

21. **(B)** The writer claims that hunting pigs to protect a golf course (A) is extreme, so this is not one of the justifications. The writer offers as justifications

both that wild pigs carry diseases dangerous to animals (B) and that they foul wildland water supplies. (C) states that pigs foul food supplies. (D) is not mentioned in the passage and (E) is extreme and not one of the justifications.

22. **(D)** The writer agrees with Hirsch that there is shocking ignorance among today's children (C). But he blames it on failure of traditional school settings to engage today's children (contrary to answer (A) which denies this failure), whereas *Hirsch's* point is that this ignorance stems from education programs that instill abstract thinking apart from knowledge (D). Contrary to Hirsch, the writer claims that the Deweyesque pedagogy (B) is uncommon, as are educational programs that instill abstract thinking apart from knowledge (E).

23. **(B)** The writer argues that Frelimo contributed to Mozambique's economic decline by embracing an inappropriate strategy of development, a socialist one. If such a strategy were appropriate (B), this would weaken the argument. As demonstration of its inappropriateness, the writer notes that such a strategy was based on large-scale development projects (A), prevailing economic conditions were not favorable for government policies (C), and the strategy could not halt economic decline (D). If these assertions are true, the argument would be strengthened. Also, if the colonial economy collapsed after independence in 1975 (E), as the writer suggests, then the argument is strengthened.

24. **(C)** The conclusion is that children are not as egocentric as Piaget asserted. Thus the claims that there is childhood egocentricism (A), and that evidence supports egocentricism (E) are not consistent with the conclusion. The argument also denies that excessive burdens upon memory are relevant difficulties (B) and that children have poor communicative abilities (D). The only statement consistent with the conclusion is that Piaget supported a notion of childhood egocentricism (C).

25. **(A)** If verbatim documentary evidence is no more reliable than oral testimony (A), this would strengthen the writer's argument that oral history is not inferior to documentary history. The book cited does appear to discuss oral and documentary evidence (B), and the writer suggests that those who use oral evidence are often faced with the issue of the respective value of documentary and oral sources (D), but these neither strengthen nor weaken the argument. And the writer never says or implies that parliamentary inquiries into industrial conditions are useful oral history sources (C), or that verbatim evidence given in parliamentary inquiries is frequently indistinguishable from documentary evidence (E).

LSAT Writing Sample – Demonstration Essay

The author argues that Jetson High School should purchase personal laptops as a means of improving test scores and better preparing students for college and beyond. His evidence consists of a study of a neighboring school district that links laptops with higher standardized test scores and a claim that computer proficiency is vital for success in today's world. Despite their apparent support for his conclusion, each item of evidence is either flawed or questionable, and does not justify purchasing personal laptops for the students.

The author's argument that laptops will improve Jetson's test scores is flawed because he incorrectly moves from a correlation to a cause. The study of a neighboring school district does suggest a relationship between laptop usage and higher test scores, but the author inappropriately assumes this to mean that the laptops caused the higher test scores. The improved test scores could have resulted from a host of other relevant factors, including better preparation for the standardized tests, superior students, new faculty hires, or other programs implemented by the schools. The author overlooks these alternative explanations for student success.

Moreover, even if the study did show a causal relationship between laptops and higher test scores, the author would need to prove the analogy between Jetson and the schools in the neighboring district in order to argue that the laptops would have similar results at Jetson. Instead, he simply assumes that there are no relevant or important differences between Jetson and the other schools. The other schools might have been better equipped to implement the new technology and integrate laptops into the curriculum. For the argument by analogy to hold, the author needs to establish that the schools are alike in the relevant ways.

Finally, the author's claim that laptops are necessary for the acquisition of basic computer proficiency is questionable. Admittedly, computers are prevalent, but it is not clear why investing in laptops for every student is necessary for students to gain those skills. The author takes for granted that the computers in the school computer lab are not sufficient to teach students the basic computer proficiency he claims is vital for student success. It is possible that the students could acquire these skills even with restricted access to old computers. Even if the computers in the lab are antiquated or too restricted, the appropriate policy might be to invest in updating and expanding the computer labs, rather than purchasing expensive and fragile laptops for every student.

The author's argument for laptops is flawed and weak. He inappropriately assumes that laptops cause higher test scores, and inadequately establishes an analogy with other schools that have had success with laptops. He also fails to articulate why laptops, as opposed to other alternatives, would not achieve the same goals. In addition, a better argument about the viability of using computers at Jetson High would address the potential unintended consequences of their use. Rather than aids

to learning, they could distract students from the lessons in the classroom. Even if Jetson High School has a surplus of funds, the cost associated with obtaining laptops for each student justifies thorough investigation of potential results.

Demonstration Essay Explanation

This is a good essay because it analyzes each piece of evidence offered to support the argument's conclusion, and does so in an organized and focused manner. In addition to identifying flaws and weaknesses in the argument, the essay explains why those flaws weaken the argument and suggests alternative explanations.

The introduction succinctly summarizes the argument and presents a thesis: the argument is flawed. The body of the essay then addresses each component of the argument in organized paragraphs. The writer makes several points: (a) The study of a neighboring school district may not mean what the argument posed in the prompt suggests it does, because it establishes a correlation and not a cause; (b) the study may not be applicable to Jetson because of distinguishing factors; and (c) personal laptops may not be necessary to achieve the desired goals. In each case, the writer uses counterexamples and even suggests different policies that might be more effective.

Finally, the conclusion not only restates the writer's position but also suggests how the argument could be improved, and what other factors should be considered by the school when making its decision. The last paragraph summarizes the author's position and restates the justification for taking that position.

LSAT

Law School Admission Test

TEST III

TEST III

Section I

Time—35 minutes
22 Questions
(Answer sheets appear in the back of this book.)

DIRECTIONS: Each group of questions in this section is based on a set of conditions. In answering some of the questions, it may be useful to draw a rough diagram. Choose the response that most accurately and completely answers the question and blacken the corresponding space on your answer sheet.

QUESTIONS 1-6

The six sections of the village parade are filled by two bands, the volunteer fire department, the pony club, clowns, and dignitaries (the mayor, the constable, and the beauty queen) in open cars. The order of march must meet the following conditions:

The clowns can be neither the first nor the last group.

Neither band can be next to the pony club.

The pony club must be just in front of the dignitaries.

1. Which of the following arrangements is an acceptable order of the sections, from first to last place?

   (A) band, ponies, dignitaries, fire department, clowns, band

   (B) clowns, ponies, dignitaries, band, fire department, band

   (C) band, clowns, ponies, dignitaries, band, fire department

   (D) ponies, fire department, dignitaries, band, clowns, band

   (E) band, fire department, clowns, dignitaries, ponies, band

2. If the bands are in second and last places in an acceptable order of march, which of the following must be true?

   (A) The ponies are in third place.

   (B) The fire department is in first place.

   (C) The dignitaries are in third place.

   (D) The fire department is in the fourth place.

(E) The clowns are in fifth place.

3. If in an acceptable order of march the ponies are in second place and the dignitaries are in third place, which of the following must be true?

(A) A band is in next-to-last place.

(B) A band is in last place.

(C) The fire department is in last place.

(D) A band is in first place.

(E) The clowns are in first place.

4. Only one order of march is possible under which of the following conditions?

(A) The bands are in second and third places.

(B) The clowns are in first places.

(C) The bands are in second and fifth places.

(D) The pony club is in last place.

(E) The dignitaries are in first place.

5. All of the following orders of march are acceptable EXCEPT

(A) fire department, band, ponies, dignitaries, clowns, band

(B) fire department, band, clowns, ponies, dignitaries, band

(C) band, fire department, clowns, ponies, dignitaries, band

(D) band, fire department, ponies, dignitaries, clowns, band

(E) ponies, dignitaries, band, band, clowns, fire department

6. If there are three or more places between the two bands in an acceptable order of march, which of the following must be FALSE?

(A) There is a band in fourth place.

(B) Either a band or the fire department is in first place.

(C) The ponies are in either third or fourth place.

(D) If the clowns are in second place, there is a band in last place.

(E) If the clowns are in third place, there must be a band in last place.

QUESTIONS 7-11

Each of three conglomerates — Amalgamated, General, and Universal — is trying to expand by attempting to take over divisions of the other companies or absorb other divisions within its larger company.

The division that takes over or absorbs the other is called an aggressor division. The other division involved is called a developed division.

When a takeover or absorption is complete, the result is a new division of the company of the aggressor division.

No division of General can either take over or be taken over by any division of Amalgamated.

No division of General can take over a division of Universal.

Currently, three mergers are pending, all meeting the conditions above.

Each conglomerate is represented at least once among the six divisions involved in these mergers.

7.   If the aggressor divisions in the pending mergers are two divisions of General and one of Amalgamated, the developed divisions must include

    (A)   one division of Amalgamated, one of General and one of Universal.

    (B)   two of General and one of Amalgamated.

    (C)   two of General and one of Universal.

    (D)   two of Universal and one of Amalgamated.

    (E)   two of Universal and one of General.

8.   If there are exactly twice as many divisions of Universal as of General among the divisions involved in the pending mergers, the three aggressors must be from which of the following conglomerates?

    (A)   Amalgamated only

    (B)   Amalgamated and General only

    (C)   General and Universal only

    (D)   Universal and Amalgamated only

    (E)   Amalgamated, General, and Universal

9.   If the pending mergers involve three divisions of General, two of Amalgamated and one of Universal, which of the following correctly describes the new divisions after the mergers have been completed?

    (A)   one of General, one of Universal and one of Amalgamated

    (B)   one of General and two of Universal

    (C)   one of General and two of Amalgamated

(D) two of General and one of Universal

(E) two of General and one of Amalgamated

10. If the pending mergers involve four divisions of Amalgamated, one of General and one of Universal, the number of divisions of Amalgamated to be taken over or absorbed can

(A) only be one.

(B) only be two.

(C) only be three.

(D) be either one or two.

(E) be either two or three.

11. If the pending mergers involve three divisions from Universal, two from General and one from Amalgamated, which of the following CANNOT be true?

(A) The division of Amalgamated is a developed division.

(B) The division of Amalgamated is an aggressor division.

(C) The three divisions of Universal are all developed.

(D) The three divisions of Universal are the aggressor divisions.

(E) The two divisions of General are both developed.

QUESTIONS 12-17

Every Wednesday, five salespeople — V, W, X, Y, and Z — check into the Dew Drop Inn.

They always stay in rooms 201 through 206.

Each takes a different room, but one of the rooms is not used by any of them.

W always takes an odd-numbered room.

Y always takes the third room in numerical order of those that the salespeople use.

Z always has a higher-numbered room than V, but none of the other salespeople takes a room between Z's and V's.

12. If V takes room 202, which of the following must be true?

(A) W takes room 201.

(B) Y takes room 204.

(C) Y takes a higher-numbered room than W.

(D) Z takes a higher-numbered room than W

(E) X takes a lower-numbered room than V.

13. If W takes room 201, which of the following is a complete and accurate list of the rooms that X might take?

(A) 202   (D) 202, 203

(B) 203   (E) 202, 206

(C) 206

14. If X takes room 201, which of the following must be true?

(A) Y takes a higher-numbered room than W.

(B) V takes a lower-numbered room than W.

(C) V takes room 202.

(D) Y takes room 203.

(E) Z takes room 204.

15. If none of the salespeople takes room 201, which of the following must be true?

I. If W takes room 203, Z takes room 206.

II. If Z takes room 203, W takes room 205.

III. X does not take room 205.

(A) I only   (D) I and II only

(B) II only   (E) I, II, and III

(C) III only

16. If W takes room 203, all of the following statements must be true EXCEPT

(A) X takes a lower-numbered room than Y.

(B) X takes room 201.

(C) Y takes room 204.

(D) V takes a higher-numbered room than Y.

(E) Z takes room 206.

17. All of the following are possible rooms for Z to take EXCEPT

    (A) 202.   (D) 205.

    (B) 203.   (E) 206.

    (C) 204.

QUESTIONS 18-22

A four-member subcommittee must be drawn from the committee composed of G, H, I, J, K, L, and M. The subcommittee is to have equal numbers of representatives from the faculty and the administration, equal numbers of men and women, and equal numbers of representatives from the undergraduate college and the professional schools.

G, J, and L are all administrators; the others are faculty members.

G, I, and L are from the college; the others are from the professional schools.

H, I, J, and M all are men; the others are women.

18. If I is chosen for the subcommittee, which of the following must also be on the subcommittee?

    (A) G   (D) L

    (B) H   (E) M

    (C) J

19. Each of the following pairs of people could be chosen to be on the subcommittee together EXCEPT

    (A) G and I   (D) H and J

    (B) G and J   (E) H and M

    (C) G and L

20. If K is chosen for the subcommittee, which of the following must also be among those chosen for the subcommittee?

    (A) G   (D) L

    (B) H   (E) M

    (C) I

21. If M is chosen for the subcommittee, the subcommittee must also include which of the following pairs of people?

    (A) G and I

    (B) G and J

    (C) G and L

    (D) I and J

    (E) I and L

22. How many four-member subcommittees meeting the conditions given but differing from one another by at least one member can be formed from this list of candidates?

    (A) 35

    (B) 17

    (C) 8

    (D) 3

    (E) 2

STOP
It time still remains, you may review work only in this section.
When the time allotted is up, you may go on to the next section.

Section II

Time—35 minutes
28 Questions
(Answer sheets appear in the back of this book.)

DIRECTIONS: Each passage in this section is followed by a group of questions to be answered on the basis of what is stated or implied in the passage. For some questions, more than one of the choices could conceivably answer the question. However, you are to choose the best answer; that is, the response that most accurately and completely answers the question, and blacken the corresponding space on your answer sheet.

A friend of mine, a novelist who was born and raised in Missouri and who has long been a student of Mark Twain, recently wrote me that he had been reading some current deep analyses of Mark Twain's works. As a result of his reading, which left him alternately astonished and numbed, he decided, "I have
(5) pretty well given up writing any book about Mr. Clemens. I am a charter member of the Mark Twain and No Hogwash Society [he used a more pithy and less polite term], and the perfessers have sifted the old man's ashes back and forth until there's nothing left but some sour-smelling talc. All the time the perfessers are trying to figure out what Mark Twain meant by this or that. Hell, he wrote
(10) about as clearly as anyone could write and I see no reason to doubt that he meant what he said. There's a perfesser wrote a book in which Huck's trip on the raft symbolized Sam's journey west in the stagecoach, and the purpose of the journey was his search for a father. Keee-rist! Another perfesser wrote a book for which he did an astonishing amount of research. Of course a lot of the research adds up
(15) to nothing important but, being a scholar, he had to put it all in."

Some of the deep analyses are removed from the reality by a distance of not less than several light-years. Mark Twain was not that remote from reality, nor did he have all those anemic theories flowing in his veins. He knew the reality as well as any writing man of his time and better than most. His works, when
(20) observed without coyness and without a succession of mirrors, show it.

The Russians are not to be found trailing the field, in this or any other area. They have made substantial contributions to the literature on Mark Twain and hogwash. They insist that America has an official line on Mark Twain, that the nation tries to suppress or forget him. Their line in general consists of this: Mark
(25) Twain is of primary significance as a social and political observer; his objects of attack are chiefly aspects of the American scene; and the United States officially and unofficially suppresses or distorts his attacks against itself.

Mark Twain is of course primarily a humorist. If he had never possessed his humorous gift, if he had only written his social criticisms, he would not now be
(30) read by millions of Russian readers and it would be useless for Russian literary

spokesmen to point to him as the great critic of democratic morals. He is also of course primarily a writer of fiction. It was through these two great gifts that he made the reputation which is so well sustained so long after his death. His American readers on the whole have no difficulty in comprehending this simple
(35) fact, and I like to think that most Russian readers have the same common sense, that they read him basically not for the lessons he teaches of the inherent "evils" of the United States but because he enlarges their lives imaginatively through a flow of pleasure. Great humor, after all, being so rare, is a very exportable commodity. When blended with wisdom and humanitarianism it is
(40) irresistible.

1. The primary purpose of the passage is to

   (A) inform the reader of Twain's humorous writings

   (B) argue that one should not overlook the obvious in Twain's writing

   (C) criticize Russian literature

   (D) suggest a solution to the trade imbalance

   (E) explain how Russians view American literature

2. As used in the passage the word *perfesser* is meant to

   (A) show the lack of education of the author's friend

   (B) give an alternative spelling of the word *professor*

   (C) show distaste for academic critics of Twain's work

   (D) highlight Twain's distaste for educated people

   (E) show the ethnic origin of the author's friend

3. The author's reference to *light-years* in line 17 is

   (A) incorrect because a light-year is a measure of time

   (B) a philosophical reference to the shape of reality

   (C) a literary reference used in evaluating critiques

   (D) related to Huck's journey

   (E) hyperbole

4. According to the author

   (A) official United States policy is to ignore Twain's work

   (B) American readers do not understand Twain's humor

   (C) Russian readers do not understand Twain's humor

    (D) the Russians have contributed their share of absurd analyses of Twain's work

    (E) Russian officials feel the United States' official policy on Twain is too tolerant

5.   The author feels Twain's sustained popularity to be the result of

    (A) increased understanding of the meaning of Twain's works

    (B) Twain's ability as a humorist

    (C) an undeserved reputation

    (D) availability of Twain's works in Russia

    (E) the ineptitude of Twain's critics

6.   From the passage, the author's attitude toward in-depth analyses of Twain's works is best described as

    (A) critical   (D) neutral

    (B) supportive   (E) resigned

    (C) distrustful

7.   From the passage, the author believes Twain's works to be

    (A) aloof

    (B) fraught with hidden meaning

    (C) simplistic

    (D) clearly written

    (E) overly critical

    As chief justice of the Supreme Court from 1801 until his death in 1835, John Marshall was a staunch nationalist and upholder of property rights. He was not, however, as the folklore of American politics would have it, the lonely and embattled Federalist defending these values against the hostile forces of
(5) Jeffersonian democracy. On the contrary, Marshall's opinions dealing with federalism, property rights, and national economic development were consistent with the policies of the Republican Party in its mercantilist phase from 1815 to 1828. Never an extreme Federalist, Marshall opposed his party's reactionary wing in the crisis of 1798-1800. Like almost all Americans of his day, Marshall
(10) was a Lockean republican who valued property not as an economic end in itself, but rather as the foundation of civil liberty and a free society. Property was the source both of individual happiness and social stability and progress.
    Marshall evinced strong centralizing tendencies in his theory of federalism

and completely rejected the compact theory of the Union expressed in the
(15) Virginia and Kentucky Resolutions. Yet his outlook was compatible with the
Unionism that formed the basis of the post-1815 American System of the Republican Party. Not that Marshall shared the democratic sensibilities of the Republi-
cans; like his fellow Federalists, he tended to distrust the common people and
saw in legislative majoritarianism a force that was potentially hostile to constitu-
(20) tionalism and the rule of law. But aversion to democracy was not the hallmark of
Marshall's constitutional jurisprudence. Its central features rather were a commitment to federal authority versus states' rights and a socially productive and
economically dynamic conception of property rights. Marshall's support of these
principles placed him near the mainstream of American politics in the years
(25) between the War of 1812 and the conquest of Jacksonian Democracy.

In the long run, the most important decisions of the Marshall Court were
those upholding the authority of the federal government against the states.
Marbury v. Madison provided a jurisprudential basis for this undertaking, but the
practical significance of judicial review in the Marshall era concerned the state
(30) legislatures rather than Congress. The most serious challenge to national authority resulted from state attempts to administer their judicial systems independent
of the Supreme Court's appellate supervisions as directed by the Judiciary Act of
1789. In successfully resisting this challenge, the Marshall Court not only averted
a practical disruption of the federal system, but it also evolved doctrines of
(35) national supremacy which helped preserve the Union during the Civil War.

8.   The primary purpose of this passage is to

    (A)   describe Marshall's political jurisprudence

    (B)   discuss the importance of centralization to the preservation of the
        Union

    (C)   criticize Marshall for being disloyal to his party

    (D)   examine the role of the Supreme Court in national politics

    (E)   chronicle Marshall's tenure on the Supreme Court

9.   From the passage we know Marshall belonged to the

    (A)   Locke Party   (D)   Federalist Party

    (B)   Republican Party   (E)   Independent Party

    (C)   Democratic Party

10.   According to the author, Marshall viewed property as

    (A)   an investment

    (B)   irrelevant to constitutional liberties

    (C)   the basis of a stable society

(D) inherent to the upper class

(E) an important centralizing incentive

11. From the passage the *compact theory* was most likely a theory

(A) supporting states' rights

(B) of the extreme Federalists

(C) of the Marshall Court's approach to the Civil War

(D) supporting centralization

(E) advocating jurisprudential activism

12. According to the author, Marshall's attitude toward mass democratic politics can best be described as

(A) hostile   (D) nurturing

(B) supportive   (E) distrustful

(C) indifferent

13. The author argues the Marshall Court

(A) failed to achieve its centralizing policies

(B) failed to achieve its decentralizing policies

(C) helped to bring on the Civil War

(D) supported federalism via judicial review

(E) had its greatest impact on Congress

14. According to the author, Marshall's politics were

(A) extremist   (D) moderate

(B) right-wing   (E) majoritarian

(C) democratic

Although February 18, 1990, marked the 60th anniversary of the discovery of Pluto, the ninth planet in the solar system has guarded its secrets well. This frigid world is so small and distant that it appears as a featureless blob even through the largest earth-based telescopes. It is also the only planet that has not yet been
(5) visited by a scientific spacecraft.

Despite these difficulties, a new picture of Pluto has begun to emerge during the past decade. Dedicated observational efforts using a variety of modern instruments, aided by some fortuitous celestial alignments, have produced a

number of surprises. Pluto has a satellite, Charon, so large that the two objects
(10) can virtually be considered a double planet. The planet has bright polar caps and
a darker, mottled equatorial region. A layer of methane ice covers most of its
surface. Pluto even possesses a thin atmosphere; when the planet is farthest from
the sun, all or part of the atmosphere may freeze and fall to the surface as snow.
Charon's surface, which appears to be quite different from Pluto's, may be a
(15) great expanse of water ice.

Pluto's size and density are much like those of Triton, the large satellite of
Neptune that was recently visited by the *Voyager 2* probe. These and other
similarities suggest that both bodies may be leftover planetesimals, relics from
the early days of the solar system that managed not to be swept up by the giant
(20) outer planets. In this scenario, Triton was captured by Neptune, whereas Pluto
was able to survive as a bona fide planet in an independent orbit about the sun.

Clyde W. Tombaugh first glimpsed Pluto in 1930 as part of a methodical
photographic survey inspired by Percival Lowell, a wealthy Bostonian with a
passionate interest in finding a possible trans-Neptunian planet. It was immedi-
(25) ately evident that Pluto is an oddball in many ways. The other outer planets orbit
the sun in roughly circular paths, but Pluto's highly elliptical orbit carries it from
30 to 50 times the earth's distance from the sun and, at times, brings it closer to
the sun than Neptune. This was the case between 1979 and 1999. Pluto's orbit
also is inclined 17 degrees to the plane in which the Earth revolves around
(30) the sun, far more than that of any other planets.

New insight into Pluto's complex nature has renewed interest for a spacecraft
mission to this distant world. Sending a pair of spacecraft increases the likelihood
that at least one encounter will be successful and because of economies of scale,
the cost would be only slightly more than for a single spacecraft. If both were
(35) successful, it would be possible to investigate time-dependent phenomena on
Pluto (such as changes in its atmosphere) and to image both hemispheres of Pluto
and Charon at high resolution.

A mission to Pluto would complete the human endeavor to perform a preliminary reconnaissance of all the major bodies in the solar system. As each
(40) planet has shed some of its secrets, the beautiful, bewildering diversity of nature
has grown ever clearer.

15. The primary purpose of this passage is to

    (A) describe atmospheric conditions on Pluto

    (B) argue for additional exploration of Pluto

    (C) detail the history of Pluto's discovery

    (D) explain Lowell's scientific contributions

    (E) criticize current spending on space exploration

16. According to the author, which of the following was farthest from the sun in 1990?

    (A) Charon   (D) Pluto

    (B) Earth   (E) Sol

    (C) Neptune

17. From the passage we know the first sighting of Pluto was

    (A) made prior to the discovery of Neptune

    (B) an unexpected surprise

    (C) part of the *Voyager* 2 fly-by

    (D) part of a systematic research plan

    (E) fortuitous

18. From the passage, the author seems to use the term ice to mean

    (A) frozen water

    (B) atmosphere

    (C) liquid methane

    (D) surface temperature

    (E) materials in their solid state

19. From the passage, planetesimals are most likely

    (A) moons

    (B) giant outer planets

    (C) small and very old astronomical bodies

    (D) spacecraft used to explore the outer planets

    (E) double planets

20. According to the author Pluto's orbit is

    (A) within that of the Earth

    (B) unknown but between 30 and 50 times that of Earth

    (C) perpendicular to that of the Earth

    (D) not circular

    (E) similar to Triton's

21. If one spacecraft was sent to explore Pluto the author would most likely feel

    (A) pleased   (D) distressed

    (B) satisfied   (E) ecstatic

    (C) relieved

      One response to the philosophic conflict between Heraclitus and Parmenides was that of the *Sophists*. The Sophists were philosophers from many different societies outside Greece who traveled about from city to city and in the fifth century B.C. came to Athens, where debate in the public assembly was open to
(5) all citizens. The Sophists argued that since reason produced such conflicting claims as those of Heraclitus and Parmenides, one must doubt the power of reason to lead to truth. Thus the Sophists became the first exponents of skepticism, the philosophic position of doubting the possibility of any true knowledge. *Protagoras*, the best known of the Sophists, appears to have made the skeptical
(10) argument that since there is no way of determining the truth about reality, reality must be said to have whatever qualities are claimed for it. Thus the Sophists threw suspicion upon all preceding Greek attempts to discover the true nature of reality.

      But, more important, the Sophists may be said to have turned Greek philoso-
(15) phy in a new direction — away from philosophizing about the physical universe and toward the study of human beings and their moral, social, and political life. The Sophists were intellectual sophisticates who had traveled about and knew many cultures and their differing customs, morals, laws, and governments. Much to the dismay of many Athenian citizens who believed that traditional Athenian
(20) morals, laws, and democracy expressed absolute truths, the Sophists were moral relativists and argued that all moral and political principles are relative to the group which believes them. None is absolutely true.

      Moreover, the Sophists claimed that the laws of cities are not natural and unchangeable but are merely the product of custom or convention. Therefore,
(25) some of the more radical Sophists argued, one is not obliged to obey the law. One should obey the law only if it is to your advantage to do so. For example, in Book I of the *Republic, Thrasymachus* the Sophist argues that might makes right, that laws serve only to protect the interests of the powerful, the ruling party. Therefore, he concludes, only a fool obeys the law if it is against his own advan
(30) tage.

      Many people in our contemporary world are very close to the Sophists in their beliefs. Like the Sophists, they are skeptics, doubtful of any claims to knowledge, especially when authorities are in conflict and fight among them-
selves — for example, about how to teach children to read or how to stop eco-
(35) nomic inflation. Like the Sophists, many people today claim that the laws protect only the right and powerful, that they are not based upon justice and need not be obeyed; they are moral relativists who deny that morality is valid other than for the group which believes in it.

22. The primary purpose of the passage is to

    (A) criticize the philosophy of Heraclitus

    (B) argue in favor of skepticism

    (C) explain the position of Protagoras

    (D) describe the philosophy of the Sophists

    (E) advocate moral enlightenment

23. From the passage, Thrasymachus would most likely agree with

    (A) Parmenides   (D) Plato

    (B) Protagoras   (E) Heraclitus

    (C) Socrates

24. According to the author skepticism

    (A) supports lawlessness

    (B) advocates divine enlightenment

    (C) does not believe in true knowledge

    (D) is untenable

    (E) originated in Athens

25. The author argues

    (A) many hold beliefs similar to those of the Sophists

    (B) skepticism cannot apply in the modern world

    (C) the Sophists were narrow-minded and uncultured

    (D) Plato was a Sophist

    (E) the Sophists were an unimportant cult

26. From the passage, Thrasymachus' position is most like

    (A) anarchy   (D) democracy

    (B) social irrelevance   (E) moral relativism

    (C) trickle-down theory

27. According to the author, Protagoras's view called into question

    (A) moral ambiguity

    (B) assertions of reality

    (C) scientific findings

    (D) urban structures

    (E) the distribution of property

28. According to the author, the Sophists emphasized

    (A) study of the physical sciences

    (B) study of human society

    (C) philosophy of the physical sciences

    (D) urban decay

    (E) legal structures

STOP
If time still remains, you may review work only in this section.
When the time allotted is up, you may go on to the next section.

Section III

Time—35 minutes
26 Questions
(Answer sheets appear in the back of this book.)

DIRECTIONS: The questions in this section are based on the reasoning contained in brief statements or passages. For some questions, more than one of the choices could conceivably answer the question. However, you are to choose the **best** answer; that is, the response that most accurately and completely answers the question. You should not make assumptions that are by commonsense standards implausible, superfluous, or incompatible with the passage. After you have chosen the best answer, blacken the corresponding space on your answer sheet.

1. These bombs are perfectly safe. For, if they were to explode, their fuses would have to be switched on, but all the fuses are safely off.

    Which of the following arguments has reasoning most like that above?

    (A) If Jim had been to the dance, Martha would have been there too. But I know she wasn't there, so Jim also stayed away.

    (B) The cake would have risen only if the baking powder were still active. So, since it did not rise, the powder must be inert.

    (C) Only the brave deserve the fair. Horace is not very brave. So he does not deserve the fair Guinevere.

    (D) If the wall had been blown up, William would have taken the stronghold. And, indeed, he did take the stronghold. So, he must have found a way to blow up the wall.

    (E) This glass will not shatter unless I drop it. I am going to drop it. Therefore, it will shatter.

2. Even the most self-serving reports of investigations of UFOs admit that at least 8% of such reports are not adequately accounted for in the standard "scientific" ways: as illusions or misperceived airplanes or stars. These genuinely unidentified flying objects must, then, be explained in some non-standard way. But the only other explanation available is that they really are crafts from another area — whether a remote planet, a remote time on this planet, or from a different physical or spiritual dimension. Thus we see that even the most hardened unbelievers covertly admit that all UFOs really come to us from the realms beyond.

    Which type of faulty reasoning does the above argument NOT contain?

(A)   Discrediting an opponent by labeling him with a derogatory level rather than refuting his claims

(B)   Inferring that something must be the case from the fact that the opposite claim has not been proven

(C)   Changing the meaning of a crucial expression in the middle of the argument

(D)   Ignoring positions intermediate between two opposed views

(E)   Refuting a misleading or exaggerated version of the opposite position, rather than an accurate one

3.   John Stuart Mill, in trying to prove that pleasure was desirable, pointed out that people did desire pleasure. This, he held, was the best evidence that pleasure is desirable, just as the fact that people see an object is the best evidence that it is visible (see-able). The usual response to this argument is that "desirable" means "ought to be desired," while "visible" means only "can be seen."

This usual response, if correct, shows that

(A)   people do not desire pleasure.

(B)   Mill has not shown that people desire pleasure.

(C)   pleasure is not desirable.

(D)   Mill has not shown that pleasure is desirable.

(E)   pleasure ought not be desired.

4.   Politics is a subject difficult to pin down, though discussions of politics have a long and venerable history. No less a figure than Aristotle propounded his views in a book called *Politics* more than 2,000 years ago. Of course, politics certainly predated Aristotle, manifesting itself, for example, in events reported in the Bible. To further complicate the subject, the politics of the 20th century are vastly different in scope and substance, if not in form, from the politics of the ancients. Thus, it is not unreasonable to be perplexed about the meaning of politics.

What is the main conclusion of this passage?

(A)   Politics is a perplexing subject.

(B)   Politics has been discussed for thousands of years.

(C)   Politics has Biblical roots.

(D)   Twentieth century politics is different from ancient politics.

(E)   Aristotle is one of the earliest authorities on politics.

5.   *Paradise Lost* was a political poem, in that it reflects Milton's view that politics is at heart a moral activity grounded in the essential liberty that affords the individual both the freedom and the responsibility to choose among personal and public alternatives which are inherently moral in nature. The source of this liberty is virtue. Hence the poem could be — and was — read also as a guide to piety and submission, and to the supposedly appropriate relations between men and women, mortal and deity, and subject and heavenly king.

What is the writer primarily arguing about Paradise Lost?

(A)   The poem shows the supposedly appropriate relations between men and women.

(B)   The poem is political because it reflects Milton's views about the relationship between politics and moral activity.

(C)   The poem shows that liberty is virtue.

(D)   The poem shows that individuals have the freedom and responsibility to choose among personal and public alternatives.

(E)   The poem was read as a guide to piety and submission.

6.   There is no need to spend much time demonstrating that Molière had contact with, and was affected by, Italian forms of comic theatre. That such influences were constantly available to him is a commonplace rather than a point of contention. Let just two facts stand for a host of others, so that we may dispose of the point. From 1658 to 1660 Molière's company shared their acting space with a resident Italian troupe. Secondly, his personal acting style was seen by contemporaries to have been modelled to some extent on that of Tiberio Fiorilli.

Which statement, if true, would weaken the writer's argument?

(A)   Molière's company shared acting space with a resident Italian troupe until 1665, not 1660.

(B)   There were several forms of comic theatre in Italy.

(C)   Moliere's acting troupe was very small.

(D)   There are other facts which the writer could note to help demonstrate his point.

(E)   Tiberio Fiorilli was born and raised in Argentina.

7.   In 1848 in France, there was a revolution by accident. If the revolution had not happened then, it may be said, it would have happened at some other time. But if it had occurred later or earlier it would have occurred in

different circumstances and would have been a different revolution. The revolution was not the foreordained result of the emergence of new social forces that could not be contained in old institutions, for none of adequate importance had yet arisen; it was rather the accidental though highly probable result of the inherent weakness of government in France.

What is the author of this passage probably trying to conclude?

(A)   Revolution was inevitable in France.

(B)   Revolution occurred because new social forces could not be contained in old institutions.

(C)   The revolution in 1848 was a probable result of inherent weakness of government in France.

(D)   The French Revolution in 1848 was accidental.

(E)   New social forces had not arisen in France by 1848.

8.   Charles S. Peirce is not an easy philosopher to read or to understand for several reasons. First, he wrote for a variety of readers without sugarcoating his encyclopedic erudition. Second, he was an original and independent investigator concerned primarily with research and pioneering in exact sciences and philosophy rather than with ladling out pleasing or consoling generalities. Third, he found it necessary to invent new technical terms. Finally, he had a steadfast faith in the power of truth to liberate men from moral confusion provided they were willing to inquire arduously and subordinate private interests to publicly verifiable knowledge.

Which of the following is consistent with the author's reasons for claiming that Peirce is not easy to read or understand?

(A)   Peirce was writing for a specific audience: people engaged in exact science and philosophy.

(B)   Peirce's writing was often technical and it frequently used technology of his own making.

(C)   For Peirce, arduous inquiry required emphasis on private interests.

(D)   Peirce avoided erudition.

(E)   Peirce believed that attempts to achieve publicly verifiable knowledge would lead to moral confusion.

9.   At some stage in a disinflation process initiated by a discrete reduction in the growth rate of the money stock, the rate of inflation must fall by more than the reduction in money growth. The reason is that the demand for real balances in the new low inflation steady state will be higher than in the

high inflation equilibrium: the economy produces real balances by causing the price level to grow more slowly than the nominal money stock.

What is the author trying to prove?

(A) Demand for real balances in the new low inflation steady state will be higher than in the high inflation equilibrium.

(B) Economy produces real balances by causing the price level to grow more slowly than the nominal money stock.

(C) At some stage in a disinflation process there is a distinct reduction in the growth rate of the money stock.

(D) Sometimes a high inflation equilibrium is lower than demand for real balances.

(E) The rate of inflation must fall by more than the reduction in money growth, if a certain stage occurs in a disinflation process initiated by a discrete reduction in the growth rate of money stock.

10. He who explores the cities of England to discover that kind of beauty in architecture which is familiar in other lands will not find it. In a satire published in London the queen reproaches her son for not taking more after his father, and interesting himself in the industrial affairs of the country. The poor Prince of Wales can only reply, "I've not a model-farming soul." A similar answer is all that England can return to the immeasurable scoldings poured out upon her because she cannot do the work of the old Italian and Dutch masters.

Which of the following is an assumption offered as support for this argument?

(A) The Prince of Wales was satirized.

(B) England's architecture is not as ugly as some people would claim.

(C) People may not find the beauty of architecture in other lands as much as they will in England.

(D) England doesn't deserve the immeasurable scolding poured out upon her.

(E) The old Italian and Dutch masters created beautiful architecture.

11. The temptation to isolate Black English and to identify it as a single cause for all black problems in America must be resisted. Many educators succumb to the temptation by postulating that Black English is the primary source of educational problems in black children in poor neighborhoods. Others suggest that the reading problems of black children are the result of lack of

facility with the language of the textbooks. Little research has been done in this area, but available data show little relationship between Black English usage and reading abilities.

What position is the author trying to defend?

(A) Black English is not the cause of all black problems in America.

(B) Black English is the primary source of educational problems in black children in poor neighborhoods.

(C) Little research has been done concerning the relationship between Black English and reading abilities.

(D) Black children lack facility with the language of the textbooks.

(E) There is at least some relationship between Black English usage and reading abilities.

12. What is civilization? An old question, and definitional games are not always fruitful. In this instance, however, we must be clear. The word "civilization" ought to be used to mean something different from and more than the term "culture" of long anthropological tradition; else why have two terms? If so, it then must be something more than a set of collective norms and values of a particular group of any size in any place.

Which of the following is an assumption that underlies the writer's argument?

(A) Anthropologists have long recognized the distinction between "civilization" and "culture."

(B) Particular groups have collective norms and values.

(C) Definitional games are useful.

(D) If we avoid old questions we can be clear about what civilization is.

(E) "Culture" refers to a set of collective norms and values of a particular group.

13. The only proof capable of being given that an object is visible is that people actually see it. The only proof that a sound is audible is that people hear it; and so of the other sources of experience. In like manner, I apprehend, the sole evidence it is possible to produce that anything is desirable is that people do actually desire it.

Which of the following, if true, would weaken this argument?

(A) It is possible for a person to desire something which she does not find desirable.

(B)   One cannot prove something is visible unless one sees it.

(C)   One cannot prove a sound is audible unless one hears it.

(D)   There are other ways, besides desirability, to prove something is desired.

(E)   Knowledge is acquired through sense experience.

14.   And deceive me as he will, he can never bring it about that I am nothing so long as I shall think that I am something. Thus it must be granted that, after weighing everything carefully and sufficiently, one must come to the considered judgment that the statement "I am, I exist" is necessarily true every time it is uttered by me or conceived in my mind.

What is the writer trying to prove?

(A)   He is certain that he exists.

(B)   He thinks he exists.

(C)   He exists only when he thinks he exists.

(D)   He exists only in his own mind.

(E)   Everyone is certain that the writer exists.

15.   For if the statement "he is sitting" is true, yet, when the person in question has risen, the same statement will be false. The same applies to opinions. For if anyone thinks truly that a person is sitting, yet, when that person has risen, this same opinion, if still held, will be false. But statements and opinions themselves remain unaltered in all respects: the statement "he is sitting" remains unaltered, but it is at one time true, at another false, according to circumstances.

According to this line of reasoning, when is the sentence "the sun is out" true?

(A)   When the sun is out.

(B)   When "the sun is out" is an opinion.

(C)   When a person believes that the sun is out.

(D)   When the statement "the sun is out" remains unaltered.

(E)   When someone really thinks that the sun is out.

16.   The second proposition is this: an action done from duty has its moral worth, not in the purpose that is to be attained by it, but in the maxim according to which the action is determined. The moral worth depends,

therefore, not on the realization of the object of the action, but merely on the principle of volition according to which, without regard to any objects of the faculty of desire, the action has been done.

Which of the following actions could not have moral worth, according to this argument?

(A) An action done by someone who wants to do what is right, regardless of the consequences.

(B) An action done by someone who is concerned about the maxim according to which the action is determined.

(C) An action done with evil intentions, that has good consequences.

(D) An action done out of appropriate volition.

(E) An action done without regard to the objects of the faculty of desire.

17. Pains and pleasures come to an end together. Good and evil do not come to an end together. The conclusion is that good is not identical with pleasure nor evil with pain. The one pair of contraries comes to an end together and the other does not, because they are different.

Which of the following propositions, if true, would make this argument stronger?

(A) If pairs of contraries are not identical, no contrary in one pair can be identical to any contrary in the other pair.

(B) Usually, something which is painful is not pleasant.

(C) Pains and pleasures cannot exist together.

(D) Good and evil may exist together.

(E) Something which is good may also be pleasant.

18. If we say that other men should see the beauties we see, it is because we think those beauties are in the object, like its color, proportion, or size. Our judgment appears to us merely the perception and discovery of an external existence, of the real excellence that is without. But this notion is radically absurd and contradictory. Beauty is a value; it cannot be conceived as an independent existence which affects our sense and which we consequently perceive. It exists in perception, and cannot exist otherwise. A beauty not perceived is a pleasure not felt, and a contradiction.

Which statement below best characterizes the writer's conclusion?

(A) The beauty of an object belongs to the object.

(B) "Beauty is in the eye of the beholder."

(C) Beauty is a value.

(D) Color, proportion, and size are properties of an object.

(E) Other men see the beauties we see.

19. Self or person is not any one impression, but that to which our several impressions and ideas are supposed to have a reference. If any impression gives rise to the idea of self, that impression must continue invariably the same through the whole course of our lives; since self is supposed to exist after that manner. But there is no impression constant and invariable.

What is the most logical inference which the writer draws from these premises?

(A) Our ideas of self come from our impressions of self.

(B) There is no impression constant and invariable.

(C) We cannot determine what self is.

(D) Our several impressions and ideas have reference to self or person.

(E) Self exists as an invariable idea.

20. If a man pretend to me, that God hath spoken to him supernaturally and immediately, and I make doubt of it, I cannot easily perceive what argument he can produce to oblige me to believe it. For to say that God hath spoken to him in the Holy Scripture, is not to say God hath spoken to him immediately, but by mediation of the Prophets or of the Church. To say he hath spoken to him in a dream, is no more than to say he dreamed that God spake to him.

What belief does the writer appear to be refuting?

(A) The belief that God speaks through the Holy Scripture.

(B) The belief that God speaks through mediation of the prophets.

(C) The belief that there is a God.

(D) The belief that one can dream about God speaking.

(E) The belief that God speaks directly to man.

21. By the fundamental law of nature, man being to be preserved as much as possible, when all cannot be preserved, the safety of the innocent is to be preferred; and one may destroy a man who makes war upon him, or has discovered an enmity to his being, for the same reason that he may kill a

wolf or a lion; because such men are not under the ties of common-law of reason, have no other rule, but that of force and violence, and so may be treated as beasts of prey.

According to this reasoning, which of the following is true?

(A) The safety of an innocent wolf or lion is preferable to the safety of destructive wolves or lions.

(B) People are not under the ties of the common-law of reason.

(C) The fundamental law of nature calls for the killing of wolves and lions.

(D) The fundamental law of nature leads to enmity between men.

(E) Capital punishment is justifiable when it will contribute to the protection of others.

22. Martin: Eventually, the resources of Earth will be exhausted. The air will be too polluted to breathe, the water too fouled to drink, the soil too contaminated to raise edible crops. If mankind is to survive, then, it must be on another planet. So, we must begin now to develop the means to travel to and live on other planets in large numbers.

    George: Nonsense. The crude rockets and habitat equipment we have could never be used to move and support more than very small expeditions to even a very near planet. Nor do we need more, since careful pollution control rules already in force or soon to be enacted will keep acceptable environmental quality for centuries.

    George misses Martin's point primarily because of

(A) a different assessment of the quality of present space program equipment.

(B) a different evaluation of the effects of environmental pollution.

(C) a different understanding of the time frame involved.

(D) a different expectation of the effectiveness of anti-pollution legislation.

(E) a different commitment to human survival.

23. A teenager claims

    When I am 16, I can be sued, but I also can drive a car.

    When I am 18 and have to register for the draft, I can vote.

When I am 21, I have to go to work, but I can drink.

Which of the following would be the most plausible conclusions from these claims?

(A)   When I am 65, I have to retire, but I get social security.

(B)   When I am 13 and have to pay adult movie prices, I should be allowed to see adult movies.

(C)   When I am six, I have to go to school, but I should not have to walk to it.

(D)   When I get married, I get enough to set up housekeeping.

(E)   When I am 35 and have my mid-life crisis, I should make a lot of money.

24.   The Greens asked the fast-food industry to comment on the environmental damage to the tropical rain forests caused by clear-cutting vast sections to make grazing land for cattle to provide hamburgers. The industry replied, "We are not interested in clearing any land that is not rich enough in natural nutrients to provide for several decades grazing without significant artificial fertilizer. Thus we are providing significant low-cost agriculture which will bring high export income to the citizens of the affected countries. And we are avoiding damage that would be brought about by the same agriculture using more expensive and polluting commercial fertilizers."

The main problem with the industry's response is that

(A)   it provides no evidence to support its generalization.

(B)   it does not discuss the original issue.

(C)   it changes the meaning of a key expression in the middle of the argument.

(D)   it attacks the questioners rather than their argument.

(E)   it misrepresents the costs of commercial fertilizer.

25.   Many people think that symbolic logic is useless because it does not present representations of real-life arguments. They believe that the usefulness of logic is directly proportional to the degree of realism. This principle is false, as the following argument shows. It is a fundamental principle that only pure studies in form have true logical value. It follows that, since every symbolic argument is a pure study in form, only arguments in symbolic form have logical value.

Which of the following arguments most closely resembles the one above in logical form?

(A)   All pines are evergreens. All cedars are evergreens. Therefore, all pines are cedars.

(B)   All warriors are human. All humans are mortal. Therefore, all warriors are mortal.

(C)   All cattle are edible. All cattle are herbivores. Therefore, all edible animals are herbivores.

(D)   All dogs bark. No non-dogs howl. Therefore, all barking animals howl.

(E)   All cats mew. No non-cats purr. Therefore, all purring animals mew.

26.   A parapsychologist investigating "lucky guesses" found that close to 30% of the major winners in state lotteries she interviewed had chosen their winning numbers as a result of some kind of "flash" — a dream or an inner voice, for example — rather than on "rational" grounds, like a loved one's birthday or some system. She claims that this data demonstrates that some people possess clairvoyance, albeit often in an indirect and uncontrolled way.

Which of the following would be most important in proving or disproving the researcher's claim?

(A)   The percentage of lottery players she interviewed who let the machines pick their numbers.

(B)   The percentage of players who are winners in the state lotteries.

(C)   The exact meaning of "major winner" in her survey.

(D)   The percentage of players who chose their numbers on the basis of a "flash" and did not win.

(E)   The percentage of the population who play the state lotteries.

STOP
If time still remains, you may review work only in this section.
When the time allotted is up, you may go on to the next section.

Section IV

Time—35 minutes

24 Questions

(Answer sheets appear in the back of this book.)

DIRECTIONS: The questions in this section are based on the reasoning contained in brief statements or passages. For some questions, more than one of the choices could conceivably answer the question. However, you are to choose the **best** answer; that is, the response that most accurately and completely answers the question. You should not make assumptions that are by commonsense standards implausible, superfluous, or incompatible with the passage. After you have chosen the best answer, blacken the corresponding space on your answer sheet.

1. Never had a leader of the Soviet Union looked so weak coming to a summit with an American president. In Moscow, political upstarts to his right and left openly ridiculed him. The Baltic states were trying to peel away; as many as four more Soviet republics opted to do the same. After five years of tinkering with the economy, he had fixed too little, too late; but more radical reforms promised inflation and unemployment.

    Which of the following is not a premise for the conclusion that the Soviet Union looked weak?

    (A) The leader was ridiculed by his own people.

    (B) America looked stronger by comparison.

    (C) Baltic republics threatened to peel away from the Soviet Union.

    (D) The economy had not been reformed enough.

    (E) Too much reform would have hurt the economy.

2. Nutrition as a discipline examines the interaction of nutrient ingestion, metabolism and utilization with the health and behavior of the organism. The ingestive phase is initiated by a complex array of factors, only some of which are directly related to the body's physiological state of need. The sensory qualities of available foods can be powerful determinants of eating behavior. Everyone is occasionally induced to eat beyond physiological need in response to a delicious taste or aroma. For some individuals, however, sensory factors assume primary importance in guiding intake, and this sensory dominance may lead to improper nutrition.

Which of the following best states the conclusion of this passage's argument?

(A) Sensory qualities of available foods can determine eating behavior.

(B) Nutrition as a discipline examines the interaction of nutrient ingestion.

(C) Everyone is occasionally induced to eat beyond physiological need.

(D) Tastes and aromas can be delicious.

(E) Sensory dominance may lead to improper nutrition.

3. The majority of socialist countries have adopted a policy of renewal, and an intensive search is going on for the model of economic management which is most appropriate for socialism. There is no single, uniform point of view in the socialist countries on the aims and methods of carrying out economic reforms, nor even on their necessity. This is quite natural, as "the strength of socialism lies in the diversity and richness of international experience."

Which of the following best states the conclusion of this passage's argument?

(A) The variety of views about aims and methods of carrying out economic reforms is natural to socialism.

(B) There is a model of economic management which is most appropriate for socialism.

(C) Socialism should seek a single, uniform point of view on the aims and methods of carrying out economic reforms.

(D) Socialism's strength derives from a diversity and richness of international experience.

(E) There is no necessity for carrying out economic reforms.

4. Small metropolises in 1840 controlled and coordinated rural regional economies, integrated intraregionally by water and by primitive roads and turnpikes. Only the East Coast metropolises — New York, Philadelphia, Boston, and Baltimore — and the southern metropolis of New Orleans had over 100,000 people; the next largest metropolis, Cincinnati, had under 50,000 people. Eleven percent of the nation's population was urban, and commodity output overwhelmingly consisted of natural resource products, principally from agriculture (72%). Natural waterways and canals provided long-distance links between a metropolis and its hinterland. Railroad trackage totaled only 3,000 miles in 1840.

Which of the following, if true, would weaken the argument's conclusion?

(A) Baltimore did not have over 100,000 people in 1840.

(B) Railroad track totalled 4,000 miles in 1840.

(C) There were few roads and turnpikes relative to today.

(D) Commodity output included non-agricultural products in 1840.

(E) Rural and regional economies controlled and coordinated themselves in 1840.

5. In a recent collection of essays, *The Tempest* is twice deemed a bad, "boring" play. Perhaps the reason for this condemnation lies not in the play itself but in our failure to imagine the conditions of Renaissance theatrical production. If recontextualized within one aspect of English history, *The Tempest*, I suggest, is a politically radical intervention in a dominant contemporary discourse. The play is constructed as a series of conspiracies, and as such it can be inserted into a vast discourse of treason that became an increasingly central response to difficult social problems in late Elizabethan and early Jacobean London.

Which of the following best summarizes this passage's argument?

(A) *The Tempest* is a bad, boring play.

(B) *The Tempest* is deemed a bad, boring play.

(C) *The Tempest* is constructed as a series of conspiracies.

(D) There were difficult social problems in late Elizabethan and early Jacobean London.

(E) It is incorrect to condemn *The Tempest* as a boring play, because it is part of the central discourse of the Renaissance.

6. Three ironies have always complicated library instruction. First of all, almost everyone who has entered — never mind "used" — more than one library concludes from the venture that each is idiosyncratic, not just in layout and collections, but in underlying logic. The same people who will go into an unfamiliar airport or grocery clear in their expectations of what they'll find and sure in their knowledge of what to do, set foot timorously in a strange library, doubtful they will come away satisfied, and uneasy about how to proceed.

Which of the following analogies best applies to the writer's argument?

(A) Since people are comfortable with unfamiliar airports, they should be comfortable with unfamiliar groceries.

(B) Since people go to unfamiliar airports and groceries, they should go to libraries.

(C)   Since people are comfortable with unfamiliar airports and groceries, they should be comfortable with unfamiliar libraries.

(D)   Since airports and groceries are idiosyncratic, libraries must be idiosyncratic as well.

(E)   Libraries have layouts and collections, just as airports have layouts and productions.

7.   Compared to his situation at home, life as a small-time drug dealer on Philadelphia's most dangerous street is a relief for the boy. His father, a junkie who died of AIDS, once tried to kill the family by burning down their house; his mother, who was hit in the arm during a recent drug shootout, spends her days locked in an upstairs bedroom avoiding her kids. The boy's older brother is in youth prison for dealing. His 16-year-old sister is pregnant. And the landlord is trying to evict all of them for not paying the rent.

Which of the following, if true, would strengthen this passage's argument?

(A)   The father failed to burn down the house.

(B)   Whenever he is in the street dealing drugs, the boy does not think about his older brother.

(C)   The mother avoids her kids.

(D)   The sister is pregnant.

(E)   In Philadelphia, landlords cannot evict people for not paying rent.

8.   The best way of making use of the terminology for causes of death during the 18th and 19th centuries is a problem often discussed among scholars in the history of medicine. It is a well-known fact that medical science in the past had a totally different concept of the functions of the human body and of the specific nature of disease. Eighteenth- and 19th-century medical philosophers based their concepts of disease and causes of death on a confusing mixture of symptoms and purely theoretical assumptions.

Which of the following is offered as a premise for the conclusion of this argument?

(A)   It is difficult to decide how best to make use of 18th and 19th century terminology for causes of death.

(B)   Medical science once had a different concept of the functions of the human body.

(C)   Medical science never had a different concept of the specific nature of disease.

(D)   Modern medical science is better than that of the past.

(E)   Scholars are totally informed of older terminology.

9.   There have been many attempts, primarily among theologians, to ascertain the contribution which Whitehead's process philosophy might make to social and political theory. Unfortunately, when one examines this growing body of literature, one becomes aware that a serious study of Whitehead's own social and political thought has been largely neglected. This neglect is no doubt due in part to the fact that Whitehead never produced a systematic political theory. While determination of his political beliefs is difficult, it is necessary if process philosophers and theologians are to assess accurately Whitehead's potential contribution to social and political theory.

Which of the following, if true, would weaken this passage's argument?

(A)   Whitehead's process philosophy has not made a contribution to social and political theory.

(B)   A serious study of Whitehead's own social and political thought has been largely neglected.

(C)   Whitehead never produced a systematic political theory.

(D)   There has been a serious study of Whitehead's social and political thought.

(E)   Determination of Whitehead's political beliefs is not difficult.

10.   In Leibniz's system, the issue of freedom occupies a prominent position. Moreover, since for him freedom does not only involve absence of external impediments, but also, among other things, the power to will as one should, it directly conflicts with weakness of will. Consequently, his views on weakness of will are to be regarded as relatively central to the system. Furthermore, systematic considerations aside, the issue of weakness of will is of considerable intrinsic interest because of its theoretical and practical aspects alike.

Of the following, which is not a premise offered as support for the conclusion that Leibniz's views on the weakness of will are central to his system?

(A)   Freedom involves absence of external impediments.

(B)   Weakness of will involves absence of external impediments.

(C)   Freedom directly conflicts with weakness of will.

(D)   The issue of freedom is important to Leibniz's system.

(E)   Freedom involves the power to will as one should.

11. Lacrosse is an amateur sport in which successful players do not follow collegiate careers with high paying professional contracts. Also most existing intercollegiate lacrosse programs either do not produce revenue or do not produce sufficient revenue to cover their operating costs. As a result, many college and university athletic administrators assign lacrosse a low priority. At the same time this situation has had the favorable consequence that lacrosse has been largely free of NCAA violations and the controversies concerning the academic progress of student athletes.

Which of the following conclusions is consistent with the writer's assertions?

(A) Lacrosse generates high revenues for colleges.

(B) Lacrosse has forced many NCAA violations.

(C) Lacrosse has remained consistent with traditional values of intercollegiate sport as a valuable extracurricular experience for serious students.

(D) Since lacrosse has many successful players, it receives strong support from college and university athletic administrators.

(E) Good lacrosse players in college often receive high paying professional contracts.

12. The literature of a nation, a time, a period, perhaps even of an individual, should be all the statements made by the culture of the time. The purpose of the student of literature, the necessity and obligation of the student of the conventional literature, is to read all these "literatures" and see how one casts light upon all the others, how each contributes to the total literature of the peoples of the time.

What is the conclusion of this passage?

(A) Students have a necessity and obligation to read conventional literature.

(B) The literature of a nation is the literature of an individual.

(C) One literature casts light upon another literature.

(D) Peoples of different times have their own literature.

(E) Students of literature should read all the "literatures" to see how each casts light on the others and contributes to the total literature of the people of the time.

13. In a trend that must remind veteran practitioners of the 1950s, the news media are criticizing the adult orientation of comic books, especially the increase in violence and sexual themes. A *New York Times Magazine* article questioned the judgment of comic book publishers, noting that "comics have

forsaken campy repartee and outlandishly byzantine plots for a steady diet of remorseless violence." *Time* went a step further, explicitly linking violence in comic books with a rise in juvenile delinquency. Such visible public criticism does not escape the notice of mainstream producers.

If the information in this passage is correct, which of the following statements is necessarily true?

(A) Contemporary criticism of comic books appears to be similar in tone to 1950s criticism.

(B) The *New York Times* linked violence in comic books with juvenile delinquency.

(C) Violence in comic books is a cause of juvenile delinquency.

(D) Comic book publishers exhibit poor judgment.

(E) Comic books have campy repartee and outlandishly byzantine plots.

14. Demographic studies indicate that the number of elderly is increasing; therefore, the total cost of caring for the elderly is also increasing. At the same time, the number of wage earners is not increasing as rapidly. The funds to care for the elderly will have to come from taxes paid by the wage earners.

Which of the following inferences can be drawn from the statements above?

(A) Unless average income increases sufficiently, the percentage of each person's income that must go to caring for the elderly will increase.

(B) The elderly will not receive adequate care.

(C) Only the rich will be able to afford health care in their later years.

(D) Younger people will vote against the increase in taxes needed to care for the growing numbers of elderly.

(E) Citizens should save their own money now to take care of their own needs during retirement, instead of depending on younger people to take care of them.

15. Important novels rarely become important films. Alfred Hitchcock often commented that a well-crafted fiction was much harder to film than second-rate writing. Great novels — those multidimensional works which explore the interior life of their characters and offer gripping emotional development — are extremely difficult to transfer to the screen. Contrast this with popular fiction, such as the gothic romance, from which entertaining movies can be made because the audience reacts on a visceral level. A good example would be Daphne du Maurier's *Rebecca*, expertly filmed by

Hitchcock.

Which of the following may we conclude, based on the assertion of the writer?

(A) Hitchcock made films other than *Rebecca*.

(B) The writer does not assume *Rebecca* to be a great novel.

(C) All well-written fiction is harder to film than second-rate writing.

(D) *Rebecca* was a great novel.

(E) *Rebecca* was an important novel.

16. All of us need adventure, though of course it's easier to handle vicariously, through the pages of a book, than when it actually arrives. The celebrated cathartic effect, that mixture of pity and fear which is supposed to refresh the soul, is better acquired by reading *King Lear*, than by being King Lear. Consider being King Lear. You have two psychotic daughters who murder each other, your best friend has his eyes torn out, and you go raving mad on a stormy heath, and end up dying of a broken heart with your third daughter's body in your arms.

Which of the following statements is inconsistent with the writer's conclusion?

(A) Vicarious adventure is easier to handle than actual adventure.

(B) It is better to read *King Lear* than to be King Lear.

(C) Actual adventure is preferable to vicarious adventure.

(D) Reading *King Lear* can arouse pity and fear in the reader.

(E) Being King Lear may arouse pity and fear in the king.

17. Meat analogies tend to be lower in protein than their real-meat equivalents, which is one unexpected reason why opting for a fake burger over a real one can be a healthy practice. Excess protein can stress the kidneys because protein is hard to digest. It can also stretch the waistline, since many meat sources of protein are high in fat calories.

Which of the following is not a premise of this passage's argument?

(A) A real burger is less healthy than a fake one, because a real burger has more protein.

(B) Protein sources can be fattening.

(C) Too much protein can harm the kidneys.

(D)   Protein can be hard to digest.

(E)   A fake burger can be more healthy than a real one.

18.   American community colleges are entering an era that in some ways parallels the 1960s in terms of the need for new staff and their development of
new skills to meet the challenges of the decade ahead. Increasingly, community college leaders are examining their future staffing needs, often with
some startling results. For example, in California, approximately 40 percent of full-time faculty will be eligible for retirement in the next six years,
with another 18 percent only a few years away. Obviously, the need to
recruit and provide staff development for a substantial new cadre of faculty
is upon us now.

If we assume the information in this passage is true, which of the following, if true, would strengthen the argument further?

(A)   Community colleges needed new staff in the 1960s.

(B)   Community college leaders are often startled by their future staffing
needs.

(C)   There is a need to recruit and provide staff development for a new
cadre of faculty.

(D)   All full-time faculty in California who become eligible for retirement
will retire immediately.

(E)   The decade ahead will be challenging for American community colleges.

19.   Aggressive behavior is a symptom of dementia that makes care-giving of
the patient more difficult. Some believe that as people become cognitively
impaired, their psychological reactions to the decline they experience often
result in aggression. Aggression appears particularly likely to occur in
response to task failure or to the conflicts that arise between care receiver
and giver, when the former becomes confused and the latter impatient. The
aggression of patients, however, may be caused not only by confusion and
hopelessness due to gradual loss of "bodily integrity," but also by structural
damage in the brain.

Which of the following is not necessarily true even if the premises of this
argument are true?

(A)   Structural damage in the brain may lead to aggression in patients.

(B)   Aggression of patients is caused by confusion and hopelessness due
to gradual loss of "bodily integrity."

(C)   Aggression may occur where a patient is confused and a care-giver is

impatient.

(D)   Loss of "bodily integrity" is different from structural damage in the brain.

(E)   Task failure is a possible cause of aggression.

20.   The number of Latino families with incomes of $50,000 or more has increased steadily during the last decade. In large part, this development is a reflection of dual- and multiple-income families whose combined earnings reach a level of affluence. In 1986, about nine percent of 500,000 Latino households were earning $50,000 or more, compared to about 17 percent of all American families. The early 1980s saw an impressive growth in Latino family income, jumping from 20,000 who earned more than $75,000 in 1980 to approximately 103,000 six years later.

Which of the following, if true, would NOT weaken the argument in the passage?

(A)   Growth in Latino family income fell from 103,000 families earning $75,000 in 1980 to 20,000 families six years later.

(B)   Twenty-seven percent, not 17 percent, of all American families, were earning $75,000 or more in 1986.

(C)   The number of Latino families with incomes of $50,000 or more has dipped slightly in the 1980s.

(D)   No dual- and multiple-income Latino families have reached a level of affluence.

(E)   In 1980, more than 20,000 Latino families made $50,000 or more.

21.   Gone are the days when the younger kids dressed in a cousin's hand-me-downs and prayed for a two-wheeler at Christmas. Spending on kids is now one of the fastest-growing sectors of America's economy. At a time when overall economic growth is crawling along at 2%, spending on and by kids 4-to-12 years old jumped an estimated 25% last year, to $60 billion. This, year the kiddie market is expected to hit $75 billion, approaching 2% of the entire U.S. economy.

If the propositions of this argument are true, which of the following assertions is also true?

(A)   The difference between spending on and by kids 4-to-12 years old last year and this year is $10 billion.

(B)   The percent of overall economic growth and the percent of growth in the spending on and by kids last year were the same.

(C)   There is no faster-growing sector of America's economy than spend-

ing on kids.

(D)   Overall economic growth is slower than spending on and by kids.

(E)   Last year's spending on and by kids 4-to-12 years old jumped 2%.

22.   Based on available information it is apparent that some housing markets are more prone than others to the impact of AIDS, for two main reasons. The first is that certain areas of the U.S. have high concentrations of AIDS cases: these cities and neighborhoods will be the first to face fears of buyers, sellers and lenders. Secondly, housing values and affordability vary from place to place in the U.S., and it follows that the financial exposure of the owners, borrowers, lenders and mortgage insurers will also vary widely in those market areas with a high incidence of AIDS.

Which of the following is the conclusion of the argument?

(A)   It is apparent that some housing markets are more prone than others to the impact of AIDS.

(B)   Housing values and affordability vary from place to place in the U.S.

(C)   Certain areas of the U.S. have high concentrations of AIDS cases.

(D)   The financial exposure of lenders will vary widely.

(E)   The financial exposure of owners will vary widely.

23.   Today, rap is a pervasive presence in popular culture, affecting not only America's musical tastes, but its fashion trends and vernacular as well. Telltale signs of rap's influence are evident everywhere. Hollywood has co-opted it, and so has Madison Avenue. Sanitized for mass appeal, rap is used to promote a wide range of products — from hamburgers to automobiles. And, in the middle-of-the-road realm of Top 40 music, rap is used to comment benignly on the human condition.

Which of the following is the best restatement of this argument's conclusion?

(A)   Rap is popular even in non-musical areas of life.

(B)   Hollywood has co-opted rap.

(C)   Rap has been sanitized for mass appeal.

(D)   Rap comments benignly on the human condition.

(E)   Madison Avenue has co-opted rap.

24. Mrs. Smith is extremely jealous with regard to the activities of her husband, a seven-foot, 300-pound professional wrestler. One day, while shopping at the mall, she sees a seven-foot, 300-pound man going into a movie theater with a young lady. Mrs. Smith follows them into the theater and, in the darkness of the theater, attacks the man with her handbag. She is mortified when, as her eyes finally adapt to the darkness, she realizes that the man is not, in fact, her husband.

Which of the following statements points out the logical flaw in Mrs. Smith's thinking?

(A) Jealousy is an irrational emotion.

(B) Mrs. Smith should have hired a detective to follow her husband.

(C) Not every seven-foot, 300-pound man is Mrs. Smith's husband.

(D) She should have waited until she saw her husband at home and discussed the matter with him in private.

(E) If she were more self-confident, she would not be so jealous.

STOP

If time still remains, you may review work only in this section.
When the time allotted is up, you may go on to the next section.

LSAT Writing Sample

(Answer sheets appear in the back of this book.)

General Directions

You will have 35 minutes in which to plan and write an essay on the topic below. Read the topic and the accompanying directions carefully. You will probably find it best to spend a few minutes considering the topic and organizing your thoughts before you begin writing. In your essay, be sure to develop your ideas fully, leaving time, if possible, to review what you have written. **Do not write on a topic other than the one specified. Writing on a topic of your own choice is not acceptable.**

No special knowledge is required or expected for this writing exercise. Law schools are interested in the reasoning, clarity, organization, language usage, and writing mechanics displayed in your essay. How well you write is more important than how much you write.

Confine your essay to the blocked, lined areas on the front and back of the separate writing sample response sheet. Only that area will be reproduced for law schools. Be sure that your writing is legible.

Sample Topic

Directions: For this essay you are presented with an argument (see next page) that offers reasons for drawing a particular conclusion. Your essay should analyze and evaluate the line of reasoning and use of evidence in the argument. For example, you may want to discuss how the logic of the argument is flawed or could be improved, or what counterexamples or alternative explanations would undermine the argument. You may also want to consider what, if any, questionable assumptions underlie the reasoning and what additional information or evidence may have been overlooked that would strengthen or weaken the argument. Note: You are NOT being asked to present your personal opinion on the subject with which the argument is concerned.

The following appeared in a letter from the Waterland Children's Water-Park's president to investors:

"Waterland Children's Water-Park had an outstanding first year, so much so that its revenues were well over the anticipated returns. This year looks even more promising. The Waterland public schools have expanded their summer vacation time. A new addition to our rides, the Super-Duper Slide, was completed this fall and will premiere on opening day. Already we've received more telephone inquires about the season than last year. Thus, you can see that in this coming year, Waterland Children's Water-Park is bound to surpass last year's huge success."

Discuss how well reasoned you find this argument.

STOP
If time still remains, you may review work only in this section.

TEST III

ANSWER KEY

Section I — Analytical Reasoning

1.	(C)	8.	(D)	15.	(E)	22.	(D)
2.	(B)	9.	(A)	16.	(B)		
3.	(B)	10.	(B)	17.	(C)		
4.	(A)	11.	(C)	18.	(C)		
5.	(A)	12.	(B)	19.	(D)		
6.	(A)	13.	(D)	20.	(C)		
7.	(C)	14.	(A)	21.	(C)		

Section II — Reading Comprehension

1.	(B)	8.	(A)	15.	(B)	22.	(D)
2.	(C)	9.	(D)	16.	(C)	23.	(B)
3.	(E)	10.	(C)	17.	(D)	24.	(C)
4.	(D)	11.	(A)	18.	(E)	25.	(A)
5.	(B)	12.	(E)	19.	(C)	26.	(E)
6.	(A)	13.	(D)	20.	(D)	27.	(B)
7.	(D)	14.	(D)	21.	(A)	28.	(B)

Section III — Logical Reasoning

1.	(A)	8.	(B)	15.	(A)	22.	(C)
2.	(E)	9.	(E)	16.	(C)	23.	(B)
3.	(D)	10.	(E)	17.	(A)	24.	(B)
4.	(A)	11.	(A)	18.	(B)	25.	(A)
5.	(B)	12.	(E)	19.	(C)	26.	(D)
6.	(E)	13.	(A)	20.	(E)		
7.	(D)	14.	(A)	21.	(E)		

Section IV — Logical Reasoning

1.	(B)	8.	(B)	15.	(B)	22.	(A)
2.	(A)	9.	(D)	16.	(C)	23.	(A)
3.	(A)	10.	(B)	17.	(E)	24.	(C)
4.	(E)	11.	(C)	18.	(D)		
5.	(E)	12.	(E)	19.	(B)		
6.	(C)	13.	(A)	20.	(B)		
7.	(B)	14.	(A)	21.	(D)		

DETAILED EXPLANATIONS
OF ANSWERS

Section I – Analytical Reasoning

QUESTIONS 1–6

The basic information about the order of march is

1	2	3	4	5	6	
						b = a band,
						c = clowns,
∦					∦ ∦p	d = dignitaries,
						p = ponies,
∦					∦ pd	f = fire department
						/ = not permitted in this space

The dignitaries cannot be in first place nor the ponies in last, since each requires the other next to it. The dignitaries after the ponies automatically keep the bands away.

1. **(C)** List (C) clearly works: the clowns are in second place, rather than at either end, and, there, separate the band from the ponies that immediately precede the dignitaries. So, all the conditions on the order of march are met. In (A), however, a band is immediately in front of the ponies and in (B) the clowns come first, both forbidden placements. So, these two are not acceptable. Neither is (D), in which the fire department comes between the ponies and the dignitaries, nor (E), in which the ponies come after, rather than before, the dignitaries.

2. **(B)** The new information makes the diagram

1	2	3	4	5	6
f	b	c	p	d	b

With a band in second place, the dignitaries cannot ride in second place, and so the ponies cannot go in first. Since the other band is in last place, only the fire department is left to go in first place, and (B) is correct and (D) is wrong. The ponies also cannot go in third place, right after a band, nor can the dignitaries

(who have to follow the ponies, not a band), so the clowns must go there. Thus, (A), (C), and (E) are wrong.

3.　**(B)**　The new information gives

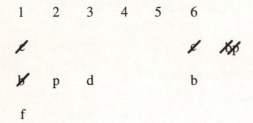

With ponies in second place, no band may be in first place. Since the dignitaries are already in place 3 and clowns also cannot be in first place, the fire department must be there, (C) has to be false. That leaves two bands and the clowns for the last three places. Since the clowns cannot be in the last place, that must be a band and (B) also has to be true. But (A) does not have to be true, for a band could follow the dignitaries without an intervening clown group. If the fire department is in first place, then (D) is false and (E) must also be incorrect.

4.　**(A)**　Putting the bands in the second and third places gives:

With the bands in positions 2 and 3, the ponies are excluded from position 1 (since a band, not the dignitaries, follows) and 4 (since a band immediately precedes). The ponies have, then, to go in position 5, with the dignitaries at the end. Since everything else is excluded from position 1 or is already placed, the fire department has to go into position 1. Then the clowns have to go into position 4, the only remaining space. In short, once the band is placed in this way, all the other positions are determined, and only one order of march is possible. So, (A) meets the condition. Answers (B) and (C) are, therefore, wrong. Choices (D) and (E) violate conditions of the problem.

5.   **(A)**   The order in (A) has a band directly in front of the ponies, contrary to the requirements. So, that is an unacceptable order and (A) is the correct answer. In all of the others, the bands are separated from the ponies by at least one other group. All of them also have the dignitaries immediately behind the ponies, and in none do the clowns come at either end of the order of march. That is, all of the others are acceptable.

6.   **(A)**   The only ways in which there could be three or more places between the two bands would be to have one band in position 1 and the other in position 5 or 6 (with 2, 3, and 4, and even 5 between). Clearly, having the first band farther right or the second farther left will result in fewer than three places between them. But in none of these three cases is a band in position 4, so (A) must be false and so is the correct answer. Each of the others can be true, as the order b c p d f b shows for all of (B), (C), and (D). As for (E), if the clowns are in third place, then the ponies and the dignitaries must be in positions 4 and 5, for one of 1 and 2 has to be a band and so does one of 5 and 6, leaving only 5 and 5 as consecutive available slots. But then position 6 does have to be filled by the second band.

QUESTIONS 7–11

From the two restrictions, it follows that a division of General can be aggressor only in absorbing another division of General and can be taken over only by a division of Universal. Any other combination involving General violates one of the restrictions.

7.　**(C)**　Since two of the aggressors are divisions of General, two of the developed divisions must be also, since General divisions can only absorb other General divisions, not take over divisions from other companies. (A), (D), and (E) must, then, all be wrong since they have fewer than two divisions of General among the developed. By the last requirement, a division of Universal must be among the developed, since all three conglomerates are to be represented but Universal is not among the aggressors. (B) is eliminated, since it contains no Universal, but (C) fits the situation exactly.

8.　**(D)**　Since all of the companies must be represented, there cannot be four divisions of Universal and two of General, for that would leave no Amalgamated. The only other way to have twice as many divisions of Universal as General is to have two divisions of Universal and one of General. There are then also three divisions of Amalgamated. The division of General cannot be an aggressor, since it could only absorb another division of General and there is not one to be absorbed in the present set of mergers. Thus, (B), (C) and (E), which have General among the aggressors, must be wrong. Since a General division is developed, it must be being taken over by a division of Universal, since no division of Amalgamated can take it over. Thus, not all the aggressors are divisions of Amalgamated, so (A) is wrong. But at least one of the aggressor divisions must be Amalgamated, for there are two aggressors yet to be assigned but only one more division of Universal. Thus, (D) is correct.

9.　**(A)**　At least one General division must be an aggressor division, since, if all were developed, there would have to be three divisions of Universal to take them over (or three more of General to absorb them), but there are not. But there can be only one General aggressor, since General divisions can only absorb other General divisions and there are not enough for two such mergers. Thus, one General division absorbs another to yield a new General division. The remaining division of General must be a developed division and, so, must be taken over by the one division of Universal (Amalgamated cannot take it over) to yield a new division of Universal. (C) and (E), which contain no new divisions of Universal, must be wrong, as must be (D), which would have two divisions formed with General as the aggressor. The final merger, then, must be the absorption of one division of Amalgamated by another, yielding a new division of Amalgamated. (B) is thus incorrect in omitting any new division of Amalgamated. But (A), which gives a new division to each company, remains and is correct.

10. **(B)** The division of General cannot be an aggressor, because such divisions can only absorb other General divisions but there is none involved in these mergers. The General division must, then, be a developed division, but this can only happen if the Universal division is taking it over, for no Amalgamated division can take it over. Thus, one merger is the Universal taking over the General. The remaining two, then, have to involve only Amalgamated divisions, one absorbing another. Thus, two divisions of Amalgamated are being absorbed, and (B) is correct. It cannot be that only one Amalgamated division is absorbed or taken over, for then the other two Amalgamated divisions would be aggressors and, so, one would have to take over a forbidden General division. (The one developed division in this hypothesis would have to be taken over by another Amalgamated division, not by a division of General, which cannot do so, nor by a division of Amalgamated but only one developed division — and that of the forbidden General.) Thus (A) and (D) cannot be correct. Three divisions of Amalgamated cannot be aggressors because, then, one would have to take over the division of General, which is forbidden. Thus, (C) and (E) are wrong.

11. **(C)** If all of three divisions of Universal are all developed, two of them must be taken over by divisions of General, for the remaining three divisions must all be aggressors. But General divisions cannot take over divisions of Universal. (C) cannot be true, so is the correct answer. As for the others, the mergers U+A–U+G–U+G (aggressor + developed) violate no restriction and make the Amalgamated division a developed one, thus making (A) true. This set of mergers also makes all three Universal divisions aggressors, verifying (D). Similarly, A+U–U+G–U+G makes (B) true. And both of these examples make (E) true. So, none but (C) must be false.

QUESTIONS 12–17
The initial information is

1	2	3	4	5	6
	W̶		W̶		W̶
Y̶	Y̶			Y̶	Y̶
Z̶				V̶	

VZ or VOZ

V can't be in 206, since Z must come in a higher-numbered room. Conversely, Z can't be in 201, since V must be in a lower-numbered room. The third room in numerical order which the salespeople occupy will be either 203 or 204, depending on whether the room they do not use is after or before, so Y will be in one of those. W is in an odd-numbered room, so is not in any even-numbered one.

12. **(B)** The added information gives

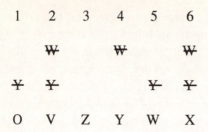

If V takes room 202, then Z must take 203 or 204 (with the unused room in 203). However, if the unused room were 203, then 204 would be the third room used by the salespeople, and, so, occupied by Y, not Z. So, Z is in 203. But this, also, cannot be the third room occupied by the salespeople, for the same reason. Thus, room 201 is unused and (A) is false. Y then is in room 204, so (B) is correct. Since 201 is empty and Z is in 203, W must be in 205, the only remaining odd-numbered room. This room is numbered higher than either 204, which contains Y, or 203, which contains Z, so both (C) and (D) are wrong. Finally, X must take 206, the only room remaining and numbered higher than 202, which contains V, so (E) is wrong also.

13. **(D)** The new information gives

```
    1    2    3    4    5    6

    Y̶    Y̶              Y̶    Y̶

         V̶    V̶              V̶    VZ or VOZ

W
```

V cannot go into 202, because then the next room occupied would be the third and, so, occupied by Y, not Z. Similarly, if the empty room is 202, V cannot go into 203 at the risk of being followed by Y, not Z; and, if 202 is occupied, V still cannot be in 203, since Y would be there already. V must, then, be in 204 or 205, with Z in 205 or 206. If V is in 204, then Y must be in 203 and 202 must be occupied — with X as the only possibility. If V is in 205, Y could be in either 203, with 204 being the empty room (it could not be 202, since 203 is the third room in order occupied), and, thus X again is in 202, or Y could be in 204 with either 202 or 203 empty and the other occupied by X. In any case, X can be in only 202 or 203, so (D) is the correct answer. (A) and (B) leave out a case each. Room 206 (in (C) and (E)) is not possible for X, since someone has to be between W and Y and she or he cannot be V or Z, so must be X before 204.

14. **(A)** The chart now is shown on the following page. With X in 201, V cannot go into 203, because it would then be followed by Y, rather than Z, for 202 must be empty. W and Y cannot be in 202, as noted originally, and V cannot,

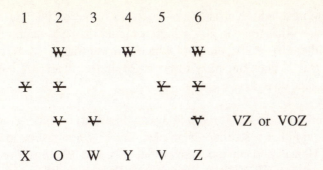

1	2	3	4	5	6	
	W̶		W̶		W̶	
Y̶	Y̶			Y̶	Y̶	
Y̶	Y̶				V̶	VZ or VOZ
X	O	W	Y	V	Z	

because the following Z would conflict with Y in third place, and Z cannot, because X, not V, would precede it. So, Y must be in 204, since the empty room is before it in the order, and V and Z are in 205 and 206, the consecutive open rooms. W, then, is in 203, the only available odd-numbered room. So, Y in 204, has a higher number than W, in 203, and (A) is correct. V, in 205, is not in 202 and not in a lower-numbered room than W, in 203, so both (B) and (C) are wrong. Y, in 204, is not in 203, so (D) is wrong and (E) fails because Z is in 206, not 204.

15. **(E)**   The new chart is

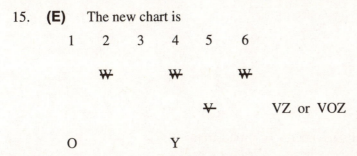

1	2	3	4	5	6	
	W̶		W̶		W̶	
			Y̶			VZ or VOZ
O			Y			

Since the first place is empty, Y will be in room 204, the third in order of the used rooms. Thus, VZ can go into either 202-203 or into 205-206. In the first case, Z will be in 203 and W will be in 205, the remaining odd-numbered room, so II is true. In the second case, W will be in 203, the odd-numbered room, and Z will be in 206. So, I is true also. In neither case will X be in 205 — but in 206 in the first case and 202 in the second. Thus, claim III is also true. So, (E), that all three are true, is the correct answer. The others omit at least one true claim.

16. **(B)**   The new information gives

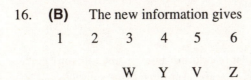

1	2	3	4	5	6
		W	Y	V	Z

If W is in room 203, Y must be in room 204, since that is the only one now available to him or her. Consequently, 201 or 202 is empty, else 203 would be the third room occupied and, so, would be Y's. V and Z cannot, therefore, occupy 201 and 202 and, so, must be in 205 and 206. So, Y has to be in 204, and

(C) is not the exception sought. Nor is (E), since Z has to be in 206. (D) is also not an exception, since V has to be in 205, which is higher than Y's required 204. And X must be in either 201 or 202, either of which is lower than Y's 204, so (A) is not exceptional. But X does not have to be in 201 rather than 202, so (B) merely might be true and so is the exception.

17.   **(C)**   If Z were in rooms 204, room 203 would have to be either empty or occupied by V. But, in either case, there is no place for Y, who must be in either room 203 or 204. Hence Z cannot occupy room 204 and (C) is the correct answer. The room sequence VZYOWX shows that 202 is a possible room for Z and thus that (A) is not the exception. OVZYWX does the same for (B), WXYVZO for (D) and WXYOVZ for (E).

QUESTIONS 18–22
   The initial information about the candidates can be summarized as

	Fac	Col	Mal
G	–	+	–
H	+	–	+
I	+	+	+
J	–	–	+
K	+	–	–
L	–	+	–
M	+	–	+

where   Fac + = faculty member, – = administrator
        Col + = from the college, – = from a school
        Mal + = male, – = female

   To be sure to get two positive and two negative from each column in just four people, the four people must be related so that each differs from each other in two columns, or else they must fall into two pairs, within which the two have complementary displays. For example, either

```
    – – –        or        – – –
  – + +                  + + +
  + – +                  – + –
  + + –                  + – +
```

If some pairs within the group differ in only column but do not fall into pairs, then there will be unequal representations of some columns. For example,

```
  + + +

  – + +
```

could be corrected only by + – – and – – –, which fall into two pairs. For convenience, the candidates can thus be presented as

```
        I      +  +  +

              (+  +  -)

     H, M      +  -  +

       K      +  -  -

              (-  +  +)

     G, L      -  +  -

       J       -  -  +

              (-  -  -),
```
with the missing items from the pattern in parentheses.

18.   **(C)**   If I, + + +, is chosen, then, since his complement, − − −, is not available, the subcommittee must consist of people who show two negatives and a positive: + − −, − + −, and − − +. The first of these, K, is not on the list of possible answers to this question, so he does not give the correct answer. The second could be either G or L, so neither must be on the subcommittee. Thus, J, the only representative of the third pattern is the required member and (C) the correct answer. Since neither G nor L must be on the subcommittee with I, (A) and (D) must be incorrect. If H or M, + − +, were on the subcommittee only − − − and − + − could make a subcommittee meeting the requirements. But, − − − is not represented among the candidates, so no subcommittee could be formed containing I and either H or M. Thus, neither (B) nor (E) can be correct.

19.   **(D)**   H and J cannot be on the subcommittee together. Their patterns, + − + and − − +, differ in only one place and so could go together only with their complements. But J's complement, + + −, is not represented among the candidates, so such a subcommittee cannot be formed. (D), then, is a correct answer. But all of the other combinations can be met: G I J K (− + −, + + +, − − +, + − −) is a possible subcommittee which shows that the pairs in both (A) and (B) can be on the subcommittee together. G H L M (− + −, + − +, − + −, + − +) shows that the pairs of both (C) and (E) might go together. So, only (D) fails.

20.   **(C)**   If K, + − −, is chosen, the subcommittee must consist of those who differ from K in exactly two categories: I, J, and either G or L, for K's complement, − + +, is not represented among the candidates. One or the other of G and L must be on the subcommittee but not either one of them in particular, so neither (A) nor (D) has to be correct. I, however, must be on the subcommittee, so (C) is correct. Putting H or M, + − +, on the subcommittee with K would require the complements of each also on the subcommittee, but, as noted, K's complement is not available. So, (C) is the sole correct answer.

21.   (C)   Once M, + − +, is chosen for the subcommittee, the possibilities are either the three patterns that differ from this in two places (+ + −, − − −, and − +

+) or the complementary pattern and some other pair of complement patterns. But, none of the patterns which differ from M's in two places is represented among the candidates. Thus, G or L, − + −, must be on the subcommittee, along with another complementary pair. However, the complement of none of I, J, or K is represented among the candidates. However, the complementation + − + and − + − is represented twice in the list, the first by H and M, the second by G and L. Thus, the only possible subcommittee with M in it is M G L H, two pairs of complementaries. Of the pairs listed, then, only G and L must be on the subcommittee that contains M. Indeed, this is the only pair both of whose members can be on such a subcommittee. All of the others involve a member whose pattern differs from M's by only one place but which cannot be involved in a complementary pair from the list of candidates. Thus, (C) is the correct answer.

22. **(D)** Within the candidates, I, J, and K have patterns whose complements are not represented among the candidates and which differ from one another in just two places. The fourth member of this set of patterns is represented twice, by G and L. So, each of I J K L and I J K G could form a subcommittee meeting the conditions. On the other hand, G L H M forms a possible subcommittee of two sets of complementary patterns, indeed, two representatives of the same complementation, + − + and − + −. Any other combination results in a pair of patterns that differ in only one place and for which at least one complement is not available and, so, cannot be a subcommittee of the sort required. Thus, just three different subcommittees can be formed and (D) is the correct answer. Admittedly, 35 different groups of four people could be pulled from the original committee, but most of these would not meet the conditions on this subcommittee, so (A) is wrong. (E) is plausible only if either the double complement set H M G L or one of the variants allowing either G or L with I J K is overlooked. (B) and (C) derive from other possible formula about possible subsets under various conditions, but do not apply in the present case.

Section II – Reading Comprehension

1. **(B)** This is emphasized in the first two paragraphs. The author notes with pleasure his friend's criticism of academics who try to read things into Twain's writing. In the second paragraph the author makes this point himself by suggesting such academic analyses do not reflect the reality of Twain's writing. The final two paragraphs also indirectly make this point by suggesting most Russian readers, like most American readers, understand the reality of Twain's work, despite government or academic interference. (A) is incorrect because the author's mention of Twain's humorous writings is only one part of the greater discussion of his clarity of writing. (C) is wrong because there is no mention of Russian literature in the passage. (D) is incorrect because the phrase *exportable commodity* is not intended to be taken literally. Rather, it is meant to imply that Twain's humor can be appreciated by non-Americans as well. (E) is incorrect

because, as with (A), this is only one part of the discussion. In addition, the author suggests in the final paragraph that it is only the Russian *government* which misunderstands Twain, and that the Russian people, he hopes, understand Twain as much as the American people.

2.   **(C)**   It should be clear from the first paragraph that the author's friend does not care for the academics who over-analyze Twain's works. *Perfesser* is often used to represent how a person with a strong accent or who is less educated might *pronounce* the word, but that is not the case here. (A) is incorrect because the author makes no suggestion that his friend is uneducated. On the contrary, by indicating his friend to be a novelist, he suggests the person probably did not write "perfesser" by accident or because he could not spell it correctly. (B) is incorrect. The correct and accepted spelling is *professor*. As indicated above, *perfesser* may be used, but not to suggest an accepted alternative. (D) is wrong because it is not Twain using the word, and the passage contains no mention of his attitude toward educated people. (E) is incorrect because we do not know the ethnic origin of the author's friend simply from the use of the word. As noted above, this spelling is often used by less educated people as well as those from certain places.

3.   **(E)**   As a measure of distance (which makes (A) wrong) the author in line 17 intends to exaggerate his opinion that the conclusion of the academics is far removed from reality. (B) is wrong because the passage does not make any references to philosophy. In addition, the phrase *shape of reality* is meaningless in this context. Although the author does use the term in evaluating academic discussions of Twain's work (not necessarily just critics), as an astronomical unit of distance it is not specifically used in literature for evaluating critiques. Thus, (C) is incorrect. (D) is wrong because the reference to Huck's journey is not made in relation to the author's mention of light-years. The author's friend mentions with disapproval that Huck's journey was compared to a journey made by Twain. The author then suggests some of the analyses of Twain's writing are far removed from reality.

4.   **(D)**   This point is made in the third paragraph, and again in the fourth. (A) is incorrect because the author is telling us it is the *Russian* belief that United States policy is to ignore Twain's work. The author does not indicate that he believes this. In fact, the reader may infer that this is part of the Russian contribution to the hogwash surrounding Twain's work. Relatedly, (E) is incorrect because the passage implies the exact opposite belief on the part of the Russians. (B) and (C) are incorrect because the author specifically indicates in the fourth paragraph that American readers have no problem understanding Twain's work. In this same paragraph he also expresses the belief or hope that Russian readers do as well.

5.   **(B)**   The author makes this point in the fourth paragraph, more specifically, in the last two sentences. (A) is incorrect because the author tells us American

readers (at least) understand Twain and there is no indication that this understanding was only recently achieved. (C) is incorrect because the author's treatment of Twain is favorable throughout the passage, and there is no indication the author believes Twain should not be highly regarded. (D) would certainly affect how many people in the Soviet Union have access to Twain's work, but the author is not concerned with the question of access. His concern is, of those with access to Twain's work, how many like what they have read and why. Thus, (D) is incorrect. As for (E), it is reasonable to infer that the author does believe some of Twain's critics to be inept, but this does not explain why Twain is popular. If (E) were correct, it would suggest a belief by the author that if the critics were better, Twain would not be so popular. This in turn leads to the conclusion that the author thinks Twain is overrated and we have seen this is not the case.

6.   **(A)**   The whole tenor of the author's discussion, including his mention of his friend's comments, leads to this conclusion. That (B) is incorrect is clear simply from the author's "light-years" remark in the second paragraph. From this same remark we can conclude the author is also not neutral to these analyses, making (D) incorrect. (C) is incorrect because there is no indication of whether the author *trusts* the analyses, rather, he believes them to be in error. Similarly, (E) is incorrect because there is no indication that the author has accepted as a fact of life that such analyses, even ones he thinks are wrong, exist. The author's point is that the analyses try to find hidden meanings in writing the author and most readers find to be very clear.

7.   **(D)**   The author makes this point via his friend's comments in the first paragraph. The author shows (A) to be incorrect in telling us how clear and realistically Twain writes, and by describing his popularity. It is unlikely these would be true if his writing was aloof. The author's critical attitude toward in-depth analyses which suggest hidden meanings in Twain's writings makes (B) incorrect. The author mentions the Russian belief that Twain was critical of democratic morals, but does not make any comments about whether he feels Twain to have been *too* critical. Thus, (E) is incorrect. One might conclude that Twain's writing was simple. If his writing was clear and realistic and humorous, suggesting it was also simple (as in not complex) is not unreasonable. Nevertheless, *simplistic* is generally used in a negative sense. Thus, even if we infer that the author believes Twain's writing to be simple, there is nothing to suggest he believes it to be *too* simple, making (C) incorrect.

8.   **(A)**   The first paragraph tells us Marshall was a Federalist, but not an extreme one, and a nationalist. The second and third paragraphs elaborate on these facts and discuss their results in the form of the decisions made by the Marshall Court. The author does suggest in the final paragraph that doctrines evolved under Marshall's centralizing tendencies helped to preserve the Union, but this is only one result of the overall theme of the passage. Thus, (B) is incorrect. (C) is incorrect because there is no indication in the passage that

Marshall was disloyal to the Federalists (disagreement does not equal disloyalty), nor that the author is criticizing Marshall for his politics. The passage does incidentally concern the role of the Supreme Court in national politics. It must if it is to discuss the politics of Marshall while he was chief justice of the Court. The focus of the passage, however, is narrowly concentrated on Marshall, rather than on the broader topic of the Supreme Court in general. Thus, (D) is incorrect. (E) is incorrect because the passage is too short to be considered much of a *chronicle* of Marshall's time as chief justice (a position we are told he held for 34 years). In addition, the passage only focuses on one aspect of Marshall's politics; too narrow a focus to be considered a chronicle.

9.   **(D)**   We are told this in the second sentence of the first paragraph. The author describes Marshall as a "Lockean republican." This is a description of Marshall's politics, not the political party to which he belonged. Locke (with an "e") was of course a noted political philosopher. Thus, to say Marshall was "Lockean" means his philosophy was like that of Locke. In addition, there was no *Locke* political party. Thus, (A) is incorrect. (B) is incorrect as well. The use of the small *r* in the description "Lockean republican" indicates that *republican* refers to a political philosophy not a political party. The author does mention the Republican Party, but only to say Marshall's politics were compatible with those of this party. By telling us this, we can conclude Marshall did not belong to this party. (C) is incorrect because, again, the small *d* indicates a political philosophy rather than the Democratic Party. (E) is incorrect because there is no mention in the passage of an Independent Party.

10.   **(C)**   We are told this in the last two sentences of the first paragraph. From these sentences, in particular where we are told Marshall believed property to be the "foundation of civil liberty," (B) is clearly wrong. In these same sentences Marshall is described as Lockean. We are then told this means he viewed property "not as an economic end in itself," making (A) incorrect. (D) is incorrect because there is no indication in the passage that property should only be held by the upper class. We are told Marshall distrusted the common people, but this is in relation to majoritarian politics, not property. Similarly, (E) is incorrect because the author does not make a connection between Marshall's view of property and his desire for a centralized government.

11.   **(A)**   In the first sentence of the second paragraph we are told Marshall strongly supported centralization and "completely rejected the compact theory." Later in the paragraph the author tells us Marshall was committed to "federal authority versus states' rights." From these comments we can conclude that the compact theory supported states' rights, which also makes (D) incorrect. (In addition, though a minor point, the resolutions the author associates with the compact theory are named for two states, Virginia and Kentucky.) (C) must be incorrect if Marshall rejected the compact theory. In addition, we are told Marshall died in 1835, well before the start of the Civil War. Although we are told Marshall

was not an extreme Federalist, it should still be clear that the Federalists, extreme or otherwise, were in favor of a strong central (federal) government. Thus, the compact theory cannot be a theory of the extreme Federalists, making (B) incorrect. (E) is incorrect because the passage makes no mention of jurisprudential activism or what that means.

12.   **(E)**   We are told this in the second paragraph when the author says Marshall "tended to distrust the common people." The author continues by indicating Marshall also saw legislative democracy as a threat to his (Marshall's) view of constitutionalism. Given this distrust, Marshall cannot be said to have been either supportive or nurturing toward mass democratic politics, making both (B) and (D) incorrect. Similarly, (C) is incorrect because by distrusting the common people and seeing a threat to constitutionalism Marshall is not being indifferent. (A) is incorrect because the author uses the word *hostile* to refer to Marshall's perceived conflict between legislative majoritarianism and constitutionalism.

13.   **(D)**   From the passage we can conclude that *federalism* is related to the policies of the Federalists, and we know that they supported a centralized government. In the third paragraph the author discusses the significance of judicial review under the Marshall Court. We are also told how Marshall's doctrines (which we were previously told had strong centralizing tendencies) supported national supremacy. From all of these pieces we can conclude judicial review was a mechanism used by the Marshall Court to support federalism. (A) is incorrect because we can conclude from the last sentence of the passage that the author believes Marshall was successful in his centralizing policies. (B) is nonsensical because it is clear from the passage that the Marshall Court did not have *decentralizing* policies. (C) is incorrect because there is no mention in the passage of the causes of the Civil War. The author only notes that doctrines developed by the Marshall Court later helped to preserve the Union. (E) is incorrect because the author tells us in the third paragraph that the practical effects of Marshall's policies were felt most strongly on "state legislatures rather than Congress."

14.   **(D)**   This can be concluded from the author's comments in the last sentence of the second paragraph where he says Marshall's "principles placed him near the mainstream of American politics." This comment also makes (A) incorrect. (A) is also incorrect because we are told in the first paragraph that Marshall did not agree with the extremist ("reactionary") wing of his own party. (B) is incorrect because there is no mention of what constitutes right- or left-wing politics. Given *current* definitions Marshall might be considered nearer to the right than the left, but this neither obviates the fact we are told his politics were "mainstream," nor is it sufficient to characterize Marshall as right-wing. (C) and (E) are incorrect because we are told in the second paragraph that Marshall distrusted the common people and saw legislative majoritarianism as a threat to constitutionalism.

15. **(B)** The author begins the passage by telling us that although Pluto was discovered many years ago, we know little about it. In the next few paragraphs the author briefly mentions what little we do know about Pluto and its satellite Charon, and how Pluto was discovered. In the final two paragraphs the author returns to the argument that further exploration is needed. To some extent, (A), (C), and (D) are mentioned in the passage. Nevertheless, each is there only to add to the overall argument in favor of additional exploration and is not the main focus. Thus, (A), (C), and (D) are all incorrect. (E) is also incorrect. From the passage we may conclude that the author does want additional funding, but there is no *criticism* of current spending levels. The author is emphasizing the positive aspects of additional spending, rather than the negative aspects of current levels.

16. **(C)** In the first sentence the author describes Pluto as the "ninth planet," but we do not know whether this refers to distance or order of discovery. Later in the passage we are given more information and can deduce that at the time Pluto was discovered it meant both. We are also told in the fourth paragraph that Pluto's highly elliptical orbit at times brings it closer to the sun than Neptune. In the next sentence the author directly states that between 1979 and 1999 Pluto had been closer to the sun than Neptune. Thus, (D) is incorrect. (E) is wrong because Sol is another name for the sun. (B) is wrong because the author tells us in the fourth paragraph that Pluto's orbit is 30 to 50 times that of Earth. Thus, at a minimum, Pluto is 30 times farther from the sun than the Earth. As a satellite of Pluto, Charon is necessarily very close to Pluto. We are not told exactly how close, but it is reasonable to assume close enough that Charon is not farther from the sun than Neptune at the same time Pluto is closer than Neptune. If this assumption was not the case, and keeping in mind the author has told us Pluto had been closer to the sun than Neptune in 1990, to correctly answer the question it would be necessary to know exactly where Charon was in its orbit around Pluto at the time of answering this question — certainly an unreasonable requirement.

17. **(D)** We are told in the fourth paragraph that Tombaugh first saw Pluto as part of a "methodical photographic survey," which can be considered a systematic research plan. We know (A) to be incorrect because the person who inspired the survey, Lowell, did so in hopes of finding a planet beyond Neptune ("trans-Neptunian"). Thus, Neptune was discovered before Pluto, not the other way around. (B) is also incorrect. We are not told whether there was any theoretical justification for expecting there to be another planet beyond Neptune, but given Lowell's interest and that the search was looking for such a planet, its discovery cannot be said to have been "an unexpected surprise." For the same reasons the discovery cannot be said to have been "fortuitous," making (E) incorrect as well. (C) is clearly wrong. We are told in the first sentence that Pluto was discovered over 60 years ago, and in the third paragraph that the *Voyager* 2 fly-by was quite recent. In addition, the author tells us in the first paragraph that no scientific spacecraft has visited Pluto, so the *Voyager* 2 could not have been involved in Pluto's discovery.

18. **(E)**   In the passage the author uses the terms "methane ice" and "water ice." Under normal room temperature methane is a gas and water is a liquid. "Water," or more accurately H_2O, is commonly known in its solid form as "ice." This should indicate that the author is talking about something in a solid form. In addition, it is common knowledge that H_2O is a gas at high temperatures. As it cools it becomes a liquid, and if cooled further a solid. Given Pluto's and Charon's distance from the sun (30 to 50 times that of earth) we can surmise it is quite cold, allowing for the possibility that materials which usually may be in gaseous form on earth (methane) are in solid form there. (A) is incorrect because the author refers to two different types of "ice," so it cannot just be frozen water. (B) is incorrect because atmosphere is a gas and the author speaks of "ice" as a solid. In addition, the author tells us Pluto's atmosphere may freeze (an indication of going to a solid state) and fall to the surface as snow, more or less a form of ice. (C) is wrong because it is clear the author is speaking of a solid so the term cannot refer to *liquid* methane. (The author's use of the term "water ice" may be confusing, but he uses it to differentiate that type of ice from methane ice. He is using *water* to refer to the chemical composition rather than the physical state of the ice.) In addition, because the author refers to two types of ice, it could not be just liquid *methane*. Materials are in their solid state at temperatures lower than their liquid or gaseous states, but because materials reach their solid states at greatly different temperatures the author could not have used the term to refer to surface temperature, making (D) incorrect.

19. **(C)**   We are told this in the third paragraph when the author defines planetesimals as "relics from the early days of the solar system." Knowing the solar system is very old makes these astronomical bodies (*astronomical* means having to do with the science of the stars, planets, and other heavenly bodies). Because the author also tells us Pluto is the approximate size of both its own satellite (Charon) and one of Neptune's (Triton), we can conclude it is small, at least compared with other astronomical bodies. (A) is incorrect because the author calls Pluto a planetesimal and notes that it has survived as a "bona fide planet." (B) is incorrect because the author's language indicates planetesimals are small. If they were the giant outer planets one may wonder why the author does not call Neptune a planetesimal or mention Saturn, Jupiter, or Uranus. Since the author clearly indicates planetesimals are left over from the early days of the solar system they cannot be spacecraft, which cannot be more than about 40 years old (at least not if they are from this planet). Thus, (D) is incorrect. The author does suggest Pluto and its satellite Charon can be considered a double planet, but the author does not mention Charon in discussing planetesimals, only Pluto, an independent planet, and Triton, a satellite of Neptune. Thus, (E) is incorrect.

20. **(D)**   In the fourth paragraph we are told that Pluto's orbit is "highly elliptical," which is essentially oval shaped, and therefore *not circular*. (A) is clearly wrong because the author tells us in the fourth paragraph that Pluto's orbit is 30 to 50 times that of earth. By telling us Pluto's orbit is 30 to 50 times larger

than the earth's, he is not suggesting that it is *unknown*, only that the distance from the sun *varies* as Pluto traces its non-circular orbit. Thus, (B) is incorrect. The author also tells us in this paragraph that Pluto's orbit is inclined 17 degrees to the plane of the earth's orbit, but perpendicular means 90 degrees so (C) is incorrect. (E) is incorrect because we are told Triton is a satellite of Neptune and can conclude its orbit follows Neptune's. Since we are also told Pluto's orbit is sufficiently different from Neptune's to occasionally bring it closer to the sun, Pluto's orbit cannot be similar to Triton's.

21.   **(A)**   In the first paragraph of the passage the author indicates Pluto has not been explored by spacecraft. In the fifth paragraph the author describes the benefits of sending *two* spacecraft to explore Pluto. If only *one* were sent, the author would undoubtedly be pleased that at least some exploration of Pluto is occurring. Nevertheless, by arguing for two, it should also be clear that the author would not be *satisfied* or *ecstatic* with only one. Thus, both (B) and (E) are incorrect. The author's tone in the passage does not suggest he is concerned about some exploration of Pluto versus *none*. By arguing for two spacecraft the author seems comfortable with the probability that at least one craft will be sent. Thus, it cannot be said that he would be relieved if only one was sent, making (C) incorrect. Certainly the author would not be distressed if Pluto was explored; this is what the author is arguing for. From another point of view, there is no indication in the passage that the author *expects* there to be more than one spacecraft sent to explore Pluto. If he did expect this, arguing for two in the passage would not make sense. Thus, (D) is incorrect.

22.   **(D)**   The author begins the passage by introducing the Sophists as a group who had an answer to a conflict between Heraclitus and Parmenides. The passage continues by describing the beliefs of the Sophists, and concludes by suggesting many in the contemporary world hold beliefs similar to those of the Sophists. (A) is incorrect because Heraclitus is only mentioned in the first sentence as being in conflict with Parmenides, and we are not told what his philosophy was. Thus, the author cannot be said to be criticizing it. (B) is incorrect because there is no indication in the passage that the author believes skepticism to be the correct view. In fact, to suggest as much would be counter to the moral relativism advanced by the Sophists. In the first paragraph we are told of one argument made by Protagoras in order to illustrate a skeptical argument. The argument is not explained in detail and is not returned to later in the passage. We cannot say, therefore, that explanation of this argument was the primary purpose of the passage, making (C) incorrect. For reasons similar to (B), (E) is also incorrect. The passage contains no indication that the author is advocating one philosophical position over another, or seeking to do anything other than describe skepticism.

23.   **(B)**   We are told in paragraph one that Protagoras was the best known of the Sophists. In the second paragraph we are told Thrasymachus is also a Sophist. In the first sentence of paragraph one we are told the Sophists had an answer to

the conflict between Heraclitus and Parmenides. This leads to the conclusion that neither Heraclitus or Parmenides were Sophists, making (A) and (E) incorrect based on the reasonable assumption that Thrasymachus is more likely to agree with another Sophist than a non-Sophist. (C) and (D) are both incorrect because neither is mentioned in the passage.

24. **(C)** This point is made in the middle of the first paragraph when the author defines skepticism as "the philosophic position of doubting the possibility of any true knowledge." The point is made again in the last two sentences of the second paragraph. (A) is incorrect because the author notes only some of the more radical Sophists argued one need not obey laws one does not believe in. In addition, by the skeptical standard, one cannot be considered lawless if one only disobeys those laws one does not believe in. (B) is incorrect because there is no mention in the passage of divine enlightenment, the gods, or the supernatural. (D) is incorrect because there is no indication in the passage that the author is critical of skepticism. The author merely describes the arguments the skeptics make. (E) is incorrect because the author notes in the first paragraph that the Sophists, the originators of skepticism, traveled from city to city and finally came to Athens in the fifth century B.C.

25. **(A)** This point is made in the first sentence of the fourth paragraph. (B) is incorrect for two reasons. First, the author does not directly comment on the applicability of skepticism. Again, he is merely describing it, not evaluating it. Second, indirectly, by noting many in the *contemporary* world hold beliefs similar to the Sophists it suggests their beliefs do apply to the modern world. (C) is incorrect because the author tells us in the first paragraph that the Sophists came from many societies and were well-traveled. (I suppose the same could be said of the Huns, but they did not travel from city to city debating philosophy.) (D) is incorrect because Plato is not mentioned in the passage. (E) is incorrect because the author gives no indication the Sophists were either short-lived or unimportant. On the contrary, by noting that many in the modern world share their beliefs it suggests they were important. In addition, the word *cult* is usually associated with religious groups, and there is no mention of the Sophists' religious beliefs in the passage.

26. **(E)** This point is made in the next to last sentence of the second paragraph where the author tells us the Sophists "argued that all moral and political principles are relative." (A) is incorrect because as described by the author the Sophists are not rejecting all forms of government (anarchy) as unjust, they only argue that moral and political principles are relative. The author notes that only some of the more radical Sophists advocated obeying only those laws it is to your advantage to obey, but this still falls short of anarchy. (B) is incorrect because it does not make sense in the context of the passage. There is no indication that all laws or society itself is irrelevant. (C) is incorrect because trickle-down theory deals with economics and there is no mention in the passage of the Sophists' position on economics. (The brief mention in the fourth paragraph of "economic

inflation" is used as an example of how the Sophists' beliefs might be used by some today.) Similarly, (D) is incorrect because there is no mention of how the Sophists felt about government in general, or various types of government.

27. **(B)** The author tells us this in the last half of the first paragraph by describing Protagoras's argument questioning any assertions of finding a true reality. (A) is incorrect because, as described, Protagoras's argument dealt with reality not morality. Nevertheless, the two are not mutually exclusive. Protagoras argues against an absolute position. Moral *ambiguity* does not suggest an absolute assertion of any kind, and, thus, must not be part of Protagoras' argument. Although *scientific* findings are not directly mentioned, it can be reasonably assumed that the Greek attempts to discover reality called into question by Protagoras included what the Greeks considered science as well as philosophy. Nevertheless, (C) is incorrect because it is too narrow and would be included in the more general option (B). (D) is incorrect because there is no mention in the passage of urban structures. Even if we read urban structures to mean society, there is no mention of how the Sophists felt about the structure of society as a whole, as opposed to specific laws. (E) is incorrect because there is no mention of how the Sophists felt about the distribution of property. Even if one were to assume this corresponded with the idea that the laws are designed to maintain the power of those who have it, it still does not suggest the Sophists advocated any particular distribution of property. According to the passage, the Sophists would only argue that *no* distribution is absolute and unchangeable.

28. **(B)** The author makes this point in the first sentence of the second paragraph when he says the Sophists turned Greek philosophy "toward the study of human beings and their moral, social, and political life." Another portion of the same sentence tells us Greek philosophy was turned away from the physical sciences, making both (A) and (C) incorrect. (D) is incorrect because, although we may reasonably assume the Sophists did not agree with all aspects of Greek society, we are not told the Sophists believed Greek society to have the kind of problems which could be characterized as *urban decay* (even if we allow for the types of problems which may have existed at that time). (E) is incorrect because we are not told specifically about whether the Sophists were interested particularly in legal structures, because it is too narrow, and since it is a part of society as a whole.

Section III – Logical Reasoning

1. **(A)** The basic argument has the form "If A then B, but not B, therefore not A," with "The bombs will go off" as A and "The fuses are on" as B. This is obviously the form of the argument in (A), with "Jim was at the dance" as A and "Martha was at the dance" as B. (Note, "only if" acts like "then" in "if ... then

..." constructions; the original claim is clearly not "If the fuses are on the bombs will go off.") The form of the argument in answer (B) is "If A then B, but not A, so not B," which is not only a different form, but also is invalid while the original argument is valid. The argument in answer (C) is valid but of a different form again, this one involving generality ("all" and the like) rather than "if ... then ..." conditionals. These other notions do not occur in the original argument. The argument in (D) has the form "If A then B, but B, so A," again involving "if ..., then ..." but different from the original argument and invalid. Finally, the argument in (E), whatever its form, is different from the original argument because it is invalid while the original is not.

2. **(E)** The argument begins by referring to a set of reports, which will turn out to be those by opponents, as "self-serving." These same opponents are later referred to as "hardened unbelievers" but no evidence is given that the reports are unreliable; they are simply dismissed with an epithet. So, (A) clearly occurs and is not the missing item. A case of (B) follows immediately, for the fact that some cases are not proven to be standard is taken as proof that they are not standard, rather than that they are still undetermined and rather than providing positive evidence that they are nonstandard. In the process, the cases which have not been proven standard are singled out as being genuinely unidentified — "real UFOs." This special status becomes a new definition of *UFO* at the end when the claim is made that all UFOs (namely that used to be called UFOs but that have not been explained in the standard way) are really nonstandard. This move is that sketched in (C), so it does occur. Finally, the only alternative to the standard explanation that is allowed is the extreme opposite of paranormal crafts, ignoring weaker nonstandard explanations like rare natural phenomena and even less extreme paranormal ones like visitors from nearby planets. This is just fault (D). The missing technique must, then, be (E). And, indeed, there is no effort in this argument to refute the views of opponents at all, let alone misrepresented views. Rather, a reasonably accurate report of what opponents say is used to appear to support the proponent's view.

3. **(D)** The test taker is being asked to find what is shown by the response that "'desire' means 'ought to be desired,' while 'visible' means only 'can be seen.'" The response, then, does not dispute that people desire pleasure (A), but it does dispute that the fact that people desire something would mean it can be said to be "desirable." (D) is the best answer because it points out that Mill does not show that pleasure "ought to be desired" and thus does not show it is desirable. (B) is incorrect; the fact that people desire pleasure is not disputed. (C) is incorrect; the response does not necessarily say that pleasure is not desirable, only that Mill has not proven that it is. Because (E) states that pleasure ought not to be desired, it is a poor choice; neither Mill nor the response necessarily tries to assert this.

4. **(A)** The passage concludes that politics is a perplexing subject (A), based on the premises that it has been discussed for thousands of years (B) and it

has a different meaning today than it had in the past (D). The passage neither claims nor implies that politics has Biblical roots (C) or that Aristotle was one of the earliest authorities on politics (E): It merely uses the Bible and Aristotle as examples of ancient sources of political views.

5.   **(B)**   The argument is that the poem is political because it reflects Milton's views about the relationship between politics and moral activity (B). It argues this on the grounds that it promotes liberty and responsibility (D), recognizes virtue as the source of this liberty, may be read as a guide to piety and submission (E), and portrays the appropriate relations between men and women (A).

The poem posits virtue as a source of liberty; it does not say liberty is virtue (C).

6.   **(E)**   The argument that Molière was influenced by Italian forms of comic theatre is based in the premises that Molière's company shared space with an Italian troupe and that Molière allegedly modelled his acting style on Tiberio Fiorilli. The assumption in the second premise is that Fiorilli was Italian, so if he was Argentinean (E), this would weaken the argument.

If Molière's troupe shared acting space with Italians for seven years instead of two (A), this would strengthen the argument, not weaken it. Whether or not there were several forms of comic theatre in Italy (B) is irrelevant to the premises that an Italian troupe and an Italian actor influenced Molière. Answer (C) is also irrelevant, since the argument is about Molière, not about his troupe or the size of his troupe. That other facts might strengthen the argument (D) does not necessarily make the argument weaker as it stands — the current premises might make the argument sufficiently probable to make further help unnecessary.

7.   **(D)**   The author is trying to conclude that the French Revolution of 1848 was an accident (D). He bases the conclusion on the premises that there were no emerging, uncontrollable social forces that would have made the revolution necessary (E), and it probably resulted from inherent weakness in government (C). Thus the author is denying that the revolution was inevitable (A) and that it occurred because new social forces could not be contained (B).

8.   **(B)**   One reason the author says Peirce was hard to understand is that Peirce was erudite and wrote for a varied audience. Thus, it would be inconsistent to claim that Peirce avoided erudition (D) or wrote for a specific audience (A).

Another reason is that Peirce promoted pursuit of publicly verifiable knowledge, rather than private interests, as the way out of moral confusion. Thus, it would be inconsistent to say Peirce emphasized private interest (C) or believed pursuit of publicly verifiable knowledge would lead to moral confusion (E).

A third reason is that Peirce creates his own technical terms, an assertion with which answer (B) *is* consistent.

9.   **(E)**   The author is trying to prove that the rate of inflation must fall by

more than the reduction in money growth, if a certain stage occurs in a disinflation process initiated by a discrete reduction in the growth rate of the money stock (E). It is evident that he is trying to prove this from the sentence which follows it, a sentence beginning "The reason is that...." The reason he offers is given in answer (A): Demand for real balances in the new low inflation steady state will be higher than in the high inflation equilibrium. The elaboration of the reason is given in answer (B): Economy produces real balances by causing price levels to grow more slowly than the nominal money stock. Answer (D) — sometimes a high inflation equilibrium is lower than demand for real balances — is implied by answer (A), and is an assumed *premise* of the argument, not what the author is trying to prove.

The author never asserts or implies that at some stage in disinflation there is a distinct reduction in the growth rate of the money stock (C).

10. **(E)** The claim is that in its ugly architecture, England has failed where the old Italian and Dutch masters succeeded in creating beautiful architecture (E). Thus, England deserves the scolding it gets, contrary to answer (D). England's architecture is ugly, contrary to answer (B). And people are more apt to find beauty in other lands than in England, contrary to answer (C).

The author does not use as support the fact that the Prince of Wales was satirized (A), although he does rely on the point of the satire as support for his argument.

11. **(A)** The author is trying to defend the claim that Black English is not the cause of all black problems in America (A) and that beliefs to the contrary should be resisted. Among those who do believe the contrary are people who claim that Black English is the primary source of educational problems in black children in poor neighborhoods (B) and that black children lack facility with the standard English found in textbooks because of their overwhelming reliance on Black English as a method of communicating (D), (E).

The author does concede that little research has been done concerning the relationship between Black English and reading abilities (C), but he states this without trying to defend it and, in fact, uses it in defense of his position.

12. **(E)** The writer is trying to justify making a distinction between "civilization" and "culture." He claims that the two are different, because civilization refers to more than a set of collective norms and values of a particular group (B), which implies that this set is what "culture" refers to (E). The writer never says or implies that anthropologists have long recognized the distinction between "civilization" and "culture" (A), only that they have long accepted a definition of "culture." He does not say definitional games are useful (C), although he states that some are not fruitful. And he does not say that avoiding old questions will allow us to be clear about what civilization is (D). Finally, while the term "culture" refers to the collective norms and values of a particular group, the writer never claims that these groups actually exist or that their existence would support his argument.

13. **(A)**   According to this argument, if something is sensible (e.g., visible or audible) then it must be sensed (e.g., seen or heard). And by analogy, if something is desirable, then it must be desired. The argument would be weakened if it were possible that a person regarded something as desirable, but didn't desire it (A) (as, for example, a recovering alcoholic who regards abstinence from alcohol as desirable, even though he desires a drink). The argument would not be weakened by the fact that one cannot prove something is visible (audible) unless one sees (hears) it ((B) and (C)), because these assertions are already offered as premises. Further, since the argument states that knowledge of sensibility is acquired through the senses, answer (E) would not weaken the argument.

Answer (D) is a bit trickier to assess. While the argument states that desirability entails desire, it does not say desire entails desirability (just as being a man entails being human, but being human doesn't necessarily entail being a man). Thus, the argument will not be weaker if it is possible that there are other ways besides desirability to prove something is desired (D).

14. **(A)**   The writer admits that he could be deceived about some things, but not about the fact that he exists. Thus he tries to prove that as soon as he thinks "I am," he necessarily knows that he exists as a thinking thing (A). The fact that he thinks (B) is offered as one of the premises to support what he is trying to prove. He makes no assumption about whether he exists only in his own mind (D) or whether he exists only when he thinks he exists (C). And he is only claiming certainty for himself; he does not argue that everyone is certain that he (the writer) exists (E).

15. **(A)**   The writer argues that a sentence is true when it corresponds to a fact, and it is false when it contradicts a fact. Thus the sentence "the sun is out" is true, if the sun really is out (A). Whether or not someone has the opinion that the sun is out (B), believes the sun is out (C), or really thinks the sun is out (E), is irrelevant: the truth of the sentence depends on the facts, not belief about the facts.

Also the writer states that even if the sentence itself remains unaltered, its truth or falsity can change, so "the sun is out" may be true or may be false, even though the words of the sentence remain unaltered (D).

16. **(C)**   The point of this passage is that the maxim (guiding principle) behind an action, not the consequences of an action, determine whether or not the action is morally good. In other words, only if an action is done with good intentions is it a good act. Thus, an action done with evil intentions, but good consequences (C) would still be bad. An action done by someone who wants to do what is right could be good, regardless of the consequences (A). An action done by someone who is concerned about the maxim of it (B) could be good, provided the maxim were good. An action done out of appropriate volition (good will) (D) would be good. And an action done without regard to desirable objects or consequences (E) could be good.

17.   **(A)**   The argument claims that good and pain are not identical because the pair of contraries good/evil is not identical to the pair of contraries pleasure/pain. This assumes (but does not state explicitly) that if pairs of contraries are not identical, no contrary in one pair (e.g., good) can be identical to any contrary in the other pair (e.g., pleasure) (A). If the proposition in answer (A) were true, therefore, it would make the argument stronger.

Whether or not something good may be pleasant (E), or something painful not be pleasant (B), is irrelevant to the argument.

The argument would be weaker if good and evil could exist together (D), since this would contradict one of the argument's premises. And since pains and pleasures could end together only if they could exist together, the argument would be weaker if pains and pleasures could not exist together (C).

18.   **(B)**   The writer is refuting the claim that the beauty of an object is in the object (A), because beauty is a value (C) and values exist in the perception of the person making the value judgment. The conclusion is, therefore, that beauty is in the eye (the perception) of the beholder (the perceiver) (B). Unlike beauty, the writer admits, color, proportion, and size are all properties of an object (D); but the writer is not trying to prove this. Similarly, he admits that we tend to believe other men see the beauties we see (E), but he is not trying to prove this either.

19.   **(C)**   The premises which the writer offers are (1) self is supposed to exist as an invariable and constant impression throughout one's whole life, and (2) there is no such impression (B). Therefore, the most reasonable inference of those listed is that we cannot determine what self is (C).

The writer does not assume or try to prove that our ideas of self come from impressions of self (A) or that self exists as an invariable idea (rather than impression) (E). And while the writer recognizes the supposition that our several impressions and ideas have reference to self (D), he does not infer this himself.

20.   **(E)**   The writer doubts, and thus tries to refute the claim that God speaks to men supernaturally and immediately, i.e., directly (E). He shows no intention of refuting the belief that God speaks through Holy Scripture (A) or through mediation of the prophets (B). Thus he is not refuting belief that there is a God (C). And he accepts the belief that one can dream about God speaking to him (D).

21.   **(E)**   The writer holds that preservation of humans is so important that we have the right to kill anything or anyone that threatens that preservation. Thus, capital punishment is justifiable when it will contribute to the protection of others (E). The fundamental law of nature calls for the preservation of all humans, if possible, and preservation of the innocent humans, where not all humans can be preserved. Such law need not lead to enmity between men (D) and does not necessarily call for the blanket killing of wolves and lions (C). Further, the law calls for the safety of humans, not the safety of wolves or lions (A).

Also, the writer implies that most people are under the ties of the common law of reason, since those who are not may be treated as beasts. Thus it is false to claim that people are not under such ties (B).

22. **(C)** Martin begins with "eventually" and talks about long-term effects. George talks about present and near future objects and activities, at most accepting solutions that will work for centuries. In short, Martin is taking a very long view and George a relatively short one. They probably do not disagree that much on the quality of the present space program equipment, for Martin urges its continued improvement and George dismisses it as inadequate for Martin's plans. So, (A) does not apply. Nor need their expectations of the effects of pollution (B) or of anti-pollution legislation (D) be that different. George merely sees that the problem can be staved off for a while, even if not forever, while Martin sees that the problem cannot be staved off forever, even if for a little while. They may even be equally committed to human survival (E) — George to getting through the present problems, Martin to the long haul. Only the time frames of their concerns are clearly different.

23. **(B)** The pattern set up in the premises is "When I am (age), I have a new obligation but also a new privilege (loosely related to the obligation)." This sets up the claim that each new obligation that comes with age should have a related privilege, the pattern of (B) — seeing R-rated movies to compensate for higher ticket prices. (C) does not demand a new privilege but only that the duty not be doubled with another duty. (A) fits the pattern of the premises exactly but is not marked as a conclusion. If taken as one, it is less plausible than (C) since nothing in the premises supports this further fact — that he will get this particular privilege — only that he ought to get some privilege. (D) does not fit because it is not age-related and, again, makes a factual claim, not one about a new privilege. Finally, (E) is about neither an age-triggered duty nor a related privilege.

24. **(B)** The question asked is about the environmental consequences of destroying the rain forest. The only environmental consequences discussed in the answer are of the use of commercial, artificial fertilizer. Thus, the original issue was not met. Since there is no general claim made, there is no generalization in need of support and (A) does not describe the case. Similarly, the industry reply does not misrepresent the cost of commercial fertilizer because it does not mention that issue. Thus, (E) is inappropriate. Nor is there any attack on the Greens in the reply (nor any evidence that the Greens had presented an argument rather than just raising an issue). So (D) does not fit. Finally, there is no case of a key word being used in what is clearly more than one meaning, so (C) does not fit.

25. **(A)** The fundamental principle is that everything with logical value is a pure study in form, since such studies are the only things allowed to have logical value: "All L are P." The other premise is that everything symbolic is a pure study in form, since nothing that is not is allowed to be symbolic: "All S are P."

The conclusion says that everything of logical value is symbolic, since only such things are allowed to have logical value: "All L are S." The argument in (A) has the same form, reading "pines" for "L," "cedars" for "S," and "evergreens" for "P." (B) has the form "All L are P. All P are S. Therefore, all L are S," which reverses the order of terms in the second premise. (C) also reverses the order of the terms in the first premise, to "All P are L." (D) might best be rendered "All P are L. All S are P. Therefore, all L are S," that is, with only the first premise turned around. Finally, (E) turns both the first premise and the conclusion, in effect reading "only" as "all": "All P are L. All S are P. Therefore, all S are L." Unlike the original argument and (A), (B) and (E) are valid.

26. **(D)** We can only begin to demonstrate a causal connection between flashes and winning if the percentage of winners was significantly higher among those who picked their numbers on the basis of a flash than among those who picked their numbers by some other means or, as in this case, if the percentage of people who picked their numbers by flash rather than other means were significantly higher among winners than among losers. And, without this possible causal connection, the question of clairvoyance does not even arise. So, (D) is needed to even start the parapsychologist's case. (C) may also play some role in demarcating the classes involved, winners and losers, but its role is merely preliminary to the major point in (D). (B) might have been an important statistic in a different experiment, one where the parapsychologist followed flash bettors to see what percentage won. The results would have been interesting if the percentage for the flash bettors was significantly greater than the percentage mentioned in (B). (A) and (E) seem to have no relevant role to play, since no claims are being made about machine bettors as a distinguished group among those who do not bet on the basis of a flash and the fact that the argument deals with percentages within the various groups makes the percentage of the total population that lies in the groups irrelevant.

Section IV – Logical Reasoning

1. **(B)** The writer supports the conclusion with three premises: the leader was ridiculed by political adversaries at home (A); Baltic republics threatened to peel away (C); and the economy had not been reformed enough (D), although too much reform would have also hurt the economy (E).

   The writer never claims that America looked stronger by comparison; thus, (B) is not one of the premises.

2. **(A)** Based on the premise that everyone is occasionally induced to eat beyond physiological need (C), because sensory dominance may lead to improper nutrition (E), the writer *concludes* that sensory qualities of available foods can determine eating behavior (A). The writer mentions, but does not try to argue, that nutrition as a discipline examines the interaction of nutrient ingestion

(B) and tastes and aromas can be delicious (D).

3. **(A)** The writer concludes that the variety of views about economic reforms is natural to socialism (A). One of the premises for the conclusion is that socialism's strength derives from diversity (D). The writer never suggests, either as a premise or as a conclusion, that there is one appropriate model of economic management for socialism (B), that socialism should seek a single, uniform point of view regarding economic reforms (C), or that there is no necessity for such reforms (E).

4. **(E)** Answer (E) is contrary to the writer's conclusion that small metropolises in 1840 controlled and coordinated rural economies. One premise is that there were few metropolises, but most of their commodity output was agricultural. If the metropolises, e.g., Baltimore, were smaller than the writer declares (A), this would not hurt the argument. Another premise is that the metropolises had access to the rural community primarily by waterways and primitive roads. An extra thousand miles of railroad track (B) or the few roads and turnpikes relative to today (C) would not hurt the argument, as long as waterways and primitive roads were the principal access routes. And the writer allows for the possibility that commodity output included 28% nonagricultural products (D), so this would not weaken the argument.

5. **(E)** The writer argues *against* the suggestion that *The Tempest* is a bad, boring play (A), (B), on the grounds that the play is a part of the central discourse of the Renaissance (E). As support for this argument, the writer notes that the play contains a series of conspiracies (C) and that it was one response to the difficult social problems in late Elizabethan and early Jacobean London (D).

6. **(C)** The writer is trying to draw an analogy between the *comfort* people feel with unfamiliar airports and groceries on the one hand, and the *comfort* they should feel with unfamiliar libraries on the other (C). The writer is not drawing any analogy between merely going to airports or groceries, and going to a library (B), between unfamiliar airports and unfamiliar groceries (A), or between the layouts and collections of one organization and the layouts and collections of any other (E). Nor is the writer arguing for the idiosyncratic nature of airports, groceries, or libraries (D).

7. **(B)** The argument implies that the boy's drug-dealing in the streets allows him not to think about troubles at home, and, therefore, life in the street must be a relief for the boy. If there is such distraction, including, e.g., a chance not to think about his brother (B), then the argument is strengthened. If there is no such distraction, the argument is weakened whether or not the mother avoids her kids (C), the sister is pregnant (D), the father failed to burn down the house (A), or Philadelphia's landlords cannot evict people for failing to pay rent (E).

8. **(B)**   The argument *concludes* that it is difficult to decide how best to make use of 18th and 19th century terminology for causes of death, thus (A) cannot be a premise, since it is the conclusion. The argument's premises include the different concepts held by medical science in the past concerning the functions of the human body (B) and the specific nature of disease (C). Neither (D) nor (E) is offered as a premise in this argument.

9. **(D)**   The argument concludes that there should be serious study of Whitehead's thought because many scholars believe this thought has contributed to social and political theory, but no one has studied Whitehead's thought itself (B). If there has been such a study (D), then the argument is incorrect and, hence, weakened. Whether or not Whitehead's philosophy has actually made any contribution (A) is irrelevant to the premise that scholars *believe* it has and that they should therefore try to support their beliefs. It is also irrelevant to this belief whether determination of Whitehead's political thought is difficult (E) and whether he produced a systematic political theory (C).

10. **(B)**   The premises are as follows: Freedom (of will) is important to Leibniz's system (D). For him, freedom, but *not* weakness of will (B), involves absence of external impediments (A) and the power to will as one should (E), and freedom conflicts with weakness of will (C).

11. **(C)**   The writer explicitly denies that lacrosse generates high revenues (A), has forced many NCAA violations (B), receives strong support from athletic administrators (D), or leads to high paying professional contracts for its players (E). So these statements would all be inconsistent with the writer's assertions. However, if the writer's assertions are true, it is quite possible that lacrosse has remained consistent with traditional values of intercollegiate sports. Hence, answer (C) is consistent.

12. **(E)**   The passage *concludes* that students of literature should read all the "literatures" (E), on the *premise* that one literature casts light upon another (C). The passage suggests, but neither as a premise nor as a conclusion, that peoples of different times have their own literature (D). And the passage addresses students of conventional literature, but does not insist that all students must read such literature (A). Nor does it assert that the literature of a nation is the literature of an individual (B).

13. **(A)**   This passage notes the 1950s style of contemporary criticism of comic books (A). If the passage is correct, then answer (A) is necessarily true. One example of the criticism is *Time* magazine's claim that comic book violence is linked with juvenile delinquency. The passage does not claim that the *New York Times* shares this view (B), nor does it claim that this view is true (C). Similarly, it notes, but does not claim as true or false, the *New York Times'* denial that comic books have campy repartee and outlandishly byzantine plots (E). And

while the passage suggests that comic book publishers may exhibit poor judgment (D), it does not suggest that this is necessarily true.

14.   **(A)**   Since the ration of elderly to wage earners is increasing, it follows that, other things being equal, each wage earner will have to pay a higher percentage of his or her income for care of the elderly. This assumes that average income does not increase to the extent that it will make up the difference.

The other answers are all possibilities, but they do not follow directly from the information given. (B), (C), and (E) are contingent upon (D). Whether the elderly receive adequate care, and whether citizens would be advised to start saving their own funds to provide for their own needs, all depends, at least in part, on the willingness of future wage earners to pay the taxes needed to care for the elderly. There is nothing in the statement that implies that voters in the future will or will not vote for such taxes.

15.   **(B)**   The writer argues that great and important novels rarely make good films, while second-rate novels can be made into good films. To support this argument, the writer cites Hitchcock's "expertly filmed" version of *Rebecca*. Thus the writer is denying that *Rebecca* is a great novel (D) or an important novel (E). We may conclude, therefore, that he does not assume *Rebecca* was a great novel (B). We cannot tell from the passage whether Hitchcock made films other than *Rebecca* (A). And we cannot tell from the passage whether *all* (as opposed to most) well-written fiction is harder to film than second-rate writing (C).

16.   **(C)**   The writer *concludes* that vicarious adventure, acquired through books, is easier to handle than (and, by implication, preferable to) actual adventure (A). Thus it would be inconsistent to claim that actual adventure is preferable to vicarious adventure (C). As proof, the writer asserts that reading *King Lear* is better than being King Lear (B). The writer allows for the possibility that reading *King Lear* and being King Lear can arouse pity and fear, so answers (D) and (E) would not be inconsistent.

17.   **(E)**   Answer (E) is the *conclusion* of the argument: a fake burger can be healthier than a real one. As premises, the passage asserts that a real burger has more protein (A), protein sources can be fattening (B), too much protein can harm the kidneys (C), and protein can be hard to digest (D).

18.   **(D)**   The conclusion is that American community colleges need to recruit and provide staff development for a new cadre of faculty. If we accept this as true, merely restating it (C) doesn't strengthen the argument further. Similarly, if we have accepted the writer's assertions that community colleges needed new staff in the 1960s (A), leaders are often startled by staff needs (B), and the decade ahead will be challenging for the colleges (E), then restating these won't strengthen the argument.

The main premise is the example that 40% of California's full-time faculty

will be eligible for retirement in the next six years. If these faculty members actually retired (D), then this would strengthen the claim that colleges need to worry about staffing.

19. **(B)** According to the argument, confusion and hopelessness due to gradual loss of "bodily integrity" *may* cause aggression, but it is not the only possible cause. Thus answer (B) is not necessarily true. The argument posits structural damage in the brain (A), patient's confusion and care-giver's impatience (C), and task failure (E) as possible causes of aggression. And it implies that there is a difference between "bodily integrity" and structural damage in the brain (D), since it regards each as a cause of aggression different from the other.

20. **(B)** The number of American families earning $50,000 or more does not weaken the argument in the passage; (B) is the correct answer. If only 20,000 families earned more than $75,000 in 1986, the passage's argument — that the number of Latino families with incomes of $50,000 or more has increased steadily — is false. (A) would weaken the argument of the passage and is not the correct answer. If the number of Latino families with incomes of $50,000 were to dip (C), it would affect the argument of the passage. Answer (D) is vague; exactly what a level of affluence is can be interpreted in many ways. Is a level of affluence $50,000 or more? Because (D) is a vague answer, (D) is not an acceptable answer. If the number of Latino families earning $50,000 or more in 1980 was greater than the number earning above $50,000 in 1986, the major argument of the passage (that the number has increased steadily) would be in error; (E) is not the best answer because the reader does not have sufficient information to make a decision.

21. **(D)** The argument asserts that spending on and by kids was $60 billion last year and will be $75 billion this year. The difference, therefore, is $15 billion, not $10 billion, so answer (A) would be false. Because the percentage of overall economic growth (2%) and the percentage of growth in spending on and by kids (25) were *not* the same, item (B) is an incorrect answer. While the argument claims spending on kids is *one* of the fastest growing sectors of America's economy, this doesn't mean there is no faster growing sector of America's economy, so answer (C) is not necessarily true. And the argument claims that last year's spending on and by kids jumped 25%, not 2% as answer (E) claims.

However, if overall economic growth is 2% and spending on and by kids is jumping at least 25%, it must be true that overall economic growth is slower than spending on and by kids (D).

22. **(A)** The argument's *conclusion* is that, apparently, some housing markets are more prone than others to the impact of AIDS. Thus, (A), which states the conclusion, is correct. The argument's *premises* are that housing values and affordability vary from place to place in the U.S. (B) and that certain areas of the U.S. have high concentrations of AIDS cases (C). Thus answers (B), (C), (D), and (E) are incorrect, and answer (A) is correct. Although (D) and (E) could be

part of the conclusion, choice (A) wholly sums up the conclusion.

23. **(A)** On the *premises* that Hollywood and Madison Avenue have co-opted rap (B), (E), rap has been sanitized for mass appeal (C), and rap comments benignly on the human condition (D), the argument *concludes* that rap is popular even in non-musical areas of life (A).

24. **(C)** There are, undoubtedly, other seven-foot, 300-pound men in addition to Mrs. Smith's husband. Thus, (C) points out the logical flaw in her thinking. Choices (A) and (E) are psychological observations. They may or may not be valid psychologically, but they do not refer to mistakes in logic. Choices (B) and (D) offer points of general advice. Again, they may or may not be valid as advice, but they do not, in any case, refer to mistakes in logic.

LSAT Writing Sample – Demonstration Essay

The president's conclusion is an overly optimistic outlook for the future of the water park in the coming year. Its past success does not directly relate to that of the coming year, and the evidence adduced to support his claim of a banner year is inconclusive and relies on unjustified assumptions.

The extra summer vacation time of the Waterland public school system will not necessarily result in increased attendance at the water park. The president assumes both that these particular children comprise the water park's customers and that they will spend their extra vacation time at the water park. If a large number of customers come from other school districts or from private schools, then attendance at the park will be largely unaffected by Waterland's public school vacation policy.

Even if the park's clientele do attend Waterland public schools, the extra vacation time may still not translate into increased attendance. For instance, many children rely on their families for transportation. To equate more vacation time with more time spent at the park supposes that transportation, not to mention money, will be just as accessible in the newly expanded vacation time, which may not be so.

The president also suggests that the increased number of telephone calls regarding the coming season is auspicious, but the president makes two errors here. First, he assumes that an increase in phone calls means an increase in interest. Second, he assumes an increase in interest will translate into increased attendance. Both assumptions are problematic. With respect to the first, the calls could have come from people who had attended last year but had forgotten the dates the park was open. Or perhaps the details of the season were not as well advertised this year, requiring more phone calls from regular customers. Thus, the phone calls may not indicate any increased interest as compared with previous years.

Moreover, even if inquiries may be generally connected to an interest in the park, they need not translate directly into attendance. Inquiries could even have come from groups who have no intention of attending but who wanted to schedule their own event such that it did not conflict with the park's season opening. Thus, the increase in phone calls does not compel the conclusion that more people will attend, or even that there is more interest this year.

Admittedly, the Super-Duper Slide could draw greater attendance, but the public would need to know about the new attraction and be sufficiently moved to act on that knowledge. The president assumes that the water slide will necessarily entice more people to the park, but if it has not been advertised, it might not attract more customers. It would be helpful to know what steps have been taken to promote the slide.

While seemingly relevant to the park's success, extra vacation time, a new water slide, and more phone calls do not necessarily mean that business in the coming year will surpass that of last year. To determine whether the evidence he cites will lead to more business and a better year, the author would need to relate the increased vacation time to the profile of his clientele, demonstrate how the Super-Duper Slide will attract new customers and cause previous customers to return, and prove that incoming telephone calls are directly related to water-park attendance.

Demonstration Essay Explanation

This is a good essay because it organizes its analysis of the argument in a clear manner, emphasizing the weaknesses of the argument and ultimately suggesting how the argument could be strengthened. In addition, the essay demonstrates a good command of vocabulary.

The introduction, while short, is effective. It concisely indicates that the evidence adduced to support the conclusion of the argument is inconclusive and rests on unjustified assumptions.

The body of the essay then delves into the assumptions by taking up each piece of supporting evidence in turn. The essay argues that the additional vacation time may not have any effect on park attendance, because the children on vacation may not be the children likely to attend the park, and the children's ability to attend the park may rely on other factors, such as transportation. The essay also discusses the ambiguity of the increase in telephone calls, as well as hidden assumptions behind the claim that a new ride will increase attendance.

The essay's conclusion is also effective. It not only contains a good restatement of the thesis, but also indicates ways in which the argument needs to be strengthened.

LSAT

Law School Admission Test

TEST IV

TEST IV

Section I

Time—35 minutes
24 Questions

(Answer sheets appear in the back of this book.)

DIRECTIONS: The questions in this section are based on the reasoning contained in brief statements or passages. For some questions, more than one of the choices could conceivably answer the question. However, you are to choose the **best** answer; that is, the response that most accurately and completely answers the question. You should not make assumptions that are by commonsense standards implausible, superfluous, or incompatible with the passage. After you have chosen the best answer, blacken the corresponding space on your answer sheet.

1. The court unanimously concluded that a 1980 law protected observations made by reporters during news gathering, in addition to undisclosed, confidential notes or tapes. But the court also ruled unanimously that the law could not be used to violate a criminal defendant's constitutional right to a fair trial, and that testimony could be compelled if there was a "reasonable possibility the information will materially assist defense."

   Based on the rulings, which sentence is necessarily true?

   (A) A reporter could not be compelled to testify about any observations made during news gathering.

   (B) A defendant does not have to compel a reporter to testify about confidential notes or tapes.

   (C) A reporter's observations made during news gathering are confidential, unless they interfere with a defendant's right to a fair trial.

   (D) A reporter has the obligation to reveal his observations made during news gathering, unless such revelations violate the defendant's right to a fair trial.

   (E) Reporters must testify whenever a defendant demands such testimony.

2. Is Britain really a democracy? The question sounds absurd: 700 years of history, the vigor of the British press and television, free elections and the merciless cut and thrust of debate in the House of Commons at Prime

Minister's Question Time all argue that of course it must be. But a provocative argument can be made that democracy in Britain begins and ends
with national elections to the House of Commons every few years. After
that, a government with a healthy majority, like those of Prime Minister
Margaret Thatcher during the 1980s, can do just about anything it wants,
with few formal checks or controls — just convention, precedent, and
common sense, which in Britain are a more powerful balancing force than
written constitutions in many other countries.

Which one of the following is not an assumption of this argument?

(A) Common sense is a check against anti-democratic government.

(B) Britain's government was established democratically.

(C) Free debate occurs in the House of Commons.

(D) Britain would be more democratic if it had a constitution.

(E) Thatcher's government was not democratic.

3. In its current economic mess, the City of Toonton can take a lesson from
the corner wine shop owner. He will tell you: "You need cash? The worst
thing to do is raise prices and cut services. The best thing to do is trim
inventory." The city should heed that advice and sell its two major airports.

Which of the following sentences offers the best restatement of the writer's
argument?

(A) Airports are like wine shops in that they shouldn't raise prices and
cut services.

(B) Toonton should cut its airports just as a wine shop which is ailing
financially should cut its inventory.

(C) Wine shop owners are more successful than Toonton.

(D) Toonton is in economic trouble because it has raised prices and cut
services at its two major airports.

(E) Wine is to a wine shop what city-owned airports are to a city.

4. If money is the sole indication, then no animal is more adored by Congress
than a cow. Congress authorized $16.2 billion in subsidies over the last 10
years to bring the supply of milk in line with demand. Nor are the rangier,
more ornery beef cattle ignored. Congress has taken special care since the
1930s to provide them grass and water, at enormous expense to the treasury. Industry executives assert that no consumers in the world pay as little
for beef and milk as Americans, and the principal reason, they say, is
government subsidies.

Which of the following, if true, would necessarily weaken the conclusion of this argument?

(A)   Congress authorized $20 billion in subsidies over the past 10 years to bring the supply of pork in line with demand.

(B)   Congress authorized only $15.2 billion in subsidies over the last 10 years to bring the supply of milk in line with demand.

(C)   Consumers in other parts of the world pay higher prices for beef.

(D)   The dairy industry is larger than the beef industry.

(E)   The treasury has been able to handle the expense of providing grass and water to beef cattle.

5.   Researchers using an amazing new "radiation" camera designed for outer space photography have photographed at least 76 individuals they believe are extraterrestrials. The photos were taken in a major European city, but they suspect aliens have infiltrated human populations worldwide — including the U.S. These individuals show up in photos of crowds very clearly, according to the inventor of the camera, and their heads are surrounded by a faint green halo which the researchers believe is caused by radiation coming out from the individuals' brains.

Assuming the photos really show 76 individuals with "faint green halos" and that the camera was designed to detect radiation in space, which of the following conclusions is the most reasonable, based on the photos?

(A)   The individuals in the photos are extraterrestrials.

(B)   The source of the halo is radiation from the individual's brain.

(C)   Extraterrestrials exist not only in Europe, but also in the U.S.

(D)   The researchers are lying.

(E)   The halos are the result of certain light reflections and the unusual sensitivity of the camera.

6.   For 40 years you have heard on this day from the mouths of my predecessors, in a number of variations, the same thing: how our country is flourishing, how many more millions of tons of steel we have produced, how we are all happy, how we believe in our government. I assume you have not named me to this office, so that I, too, should lie to you.

Which of the following, if true, would support the speaker's assumption?

(A)   The country has been flourishing.

(B)   The people believe in the government.

(C) The citizens in the audience have not been happy.

(D) The speaker is not an official.

(E) The country has produced steel for 40 years.

7. The case against the defendant was as much the work of the prosecution's feverish imagination as a construction of the law. The circumstances that resulted in her arrest, trial, and imprisonment bespeak a condition of national hysteria not unlike the hysteria that seized the Massachusetts Bay Colony in the 17th century during the Salem witch trials. If the defendant was unjustly convicted, it is because we live in an age of trial by accusation. Our society at the moment is quick to condemn anybody and everybody charged, on the flimsiest of evidence, with the crime of abusing or molesting children.

Which of the following probably is the conclusion that the writer is attempting to support?

(A) The defendant is innocent of the crime for which she was convicted.

(B) The defendant was convicted of child abuse.

(C) Modern day trials have not advanced much since the Salem witch trials of the 17th century.

(D) Society is more tolerant of child abuse and molestation than murder.

(E) The prosecutor acted illegally.

8. For those who suffered in Hitler's death camps, and for those whose families died there, the suffering is never over. Bettelheim ended his own life on March 13. It could have been a case of simply having had enough, except that the date he chose was the date the Nazis entered Austria in 1938. He was a Viennese Jew who had spent 18 months in Dachau and Buchenwald. Like fellow author Primo Levi, who killed himself in 1987, and like hundreds of others, he never overcame survivor's guilt.

Which of the following assumptions is the writer making?

(A) Bettelheim committed suicide because he suffered so much in Hitler's death camps.

(B) Bettelheim committed suicide because he had enough of life.

(C) Bettelheim committed suicide because fellow author Primo Levi killed himself in 1987.

(D) Bettelheim was a Viennese Jew.

(E) Levi was in a Nazi death camp.

9. Every Chinese democrat shares the joy of the East European peoples who witnessed the collapse of communist totalitarianism in 1989. We also realize that the blood spilled in Tiananmen Square was the actual prelude to that great revolution. The Beijing Spring provided an example to the leaders of Eastern Europe, who surrendered to the popular will. The only way to explain the mostly peaceful climate in which the events took place is that the Tiananmen Square massacre aroused such indignation throughout the world that the governments of Eastern Europe did not dare repeat such horrors.

Which of the following is not an assumption of this argument?

(A) The event in Tiananmen Square led Eastern European countries to reject communism.

(B) The event in Tiananmen Square led to a peaceful revolution in Eastern Europe.

(C) Chinese democracy has led to the collapse of communist totalitarianism in China.

(D) The event in Tiananmen Square was a massacre.

(E) The Eastern European rejection of communism was in response to popular will.

10. It is common to hear Cubans say in one breath, "I would give my life for Fidel," and in the next, "I don't know how we put up with all the shortages." All positive aspects of the revolution are credited to Castro himself and kept in a separate compartment. A couple in line for ice cream echoed a refrain that has been familiar for several years: "If only Fidel knew how badly things worked, such as the buses or the telephones, he would chase out the incompetent officials." Fidel Castro has been chasing out incompetent officials in one speech after another for three decades.

Which of the following is the conclusion of this passage?

(A) Castro is not responsible for shortages.

(B) Castro has chased out incompetent officials.

(C) The buses and the telephones don't work in Cuba.

(D) The Cubans are giving Castro unjustified credit for chasing out incompetent officials.

(E) Cubans like Castro.

11. Israel's present system of high taxes, low wages, and a tortuous bureau-cracy stifles initiative, but it also makes us better fathers. Israel's ineffi-cient economy and relative lack of economic opportunity prevent most Israelis from sacrificing family values for the material rewards of financial success. True success to an Israeli father is getting the kids out the door each morning feeling good about themselves.

What is the main reason, offered in this passage, for the claim that Israelis are better fathers?

(A) Lack of economic opportunity allows Israelis to focus on family values rather than on material gain.

(B) Israeli children feel good about themselves.

(C) Israelis have economic opportunities that allow them material re-wards of financial success.

(D) Israelis have no initiative to reduce high taxes.

(E) Israelis have a tortuous democracy.

12. Mental illness is on the rise in Latin America, according to one theory, due to the worsening national economies and their attendant instability, unem-ployment, and lower living standards. Psychiatric disorders will continue to rise in the coming years, especially if the foreign-debt crisis is not solved. Twenty-five percent of Latin America's adult population suffers from psy-chological disorders, and 1.7 percent suffers from serious mental illness. The attribution of these ills to foreign debt cannot be scientifically de-duced, but the theory is a possible explanation and the region's govern-ments should be apprised of the problem.

Which of the propositions below is not consistent with this argument?

(A) One in four adult Latin Americans suffers from psychological disor-ders brought on by economic woes.

(B) The theory that mental illness in Latin America is caused by foreign debt can be scientifically deduced from the worsening national econo-mies and their attendant instability.

(C) Unemployment and lower living standards among adult Latin Ameri-cans have contributed to a rise in psychological disorders.

(D) Latin American governments are not fully aware of the connection between economic crisis and mental illness.

(E) Psychiatric disorders may continue to rise even if the foreign-debt crisis is solved.

13. The causes for intellectual alarm about the formation of the universe began in the mid-1980s. In 1987, the general acceptance of the Big Bang theory received a shock when a probe sent up by U.S. and Japanese researchers found distant energy emissions that suggested a series of secondary Big Bangs. The previous year, it was first noted that in addition to the uniform outward expansion of the universe, there seemed to be a gravitational pull toward a vast region subsequently named the Great Attracter. In April 1989, an Italian group identified another giant agglomeration of galaxies three times farther away.

Which statement best summarizes why the writer thinks there is intellectual alarm about the formation of the Universe?

(A)   Recent astronomical discoveries, including secondary Big Bangs and a giant agglomeration of galaxies, have caused people to question the Big Bang theory.

(B)   U.S. and Japanese researchers have found distant energy emissions.

(C)   There is a uniform outward expansion of the universe.

(D)   There are unexplained gravity pulls.

(E)   Italian researchers identified galaxies three times farther away than the Great Attracter.

14. Research suggests that analysis is frequently distorted, suppressed, or selectively represented in policy discussions. Administration officials have felt free to ignore or distort technical advice when it hasn't been compatible with their bureaucratic or political convenience. Similarly, analyses are cited when they bolster a particular ideological position, sealed when they are likely to embarrass persons in power. Analysis is a political instrument to be trotted out when it supports one's objectives or undercuts one's opponents, and to be suppressed, if possible, when it opposes one's objectives or strengthens one's opponents.

Which of the following best states the conclusion that this passage is supposed to support?

(A)   Sometimes technical advice is not compatible with bureaucratic or political convenience.

(B)   Persons in power often seal analyses, if such analyses will be embarrassing.

(C)   Analysis should be suppressed if it opposes one's objectives.

(D)   People who wish to arrive at the truth in policy discussions will not get much help from analysis.

(E)   Analysis should be trotted out if it undercuts one's opponents.

15. To control automobile speeding within a 65-mile-an-hour limit or to enforce a $1.15 minimum wage provision are concrete administrative objectives. In these and similar cases the administrator's problem is to maximize compliance and cooperation, for there will always be resistance, footdragging, and some overt defiance. If there were no resistance, there would be no need for the administrative program at all; and if it were impossible to increase the frequency of compliance through governmental action, there would equally obviously be no reason for administrative action.

According to this passage, under which of the following circumstances would there be a need for administrative action?

(A) if there were no resistance

(B) if it were possible to increase frequency of compliance through governmental action

(C) if the speed limit were 65 miles per hour and the minimum wage were $1.15

(D) All of the above.

(E) None of the above.

16. As Lockard points out, frustration is a function of two related factors. The first is the perception that secured rights may be lost in the future. The second is the perception that future advancement (be it economic, social, or political) is artificially limited by factors other than a man's ability or skill. This condition is the crux of the Kern Commission's indictment of white America and forms the basis for the continuing frustration and alienation of the black man in America today.

Which of the following is not one of the assumptions of this argument?

(A) Lockard is correct.

(B) Future advancement is limited by man's ability or skill.

(C) The Kern Commission found fault with white America.

(D) Rights considered secured are not guaranteed.

(E) The black man in America is alienated.

17. A more aggressive prosecution of antitrust cases is needed in order to reduce monopolistic tendencies in some industries. Even when no one company enjoys a total monopoly, a tendency toward monopoly still results in decreased competition. This reduces production and increases prices. Thus, a tendency toward monopoly is a principal cause of inflation.

Which of the following conclusions can most properly be drawn from the above assumptions?

(A)   Antitrust prosecution only benefits foreign competition.

(B)   Antitrust prosecution reduces inflation.

(C)   Antitrust prosecution results in a decrease in production.

(D)   Antitrust prosecution causes unemployment.

(E)   Foreign competition causes unemployment.

18.   The conflict in the townships is a lamentably dramatic illustration of the more general inability of the state to control the African majority. The police and army simply are incapable of maintaining order. The state of emergency which provided an umbrella for the unrestrained use of state power, brought greater conflict, not peace and stability. But the mere fact that force is used to maintain order is testimony to a breakdown in governance. Those institutions designed to nourish conformity and obedience — that is, the new tricameral Parliament and the African community councils — met with widespread rejection by blacks.

Which of the following is the main conclusion of the argument?

(A)   The police and army cannot maintain order.

(B)   The government cannot control the African majority.

(C)   Institutions designed to nourish conformity and obedience should be rejected.

(D)   Unrestrained use of state power brings conflict, not peace and stability.

(E)   There is conflict in the townships.

19.   A variable which may confound studies of addiction is that of availability or access. The situation in Yemen is very interesting because qat is legal, and it is harvestable over a period of several months. In addition, the staggered planting practices, differences in microclimate, irrigation in some areas and the construction of new roads all have worked to create a situation in which qat is virtually always available in most parts of the country. Contributing to this availability is the fact that in almost any qat market one can find a cheap kind of qat as well as an expensive one, with a complete range of prices in the larger markets.

Which of the following is a conclusion of this argument?

(A)   The availability of qat makes it difficult to study addiction.

(B)   Qat is harvestable over a period of several months.

(C)   Qat is available in most parts of the country.

(D)   It is possible to purchase inexpensive qat.

(E)   Qat is legal in Yemen.

20.   "Governance" is different from "management." Governance has two chief elements: overall supervision of management, and accountability for the conduct and policies of the organization to all those who have a stake in it. In a company, the "stakeholders" comprise shareholders, creditors, managers, workers, consumers, suppliers, and also the general public. The board of directors is the instrument of corporate governance. It stands midway between corporate executives and various "stakeholders." The clearest recognition of the functional difference between governance and management is found in the two-tier board system of Germany, which comprises a "supervisory" board and a "management" board.

If the inference in this passage is correct, which statement below must also be correct?

(A)   Governance is accountable to management.

(B)   Management is a chief element in governance.

(C)   Management is accountable to governance.

(D)   Governance, being higher than management, is accountable to no one.

(E)   The "stakeholders" are corporate executives.

21.   There is a great difference between the Russians and the Japanese in the way they proceed with negotiations once under way. The Russians often start by launching a strong offensive action; then they tend to retreat gradually in the face of strong resistance by the other side, frequently ending up with what amounts to being a substantial compromise. The Japanese, on the other hand, follow almost the opposite behavioral pattern. They start reflectively, unite themselves slowly, and then manage the crisis fairly well.

Which one of the following is not one of the premises offered for the conclusion?

(A)   The Russians start out uncompromisingly, but eventually soften their stance.

(B)   The Japanese start out compromisingly, but strengthen their stance as negotiations proceed.

(C)   There is a great difference between the Russians and the Japanese in the way they proceed with negotiations.

(D)   The Japanese tend to unite themselves slowly.

(E)   The Russians tend to retreat gradually.

22.   Why have the metropolitan areas of the United States suburbanized so quickly? One thinks of the plentiful land around most cities, of the wealth of the nation, of the heterogeneity of the American people, of cheap energy and its inducement to decentralization, of the attractiveness of the domestic ideal, and of rapid technological advances which made long-distance commuting feasible. But government has not been an impartial observer. Federally financed interstate highways have undermined the locational advantages of inner-city neighborhoods, while income-tax deductions have encouraged families to buy houses rather than rent apartments.

What appears to be the main point of this passage?

(A)   Metropolitan areas have suburbanized so quickly.

(B)   The American people are heterogeneous which has led them to seek the suburbs.

(C)   Government has contributed to the suburbanization of America.

(D)   Rapid technological advances have made long-distance commuting feasible and, hence, the suburbs have become more attractive.

(E)   Income-tax deductions have encouraged families to buy houses rather than rent apartments.

23.   There are 150,000 miles of railway in the United States: 300,000 miles of rails — in length enough to make 12 steel girdles for the earth's circumference. This enormous length of rail is wonderful — we do not really grasp its significance. But the rail itself, the little section of steel, is an engineering feat. The change of its form from the curious and clumsy iron pear-head of 30 years ago to the present refined section of steel is a significant scientific development.

Which of the following is not one of the writer's premises for the conclusion that the rail is an engineering feat?

(A)   There are 150,000 miles of railway in the United States.

(B)   The rail is a significant scientific development.

(C)   There is enough rail to encircle the earth 12 times.

(D)   The rail has changed from its curious and clumsy iron pear-head of 30 years ago.

(E)   The rail itself is a little section of steel.

24. Even in a country in which a low national income and a scarcity of technical skills make analysis relatively difficult, the role of analytic policy-making is not to be underestimated. India, for example, has been wrestling for a number of years with policy on irrigation. In general, Indian policy has been to distribute water thinly. Millions of Indian farmers therefore receive water supplies helpful for forestalling drought in dry years even if it is insufficient to achieve a steady annual increase in yields.

Which of the following, if true, would not weaken the conclusion that the role of analytic policy making in countries of low income and scarce technical skills is not to be underestimated?

(A) India's policy of water distribution is not analytic.

(B) The water supplies are insufficient to achieve a steady annual increase in yields.

(C) Analytic policy making doesn't work in countries with low national income and scarcity of technical skills.

(D) The water supplies that India distributes have not forestalled drought in dry years.

(E) India has failed to establish a policy on irrigation.

STOP

If time still remains, you may review work only in this section.
When the time allotted is up, you may go on to the next section.

Section II

Time—35 minutes
24 Questions

(Answer sheets appear in the back of this book.)

DIRECTIONS: Each group of questions in this section is based on a set of conditions. In answering some of the questions, it may be useful to draw a rough diagram. Choose the response that most accurately and completely answers the question and blacken the corresponding space on your answer sheet.

<u>**QUESTIONS 1–6**</u>

In the Classics Corner of the auto show, the Avanti, Bugatti, Cord, Dusenberg, and Edsel line up. Each has a special ornament: a hood statue, a monogrammed door, a chromed spare-tire cover, a rhodium-plated engine, or eel-skin upholstery. Their order from left to right meets the following conditions:

> The Cord is immediately left of the car with the chromed spare-tire cover and immediately right of the car with the rhodium-plated engine.

> The Bugatti is immediately left of the car with the monogrammed door.

> The only car next to the Avanti is the one with the hood statue.

> The car with the monogrammed door is immediately to the left of the one with the eel-skin upholstery.

> There are exactly two cars between the Avanti and the Dusenberg.

1. Which car must be fourth from the left?

    (A) Avanti
    (B) Bugatti
    (C) Cord
    (D) Dusenberg
    (E) Edsel

2. Which car must have the monogrammed door?

    (A) Avanti
    (B) Bugatti
    (C) Cord
    (D) Dusenberg
    (E) Edsel

3. Suppose that it is no longer required that the only car next to the Avanti be the one with the hood statue. Suppose further that the Bugatti need not be immediately to the left of the car with the monogrammed door and that the

Avanti need not be separated from the Dusenberg by exactly two cars. If these conditions hold, which of the following must be true?

(A) The Cord has the hood statue.

(B) The leftmost car in the line is either the one with the eel-skin uphol-stery or the one with the rhodium-plated engine.

(C) The car third from the left has the chrome spare-tire cover.

(D) The Cord has the rhodium-plated engine.

(E) The Avanti has the hood statue.

4. If the Cord is immediately left of the car with the chromed spare-tire cover and immediately to the right of the car with the rhodium-plated engine, and if the only car next to the Avanti is the one with the hood statue, and if none of the other conditions holds, which car may be third from the left?

(A) the Bugatti or the Dusenberg only

(B) the Bugatti, the Dusenberg or the Edsel only

(C) the Bugatti, the Cord, the Dusenberg, or the Edsel only

(D) the Avanti, the Bugatti, the Dusenberg, or the Edsel only

(E) the Avanti, the Bugatti, the Cord, the Dusenberg, or the Edsel

5. If the Cord is immediately left of the car with the chromed spare-tire cover and immediately to the right of the car with the rhodium-plated engine, and if none of the other conditions holds, then which of the following must be true?

(A) The second car from the left is not the one with the chromed spare-tire cover.

(B) The third car from the left is not the one with the rhodium-plated engine.

(C) The third car from the left is not the one with the hood statue.

(D) The Cord is not the second car from the left.

(E) The Dusenberg is not the fourth car from the left.

6. If the only car next to the Avanti is the one with the hood statue and if none of the other conditions holds, which position(s) may be occupied by the car with the hood statue?

(A) second from the left or second from the right only

(B)   leftmost, middle, or rightmost only

(C)   second from the left, middle, or second from the right only

(D)   any but the rightmost

(E)   any but the leftmost

QUESTIONS 7–12

An airline serves seven towns — A, B, C, D, E, F, and G — with three round-trip flights. The complete listing of the flights is:

Flight One is between A and C, with a stop at B.

Flight Two is between B and C, with a stop at D.

Flight Three is between E and G, with a stop at F.

Two towns are said to be connected non-stop if there is a flight from one to the other with no intervening stop.

The fare for a flight between any two towns connected non-stop is the same, and the fare for a trip that involves stops or even changes of flight is the sum of the non-stop fares involved.

7.   Which of the following towns is connected non-stop to the most other towns?

(A)   B   (D)   E

(B)   C   (E)   F

(C)   D

8.   Which of the towns in the list below is connected by the airline — non-stop or with stops or change of planes — to fewer other towns than any other on the list?

(A)   A   (D)   D

(B)   B   (E)   E

(C)   C

9.   If the airline added a new flight connecting C and F non-stop, which of the following is a pair of towns of which *neither* is a stop on the cheapest trip from A to G?

(A)   B, C   (D)   D, E

(B)   B, D   (E)   E, F

(C)   C, D

10. If the airline added to the original three flights a new flight connecting A and G non-stop, which of the following would still be connected non-stop to only one other town?

    (A) C   (D) F

    (B) D   (E) G

    (C) E

11. If the airline added to the original three flights a new one connecting C and G non-stop, to which town would the trip from E be most expensive?

    (A) A   (D) F

    (B) B   (E) G

    (C) C

12. If the airline added to the original three flights a new flight which connected A non-stop to E, E non-stop to D and D non-stop to G, which of the following could NOT possibly be a complete and accurate list of all the towns stopped at on a single airline trip from B to E?

    (A) A   (D) D, F

    (B) D   (E) C, D, G, F

    (C) C, D

QUESTIONS 13–16

Around Fashion Circle stand an A-frame house, a Bauhaus, a Cape Cod, a Dymaxion, an Ergonometric, a Federalist, a Georgian, and a Half-timbered, each on one of the ten evenly spaced lots of the outer periphery of the circle. Broad access roads fill the remaining two lots.

The Federalist is directly across the circle from the Georgian, with an equal number of lots separating them on both sides of the circle.

The A-frame and the Half-timbered are next door to the Georgian.

The A-frame and the Bauhaus are not next door to each other.

The Ergonometric and the Bauhaus are next door to each other.

Neither access road is on a lot next door to the Federalist.

13. If the Ergonometric is next door to the A-frame, which of the following must be true?

    (A) The access roads are on adjoining lots.

    (B) An access road runs through a lot next to the Bauhaus.

    (C) The Cape Cod is next door to the Dymaxion.

(D) The A-frame is next door to the Bauhaus.

(E) The Federalist is next door to the Georgian.

14. If the Dymaxion is immediately to the right of the Federalist and the A-frame and the Half-timbered are both next to an access road, then all of the following statements must be true EXCEPT

(A) the Cape Cod is next to an access road.

(B) the Bauhaus is next to the Cape Cod.

(C) the Ergonometric is to the left of the Federalist and to the right of the Georgian.

(D) the Bauhaus is to the left of the Federalist and to the right of the Georgian.

(E) the Cape Cod is next door to the Dymaxion.

15. If the Cape Cod is immediately to the left of the Federalist and the Dymaxion is two places to the right of the Georgian, which of the following must be true?

(A) The Half-timbered house is next to an access road.

(B) The Dymaxion is next door to the Federalist.

(C) The Ergonometric is next door to the Cape Cod.

(D) There is an access road immediately to the right of the Dymaxion.

(E) The two access roads are next to each other.

16. Which houses can occupy the three lots directly to the right of the Georgian in the order given?

(A) A-frame, Bauhaus, Ergonometric

(B) A-frame, Cape Cod, Dymaxion

(C) A-frame, Dymaxion, Ergonometric

(D) A-frame, Half-timbered, Cape Cod

(E) Half-timbered, Ergonometric, Dymaxion

QUESTIONS 17–20

The Tetrad, a committee of four, is to be chosen from a group of 10 experts in the Arts — Memory, Agency, and Prophecy. Each candidate is either a Wizard or not and each is either a Mage of one Art or a master of two Crafts within the Arts, but not both. Each Art must be represented in the Tetrad by at least one

member who is either a Mage of that Art or a master of one of the Crafts that falls within that Art. At least three members of the Tetrad must be either Wizards or masters of two Crafts. The qualifications of the candidates are as follows:

Z, Y, and X are Mages of Memory.

V and U are Mages of Agency.

S and R are Mages of Prophecy.

W is a master of a Craft in Memory and a Craft in Agency.

T is a master of a Craft in Agency and a Craft in Prophecy.

Q is a master of two Crafts in Prophecy.

Y, V, and U are wizards; the others are not.

17. Which of the following is a possible composition of the Tetrad?

    (A) Z, Y, X, U

    (B) Y, X, R, Q

    (C) X, W, S, R

    (D) W, U, S, Q

    (E) V, T, S, Q

18. If Y, W, and R are selected for the Tetrad, which of the following lists all and only those who could be selected as the fourth member?

    (A) X, V, S

    (B) V, U, S

    (C) Z, X, U, T

    (D) V, U, T, Q

    (E) Z, X, V, U, S, Q

19. Which of the following groups of three can serve together with any one of the remaining seven candidates?

    (A) Z, W, R

    (B) Y, X, T

    (C) W, V, Q

    (D) V, U, R

    (E) U, T, Q

20. Which of the following statements is true?

    (A) More than one Wizard must be in the Tetrad.

    (B) The Wizard(s) in the Tetrad must represent more than one Art.

    (C) A Wizard from each Art must be in the Tetrad.

    (D) U can be a Mage of Prophecy.

    (E) A Tetrad can have no wizards.

QUESTIONS 21–24

The noble tribe goes to the ball in a rainbow of body-concealing, hooded robes. Concealed within the red, orange, yellow, green, blue, indigo, and violet raiments were the Earl and his Countess, their son and their two daughters, the children's uncle, and the Earl's son-in-law. Because the family runs to a type, even in the choice of mates, it is not obvious who is who. However, it is known that:

Orange and yellow conceal members of the same sex.

Green and blue conceal members of different sexes.

The person in indigo is older than the one in green.

The person in yellow is not the father of the person in red.

The red cape covers the married daughter.

21.   How many of the seven people in the party are male?

(A)   2   (D)   5

(B)   3   (E)   6

(C)   4

22.   Which of the following must be true?

(A)   The person in yellow is male.

(B)   The person in green is male.

(C)   The person in blue is female.

(D)   The person in indigo is female.

(E)   The person in violet is female.

23.   Which of the following must be true?

(A)   Orange and green conceal people of the same sex.

(B)   Yellow and blue conceal people of the same sex.

(C)   Orange and blue do not conceal people of the same sex.

(D)   Blue and indigo do not conceal people of the same sex.

(E)   Indigo and violet do not conceal people of the same sex.

24.   If the people in yellow and blue are brothers, which of the following must be true?

(A)   The person in green is female.

(B)   The person in green is male.

(C)   The person in indigo is female.

(D)   The person in indigo is male.

(E)   The person in violet is female.

STOP

If time still remains, you may review work only in this section.
When the time allotted is up, you may go on to the next section.

Section III

Time—35 minutes
25 Questions

(Answer sheets appear in the back of this book.)

DIRECTIONS: Each group of questions in this section is based on a set of conditions. In answering some of the questions, it may be useful to draw a rough diagram. Choose the response that most accurately and completely answers the question and blacken the corresponding space on your answer sheet.

QUESTIONS 1–2

All basketball players are athletic. Some teenagers are basketball players. Some athletic persons are skaters. No teenagers are skaters.

1. If the statements above are true, which of the following must also be true?

    (A) All skaters are athletic.

    (B) No basketball players are skaters.

    (C) Some teenagers are athletic.

    (D) Some teenagers are skaters.

    (E) All athletic persons are basketball players or skaters.

2. If it is also true that all athletic persons and teenagers are thin, all of the following must be true EXCEPT:

    (A) Some basketball players are skaters.

    (B) Some thin people are skaters.

    (C) All athletic adults are thin.

    (D) All basketball players are thin.

    (E) Some athletic persons are skaters.

3. Whether or not you can tell a person's level of intelligence by the excellence of his grammar is not clear to me. However, most people seem to believe that you can.

    The author of the preceding passage would be most likely to agree with which of the following?

(A)   Good grammar is not important unless you work in the communications field.

(B)   Good grammar is not important because it is not clear what effect it has on the perceptions of others.

(C)   Good grammar is not important because you should judge a person's intelligence by what he says, not how he says it.

(D)   Good grammar is important because it affects the behavior of others.

(E)   Good grammar is important because it may indicate one's level of intelligence.

4.   Tiffany: In none of the volleyball games in which I have played did Lisa make a mistake.

Jon: That's not true. Lisa made several mistakes in the game on Tuesday night.

Jon's response implies which of the following?

(A)   Tiffany has not played in any games in which Lisa also played.

(B)   Tiffany believes that Lisa is the best player on the team.

(C)   Tiffany has played in every game that Lisa has played in.

(D)   Tiffany played in the game on Tuesday night.

(E)   Tiffany has not watched Lisa's play very closely during the season.

5.   Only if there is oxygen in the chamber will the match burn. The match is burning; therefore, there is oxygen in the chamber.

Which of the following arguments most closely resembles that in the passage above?

(A)   Without the existence of God there can be no miracles. I witnessed a miracle; therefore, God exists.

(B)   Cars cannot run without fuel. That car is running, therefore, it must have gasoline in its tank.

(C)   Trees cannot grow without water. I am watering this tree; therefore, it will grow.

(D)   Ninety percent of the people bitten by cobras die. Amil was bitten by a cobra; therefore, he will die.

(E)   I cannot work without a secretary. Heather was recently hired as my secretary; therefore, now I can work.

QUESTIONS 6–7

Since 1980, the starting salaries of those with Master's Degrees have failed to keep up with increased costs associated with graduate tuition, books, and fees. While it is true that the differential between the starting salaries of those who have Master's Degrees and those who do not is still large enough to make going to graduate school financially advantageous, the differential is now fairly small. Therefore, those who do not wish to continue their education, should enter the work force rather than go on to graduate school.

6. Assuming that all of the premises in the above argument are true, which of the following, if also true, would most seriously weaken the conclusion?

   (A) Since 1980, the percentage of persons who go on to graduate school has risen sharply.

   (B) Since 1980, the percentage of persons who go on to graduate school has fallen sharply.

   (C) Since 1980, the employment rate for those who have Master's Degrees has fallen more sharply than the rate for those who do not.

   (D) Since 1980, the unemployment rate for those who have Master's Degrees has fallen more sharply than for those who do not.

   (E) The author of the passage never went to graduate school, and is biased against doing so.

7. Assuming all of the premises in the above argument are true, which of the following, if also true, would most strengthen the conclusion?

   (A) Studies show that many people who do not wish to go to graduate school, but who go anyway, suffer extreme emotional distress.

   (B) Studies show that those who have gone to graduate school report greater job satisfaction than those who have not.

   (C) Studies show that those with no college preparation have less difficulty landing their first job than do those with Master's Degrees.

   (D) Studies show that the nation's graduate schools have the capacity to enroll 10% more people in graduate studies.

   (E) Since 1980, the percentage of college graduates entering the job force has risen sharply.

QUESTIONS 8–9

The life expectancy of persons in positions of authority is greater than that of the general population. This is, I believe, because those people can afford better than average diets and health care. One study in particular showed that military personnel at the rank of colonel or above have a greater than average life expectancy.

8. Which of the following, if true, fails to weaken the evidence about the military which is supplied by the author?

    (A) High ranking officers in the military are much less likely to smoke or drink than is the general population.

    (B) High ranking officers in the military get more exercise than does the general population.

    (C) High ranking officers in the military have the same diet and health care as do enlisted men, whose life expectancy is not greater than that of the general population.

    (D) The study in question is five years old.

    (E) All of the officers in the study were women, and everybody knows that women have a longer life expectancy than men.

9. Which of the following unspoken assumptions does the author of the passage make?

    (A) Better diet and health care increases life expectancy.

    (B) People in positions of authority make more money than does the average person.

    (C) Military officers at or above the rank of colonel have positions of authority.

    (D) None of the above.

    (E) All of the above except (D).

10. Research shows that mental imaging often has a beneficial effect on performance. After much testing with many different types of individuals, it has been shown that, in most cases, mental imaging leads to improved performance in everyday activities that require the development of a person's special skills. Driving is an everyday activity which requires the development of special skills. Therefore,

    Which one of the following is the best completion of the above argument?

    (A) mental imaging alone will not prevent traffic accidents.

    (B) mental imaging may help to improve driving performance.

    (C) mental imaging is no more effective than actual hands-on practice in developing driving skills.

    (D) mental imaging is the best method for training new drivers.

    (E) mental imaging is the best method for developing new skills.

11. Just a few years ago, high school students in Metropolis were more likely to commit a crime than to graduate. This was because the local culture placed too little emphasis on getting a high school diploma. But now after years of concerted effort by school board officials, parents, and community leaders to change this, students are graduating in record numbers. This is a sure sign that the local groups have been successful in changing the local culture.

Each of the following indicates a possible flaw in the reasoning in the passage above EXCEPT:

(A) The economy was very bad a few years ago and, unlike now, there was little opportunity for anyone, graduate or non-graduate, to find a job.

(B) The language requirements for graduation have been dramatically lowered in the past few years.

(C) Parents have not been as effective in changing the local culture as community leaders have been.

(D) The state legislature passed a law a few years ago which made possession of a high school diploma a requirement for obtaining a driver's license.

(E) Students entering high school in Metropolis are better prepared to do high school work than they were a few years ago.

QUESTIONS 12–13

The United States Department of Agriculture's (USDA's) approval requirements for the use of pesticides are counterproductive. Ted, a farmer I know, used to combat corn borers by using popalexine 10. It was environmentally safe, but the USDA required so much documentation about its use that Ted stopped using it. Another acquaintance, Joe, uses xenophine, which is potentially harmful to plants and animals, but requires minimal paperwork. Joe wants only to reduce his paperwork and make a profit. He knows that over the course of time he will probably harm plants and animals around his farm by using xenophine.

12. The author of the passage argues by

(A) providing examples to support two opposing positions.

(B) basing a conclusion on specific cases.

(C) disputing evidence cited by those with an opposing point of view.

(D) predicting personal experience from a general principle.

(E) using a generalization based on observation to undermine a theoretical principle.

13. We may infer from the passage that by counterproductive requirements, the author means:

    (A) Those that discourage environmentally safe practices.

    (B) Those that put his friends to a lot of trouble.

    (C) Those that do not encourage environmentally harmful practices.

    (D) Xenophine should be banned.

    (E) Making a profit.

14. Everyone knew that if the professor put a question on the test about astrophysics, no one would pass. Since half the class passed, the professor must not have put a question about astrophysics on the test.

    Which one of the following is most similar in logic to the argument above?

    (A) The team always loses when Pete plays. Therefore, if the team is to win Thursday night, the coach had better not let him play.

    (B) Eating hot peppers is the cause of sarpogus of the stomach. Jim does not eat hot peppers, so his ailment cannot be sarpogus.

    (C) If Hank had forgotten to pay a $40 fine, he would have lost his license. He has not lost his license, so he did not forget to pay the fine.

    (D) A red sunset means good weather tomorrow. This is a red sunset, so tomorrow's weather will be good.

    (E) An applicant could get the job only if she had experience or an advanced degree. Emmy has neither, so she won't get the job.

15. A Canadian cold front will hit Eureka in about four hours. Precipitation results from about 75% of such fronts in the Eureka area. Moreover, the current season, winter, is the time of year in which Eureka is most likely to encounter snowfall.

    Which of the following, in addition to the information above, would be most helpful in determining how likely Eureka is to get snowfall in the next several hours?

    (A) the percentage of snowfalls that occur in Eureka in the winter, as opposed to the fall

    (B) the percentage of snowfalls in the Eureka area that occur during winter cold fronts

(C) how many Canadian cold fronts hit the Eureka area, on average, in a year

(D) the percentage of wintertime Canadian cold fronts hitting the Eureka area that cause snowfall

(E) whether Eureka has more or fewer snowfalls during the winter than do nearby towns

16. No club member ran in the 600 meter race unless he or she wore white shoes. No club member ran in the 600 meter race or wore white shoes.

Which one of the following conclusions can be correctly drawn from the statements above?

(A) No one but club members ran in the 600 meter race.

(B) No person wearing white shoes ran in the 600 meter race.

(C) Only club members ran in the 600 meter race.

(D) No club member ran in the 600 meter race.

(E) Some club members wearing white shoes ran in the 600 meter race.

17. Dr. James: Ms. Jones, I believe that we'll have to increase the dose of Torozan to control your symptoms.

Ms. Jones: But I don't like the side effects of Torozan. I've decided not to take any more of it.

Dr. James: Very well, we'll keep the dose the same.

Which one of the following words or phrases has been misinterpreted in the conversation?

(A) increase   (D) the same

(B) any more   (E) Torozan

(C) symptoms

18. If Bob was a history professor at a major university, his works would be widely read. He is not a history professor since his works are not widely read.

The above conclusion is unsound because the author does not consider that

(A) Bob could be a science fiction writer whose works are widely read.

(B) Bob could be a biology professor.

(C)   Bob's works could be widely read for another reason.

(D)   Bob could be a history professor at a small college.

(E)   Bob could be a historian who works in the national archives.

19.   The European Union should demand that member nations stop giving cash subsidies to farmers. The Union has already abolished protective tariffs on manufacturers. This action was based on the belief that market forces are the only reliable indicators of which nations should produce which products and in what amounts. When member nations subsidize farm products, they upset natural market forces and artificially determine production.

In arguing that member nations of the European Union should stop giving cash subsidies to farmers, the author relies on

(A)   a comparison between the effects of farm subsidies and protective tariffs.

(B)   the principle that farmers need to be protected from unfair competition.

(C)   the use of emotionally charged descriptions of tariffs and subsidies.

(D)   the idea that farm subsidies upset the natural cycle of production and consumption within a country.

(E)   the fact that farm subsidies are counterproductive for the nations which use them.

20.   Writing beautiful operas requires a talent for music composition and a flair for the dramatic. Bach, however, was the greatest of all composers. Though he did not have a flair for the dramatic, he could have excelled at writing operas.

Which of the following contains a logical error that most closely resembles the logical error contained in the passage?

(A)   The question is whether Angela could be the author of this short story. The episode described as occurring on the night of September 10 is like nothing she has actually experienced, so we can eliminate her as the author.

(B)   It is true that it is necessary to feel great passion in order to be a true artist. However, Friedmann has a very vivid imagination, so she could be a true artist without feeling great passion.

(C)   Whenever I talk to Lynn on the phone I enter it in my phone log. I did not enter a conversation for last Thursday in the log, so I know that I did not talk to her on the phone that day.

(D)　Only if I can make my payment before next week can I prevent foreclosure on the property. However, I cannot possibly get the money for the payment together this week, so I cannot prevent foreclosure.

(E)　Only the brightest deserve to be on the advisory committee. Sally is clearly among the brightest, so she deserves to be on the committee.

QUESTIONS 21–22

President:　Dr. Kesler, I have been told that developing an initial climate of trust, which is the first step in building a strong and lasting relationship with our new treaty's signatory, will be impossible because we have not appointed a special team of representatives to be stationed in Edenia. Can you assure me that our relations with Edenia have not been permanently damaged by our failure to appoint such a team?

Presidential
advisor:　Mr. President, our relations with this nation have not been permanently damaged by our failure to appoint such a team. An initial climate of trust between nations is not some sort of fail-safe device that guarantees good relations forever. An initial climate of trust does give the relationship between two nations a head start, but many factors are involved in our building a strong and lasting relationship with this nation.

21.　If everything the advisor says is true, which of the following must also be true?

(A)　The best relations between nations are developed by immediate actions such as one nation's appointing representatives to be stationed in the country with which it has signed a treaty.

(B)　There is a high degree of correlation between the best relations between nations and those relations that begin with a climate of trust between the nations.

(C)　A strong and lasting relationship is necessary for one nation to develop a climate of trust between itself and a nation with which it has signed a treaty.

(D)　Where immediate actions such as the appointment of representatives to the other nation takes place, a strong and lasting relationship between two treaty nations will be assured.

(E)　An initial climate of trust is not necessary for the development of a strong and lasting relationship between nations which have signed a treaty.

22. The advisor does which of the following in his reply to the president?

   (A) He rejects an analogy in an attempt to reduce the president's concern.

   (B) He cites evidence to show that the president's worry is unfounded.

   (C) He misinterprets the president's explanation of his concern.

   (D) He establishes that the information the president was told was in error.

   (E) He names other factors that are more important in creating an initial climate of trust.

23. Hinklemore: Initiative, referendum, and recall are regarded by experts as interferences outside the legislative process, but I believe they are indispensable because they are often the voters' only protection against legislators' tendency to play politics with sensitive issues.

   Bullfinch: I don't agree. Politics requires compromise among various factions in a legislative body. Initiative, referendum, and recall upset the delicate balance of forces within the legislature which makes maneuvering and compromise possible.

   Hinklemore and Bullfinch will not be able to resolve their disagreement logically unless they

   (A) define a key term.

   (B) rely on the opinions of established authorities.

   (C) question an unproved premise.

   (D) present supporting data.

   (E) distinguish fact from opinion.

24. Abolish increased wages for overtime, and workers would find that their take home pay has decreased. Abolish increased wages for overtime, and employers would find that increases in production have disappeared.

   Which of the following is a logical conclusion that depends on information in both of the statements above?

   (A) Overtime work should be abolished so that employers can save money that would otherwise be paid for overtime.

   (B) The best workers are those who would be willing to work overtime

for regular pay.

(C)   Increases in production depend in part on workers' take home pay not decreasing.

(D)   Increased wages for overtime are essential to healthy corporations.

(E)   Increases in production depend on increased wages for overtime.

25.   Scientists have concluded that exposure to the sun is responsible for 45% of all cases of melanoma. Since last June, more reliable methods of identifying melanoma have been developed, accounting for the fact that reports of melanoma have increased by 30% since last June.

Which of the following is an assumption underlying the argument in the passage?

(A)   Sunbathing is still relatively safe, despite the increase in the number of cases of melanoma.

(B)   Exposure to the sun has increased dramatically since last June.

(C)   The incidence of melanoma has not increased since last June.

(D)   Doctors are less reluctant to report cases of melanoma than they previously were.

(E)   Methods of reporting melanoma have become more convenient since last June.

STOP

If time still remains, you may review work only in this section.
When the time allotted is up, you may go on to the next section.

Section IV

Time—35 minutes
26 Questions

(Answer sheets appear in the back of this book.)

DIRECTIONS: Each passage in this section is followed by a group of questions to be answered on the basis of what is **stated** or **implied** in the passage. For some questions, more than one of the choices could conceivably answer the question. However, you are to choose the **best** answer; that is, the response that most accurately and completely answers the question, and blacken the corresponding space on your answer sheet.

Now that brings me to what I must say a word about the distinction between what have been called reason and understanding. Reason is the way of
looking at things which *comprehends,* while understanding merely *apprehends.*
They are not two different faculties. It is only darkening counsel to speak of them
(5)   as though they were. They are two different modes of thinking about things,
determined in their differences by the purposes which we have in view. If I want
to make a hard-and-fast distinction it is, of course, natural that I should express
myself in a way that makes the distinction very definite, hypostatises it, if I may
use the expression. But if, upon the other hand, what I want to do is really to see
(10) how this distinction looks from the point of view of the mind which made it, and
which, just because it made it, is capable of expressing it, then I look from the
standpoint of the comprehension which seeks to resolve the differences. Reason
is, therefore, a way of looking at things which is larger than the mere understanding which made and set fast the differentiation. Reason and understanding are not
(15) thoughts of two different natures, two faculties. They are thought pursuing
different ends. We make our own experience present different appearances
according as our ends differ.   That is a very familiar observation. Long ago
Montaigne put it in one of his Essays, that on Democritus and Heraclitus, in very
simple language. "Wherefore," he says, " let us no longer excuse ourselves by
(20) laying the blame on the quality of external things. It belongs to us to give ourselves an account of them. Our good and our evil had no dependency except from
ourselves. To ourselves let us make our offerings and our vows, and not to
fortune. She hath no power over our character. On the contrary, character draws
fortune in its train, and moulds her to its own form." In other words, what to the
(25) man whose spirit is cast in a narrow mould seems final and irresoluble in ill-
fortune, may seem to the man, of larger comprehension a very different thing. It
depends on our end and purpose, it depends on whether we are at the standpoint
of comprehension or merely of apprehension in difference, how the things
present themselves. Well, the essence of understanding is to separate. If I look at
(30) marbles in a row my purpose is to count them, to enumerate them, and therefore I

am seeking to apprehend them, each in its difference from the other. If I am trying to comprehend I do not dwell upon the distinctions, but I search for the larger whole, the unity in which the differences are comprehended.

(35) Now for apprehension, for understanding, the leading mode of operation is distinction in space and in time. Between space and time there is a considerable difference. In space things are regarded as just as completely independent of one another as they can possibly be. The very essence of space is mutual exclusion of parts. You have got the very hardest of distinctions there. But in time the now only has meaning as distinguished from a past and from a future. These never co-
(40) exist. The essence of them is that the one should be actual and real in contrast with the other two, the past and the future, which are not actual. Therefore in time you have got a stage on towards comprehension, towards the comprehension of the past, the present, and the future as in a unity in which they are not indepen-dent but related, and which is more than any one of them. Just so in a piece of
(45) music you have the notes, no doubt capable of being taken in their separation, but also getting their meaning, and each one getting its meaning, from the musical whole which is the form in which full comprehension appears.

Now the truth about space and time is that they are modes in which the mind presents phenomena, space the hardest and most abstract form of distinc-
(50) tion, time the form in which that distinction is less hard and abstract, but is still one in which separations are made. But it is plain, if the view of thought which I have been presenting to you is right, that thought not only must have, but actually has, other and higher forms, from the standpoint of which presentation in space and time is deficient and inadequate to the truth.

1.   What has the author confirmed in the above presentation?

    (A)   Reasoning and understanding seek to attain the same goals.

    (B)   The lines between reasoning and understanding are blurred because the distinctions between them are unclear.

    (C)   Although reasoning and understanding are two different faculties, they pursue the same ends.

    (D)   Reasoning and understanding are not different faculties, but their purposes are totally different.

    (E)   Although the faculties of reasoning and understanding are different, their ultimate purpose is the same.

2.   What important conclusion can be drawn from the author's presentation?

    (A)   Presentation of thought in space and time is real and necessary and is the only mode available at this time.

    (B)   There is a considerable difference between space and time, but there

may be co-existence between parts in space.

(C)   Space and time are very much alike; just as the now, the past, and the future may co-exist in a given time, the parts in space may likewise be separate and blurred.

(D)   Understanding seeks to unify, to consolidate; reason seeks to celebrate the distinctions and to focus not just on the whole.

(E)   Comprehension and reasoning seek to find the larger whole; apprehension and understanding tend to focus on the differences and distinctions in both time and space.

3.   Which factor was not used in supporting the passage?

(A)   marbles

(B)   musical notes

(C)   constellations

(D)   man's character

(E)   past, present, and future

4.   The writer seems to imply that

(A)   the whole may be greater than the sum of the parts.

(B)   Montaigne omits many important reasoning techniques in his philosophy of blaming what we are on external things.

(C)   nurture is more important than nature.

(D)   focusing on relationships in a society would be at a lower thinking level than noting similarities and differences among people.

(E)   we are what we eat.

5.   A completed recipe is comparable to which of the following?

(A)   understanding

(B)   comprehending

(C)   rationalizing

(D)   analyzing

(E)   both understanding and analyzing

6.   Which of the following choices best describes how the writer views thinking?

(A)   a vertical structure with various levels

(B)   comparable to a Venn diagram with many similarities

(C)   impossible to analyze

(D)   different faculties

(E)   a way to pinpoint differences

Americans who enjoyed the movie "Shogun" would find the role of warriors who were devoted followers of the shogun an interesting part of Japanese history. During the feudal period, warriors were intensely loyal to their leaders. Faithfully fulfilling orders of their lord was an honorable duty. The warriors (*samurai*)
(5) expected their wives to make similar sacrificial efforts to ensure victory. Samurai wore two swords and at times were feared by the commoners. During those feudal years, an insensitive warrior could without hesitation cut down a person who stood in his way. Yet not all samurai were crude fighters. In fact, many of them developed a number of cultural skills. Great interest in writing poetry by
(10) samurai was passed from generation to generation. To this day, ordinary Japanese citizens find pleasure in writing poems. After feudal wars ended and lords no longer needed their protective services, the educated warriors were frequently transferred to urban centers and appointed to carry out bureaucratic duties.
During the Tokugawa Period, many people were educated through a private
(15) tutoring system. Samurai and commoners participated in the educational process. Domain schools for samurai were established. Private academies enrolled samurai and other members of the community. Buddhist temple schools also figured prominently in educating common people, including a small percentage of women. Toward the latter part of the 19th century during the Meiji Period, the
(20) first Ministry of Education was established. Today, Japan's educational standards and policies are widely debated. Those who admire the educational system point to the high literacy and productivity of the Japanese people. Those who criticize the system complain about the high stress placed on young people who are pressured to pass key tests at certain intervals. The tests determine whether or not
(25) students can enroll in top-rate kindergartens, elementary schools, high schools, and elite universities. Japanese mothers devote their lives to the educational progress of their children. Completion of heavy homework assignments and class ranking are central concerns of the family. Many children attend private afterschool schools or cram schools (*juku*) and/or are taught by private tutors in
(30) the afternoons and evenings. Rote learning is a necessity for preparation for tests. Pressure on the students stems from the fact that only those students who emerge from elite universities have opportunities to be groomed for top positions in government and business. Some observers believe that the time and cost of preparing children for the best positions account for the low birthrate and many

(35) abortions in Japan. Thus with only a child or two, parents can closely guide each one toward "success." Others also feel that the stress and strain placed on young people to make the highest scores in their classes may explain the high rate of suicide among teenagers.

Japanese group interaction is a topic often considered by students of manage-
(40) ment. Unlike the American bureaucratic style where the boss is prone to make policy and announce policy to personnel on the lower rungs of the hierarchy, the Japanese system is based on group decision making and implementation. Upon graduation, new employees enter government as a group and work as a group during their long tenure. Groups function quite well in Japan due to a number of
(45) reasons. With the exception of a few citizens who have Korean ancestors, the country is composed of a homogeneous population. A long tradition of good manners and a uniform education curriculum necessary for students to prepare for key exams are important elements required for adults to work harmoniously. The style of communication leads to reduced friction. Japanese feel no compul-
(50) sion to strike a deal in a hurry. Rather, they talk around a topic without brusque collision of ideas and personalities. Indirect, vague communication which is called "belly talk" frustrates Americans who are accustomed to being direct, targeting key points, and quickly making decisions. Japanese operate on a basis of group consensus. When details are eventually completed, the group transmits
(55) the suggested policy to their superior. Unlike Americans who prefer "top down" communication in the organization, Japanese prefer "bottom up" communication. Unlike Americans who strive to be identified as "the leader" with subsequent promotions, the Japanese group that originated when first hired is rewarded as a group. The group rises intact in the hierarchy until one individual is appointed to
(60) a top position. By this time, the other members of the group are eligible for retirement, or they move out of that particular organization. While most American industries have not attempted to copy Japanese management styles, elements of group decision making have been incorporated.

7. How did ideas about the role of warriors change over a period of time?

    (A) Samurai were at first among the best educated citizens until war broke out. At that point they turned against their own people. After the war, philosopher kings requested assistance of Buddhist priests in taming young warriors.

    (B) Theoretically, warriors with their history of cruelty and loyalty could not be retrained.

    (C) Samurai and their lords experienced mutual dependence until peace no longer required a warrior class. The samurai's educational foundation made them natural candidates for bureaucratic positions.

    (D) Shoguns and their warriors were defeated in battles and one by one left the rough country to explore civilization. Uneducated, the warriors

were at first ill-equipped to function in the more sophisticated hierarchy of organized government.

(E) The author infers that the teachers in private and religious schools were fearful of the two-sworded warriors who, the reader might envision, were similar to modern-day gangs in the halls of the temple schools. Once graduated, it appears that the warriors' attempt to take over government offices was successful.

8. What seems to be the purpose of the author's presentation on Japanese education?

(A) The author overwhelmingly rejects the Japanese educational system.

(B) The author has attempted to present the merits of the educational system while at the same time exposing serious defects.

(C) The author is trying to convince Americans that more pressure on parents and children should be exerted by educators in public schools, private schools, and juku.

(D) The author's jaded view of the educational system in Japan is at best a paradox because he seems to advocate sacrifices which must be made in order to elevate the rate of literacy and productivity in American schools.

(E) The author is only trying to present an historical analysis of the education system in earlier periods and modern times in an objective manner without subjective imposition of personal views on the reader.

9. What are commonplace experiences of young women in Japan?

(A) As in early years when women were dominated by samurai husbands, wives and mothers today must make personal sacrifices in order to be successful "education moms" who guide their children through the maze of assignments and exams.

(B) As in early years when a few women enrolled in Buddhist temple schools, young females generally have little education because education is mostly for young boys, commonly known as juku.

(C) The author infers that young mothers actually complete some of the heavy homework assignments of their children so that the children will have time to study under a tutor who prepares them for the next test.

(D) Young women have no future and no happiness unless they themselves make top scores on tests, enter an elite university so that they can marry a successful man, and rear a large family of brilliant children.

(E) Only lower class women undergo abortions. Unfortunately, mothers in the lower economic class with children of average or below average mental abilities must deal with a higher rate of teenage abortions and teenage suicides.

10. Which statement best describes the educational philosophy in Japan?

(A) Students must spend a great deal of time learning long lists of facts. Teaching preparations must be geared to teaching reading skills to all students. Extensive written exams are the best method for determining who should later lead the country in business, industry, and government.

(B) Education is of great value, but social contacts with other children in informal after-school classes are more important.

(C) Despite great emphasis on the part of the Minister of Education to incorporate Meiji teaching techniques, mothers dominate school policies in ways that will promote recognition of the most talented children.

(D) The Japanese education philosophy stresses "practical education" in scientific and mathematical subjects.

(E) The author suggested that warriors' domination of the early educational process has influenced educational curricula today with great emphasis on creativity and decreased emphasis on memorization.

11. What is the management philosophy in Japan today?

(A) Given the difficulty of Japanese individuals to get to the heart of the matter and to make fairly quick decisions, it is best to appoint a supervisor of a group who can tie the ends together when the group bogs down. Supervisors often suffer from ulcers (belly talk) during periods of tension.

(B) Management is forced to react to the difficulty of hiring young graduates of elite universities. The situation is further complicated due to inflated egos. Management must spend a great deal of time supervising heterogeneous groups and avoiding friction among leadership-prone men who were stars throughout their educational experience.

(C) Disgusted with the slow pace of group decision making, the Japanese will most likely change their management style and look more to the American single-administrator-type system where things are accomplished on a faster pace and where the boss makes all decisions.

(D) The education philosophy of Japan, with its emphasis on rote learning and competition, is in direct contrast with Japanese management

style, which places emphasis on group problem-solving and cooperation.

(E)   As a part of their bid for global economic dominance, the Japanese
managers will continue trying to increase efficiency at all costs.

12.   How does the author view modern Japanese society?

(A)   Society functions best when highly intelligent young people and their
families feel that ultimate success is promotion to a position of responsibility in government, business, or industry by the time a man
has passed middle age.

(B)   It is obvious that social needs are accommodated when examinations
and entry levels to good jobs are structured so that a class of illiterate
people will be available to clean and sweep.

(C)   Although education stresses eliminate the lazy, faint-hearted, and
emotionally insecure, rote learning and striving for the best jobs will
automatically produce the best social order.

(D)   Although there are many admirable traits of Japanese society, such
as high literacy, ability to work long hours, and courteous interaction
among people, questions must be raised about several issues: the
high rate of suicides and abortions, stress imposed on all members of
families, late-bloomers in schools who have shifted to educational
tracks that fail to develop their full potential in the marketplace, etc.

(E)   There are many admirable traits of Japanese society, such as literacy
and work patterns. Detractors who raise such points as suicide and
educational pressures on society are most often jealous or critical
Americans, such as the author, who are apologists for defects in the
American system and who ascribe to America the one and only way
of life.

Incremental changes in federal government personnel management practices
are the result of a long struggle which is chronologically documented. When our
constitution was written, the framers focused on such important factors as
separation of powers and sovereignty of "we the people." They left to future
(5) policymakers the task of deciding manager/employee relationships. At first our
national government, composed of small agencies, attracted social elites who had
prior management experience in either a business or farming. Generally speaking, people who worked in government during those first years maintained high
ethical standards and were among the best educated group of citizens. Federal
(10) government employees in the earliest years felt responsible for providing excellent service with public interest a central theme. The distinct management
philosophy was classified the trustee period.
As political philosophies changed, the characteristics of federal employment

(15) changed. Political parties clashed. Bitter feelings toward the other party led to distrust in government employment. Winners felt that they should reward party workers, regardless of educational preparation for the job, with appointment to government positions. By 1820, the patronage system was born. Loyalty to the elected politicians was the governing principle in hiring and firing practices. Unfortunately, some of the party faithful fostered corruption and other abuses.

(20) By 1883, disenchanted constituents pressured members of Congress to change the federal personnel system. The Civil Service Reform Act readily became law after President Garfield was shot by an office-seeking party worker who failed to acquire a job after the election. The new law, commonly known as the Pendleton Act, was a cautious step at best, but it did provide a foundation on

(25) which to build a more stable civil service cadre. Patronage as a mode for acquiring a job was eliminated in some of the agencies. A three-person Civil Service Commission provided leadership in moving recruitment and hiring practices away from politics and toward hiring based on qualifications which matched job descriptions. The jurisdiction of the commission at first was quite small. By the

(30) time the second federal law was passed, the authority of the Commission had expanded, and government employees could not be fired unless the employer substantiated that there was good cause to fire the employee. Employees' Fifth Amendment due process guarantees were a crucial barrier to unfair administrative practices.

(35) Among other laws that affected federal government personnel practices was the Hatch Act. The new law provided additional protections against removal for political purposes. Critics assert that the law invaded First Amendment rights by denying civil service employees the opportunity to work actively in political campaigns, run for public office, or serve as party officers.

(40) Racial prejudices, common in the private sector, led to discrimination in federal hiring, promotion, and firing practices. The Civil Service Commission was ineffective in monitoring and enforcing equal protection. Power of enforcement was transferred to the Equal Employment Opportunity Commission in 1978. Federal judges also played a prominent role in getting to the root of

(45) inequities in such cases as *Griggs v. Duke Power Company* in 1971 where the Supreme Court ruled that test questions must be related to expected job qualifications and performance.

13. Which statement best summarizes the history of personnel management in the United States?

(A) The values of late 18th century public administrators are not and cannot be applicable to modern government.

(B) Benefits of patronage practices outweigh problems. The author implies that civil servants who are loyal to the president, his party, and his policies will work harder in order to win the next election.

(C) As science and technology change, the definition of honesty and merit should change accordingly.

(D)   The original basic values of public personnel managers under President Washington have remained intact, for the most part, similar to the values of 20th century personnel management although other values have been introduced.

(E)   Due to the wide variety of intelligence and skills, it is impossible to develop fair personnel policies.

14.   What becomes apparent under close examination of the author's analysis?

(A)   The author illustrated how tension exists between standards of a professional, non-patronage personnel system and constitutional rights of free speech and association of governmental employees.

(B)   The author has become bitter about political party conflicts and personnel loyalties.

(C)   The author adheres to the theory that government administrators must never question strict obedience to agency rules.

(D)   The author advocates legislative delegation of unlimited discretion to administrators in hiring and firing.

(E)   It is apparent that the author sympathizes with industry in the *Griggs* case.

15.   Which analysis by the author is valid according to passages above?

(A)   The analyst is squarely in the camp of modern day philosophers who adhere to the theory that popular sovereignty can never lead to good personnel practices in government.

(B)   The writer disagrees with the Supreme Court's interpretation of the equal protection clause and implies that tests are indeed valuable in personnel placement regardless of impact of scores on racial groups.

(C)   The author carefully analyzes problems which developed during the affirmative action movement when President Garfield meddled unfairly in hiring practices of the Civil Service Commission.

(D)   The author objectively describes an instance when the EEOC and the Supreme Court justices found common ground in constitutional interpretation that brought about changes in personnel policy standards.

(E)   The author rejects incrementalism as an explanation for what has happened in personnel management.

16.   What details did constitutional framers incorporate into our fundamental law?

(A)   The constitutional provisions are broadly worded and do not provide

specific personnel policies for government bureaucracies.

(B) The framers' legal philosophy "We the people..." was grounded in patronage rewards of government jobs for political campaign workers.

(C) The Civil Service Provision of the constitution was dormant until President Garfield enforced that section of the constitution.

(D) The constitutional separation of powers doctrine, important to the personnel management, was struck by the court in the "separate but equal" case.

(E) The author fails to discuss the spoils system, a once popular method of hiring people based on the wishes of winners of elections who wanted to offer jobs to people who showed the greatest support during the campaign.

17. What was the philosophy behind the Hatch Act discussed in lines 35–39?

(A) Civil servants appointed on a system of merit are in a strategic position to be pressured to work actively to reelect whoever holds office at the time with threat of job loss if they refuse.

(B) The Hatch Act was passed to provide affirmative action in protecting black governmental employees after the election.

(C) Congress, as punishment to those governmental employees who would not work in election campaigns, took revenge by denying civil servants the privilege of active participation in the next election.

(D) The philosophy behind the Hatch Act was rather vague and puzzles political observers who have not discovered the real reason the law was passed.

(E) Civil servants are in a position to know secret data in files which could harm an incumbent seeking election. It appears that under the old law, it is illegal to disclose fraud during elections.

18. What kinds of regulations apply to personnel managers to govern equality during the hiring process?

(A) Prior to 1883, personnel managers had a fairly free hand in deciding whom they would hire, but politics did not count.

(B) The author implies that before a person is hired the *Griggs* case mandates employers perform what is known as "mixed scanning" — a system of evaluating a large amount of data.

(C) In recent years, employment-screening tests may be challenged by applicants as violating the equal protection clause if the questions

have no specific application to skills that are required for the position.

(D) The constitutional requirement of fair procedures has yet to protect a civil servant from losing his job due to racial prejudice of his supervisor.

(E) Under the balance of power theory, Congress has no formal power to govern personnel policies of the federal executive branch.

19. How can the above paragraphs be evaluated?

(A) The author has demonstrated that he does not fully understand the philosophy of separation of powers and the federal system of government.

(B) The author has developed a systematic frame of reference for analyzing how the three branches of government have succeeded and failed in resolving critical issues of personnel management.

(C) It is evident that the author is dismayed with "big government" which is highlighted by too many new agencies.

(D) The author's philosophy is apparent in his support for centralization of government with personnel rule-making transferred back to Congress.

(E) Formal study of public administration is hampered because our system of government operates under rules of strict confidentiality, similar to the difficulty of studying decision making within big business.

The Civil Service Commission authorized tests and other forms of screening. Applicants are ranked according to test scores and other criteria, such as experience. Secretaries, plumbers, and other skilled laborers are required to take specialized tests. In earlier years professionals were given PACE examinations,
(5) but these exams are no longer administered. According to the ranking scale, the top three applicants become finalists who will compete for the job vacancy. Once on the job, the employee must deal with other forms of classification. For years, the Civil Service Commission made policy with regard to pay scales based on job descriptions. The procedure proved unwieldy. Currently, agencies handle their
(10) own classification systems. Controversies surfaced from time to time. After the Watergate scandal, Congress decided that change was in order. In 1978, Congress passed the Civil Service Reform Act. The legislators defined merit and cited nine principles that serve as guidelines today. Merit pay was initiated. New structural changes led to division of duties among the Office of Personnel
(15) Management, the Merit System Protection Board, the Office of Special Counsel, the Federal Labor Relations Authority, and the Senior Executive Services.

The new system was designed to improve working conditions. Proponents pointed to flexibility and rewards for excellent service. To protect the honest,

hardworking civil servants from dishonest and/or unfair supervisors or fellow
(20) employees, the Merit System Protection Board promulgates rules and sees that
they are administered by other agencies. Federal employees may bring their
complaints to the Office of Special Counsel. After investigation and hearings, the
case may go before the Merit System Protection Board. Cases that deal with
violations of the law may be investigated by Congress, or the federal courts.
(25) Analyst Ronald D. Sylvia found that the Office of Special Counsel has not
functioned well. Few cases have been appealed to the board or to court.
Whistleblowers have experienced little protection in the way the Office functions.

Despite changes in laws, system, rules, procedures, and practices, federal
(30) government has yet to resolve many problems that beset both private and public
sectors. For example, it has been hard to eliminate different kinds of discrimination in state and federal agencies: sex, age, race, religion, and members of ethnic
groups. Policymakers are generally puzzled on how to deal fairly with employees
who are pregnant, new parents, victims of sexual harassment, drug abusers,
(35) alcoholics, and AIDS victims. Proponents are calling for changes in philosophy
with regard to employee rights on the job and as politically active citizens. If
Congress and/or the president as chief executive fail to address the controversies,
agency managers must rely on legal staffs to aid them on a case-by-case basis in
developing rules or deciding employee complaints. Eventually, questionable
(40) personnel management policies are challenged in courts of law or in arbitration
and mediation processes.

The values of the 18th century practitioners included striving for honest
government manned by highly ethical, educated citizens. Public service was
performed by capable persons whose loyalty to the constitution was seldom
(45) questioned. Although many other principles have become woven into the fabric
of public administration today, Congress and recent presidents through their
executive orders have tried to maintain these values and incorporate higher goals.
As we have seen, the tasks have not been easy. Much remains to be envisioned,
crafted, and implemented.

20. What is the intent of the author in discussing personnel problems?

(A) He attempts to place in perspective difficult management problems
that government has power to rectify.

(B) The author promotes the idea that laws are useless and that efforts to
change human beings are futile.

(C) The author summarizes the roles of state legislatures and state courts
in correcting federal problems.

(D) He ignores the important role of constitutional due process guarantees in administering federal policies on agency clients.

(E) He wants to show how a unitary government (all national power is
centralized) actually works in our federal system of government.

21.   What current management problems has the author identified?

   (A)   Recent problems have been generally ignored in the development of jurisprudence of our constitutional system of government.

   (B)   Flaws in the system mostly stem from the fact that the public school systems have failed to incorporate into the curriculum knowledge needed to pass today's more difficult PACE tests.

   (C)   Present-day personnel problems could be eliminated if, as the author implies, liberalism and "an open society" were abandoned.

   (D)   Laws and administrative rules must reflect changes in sociological conditions as minority members of society wish to enter more responsible positions in the work force.

   (E)   All personnel offices must deal with pay scales ratified by a centralized federal office in Washington, D.C.

22.   What major management problem in federal government remains unresolved today?

   (A)   Government has attempted, but so far has failed to protect adequately employees who report illegal activities of superiors or fellow employees.

   (B)   Despite frequent pressure on political leaders to appoint business leaders top public administrators, government management positions have not been fully restored to administrators who have expertise on for-profit enterprises.

   (C)   The Civil Service Commission should, according to the author, regain its authority to determine pay classifications.

   (D)   The author has implied that a serious administrative problem is open clashes between the senior executives and the Office of Personnel Management with regard to ranking scales of applicants.

   (E)   The author is rather complacent about the way government is operated today.

23.   What is the significance of classifications in the federal civil service?

   (A)   Locked into a ranking system, policymakers soon recognized that good performance on the job might go unrewarded.

   (B)   Classifications are the best route to fairness and equal treatment of employees.

   (C)   Featherbedding (hiring more people than are needed to perform the

work) was encouraged through a system of pay scales based on job description.

(D)   Classifications encourage enthusiastic responses from agency lawyers.

(E)   Applicants for jobs that require manual skills receive ranking before undergoing special tests to show that they can perform the skills.

24.   How does the author describe the role of public administration in oversight of management practices?

(A)   The major task of government is to make rules that govern workers and strictly enforce those rules.

(B)   The major task of public administration is quasi-legislative (rule making powers).

(C)   The major task of public administration, as the author demonstrates, is quasi-judicial (hearing and deciding cases initiated by the agency itself, government employees, or by agency clientele).

(D)   The agency does not oversee management practices. The author maintains that courts of law are charged with oversight duties.

(E)   Due process demands procedural guidelines and a bureaucracy designed to enforce rules and to defend employees who believe that they have been unfairly treated under those rules.

25.   What kinds of challenges in the workplace identified by the author remain for government to solve?

(A)   Perhaps the greatest problem that remains in America is racial prejudice.

(B)   Rude behavior, such as smoking in crowded places, has been solved by airlines and thus, according to the author, must be handled by Congress since employers are intimidated by their employees.

(C)   The author sees quick resolution of management problems in hiring people whose AIDS tests are positive because of such administrative mechanisms as the Office of Special Counsel.

(D)   Policies are needed to account for human nature which, unfortunately, is inclined to develop other kinds of prejudices in addition to biases against race and religion. These attitudes foster ill-advised behavior of managers.

(E)   Solving social ills in the workplace is not considered part of the job

description of management in business or government.

26. How did Watergate affect personnel management policies in federal government?

    (A) The number of specialized tests was increased to include people who were classified "professionals."

    (B) Effort was made to accommodate federal employees with special needs, such as protection from unscrupulous employers and/or difficulty working under arbitrary employers.

    (C) Pay scales became the central focus of the executive branch with increased authority allocated to a centralized national commission.

    (D) The number of guidelines designed to ensure honest government was decreased by executive fiat after the president associated with the Watergate fiasco resigned.

    (E) Actually, government remained structurally the same with only one minor change — broadened jurisdiction and an increased number of Civil Service Commissioners.

STOP

If time still remains, you may review work only in this section.
When the time allotted is up, you may go on to the next section.

LSAT Writing Sample

(Answer sheets appear in the back of this book.)

General Directions

You will have 35 minutes in which to plan and write an essay on the topic below. Read the topic and the accompanying directions carefully. You will probably find it best to spend a few minutes considering the topic and organizing your thoughts before you begin writing. In your essay, be sure to develop your ideas fully, leaving time, if possible, to review what you have written. **Do not write on a topic other than the one specified. Writing on a topic of your own choice is not acceptable.**

No special knowledge is required or expected for this writing exercise. Law schools are interested in the reasoning, clarity, organization, language usage, and writing mechanics displayed in your essay. How well you write is more important than how much you write.

Confine your essay to the blocked, lined areas on the front and back of the separate writing sample response sheet. Only that area will be reproduced for law schools. Be sure that your writing is legible.

Sample Topic

Directions: For this essay you are presented with an argument (see next page) that offers reasons for drawing a particular conclusion. Your essay should analyze and evaluate the line of reasoning and use of evidence in the argument. For example, you may want to discuss how the logic of the argument is flawed or could be improved, or what counterexamples or alternative explanations would undermine the argument. You may also want to consider what, if any, questionable assumptions underlie the reasoning and what additional information or evidence may have been overlooked that would strengthen or weaken the argument. Note: You are NOT being asked to present your personal opinion on the subject with which the argument is concerned.

The following appeared in a memorandum from the owner to the manager of Quicksilver Gym:

"A recent survey of commercial gyms that offer rock-climbing reported that 25 percent fewer accidents occurred in gyms that required an annual training session for members versus those with a onetime training session. Our competitor across town, Slade's Gym, has annual rock-climbing certification, and they have fewer rock-climbing accidents than we do. In the past three years, the majority of accidents at Quicksilver have involved rock climbing. In order to improve our safety record, we should require an annual certification for our rock-climbing customers."

Discuss how well reasoned you find this argument.

STOP
If time still remains, you may review work only in this section.

TEST IV

ANSWER KEY

Section I — Logical Reasoning

1.	(C)	8.	(A)	15.	(B)	22.	(C)
2.	(D)	9.	(C)	16.	(B)	23.	(A)
3.	(B)	10.	(D)	17.	(B)	24.	(B)
4.	(A)	11.	(A)	18.	(B)		
5.	(E)	12.	(B)	19.	(A)		
6.	(C)	13.	(A)	20.	(C)		
7.	(A)	14.	(D)	21.	(C)		

Section II — Analytical Reasoning

1.	(D)	8.	(E)	15.	(D)	22.	(A)
2.	(D)	9.	(D)	16.	(C)	23.	(E)
3.	(A)	10.	(C)	17.	(D)	24.	(A)
4.	(B)	11.	(A)	18.	(D)		
5.	(A)	12.	(D)	19.	(C)		
6.	(A)	13.	(A)	20.	(E)		
7.	(A)	14.	(B)	21.	(C)		

Section III — Logical Reasoning

1.	(C)	8.	(D)	15.	(D)	22.	(D)
2.	(A)	9.	(E)	16.	(D)	23.	(A)
3.	(E)	10.	(B)	17.	(B)	24.	(C)
4.	(D)	11.	(C)	18.	(D)	25.	(C)
5.	(A)	12.	(B)	19.	(A)		
6.	(D)	13.	(A)	20.	(B)		
7.	(A)	14.	(C)	21.	(E)		

Section IV — Reading Comprehension

1.	(D)	8.	(B)	15.	(D)	22.	(A)
2.	(E)	9.	(A)	16.	(A)	23.	(A)
3.	(C)	10.	(A)	17.	(A)	24.	(E)
4.	(A)	11.	(D)	18.	(C)	25.	(D)
5.	(B)	12.	(D)	19.	(B)	26.	(B)
6.	(A)	13.	(D)	20.	(A)		
7.	(C)	14.	(A)	21.	(D)		

DETAILED EXPLANATIONS OF ANSWERS

Section I – Logical Reasoning

1. **(C)** The court's rulings, taken together, hold that a reporter's observations are confidential, *except* when keeping them confidential would violate a criminal defendant's right to a fair trial. Answer (A) contradicts the court's ruling by claiming that a reporter can never be compelled to testify. (D) says that the reporter must always reveal information, with one exception; the court said that only in one exception must a reporter reveal information. According to (E) the defendant may compel testimony whenever he wants, but the rulings permit the defendant to compel testimony only under certain conditions.

  (B) is neither true nor false based on the court's rulings. The rulings have to do with the circumstances under which a *reporter* may be *compelled* to testify, not with the circumstances under which a *defendant* may *choose not* to compel a reporter to testify.

  (C) captures both rulings: the claim that the law ensures a reporter's confidentiality and the exception that a reporter must testify when such testimony is necessary to preserve a defendant's right to a fair trial.

2. **(D)** The argument is that while the Thatcher government of Britain was established democratically (B), it had freedoms uncharacteristic of democracies. So in spite of certain balances, it may not have been democratic (E).

  Answer (A) is one of the assumptions of the argument, since the final sentence of the argument implies that common sense is one of several checks (along with convention and precedent) against anti-democratic government. (C) is assumed in the writer's acknowledgement of "the merciless cut and thrust of debate in the House of Commons...." as evidence that the British government might be democratic.

  (D) is contrary to the writer's assumption that convention, precedent, and common sense can provide a more balancing force than any constitution and that a balancing force is essential to a healthy democracy, since it provides formal checks and controls.

3. **(B)** The writer draws an analogy between a wine shop and its inventory, on the one hand, and Toonton and its "inventory" (the airports), on the other: the suggestion is that Toonton should refrain from raising prices and should cut services, just as financially ailing wine shops do. Thus, answer (A) is incorrect, because it draws an analogy between wine shops and airports, not between wine shops and the city. Answer (E) recognizes the analogy that the writer is trying to

draw, but states this as the argument, whereas the writer is using the analogy as *support* for the argument. Similarly, the writer implies that wine shops are better off than Toonton (C), as *support* for the argument, not as the argument itself.

Answer (D) is incorrect, because the writer says nothing about what Toonton does *at* its airports; rather, he asserts something about what the city should do *with* its airports.

The writer's purpose is not merely to draw the analogy he does, but to use it in support of his claim that the city should sell the airports. Answer (B) notes both the analogy and the conclusion the analogy is meant to support.

4.　**(A)**　The argument's point is that since Congress has spent more money on the cow than on other animals, Congress must like the cow better than it likes other animals. Answer (B) does not weaken the argument, as long as the amount of money spent ($15.2 billion, instead of $16.2 billion) is still more for cows than for other animals. (C) strengthens the conclusion; it verifies that consumers elsewhere do pay more for beef than American consumers do. (C) could not be the correct answer because we are looking for an item that would WEAKEN the argument. (D) is also irrelevant, since the argument is not about which sort of cow (beef or dairy) is the more popular. And (E) is irrelevant because the argument is not about what Congress can afford but rather what proportion of its allotment for animals has gone to cows.

(A) would weaken the argument, if it were true, because Congress would have spent more on pigs than on cattle and, according to the principle of the argument, this would indicate that Congress has a greater fondness for pigs than for cattle.

5.　**(E)**　The problem here is to decide how much one may infer from the fact that some images in the photograph are images of people with green halos around their heads. Answer (A) requires us to jump to a conclusion that is not supported by the photograph: there is no obvious connection between an image of a green halo and extraterrestrial life. For this reason we may also reject (C): if the photo does not support the claim that there are extraterrestrials in the photo, then it does not support the claim that there are extraterrestrials elsewhere. Nor is there any obvious connection between a green halo and the unlikely possibility that radiation could emanate from a person's brain (B). One might be tempted to accept (B), since the camera is meant to detect radiation, but (1) there is no previous observation to support the possibility of such radiation and (2) answer (E) is simply more probable.

Answer (D) is tempting, but unfounded, since (1) the question assumed the photos really show the images as described and (2) there is no evidence to contradict the researchers' assertion that they *believe* what they claim.

Answer (E) is the most reasonable by default — all of the other answers are less reasonable. It is also more reasonable because photos can be affected by unusual lighting and, one may presume, such effects can be more startling when the camera is extra sensitive.

6.   **(C)**   The speaker, apparently a recently elected official, implies that his predecessors have lied and that he has been elected, in part, because voters want him to tell the truth about their country. If the country has been flourishing (A), or the people believe in government (B), then the speaker's predecessors were not lying about these. Hence, (A) and (B) could not support the speaker's assumption. If the speaker is not an official (D), then he was named to the office and his assumption is meaningless; it is not given further support. The country may have produced steel (E), with or without producing the millions of tons claimed by the predecessors. This statement, therefore, neither weakens nor supports the writer's assumption.

If the citizens in the audience have not been happy (C), then this confirms one of the lies alleged to be told by the predecessors. Each confirmation of a lie will lend support to the writer's assumption.

7.   **(A)**   The writer is arguing that the defendant was unjustly convicted of child abuse and that this resulted from society's tendency to presume accused child abusers are guilty before such guilt has been proven. That the defendant was convicted (B) is a given fact, and is not the writer's conclusion. While the writer draws an analogy between today's national hysteria and the hysteria of the Salem witch trials (C), she is not making the broader claim that all modern trials are similar to the witch trials. Nor is she trying to *conclude* anything about the similarities of the two kinds of trials. She does draw an analogy between the case in question and the witch trials as *support for* her conclusion. The writer does not admit that society is more tolerant of the crimes of child abuse and molestation than of murder, so (D) is not an acceptable answer. And although the writer is obviously unhappy with the prosecutor's "feverish imagination," she stops short of claiming that the prosecutor acted illegally (E).

The best answer is that the defendant is innocent of the crime (A), because all of the assertions made by the writer point to this conclusion.

8.   **(A)**   The writer argues that Bettelheim's "survivor's guilt," arising from his imprisonment in Hitler's death camps, led him to commit suicide (A). The writer cites as evidence (1) the date that Bettelheim chose to kill himself: the same date that the Nazis entered Bettelheim's country, and (2) the fact that others suffering from survivor's guilt, such as Primo Levi, have killed themselves. Thus, the writer is not claiming that Bettelheim's motive was loss of interest in life (B). And the writer never suggests that Levi's death caused Bettelheim's suicide (C). So the first assumption is the only one the writer is making. (D) is irrelevant because Levi could have been in Nazi prison for several reasons, not just because he was a Viennese Jew. (E) does not necessarily have to be an assumption, because Levi could have survivor's guilt from another incident.

9.   **(C)**   The writer, a Chinese democrat, argues that the massacre in communist China was a prelude to (A), and a contributing factor in the peaceful collapse (B) of communism in Eastern Europe. The writer refers explicitly to the "Tiananmen Square Massacre" (D) and to the popular will of the Eastern Europeans (E).

Nowhere, however, does the writer suggest that communism has collapsed in China, thus (C) is not an assumption of the argument.

10. **(D)**   The writer argues that Castro deserves less credit and more blame than Cubans are willing to give him, at least to the extent that the Cubans and Castro (in his speeches) have given him credit for getting rid of incompetent officials that are actually still around (D). According to the writer, the Cubans incorrectly assume that Castro is not responsible for shortages (A) and has chased out incompetent officials (B): neither of these assumptions is a conclusion of the passage, but the incorrectness of both is offered in support of the conclusion. The writer acknowledges, but is not trying to prove, that the buses and telephones don't work (C) and that Cubans like Castro (E).

11. **(A)**   The conclusion of the passage is that Israeli fathers are exceptionally good fathers. The main reason, or premise, is that Israel's economy is so poor, that Israelis have no incentive to pursue economic gains. This lack of interest permits Israeli fathers to focus on family values (A).

    Answer (B) illustrates the goodness of the Israeli father, but is not the main reason why these fathers are good.

    By claiming that Israelis have good economic opportunities, answer (C) contradicts the main premise of the passage. The passage does not claim that Israelis have no initiative to reduce high taxes (D) or that Israelis have a tortuous democracy (E).

12. **(B)**   The general premise here is that in Latin America, mental illness increases as the economy becomes worse. Thus, economic woes must be causing the mental illness. An indication of this is that 25 percent of Latin Americans suffer from psychological disorders (A). Unemployment and lower living standards are part of the worsening economy that is claimed to contribute to the rise in mental illness (C). The writer suggests that Latin American governments need to become aware of the connection between crisis and mental illness (D). And while the passage singles out the foreign debt crisis as an "especially" significant factor in psychiatric disorders, it allows for the possibility that such disorders will rise even if the debt crisis is solved (E). However, the passage claims that the connection between mental illness and foreign debt *cannot* be scientifically deduced, an assertion which is contradicted by answer (B).

13. **(A)**   The writer claims that there is intellectual alarm about the formation of the universe because the widely accepted Big Bang theory is inconsistent with recent astronomical discoveries (A).

    Among the discoveries cited as examples for questioning the Big Bang theory is that U.S. and Japanese researchers have found distant energy emissions (B). There are also unexplained gravity pulls (D), and Italian researchers have identified galaxies three times farther away than the Great Attracter (E). None of these is a summary of the argument.

    While the writer acknowledges there is uniform outward expansion of the universe (C), it is partly because there is more than this (a gravitational pull) than there is intellectual alarm. Answer (C), therefore, is not even one of the reasons for the writer's claim, let alone a summary of the reasoning.

14. **(D)**   This passage argues that, because analysis can be distorted to suit the needs of the person using it, it is of no use in determining the truth in policy discussions (D). The possible incompatibility of technical advice with bureaucratic or political convenience (A) and the occasional sealing of embarrassing analyses (B) are cited as examples of the *premise* that analysis is often distorted.

Further, while the writer says analysis is suppressed when it opposes one's objectives and trotted out when it undercuts an opponent's objectives, the writer never says that it *should* be suppressed (C) or trotted out (E).

15. **(B)**   The argument claims that if there is resistance (A), footdragging, and overt defiance, there is need for administrative action to maximize compliance and cooperation (B). That the speed limit is 65 miles per hour and the minimum wage is $1.15 (C), is not by itself occasion for administrative action. Choice (A) states there is no resistance. (D) and (E) cannot be applied.

16. **(B)**   The writer agrees with Lockard (A) that black men are frustrated and alienated (E), because, in part, they feel insecure about their rights (D) and they feel their further advance is limited by factors having nothing to do with their abilities or skills. The writer also cites the Kern Commission's indictment of white America (C) as support for his argument.

The writer neither suggests nor assumes that further advancement is limited by man's ability or skill (B).

17. **(B)**   The reasoning of the argument is as follows: a tendency toward monopoly reduces competition, leading to an increase in inflation. By implication, aggressive antitrust prosecution reduces the tendency toward monopoly, thus increasing competition and reducing inflation. Therefore, (B) is the correct choice. Choices (A), (D), and (E) are irrelevant since they involve factors that are not mentioned in the argument — unemployment and foreign competition. Choice (C) is directly contradicted by the argument.

18. **(B)**   The writer offers several premises to support his conclusion that the government cannot control the African majority (B). Two of these premises are that the police and army cannot maintain order (A) and there is conflict in the townships (E). Another premise is that institutions designed to nourish conformity and obedience are being rejected by blacks, although the writer never says that these institutions should be rejected (C).

Answer (D) is a broader claim than the conclusion of the passage, since this answer condemns all unrestrained use of state power, while the passage claims only that such use of power is failing when it occurs against the African majority.

19. **(A)**   The writer concludes that widespread availability of or access to qat makes studies of addiction difficult (A). As premises, the writer notes qat's widespread availability in most parts of Yemen (C), its harvestability (B), its low cost (D), and its being legal (E).

20. **(C)** One reason this passage infers that governance and management differ from each other is that one of the roles of governance is to supervise management. Thus, management is accountable to governance (C), but it is not true that governance is accountable to management (A). Nor, therefore, is it true that management is a chief element in governance (B), since the two are separate and distinct.

A second reason for this passage's inference is that governance, but not management, is accountable to the "stakeholders." Thus, it is not true that governance is accountable to no one (D). Further, since corporate governance stands between the "stakeholders" and corporate executives, stakeholders must be distinct from the corporate executives. Thus answer (E) is incorrect.

21. **(C)** The conclusion is that there is a great difference between the Russians and the Japanese in the way they proceed with negotiations. Thus answer (C), a statement of the conclusion, is not one of the premises of the conclusion.

The writer offers as premises for the conclusion the claims that the Russians retreat gradually (E), moving from an uncompromising stance to a softer stance (A); and that the Japanese tend to unite themselves slowly (D), moving from a compromising stance to a stronger stance (B).

22. **(C)** The main point of this passage is that, among the many reasons one might offer for the suburbanization of U.S. metropolitan areas, one must include government involvement (C).

Other reasons acknowledged by the writer, but as secondary to the main point, include the heterogeneity of Americans (B), rapid advances in commuting technology (D), and income-tax deductions for homeowners (E).

Answer (A), which refers to the rapid suburbanization of metropolitan areas, is assumed as a given fact by the writer — it is not what the writer is trying to prove.

23. **(A)** The writer argues that the rail is an engineering feat because the rail is a significant scientific development (B), there is enough rail to encircle the Earth 12 times (C), the rail is no longer the clumsy pear-head it was (D), and for all its significance it is just a little section of steel (E).

In addition, the writer claims that there are 300,000 miles of rail, not 150,000 miles of rail (A), so answer (A) is not one of the premises.

24. **(B)** The writer defends his conclusion — that the role of analytic policy making must not be underestimated even in countries of low income and scarce technical skills — by using the example of India's irrigation policy. This policy distributes water thinly, thus forestalling drought, but not increasing yields.

This argument would be weaker if India's policy were not analytic (A), the water supplies that India distributes had not forestalled drought (D), or India had no policy on irrigation (E), since each of these contradicts a premise of the argument. Also, answer (C), if true, would weaken the argument, because it contradicts the conclusion by claiming that analytic policy will not work in countries with low national income and scarce technical skills.

Answer (B), however, would not weaken the argument, since the writer acknowledges that the water supply will not increase yields. It is sufficient for the writer's purposes if the water supplies are helpful and are the result of analytic policy.

Section II – Analytical Reasoning

QUESTIONS 1–6

The initial information is summed up as

    eCc
    Bd
    | Ah or hA |
    du
    A—D or D—A

(Capital letters for the car names, lower case for the ornaments: c = chromed spare-tire cover, d = monogrammed door, e = rhodium-plated engine, h = hood statue, u = eel-skin upholstery.)

Collecting these together gives

	1	2	3	4	5
eCc					
Bdu		A̶	A̶	A̶	
| Ah–D or D–hA |	C̶				C̶

Placing that on a single diagram gives

	1	2	3	4	5
	D̶		D̶	D̶	
				B̶	B̶
	d̶	d̶		d̶	d̶
	u̶	u̶			
	d̶				d̶
	h̶		h̶		h̶
	e	C	c		
				D	
	A	h	B	d	u
					E

The negative entries come from the impossibility of fitting one or another of the lists into the space with the denied item in that space. The first line comes from the Avanti's being at one end or the other. The second is from the fact that there is a car on either side of the Cord. The third is from the fact that the Dusenberg is fourth from one end or the other. The fourth from the fact that there are two cars right of the Bugatti. And so on. When all of the negative entries have been made, it appears that only the car with the rhodium-plated engine can go into position 1, since all the other special

features have been excluded from that place. But that brings the Cord in position 2 and the car with the chromed spare-tire cover in 3 with it. Since the Cord is in position 2, the Dusenberg is not and must, therefore, be in position 4. This forces the Avanti to be in position 1 (and to have the plated engine) and, with that, the hood-statue in position 2 (and, so, to be the Cord). This leaves the second string of 3, starting with the Bugatti, and it has to go from position 3 rightward: 3 — Bugatti — Chromed spare-tire cover, 4 — monogrammed door — Dusenberg, 5 — eel-skin upholstery. By default, this last has to be the Edsel.

1. **(D)** See the initial reasoning. The Avanti is in an end position in any case, so it is not position 4. Thus, (A) is wrong. The Bugatti has two items to its right, so it cannot be next to the right end. So, (B) is wrong. (C) cannot be right because, if the Cord is in position 4, the Dusenberg has to be in position 2 and the Avanti in position 5. But, then, the Bugatti cannot be in position, for then position 3 contains both the car with the eel-skin upholstery (two right of the Bugatti) and the one with the chromed spare-tire cover (just left of the Cord). Nor can the Bugatti be in position 3, since, then the Cord would have both monogrammed doors (just right of the Bugatti) and a hood statue (next to the Avanti). So, since the Bugatti must go into either position 1 or position 3, if the Cord is in position 4, but can go into neither, the Cord cannot go into position 4. The case against (E) is similar: if the Edsel is in position 4, the Dusenberg again has to be in 2 and the Avanti in 5. Then, the Bugatti must be in 1 (since the Cord cannot be) and the Cord in 3. But then, the Dusenberg, in 2, has both the monogrammed door (right of the Bugatti) and the rhodium-plated engine (left of the Cord). Since this is impossible, so is putting the Edsel in position 4. Thus, only (D) is left.

2. **(D)** See the initial reasoning. (A) must be wrong because the Avanti is on an end of the row but the monogrammed doors are on a car between two others — the Bugatti and the car with eel-skin upholstery. (B) has to be wrong because the Bugatti is just left of the car with monogrammed doors. (C) is wrong because, were it correct, the car to its right would have both the eel-skin upholstery and the chromed spare-tire cover, contrary to the condition that each car has just one feature. Finally, (E) must be wrong, for if the Edsel has the monogrammed door and so is just right of the Bugatti, the two ordering patterns would have to combine as eC(cB)(dE)u. (The other order would make the third car in order have both the plated engine and the eel-skin upholstery.) But then the Avanti must be in position 1 (else the Edsel would have the hood statue as well as the monogrammed door). But that means that the Dusenberg has to be in position 4, which the Edsel already occupies. Since this is impossible, the Edsel cannot have the monogrammed door, so (E) is wrong. This leaves only (D) as correct.

3. **(A)** The new conditions reduce the list of known items to eCc and du, which must go together either as eCcdu or dueCc. In either case, the Cord must have the hood statue, because it occupies the only place for which no special feature is given and the hood statue is the one missing feature. So, (A) is true. The leftmost car may be the one with the rhodium-plated engine, but the

monogrammed door is still left of the eel-skin upholstery, so that cannot be leftmost in the row. Thus, (B) is not true. (C) is true on one possible arrangement of the cars within the new rules, but not on the other, so it does not have to be true. (D), which goes against (A), is wrong. This leaves (E), which also goes against (A) and is incorrect.

4.   **(B)**   All the possible orders of the given information are eCchA, AheCc, —e(Ch)(Ac), and (Ae)(Ch)c—. So, the Avanti clearly cannot be third from the left, since it is always at an end. Thus, (D) and (E), which include the Avanti among the possibilities, must be wrong. So must (C), which includes the Cord, for it is always in either position 2 or position 4, never position 3. Since (De)(Cd)Ec)(Bh)(Au) is possible within the new restrictions, the Edsel can be in position 3. So, (B), rather than (A), is the correct answer. In the suggested sequence, the two positive restrictions are met and others given originally are not — the Dusenberg sits three cars, not two, from the Avanti, the Bugatti is not just left of the car with the monogrammed door, and the monogrammed door is not just left of the eel-skin upholstery. (Be)(Cu)(Dc)(Eh)(Ad) similarly show that the Dusenberg can indeed go into position 3, and (De)(Cu)(Bc)(Eh)(Ad) does the same for the Bugatti. So, (B) is indeed the correct answer.

5.   **(A)**   Because the car with the chromed spare-tire cover has two cars to its left, the Cord and the other car with the rhodium-plated engine, it cannot be farther left than the third car from the left. So, (A) must be true and the correct answer. (B) need not be true, since the cars could be arranged udeCc, for example, putting the car with the plated engine in position 3. (C) need not be true, for nothing prevents the Cord from being the car with the hood statue, or the cars' being arranged ue(Ch)cd. (D) is falsified by eCcud and (E) by eCc(Du)(Ad), for example.

6.   **(A)**   Since there is only one car next to the Avanti, the Avanti is either rightmost or leftmost. The car with the hood statue is next to it, so it is second from the right or left. Thus, (A) is the correct answer. In any other place, the Avanti, next to the hood-statued car, would also have a car on the other side, so each of the remaining answers includes an unacceptable position. (B) also excludes the two real possibilities.

QUESTIONS 7–12
    An initial map might be

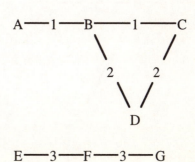

7.   **(A)**   B is connected non-stop to both A and C, by Flight One, and, by Flight Two, to D as well, that is, to three other towns in total. A is connected non-stop only to B. C and D are connected non-stop only to one another and B. Similarly, E and G are connected non-stop only to F, while F is connected non-stop only to the two of them. So B is so connected to the most, that is, three; C, D, and F are so connected to two, and E, A, and G are connected non-stop to only one. Thus, (A) is the correct answer.

8.   **(E)**   Each of A, B, C, and D is connected to all of the other three eventually: B non-stop, the others either non-stop or with a stop or flight change at B (A1B1C, A1B2D and the reverses). E, however, is connected only to F (non-stop) and G (with a stop at F). Thus E connects to fewer, two to the others' three. So, (E) is the correct answer.

9.   **(D)**   The diagram would now look more like

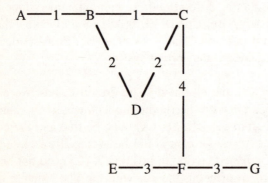

The cheapest trip, which is the one which involves the fewest stops, would be A–B–C–F–G. The two towns left out of this trip are D and E, so answer (D) is correct. The only flights out of A go to B, so any trip from A must go through B. Thus, answers (A) and (B) must be wrong. Similarly, any trip that moves from the upper four towns to the lower three (in this diagram) has to pass through C, so answer (C) must be wrong. For the same reason — that any trip between the two groups has to pass through F — answer (E) is wrong.

10.   **(C)**   Now the map might be

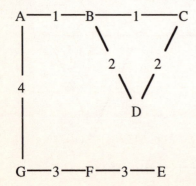

Originally, A, E, and G were connected non-stop to only one other town. However, A and G are now connected non-stop to one another, as well as to the other town (B and F, respectively) to which they were originally so connected. This leaves only E still connected non-stop to one other town, F. The others listed remain connected to two other towns: C to B and D (so (A) is wrong), D to B and C (contrary to (B)), F to G and E (against (D)) and G to F and A (denying (E)). Thus, (C) remains the right answer.

11.　**(A)**　A useful map now might be

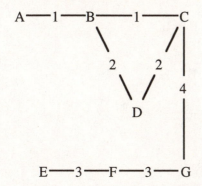

The expense of the trip is related directly to the number of stops, so we need only list these figures for trips from E, even taking the shortest route each time: F : 1, G : 2 (so (D), which has F most expensive, is wrong), C : 3 (so (E) is wrong), B : 4 (so (C) is wrong) A : 5 (so (B) is wrong, too). D, like B, takes 4 stages, so A is the most expensive of all, not merely of those listed.

12.　**(D)**　Now a map would seem to require

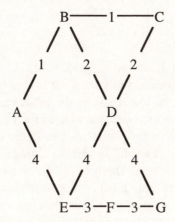

Since B1A4E is clearly a flight from B to E which stops only at A, (A) provides a complete and accurate list of stops on such a flight. Similarly, B2D4E shows (B) to meet the conditions and so not be the failing case sought. B1C2D4E does the

same for (C) and B1C2D4G3F3E does for (E). (D), however, is incomplete, since to get to F from D requires going through either G or (unlikely on this trip) E, so that one stop has been omitted. Thus, (D) is the correct answer: the list that does not meet the conditions.

QUESTIONS 13–16

The initial arrangement is approximately

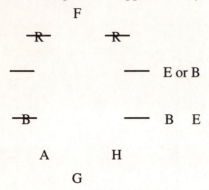

13. **(A)** The new information gives

F

    R   R

B   — E or B

E   — B E

    A   H

      G

The Ergonometric house goes next to the A-frame on the side away from the Georgian, as required, and the Bauhaus then goes on the side of the Ergonometric away from the A-frame (D). Because the roads do not adjoin the Federalist, the Cape Cod and the Dymaxion must go onto the lots on either side of the Federalist. Thus, they are not next door to each other and (C) is false. The Bauhaus has houses on each side — Ergonometric and one of the Cape and the Dymaxion — so a road runs on neither side of it, and (B) is false. The roads, then, must be in the remaining two places, which are next to one another between the Half-timbered and one of the Cape Cod and the Dymaxion. (A) is then the correct answer. (E) The Federalist and Georgian are opposite one another.

14. **(B)** The new information gives

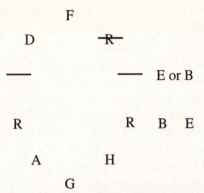

```
        F
  D        R

  ──          ──   E or B


  R          R   B   E

    A        H
        G
```

Since the Ergonometric house and the Bauhaus have to be on adjacent lots, the houses must occupy the two lots immediately to the left of the Federalist, for only one lot is unassigned on the right. Thus, (C) and (D) both have to be true, since these lots are also on the Georgian's right. The remaining unassigned lot is the one between the Dymaxion and a road. That lot must be occupied by the Cape Cod, so (A) and (E) have to be true. (B), however, must be false, since the Cape Cod is between the Dymaxion and a road, and the Bauhaus is between the Ergonometric and either the Federalist or the other road. (B) is, therefore, the correct answer.

15. **(D)** With these houses located, the map is

```
           F
    R          C

    ──          R   E or B


    R          D   B   E

      H        A
        G
```

or maybe (since the sides for the A-frame and the Half-timbered were not given)

```
           F
    R          C

    ──          R   E or B


    R          D   B   E

      H        A
        G
```

In either case, the Ergonometric and the Bauhaus must be in the two lots immediately right of the Federalist, since they have to go into adjoining lots with one of them in this place. The remaining two places must, then, be roads. Thus, (D), that a road runs immediately to the Dymaxion's right, must be true and the correct answer. (A) is true in one arrangement of the Half-timbered and the A-frame houses, but not the other and, so, does not have to be true. (B) must be false, since there are four places between the Georgian and the Federalist and the Dymaxion is only half-way along that space. (C) must be wrong because the given houses on the Cape Cod side of the Federalist leave only one lot, and the Ergonometric can go only where the Bauhaus can go next to it. Finally, (E) is false because the arrangement of houses does not allow a solid line of houses around either side to permit a double gap on the other.

16. **(C)** The arrangement in (C) would be

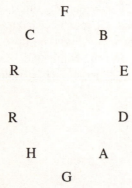

The Bauhaus would have to go immediately to the left of the Federalist to meet the condition that it is next to the Ergonometric. The Cape Cod would have to go to the right to meet the condition that both lots adjacent to the Federalist have houses. The two roads go into the remaining lots. Thus, all the conditions are met and (C) is the correct answer.

The arrangement in (B)

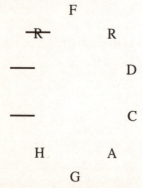

fails because once the three specified houses have been placed, only one lot is left on that half circle, so neither the Bauhaus nor the Ergonometric can occupy it, for these two must be on adjacent lots. Since they were the only houses left,

this lot must have a road on it. But this lot is also next to the Federalist, and no road runs on a lot next to the Federalist, So, (A) is not a possible arrangement.

(D) is not possible because the Half-timbered house is already placed, just to the left of the Georgian (in this pattern), and cannot be relocated. (E) also fails immediately, since, in it, the Ergonometric house is between two houses other than the Bauhaus. And (A) fails because the Bauhaus cannot go next to the A-frame by an initial condition.

QUESTIONS 17–20

Z = M
Y = MW
X = M
W = ma
V = AW
U = AW
T = ap
S = P
R = P
Q = pp

(Capital letters for Arts, lower case for crafts within arts.)

17. **(D)** (D) gives (ma)(AW)(P)(pp), all Arts represented and a Wizard and two double masters, to meet all the conditions. Thus, (D) is the correct answer. (A) gives (M)(MW)(M)(AW) and so lacks any representative of the Art of Prophecy. (A) is also short one Wizard/double master. (B) covers (MW)(M)(P)(pp) but, similarly, lacks a third Wizard/double master and also lacks a representative of Agency. In (C), the members represent (M)(ma)(P)(P), covering all the Arts but lacking two Wizard/double masters. (E) gives (AW)(ap)(P)(pp), missing both a representative of Memory and a Wizard/double master.

18. **(D)** The given triad, (MW)(ma)(P), represents all three Arts and provides two of the needed three Wizard/double masters. Thus, all that is required is a fourth member who is a member of this last group. Thus, V and U (a pair of Wizards) and T and Q (a pair of double masters) could each fill the last post, but no one else can: Z, X, and S are all Mages but not Wizards. So, (D) is the correct answer. The others either include people who are not Wizards/double masters or exclude some who are and, indeed, do both.

19. **(C)** To meet the conditions given, the three must all be Wizards/double masters and must represent all three Arts. The triad WVQ, (ma)(AW)(pp), does this with a Wizard and two double masters, a Mage in Agency and a master of a craft in Memory and one in Prophecy. Thus, (C) is the correct answer. The triad in (A), representing (M)(ma)(P) cannot occur together in a possible Tetrad, because the three lack two Wizards/double masters. (B)'s triad, representing (MW)(M)(ap), could be completed by any Wizard or double master, but not by

just any candidate. The triple in (D), representing (AW)(AW)(P), needs a representative of memory and a Wizard or double master — Y or W, in short — to make a complete Tetrad; nothing else will do. Finally, (E) shows (AW)(ap)(pp) can be completed only by a representative of Memory, though no further qualifications are needed.

20. **(E)** (C) is clearly not true, because no Wizard represents Prophecy on the list and, so, there cannot be a Wizard from each Art in the Tetrad. Yet the Tetrad can be formed. (A) is also clearly false, since ZWTQ [(M)(ma)(ap)(pp)] is a possible Tetrad by the rules, yet contains *no* Wizards (E). Consequently, (C) must be false, because there does not have to be any wizard at all — let alone several, from different arts — in the group. But even if there are Wizards, they need not be from different Arts, since ZVUQ [(M)(AW)(AW)(pp)] is a possible Tetrad in which there is more than one Wizard, yet only one Art represented by a Wizard. So (A), (B), and (C) are not true, and (E) is the correct answer. (D) is incorrect because we are told U is a Mage of Agency.

QUESTIONS 21–26

The initial information is only

R O Y G B I V

m ~~e~~   M = e/s/u/l F = c/m/d I > G O = Y G ≠ B

F

(Capital letters for colors, lower case for people: c = the Countess, d = the unmarried daughter, e = the Earl, l = the son-in-law, m = the married daughter, s = the son, u = the uncle.)

21. **(C)** The Earl, his son, his son-in-law, and the children's uncle add up to four. So answer (C) is correct. Any lower number would have one of these female, any higher would make the Countess or one of her daughters male.

22. **(A)** Since orange and yellow are worn by members of the same sex, that sex must be male. For, one of the wearers of green and blue must be female and the married daughter, in red, is female, so, if the wearers of yellow and orange were also female there would be four females. But there are only three females. Thus, the wearers of orange and yellow must be male. So, in particular, the wearer of yellow is male and (A) is the correct answer. Either the green-wearer or the blue-wearer must be male and the other female, but nothing so far requires that the distribution be that laid out in (B) and (C). These might be true, but need not be. Similarly, either the indigo or the violet robe is worn by a female (since one is in red, one is in either blue or green, and none is in yellow or orange, the remaining one must be in this pair); but there is no way to tell which from the information given. One of (D) and (E) is true, but neither one has to be.

23. **(E)**   If the people in indigo and violet were both male, they, together with the two in yellow and orange and the one in either blue or green would make five males. But there are only four. So, they cannot both be males. Similarly, they cannot both be female, since the two of them, together with the one in red and the one in either green or blue, would make four females. But there are only three females. So, the people concealed by indigo and violet must be different sexes and (E) is correct. Since the information so far does not determine which of the blue-wearer and the green-wearer is male, it does not determine which of (A) and (B) is true. Although one of them is, neither one has to be. Similarly, (C) may be true (if a female wears blue) but need not be. The same applies to (D), only more so, because the sex of neither part is determined.

24. **(A)**   If the people in blue and yellow are brothers, then both are male. Since one of the people wearing blue or green is not male, that must be the person in green, who is, therefore, female, as (A) says. (B) has to be false, since (B) would have both the person in blue and the person in green, the same sex, against the original restriction. (C) might be true, as might both (D) and (E) together, because the wearers of indigo and violet have to be of different sexes (see the discussion of 23). However, none of these latter three has to be true, as (A), the correct answer, does.

Section III – Logical Reasoning

1.   **(C)**   Since all basketball players are athletic, and some teenagers are basketball players, it follows that those teens who are basketball players are athletic. Answer (C) must be true.

Answer (A) is not necessarily true. Sentence three says that some athletic persons are skaters, which leaves open the possibility that some nonathletic persons are also skaters.

Since all basketball players are athletic, and some athletic persons are skaters, some of the athletic persons who are basketball players may also be skaters. Thus, (B) is not necessarily true.

The last sentence of the passage states that no teenagers are skaters. Therefore, answer (D) is wrong.

Just because all basketball players are athletic does not mean that all athletic persons are basketball players. Some athletic persons may play baseball. That some athletic persons are skaters does not mean that all are. Again, some may play baseball. Therefore, answer (E) is not necessarily true.

Sometimes it is helpful to use Venn diagrams to answer questions like this one. First, draw a circle to represent athletic persons. Mark it with an A (for athletic). Next, draw a smaller circle within the A circle. Mark it BB for basketball players.

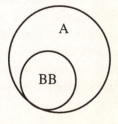

We know that A is at least as large as BB, since all BB are A, but we don't know if all A are BB. Next, draw another circle which partially intersects BB, and mark it T for teenagers. In the part of T which intersects A only, place a question mark, since we cannot say for sure whether any Ts are A but not BB. Next, draw a circle which intersects A and BB. Mark it S for skaters. On the part of S which intersects BB draw a question mark, since it is not clear from the passage if S intersects BB. S and T should not intersect, based on the last sentence of the passage. Your final diagram should be:

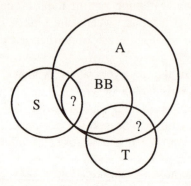

Now it is easy, using the diagram, to answer question one. Go through the answer choices one at a time while looking at the diagram. (A) need not be true, since part of S is outside circle A. (B) need not be true, since we don't know if S intersects BB. (C) must be true, since part of T is in BB, which is in A. (D) is obviously false, since T and S do not intersect. (E) is not true, since part of A is in neither S nor BB.

2.   **(A)**   Answer (A) is not true and, thus, the correct response. All basketball players are athletic, but all athletic persons are not necessarily basketball players. Some athletic persons may skate but not play basketball.

If all athletic persons are thin, and some athletic persons are skaters, then there are some thin persons who are skaters (the skaters who are athletic). Answer (B) must be true.

Question two states that all athletic persons are thin, so all athletic adults, a subcategory of all athletic persons, must also be thin. Answer (C) must be true.

If all basketball players are athletic, and all athletic persons are thin, all basketball players must be thin. Answer (D) must be true.

The original passage stated that some athletic persons are skaters, so answer (E) must be true.

We could use our Venn diagram above to answer this question. Shade everything within the A and T circles to represent thin. Now look for the answer choice which must be true. (A) need not be true, since we have a question mark at the intersection of S and BB. (B) must be true, since part of S is shaded. (C) must be true, since ALL athletic persons are thin. (D) must be true, since all of BB is shaded. (E) must be true, since part of S is in A.

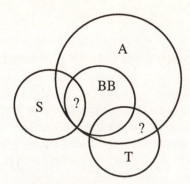

3. **(E)**   (E) is the best answer. The author is not willing to rule out the possibility that good grammar does indicate high intelligence. He implicitly concedes that it may in fact do so. The fact that most people think it does certainly strengthens the possibility that it does. Therefore, he would likely say that good grammar is important for that reason.

(A) is not the correct answer, because the author says nothing about the importance of good grammar for success in various professions.

(B) is not correct because the author clearly states that most people seem to believe that they can judge a person's intelligence by the excellence of his grammar. The author obviously thinks that those with good grammar are perceived by most people as being more intelligent than those with bad grammar.

The author is not sure whether or not good grammar indicates a higher level of intelligence. He does say that most people seem to think that it does. Therefore, he probably would not say that good grammar is unimportant. (C) is not the best answer.

(D) is not correct because the author does not say anything about how people's perceptions of another's intelligence affects their behavior toward that person.

4. **(D)**   Jon's response has two parts. First is the assertion that Tiffany is wrong in saying that Lisa has not made a mistake in any game in which both of them played. Second is the proof of the assertion, that in the game on Tuesday night Lisa made mistakes. For the proof to be valid, Tiffany and Lisa must both have played in the Tuesday night game, (D). If Tiffany has not played in any games with Lisa (A), the fact that Lisa made mistakes on Tuesday night does not prove Jon's assertion. Tiffany may or may not believe that Lisa is the best player on the team, (B). Either way, Tiffany's opinion has nothing to do with the validity of Jon's proof. Jon does not imply that Tiffany has played in every game that Lisa has played in, (C), only that they both played on Tuesday night. There may well have been games in which Tiffany did not play and in which Lisa made mistakes. Tiffany does not say otherwise, so proving otherwise would not weaken her statement. Jon has nothing to say about other games during the season, only the one on Tuesday night, so (E) is not the correct answer.

5. **(A)**   The form of the argument is:

1. Only if X then Y.
2. Y.
3. Therefore X.

In other words, Y can exist (or be true) only if X does (or is). Y exists (is true), therefore X exists (is true).

The only answer that follows this format is (A). Only if God exists can there be miracles. There are miracles (the speaker has seen one). Therefore, God exists.

In (B) it is stated that cars cannot run without fuel; that car is running, so it must have gasoline. However, gasoline and fuel are not synonymous. Cars can run on propane and natural gas, as well as electricity. That the car is running does not necessarily mean that it is running on gasoline.

The form of the argument in (C) is:

1. Only if X (water) then Y (tree will grow).
2. X.
3. Therefore Y.

This is not a valid form of argument, and it is a different form of argument than the passage. Although water is necessary for the growth of the tree, growth requires other things as well, such as soil and sunlight. We cannot say from the information given in (C) that the tree is receiving these things in addition to water.

Answer (D) is in the form of a probability, and it too is not a valid argument. Just because ninety percent of the people bitten die does not necessarily mean that Amil will die. It is probable, but not certain, that he will.

Answer (E) has the same form as answer (C). It fails for the same reason, namely that other things besides a secretary may also be necessary for me to work.

6.   **(D)**   Answer (D) weakens the argument. If (D) is true, going to graduate school is likely to accomplish two things: increase one's starting salary and increase one's chances of being employed.

The premises in the passage are:

1. that the financial rewards from getting a Master's Degree were greater in the past than they are now;
2. getting a Master's Degree is still a good financial investment;
3. however, the financial benefit accrued from a Master's Degree is now relatively small.

The conclusion is that, given the premises, one should not go on to graduate school if one is not so inclined.

Since we are to assume that the author's premises are correct, no other information should make them incorrect. Therefore, answers (A) and (B) have little or nothing to do with the conclusion. Whether or not more people are going to graduate school than before, a person's decision will still be made on a cost-benefit basis and on personal preference.

Answer (C) would strengthen the argument, not weaken it. If going to graduate school lessens one's chances of getting a job, one should obviously hesitate before deciding to go.

Answer (E) has no bearing on the conclusion because, whether or not the author of the passage is biased, we are told to consider his premises as true.

7.   **(A)**   The conclusion of the passage is that college graduates who do not wish to continue their education should enter the work force rather than attend graduate school. Answer (A) supports this conclusion by adding new information that those who do not wish to go to graduate school may suffer emotional distress if they go anyway.

Answer (B) weakens the conclusion by adding the information that going to graduate school may add to greater job satisfaction later.

Answer (C) talks about high school graduates while the author speaks only to the question of whether or not college graduates should go on to graduate school. Therefore, answer (C) is irrelevant to the argument.

Answer (D), if it does anything, strengthens the conclusion by showing that places are available for those who might consider going to graduate school.

Answer (E) suffers the same difficulty as answer (B) in question 6 [see explanation for answer (B) in question 6]. Since we are told to accept the truth of the premises, answer (E) cannot negate them. Therefore, it neither supports nor detracts from the conclusion.

8.   **(D)**   The passage identifies an effect (or phenomenon), namely that persons in positions of authority have greater than average life expectancies. The author posits as the cause (explanation of the effect) the fact that they have better than average diets and health care. He cites the study of military officers to prove he has identified the correct cause. (D) is a judgment call, but five years does not seem a long enough time to invalidate the findings of the study, unless we can assume that major changes in all the relevant factors have taken place in the intervening time. Answers (A) and (B) offer alternative explanations for the greater life expectancy of officers. We know that smoking, drinking, and lack of exercise can contribute to early death. Therefore, it may be that the officers' increased life expectancy is due not to better diet and health care, but to the other factors. If so, this weakens his use of the study to support his particular explanation of why persons in authority have longer life expectancies. Answer (C) does not offer an alternative explanation for the officers' increased life expectancy. But it does call into question the link between health care and diet, on the one hand, and increased life expectancy of officers, on the other hand. If officers and enlisted men have the same diet and health care, but different life expectancies, another factor must account for it. Answer (E) weakens the argument of the writer. If all the officers in the military are women, the argument that the long life span of those in authority is because of good diets and the good health care they receive has not been proven. The average life span of women in authority *and* out of authority is above that of men.

9.   **(E)**   The author does not specifically state that better diet and health care increase life expectancy, but he clearly assumes it to be true (A).

The author states that people in positions of authority can afford better health care than can the general population. He must assume, therefore, that they make more money than does the general population (B).

Since the author cites the study of officers to support his conclusion that the group in question (persons in positions of authority) has a longer life expectancy, he must assume that military officers are members of the group (C). If they were not, the facts about them would not be relevant to his argument.

Therefore, answer (E) is correct.

10.   **(B)**   The passage is in the form of a syllogism, and the reader is asked to choose which of the answers supplies the proper conclusion. The syllogism is:
  1. major premise — mental imaging leads to improved performance in some activities which require the development of special skills;
  2. minor premise — driving is such an activity;
  3   conclusion — therefore mental imaging may lead to improved performance in driving. That, of course, is answer (B).

Answer (A) is not correct because the major premise is in the positive form. It states what mental imaging can accomplish, not what it fails to accomplish.

Answer (C) brings in a new element, a comparison between mental imaging and forms of training. This is outside the scope of the argument.

(D) makes a claim which the premises do not support. The major premise did not assert that mental imaging was the BEST method of developing skills. One could say, consistent with the major premise, that mental imaging is one of many methods of improving performance, but not necessarily the best method.

The major premise does not support the conclusion that mental imaging is (E) the best method of developing NEW skills. The major premise asserts that it leads to improved performance. One might infer from this that mental imaging works only for those who already have the skill in question and merely wish to improve it. A more powerful argument against (E) is that the minor premise introduces the concept of driving into the argument. It would be unnecessary for the author to do this unless he wished to state a conclusion about how mental imaging can apply to driving.

11.   **(C)**   The argument in the passage is a causal one: that X caused Y, and that by changing X we have changed Y. The X in question is too little emphasis by the local culture on graduation; the Y is low graduation numbers.

All of the answers except (C) give an alternative explanation of Y. If any of those statements were true, the argument of the passage would be weakened or destroyed. It could be that the real explanation for Y is that (A), the economy used to be bad, so there was little personal incentive to graduate; but now, with an improved economy, incentive has increased. Or, (B) the high language requirements of the past were the real reason for Y. By lowering them, we change Y. Or, perhaps, an action of the state (D), which has nothing to do with the local community, has changed Y. Perhaps students are now better prepared for high school, (E), so changes in emphasis by the local culture was not the decisive factor.

Only answer (C) fails to weaken the argument. The author of the passage says nothing about which of the three groups mentioned was the most effective in

changing local culture. In fact, it is irrelevant to the argument which group was most or least effective in doing so.

12. **(B)**   The best answer is (B). The author cites two cases which support his conclusion.

Both of the author's examples support the same conclusion, namely that the USDA's requirements are counterproductive. The first example shows how the requirements discourage some activities that are environmentally safe. The second shows how the same requirements encourage activities that are environmentally harmful. Since both examples support the same conclusion, (A) cannot be the answer.

(C) fails because those with an opposing viewpoint are not mentioned, so the author does not specifically dispute any evidence cited by them.

Rather than predicting personal experience from a general principle, (D), the author is using personal experience (observation of his friends' actions) to prove a general principle (the regulations are counterproductive). Therefore, (D) fails.

The author does generalize based on observation, (E), but he does not use that generalization to undermine a theoretical principle. He uses it to argue against an action (the regulations) of the USDA.

13. **(A)**   To show that the requirements are counterproductive, the author cites one example. This example shows how the regulations discourage environmentally safe practices, as in (A). (C) states the opposite of what is given in the passage. It is likely that the author would applaud requirements that put his friends to a lot of trouble as long as the result of those requirements discouraged harmful and encouraged safe practices. So (B) must be rejected. The answer, then, is (A). (D) and (E) cannot be inferred as falling under the author's definition of counterproductive.

14. **(C)**   The form of the argument in the passage is:
  If X then Y;
  Not Y, so not X.
  X is: an astrophysics question is on the test.
  Y is: no one would pass.
The form of the argument in (C) is identical to that in the passage. 'If Hank forgot to pay' is X. 'He would have lost his license' is Y. Not Y so not X.

The form of the argument in (A) is: If X then Y. So if you don't want Y then eliminate X. X is the team losing; Y is Pete playing. This is similar to the argument in the passage, except that it implies that someone who is personally interested in the result can do something to avoid it. This element is missing from the passage.

The form of the argument in (B) is: Only if X then Y. Not X, so not Y. Eating peppers is the cause of sarpogus, so only if you eat peppers can you have sarpogus. You don't eat peppers, so you can't have sarpogus.

The form of the argument in (D) is: if X then Y. X, so Y. If we have a red sunset we will have good weather tomorrow. We have a red sunset; so we will have good weather tomorrow.

The form of the argument in (E) is: only if W or X then Y. Neither W nor X, so not Y.

15. **(D)** Answer (D) tells us exactly what we need to know, namely, what percentage of Canadian cold fronts that hit Eureka in the winter cause snow. When we know this, we can make an informed estimate of the probability that this wintertime Canadian cold front will cause snow in Eureka.

Answer (A) has little to do with whether this particular type of cold front is likely to cause snow. This type may always cause sleet, regardless of whether it hits in the fall or winter.

Answer (B) may tell us very little. It could be that 90% of winter cold fronts cause snow in Eureka. This alone would make us think that this front was almost certain to cause snow. But it could be that the 10% of winter cold fronts which do not cause snow are the Canadian fronts, and they, for example, may always cause sleet.

Answer (C) may also tell us very little. Canadian cold fronts may hit the area at all times of the year, resulting in snow, rain, sleet, or hail. What we need to know is not how many such fronts hit in a year, but what kind of precipitation they are likely to cause in the winter.

We are not interested in how often Eureka gets snow relative to the surrounding areas, answer (E). What we are interested in is how likely it is that a specific weather pattern causes snow in Eureka in winter.

16. **(D)** This is a fairly straightforward question. Sentence one states that to run in the 600 meter race a club member had to wear white shoes. We see from sentence two that no club member who wore white shoes ran in the race. The necessary conclusion is that no club member ran in the 600 meter race, (D). It is entirely possible that nonclub members ran in the race, so (A) is out. That no club member wearing white shoes ran in the race does not mean that no nonclub members wearing white shoes ran in the race, (B). We know it is logically impossible for any club member to have run in the race, (C). We also know from sentence two that no club members both wore white shoes and ran in the race, so (E) is eliminated.

17. **(B)** Ms. Jones' statement that she has decided not to take 'any more' Torozan can mean either that she is not willing to take an increased dose of the drug, or that she intends to take none of the drug at all. She obviously means the latter, though Dr. Jones has interpreted her statement to mean the former. The term 'increase,' (A), can mean only one thing, for the doctor to prescribe a larger dose. They both evidently know what her symptoms are, (C), and this is not at issue in the passage. Since both obviously know what the present dose is, 'the same' is not the misunderstood phrase (D). Since the doctor prescribed it and Ms. Jones is taking it, both evidently know what (E), Torozan, is.

18. **(D)** The argument in the passage is this:

Major premise: the works of a history professor at a major university would be widely read.

Minor premise: Bob's works are not widely read.

Conclusion: Bob is not a history professor.

The conclusion does not follow from the premises. The only conclusion which can logically be inferred is that Bob is not a history professor at a MAJOR university. He might well be a history professor at a minor university or college, (D). Answer (A) is incorrect because the minor premise states that Bob's works are not widely read, and (A) contradicts this. Answer (B), that Bob might be a biology professor, is entirely possible based on the premises, but it does not help to explain why the author's conclusion is wrong. It does not get to the root of the problem which is that Bob might be a history professor without his works being widely read. Answer (C) fails for the same reason as (A). Answer (E) fails for the same reason as (B).

19. **(A)**   The best answer is (A). The author implies that the rationale for abolishing protective tariffs applies also to abolishing farm subsidies. Each of the policies interferes with market forces which are the only reliable means of determining production. The author does not argue that farmers need to be protected from unfair competition, (B), although one might make that argument using the author's premises. Nor does the author use emotionally charged language, (C). The only descriptive phrases are 'reliable indicators,' 'upset market forces,' and 'artificially determine production.' These are hardly emotional. Answer (D) must be eliminated because the argument refers to international trade, not to market forces operating within a single country. Answer (E) must also be eliminated, since the author does not state specifically that farm subsidies are counterproductive for the nation using them. This argument could, however, be made on the basis of the premises.

20. **(B)**   The argument is:

Major premise: both A and B are necessary for C.

Minor premise: Bach had an excess of A but did not have B.

Conclusion: Bach could do C anyway.

This is an invalid argument.

The argument in (B) is:

Major premise: One must feel great passion to be an artist.

Minor premise: Friedmann has a vivid imagination.

Conclusion: Friedmann could be a true artist without feeling great passion.

As in the example, the conclusion contradicts the major premise.

The argument in (A) is:

Major premise: Angela could have written the story only if she has experienced all the events described in it.

Minor premise: she has not experienced X, which is an event described in the story.

Conclusion: She cannot be the author.

This is a valid argument.

The argument in (C) is:

Major premise: a phone conversation means an entry in the phone log.

Minor premise: there is no entry for last Thursday.

Conclusion: there was no phone conversation for last Thursday.

This is a valid argument.

The argument in (D) is:

Major premise: a payment before next week means I can prevent foreclosure.

Minor premise: no payment before next week.

Conclusion: I cannot prevent foreclosure.

This is a valid argument.

The argument in (E) is:

Major premise: only bright people deserve a place on the advisory committee.

Minor premise: Sally is bright.

Conclusion: Sally deserves to be on the committee.

A careful reader would note that this is NOT a valid argument. That only x's deserve y does not mean that being an x is the only criterion for deserving y. (Perhaps you have to be an x over the age of 21.) Therefore, we cannot say with certainty that Sally deserves y. Answer (E) differs enough from the passage to eliminate it as the answer. The passage specifically states that quality P is necessary for Q. It then says that someone lacking quality P can have Q anyway. Answer (E) does not specifically mention a quality which is necessary for y, then assert that person x can have y without having the necessary quality.

21. **(E)**   The argument which the president wants the advisor to attack is this:

Premise 1: appointing a team of representatives is necessary to an initial climate of trust.

Premise 2: an initial climate of trust is necessary for a lasting relationship.

Conclusion: since no representatives were appointed, there will be no lasting relationship and permanent relations have been damaged.

The advisor complies. First he contradicts the conclusion that the relations have been permanently damaged. Then he indicates the conclusion is false because premise 2 is false. He admits that an initial climate of trust is helpful in developing a lasting relationship, but he implies that it is not a necessary condition of such a relationship. Therefore, the answer is (E). Answer (A) is wrong because it appears from what the advisor says that the best relations depend on many factors other than the one mentioned in (A). Answer (B) is wrong, since it is impossible to say, based on the advisor's statements, what the correlation is between an initial climate of trust and lasting relations. It is impossible to say because there are other factors involved in developing a lasting relationship. Answer (C) is wrong because it confuses the effect desired with one of its possible causes. Answer (D) is wrong because it treats the immediate actions

mentioned as both necessary and sufficient to produce the effect, whereas the advisor clearly states that other causes are necessary to produce that effect.

22. **(D)** It should be evident from the above explanation that what the advisor does is (D), establish that the information was in error. The answer cannot be (A), since no analogy was used by the president. (An analogical argument is one which states or implies that an example is somehow like the present case.) Answer (B) is wrong since the advisor cites no evidence at all. Answer (C) cannot be true since the advisor addresses the president's argument very well. Answer (E) may seem the best to some, but it fails also. The advisor argues not that other factors are important for an initial climate of trust, but that an initial climate of trust is not necessary for a lasting relationship.

23. **(A)** This question is harder than average because several of the answers seem to apply. In the passage, Hinklemore uses the word 'politics' in a decidedly pejorative way. By 'playing politics' he means something like 'avoiding the issue' or 'using the issue for personal gain.' Bullfinch, on the other hand, does not use the word in a pejorative way. By 'politics' he means 'a process of compromise for resolving problems.' If Hinklemore is right, politics involves avoiding the issue, so the mechanisms mentioned may well be necessary to protect the public interest. If Bullfinch is right, politics involves delicate compromise between the representatives of the people, so the mechanisms may be detrimental to the public good. To reach an agreement, then, the two must first clear up the confusion over the meaning of the word 'politics,' answer (A). Basing the arguments on authority, (B), would not clear up the disagreement until both understand the crux of the problem, which is the two different meanings of 'politics.' The unproved premises in the arguments are the two meanings assigned to 'politics.' Establishing the meaning of the term is a matter of definition, not of logical proof. Therefore, (C) is not the best answer. The two debaters may present data to support their positions (D). Yet this will solve nothing until they establish the meaning of the term, so they can each address the same issue. Answer (E) is not the best because the examinee is not asked how the arguments may be made factual, only how the disagreement may be resolved. This leaves open the possibility that the two could agree to an argument that is factually wrong, but develops logically from the premises.

24. **(C)** This is a fairly difficult question. The examinee is asked to choose the answer which depends on facts from both statements.

Answer (C) is the best answer. Statement one establishes that abolishing increased pay for overtime leads to decreased take home pay. Statement two establishes that abolishing increased pay for overtime means increases in production will disappear. The implied connection between the two statements is that workers will not work overtime if they do not get increased pay for it. The complete argument is this:

Premise 1: abolish increased pay for overtime and workers' take home pay
   will decrease because:
Premise 2: (implied assumption which is derived from both statements)
   workers will be unwilling to work overtime, as they presently do, if
   they are not compensated for it at an increased rate, as they presently
   are.
Premise 3: (implied assumption from statement two) if workers do not
   work overtime, increases in production will disappear.
Conclusion: therefore, in order to have increases in production, workers
   must not cease to be compensated at an increased rate for overtime.

We can see that there is a logical connection between workers' take home pay
decreasing (x) and failure to maintain increases in production (y). The connection
is this: failure to pay increased wages for overtime will cause x, which will
indirectly lead to y. If we do not want y we must remove its indirect cause, x.

Answer (A) is a value judgement which the premises do not support. (A
value judgement is a statement that contains words like 'should' or 'ought.') The
premises are statements of fact, not statements of how things ought to be.

Answer (B) is not the best because the premises say nothing about the difference between the best workers and other workers.

Answer (D) goes beyond the premises. It requires another premise, that increases in production are essential to a healthy corporation. Nor does it depend
on statement one. The argument required for it is:

Premise 1: increased wages for overtime are required for increases in
   production.
Premise 2: increases in production are required for healthy corporations.
Conclusion: increased wages for overtime are required for healthy corporations.

As you can see, statement one of the passage is not necessary to this argument.

Answer (E) may appear to be the best answer, and it is a logical conclusion
from statement two. However, it receives no support from statement one. Since
the instructions require the conclusion to depend on both statements, we may
eliminate (E) as the answer.

25. **(C)**   Answer (C) is the underlying assumption. If the author is going to
attribute increased reports of melanoma to one cause, improved detection methods, he is implicitly ruling out other explanations of the phenomenon. The most
logical alternative explanation is that cases of melanoma have increased at a rate
equal to the rate of increase in reports of the disease.

Answer (A) is not the best because the passage deals with methods of identifying and reporting melanoma, not with the danger or safeness of sunbathing. If
one were to infer anything about sunbathing from the passage, it would be that
sunbathing is NOT relatively safe.

Answer (B) is seemingly correct, based on the greater number of reports of
melanoma. So exposure to the sun, which causes a high percentage of melanomas,
must also have increased. However, (B) contradicts the conclusion of the passage

that reports of melanoma have increased because methods of identifying it have improved. Answer (B) offers an alternative explanation which, if true, weakens the author's conclusion.

Answer (D) is a possible alternative explanation for increased reports. However, it cannot be an underlying assumption because it contradicts the author's conclusion.

Answer (E) is also a possible alternative explanation. It fails for the same reason as (B) and (D).

Section IV – Reading Comprehension

1.   **(D)**   Answer (D) is correct. The author is adamant that the two are not different faculties but that their processes and their ends are separate.

(A) is incorrect because reasoning and understanding do not seek to attain the same goals; according to the passage, reasoning "comprehends" but understanding "apprehends." (B) is not the right answer. The author is certain that the lines between reasoning and understanding are *not* blurred; the distinctions between the two are clear. (C) is incorrect. They are *not* two different faculties. (E) is incorrect. Not only are the faculties of reasoning and understanding the same, but their purposes are totally different.

2.   **(E)**   Answer (E) is correct. The author states in the first five lines that reasoning/comprehension look at things in one manner while understanding seeks to separate, to apprehend. The author notes that in time and space there is considerable difference and that in space things are independent of one another.

(A) is incorrect. The view of thought as being limited to space and time alone is erroneous. The author states that thought has other and higher forms; space and time alone are "deficient and inadequate to the truth." (B) is false. The author states that in space one has the very hardest of distinctions; "...things are regarded as just as completely independent of one another as they can possibly be." (C) cannot be true. The author states that space and time have considerable differences. The now, the past, and the future may never co-exist. (D) is false. The author states that the "essence of understanding is to separate"; reason, on the other hand, is "a way of looking at things which is larger than the mere understanding which made and set fast the differentiation."

3.   **(C)**   Answer (C) is correct. Even though the author does talk about space in the passage, he does not specifically mention constellations. So while it may have made a good example, it was not used in the passage and is therefore wrong.

(A) is incorrect. In describing that the "essence of understanding is to separate," the author cites counting a row of marbles as an example. (B) and (D) are

not the right answers. The author uses both of these choices in describing a unity in which the parts that constitute it are not independent but related. (E) is incorrect. When explaining "thought pursuing different ends," the author cites an essay by Montaigne that discusses blaming man's actions on character rather than fortune.

4.   **(A)**   Answer (A) is correct. The philosopher considers comprehension a superior intellectual process to separating the parts and examining them (understanding).

Answer (B) is wrong, for the author agrees with Montaigne, who attributes what we are to things within us, as opposed to the quality of external things. Thus, (B) implies the opposite of the author's opinion. (C) is incorrect. The writer believes that character is the result of ourselves and is not dependent from without. (D) is the wrong answer. The author observes that analyzing and noting differences is at a lower level than comprehending and not dwelling upon distinctions. (E) is false. The author would emphasize that external factors are less important than one's character.

5.   **(B)**   Answer (B) is correct. A completed recipe is not dependent on the distinctions but on the larger whole or the unity in which the differences are comprehended.

Answer (A) is incorrect. Understanding is more like the individual ingredients, which are distinct, than like the completed recipe. (C) is the wrong answer. Rationalizing is a way of thinking not described in the passage at all. (D) is not analogous to the completed recipe because analyzing is considering parts, not the whole. (E) is incorrect. Both understanding and analyzing look at parts and distinctions rather than the whole.

6.   **(A)**   Answer (A) is correct. The author sees thinking as having various levels; comprehension is superior to mere understanding.

Answer (B) is wrong. Comprehension and understanding are different. (C) is incorrect. Thinking can be analyzed; analyzing is a part of thinking. (D) is not the right answer. The author is adamant about the fact that comprehending and apprehending are not two different faculties; they just have different purposes. (E) is incorrect. Thinking can be more than just pinpointing differences.

7.   **(C)**   Answer (C) traces one of the most interesting developments in Japanese government where warriors were able to adapt to new positions of responsibilities.

Answer (A) is incorrect. Samurai were fairly loyal to Japanese lords, although they could be cruel and crude on occasion. "Taming" is too harsh. However, warriors obtained their education in the Buddhist temples. Answer (B) ignores the fact that samurai were educated to become civil servants. Answer (D) overstates the case with regard to lack of education of warriors. Although some

warriors were less educated than others, it should be remembered that samurai were quite good poets and many attended school. Answer (E) has not interpreted the text correctly. The author provides no evidence that schools were places of roving gangs of warriors. The author does explain that samurai were assigned to governmental offices.

8. **(B)** Answer (B) illustrates how analysts should consider both weaknesses and strengths of the topic under investigation, such as education.

Answer (A) is an exaggeration. Criticism does not necessarily mean that that author "overwhelmingly" rejected the process. Answer (C) misinterprets the analysis. In fact, the author questions the desirability of the kind of pressure exerted on children in Japan. Answer (D) assumes that the author's analysis is prescriptive. Rather, he examines and comments without suggesting that Americans copy the exact system. Answer (E) is partially correct. However, readers can easily detect negative reaction to the high tension routine in school and at home.

9. **(A)** Answer (A) is correct. Japanese wives are caught in a daily schedule that is geared to the needs of their children and the demands of the educational system, as the author vividly portrays.

Answer (B) is incorrect. The author does not imply that only males receive formal education. Answer (C) is wrong. The purpose of the heavy assignments is for students to prepare for the tests — not in any way could they be classified as "busy work." Answer (D) has come to the wrong conclusion that the author has not suggested. Although young women experience the same educational pressures to enter elite universities, certainly future happiness does not entirely depend upon that feat. Answer (E) cannot be inferred from the statements above. In fact, abortions and small families cut across social and economic levels.

10. **(A)** Answer (A) is correct because Japan places a great deal of emphasis on factual information that can be tested on a massive scale. A great deal of faith for choice of leadership tracks is placed on the ability to make top score on exams.

Answer (B) is wrong because the classes after school which are designed to improve skills for tests have no time for social activities. Answer (C) is incorrect. The author does not imply mothers have great power over school policies, nor does he provide a clue that there is such a technique as Meiji! Answer (E) improperly gives credit to the power of warriors over the early educational process. Rather the educational process influenced warrior-students. Answer (D) is wrong. The passage makes no mention of Japanese educational policies stressing one subject over another.

11. **(D)** Answer (D) is correct. In Japan, the education philosophy and the management philosophy contradict one another. (D) summarizes this conflict well.

Answer (A) has missed the entire point of the supervisor's role and has not understood "belly talk," which is a term that describes vague, non-decisive communication. Answer (B) is incorrect. The author does not mention young graduates with inflated egos. Furthermore, the author states that the groups are homogeneous and their style of communication leads to reduced friction. Answer (E) is not the correct answer; the passage never mentions "global dominance" or the phrase "at all costs." Answer (C) is a poor choice because the author does not imply that Japanese are impressed with American management style.

12.   **(D)**   Answer (D) is correct. The author, without prescribing the best educational goals, stimulates readers to further consider the process that may go beyond his own observations about stress and suicide.

Answer (A) is incorrect. Although the author traces the method for selection of leaders of the Japanese society, he does not embrace the idea that society functions best if only the most intelligent hold power positions. Answer (B) is incorrect. The text does not support the idea that a conscious effort is made to create a pool of poorly educated people for the worst kinds of jobs. Answer (C) is incorrect. While the author describes what has taken place in Japan over a long period of time, he has not made the subjective statement that Japan has produced the best social order. Answer (E) is an overstatement which assigns bias where there is no evidence of bias on the part of the author.

13.   **(D)**   The correct answer is (D). The author examines the trustee period when educated, highly ethical people managed government during President Washington's administration. He traces the deterioration of values under presidential administrations between 1820 and 1883, when party affiliation and loyalty were the controlling factors in hiring and firing government personnel. He examines how in recent years Congress and federal agencies have taken positive steps to ensure quality management based on education and to eliminate unethical practices based on self-interest and corruption.

Answer (A) is incorrect. The author does not imply or specify that honesty, education, and public interest have gone out of style. He does recognize that while high achievement in education is important, many jobs do not require broad knowledge. For those positions, specific knowledge needed to perform a job well is the basic requirement. Thus, the early values that he identified remain important today. Answer (B) is wrong. If the reader thought that the author implied that civil servants who are loyal to the president, his party, and his policies will work harder in order to win the next election, the author's point of view was missed. The author pointed out that under the patronage system, unqualified people working in government damaged the reputation of public service, especially when fraud and other corruption were reported in many localities. Answer (C) is incorrect. Although the author said that additional values have governed modern governmental processes, he certainly did not prove that as science and technology change, the definition of honesty and merit should change accordingly. In fact, ethical administrators will remain the bulwark of good government. Standards for measuring and rewarding

meritorious service may change, but merit itself remains a basic value under the scrutiny of the author. Answer (E) does not reflect the views of the author who recognizes that differences require development of fair procedures.

14. **(A)** Choice (A) is the correct answer. The author discusses the need to reduce the pressure of politics often exerted on government employees. He noted that Congress passed the Hatch Act, which denies federal employees opportunity to participate actively in political party campaign strategies. At that point tension develops when government employees who want to play a prominent role in party politics face loss of jobs. The Bill of Rights protects citizens who wish to participate in the political process. Specifically, First Amendment free speech and association limit governmental power on citizens' political activities. Federal employees are caught between the Hatch Act limitations and First Amendment freedoms.

Answer (B) is incorrect. Bitterness is not an appropriate description of the way the author portrayed his examination of political pressure on employees. Perhaps analytical precision would be the term that better describes the author's style of writing. Research findings showed party battles and jealousies made it desirable for politicians to appoint party faithful to government positions. But under these conditions, governmental purposes were compromised. The author illustrated the case in point by reminding readers that President Garfield lost his life under the patronage system. Answer (C) is incorrect. The author, while respecting rules and lamenting the fact that some agencies failed to follow rules, did not call for blind obedience to agency rules. He reported that the Civil Service Commission and the Office of Legal Counsel failed to carry out policies to protect applicants and employees, but he also left room for agency interpretation of the constitution in application of the rules. The author called for revision of old rules and promulgation of new rules in order to remedy problems which exist in personnel practices. Answer (D) is incorrect. Unlimited discretion of administrators in hiring and firing is a return to the old patronage system and the days before affirmative action. The author does not propose an unconstitutional law. Answer (E) stated an opinion where there is no evidence how the author feels about the case. His statement about the results of the *Griggs* case was neutral.

15. **(D)** Answer (D) is correct. The Supreme Court provided leadership when in a 1971 landmark case it made illegal tests that measured *general educational achievement* of job applicants rather than *specific knowledge required of the job description*. The discriminatory practice was a clear violation of the equal protection clause. A few years later, the Equal Employment Opportunity Commission (EEOC) acquired power to protect employees against discrimination after the Civil Service Commission defaulted in enforcing equal protection guarantees of the constitution. Thus, the authority of the EEOC for providing equity in personnel practices, which would include content of tests and the negative impact on disadvantaged groups, was reinforced in the court's interpretation of equal protection in *Griggs v. Duke Power Company*. From this example, readers can

conclude that court precedents are valuable tools of agencies that enforce equal protection.

Answer (A) is incorrect. Our constitution is based on popular sovereignty or "We the people..." Under popular sovereignty, citizens have power to change the constitution that governs our country. The author has vividly shown how personnel standards have varied over the years according to the ideas and wishes of the people. For example, the patronage system was permitted by the public until it became tired and disillusioned with the whole process. At that point Congress felt compelled to change the system by passing laws and authorizing mechanisms which monitor and punish wrongdoing by employers and employees. Answer (B) is incorrect. The reader may have misread the paragraphs and made the wrong choice. The conclusion stated in (B) is erroneous. In fact, the author calls for alleviation of numerous grievances of employees in instances where the equal protection clause does not govern the process. Answer (C) is incorrect. The statement shows failure to grasp the historical setting provided by the author. For example, President Garfield's death preceded the Civil Service Commission and affirmative action. Answer (E) misinterprets the author, who recognized and understood how policies were made in small steps which were governed by how much change was politically possible during various stages of history.

16. **(A)** Answer (A) is correct. The author clearly states that the constitutional framers "focused on such important factors as separation of powers and sovereignty of 'we the people.'" They left it to future policymakers to decide specific personnel policies for government bureaucracies. Answer (B) is incorrect. The patronage system, according to the author, was born in 1820 and has no relation to the phrase, "We the people." Answer (C) is also incorrect. President Garfield never enforced the Civil Service Reform Act; the law was enacted as a result of his being "shot by an office-seeking party worker who failed to acquire a job after the election." Even if Garfield had proposed the legislation, (C) would be wrong. The constitutional framers incorporated no such provision into our fundamental law. Answer (D) is wrong. The constitutional separation of powers doctrine is the foundation of the government and was never struck. The "spoils system" was not incorporated into the Constitution by the framers, making (E) an incorrect answer.

17. **(A)** Answer (A) is correct. The law was to protect employees from job losses if they refused to campaign in a political election.

Answer (B) is wrong. Although affirmative action has great merit, the author has not implied that the law was designed to protect any one race. Answer (C) is not correct. As the author stated, the law was designed to protect government workers. Answer (D) is incorrect. The author forthrightly states what is a well-known purpose of the Hatch Act. Answer (E) has fabricated the purpose of the law and the way that the law is enforced.

18.   **(C)**   Answer (C) is correct. The *Griggs* case is a good example of how a job applicant successfully challenged questions used on a test by a power company, irrelevant to the position being discussed, to screen him out of a job.

Answer (A) is wrong. If government should arbitrarily decide whom to hire, it is an erroneous assumption that political shenanigans led to unfair decisions. In fact, one of the purposes of the Civil Service Commission was to move away from politics. Answer (B) wrongly concludes that the law requires massive red tape before a person is eligible to work in either the private or public sector. Answer (D) is wrong. The author explained the role of the Civil Service Commission was expanded in order to make the Fifth Amendment viable in federal government. Answer (E) ignored a good example of congressional power over personnel policies when it passed the Pendleton Act.

19.   **(B)**   Answer (B) is correct. In an orderly way, the author considered the values of the framers of the constitution, the quality of early public administrators, and the deterioration of quality until pressure was exerted on Congress to regulate the hiring and firing practices of government managers. He continued his analysis by commenting on Fifth Amendment due process guarantees in personnel management and the effort Congress made to remove government employees from the stress and strain of working for politicians. He explained the creation of important agencies chartered to protect employees, and he identified grave problems which remain. Finally, he showed how values of the first federal government administrators are similar to standards that govern the process today.

Answer (A) is incorrect. Separation of powers does not mean that Congress and the courts have no roles in governing personnel practices in the executive branch of government. Although legislative powers are lodged in Congress and judicial powers are lodged in the judicial branch, authority to carry out executive policy comes from laws passed by the legislature, and conflicts are settled in the courts. The author shows how the three branches have interacted over the past two centuries in the substantive area of personnel management. Answer (C) is incorrect. The statement is a misinterpretation of the author's criticism of flaws in the federal system. He does not call for elimination or reduction of agencies or personnel. Rather he recommends improvement so that established agencies will function more effectively. Answer (D) is incorrect. While the author does not call for centralization of government for personnel rule making, he does recognize the important role Congress plays in making laws which will prompt governmental agencies to provide equal protection and due process in all phases of administering personnel regulations. Answer (E) is refuted by the tremendous number of facts made from study and observation of students of government which the author reports. Such details could not be examined if government were protected from public scrutiny.

20.   **(A)**   Answer (A) is correct. While the author has found that unfairness still exists, his viewpoint is optimistic in that he reports what is lacking and how due process and equal protection can serve as the constitutional basis for further improvement.

Answer (B) is incorrect. The author does not hold to this philosophy in analyzing personnel management in the past and proposes new rules and laws for the future. Answer (C) is wrong with regard to facts. The author's main thrust in these paragraphs is toward federal processes. Answer (D) is incorrect. The author grounds much of his work in procedural fairness. Answer (E) is an error because our federal system of government cannot exercise all authority over state and local governments, and the author makes no assertion that such a unitary system exists or should exist.

21.   **(D)**   Answer (D) is the correct answer. Not until the middle of the 20th century, as the author's essay reflects, have changes occurred in society to the point that minority expectations include working in responsible positions in government. As he traces customs, mores, and laws governing personnel management, it soon becomes apparent that Congress and the Supreme Court did not make meaningful policies along this line until well into the 20th century. Employment practices were repressive, and minorities did not find relief until Congress passed laws and authorized agencies that were intended to protect minorities in their attempt to be hired and to move upward. Thus pressure to change laws were due to sociological changes in our country, and in turn, new laws and precedents generated further sociological changes that greatly affected personnel policies.

Answer (A) is incorrect. The author cited a major case and then alluded to the role of courts in the development of equality and fair procedures. Court opinions that provide interpretations of the constitution, rules, and laws are the substance of jurisprudence. It is interesting to note, however, that the author suggests additional modes of out-of-court dispute resolution. Arbitration and mediation are becoming attractive methods for handling personnel conflicts. Answer (B) is incorrect. Review the paragraphs above, note that PACE exams are no longer administered. Nowhere does the author advocate the designing of a curriculum for public schools which will prepare students for specific government tests. Answer (C) is wrong. Actually, the thrust of the author's essay implies a rejection of a narrow political philosophy which would close doors to minorities and women. Rather, he supports protections which would lead to hiring a cross section of the national community. Answer (E) is incorrect with regard to facts presented by the author.

22.   **(A)**   Answer (A) is correct. When a federal employee blows the whistle on another federal employee who has violated the law, the whistleblower may be in jeopardy of demotion or losing his job. As the author pointed out, the Office of Special Counsel has done very little to protect this small group of courageous government workers. The lack of aggressive action on the part of the Office is a major problem because whistleblowers are a valuable source of keeping government honest and accountable for serving the public interest.

Answer (B) is incorrect. The statement reflects an erroneous conclusion that the author thinks businessmen should be appointed to administrative positions in

order to restore good government. Although he admired the work of the business/agricultural-oriented administrators in earliest years of our government, he does not suggest such a criteria. His philosophy is grounded on hiring high caliber men who abide by sound principles, such as ethics, fairness, public service, and equity. Answer (C) is incorrect. The author traces portions of the historical development of civil service, explains the Civil Service Commission's authority to determine pay classifications and then its loss of authority. He describes the event without explaining his personal preferences. Answer (D) is incorrect. While the possibility that a few senior executives may disagree with how applicants are ranked during the hiring process, the author's descriptive narrative fails to explain whether or not the top executives would have much interest in the procedures for choosing entry-level applicants. Answer (E) ignores the final comment by the author who thinks that much work remains before much-needed solutions are created with regard to personnel management in business and government.

23. **(A)** Answer (A) is correct. Evidently, the author's research showed that other methods of evaluation and rewards introduced by the merit system were introduced because old-style rankings were not viable for special recognition when work was performed exceptionally well.

Answer (B) is wrong. Actually, as the author notes, early personnel policy makers operated under this philosophy, but eventually made revisions and adjustments in order to provide equality and fairness. Answer (C) is not supported by anything that the author relates. Answer (D) is incorrect. According to the author, government attorneys have been quite lax in their duties along this line. Answer (E) is chronologically erroneous. Ranking of applicants for jobs requiring skilled manual labor is based on test scores.

24. **(E)** Answer (E) is correct. For example, the author systematically describes the role of the Merit System Protection Board, the Office of Special Counsel, and other agencies.

Answer (A) is only partially correct. Although rules and enforcement of rules are important, the author has shown that management oversight includes other duties. Answer (B) is only partially correct. Rule making is a large part of the bureaucracy, but not the entire scope. Answer (C) is partly true. Cases are tried, for example by the Merit System Protection Board, but equally important are other activities of the agencies. Answer (D) has misinterpreted the author's presentation. While he acknowledges the necessity of judicial process, he has not suggested that oversight be lodged within the judicial system.

25. **(D)** Answer (D) is correct. The author points out issues that are on the policy agenda, but rules that would eliminate all forms of discrimination have not yet been promulgated.

Answer (A) is not entirely true. It is true that racial prejudice remains a grave problem, but other kinds of problems include elimination of rules that punish pregnant women, victims of alcoholism and AIDS, etc. Answer (B) is wrong as

far as the author's discussion. He does not address behavior considered rude by some people and considered by smokers a matter of free choice. Answer (C) is wrong on two counts. The author soundly criticized the Office of Special Counsel for its plodding ways and acknowledged that a satisfactory AIDS policy has not yet been devised. Answer (E) is incorrect. The author has identified a number of social ills which impinge upon the workplace and must be addressed by administrators if business and government attempt to deal fairly with all employees.

26. **(B)**   Answer (B) is correct. The author listed five agencies that were established. The agencies were assigned certain areas of authority: personnel management, merit system protection, legal expertise, management/labor relations, and services of top administrators.

Answer (A) is incorrect. The author noted that the PACE exams administered to professionals were discontinued. Answer (C) fails to take into consideration the fact that policymaking with regard to pay scales was eventually decentralized. Answer (D) is in error. In fact, the Watergate scandal led to increased emphasis on ethics in government with a special board established for the purpose of promoting integrity in government. Answer (E) is wrong. A frontal attack was made on the Civil Service Commission when Congress passed the Civil Service Reform Act.

LSAT Writing Sample – Demonstration Essay

The owner's conclusion that Quicksilver Gym should change its safety policy on rock-climbing from onetime certification to annual certification for its members is initially compelling, because it relies on diverse evidence, ranging from statistics and examples from other businesses to select data taken from Quicksilver Gym. The argument is flawed, however, because it relies on fallacious assumptions that undermine each of its premises.

The owner initially appeals to a study to justify his conclusion, but the survey data is ambiguous and potentially misleading. The survey establishes a correlation between the number of accidents and annual climbing training. The owner, however, assumes that the lower number of accidents is a result of the safety policy. There may be some other factor common to gyms that require annual training sessions that decreases the likelihood of accidents.

The survey also does not indicate the nature of the accidents that occurred, or whether they were associated with rock climbing. The accidents could have been entirely unrelated to rock-climbing, and therefore the rock-climbing training would not affect the accident rates. In addition, some of the gyms surveyed might be exclusively rock-climbing gyms, and although they have annual training sessions, they would necessarily lack the accidents associated with other gym activities, thereby skewing the results of the survey.

The owner also assumes that Slade's fewer rock-climbing accidents directly relate to their policy on rock-climbing safety classes. Slade's position on rock-climbing certification might not be the cause of fewer accidents. Instead, they might have other safety policies that reduce accidents, such as mandatory protective gear or age restrictions. Or the number of accidents at Slade's may have no relation to policies at all. Slade's may have better equipment, better instructors, and better facilities that provide a safer rock-climbing environment.

Furthermore, the owner's comparison of Quicksilver with Slade's assumes an analogous relationship between the two. Gym size has a direct bearing on whether it is appropriate to compare the number of rock-climbing accidents at the two gyms. Instead of comparing the absolute number of accidents that occurred at each of the gyms, the ratio of accidents to number of rock climbers from each gym would be a more incisive gauge of comparison.

The most ostensibly significant justification for changing the safety policy—namely, that the majority of accidents at Quicksilver have involved rock climb-

ing—assumes that Quicksilver's change in policy would reduce these accidents. The safety certification, however, might have no relation to the rock-climbing accidents that occur. For instance, the accidents might be the result of faulty equipment. In that case, better and more frequent training would do nothing to prevent these mishaps.

Although the owner's concern for safety is estimable, he could strengthen his argument by expanding his correlations, which requires a better understanding of Quicksilver and the businesses with which he compares it. The connections between Quicksilver Gym, the gyms in the survey, and Slade's Gym need to be made more precise in order to be relevant to Quicksilver's potential course of action.

Demonstration Essay Explanation

This is a good essay that exposes several points that undermine the argument. The essay begins with a short introductory paragraph that provides a recap of the argument and the nature of the supporting evidence. The thesis is clear: the argument is flawed because it rests on fallacious assumptions.

The body of the essay then develops this thesis by discussing in separate paragraphs each piece of supporting evidence: the survey data, the comparison to Slade's Gym, and Quicksilver's injury statistics. Each paragraph pokes holes in the argument by presenting alternative explanations and interpretations of each of these items of evidence. The overall effect is to substantially undermine the argument's conclusion.

The concluding paragraph reiterates the thesis and suggests what changes need to be made to strengthen the argument.

LSAT
Law School Admission Test

TEST V

ZZZ's

2.9.07 FRI
~3PM

TEST V

Section I

Time—35 minutes
22 Questions

(Answer sheets appear in the back of this book.)

DIRECTIONS: Each group of questions in this section is based on a set of conditions. In answering some of the questions, it may be useful to draw a rough diagram. Choose the response that most accurately and completely answers the question and blacken the corresponding space on your answer sheet.

QUESTIONS 1–6

The five-member Women's Junior Varsity Fencing Team is to be selected from a pool of five freshmen, Alicia, Beth, Carlotta, Denise and Ellen, and four Sophomores, Faith, Grace, Helen and Irene. Only four members of the pool have competitive experience, Grace, Helen, Ellen and Alicia, at least three of whom will make the team. The coach, planning to build future Varsity Team members, will select three Freshmen and two Sophomores for the Junior Varsity Team. Unfortunately, personality difficulties make selecting the team members a bit more difficult.

Beth and Ellen will not fence on the same team.

Faith and Helen will not fence on the same team.

Grace and Carlotta will not fence on the same team.

1. If all four fencers with competitive experience make the team, which of the following *must* make the team?

    (A) Beth   (D) Irene

    (B) Denise   (E) Faith

    (C) Carlotta

2. If the team is considered as a whole, which of the following fencers must make the team?

    (A) Denise   (D) Grace

    (B) Alicia   (E) Helen

    (C) Irene

333

3. If Grace does not make the team, the only decision as to team members is whether to choose:

    (A) Denise or Carlotta   (D) Beth or Ellen

    (B) Faith or Helen   (E) Faith or Irene

    (C) Beth or Faith

4. Which of the following pairs of fencers cannot make the team?

    (A) Beth and Denise   (D) Carlotta and Beth

    (B) Denise and Ellen   (E) Alicia and Denise

    (C) Ellen and Carlotta

5. Each of the following pairs of fencers could make the team EXCEPT

    (A) Faith and Irene   (D) Irene and Grace

    (B) Grace and Helen   (E) Grace and Faith

    (C) Helen and Irene

6. If Irene does not make the team, which of the following fencers will make the team?

    (A) Beth   (D) Alicia

    (B) Faith   (E) Carlotta

    (C) Helen

QUESTIONS 7–11

   Six friends, Alfonso, Barbara, Chris, Darnell, Esther, and Frank, have lunch together every day and sit at a hexagonal table. The following rules always apply to the seating arrangements:

   Alfonso always sits immediately to the left of Darnell.

   Chris never sits next to Barbara.

   Esther always sits directly across the table from Barbara.

7. If Alfonso is seated next to Barbara, which of the following *could* be true?

    (A) Chris is seated directly across from Darnell.

    (B) Frank is seated next to Esther.

    (C) Alfonso is seated directly across from Chris.

(D)   Frank is seated directly across from Alfonso.

(E)   Chris is seated immediately to the left of Alfonso.

8.   If Esther is seated next to Alfonso, which of the following *could* be true?

(A)   Chris is seated directly across from Darnell.

(B)   Frank is seated next to Esther.

(C)   Alfonso is seated directly across from Chris.

(D)   Frank is seated directly across from Darnell.

(E)   There is exactly one seat between Chris and Esther.

9.   Which of the following *cannot* be true?

(A)   Alfonso is seated directly across from Chris.

(B)   Chris is seated next to Alfonso.

(C)   Chris is seated directly across from Darnell.

(D)   Barbara is seated immediately to the right of Darnell.

(E)   Frank is seated directly across the table from Alfonso.

10.   If Chris is seated directly across the table from Alfonso, which of the following *could* be true?

(A)   Barbara is seated immediately to the right of Darnell.

(B)   Frank is seated next to Esther.

(C)   Frank is seated immediately to the left of Chris.

(D)   Esther is seated next to Alfonso.

(E)   Barbara is seated immediately to the left of Alfonso.

11.   If Barbara is seated immediately to the right of Darnell, which of the following *cannot* be true?

(A)   Frank is seated immediately to the right of Barbara.

(B)   Esther is seated immediately to the left of Alfonso.

(C)   Chris is seated directly across from Darnell.

(D)   Chris is seated directly across from Alfonso.

(E)   Chris is seated next to Esther.

QUESTIONS 12–18

The 7 members of the Quality Control Division, Mr. Rodriguez, Ms. Unger, Ms. Queen, Mr. Singer, Mr. Thomas, Ms. Winters and Ms. Vellars, are going to have a group photograph taken, and they will be arranged in a line according to height.

Ms. Queen is taller than Mr. Thomas

Ms. Winters is shorter than Ms. Queen

Mr. Rodriguez is taller than Mr. Singer

Ms. Vellars is shorter than Ms. Winters

Mr. Singer is taller than Ms. Winters

Ms. Unger is taller than Ms. Queen

12. Which of the following is impossible?

    (A) Ms. Vellars is the shortest

    (B) Mr. Rodriguez is the tallest

    (C) Ms. Winters is the shortest

    (D) Mr. Thomas is the shortest

    (E) Ms. Unger is the tallest

13. If Ms. Unger is not the tallest, who must be?

    (A) Mr. Rodriguez   (D) Mr. Thomas

    (B) Ms. Queen   (E) Ms. Vellars

    (C) Mr. Singer

14. If there are two individuals taller than Mr. Rodriguez, who is the second tallest?

    (A) Mr. Singer   (D) Ms. Queen

    (B) Mr. Thomas   (E) Ms. Winters

    (C) Ms. Unger

15. If Mr. Singer is in the exact middle of the group, which of the following is impossible?

    (A) Ms. Queen is taller than Ms. Winters

    (B) Mr. Thomas is shorter than Ms. Vellars

(C)   Ms. Winters is shorter than Ms. Vellars

(D)   Mr. Rodriguez is the tallest

(E)   Ms. Unger is the tallest

16.   Which of the following orderings, going from tallest to shortest, is impossible?

(A)   Rodriguez, Unger, Singer, Queen, Winters, Thomas, Vellars

(B)   Rodriguez, Singer, Unger, Queen, Thomas, Winters, Vellars

(C)   Rodriguez, Unger, Queen, Singer, Winters, Thomas, Vellars

(D)   Unger, Queen, Rodriguez, Singer, Winters, Vellars, Thomas

(E)   Rodriguez, Unger, Queen, Singer, Vellars, Winters, Thomas

17.   If the three tallest members of the group are Mr. Rodriguez, Ms. Unger and Mr. Singer, who must be in the exact middle of the group?

(A)   Ms. Winters

(B)   Ms. Queen

(C)   Mr. Thomas

(D)   either Ms. Queen or Mr. Thomas

(E)   either Mr. Thomas or Ms. Winters

QUESTIONS 18–22

The following facts are known about a certain family:

Pete is Ramon's father and Angela's son.

Pete has more daughters than he has sons and he has more sons than he has sisters and all of his children come from his marriage to Sylvia.

Rachel is Ramon's aunt and Pete's sister, and she has several children.

Ramon's mother, Sylvia, has no siblings. Ramon has at least one brother.

18.   Which of the following is impossible?

(A)   Ramon has more brothers than he has male cousins

(B)   Ramon has more male cousins than he has brothers

(C)   Ramon has more aunts than he has uncles

(D)   Ramon has more aunts and uncles than Pete has brothers

(E)   Ramon has more cousins than Angela has grandchildren

19. If Juan is Pete's brother, then Sylvia is Juan's

    (A) sister   (D) niece

    (B) sister-in-law   (E) daughter

    (C) aunt

20. The minimum number of children that Pete and Sylvia have is

    (A) two   (D) five

    (B) three   (E) six

    (C) four

21. Rachel's children are

    (A) Ramon's nieces and nephews

    (B) Ramon's cousins

    (C) Pete's cousins

    (D) Angela's nieces and nephews

    (E) Sylvia's siblings

22. Angela's grandchildren, apart from Ramon and his siblings, are

    (A) Pete's nieces and nephews.

    (B) Ramon's children.

    (C) Sylvia's children.

    (D) Pete's children.

    (E) Rachel's cousins.

STOP

If time still remains, you may review work only in this section.
When the time allotted is up, you may go on to the next section.

Section II

Time—35 minutes
28 Questions

(Answer sheets appear in the back of this book.)

DIRECTIONS: Each passage in this section is followed by a group of questions to be answered on the basis of what is **stated** or **implied** in the passage. For some questions, more than one of the choices could conceivably answer the question. However, you are to choose the **best** answer; that is, the response that most accurately and completely answers the question, and blacken the corresponding space on your answer sheet.

British film critic Robin Wood, in his provocative book, *Hitchcock's Films*, calls *I Confess* "earnest, distinguished, very interesting, and on the whole a failure." He points briefly to some parallels with *Strangers on a Train* and then examines the character played by Anne Baxter. But in this case his analysis of
(5) Hitchcock's work — elsewhere frequently compelling — seems to me earnest, distinguished, very interesting, and on the whole a failure. *I Confess* is not flawless; but the genius which had produced *Strangers on a Train* the previous year is not entirely eclipsed in this effort. Hitchcock has expressed regret that "the final result was rather heavy-handed ... lacking in humor." Agreed. But
(10) when he says it lacks subtlety, he is too modest. The treatment of the characters shows remarkable precision and subtlety. The structure of the film is admirable, and the sense of contrast between idealism and romantic fantasy (which lies but a hair's breadth beyond idealism) is finely delineated.

The thematic development of *I Confess* is directed toward the confession of
(15) Father Logan (Montgomery Clift) that he was once in love with Ruth Grandfort (Anne Baxter). The title of the film, in fact, refers only superficially to Keller's (O. E. Hasse) words at the beginning and at the end. Everyone in the film is forced to make a confession, an admission of feeling if not of guilt — Father Logan most of all. Therein lies the essential irony of the tale. Logan does not
(20) confess that he had an affair, but that he is a man with feeling and emotion, traits which his manner belies. The outrage of the citizens is puritanical and self-righteous. (Only a rigidly old-world morality could be offended at the discovery that a priest has feelings!) But both the people and Logan must learn that there is a humanity underneath the black cassock — a humanity not obliterated by the
(25) ecclesiastical role a man plays. That *I Confess* is psychically his, he must confess his humanity. (In this regard, it is interesting that his brother priests are far more relaxed, witty and even playful. The youngest priest, for instance, has a mania for bicycle riding, which leads to humorous punctuations of rectory scenes by the bicycle's clash and clatter.) The final irony is that the priest's humanity must be
(30) established by confrontation with Ruth's unfounded romantic fantasies.

The occasional heaviness and overdrawnness of *I Confess* are due to some unfortunate casting. Clift's method acting comes across as merely wooden, and Miss Baxter, whom Hitchcock had not wanted for the role, overacts distressingly. There is too overt a use of religious symbolism. Crosses abound like birds
(35) elsewhere; Logan, walking the street reflectively, is even photographed against a foreground of a statue of Christ carrying his cross. It is all a bit too obvious to have much emotional weight or effect.

But the film on the whole is certainly not a failure. It is a minor Hitchcockian exercise in the examination of a sealed fantasy life, the analysis of role playing,
(40) and a reflection on the delicate balance necessary to achieve a healthy spiritual life.

1.   The primary purpose of this passage is to

   (A)   criticize Hitchcock's lack of directorial humor

   (B)   examine Hitchcock's directorial style

   (C)   develop the characters of *I Confess*

   (D)   show the value and subtlety of *I Confess*

   (E)   compare *I Confess* with *Strangers on a Train*

2.   The author believes Wood's analysis of *I Confess* to be

   (A)   perceptive

   (B)   off the mark

   (C)   of no value

   (D)   correct

   (E)   superficial

3.   When the author uses the word *eclipsed* in line 8 he suggests

   (A)   Hitchcock really was not a genius

   (B)   *I Confess* was a failure

   (C)   *I Confess* was better than *Strangers on a Train*

   (D)   some of Hitchcock's genius shows in *I Confess*

   (E)   Hitchcock's personal interest in astrology

4.   According to the author, who confesses in *I Confess*?

   (A)   everyone   (D)   Hasse

   (B)   Clift   (E)   Logan

   (C)   Grandfort

5.   The author argues that Father Logan must confess his

   (A)   sins   (D)   breach of faith

   (B)   lust for Grandfort   (E)   murder

   (C)   humanity

6.   From the passage, which of the following is a complaint the author has with *I Confess?*

   (A)   thematic development

   (B)   lighting

   (C)   criticism

   (D)   subtlety

   (E)   acting

7.   On the whole the author feels *I Confess* to be

   (A)   a failure

   (B)   flawed but interesting

   (C)   an unqualified success

   (D)   pretentious

   (E)   boring

Restoring the seceded states to the Union was the central issue in American politics from 1865–1869. This was pre-eminently a constitutional question involving the distribution of power between the states and the federal govern-ment. Considered from a strictly legal standpoint reunification presented perplex-
(5) ing difficulties. Social and economic turmoil resulting from the destruction of slavery vastly complicated the problem, if it did not make a peaceful solution virtually impossible. Behind the rhetoric of states' rights and federal supremacy the core elements in the Reconstruction problem were the status and rights of the former Confederates, on the one hand, and the status and rights of the emanci-
(10) pated slaves, on the other. The task of postwar Union policy was to reconcile the demands of these conflicting groups while restoring the federal system according to Northern republican principles.

Reconstruction as a problem in constitutional politics began with the disrup-tion of the Union in the months before Sumter and continued throughout the war.
(15) The first ideas on the subject to be given practical expression were those ad-vanced by President Lincoln at the beginning of the war. In his message to Congress in July 1861 and in a series of executive actions in subsequent months, Lincoln held that secession was null and void, and that the so-called seceded

(20) states were, therefore, still in the Union. He admitted that the Southern states were out of their normal relationship to the other states and the federal government since they had no loyal governments and were controlled by persons in rebellion against federal authority. But the states, as political entities distinguished from their governments, still were in the Union. Hence all that was necessary for Reconstruction was the suppression of actual military rebellion, the

(25) creation of loyal state governments by loyal citizens, and the resumption of normal relations with the federal government.

Lincoln assumed that it was the duty of the federal government to assist the states in Reconstruction. The justification for this assumption he found in Article IV, Section 4, of the Constitution, by which the United States guaranteed every

(30) state a republican form of government. All subsequent Reconstruction schemes drew upon this constitutional provision as justification for federal controls.

Finally, Lincoln assumed that the president had authority to carry through a competent Reconstruction program with little congressional assistance. A principal step in the plan was the suppression of rebellion, already being accomplished

(35) under the president's war powers. Lincoln admitted that in practice Congress would have final authority to pass upon presidential Reconstruction, since it could seat delegates from southern states at its discretion.

Lincoln's plan had two great virtues. It was consistent, for it rested upon the same premise of the nullity of secession upon which the administration had

(40) prosecuted the war. And it was simple of execution and promised a rapid restoration of a normally functioning constitutional system. Its great practical weakness was that Congress could destroy it merely by refusing to seat delegates from the reconstructed states.

8. The primary purpose of this passage is to

   (A) criticize Congress for refusing Southern delegates

   (B) describe Lincoln's reconstruction plan

   (C) explain the failure of Reconstruction

   (D) highlight the causes of the Civil War

   (E) argue against federal supremacy

9. From the passage, Reconstruction is most likely

   (A) the rebuilding of destroyed southern cities

   (B) the process of reintegrating the seceded states

   (C) another name for the Civil War

   (D) the seating of Southern delegates to Congress

   (E) the suppression of military rebellion

10. According to the author, one of the most important parts of the Reconstruction problem involved

   (A)   the rights of former slaves

   (B)   states' rights advocates

   (C)   suppression of military rebellion

   (D)   congressional support

   (E)   the distribution of federal power

11. From the passage, under Lincoln's view the seceded states

   (A)   could only rejoin the Union by petitioning Congress

   (B)   were constitutionally removed from the Union

   (C)   had fewer powers than other states

   (D)   were under martial law

   (E)   were still part of the Union

12. The author tells us Lincoln believed the federal government should

   (A)   leave Reconstruction to Congress

   (B)   let the states develop a Reconstruction plan

   (C)   stay out of Reconstruction

   (D)   assist states in Reconstruction

   (E)   allow Reconstruction during military rebellion

13. The author argues Lincoln's plan was good because it

   (A)   brought an end to the Civil War

   (B)   relied on presidential action

   (C)   it coincided with war-time Union policy

   (D)   was pro-states' rights

   (E)   was consistent with the Constitution

14. Lincoln justified his plan based on

   (A)   congressional authority

   (B)   a constitutional provision

   (C)   federal supremacy

(D)   administrative expertise

(E)   the economic problems in the South

The intensely hot conditions that prevailed at the universe's birth probably lie forever beyond the reach of even the largest particle accelerators. Investigators of low-temperature physics, however, have long surpassed nature. In the 15 billion years since the big bang, no point in the universe at large has reached a tempera-
(5)   ture cooler than three kelvins (the temperature of the cosmic microwave background). In laboratories, however, temperatures measured in nanokelvins and picokelvins are being achieved. The phenomena being studied at such temperatures are not only new to physicists, they have never occurred before in the history of the cosmos.
(10)   Of all the unusual phenomena that ultralow temperatures elicit, perhaps the most spectacular are superfluidity — the frictionless flow of a fluid — and its electronic analogue, superconductivity. Superfluidity in liquid ^{4}He, the common isotope of helium, has been known since 1938. In 1972 Douglas D. Osheroff, Robert C. Richardson and David M. Lee of Cornell University found that the rare
(15)   isotope ^{3}He could also become superfluid. Exploration of the properties of this new kind of matter has been a central project of ultralow-temperature physics for the past decade and a half.

The behavior of superfluid ^{3}He can be very intricate even though its structure is that of a simple liquid, composed of identical, chemically inactive, rare gas
(20)   atoms. In addition to being worthy of study for its own sake, this combination of the simple and the complex makes superfluid ^{3}He an ideal substance in which to study many other condensed-matter problems, ranging from the properties of neutron stars to those of high-temperature superconductors.

Laboratory studies of the behavior of superfluid ^{3}He may eventually yield
(25)   insight about forms of matter found nowhere on the earth. It is conjectured, for example, that the neutron matter (neutronium) in rapidly rotating pulsars is superfluid, even though the temperature in neutron stars is about 100 million kelvins. Neutron matter clearly cannot be studied in the laboratory, but it may be possible to mimic its behavior by means of rotating superfluid ^{3}He or ^{4}He.
(30)   Neutrons, like ^{3}He atoms, are fermions, and it is believed that neutronium becomes superfluid by the same Cooper-pair mechanism operating in ^{3}He. Only detailed theoretical calculations can tell whether the correspondence between superfluid ^{3}He and neutronium is sufficiently close for such models to yield useful results. If so, experiments will be performed on ^{3}He with neutron stars in
(35)   mind.

The experimental verification of such a possibility may lie far in the future, because such a transition may take place only at temperatures well below those to which liquid helium can be cooled at present. Nevertheless, there is little doubt that those temperatures will eventually be reached.

15.   The primary purpose of the passage is to

(A)   discuss properties of neutron stars

(B)   identify isotopes of helium

(C)   explain the value of ultralow temperature experiments

(D)   describe how superfluids are formed

(E)   contrast alternative theories of the temperature of the universe

16.   The authors argue the temperature of the cosmic microwave background

(A)   can never be duplicated in an experiment

(B)   is too hot for particle accelerators

(C)   results in neutron stars

(D)   is unimportant to high-temperature superconductivity

(E)   has been surpassed in laboratories

17.   From the passage, a *picokelvin* (line 7) is most likely

(A)   a very small unit of temperature

(B)   an isotope of helium

(C)   a temperature associated with neutron stars

(D)   a superfluid

(E)   a laboratory experiment

18.   From the passage, *superfluid ^4He* is most likely

(A)   a very cold form of the element helium

(B)   an isotope of hydrogen

(C)   superconductive matter

(D)   a form of neutronium

(E)   a nanokelvin

19.   The authors argue that by studying superfluid ^{3}He, we can learn something about

(A)   superfluid ^{4}He

(B)   other matter found on the earth

(C)   laboratory studies

(D)   condensed matter

(E)   the temperature of the universe

20. The authors tell us experimentation is not complete because

    (A) sufficiently low temperatures have not been reached

    (B) another isotope of helium needs to be found

    (C) Osheroff, Richardson, and Lee abandoned their project

    (D) of a lack of funding

    (E) such high temperatures cannot be duplicated in the laboratory

21. We know from the passage that neutron matter

    (A) exists at only very low temperatures

    (B) is not found on earth

    (C) can only be produced in experiments

    (D) does not exist in nature

    (E) has been experimentally verified

All of Plato's philosophical writing was done in the form of dialogues, conversations in which almost always the principal speaker is Socrates. These are the first philosophical dialogues of the Western world. So far as we know, Plato himself invented the dialogue as a literary form, apparently from his actual
(5) experience of listening to Socrates in his characteristic conversations. Socrates wrote nothing, but all the philosophy Plato wrote is attributed to him, with the result that it is impossible to disentangle with complete certainty the Socratic from the Platonic element in the dialogues. Most scholars agree that aside from the very early dialogues in which Plato was seeking to present the true teaching
(10) of Socrates in order to defend him and to honor his memory, the dialogues represent Plato's own views. Plato wrote more than 20 dialogues, many of them of fine literary quality. Since they depict actual conversations, they are open-ended, flowing, informal, very different from the tight, systematic, rigorously deductive argumentation which we will find, for example, in Descartes. The
(15) persons who take part in the dialogues become three-dimensional as Plato sketches them — the pompous, blustering Thrasymachus; the polite reasonable-ness of Adeimantus and Glaucon; the handsome and clever Alcibiades; and Socrates himself, master of the put-down, making fools of those who ventured to offer their opinions in response to his prodding, and making enemies of those he
(20) disagreed with in politics and philosophy.
Most of the dialogues use the philosophic method which Socrates invented — the *Socratic Method*. It is a form of seeking knowledge by question and answer. The question is put by Socrates, and is usually a general question: What is courage? What is justice? The answer offered by the respondent takes the form
(25) of a definition: Courage is ——. Socrates then proceeds to refute each definition by offering a counterexample designed to show that the definition which was

offered is too narrow, too restricted, or is biased or uninformed. Plato uses Socratic Method superbly in Book I of the *Republic*. Socrates asks Cephalos, a wealthy and honorable old merchant, "What is justice?" Cephalos replies from
(30) the narrow point of view of the ethics of a businessman: Justice is speaking the truth and paying one's debts. But Socrates replies with a counterexample: "Sometimes paying one's debts may be unjust, as when you owe a friend a weapon, but since he has subsequently become insane, would it not be unjust to return it to him?" Cephalos agrees; his own definition is demolished. A new
(35) definition must be constructed to cover this type of case.

The Socratic Method uses the technique of the counterexample to mount a series of questions expanding the number of examples, cases, particulars, to be included in the definition. A definition must state what all the examples, cases, instances, particulars, have in common as examples of courage, justice, and so
(40) forth. Sometimes the definition arrived at shows the falsity of the original defini- tion by completely reversing it. Sometimes, as at the end of Book I of the *Repub- lic*, no definition is reached although many are rejected.

Under the influence of Socrates' emphasis upon the importance of universal and unchanging definitions, Plato's primary intention as a philosopher was to
(45) find definitions for the concepts of justice and of the state.

22. The primary purpose of the passage is to

   (A) describe the structure of Plato's writing

   (B) examine Socrates' contribution to the dialogues

   (C) explain the Socratic Method

   (D) discuss the importance of the *Republic*

   (E) define justice

23. According to the author, Socrates

   (A) failed to influence Plato

   (B) only wrote in dialogues

   (C) disdained the question and answer format

   (D) tried to defend the memory of Plato

   (E) was not a writer

24. The author suggests the style of the dialogues

   (A) is similar to the style used by Descartes

   (B) concentrates on straight-forward definitions

   (C) is highly structured

(D)   has a fluid structure

(E)   is rigorously deductive

25.   From the passage, the *Socratic Method* is most likely

(A)   outmoded

(B)   a style developed by Plato

(C)   an indirect search for knowledge

(D)   useful only for general questions

(E)   the style used by Cephalos

26.   According to the author, Plato's role in the dialogues is that of

(A)   questioner   (D)   foil

(B)   writer   (E)   student

(C)   critic

27.   From the passage, the use of counterexamples is intended to

(A)   confuse the student

(B)   highlight additional considerations

(C)   test the student's memory

(D)   exercise caution

(E)   direct the student

28.   The author suggests that other than Socrates the speakers in the dialogues are

(A)   straw men   (D)   cowards

(B)   fully developed   (E)   two-dimensional

(C)   portrayed as fools

STOP

If time still remains, you may review work only in this section.
When the time allotted is up, you may go on to the next section.

Section III

Time—35 minutes
24 Questions

(Answer sheets appear in the back of this book.)

DIRECTIONS: The questions in this section are based on the reasoning contained in brief statements or passages. For some questions, more than one of the choices could conceivably answer the question. However, you are to choose the **best** answer — that is, the response that most accurately and completely answers the question. You should not make assumptions that are by common-sense standards implausible, superfluous, or incompatible with the passage. After you have chosen the best answer, blacken the corresponding space on your answer sheet.

1.   The boyhood dream of one day becoming a professional athlete — a dream shared by nearly all the men interviewed in this study — is rarely realized. The sports world is extremely hierarchical. The pyramid of sports careers narrows very rapidly as one climbs from high school, to college, to professional levels of competition. In fact, the chances of attaining professional status in sports are approximately 4/100,000 for a white man, 2/100,000 for a black man, and 3/1,000,000 for a Hispanic man in the United States.

Which of the following is necessarily true, if all the information in this passage is correct?

(A)   All the men interviewed were professional athletes.

(B)   A person stands a better chance of being a high school athlete than of being a college athlete.

(C)   A black man stands a good chance of being a professional athlete, relative to the chances of a white man or a Hispanic man.

(D)   A Hispanic man has a better chance of being a professional athlete than a white man.

(E)   A person stands a better chance of being a professional athlete than of being a college athlete.

2.   What is needed at this point, before proceeding to any further analysis, is a definition of bourgeois liberal democracy. The term is used here to denote (1) a representative government elected by (2) an electorate consisting of the entire adult population, (3) whose votes carry equal weight, and (4) who are allowed to vote for any opinion without intimidation by the state apparatus. Such a form of government would be bourgeois to the extent

that it organized, unified, and reproduced the political and economic dominance of the bourgeoisie.

Which of the following, if true, would weaken this argument?

(A) Sometimes an electorate excludes certain members of the adult population.

(B) Not all liberal democracies are bourgeois.

(C) No present government is dominated by the bourgeoisie.

(D) No democratic form of government could organize the political and economic dominance of the bourgeoisie.

(E) A government cannot achieve political and economic dominance simultaneously.

3. Everyone knows that correlations do not establish causal relationships among the variables they measure. And yet the examples of precisely such relationships being inferred are too numerous to require documentation. It has become commonplace, for example, to conclude that, because a given group of rich or successful men with few exceptions had rich or successful parents, the achievements of the sons were due to the good things conferred on them by their fathers. Perhaps they were. Unfortunately, the aggregate data are unrevealing.

Which example would add support to the conclusion of this argument?

(A) A woman born of wealthy parents who has succeeded because of good things conferred on her by her father.

(B) A poor and unsuccessful woman who has rich parents.

(C) A group of rich or successful women who had rich or successful parents.

(D) Rich fathers who conferred good things on their daughters.

(E) A woman born of wealthy parents who has made a success of herself without help from her parents.

4. Besides the obvious influence of Hegel, two principal influences may be discerned in Hinrich's first book, i.e., Neo-Platonism and, to a lesser extent, chiefly as regards the terminology filtered through Schelling and Hegel, Boehme. Hinrich is much more of a Neo-Platonist than Hegel, and these closer ties to Augustine, Pseudo-Dionysius, and Eirgena allow his religious thought to be more integrated, more systematic, more complete-in-itself, than Hegel's, while at the same time, by the implicit comparison, it points out certain shortcomings in Hegel's theory.

Which of the following is the most reasonable conclusion based on this passage?

(A)   Augustine was a Neo-Platonist.

(B)   Boehme was influenced by Hegel.

(C)   Schelling and Hegel used the same terminology.

(D)   Hinrich's book represents a revision and in some respects an advance over Hegel's views.

(E)   Hegel's work was an improvement over Hinrich's.

5.   If *all* beliefs were not the result of rational deliberation or enlightened evaluation but rather were the result of the social situation of the believer, then the whole enterprise of cognitive sociology would be self-indicting. For if *all* beliefs are socially caused, rather than rationally well-founded, the beliefs of the cognitive sociologist have no relevant rational credentials and no special claims to acceptability. In other words, the thesis that all thought is socially determined and thus cannot claim to be true does itself claim to be true.

What appears to be the point of this passage?

(A)   Beliefs are socially determined rather than rationally well-founded.

(B)   The claims of the cognitive sociologist are unacceptable if beliefs are socially caused.

(C)   The enterprise of cognitive sociology is not self-indicting because all beliefs are the result of rational deliberation.

(D)   The thesis that all thought is socially determined is true.

(E)   Beliefs are rationally well-founded rather than socially determined.

6.   It has been commonly believed that most work careers follow the temporal sequence of occupational choice, preparation and training, and entry and retention. However, most individuals do not make stable occupational choices as the first step in their work careers, nor do they show a strong commitment to a particular occupation during their work careers. Rather, occupational mobility is far more characteristic of most work careers than occupational stability. One possible explanation of the high rates of occupational mobility is that individuals are responding to opportunities that develop during the course of their careers.

Which of the following statements best states the conclusion which this argument is trying to prove?

(A) It's a common belief that most work careers follow a temporal sequence.

(B) Work careers tend to be mobile, rather than stable.

(C) Individuals respond to opportunities that develop during the course of their careers.

(D) People tend not to make strong commitments to a particular occupation during their work careers.

(E) Occupational choices are not usually the first step in people's work careers.

7. After years of neglect, the poor child has come to the forefront of research in education. The national conscience is twinging and the rush for remediation is on. Studies focusing on the poor child are abundant and a thorough review of the literature would be exhausting, as well as futile. It would be futile because the literature on the poor child tends to lack imagination and illustrates an unwillingness to test out a variety of interpretations. The literature tends to present a hit-and-run approach to the learning problems of the poor.

Which of the following best states the main point of this passage?

(A) Remediation is becoming more popular in an attempt to solve poor children's problems.

(B) Studies focusing on poor children are too numerous to review.

(C) The poor child, once neglected, is now being studied a great deal.

(D) Researchers appear to be seeking a one-shot method for dealing with poor children's problems.

(E) Literature on poor children is boring.

8. The first thing to know about the Foreign Service is its long-standing pride in exclusivity, a pride that necessarily requires excluding somebody. For many years, Foreign Service officers earned a reputation, still not completely eliminated, of being drawn primarily from elite circles. Even today, the Foreign Service continues to have a low number of blacks and women. Increasingly, however, this sense of exclusivity has been shifted to career background rather than social class.

If the information is correct, which statement below cannot be true?

(A) The Foreign Service is proud of its exclusivity.

(B) The Foreign Service's exclusivity extends to minorities.

(C)   Many Foreign Service officers are drawn from elite circles.

(D)   In maintaining its exclusivity, the Foreign Service is paying more attention to career background than to social class.

(E)   The Foreign Service's exclusivity does not extend to careers.

9.   In the early ages of the world, according to the scripture chronology, there were no kings; the consequence of which was there were no wars; it is the pride of kings which throws mankind into confusion. For all men being originally equals, no one by *birth* could have a right to set up his own family, in perpetual preference to all others forever, and though he himself might deserve some degree of honors from his contemporaries, his descendants might be far too unworthy to inherit them.

This statement is most apt to be made by a person who

(A)   considers monarchy to be acceptable, although not natural.

(B)   considers monarchy to be an unacceptable form of government, because all people are equal by birth.

(C)   considers monarchy to be unacceptable, because the Bible does not speak of kings favorably.

(D)   considers monarchy to be acceptable, as long as the monarch doesn't start any wars.

(E)   considers the monarchy to be acceptable, as long as the monarch's pride doesn't throw mankind into confusion.

10.   The majority of women who divorce eventually remarry. However, the proportion remarrying appears to be declining. Recent analyses of this topic have indicated that about three-quarters of the women who divorce ultimately remarry. The results of the 1985 survey imply that remarriage following divorce will be somewhat less common in the future than in the recent past. An informed guess about the percentage of divorced women who eventually remarry would be that the overall proportion will fall to at least 70%. This speculation is based upon inspection of results of the 1975, 1980, and 1985 surveys.

Which of the following is not an assumption of the writer's position?

(A)   At the time the writer was writing this passage, 75% of women who divorced were apt to remarry.

(B)   It is not definite that remarriage following divorce will be somewhat less common in the future than in the past.

(C)   In the future, divorced women who remarry will no longer constitute the majority of divorced women.

(D)   The information in the 1975, 1980, and 1985 surveys allows speculation concerning the drop in the percentage of divorced women remarrying.

(E)   The results of the 1985 survey are consistent with the results of the two previous surveys.

11.   The dating culture in Japan is backward compared with the Western standard. The majority of young people have dating experiences but the dating code has yet to be established. It, in turn, signifies the fact that dysfunctional aspects of dating are likely to exert a severe impact on the participants. And therefore, it is urgently requested that a clarification be made of the pattern of mate selection in Japan; the developmental stages as well as the assigned tasks at each stage.

What appear to be the elements of the dating code which the writer seeks?

(A)   The dating experiences of the young people.

(B)   The dysfunctional aspects of dating.

(C)   The development stages of the pattern of mate selection, as well as the assigned tasks at each stage.

(D)   The impact on dating participants.

(E)   Western standards of dating.

12.   The Nazis will never destroy us. Even if, to suppose the impossible, they win the military decision, they still cannot destroy us. A free people may be disarmed and tormented. They can never be conquered by an external foe. But these slippery borers-from-within, these plausible pseudo-democrats, the Communists, are something else. They are dangerous because they are not recognized as dangerous. Cleverly they seize on the weaknesses and inconsistencies of 'The democratic way.'

Based on this passage, which of the following is not one of the writer's reasons for fearing Communists more than Nazis?

(A)   The Nazis will never destroy us.

(B)   Communists may disarm and torment democratic people.

(C)   People who are not recognized as dangerous can be dangerous.

(D)   The "democratic way" suffers from inconsistences and weaknesses.

(E)   The Communists are foes, but not external foes.

13. Historical and comparative research has shown the relative invariance of household size, the prevalence of nuclear household structure, and the concentration of household extension in only limited segments of the life course. These findings do not contradict the claim that extended kinship ties beyond the household may decline with modernization, but they have led to more refined theories about the decline of extended households and the rise of the nuclear family.

Which of the following is consistent with the findings accepted by the writer?

(A) The nuclear family is more common than the extended household.

(B) Household size tends to vary.

(C) Extended kinship ties beyond the household will not decline with modernization.

(D) Concentration of household extension is widespread.

(E) Historical and comparative research conflicts with claims about the decline of extended kinship ties.

14. The upsurge of interest in the Marxist theory of the state seems to be the result of the conjunction of two trends. First, existing theories of the state were found by scholars to be heavily ideological and therefore poor guides for understanding political reality. Second, the political activism of the 1960s failed to think through the ends of action itself. As existing theories lost their credibility and the New Left withered away, it became clear to scholars that some serious thought had to be devoted to developing a theory of the nature of political power in advanced capitalist societies.

Which of the following, if true, would weaken the writer's argument?

(A) Political activism of the 1960s withered away.

(B) The nature of political power in advanced capitalist societies cannot be explained by existing theories of the state.

(C) The failures of existing theories of state to explain political reality, combined with the withering away of the New Left, have led to an upsurge in interest in Marxist theory.

(D) Heavily ideological theories could be good guides for understanding political reality.

(E) Too much ideology in a theory makes it a poor guide for understanding the reality it purports to explain.

15. The World Bank has recently estimated the number of people in absolute poverty in the Third World at around 780 million. Half of them are in South Asia. The other half lives in East and Southeast Asia, sub-Saharan Africa, Latin America, North Africa and the Middle East. Roughly 80 percent of these poor live in the countryside, mostly as small farmers and landless laborers. Poverty is thus an essentially rural phenomenon.

What is a more reasonable conclusion based on the premises, than the one the writer draws?

(A) Poverty in the Third World is essentially a rural phenomenon.

(B) Most poverty occurs in the Third World.

(C) Most of the rural poverty in the world occurs in the Third World.

(D) The World Bank is concerned more with the poor in the Third World than it is with poor in other parts of the world.

(E) Approximately 390 million people live in East and Southeast Asia.

16. The Biological Weapons Convention, which was signed in 1972, forbade signatories "to develop, produce, stockpile, or otherwise acquire or retain" biological weapons — specifically, "microbial or other biological agents, or toxins whatever their origin or method of production." But today it is possible to produce various toxins synthetically; toxins are not living substances and in this sense are chemicals. Thus they would not be covered by the Convention, but by the Geneva Protocol of 1925 which forbids the use of chemicals in war and not their production.

Which of the following conclusions is supported by the passage?

(A) Biological weapons are worse than chemical weapons.

(B) "Toxin" is more difficult to define than it used to be.

(C) Chemical weapons are worse than biological weapons.

(D) Weapons containing toxins are worse than biological weapons.

(E) Concern about biological weapons is more recent than concern about chemical weapons.

17. The reader knows that a story is being told by someone. Who the author is determines what is written and how the story is told, and so also determines in large measure the way in which the reader is likely to react to the story. All novels are told by an implied author who is created by the biographical author and is necessarily part of the formal experience of reading the novel. You cannot, after all, tell the dancer from the dance.

According to this argument, which sentence would be true?

(A)   The implied author of a story creates a biological author.

(B)   One cannot understand *Huckleberry Finn* without understanding Mark Twain.

(C)   One cannot understand Mark Twain without understanding *Huckleberry Finn*.

(D)   Readers often fail to recognize that the author has something to do with the story.

(E)   All novels are written by an implied author.

18.   Sun recalls his impressions about the order and peace of the West by saying "the old Honolulu post office (which delivered daily mail without fail, to his surprise) stands out in my mind very clearly." Everywhere in Hawaii he saw evidence of respect for laws which led him to believe that comfort, abundance and progress resulted from the orderly maintenance of these laws. Admiring Americans with their "land of the free and home of the brave," he soon came to believe that it was the American sort of law that China sorely needed.

Which statement, if true, would weaken Sun's argument?

(A)   The old Honolulu post office no longer exists.

(B)   China had its own laws.

(C)   China had its own methods for delivering the mail.

(D)   It's possible to respect the law, even if the law is not maintained in an orderly fashion.

(E)   Comfort, abundance, and progress may result even in the absence of orderly maintenance of laws.

19.   By "materialism" I mean the theory that there is nothing in the world over and above those entities which are postulated by physics. Thus I do not hold materialism to be wedded to the billiard-ball physics of the 19th century. The less visualizable particles of modern physics count as matter. Note that energy counts as matter for my purposes: indeed in modern physics energy and matter are not sharply distinguishable.

Which of the following is an inference that we may draw from this passage?

(A)   Only physicists are materialists.

(B)   Matter is nothing but energy.

(C) The writer doesn't like billiards.

(D) There are fewer visualizable particles in modern physics than in 19th century physics.

(E) Nineteenth century materialism was limited to the visualizable.

20. There are two issues that people concerned about the liberation of women and men from rigid and limiting sex roles must consider. One is whether there is any basis to the claim that there are biologically derived characteristics which universally differentiate men and women. The other is to understand why in almost every society women are dominated by men and are thought to be inferior to men. This essay refutes the claim for universal and necessary differentiation based on a comparison of cultures and socialization practices to account for such differences where and when they occur.

Which statement best summarizes the writer's argument?

(A) One must consider rigid and limiting sex roles, because people are concerned with the liberation of men and women.

(B) Differences between men and women are universal, but not necessary.

(C) Differences between men and women are necessary, but not universal.

(D) Differences between men and women are based on culture and socialization and hence are neither universal, nor necessary.

(E) In almost every society women are dominated by men.

21. During the 19th century, and through much of the early 20th, *Hamlet* was regarded as Shakespeare's central and most significant play, because it dramatized a central preoccupation of the age of Romanticism: the conflict of consciousness and action, the sense of consciousness as a withdrawal from action which could make for futility, and yet was all that could prevent action from becoming totally mindless. Perhaps, if we had not had *Hamlet*, we might not have had the Romantic movement at all.

Which of the following, if true, would weaken this argument?

(A) Actions cannot be prevented from being totally mindless.

(B) Romanticism was not preoccupied with the conflict of consciousness and action.

(C) *Hamlet* was not Shakespeare's central and most significant play.

(D) Shakespeare was not a Romantic.

(E) The Romantic movement did not occur until after *Hamlet* was written.

22. I know of a man who, going to a dentist, was proud of the calmness with which he took his punishment. But after the session was ended, the dentist said to him: "I observe that you were very much afraid of me. For I have noted that, when patients are frightened, their saliva becomes thicker, more sticky. And yours was exceptionally so."

Which of the following is an assumption of the dentist's argument?

(A) Thickening saliva causes fear.

(B) One cannot be calm and afraid at the same time.

(C) Thickening saliva causes stickiness.

(D) The patient was not afraid until the session was over.

(E) There is a causal connection between a patient's fear and a patient's thickening saliva.

23. In the King James version of the Bible we encounter the Psalmist's injunction to "worship the Lord in the beauty of holiness." It is significant, however, that other versions translate the passage "in the splendour of Holiness," and others render it "in holy array" or "festive attire." Immediately we are made aware of the fact that the biblical word translated as "beauty" in the King James version is not synonymous with that which originated in Greek thought, and eventually became the original definitive category of aesthetics.

Which of the following is *not* one of the writer's reasons for concluding that "beauty" in the King James version is different from beauty studied in aesthetics?

(A) "Splendour" and "aesthetic beauty" are not synonymous.

(B) "Holy array" is not synonymous with "beauty of holiness."

(C) Greek thought was developed from aesthetics.

(D) The word "beauty" in the King James Version is not synonymous with the Greek word for "beauty."

(E) English translations of the Psalms differ from each other.

24. In a word, Cleanthes, a man who follows your hypothesis, is able, perhaps, to assert or conjecture that the universe sometime arose from something like design; but beyond that position he cannot ascertain one single circumstance, and is left afterwards to fix every point of his theology by the utmost license of fancy and hypothesis. This world, for aught he knows, is very faulty and imperfect, compared to a superior standard; and was only

the first rude essay of some infant deity who afterwards abandoned it, ashamed of his lame performance.

What appears to be Cleanthes' hypothesis, which the writer is refuting?

(A) The world was designed by an infant deity.

(B) The world is faulty and imperfect.

(C) The universe arose from something like a design.

(D) The universe was designed by a perfect designer.

(E) Theories about the universe are based on fancy and hypothesis.

STOP

If time still remains, you may review work only in this section.
When the time allotted is up, you may go on to the next section.

Section IV

Time—35 minutes
25 Questions

(Answer sheets appear in the back of this book.)

DIRECTIONS: The questions in this section are based on the reasoning contained in brief statements or passages. For some questions, more than one of
the choices could conceivably answer the question. However, you are to choose
the **best** answer; that is, the response that most accurately and completely
answers the question. You should not make assumptions that are by
commonsense standards implausible, superfluous, or incompatible with the passage. After you have chosen the best answer, blacken the corresponding space
on your answer sheet.

QUESTIONS 1–2

Before the time of the scientific revolution of the seventeenth century,
astronomers held the so-called geocentric theory. The fundamental claim of this
theory is that a celestial body moves around the Earth. These astronomers, of
course, agreed with everyone else that the sun is a celestial body.

1.   From these two claims, which of the following conclusions follows from
     the premises?

     (A)   the Earth moves around the sun.

     (B)   the Earth is stationary.

     (C)   the sun also moves around the Earth.

     (D)   the sun is stationary.

     (E)   only some celestial bodies move around the Earth.

2.   In this argument, the premise "a celestial body moves around the Earth"
     means

     (A)   only some celestial bodies so move, while some do not.

     (B)   no celestial bodies move around the Earth.

     (C)   all celestial bodies move around the Earth.

     (D)   some celestial bodies do not move around the Earth.

     (E)   the sun is not a celestial body.

QUESTIONS 3–4

Neuroscientists notice that often healthy teenage boys who are normally calm, reasonable, and well-mannered commit acts of violence. These scientists attribute the cause of the violent behavior to some or all of the following factors.

    I.   watching violent movies or TV shows

    II.   being deprived of water and nourishing foods

    III. having abnormally low concentrations of neurotransmitters

John is just such a teenage boy who has suddenly displayed violent actions, even though he is normally calm, reasonable, and well-mannered.

3.   If the claims of the neuroscientists are true, and if John has not been watching violent movies or television shows, his violent actions are caused by

    (A)   being deprived of water and nourishing foods.

    (B)   having abnormally low concentrations of neurotransmitters.

    (C)   either being deprived of water and nourishing foods, or having abnormally low concentrations of neurotransmitters, or both.

    (D)   either being deprived of water and nourishing foods, or having abnormally low concentrations of neurotransmitters.

    (E)   being deprived of water.

4.   Which of the following is an inference that can be drawn from the information on violent behavior in teenage boys and about John?

    (A)   All teenage boys will display violent behavior at some time or another.

    (B)   Violent behavior will never occur in teenage girls.

    (C)   If the violent behavior results only from abnormal concentrations of neurotransmitters, the restoration of the correct concentration will cure the violent behavior.

    (D)   No teenage boys will display violent behavior.

    (E)   Deprivation of water and nourishing foods will result in violent behavior amongst teenage boys.

QUESTIONS 5–6

Margaret Brown, a juror in a recent court case, reasons to her fellow jurors that if Donald Smith committed the murder of Janice Scott, then he hid the gun. In court, Smith finally admitted hiding the gun.

5.   From this argument, we can conclude that

(A)   Smith is guilty.

(B)   Smith committed the murder.

(C)   Smith owns a gun.

(D)   We can't say if Smith did or did not commit the murder.

(E)   Smith did not commit the murder.

6.   Given that the facts stated by juror Brown are true, and that these are the only known facts, we can conclude that

(A)   Smith is innocent.

(B)   Smith has been proven guilty beyond any doubt.

(C)   Smith is guilty beyond a reasonable doubt.

(D)   it is 90% probable that Smith is the murderer.

(E)   there is not enough information to convict Smith.

QUESTIONS 7–8

Ms. Carolyn Jones is one of several jurors weighing the evidence in a murder trial. She reasons to her fellow jurors that if Ronald Clark killed Rebecca Dunne, then he hid the murder weapon — the gun. But, we have conclusively established that Ronald Clark was 5,000 miles away from the scene of the crime at the time it was committed.

7.   From this, we can conclude that

(A)   Clark hid the gun.

(B)   Clark did not hide the gun.

(C)   Clark owns the gun.

(D)   Clark owns a gun.

(E)   Clark may or may not have hidden the gun.

8.   From the information given, and assuming that Clark did not pay to have Ms. Dunne killed, we can conclude that

(A)   Clark is guilty and he owns a gun.

(B)   Clark is innocent and he did not hide the gun.

(C)   Clark is innocent, but he did hide the gun.

(D)   Clark is innocent and he may have hidden the gun.

(E)   Clark does not own a gun.

QUESTIONS 9–10

Only American citizens can vote in U.S. Presidential elections.

9. From this claim, we can infer that

   (A) all American citizens can vote in U.S. Presidential elections.

   (B) all people who can vote in U.S. Presidential elections are American citizens.

   (C) some American citizens can vote in U.S. Presidential elections.

   (D) all voters in U.S. elections are American citizens.

   (E) U.S. nationals can vote in U.S. elections.

10. Consider the following:

    X is a *necessary* condition for Y when, without X, there is no occurrence of Y. Note, however, that X is not the only factor that is necessary for the occurrence of Y.

    X is a *sufficient* condition for Y, if when X occurs, then Y occurs.

    Given the above information and that "only American citizens can vote in U.S. Presidential elections," we can conclude that being an American citizen is a _____ condition for being able to vote in U.S. Presidential elections.

    (A) sufficient

    (B) necessary

    (C) sufficient and necessary

    (D) neither sufficient nor necessary

    (E) sufficient, if the person is born outside of the U.S.

11. Consider the claim: "None but the brave deserve the fair maidens." From this claim we can conclude that

    (A) all people who deserve the fair maidens are brave people.

    (B) all people who are brave deserve the fair maidens.

    (C) some people who are brave deserve the fair maidens.

    (D) some people who deserve the fair maidens are brave people.

    (E) no one deserves the fair maidens.

12. Before the time of the scientific revolution of the sixteenth century, astronomers held that the Earth is a heavenly body. Moreover, they all held, of course, that the Earth moves in a perfect circle.

    The conclusion of this argument follows from which premise?

(A)   Some heavenly bodies move in perfect circles.

(B)   Some heavenly bodies do not move in perfect circles.

(C)   No heavenly bodies move in perfect circles.

(D)   All heavenly bodies move in perfect circles.

(E)   Most heavenly bodies move in perfect circles.

13.   Consider the claim: "No human being has free will."

Which of the following sentences denies this claim?

(A)   All human beings have free will.

(B)   Some human beings do not have free will.

(C)   Some human beings have free will.

(D)   All human beings have genuine choice.

(E)   No human being has genuine choice.

14.   Garage owner: "I would like to raise the price of a Handy Dandy Automobile Tune-Up by 20%." Paid Consultant: "If you raise your price you'll almost certainly lose 20% of your current business. Since you cannot afford to lose any business, you will have to mount an advertising campaign. An advertising campaign will cost you about two months' gross income, but could increase business by as much as 10%. This means you could break even in 13 months, if you raise your price and have excellent results from the advertising campaign. However, your last advertising campaign produced no measurable positive results, so you should not expect positive results from a future one.

The consultant's advice is structured to lead to which of the following conclusions?

(A)   Advertising campaigns are usually not cost effective.

(B)   The advertising campaign will probably not increase business.

(C)   The owner should not increase his price for tuning up automobiles.

(D)   Advertising campaigns cannot overcome the effects of an increase in prices.

(E)   The owner should increase his price for tuning up automobiles, but not run an advertising campaign.

15. These days police agencies claim the nationwide per capita crime rate is down. However, it is no safer to walk down the streets of New York, Chicago, or Los Angeles than it was a decade ago. Just as many robberies, muggings, and burglaries are occurring there, per capita, as at any time in the recent past. Therefore, the crime rate must not be any lower than it has ever been.

Which of the following, if true, would most seriously weaken the conclusion in the passage above?

(A) There are more people now living in the three cities mentioned than there were a decade ago.

(B) The per capita incidence of nonviolent crime has dropped dramatically in the past five years, nationwide.

(C) The per capita rural crime rate is less than it was a decade ago.

(D) There are just as many criminals now as a decade ago.

(E) Just as many crimes are now committed as a decade ago.

16. The recent increase in the number of accidents involving tractor-trailer rigs is due to driver inexperience. Rising air freights have caused the trucking industry to expand rapidly, resulting in a great demand for truck drivers. As a result, driver training schools have shortened their training courses from six to five months, in order to turn out more graduates. This means that graduates do not get enough hands-on training before receiving their driving certifications.

The author's conclusion that the increase in the number of accidents involving tractor-trailer rigs is due to driver inexperience is most weakened by the fact that the author has

(A) not specified what percentage of the recent accidents have involved graduates of the five-month courses.

(B) not demonstrated that the six-month training course adequately prepares drivers for the open road.

(C) not demonstrated that increased air fares have resulted in an expansion of the trucking industry.

(D) not demonstrated that if the airline industry had expanded as much as the trucking industry has, it too would not have experienced an increase in accidents.

(E) attempted only a partial explanation for the increase in trucking accidents.

17. Blue refuses to ride with the car pool only if Red rides. If Blue does not ride with the car pool, either White or Green asks to sit by Yellow. If Yellow is asked to sit by White or Green and Blue does not ride, he agrees. If Yellow is asked to sit by White or Green, and Blue does ride with the car pool, Yellow does not agree.

If Blue refuses to ride with the car pool, which of the following can be logically deduced from the information given?

(A) White asks to sit by Yellow.

(B) Green asks to sit by Yellow.

(C) Yellow refuses to sit by either White or Green.

(D) Red rides with the car pool.

(E) Yellow does not ride with the car pool.

18. If nation X does not agree to lower its trade barriers, we will run the worst trade deficit since World War II, domestic jobs will be lost, we will experience an economic slowdown, and our European allies will stop looking to us for economic leadership. In view of these facts, it is clear that we must force nation X to lower its trade barriers.

Which of the following beliefs can reasonably be attributed to the author of the above passage?

(A) It is undesirable for us to run the worst trade deficit since WW II.

(B) It is desirable for domestic jobs to be lost.

(C) It is desirable for every nation to run a trade surplus.

(D) It is desirable to have European allies stop looking to us for economic leadership.

(E) It is undesirable for us to trade with nation X.

19. A study published by a noted scholar says that desire for territorial acquisition is the leading cause of war. I disagree. Most wars are the result of ideological differences between the leadership of the warring countries. From the Peloponnesian War between aristocratic Sparta and democratic Athens, to World War II between the fascist Axis and democratic Allies, ideology has been at the root of most human conflict.

Which of the following best describes the form of the argument above?

(A) It argues from analogy.

(B) It offers an alternative explanation.

(C)   It attempts to discredit the noted scholar's study by challenging its methodology.

(D)   It attacks the credibility of the noted scholar.

(E)   It cites evidence that the scholar overlooked.

20.   A free democratic political system is the best form of government there is. Therefore, it is well worth defending, and we should all be willing to do our part to preserve it. Because a free democratic system is well worth defending, it is clearly the best form of government there is.

Which one of the following illustrates the same weak reasoning as found in the passage?

(A)   A free market economy is the best type of economic system there is. It allows the distribution of wealth based on the talents and abilities that individuals bring to the market. This means that one's contribution to the health and welfare of society determines one's reward.

(B)   To live a virtuous life is the best thing that there is. If one avoids vice, one is sure to be happy.

(C)   This book is very boring. I tried to read it last night, and I almost fell asleep.

(D)   Every time I wake up the alarm clock goes off. Therefore, when I wake up tomorrow, the alarm clock will go off.

(E)   I love sports, and that's why I play them all the time. I hope to play sports until I'm 70 years old. Since I play sports all the time, I must really love them.

21.   I am against any speed limits on freeways. I feel that people should be allowed to drive as fast as they want to on these modern, smoothly surfaced thoroughfares. Speed limits have the effect of telling drivers, "You are not a good judge of your own driving skills, or of how quickly you need to get somewhere." To be sure, the right of one person to drive at excessive speeds may infringe on the rights of others to be safe on the public highways, but we must try to balance these rights to afford maximum protection to each. For example, under no condition should someone be allowed to drive faster than 55 miles per hour in or near any city, even on a freeway.

The reasoning in the above passage is flawed because it

(A)   contains an inconsistency about whether there should be speed limits on freeways.

(B)   does not establish that citizens have a right to be safe on the public highways.

(C)   assumes that the right to be the judge of your own driving skills takes precedence over the right of others to be safe on the public highways.

(D)   Argues for a 55 mph speed limit.

(E)   States everyone's rights are equal.

22.   Ever since Lucky Silas stopped appearing on national television, the communist world has fallen deeper and deeper into disarray and the democratic, capitalist world has moved from triumph to triumph. Getting rid of the liberal bias in our media sure makes a difference in the success of our foreign policy.

Which of the following best characterizes the argument above?

(A)   It attacks an opponent rather than his argument.

(B)   It recommends an act by pointing to good consequences it will lead to.

(C)   It infers a cause from its effects.

(D)   It uses loaded language in place of argument.

(E)   It supports a causal claim by pointing to a temporal sequence.

23.   Some music lovers pride themselves on their knowledge of classical and baroque compositions. Some music lovers prefer the big band sound. They know the title of every tune ever played by the Glen Miller band. Other music lovers concentrate on the works of great blues artists such as B.B. King. But even though not all music lovers can read music, they all enjoy playing and interpreting their favorite music for their friends.

If the information in the passage is true, which of the following CANNOT be true?

(A)   Most music lovers do not pride themselves on their knowledge of baroque and classical music.

(B)   Everyone who enjoys playing and interpreting his favorite music for his friends is a music lover.

(C)   Music lovers who prefer the big band sound are more likely to memorize the names of their favorite tunes than are music lovers who concentrate on the works of blues artists.

(D)   There are fewer music lovers who enjoy playing and interpreting

369

their favorite music for their friends than there are music lovers who can read music.

(E) All three types of music lovers mentioned in the passage can read music.

24. Changing your car's oil regularly, no matter what type of motor oil you use, will reduce engine wear. Scientists have concluded that regular oil changes reduce engine wear by purging the engine of dust and tiny metal fragments. So you can forget about buying oil with special lubricating additives: change your oil regularly and say goodbye to premature engine wear.

Which of the following is a criticism of the reasoning in the argument?

(A) Regular oil changes using oil with special lubricating additives has been shown to reduce engine wear.

(B) The fact that regular oil changes will reduce engine wear does not show that special lubricating additives in oil are of no value.

(C) Few people change their oil regularly enough.

(D) Engine wear occurs all of the time during engine use.

(E) Scientists have been wrong about special lubricating additives in oil.

25. A recent survey showed that many consumers of company A's products are dissatisfied with them. The survey also showed that most of the dissatisfied customers believe that the products are of low quality. Therefore, to increase consumers' satisfaction with its products, the company need only concentrate on changing consumers' beliefs regarding the quality of its products.

Which one of the following, if also shown by the survey, would most seriously weaken the conclusion drawn by the author of the passage?

(A) The dissatisfied consumers feel that the products are too expensive.

(B) Consumers who are satisfied with the products slightly outnumber those who are dissatisfied.

(C) Consumers of company A's products are more dissatisfied than consumers of other companies' products.

(D) Most people in advertising in company A believe that their company's products are of a higher quality than those of other companies.

(E) The consumers who are satisfied with company A's products believe that the products are of high quality.

STOP

If time still remains, you may review work only in this section.
When the time allotted is up, you may go on to the next section.

LSAT Writing Sample

(Answer sheets appear in the back of this book.)

General Directions

You will have 35 minutes in which to plan and write an essay on the topic below. Read the topic and the accompanying directions carefully. You will probably find it best to spend a few minutes considering the topic and organizing your thoughts before you begin writing. In your essay, be sure to develop your ideas fully, leaving time, if possible, to review what you have written. **Do not write on a topic other than the one specified. Writing on a topic of your own choice is not acceptable.**

No special knowledge is required or expected for this writing exercise. Law schools are interested in the reasoning, clarity, organization, language usage, and writing mechanics displayed in your essay. How well you write is more important than how much you write.

Confine your essay to the blocked, lined areas on the front and back of the separate writing sample response sheet. Only that area will be reproduced for law schools. Be sure that your writing is legible.

Sample Topic

Directions: The scenario presented below describes two choices, either one of which can be supported on the basis of the information given. Your essay should consider both choices and argue for one and against the other, based on the two specified criteria and the facts provided. There is no "right" or "wrong" choice: a reasonable argument can be made for either.

Mark Chaser, 26, has just graduated in the top fifth of his class at a prestigious law school. He has just received entry-level job offers from the two law firms described below. Argue for his accepting one of the offers over the other given the following long-term career goals Chaser has held for many years:

• To be a wealthy senior partner in a prominent law firm by the age of 40
• To someday enter national politics, most likely as a senator or congressman

Chaser received the first offer from the prestigious Wall Street law firm Doran, Reilly and Doran. This corporate law firm, with offices in New York, Washington, D.C., and Los Angeles, offered Chaser an associate position starting at $85,000 a year and a cubicle in the basement of their Manhattan offices. Most of Chaser's work will involve doing research with 20 to 30 other young associ-

ates on merger and antitrust cases for major companies. The firm hires about 100 top graduates from the best law schools every year and promotes from within the firm. Currently, there are 5 senior partners, 25 junior partners, and 475 associates.

The second job offer was from Smith, Tyler and Hyde, a prominent law firm in Cedar Rapids, Iowa. The firm handles a wide range of cases, civil and criminal, throughout the Midwest. Smith, Tyler and Hyde has never hired such a promising law school graduate in the firm before and is very interested in upgrading its national image. It offered Chaser a starting salary of $50,000 a year, early promotion to junior partner, a broad range of legal experiences, use of a 15-room Victorian house near the firm's offices, and a free membership in a private club. The firm consists of 3 senior partners, 15 junior partners, and 90 associates. Each of the senior partners has been politically active in the state. One is a former U.S. senator, and the other two are sitting members of Iowa's state legislature.

STOP

If time still remains, you may review work only in this section.

TEST V

ANSWER KEY

Section I — Analytical Reasoning

1.	(B)	8.	(A)	15.	(C)	22.	(A)
2.	(B)	9.	(B)	16.	(E)		
3.	(A)	10.	(E)	17.	(B)		
4.	(D)	11.	(D)	18.	(E)		
5.	(A)	12.	(C)	19.	(B)		
6.	(D)	13.	(A)	20.	(D)		
7.	(C)	14.	(D)	21.	(B)		

Section II — Reading Comprehension

1.	(D)	8.	(B)	15.	(C)	22.	(A)
2.	(B)	9.	(B)	16.	(E)	23.	(E)
3.	(D)	10.	(A)	17.	(A)	24.	(D)
4.	(A)	11.	(E)	18.	(A)	25.	(C)
5.	(C)	12.	(D)	19.	(D)	26.	(B)
6.	(E)	13.	(C)	20.	(A)	27.	(E)
7.	(B)	14.	(B)	21.	(B)	28.	(B)

Section III — Logical Reasoning

1.	(B)	8.	(E)	15.	(A)	22.	(E)
2.	(D)	9.	(B)	16.	(B)	23.	(C)
3.	(E)	10.	(C)	17.	(B)	24.	(D)
4.	(D)	11.	(C)	18.	(E)		
5.	(B)	12.	(B)	19.	(E)		
6.	(B)	13.	(A)	20.	(D)		
7.	(D)	14.	(D)	21.	(B)		

Section IV — Logical Reasoning

1.	(C)	8.	(D)	15.	(B)	22.	(E)
2.	(C)	9.	(B)	16.	(A)	23.	(D)
3.	(C)	10.	(B)	17.	(D)	24.	(B)
4.	(C)	11.	(A)	18.	(A)	25.	(A)
5.	(D)	12.	(D)	19.	(B)		
6.	(E)	13.	(C)	20.	(E)		
7.	(E)	14.	(C)	21.	(A)		

DETAILED EXPLANATIONS OF ANSWERS

Section I – Analytical Reasoning

QUESTIONS 1–6

This is a selection task in which the members of one group are to be drawn from two disparate pools under certain restrictions. Begin by identifying the pools and the members of each pool and whatever restrictions are known about use of the pools. In this case there are actually three pools (the members overlap) with the following restrictions:

Freshmen — A, B, C, D and E (choose *exactly* 3)
Sophomores — F, G, H and I (choose *exactly* 2)
Experience — A, E, G and H (choose *at least* 3)

Now, list the other restrictions on the final group that are known:

Not both B and E
Not both F and H
Not both C and G

By plugging in the data given in the stem to each question, the correct answers can be determined.

1.   **(B)**   (A) cannot be correct for, if E makes the team, then B doesn't. (C) is incorrect for, if G makes the team, then C doesn't. Both (D) and (E) are incorrect since either of those answers would place 3 sophomores on the team. Thus, (B) is the correct answer.

2.   **(B)**   This question is slightly more difficult, for it involves excluding possibilities. Try to generate combinations omitting the person named. If that can be done within the rules, then that person is not a necessary member of the team. (A) is incorrect — A, E, G, H and D (from question 1) is a possible team. (C) is incorrect — A, E, H, I and C is a possible team. (D) is incorrect — A, E, G, D and F is a possible team. (E) is incorrect — G, H, I, A and E is a possible team. Thus, (B) is correct.

3.   **(A)**   A, E and H must make the team, as must I (to account for 3 experienced fencers and 2 sophomores) so only one slot remains. (B) is incorrect, H has been chosen and won't fence with F. (C) is incorrect, B has been chosen and F

can't be on the team with H. (D) is incorrect, B has been chosen and E can't be on the team with B. (E) is incorrect, F can't be on the team with H and I has already been chosen. Thus (A) is correct, either D or C will make the team.

4. **(D)** Here, try to construct a team *including* the pairs in the answer. (A) is incorrect — A, G, H, B and D is a possible team. (B) is incorrect — A, E, G, H and D. (C) is incorrect — A, E, H, C and I. (E) is incorrect — A, B, D, G, and H. Thus, (D) is the correct answer — you cannot construct a team with both B and C.

5. **(A)** This is the same task as in problem 4. The team A, E, G, H and D accounts for (B); the team A, G, H, B and I for (C) and (D); and the team A, E, G, F and D for (E). Thus, (A) is correct, no team can contain both F and I.

6. **(D)** Two sophomores and three freshmen are to be selected. If F and G make the team, H and C will not play and we have one player with experience. (C) and (E) have been ruled out. Helen could play instead of F, so (B) is not definitely the answer. The same could be said for Beth (A). So (D) is the only player to definitely make the team.

QUESTIONS 7–11

This is an ordering problem in which certain features of the order are given by the rules. Begin such a problem by setting down all of the known data. In this particular problem, draw a hexagon and randomly place A immediately to the left of D. When you add the information that B is always directly across from E, and that C is never next to B, it becomes clear that there are only two possible seating arrangements: A – D – E – C – F – B and A – D – B – F – C – E. Use your test booklet as scratch paper to draw these arrangements for quick reference:

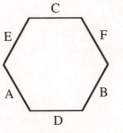
First Ordering

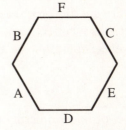
Second Ordering

Whether or not you choose to draw these arrangements, be sure to remember them and to refer to them in the solution of the problems. Any other arrangement violates one or more of the stated rules. The answers to the questions are now obvious.

7. **(C)** This question requires the second ordering, since A is next to B. In this ordering, C cannot be seated across from D, for that would place C next to B, in violation of a rule. Thus (A) is not the correct answer. (B) cannot be the

correct answer, for that too would place C next to B. (D) cannot be correct for that, too, would place C next to B. And (E) cannot be correct for to the left of A must be either B or E. Thus (C) is the correct answer, as C must be directly across from A.

8.   **(A)**   This question requires the first ordering, since E is next to A. (B) could not be true, for that would place C next to B. (C) cannot be true for that, too, would place C next to B. (D), for the same reason, cannot be true. (E) cannot be true for, again, it would place C next to B. Thus (A) is the correct answer, in fact, (A) *must* be true.

9.   **(B)**   For this question, either ordering is possible, so you need to refer back to each diagram. And note that this question asks which solution *must* be false. Since neither ordering is specified, you can utilize your answers to previous questions as an aid in answering this question, for a correct answer to a previous must be capable of being true, and it thus could not be a solution that *must* be false. (A) could be true, as it is the correct answer to (1). (C) could be true as it is the answer to (2). (D) could be true, as is seen in the second ordering. (E) could be true, also shown in the second ordering. (B) however, could not be true, as its truth would make it impossible to have both A immediately to the left of D and E seated directly across from B.

10.   **(E)**   This question requires the second ordering, as C is directly across from A. (A) could not be true as that would place B next to C. (B) could not be true, for the same reason. (C) could not be true, for the same reason. (D) could not be true, again for the same reason. (E) could, in fact, *must* be true, and is thus correct.

11.   **(D)**   This question requires the first ordering and asks which solution *must* be false. (A) is incorrect, as it must be true. (B), (C), an (E) share the same fate. (D), however, could not be true, as it would place B next to C. (D) is correct.

QUESTIONS 12–17

This is a set of linear ordering problems. Begin by collecting all the data at your disposal. Remember, "taller than" and "shorter than" are transitive relations — if *x* is taller than *y* and *y* is taller than *z*, you can derive that *x* is taller than *z*. In these problems, certain features of the ordering are guaranteed. The following *sequences* cannot be violated, although there can be additional letters between the members of these sequences:

$$U - Q - T$$
$$U - Q - W$$
$$R - S - W - V$$

taller   shorter

All correct answers *must* satisfy those sequences. Draw 7 spaces and indicate the progression from tallest to shortest (I move from left to right with left being the tallest, but you need not do so) and fill in the blanks as needed.

12. **(C)** For this problem, the correct answer (C) is obvious. V is shorter than W, as the third data line above shows. (A) is incorrect, V could be the shortest (in fact, either V or T must be) so (D) is also incorrect. (B) and (E) are both incorrect, for either U or R must be the tallest.

13. **(A)** Since we have determined that either U or R must be the tallest, if it is not R it must be U, so (A) is the correct answer. Remember to make full use of all of the information at your disposal. (B) – (E) clearly violates one of the restrictions on order.

14. **(D)** For this problem place R in the third spot and begin experimenting with possible combinations. All of the acceptable solutions begin U – Q – R – x – x – x – x. Thus Q is the second tallest, and (D) is the correct answer.

15. **(C)** Here there are many different orderings that are possible. Before examining all of them, note that (C) must be the correct answer for it makes W shorter than V in violation of one of the conditions. If this is not immediately obvious to you, begin by constructing orderings that satisfy the conditions given in the problem. The orderings R – U – Q – S – W – V – T and U – R – Q – S – W – V – T satisfy (A), (B), (D) and (E), so, again (C) is the correct answer.

16. **(E)** For this problem, simply scan each of the orderings provided to see whether it conforms to the rules. There is no shortcut here. Carefully examine each line. (E) is defective (and the correct answer) because it has W shorter than V.

17. **(B)** If the three tallest members of the group are R, U and S, Q must be in the exact middle and (B) is the correct answer. Since Q is taller than either T or W, (A) and (C) are incorrect. And since both (D) and (E) include incorrect answers as options, they, too, are incorrect.

QUESTIONS 18–22

These problems involve multiple relations, all centered on a family tree. Begin by diagramming all that you know about the family.

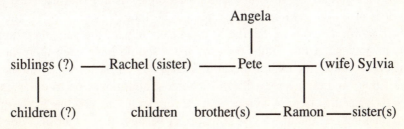

Remember, Pete has more daughters than sons (which means that Ramon has more sisters than brothers) *and* Pete has more sons that he has sisters. Also note that since Sylvia has no siblings, all of Ramon's cousins are on his father's side of the family and thus grandchildren of Angela. We do not know how many sisters Pete has, nor how many, if any, brothers he has.

18. **(E)** Since this question asks which is impossible, there must be enough data in the problem to get a firm answer. (A) is incorrect because there is insufficient data to make a decision. (B), (C) and (D) are all incorrect for the same reason. (E) is the correct answer. All of Ramon's cousins are grandchildren of Angela, as are Ramon and his siblings, and the number of siblings of Ramon cannot exceed that number plus the number of his cousins.

19. **(B)** This question is simply one of family relations. The wife of one's brother is one's sister-in-law. Thus, (B) is the correct answer.

20. **(D)** Pete has at least 1 sister and, since he has more sons than sisters, he has at least 2 sons. And since he had more daughters than sons, he has at least 3 daughters. Thus he and Sylvia have at least 5 children, and (D) is the correct answer.

21. **(B)** As with question 21, this is a matter of family relations. The children of one's aunt are one's cousins. The sister of one's father is one's aunt. Thus, Rachel's children are Ramon's cousins and (B) is correct. (A) is incorrect, one's nieces and nephews are the children of one's siblings. (C) is incorrect, Rachel's children are Pete's nieces and nephews. (D) is incorrect, they are Angela's grandchildren. (E) is incorrect, Sylvia has no siblings.

22. **(A)** According to the diagram, we see that Angela's grandchildren are Pete's nieces and nephews (A). Ramon's children are not given (B). (C) Sylvia's children are Ramon and his siblings. Pete's children (D) are also Ramon and his siblings. Rachel's cousin (E) does not play into this diagram.

Section II – Reading Comprehension

1. **(D)** In the first paragraph the author criticizes Robin Wood's analysis of *I Confess*. The author suggests that though *I Confess* is not flawless (first paragraph), it is also not a failure (last paragraph). Although the author agrees with Hitchcock's own assessment that the film is heavy-handed and lacking in humor, there is no indication the author believes there should have been more humor. Even if one assumes the use of the term *heavy-handed* has a negative connotation, the author merely agrees with the statement and moves on to other points. Thus, it is clear the lack of humor is a minor point and not the focus of the passage, making (A) incorrect. (B) is incorrect because the author also does not

dwell on Hitchcock's directorial style. The author does mention some obvious problems, such as the overt use of religious symbols, but this is just one portion of the author's discussion of the film, rather than Hitchcock's directing. Certainly the two are intimately related, but it would be difficult to examine Hitchcock's directorial style by briefly discussing only one film, mentioning another, and alluding to a third (*The Birds*). (C) is incorrect because the author does not *develop* characters in the passage. The author does point out some of their qualities and characteristics in order to show the reader they have some depth and subtlety. (E) is incorrect because the author tells us Wood compared the two movies. The author does mention *Strangers on a Train*, but only in passing, and certainly not to a sufficient extent to be considered a comparison.

2. **(B)** The author makes this point by telling us Wood's analysis is "earnest, distinguished, very interesting, and on the whole a failure." From these words the author certainly does not think it to be either correct or perceptive. If it had been either, it would not have been a failure. Thus, (A) and (D) are both incorrect. On the other hand, the language the author uses also suggests he believes there to be some merit in Wood's analysis, making (C) incorrect. The author does not specifically indicate why he believes Wood's analysis to be a failure. So we cannot say with certainty the author believes it to be superficial. In addition, it is unlikely the author would describe the analysis as earnest, distinguished or interesting if he also believed it to be superficial. Thus, (E) is incorrect.

3. **(D)** Where this language appears in line 8 the author is telling us he believes Hitchcock's genius to have been fully evident in *Strangers on a Train*. Although the author admits *I Confess* has its flaws, by saying the genius which had made *Strangers on a Train* was "not entirely eclipsed" in *I Confess* he is suggesting that some of Hitchcock's genius does show in the later film. From this we can conclude (C) is incorrect. (A) is incorrect because the author does not suggest in the passage that Hitchcock was not a genius, only that *I Confess* was not up to his usual standards. In the first sentence of the last paragraph the author directly states that he does not believe *I Confess* to be a failure, making (B) incorrect. (E) is incorrect because *eclipse* is used as a metaphor, and there is no mention in the passage of Hitchcock's astrological beliefs.

4. **(A)** In the second paragraph the author tells us the thematic development is directed toward Father Logan (played by Clift) and his confession of having had an affair. Nevertheless, in the third sentence of this paragraph the author tells us, "Everyone in the film is forced to make a confession." Thus, although the film is directed toward Logan (Clift) who does confess, he is not the only one to do so. Thus, both (B) and (E) are incorrect. For similar reasons, (C) and (D) are also incorrect. According to the author's statement they did confess, but by picking any one individual it implies the others did not confess which is incorrect.

5.   **(C)**   The author tells us this in the middle of the second paragraph where he says "Logan must learn that there is a humanity underneath the black cassock." The author tells us Logan once loved Grandfort, but there is no mention of continuing affection, let alone lust, making (B) incorrect. In addition, at the end of the second paragraph we are told Grandfort's romantic fantasies, presumably directed toward Logan, are "unfounded," suggesting her affections are unrequited. Similarly, we are not told of any *sins* which Logan has committed, making (A) incorrect. The author does use the word *affair* to describe Logan's previous relationship with Grandfort, but he also uses the word *love* so we cannot be sure if anything occurred in the relationship to warrant a confession. Given the uncertainty, (C) is the better answer. There is also no suggestion of a breach of faith on Logan's part, making (D) incorrect. (E) is incorrect because there is no mention of murder in the passage. (Those familiar with the film will recall Logan was accused of a murder he did not commit.)

6.   **(E)**   In the first paragraph the author agrees with Hitchcock that the film is heavy-handed and lacks humor. In the third paragraph the author attributes the heaviness to the acting. In particular, Clift's method acting and Bancroft's overacting. In this paragraph the author also mentions problems in overt use of religious symbols, but this is not one of the options to the question. Thematic development is discussed in the second paragraph. In this paragraph the author is showing us the subtlety of the plot and characters in order to show why Wood's analysis (noted in the first paragraph) is a failure. It is clear the author does not believe thematic development to be a problem, making (A) incorrect. At the end of the first paragraph the author disagrees with Hitchcock that the film lacks subtlety, and tells us why in the second paragraph. Thus, (D) is incorrect. (B) is incorrect because there is no mention in the passage of lighting techniques used in the film. Although the author does think Wood's analysis is a failure, this is a complaint with the *analysis* not the *film*, making (C) incorrect.

7.   **(B)**   The author admits *I Confess* is flawed in the first paragraph. In the final paragraph the author also tells us he believes the film is not a failure, as argued by Wood, and summarizes why. Thus, (A) is clearly incorrect, as is (C). (D) is incorrect because the author gives us no reason to believe he thinks the film to be pretentious. He tells us in the third paragraph some of the problems with the film, and this is not one of them. For the same reasons (E) is incorrect. The author does suggest that Clift's acting comes off as wooden, but this does not imply that it was boring.

8.   **(B)**   The passage begins with a description of the Reconstruction problem then tells us of Lincoln's plan and how he justified it and concludes by explaining the plan's virtues. (A) is incorrect because the author does not say Congress *did* refuse to seat Southern delegates, he only informs us this was a weakness of the plan that *might* occur. (C) is incorrect because Reconstruction did not fail (the Southern states once again became a functioning part of the

Union), and there is nothing in the passage to suggest otherwise. (D) is incorrect because the author does not attempt to highlight or otherwise consider what *caused* the Civil War. Instead, he is concerned with what happened *after* the war. (E) is incorrect because the author only mentions federal supremacy as a part of the problem, and suggests it is not an important part.

9. **(B)** The author begins the passage by discussing the restoration of the seceded states to the Union. The second paragraph continues this discussion, but attaches the word *Reconstruction* to the problem. The plain meaning of the word should suggest putting something back together again (reconstructing it), which was what needed to be done to the Union. (A) is incorrect because there is no mention in the passage about rebuilding destroyed Southern cities. In addition, it was not just the cities which needed rebuilding, which would make (A) too narrow. (C) is incorrect because Reconstruction necessarily took place *after* the war which caused the need for putting the Union back together again. The author does indicate that the Reconstruction *problem* began with the initiation of hostilities. By this the author means that once the Union was torn apart it would eventually have to be put back together. The author mentions the seating of Southern delegates as a potential problem with Lincoln's reconstruction plan, but it is not part of the plan itself, making (D) incorrect. Along the same lines, (E) is incorrect because the suppression of military rebellion was only a *part* of the plan.

10. **(A)** The author tells us this in the first paragraph when he uses the words "core elements" then lists the status and rights of emancipated (i.e., former) slaves. In this same sentence the author suggests the discussion of states' rights and federal supremacy is rhetoric. In this sense the author is using *rhetoric* with a slightly negative connotation, meaning they are not the important parts of the Reconstruction problem. Thus, both (B) and (E) are incorrect. (C) is incorrect because this was part of Lincoln's plan. Certainly the suppression of military rebellion is important, but the author only mentions it in passing and does not indicate it has particular significance. (D) is incorrect because congressional support would be for the Reconstruction *plan* and not part of the *problem* for which the plan is being developed.

11. **(E)** This point is made clear in the middle of the second paragraph. (A) is incorrect because the author's discussion of Lincoln's plan does not include a requirement that Southern states petition Congress to rejoin the Union. (B) is incorrect because there is no indication in the passage of any Constitutional mechanism for removal of states from the Union. (C) is incorrect because there is no mention of the seceded states being distinguished from other states except for the fact that they had tried to secede. (D) is incorrect because there is no mention of martial law in the passage.

12. **(D)** This point is made in the first sentence of the third paragraph. (A) is

clearly wrong because the author tells us of Lincoln's plan for Reconstruction and notes the plan could be destroyed by Congress. For the same reasons, (B) is also wrong. If Lincoln believed Reconstruction should be left to either Congress or the states he would not have bothered to formulate his own plan. This same reasoning also makes (C) incorrect. (E) is incorrect because we are told in the last sentence of the second paragraph that one of the parts of Lincoln's plan was the suppression of actual military rebellion. Thus, contrary to what is suggested by the language of (E), Reconstruction could not proceed during military rebellion — at least not past the point of suppressing the rebellion.

13. **(C)** The author tells us the virtues of Lincoln's plan in the final paragraph. One of these virtues is that the plan was consistent with administration policy during the war. (A) is incorrect because the plan was not *designed* to end the war. We are told one part of the plan was the suppression of military rebellion. We are not told whether this just means formal large-scale hostilities or also includes smaller bands of soldiers continuing to fight after formal surrender has occurred. In either case, the plan, as presented in the passage, only indicated that rebellion needed to be suppressed, and did not suggest how that was to be accomplished. To the extent the plan was formulated by Lincoln, it did rely on presidential action, but this is not one of the virtues mentioned by the author in the final paragraph, making (B) incorrect. Similarly, (D) is incorrect because this is simply not one of the virtues mentioned by the author. Lincoln undoubtedly formulated his plan to be consistent with the Constitution, and we are told that he justified the plan under Article IV. Nevertheless, (E) is incorrect because, again, this is not mentioned by the author as one of the plan's two great virtues.

14. **(B)** In the third paragraph we are specifically told Lincoln justified his plan under Article IV, Section 4 of the Constitution. Congressional authority, in particular the ability to seat Southern delegates, certainly could affect the plan, but it was not a *justification* for the plan, making (A) incorrect. Along the same lines, federal supremacy is an issue to be considered, but not a justification for the plan. Thus, (C) is incorrect. (D) is incorrect because there is no mention in the passage of administrative *expertise*. The only direct mention of the administration is when the author tells us Lincoln's plan was consistent with the way the administration prosecuted the war. The post-war economic situation in the South was certainly a reason for needing a plan in the first place, but the passage discusses *justification* in terms of *authority* not reasons. Thus, (E) is incorrect.

15. **(C)** After giving some background information in the first three paragraphs, the authors tell of the value of ultralow-temperature experiments in the fourth. In particular, such experiments will provide further information on condensed-matter problems such as the properties of neutron stars. (A) is incorrect because the passage suggests we do not know the properties of neutron stars. In fact, it is this information which researchers hope to gain by ultralow-temperature experiments. Two isotopes of helium are mentioned in the passage: ^{3}He and ^{4}He. Nevertheless, the authors give no indication that their discovery was either made

recently or as the result of these experiments. These particular two isotopes are mentioned simply because they form superfluids at ultralow temperatures. Thus, (B) is incorrect. Despite discussing superfluids throughout the passage, we are not told *how* superfluids are formed in experiments, except that it requires ultralow temperatures. Thus, (D) cannot be the primary purpose of the passage. (E) is incorrect because the passage does not present more than one theory of the universe (the Big Bang) and does not discuss alternative explanations of temperature.

16.   **(E)**   The authors make this point twice in the first paragraph by saying investigators of low-temperature physics have surpassed nature, and that temperatures attained in the laboratory have never occurred in nature. It is clear from these statements that (A) is incorrect. The first paragraph also uses the terms "low temperature" and "temperature cooler than three kelvins" indicating the passage is concerned with very cold temperatures, making (B) incorrect. The particle accelerators mentioned in the passage cannot attain the *high* temperatures that occurred during the Big Bang. (C) is incorrect because the authors make no connection between the temperature of the cosmic microwave background and the formation of neutron stars. The mention of the background temperature is simply to show how science has progressed beyond nature in achieving low temperatures. The authors then make a different connection between ultralow-temperature experiments and how matter behaves in neutron stars. There is no connection between the background and the stars. The authors mention the study of high-temperature superconductors as something which may benefit from ultralow-temperature experiments. The authors do not, however, make any connection between the cosmic microwave background and these superconductors, making (D) incorrect.

17.   **(A)**   *Picokelvins* are mentioned in line 7 where the authors are telling us of *ultralow* temperature experiments. It is clear from the passage that *kelvins* are units of temperature. Even if one did not know the prefixes *nano* and *pico* mean one-billionth (10^{-9}) and one-trillionth (10^{-12}), it can be inferred from the context that they must be very small units of temperature. (B) is incorrect because only two isotopes of helium are mentioned and they are not given names other than ^{3}He and ^{4}He. There is no basis to assume a picokelvin is related to either of these isotopes. From the first paragraph it is clear that a picokelvin is related to a very low temperature. From the third paragraph it is clear the temperature of neutron stars is very high. The combination of these two makes (C) incorrect. It is clear from the language in the first paragraph that picokelvins are a measure of temperature. In the second paragraph the authors indicate that superfluids are formed at ultralow temperatures, but this does not mean a unit of temperature is a superfluid. Thus, (D) is incorrect. (E) is also incorrect because the authors tell us that temperatures measured in picokelvins have been *achieved* in laboratory experiments, from which one can conclude picokelvins are not experiments themselves.

18.   **(A)**   In the second paragraph the authors tell us that ^{4}He is the common isotope of *helium* — not *hydrogen*, making (B) incorrect. From the first sentence

of the second paragraph we also know superfluids are formed at ultralow temperatures. Thus, superfluid ^{4}He is a very cold form of helium. (C) is incorrect because the authors never suggest that superfluids and superconductors are the same thing. In fact, they make an explicit distinction in the second paragraph. From the passage one can conclude neutronium is highly condensed matter found in stars (if one did not already know this). In the fourth paragraph the authors tell us that "Neutron matter clearly cannot be studied in the laboratory." Since superfluid ^{4}He *is* studied in laboratory experiments, it is clear it cannot be a form of neutronium (neutron matter). For the same reason (D) was incorrect in question 17, (E) is incorrect here.

19. **(D)** This point is made in the fourth paragraph. Although it is probably true that the study of superfluid ^{3}He will yield results applicable to superfluid ^{4}He, this is not the focus of the authors' arguments. From the fourth and fifth paragraphs it is clear the authors are concerned with condensed matter, specifically, neutronium and neutron stars. Thus, (A) is incorrect. From the first sentence of the fourth paragraph the authors make it clear they are interested in what experiments with superfluid ^{3}He may reveal about "forms of matter found nowhere on the earth." Thus, (B) is incorrect. (C) is incorrect because the process is reversed. It is through the laboratory studies that we learn about superfluid ^{3}He. (E) is incorrect because there is no indication the authors are interested in learning more about the temperature of the universe in general. The relevance of temperature is in how matter behaves at very high and very low temperatures.

20. **(A)** This point is clearly made in the final paragraph. (B) is incorrect because there is no indication in the passage either that additional isotopes of helium do not already exist, or that the authors care whether they do or not. (C) and (D) are both incorrect because there is no suggestion in the passage that the named researchers abandoned their project or that a shortage of funding is inhibiting attaining sufficiently low temperatures. (E) is incorrect because the problem is in achieving ultralow temperatures, not high temperatures.

21. **(B)** We are told this in the fourth paragraph. We are also told neutron matter is found in stars. Since stars have very high temperatures, (A) is incorrect. From the fourth paragraph we know neutron matter is not found on earth and are told it cannot be studied in the laboratory. From these two items, we can conclude (C) is incorrect. Similarly (E) is incorrect. It may have been possible that an experiment verified the existence of neutron matter without having to produce any on earth, but this is not mentioned in the passage. (D) is incorrect because we are told neutron matter is found in stars and there is no suggestion stars are not found in nature.

22. **(A)** The author begins the passage by telling us about Plato's writing and concludes it by telling us Plato's primary intent as a philosopher. In the course of the discussion the author tells us about both Socrates' contribution to

Plato's writing and the Socratic Method, but these are only parts of the greater theme of Plato's writing. The author does not discuss either of these two sufficiently to be considered the main focus of the passage. Thus, both (B) and (C) are incorrect. Although the *Republic* is mentioned twice in the passage, it is only to tell us where we can find particular examples of Plato's writing, so (D) is incorrect. (E) is incorrect because the example where justice is defined is used by the author only to show how Socrates used his method, *not* to actually define justice.

23. **(E)**   This point is clearly made in the first paragraph where the author states: "Socrates wrote nothing." Occasionally, one might say someone was not a writer, but mean that person was not a *good* writer. Because we are told Socrates did not write *anything*, we do not have to worry about resolving this possible ambiguity. This also makes (B) incorrect. (A) is clearly wrong from a reading of the first paragraph. The author tells us several of Plato's dialogues were written to defend and honor Socrates. This would not be the case if Socrates had no influence on Plato. This also shows (D) to be incorrect because it reverses the two; Plato defended Socrates, not the other way around. We are told in the first sentence of the second paragraph that Socrates invented the Socratic Method which relies on a question and answer format. This clearly makes (C) incorrect.

24. **(D)**   The author makes this point in the middle of the first paragraph by telling us the dialogues are "open-ended, flowing, informal" and so on. The author then contrasts this fluid style with the "tight, systematic, rigorously deductive argumentation which we will find, for example, in Descartes." Thus, (A) is incorrect because the author uses the writing of Descartes as an example of a style of writing vastly different from that of the dialogues. In addition, (C) and (E) are incorrect because they describe the writing of Descartes rather than that of the dialogues. From the example provided in the second paragraph (Cephalos and justice) and the third paragraph, we can conclude that Socrates, and therefore the dialogues, rely on a circuitous path to reach the desired definition. Thus, (B) is incorrect.

25. **(C)**   Searching for definitions is certainly a search for knowledge. The Socratic Method is indirect because it makes use of the counterexample and forces the student to continually reassess the given definition in light of counterexamples. (A) is incorrect because the author makes no comment in the passage as to whether the Socratic Method is of any use today. (It is, since it is used by most law schools.) (B) is incorrect because we are told in the first sentence of the second paragraph that the Socratic Method was developed by Socrates. In the second paragraph the author tells us the question asked is *usually* a general one. Nevertheless, *usually* does not mean *always*, and there is nothing elsewhere in the passage which can support such a meaning. Thus, (D) is incorrect. (E) is incorrect because Cephalos is only mentioned as a speaker in one of the dialogues, not as a proponent of the Socratic Method.

26. **(B)** This is clear from the first sentence of the passage. In the second paragraph we are told questions are put by *Socrates*, making (A) incorrect. As both the inventor and writer of the dialogues, Plato is not likely to also be their critic (and we are given no evidence that he was critical of them). Thus, (C) is incorrect. (D) is incorrect because we are told of several of the speakers in the dialogues who answer the questions of Socrates (first paragraph), and Plato is not one of them. Those familiar with the relationship between Plato and Socrates will know that Plato was a student of Socrates'. Nevertheless, (E) is incorrect because the question is asking about Plato's role *in the dialogues*. In addition, the student in the dialogues is generally the one answering the questions, and it has been shown for (D) why this does not include Plato.

27. **(E)** The important distinction here is between (B) and (E). The first sentence of the third paragraph would seem to suggest (B) is the correct answer. The point of providing counterexamples, however, is not simply to accumulate additional considerations. The additional considerations are important because of the search for a definition. As the questioner, Socrates *directs* the student in the search for a definition via the use of counterexamples. Thus, (E) is correct, and (B) is not. Although students may become confused when confronted with the Socratic Method, this is not the *intent* of the counterexamples, making (A) incorrect. (C) is incorrect because there is no mention in the passage of trying to develop the memory of students. As already noted, the purpose of the counterexamples is to direct the student toward a definition. The several "examples, cases, instances, [and] particulars" included in the definition are not there because of a need to exercise caution. The author does not indicate that there is any need to exercise caution in formulating the definitions. Thus, (D) is incorrect.

28. **(B)** This point is made in the first paragraph where the author tells us "the persons who take part in the dialogues become three-dimensional." This clearly makes (E) incorrect. *Straw men* would not be fully developed, since they are generally used to provide only token arguments which lack real substance. Thus, (A) is incorrect. (C) and (D) are both incorrect because the speakers noted by the author each has his own personality, and none of them is noted as being either a coward or a fool. The author does suggest that Socrates can make "fools of those who ventured to offer their opinions in response to his prodding." Socrates making someone look foolish through his questioning is different from how they are portrayed by Plato in the dialogues. In addition, there is simply a fundamental difference between being a fool and being made to look foolish (which is what Socrates does, he cannot literally make a fool of someone).

Section III – Logical Reasoning

1. **(B)** The passage argues that it is extremely difficult for men to become professional athletes and cites the hierarchical nature of sports and specific statis-

tics as evidence. The author claims to have interviewed men who dreamed of being professional athletes, but he does not say whether any or all of these men were athletes, so (A) is not necessarily true. (C) is a false statement; a white man — not a black or Hispanic man — stands a better chance of being a professional athlete. (D) is incorrect; a Hispanic man has less of a chance of being a professional athlete than a white man.

However, if "the pyramid of sports careers" really "narrows very rapidly" from high school to college, then it must be true that a person stands a much better chance of being a high school athlete than of being a college athlete (B), and not a better chance of being a professional than collegiate (E).

2. **(D)** The argument is that a government which meets the four criteria stated is bourgeois, because it organizes, unifies, and reproduces the political and economic dominance of the bourgeoisie.

The argument never suggests or assumes that all liberal democracies are bourgeois, thus answer (B) would not weaken the argument. Nor does the argument assume that all electorates must consist of the entire adult population, so answer (A) would not weaken the argument.

In addition, the author never declares that a liberal bourgeois government exists, so the argument would not be weakened by the fact that no government is dominated by the bourgeoisie (C). In the same vein, the author never says that it is possible for such a government to exist; he only implies that if one existed, it would entail both the political and the economic dominance of the bourgeoisie. That such political and economic dominance couldn't occur simultaneously (E), would not weaken the argument. It would merely render impossible the existence of such a government.

The writer is claiming that a liberal bourgeois democracy could organize the political and economic dominance of the bourgeoisie. Thus, if such organization were impossible (D), it would weaken the argument.

3. **(E)** The conclusion is that many people *incorrectly* infer that correlations establish causal relationships among the variables they measure. The writer notes and rejects any belief in any necessary causal connection between a group of rich or successful men and the men's rich or successful parents: just because both child and parents are rich and successful, does not mean the parents' wealth or success caused the child's wealth or success.

A woman whose success was caused by her father's gifts (A), would show that a causal connection is possible and thus would weaken the argument. A poor and unsuccessful woman who has rich parents (B) would not exemplify the correlation in question and thus would be irrelevant to the argument. A group of rich or successful women with rich or successful parents (C), and rich fathers who confer good things on their daughters (D), exemplify the correlation in question, but the examples do not make any assertion about a causal connection. Thus, the examples neither weaken the argument nor support the conclusion.

A woman who was successful without help from her wealthy parents (E), would be evidence that a correlation is possible without a causal connection and

thus would support the passage's conclusion.

4.   **(D)**   According to the passage, Hinrich's book (1) is influenced by Hegel, (2) is more integrated, systematic, and complete-in-itself than Hegel's, and (3) points out certain shortcomings in Hegel's theory. If so, then we may conclude that Hinrich's book is a revision and an advance over Hegel's views (D). This is contrary to the assertion that Hegel's work was an improvement over Hinrich's (E).

The writer suggests that Augustine (along with Pseudo-Dionysius and Eirgena) was a Neo-Platonist (A) and that Schelling and Hegel used the same terminology (C), but he suggests these as support for the conclusion, not as conclusions themselves.

And since, according to the passage, Boehme's terminology was filtered through Schelling and Hegel, it is more likely that Hegel was influenced by Boehme than that Boehme was influenced by Hegel (B).

5.   **(B)**   If beliefs are socially caused — and the writer does not provide sufficient proof of this — cognitive sociologists are unacceptable. (B) is the best answer. The writer does not convince the reader that all beliefs are socially caused (A) or rationally well-founded (E); neither (A) nor (E) is an adequate answer. Because all beliefs are not the result of rational deliberation, (C) is not true; cognitive sociology is not self-indicting because all beliefs are not the result of rational deliberation or socially caused. The thesis is NOT that all thought is socially determined; (D) is not an acceptable answer.

6.   **(B)**   The conclusion is that occupational mobility is more common than occupational stability (B). This is contrary to the belief that most work careers follow a temporal sequence (A). As *premises* for this conclusion, the writer claims that individual's respond to opportunities that develop during their careers (C), that people tend not to make strong commitments to a particular occupation during their work career (D), and that occupational choices are not usually the first step in people's work careers (E).

7.   **(D)**   The writer finds fault with researchers who, unwilling to test a variety of interpretations, appear to be seeking a one-shot method for dealing with poor children's problems (D). To support this point, the writer notes the enthusiasm of the researchers for a solution as indicated by increased popularity or remediation (A) and the vast number of studies (B and C). And he notes how unimaginative the literature is (E).

8.   **(E)**   The passage argues that the Foreign Service continues to be proud of its exclusivity (A), an exclusivity which requires drawing officers from elite circles (C) and excluding minorities (B). It argues further that the Service is shifting its sense of exclusivity from social class to career background (D). Thus,

if this information is correct, it cannot be true that the Foreign Service's exclusivity does not extend to careers (E).

9.   **(B)**   This passage claims that monarchy is unacceptable, in part, because kings believe they have a right by birth to put themselves and their families above the others, when actually all people are equal by birth (B). The passage never says that the Bible spoke of kings unfavorably (C). And obviously the passage does not consider the king to be acceptable for any reason (A), (D), (E).

10.   **(C)**   The writer assumes that the majority of women who divorce will eventually remarry, although the percentage of remarriages will drop from the current rate of 75% (A) to about 70%. The writer admits that his assumption is "an informed guess" and a "speculation" and is thus not definite (B). He bases his assumption on the 1975, 1980, and 1985 surveys (D), each of which appears to offer information consistent with the others (E).

Since the writer assumes that a majority (70%) of women will remarry, he must not be assuming that divorced women who remarry will no longer constitute the majority of divorced women (C).

11.   **(C)**   Having noted that the dating code in Japan has yet to be established, the writer goes on to request clarification about the developmental stages of the pattern of mate selection and the assigned tasks of each stage (C), implying that these will provide a foundation for the dating code. Once established, this code should help limit or eliminate the dysfunctional aspects of dating (B) and their severe impact on dating participants (D) these aspects and their impact are not part of the code itself.

While the dating code may be based on information gathered from dating experiences of young people (A), it is the patterns, not the experiences themselves, which are elements of the code.

Finally, the writer is interested in Japanese standards of dating, not western standards as suggested in answer (E).

12.   **(B)**   The writer fears Communists more than Nazis in part because the Nazis cannot destroy "us" (A), while the Communists can. The Communists can destroy us because "our democratic way" suffers from inconsistencies and weaknesses (D); they are dangerous because they are not recognized as dangerous (C); and they are internal, not external foes (E).

The writer does not declare that the Communists may disarm and torment democratic people (B), although he does say this about the Nazis.

13.   **(A)**   According to the writer, historical and comparative research shows the prevalence of nuclear families over extended households (A), therefore, it is inconsistent to claim that extended households are widespread (D). Research also shows the relative invariance of household size, thus it is inconsistent to say household size varies (B).

This research does not, the writer states, conflict with claims about the decline of extended kinship ties (E). And contrary to answer (C), the research is consistent with the claim that extended kinship ties may decline with modernization.

14. **(D)**   The writer argues (C) that increased interest in Marxist theory is based on failures of existing ideological theories to explain political reality (B and E) and on the withering away of 1960s political activism (A).

Since the argument relies in part on the belief that heavily ideological theories are not good guides for understanding political reality, it would be weakened by answer (D), which holds that such theories are good guides.

15. **(A)**   The writer claims only that poverty is an essentially rural phenomenon, but he bases this only on information about poverty in the Third World. Therefore, a better conclusion would be that poverty *in the Third World* is a rural phenomenon (A). The premises do not permit so sweeping a conclusion as the sentence that most poverty occurs in the Third World (B) or that most rural poverty occurs in the Third World (C); the premises discuss poverty in the Third World, not poverty in general or even rural poverty in general.

Although the World Bank has apparently studied the Third World, this does not mean the bank is more concerned with poor in the Third World than it is with poor elsewhere (D).

The passage does imply that 390 million people live in East and South Asia (E), but this implication is a premise of the passage, not the conclusion.

16. **(B)**   The passage indicates that it is now difficult to tell whether a toxin is a biological entity or a chemical entity, although in 1972 it was assumed to be biological, as implied by the Biological Weapons Convention. Thus, "toxin" is more difficult to define than it used to be (B).

The passage offers no comparison of biological weapons that would allow us to claim one is worse than the other (A) or (C). Nor does it offer a comparison between toxins and biological weapons that would support the conclusion that toxins are worse than biological weapons (D).

Finally, while the Biological Weapons Convention was signed more recently than the General Protocol, this does not mean that the writer believes that concern about biological weapons is more recent than concern about chemical weapons (E).

17. **(B)**   The passage argues that the author is an integral part of the story and of the experience of reading the story — one cannot understand the story, therefore, without understanding its author. Thus, one cannot understand *Huckleberry Finn,* for example, without understanding Mark Twain (B). The passage does not imply the converse, that one cannot understand Mark Twain without understanding *Huckleberry Finn* (C). Nor does it imply that readers fail to recog-

nize the role of the author in the story (D).

Further, while it claims that novels are *told* by an implied author, it does *not* imply that novels are *written* by an implied author (E). And it does not claim that the implied author creates the biological author (A), but rather that the biological author creates the implied author.

18. **(E)** Sun's argument is that because there is respect for law in America and because there is comfort, abundance, and progress, the former must be the cause of the latter. This argument would be weakened if comfort, abundance, and progress could happen without orderly maintenance of laws (E).

Although Sun prefers American law to Chinese law, his argument allows for the possibility that a law could be respected without being maintained in an orderly fashion (D) and that China had its own laws (B).

A symbol, for Sun, of American law and prosperity is the Honolulu post office. It illustrates his point, but is not a necessary premise of his argument. Thus, his argument would not suffer if the post office no longer existed (A) or if the Chinese delivered their mail differently from the Hawaiians (C).

19. **(E)** The writer offers a definition of materialism which allows for the existence of unseen matter such as energy. This allowance, distinguishes his definition from the 19th century definitions which, he implies, limited matter to the visualizable (E).

Although the writer limits the world of existing things to the entities studied by physicists, he does not imply that *only* physicists can believe in such entities. Thus, we may not infer that only physicists are materialists (A). While the writer says energy and matter are not *sharply* distinguishable, they may be distinguishable to some degree, so we may not infer that matter is nothing but energy (B).

The writer's use of the term "billiard-ball" is as a metaphorical description of 19th century physics, it does not refer to the game of billiards. So while the writer may find fault with 19th century physics, he says nothing which permits us to infer that he does not like billiards (C).

Finally, the writer says that modern physics studies particles less visualizable than those studied in 19th century physics, but this does not imply that there are fewer such particles (D).

20. **(D)** The writer argues that differences between men and women are neither universal (B) nor necessary (C), because they are based on cultural and social practices (D).

The writer is addressing people concerned about rigid and limited sex roles, but he is not arguing that one must consider such roles (A). And the writer is not arguing that women are dominated by men in most societies (E), rather he accepts this as a given fact and proposes to argue for one explanation of it.

21. **(B)**   The argument is that *Hamlet* was important to and perhaps influential on Romanticism, because *Hamlet* grapples with the conflict of consciousness and action — a conflict significant to Romanticism. If Romanticism were not particularly interested in this conflict, then the writer's argument would be weakened (B).

Although the play might have been significant to the Romantics, the writer's argument would not be weakened if *Hamlet* were not the most significant of all Shakespeare's plays (C), if it were written before the Romantic movement started (E), or if Shakespeare himself were not a Romantic (D). All these would be irrelevant to the argument that the Romantics found *Hamlet* to be significant. Also irrelevant to the argument would be the claim that actions cannot be prevented from being totally mindless (A); the argument assumes the Romantic's interest in such prevention, but not necessarily the possibility of such prevention.

22. **(E)**   The dentist assumes that fear causes one's saliva to become thicker and more sticky (E), not that the thickening saliva causes the fear (A). Nowhere does the dentist claim that thickening saliva causes stickiness (C) or that one cannot be calm and afraid at the same time (B). And the dentist implies that the patient was afraid during the session; he did not become afraid only after the session was over (D).

23. **(C)**   The writer's conclusion is that "beauty" in the King James version of the Bible is not the same as beauty studied in aesthetics, because aesthetics gets its concept of beauty from Greek thought and the word "beauty" in the King James version is not synonymous with the Greek word for "beauty" (D). The King James version's word is different, according to the writer, because "beauty of holiness" appears in different English translations of the Psalms (E) as "Holy array" (B) or "splendour of Holiness" (A), but presumably the Greek word for "beauty" could not be similarly translated.

Note the writer's implication that Greek thought preceded aesthetics, thus Greek thought could not have come from aesthetics (C).

24. **(D)**   The writer acknowledges Cleanthes' hypothesis that the universe has a design, and that others might be able to demonstrate something close to this. But the writer goes on to find fault with Cleanthes' position by suggesting that the universe could be a faulty, imperfect design. The implication here is that Cleanthes believes the world was designed by a perfect designer (D). Cleanthes' position is contrary to the hypothesis that the world is faulty and imperfect (B) and that the universe arose from something *merely like* a design (C). It says nothing about whether the designer was an infant deity (A) or whether theories about the universe are based on fancy and hypothesis (E).

Section IV – Logical Reasoning

1. **(C)**   is the correct response. This conclusion follows from the premises, and

can be proven to follow from the two premises even though this conclusion is false. This only emphasizes, however, that logical validity or "derivability" is not the same as truth. One can logically reason to a false conclusion if at least one of the premises, in this case the first claim, is false. (A) is incorrect. Though this is factually true, this statement cannot be derived validly from the two premises that are given. Answer (B) is incorrect because this false statement cannot be derived from the information given, i.e., the two claims (premises). (D) is also incorrect. This cannot be inferred logically from the two premises given. Answer (E) is incorrect because this cannot be logically derived from the premises given. Note that the premise "A celestial body moves around the Earth" does not mean that only one celestial body does so. Sometimes the indefinite article has the meaning of "all," as in this example.

2.   **(C)**   is the correct response. Since "a celestial body moves around the earth," and the geocentric theory holds that all things revolve around the Earth, then all celestial bodies must move around the Earth. (A) is incorrect. Here the force of the "a" is "all," although sometimes "a" has the force (meaning) of "some." For example: "A cat came into my bedroom" means at least one cat so moved, but not that all cats in the world came into my bedroom. One must read carefully for meaning. (B) is incorrect. When "a" has the meaning of "no" there must be another negative word, usually "not." Thus "A cat is not a bird" means "No cats are birds," while "A dog is a mammal" means "All dogs are mammals." (D) is incorrect because sometimes "a" can mean "some," but not in this example. Answer (E) is also incorrect because the premise in question says nothing about the sun being a celestial body or not. Besides, the second premise in the argument has established that the sun *is* a celestial body.

3.   **(C)**   is the correct response. The question asks you to identify the cause of a personality disorder when three possible causes have been listed. The key concept is that the scientists attribute the cause of violent behavior in teenage boys to some or all of the causes. This means that all three causes may be acting together; or any two of them may be acting together; or just one of them may be acting. Since we are told that John has not been watching violent movies or TV shows, John's violent behavior was caused by either or both of the remaining factors.

4.   **(C)**   is the correct response. Given that there is definitely only one cause identified, removal of that cause presumably will result in a cure. (A) is incorrect. From the fact that John, a teenager, displays violent behavior, it does not follow that all teenagers will so act. Answer (B) is also incorrect. From the fact that John displays violent behavior, it does not follow either from this, or from the fact that only teenage boys were considered in the study, that no girls will ever display violent behavior. (D), of course, is incorrect given the scenario that John is a teenage boy and he does display violent behavior. (E) is also incorrect. A teenage boy may be deprived of water and nourishing foods, but may have a body chemistry that can tolerate these deprivations for long periods of time.

5.   **(D)**   is the correct response. The fact that Smith had the gun does not tell us whether or not he committed the murder. Concluding that he is guilty, from the premises given, would be an error known as the fallacy of affirming the consequent. In general terms, this fallacy can be understood as follows:

1) If Hypothesis (A) is true, then the consequence of this hypothesis, (B) is true.
2) Consequence (B) of Hypothesis (A) is true.
3) Therefore, Hypothesis (A) is true.

For example, "If Anna eats her vegetables, she will get dessert. Anna will get dessert. Therefore, she will eat her vegetables." But, Anna may get dessert for another reason. She may trick her mother and take the dessert when her mother is not looking. This type of reasoning can be proven to be invalid. From the information given, (A) and (B) are incorrect because we cannot know if Smith killed Ms. Scott, since he may have hidden the gun *for someone else*. (C) does not follow, since Smith may have hidden the gun belonging to someone else. Answer (E) is also incorrect because we cannot conclude this either, since he *may have* committed the murder.

6.   **(E)**   is the correct response. All the other answers do not follow logically from the facts provided. Given that Smith had a gun, even if it is the gun used to murder Ms. Scott, it follows that Smith may or may not have committed the murder.

7.   **(E)**   is the correct response. (A) is incorrect given that Clark was 5,000 miles away, and therefore, could not have killed Ms. Dunne. But, he may have returned the day after, found the murder weapon used by someone else, and then hidden it; or he may not have hidden it (B). (C) and (D) cannot be inferred from just the information given. The argument given by Ms. Jones is an example of a well-known fallacy called denying the antecedent. In general terms, this fallacy can be understood as follows:

1) If P, then Q
2) Not P
3) Therefore, not Q

But, this conclusion is mistaken. Even if (P) turns out to be false, (Q) could still be true. For example, if you study, you will pass the test. You did not study. Therefore, you will not pass the test. However, you may cheat on the test and pass it that way.

8.   **(D)**   is the correct response. We have established that he couldn't have pulled the trigger on Ms. Dunne; and we are given the information that he did not pay to have someone kill her. Whether Clark hid the gun or not, or whether he owns a gun or not, cannot be determined on the basis of the information given.

9. **(B)** The original sentence claims that a necessary condition for a person to be able to vote in U.S. Presidential elections is that he or she be an American citizen. (B) is the correct answer. (A) says that the moment a person is an American citizen, he or she can vote, which is obviously false for a person five years of age born in the U.S. To take this further, if all citizens of the U.S. happen to be five years of age, then none can vote (C). The original sentence speaks only of the U.S. Presidential elections, unlike (D), which includes all U.S. elections. Therefore, (D) goes beyond the scope of the original claim and must be wrong. (E) is incorrect given that no mention is made of U.S. nationals.

10. **(B)** (B) is the correct response. For if one were not an American citizen, one could not vote in U.S. Presidential elections, according to the original claim. If it were a sufficient condition, as claimed in answer (A), this would mean that the moment one is an American citizen, one could vote in such Presidential elections, which is false. Surely, a newborn infant born in Ohio is an American citizen, although he or she cannot vote yet in an American Presidential election. Given the correctness of (B), (C) and (D) are obviously incorrect, as is (E).

11. **(A)** (A) is the correct response, for being a brave person is a necessary condition for deserving the fair maidens. (B) states a sufficient condition, such that the moment one is brave, he deserves the fair maidens, which may be false. There may be other conditions that he has to fulfill, such as being of noble birth. If noble birth is a condition and no brave people are of noble blood, then none of the brave people deserve the fair maidens. Thus, (C) is incorrect. (D) implies that other people, who are not brave, deserve the fair maidens. This is wrong. (E) is obviously incorrect given the correctness of (A).

12. **(D)** (D) is the correct response. And so, if the Earth is a heavenly body, which it clearly is, then the Earth moves in a perfect circle. This argument is thus valid, even though the supplied premise and the conclusion are both false. (A) could not be the correct answer, for if only *some* heavenly bodies move in perfect circles, the Earth might not be one of them, and the conclusion would not follow. A similar situation is presented in (E); for the Earth, again, might not be one of the heavenly bodies that so move. Given that (D) is correct, (B) and (C) are incorrect.

13. **(C)** (C) is the correct response; it is the contradictory of the original claim, i.e., both sentences cannot be true or false together. (A) is incorrect, because while (A) cannot be true when the original is true, both the original and (A) can be false together. (B) is implied by the original claim, i.e., if the original claim is true, (B) must also be true. Therefore, (B) is not the denial of the original. (D) is incorrect. Since "free will" and "genuine choice" mean the same, (D) is equivalent to (A), and as (A) is incorrect, so is (D). Given that (C) is correct, (E) is obviously false.

14.   **(C)**   The consultant says nothing about advertising campaigns in general, so eliminate (A). That the advertising campaign will probably not increase business (B) is not the conclusion of the argument, but one of the premises of it. (C) has to be the answer. If the owner increases the price he will almost certainly lose 20% of his business, which he cannot afford to do. An advertising campaign could be expected to replace only half of the lost business, and probably not even that. Therefore, he should not increase the price. Eliminate (D) for the same reason as (A). Eliminate (E) since the owner cannot afford the lost business.

15.   **(B)**   It could be that the crime rate per capita has not gone down in the three cities named, but has gone down in the nation as a whole, so eliminate (A). (B) seriously weakens the conclusion. The speaker considers only three types of violent crime, and those only in three cities. If the nonviolent crime rate has dropped dramatically, there is a good chance it has pulled the overall per capita crime rate down with it. Eliminate (C) because the drop in the rural rate may be offset by an increase in the urban rate. (D) and (E) do not include the words "per capita." If the population has increased and the number of criminals and crimes has remained constant, the per capita incidence of both has dropped.

16.   **(A)**   The author argues that the increase in accidents is due to driver inexperience, which in turn is due to the shortening of the training courses. The problem is, the author does not tell us what percentage of the accidents are being caused by the undertrained (as he says) drivers. It could be that accidents have increased, but none of the five-month trainees have been involved. Eliminate (B) and (D) because they do not address the central point of the passage, which is that the shorter courses are causing more wrecks. Eliminate (C) because the reason why the trucking industry expanded is not crucial to the argument. Eliminate (E) because the author is attributing all of the increase in accidents to the shorter courses, and has thereby attempted a full explanation of the phenomenon.

17.   **(D)**   This is a question which one can answer by reading the first sentence of the passage. We are told that Blue refuses to ride only if Red rides. Then we are asked, if Blue refuses to ride, which of the following may be logically deduced (must be true)? The answer is (D), Red rides. Eliminate (A) and (B) because EITHER White or Green asks to sit by Yellow, and we cannot deduce which it is. Eliminate (C) because that would happen only if Blue did ride. Eliminate (E) because the passage lists no circumstances under which Yellow will not ride.

18.   **(A)**   The author wants us to force nation X to lower its trade barriers in order that we may avoid four things: the worst trade deficit since WWII (A); loss of domestic jobs; an economic slowdown; and loss of economic leadership. We may infer that he thinks these things are undesirable, since he wishes to avoid them. The author says nothing about the desirability of any nation's running a trade surplus, much less the impossible feat of all nations' doing so (C). The answer is (A). (B), (D), and (E) are not beliefs we can attribute to the author.

19. **(B)**   The author does not argue from analogy, (A), but cites two wars as examples which support his interpretation (B). Webster's *Collegiate Thesaurus* gives the following definition of analogy: "… expression involving explicit or implicit comparison of things basically unlike but with some striking similarities…." (G. and C. Merriam Co: Springfield, Mass., 1976). An analogy, then, is based on the similarity of certain attributes of two things, when the things themselves are essentially different. One war is not essentially different from another, as an athletic contest is from a war. One war would not, then, normally serve as an analogy for another. The author does not (C) try to discredit the scholar's methodology. In fact, nothing is said about the methodology of the study. It may rely heavily on statistical techniques, or it may be a survey of previous accounts of war. We are not told which. The author does not say that the scholar should be disbelieved because he is not trustworthy (D). We cannot tell from the passage if the scholar overlooked the wars cited by the author of the passage (E). Perhaps he did not, but rather gave a different interpretation of what caused them.

20. **(E)**   Is it the best form of government there is because it's worth defending, or is it worth defending because it's the best form there is? This is a type of circular reasoning. A premise is offered in support of a conclusion. The conclusion is then offered to prove the premise. The argument turns back on itself, instead of moving forward. Arguments (A), (B), and (C) begin with a conclusion, then offer statements in support of the conclusion. Argument (D) is a (weak) form of inductive reasoning, where the person argues that one thing always follows another in his experience, so it will do likewise tomorrow. (E) is like the passage. Does he love sports because he plays them all the time; or does he play them all the time because he loves them?

21. **(A)**   The author starts out arguing one thing, that there should be no speed limits on freeways, and finishes by arguing the opposite, that there should be speed limits in some cases (D). The answer, then, must be statement (A). The author does not establish that citizens have a right to be safe on the public highways, but that is a premise any reasonable person would grant without a supporting argument. Therefore, we would not include (B) as a flaw in the argument. With regard to (C), the author first appears to think that the right to judge your own driving skills takes precedence over the right of others to be safe. But then he says that these rights must be balanced (E). It is not clear, then, which of the two he would support when shown the contradiction. The best answer is (A).

22. **(E)**   The argument is that the resignation of Lucky Silas was followed by the triumph of the West, therefore, the resignation of Silas (and his ilk) caused (or at least permitted) the triumph of the West. This is basing the claim that A caused B merely on the fact that A came before B, as (E) says. Silas is not attacked directly in this argument, nor is there any evidence that he has presented an argument, so (A) does not fit. (B) has some merit, for the argument does implicitly praise Silas's resignation by pointing to what the speaker takes to have

been its effects. However, the act and the effects are both in the past, so the act is not being recommended and (B) does not fit the case. In both of these latter, the argument does use loaded language of a mild sort ("liberal bias," "triumph," etc.) but these do not replace the argument and are not even on the same topic as the argument seems to be. So (D) does not apply. While the conclusion of this argument is a claim that one event caused another, it is not inferring a cause from its effects. That would be to infer that A occurred because B did and A is known to cause B. Here the supposed cause is already known to have occurred and what is inferred is that it was a cause of B, an event also known to have occurred. So, (C) also does not describe this case.

23.   **(D)**   This is a difficult question. It asks you which of the answers cannot be true. It will be easier for you to find the answer if you ask yourself which of the answers must be false.

(D) is the best answer. If ALL music lovers, (ml), enjoy playing and interpreting their favorite music for their friends, (p), but not all can read music, (r), then more ml are p than r. The statement that more ml are r than p must be false.

We cannot say that (A) is false. The passage does not give us a numerical breakdown of music lovers by category. Nor is it necessary that all types of music lovers have been mentioned in the passage. We do not know, therefore, how many music lovers are in the first category discussed in the passage.

The final sentence of the passage establishes that all music lovers enjoy playing and interpreting their favorite music for their friends. That all x's do and y does not mean that everyone who does y is an x. Therefore, (B) is not necessarily false.

The passage lends some small support to the truth of (C), although it does not necessarily establish it as fact. Therefore, (C) is not necessarily false.

It is not necessarily false that (E), all three types of music lovers mentioned in the passage can read music. If the three types mentioned are the only types of music lovers that there are, then the statement would be false. However, one cannot establish on the basis of the passage that the author has given an exhaustive list of the types of music lovers. Perhaps all of the types mentioned can read music, but others not mentioned cannot.

24.   **(B)**   The conclusion of the passage is that special lubricating additives in oil are either unhelpful or unnecessary for reducing engine wear. Answer (B) gets to the heart of the matter. It may be true, as the author of the passage states, that regular oil changes alone will reduce engine wear. This does not establish that additives do not provide additional protection against engine wear. If they do, the conclusion of the passage is wrong.

Answer (A) does not necessarily contradict the conclusion, because we cannot tell from (A) whether the oil change alone or the special additives are responsible for reducing engine wear.

Even if we grant (C), it is unclear what effect it has on the conclusion. Perhaps the special additives are extremely helpful in reducing engine wear in cases where the oil is not changed regularly. On the other hand, the benefit, if any, of special additives may not be such as to prevent engine wear in cases

where the oil is not changed regularly. Therefore, (C) is not the best answer.

Perhaps it is true that (D), engine wear, occurs all of the time. The effect of this on the conclusion is uncertain. Therefore, (D) fails for the same reason as (C).

The passage makes no claim about scientists' conclusions regarding special additives. Therefore, even if we grant that scientists have made a mistake about the additives (E), we do not know what the mistake might be or what effect it will have on the author's conclusion.

25. **(A)** The argument in the passage is this:

Premise 1:   Consumers are dissatisfied with the products.

Premise 2:   The dissatisfaction results from consumers' perception that the products are of low quality.

Conclusion: To alleviate dissatisfaction we must change consumers' perceptions regarding the quality of the products.

The question asks for another premise which would weaken the conclusion. We are looking, then, for a premise that contradicts the conclusion.

Answer (A) satisfies the requirement. The argument assumes that the only source of dissatisfaction is the perception of low quality. Therefore, the solution is to change that particular perception. If, however, there is another perception which also leads to dissatisfaction, the conclusion is wrong and another perception must also be changed in order to alleviate dissatisfaction.

Answer (B) has no effect on the conclusion. The premises make no mention of the relative number of consumers who are satisfied versus the number who are dissatisfied. Granting (B) as a premise does not change the conclusion.

Answer (C), likewise, has no effect on the conclusion. The solution for the dissatisfaction is still the same.

Answer (D) is simply beside the point. The problem does not arise from the perceptions of those in advertising, so their opinions have no bearing on the problem.

Answer (E) is also beside the point. The problem is not with consumers who are satisfied with the products, but with those who are not. The solution, then, has nothing to do with those who are satisfied.

LSAT Writing Sample – Demonstration Essay

Chaser should accept the job offer from Smith, Tyler and Hyde in Iowa, because it would provide him with the greater opportunity to fulfill his two goals of becoming a wealthy senior partner in a prominent law firm and someday entering national politics.

Although the Wall Street law firm Doran, Reilly and Doran offers Chaser an initially higher salary than the Cedar Rapids firm, he would have to live in the New York City area, where the cost of living is much higher than that of a small Midwestern city. The Iowa firm also offered Chaser free use of a house; thus, he is saved the expense of paying rent or a mortgage. From a financial standpoint, Chaser would actually be better off with the lower-paying job in Iowa, where his standard

of living would be higher than in the New York City area as a result of the lower cost of living and the benefits offered by the Iowa firm.

Smith, Tyler and Hyde also offered Chaser a greater chance of becoming a senior partner by age 40. While the Wall Street firm is very prominent, Chaser would be just one of many equally qualified law school graduates hired by the firm. One's chances of being promoted to senior partner are limited at best, especially given the current structure of 5 senior partners in a firm of 505 attorneys. Furthermore, the conditions that would allow Chaser's work and abilities to be noticed are not present in the Wall Street firm. He would be working among 20 to 30 other associates, and his contributions would be difficult to isolate. By contrast, Chaser's chance of becoming a senior partner at Smith, Tyler and Hyde is virtually assured, as he is being deliberately recruited from his school to upgrade the firm's image, and has been promised early promotion. In terms of his goal to become a senior partner by age 40, Chaser's interests are again better served by joining the Iowa firm.

Chaser's goal of entering national politics would also be advanced by joining the Cedar Rapids firm. While Doran, Reilly and Doran enjoys national prestige and has offices in Washington, D.C., it is just one of several nationally known law firms in New York handling major corporate cases. In addition, Chaser would just be one qualified attorney among many with little chance to make a name for himself. The Cedar Rapids firm, by contrast, handles a wide range of cases in the Midwest and would stand out more from the crowd. Essentially, it is still better to be a big fish in a small pond than a big fish in a big pond. The partners at the Iowa firm also have a strong history of political involvement at both the state and the national levels. Building strong relationships with a former U.S. senator and two current members of the state legislature would no doubt boost Chaser's access to politics and help prepare him for his future political goals.

Because the Iowa offer would better enable Chaser to achieve his goals, he should join Smith, Tyler and Hyde. He would be able to advance faster, live better, and acquire a better political base by joining the Iowa firm.

Demonstration Essay Explanation

This is a good essay, because it organizes the arguments in a clear and orderly manner, emphasizes the pros of the choice made while acknowledging the strengths of alternative positions. The author's position is effectively and clearly presented. The essay is of sufficient length, and the variation of sentence structure helps retain reader interest.

The opening paragraph of the essay states the author's position and summarizes the reasons for taking that position. The second paragraph tackles the issue of the apparently higher salary that the New York law firm offered. It refutes the seeming advantage of a higher salary with outside common knowledge about the cost of living in different regions of the United States. This paragraph also makes use of the details given in the topic statement to support the author's position.

Paragraph 3 directly addresses one of the goals of Mark Chaser provided in the topic statement, that of becoming a senior partner in a prestigious law firm by age 40. Outside information is again used to support the author's position and is useful, because it demonstrates the author's ability to think and reason independently

within the framework of the given facts.

The fourth paragraph speaks of Chaser's second primary goal of one day entering national politics. It points out that Chaser will have a much easier time making himself noticed in a smaller community like Cedar Rapids than he would in a
metropolis like New York City.

The last paragraph reiterates the author's position and summarizes the three
basic reasons behind the decision.

LSAT
Law School Admission Test

TEST VI

Part of
no 26
comes

卌
卌

TEST VI

Section I

Time—35 minutes
26 Questions

(Answer sheets appear in the back of this book.)

DIRECTIONS: The questions in this section are based on the reasoning contained in brief statements or passages. For some questions, more than one of the choices could conceivably answer the question. However, you are to choose the **best** answer; that is, the response that most accurately and completely answers the question. You should not make assumptions that are by common sense standards implausible, superfluous, or incompatible with the passage. After you have chosen the best answer, blacken the corresponding space on your answer sheet.

1. During the 60s and 70s there was much reaction against "hippies," particularly men with long hair. During the same period, the voting age was being lowered in many states. In one state these two trends came together in a law that lowered the voting age to 19 for all except men with long hair. "They just don't look like citizens," a legislator explained his vote in favor of the law.

    The legislator assumes which of the following?

    (A)   People who look like citizens should be allowed to vote.

    (B)   Only people who look like citizens should be allowed to vote.

    (C)   People who are allowed to vote look like citizens.

    (D)   Only people who are allowed to vote look like citizens.

    (E)   Hippies cannot be trusted with the vote.

2. In a recently completed test, two groups of rats were fed the same diet except that for one group the amount of vitamin E was reduced significantly below normal. As the experiment progressed, the rats receiving the feed with lowered levels of vitamin E displayed the signs of aging significantly earlier than did the rats whose diet contained normal amounts of vitamin E. The signs involved covered the range of characteristic aging — hair loss, menopause, osteoporosis, and senility, to name a few. The experimenters concluded that lowering the intake of vitamin E accelerates the

aging process. Although the exact connection between vitamin E and the aging process has not been determined, we may expect that a regime involving many times the normal dose of vitamin E will soon be shown to slow the aging process markedly.

The principle that leads from the experimental results to the expectation above is most like which of the following:

(A) If one pill a day will cure this fever in a week, two a day will cure it in half a week.

(B) If lack of vitamin C in the diet causes scurvy, then restoring vitamin C to the diet can prevent scurvy.

(C) If drinking more than my normal amount of coffee makes my heart race, drinking a lot less than my normal amount might make it beat dangerously slow.

(D) If three hours sleep less than my normal makes me drowsy all day, then three hours more should make me really alert.

(E) If letting up on the brake lets the car speed up going down hill, then pressing harder on the brake will slow it down.

3. Though often condemned, the loaded question is a useful device for speeding the legal process. In the classic example, "Have you stopped beating your wife?," either a "Yes" or a "No" answer concedes that the person has beaten his wife, thus giving a confession to an actionable offense. Similar results may be obtained generally with questions which begin, for example, "Do you regret...?," where the blank is filled with a description of the crime at issue — "murdering your grandmother," for instance.

This recommendation would most strongly appeal to someone who held that

(A) the purpose of questioning in a legal process is to arrive at the truth, as quickly as possible.

(B) the purpose of questioning in the legal process is to assign blame for a crime, as swiftly as possible.

(C) the purpose of questioning in the legal process is to achieve justice, as quickly as possible.

(D) questioning in the legal process is not to be guided by ethical considerations.

(E) logical considerations are not relevant to questioning in the legal process.

4. One of the most interesting discoveries of the Golden Age of Explanation was an island on which the population was divided into two tribes, the Truves, who always told the truth, and the Falls, who always lied. The discoverer of this island left a record of one of his encounters there. He met two natives and asked them which tribe they belonged to. One answered by saying that they were both Falls.

From this answer, the explorer

(A) could tell that they were both Falls.

(B) could tell that the speaker was a Fall and his companion a Truve.

(C) could tell that the speaker was a Truve and his companion a Fall.

(D) could tell that both natives were Truves.

(E) could not determine the tribes of the two natives.

5. Getting good nutrition is a complex matter. You have to consider getting the right amount of a number of vitamins and minerals, the right balance of fats of different kinds, of proteins of different kinds, the right number of calories from the right sources, and much more. Yet getting a properly balanced diet is the most important thing you can do. Fortunately, PerFooD Plus, the perfect food and then some, is now available. Three designated servings a day guarantees the very best balanced diet in every respect. You owe it to yourself to start on PerFooD Plus today.

Which of the following would NOT be an objection to the above argument?

(A) A well-planned diet of ordinary food does as well as PerFooD Plus in providing proper nutrition.

(B) A well-planned diet of ordinary food costs less than PerFooD Plus, even taking planning time into account.

(C) A well-planned diet of ordinary food tastes better than PerFooD Plus.

(D) In laboratory tests, some of the ingredients of PerFooD Plus have combined with stomach acids to form highly toxic compounds.

(E) The manufacturer of PerFooD Plus has been cited for inhumane treatment of test animals in its cosmetics division.

6. The so-called Personal Banker is a scam. Every time I go to my bank, I get sent to a different person, none of whom have known me nor been familiar with my financial situation and most of whom have obviously been very new to banking.

The speaker above obviously assumes that

(A) "personal" involves an enduring relationship of familiarity.

(B) he deserves the services of an experienced banker.

(C) his financial situation requires expert care.

(D) he will get better assistance from an acquaintance.

(E) his bank is trying to mislead him.

7. At least one argument that marijuana is a dangerous drug does not establish its claim. If you accept the argument that smoking marijuana leads to using hard drugs because, even though not all marijuana smokers go on to using hard drugs, almost all hard-drug users started by smoking marijuana, then you ought also accept that drinking water leads to hard-drug use, since, although not all water drinkers go on to using hard drugs, almost all hard-drug users started by drinking water.

The speaker here refutes an earlier argument by

(A) pointing to another argument of the same form and with equally good premises which has a false conclusion.

(B) pointing out that it is a case of the unreliable argument from the fact that A follows B to the claim that B causes A.

(C) pointing to an inaccurate version of the original argument and refuting that as though it were the original argument.

(D) pointing out that the original argument, while a sketch of a good one, is inadequately detailed to be decisive.

(E) pointing to an exception to the general claim that the original argument tries to establish.

8. Boy, the rules are sure unfair to us teenagers. We have to pay an adult ticket price to see a movie but then we can't see adult movies. Six bucks to see the same thing my kid sister can see for two! And then it is four years of adult prices before we can drive and six before we can vote and nine before we can drink and for more than half of that we are still paying the price for movies we can't see. It is really unfair! So, we ought to demand that they ___

Which is the most likely completion of the last sentence above?

(A) lower the voting age.

(B) lower the drinking age.

(C) lower the driving age.

(D)   lower the teenage movie price.

(E)   raise the movie price for younger people.

9.   Evan: Boy, am I relieved! My aunt is going to have thoracic surgery, which is really major surgery, but I just learned that over 85% of patients who have thoracic surgery recover fully.

   Yvonne: Don't get your hopes up. Your aunt is almost 80 and less than 15% of patients that age who have thoracic surgery recover fully.

On the basis of the information supplied by both Evan and Yvonne, which we assume to be correct, what is the most reliable estimate of the chances that Evan's aunt will recover fully?

(A)   Her chances are about 100%.

(B)   Her chances are about 85%.

(C)   Her chances are about 50%.

(D)   Her chances are about 15%.

(E)   Her chances are about 12.75%.

10.   Current problems in the Middle East are the result of British and French interference in the breakup of the Ottoman Empire at the end of World War I. They divided the territory up to suit their national interests, without taking into account the concerns of the inhabitants of the area. They, not the United States, should, therefore, be the ones to bring about a just and peaceful solution to the present conflicts.

Which of the following is most like the argument above?

(A)   Hangovers are caused by alcohol in the blood, so another drink in the morning will cure the hangover.

(B)   The problem in this car originated in the factory, so the manufacturer ought to fix it.

(C)   The child, not her mother, should wash the car.

(D)   Criminals cause a lot of pain and suffering to their victims, so they, not the government, ought to reimburse the victims.

(E)   This book was borrowed from the public library, so it ought to be returned.

11.   A number of apes of various species have been said to have learned to carry on at least simple conversations in a human language, American Sign Language. However, many of these claims turn out to be based on anecdotal

evidence, rather than rigorous testing. What tests were conducted allowed the testers to provide (probably unconscious) cues to guide the apes' behavior to resemble conversation.

These claims lead most correctly to what further claim?

(A) No ape has ever learned a human language.

(B) No ape has ever learned American Sign Language.

(C) No ape tested had learned American Sign Language.

(D) No ape has been shown to have learned American Sign Language.

(E) No ape that learned American Sign Language was properly tested.

12. Claude Bernard randomly divided a population of rabbits into two groups, one fed a vegetarian diet, the other fed meat. When he analyzed the urine from these two groups, he found that the urine from the meat-eating group contained significant amounts of ketone, while that of the vegetarian group was free of ketone. From this he concluded that metabolizing meat caused the ketone in the urine. He then analyzed the urine of rabbits that had been deprived of food and found that the urine of starving rabbits also contained considerable ketone. From this he concluded that starving rabbits are also metabolizing meat — their own stomachs!

The principle underlying this latter conclusion was most nearly

(A) like causes produce like effects.

(B) like effects arise from like causes.

(C) extremely deviant situations tend to be very similar.

(D) the simplest explanation is the best.

(E) a surprising conclusion is more likely correct.

13. "A student may request permission to submit extra credit work only if he has properly completed all the regular work. Regular work is properly completed only if it is either handed in on time or is handed in late with prior permission."

Charles will get no better than a C on the basis of his regular work; with extra credit work he might receive a B.

Which of the following is certain under the rules cited above?

(A) If he has no late regular work and does the extra credit work, he will get a B.

(B) If he has unexcusedly late regular work, he has no chance to get better than a C.

(C) If he has regular work that is late, but with prior permission, he can do extra credit work.

(D) If he has no late regular work, he has a chance to get a B.

(E) If he receives a C, then he did not do extra credit work.

14. Joe and Bob are cutting cards. The suits have been ordered as well as the cards within the suit, so there can be no ties. Joe has won the first three cuts. Bob decides to raise his ante considerably on the next cut, reasoning that it is very unlikely that Joe could win four cuts in a row.

Which of the following is the best summary of the principle underlying Bob's reasoning?

(A) He follows the unreliable principle that if three similar events are jointly unlikely, then a fourth similar event is also unlikely.

(B) He follows the reliable principle that if each of four events is unlikely, then their joint occurrence is unlikely.

(C) He follows the unreliable principle that if the joint occurrence of four events is unlikely, each of them separately is unlikely.

(D) He follows the reliable principle that if three similar events are each unlikely, then a fourth similar event is unlikely as well.

(E) He follows the unreliable principle that if four events are jointly unlikely, then the fourth is unlikely given that the other three have occurred.

15. Positive emotions may have beneficial effects during exercise. Dr. Schwarz asked thirty-two college volunteers who had acting experience to imagine events that would evoke happiness, sadness, anger, fear, and neutral emotion, and then had them sustain those emotions while exercising. Each emotion produced different blood pressure, heart rate and body movement patterns during imagery alone and with exercise. Anger during exercise raised the participants' heart rates an average of 33 beats per minute — more than double the increase during neutral (normal) exercise; a context of happiness raised heart rates less than half the average increase of normal exercise.

Which of the following, if true, would weaken the writer's argument?

(A) Some people do not have positive emotions when they exercise.

(B) Anger during exercise actually raised the participants' heart rates an average of 66 beats per minute.

(C) Normal exercise resulted in one half the heart rates of exercise done during anger.

(D) Not every college volunteer was able to evoke fear.

(E) Heart rates during normal exercise were half that of heart rates during relaxation.

16. How is Paxamar to survive in its contentious environment? Paxamar's survival depends on a "qualitative edge." As long as Paxamar employed top-line weapons systems many years before its surrounding enemies acquired them, *qualitative edge* was a meaningful term. Recently, however, many countries have been supplied with the most sophisticated weapons. Eroding deterrence is an added destabilizer to peace. Should war ever occur, Paxamar must be able to produce its own secret weapons so that it can surprise its enemies.

Which of the following is *not* a premise of this passage's argument?

(A) Deterrence is a stabilizing force in the area around Paxamar.

(B) Paxamar once had a qualitative edge.

(C) Paxamar is surrounded by its enemies.

(D) Secret weapons would allow Paxamar to surprise its enemies.

(E) Paxamar has less sophisticated weapons than its enemies.

17. Mankiw and Weil found that demand for housing climbs between ages 20 and 30, levels off through age 40, and then declines about 1 percent per year. The economists said real estate boomed in the 1970s because that's when the first wave of baby boomers began to look for a place of their own. And the boom has ended because the smaller baby-bust generation, born in the late 1960s, is entering its house-buying years.

Which of the following is a conclusion supported by the economists' findings?

(A) Housing demand will grow more slowly than before.

(B) The smaller baby-bust generation is in its house-buying years.

(C) Real estate boomed in the 1970s.

(D) Demand for housing declines after 30.

(E) Baby boomers are entering their house-buying years.

18. Of the cities and the towns in the Central Valley, none is more charged with the spirit of change than Fresno. Detractors like to point out that in a national poll taken about 20 years ago to determine the most desirable place in the country to live, Fresno placed dead last. And indeed there have been times when the city seemed to have all the ambience of a bus station. But results of the 1990 census showed Fresno to be the fastest-growing big city in the nation, having a population increase of 61% during the 1980s. Furthermore, between 1990 and 2000, Fresno County experienced a population growth rate of 19.8%, as opposed to California's 13.9% and the U.S.A.'s 13.1% growth rates.

What is the conclusion of this passage?

(A) Fresno had a population increase of 61% in the 1980s.

(B) Fresno is the least desirable place to live.

(C) Detractors like to point out that Fresno is like a bus station.

(D) Fresno is a big city.

(E) Fresno is one of the fastest improving cities in the Central Valley.

19. Signs of Freemasonry are everywhere. At a stoplight, you pull up behind a new automobile sporting the Masonic square and compasses above its bumper. At the Towson Fourth of July parade, you watch white-haired men in tasseled fezzes ride down the street in go-carts. The three temples of Charles Street — the Grand Lodge at Saratoga, the Scottish Rite at Thirty-ninth, and the Boumi Temple at Wyndhurst — are imposing monuments on the city's landscape. Even the U. S. dollar bill bears a Masonic symbol — an ancient pyramid capped by a radiant, all-seeing eye.

Based on this passage, which of the following may we infer?

(A) The Boumi Temple at Wyndhurst is a sign of Freemasonry.

(B) The Towson Fourth of July parade is a Freemason parade.

(C) All Freemasons have new automobiles.

(D) Only white-haired men wear tasseled fezzes.

(E) Charles Street has too many temples.

20. Environmental groups argue that incineration doesn't make garbage disappear, but converts it into poisonous gases and residue ash full of toxic heavy metals. As for recovering energy from burning garbage, so far, it's a wash. Operational problems have prevented many plants from processing their garbage at their designed capacity. The Office of Technology Assess-

ment, Congress' analytical arm, estimates that trash-to-energy facilities generate only about 0.2 percent of the nation's total energy production.

Which of the following, if true, would weaken the environmental groups' arguments?

(A)   More plants than previously thought are unable to process garbage at their designed capacity.

(B)   Trash-to-energy facilities generate less than 0.2 percent of the nation's total energy production capacity.

(C)   The poisonous gases and residue ash from incinerated garbage eventually disappear.

(D)   The Office of Technology Assessment usually makes accurate estimations.

(E)   Some plants have no operational problems.

21.   I think that by now I know a good deal of the world around me. I have given credence only to the confirmation of my senses, only to consistent experience. I have touched what I have seen, I have taken apart what I have touched; I have repeated my observations again and again; I have compared the various appearances with each other; and I was satisfied only after I had insight onto their exact connection.

Which proposition below, if true, would weaken the author's argument?

(A)   Some appearances cannot be deduced from others.

(B)   The senses can be deceiving.

(C)   The speaker trusts only his senses.

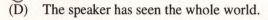

(D)   The speaker has seen the whole world.

(E)   Some appearances cannot explain others.

22.   A feminist believes a world where socioreligious and legal systems are governed by women would be a more human world than the present one, which is governed by men. There would be less greed, injustice, exploitation, and warfare. There would be more concern for posterity and also for the quality of life in the here and now. Sound biological evidence supports these views. Among most mammals only females bear responsibility for the survival of individuals other than themselves. The survival of any species really depends on the caring behavior of its females, not the aggressive behavior of its males.

Which of the following, if true, would not weaken the feminists' argument?

(A) Current socioreligious and legal systems are governed by women.

(B) Among a majority of mammals males share the responsibility for survival of individuals other than themselves.

(C) Female behavior can be as aggressive as male behavior in most species.

(D) A more human world would be greedier and more unjust.

(E) Available biological evidence is limited to information about which mammals bear responsibility for the survival of individuals other than themselves.

23. To most people who have been educated in philosophy the idea that there are things psychical which are not also conscious is so inconceivable that it seems to them absurd and refutable simply by logic. I believe this is only because they have never studied the relevant phenomena of hypnosis and dream, which — quite apart from pathological manifestations — necessitate this view. Their psychology of consciousness is incapable of solving the problems of dreams and hypnosis.

Which of the following is the author arguing?

(A) There is nothing psychical which is not also conscious.

(B) The phenomena of hypnosis and dreams necessitates the view that there are psychical phenomena which are not conscious.

(C) The problems of dreams and hypnosis cannot be solved.

(D) The proposition that there is anything psychical which is not also conscious is an absurd proposition.

(E) The proposition that there is anything psychical which is not also conscious is refutable by logic.

24. Many politicians, gerontologists, and editorial writers deplore the trend toward early retirement. This trend, which began after World War II and accelerated in the 1960s and 1970s, has led to a dramatic decline in work effort and earnings among the elderly. Opponents of earlier retirement believe that keeping people in the work force longer will raise the nation's output, reduce the costs of Social Security, and improve the well-being of older Americans. In contrast, the groups most directly affected by retirement patterns — employers, labor unions, and especially older workers themselves — are not interested in reversing recent retirement trends.

Which of the following propositions is NOT supported by the premises of this passage?

(A) Gerontologists are against earlier retirement.

(B) Work effort among the elderly has declined since World War II.

(C) Labor unions favor earlier retirement.

(D) Many gerontologists and employers differ with each other about earlier retirement.

(E) Earnings among the elderly have declined as earlier retirement has increased.

25. Over and over we have heard it said that Vico was ahead of his time and that he anticipated nearly everything in our own time. What we would seem to require before anything else, however, is a contemporary setting rich enough so that we can see Vico addressing his own time and trying to solve his own problems before he anticipates any of ours. Even then, some obscurity will likely remain, because Vico was a truly original thinker who discovered his own originality only slowly and tortuously and perhaps never completely or clearly.

Which of the propositions below best characterizes the writer's conclusion?

(A) Vico was ahead of his time.

(B) Vico scholars should devote more attention to Vico's views of his own time.

(C) Vico was an original thinker.

(D) Vico anticipated nearly everything in our time.

(E) Vico discovered his own originality only slowly and tortuously.

26. Although the church held a virtual monopoly over marriage and divorce in medieval Russia, it did not realize that nominal authority until the eighteenth century. The reason was not lack of will but institutional backwardness: the church simply lacked the instruments — unambiguous law, parish documentation, bureaucratic infrastructure — that would have enabled it to translate its formal authority into real power. As a result, the medieval church could only exercise episodic control over marriage and divorce; matrimony was more a secular contract than a church sacrament.

Which of the following is a premise of the passage's argument?

(A) The church in medieval Russia lacked the will to exercise its authority over marriages.

(B) The church held a virtual monopoly of power over marriage and divorce in medieval Russia.

(C)   The church could translate its formal authority into real power.

(D)   The pre-eighteenth century church couldn't exercise real power over marriage and divorce.

(E)   The church had a bureaucratic infrastructure.

STOP

If time still remains, you may review work only in this section.
When the time allotted is up, you may go on to the next section.

Section II

Time–35 minutes
27 Questions

(Answer sheets appear in the back of this book.)

DIRECTIONS: Each passage in this section is followed by a group of questions to be answered on the basis of what is **stated** or **implied** in the passage. For some questions, more than one of the choices could conceivably answer the question. However, you are to choose the **best** answer; that is, the response that most accurately and completely answers the question, and blacken the corresponding space on your answer sheet.

Incrementalism is a strategy used to reduce the enormous problems of decision making and calculation arising during the budgetary process. Incrementalism assumes the calculation of each year's budget uses some base as a starting point, such as last year's budget, and focuses attention on the marginal changes.
(5) In a broad sense this base can be zero, as in Zero Base Budgeting. The usual case, however, is to use the previous year's budget as the base, with the expectation that the next budget will be an expansion of it.

The first test of incrementalism considers the continuity of the organization requesting the budget. Many organizations continue their activities from year to
(10) year without a great deal of fluctuation. Their requirements for funding are relatively stable, and their ongoing programs are continued as long as constituency needs are being met. Such organizations do not need to consider alternatives beyond those required to maintain their services. Only when the organization is not meeting its constituency's needs is it necessary to adapt procedures and
(15) strategies and consider new alternatives.

When new alternatives are proposed they usually come in the form of new programs or an expansion of old programs. For the organization making a budgetary decision, the additional or expanded programs are those that will receive the greatest attention since they are the items which have not been
(20) previously discussed. The other items appearing in the request have been discussed and settled, and unless there are specific reasons for doing so, they need not be considered again. This strategy benefits those who must process large amounts of information by substantially reducing the items needing consideration. The information necessary to adequately consider even one or two programs
(25) can be enormous. Reconsideration of the entire budget on a yearly basis would make the task impossible.

The behavioral approach helps to explain why budgeting is done incrementally. The first problem facing a consideration of the entire budget is the nonintegration of the organizational goals. Each subunit of an organization can have its
(30) own goals which may not always be in line with the goals of the organization as a

whole. Thus, the organization at times pursues conflicting goals. Rather than attempting to resolve this situation all at once, the goals are dealt with one at a time. This approach limits the number of decisions which must be made at a given time.

(35)   Second, in problem solving there is a tendency to look in one's own back-yard first, i.e., trying something similar to what has been done previously, but different enough to solve the problem. This looks at the problem in small incre-ments in an attempt to keep costs down. The search is not for the best solution to the problem, only an adequate one. Thus, the chances are better that small

(40) changes will adequately solve the problem at less cost than will a complete reconsideration of the problem to find the best solution.

1. The primary purpose of the passage is to

    (A)   describe the federal budgetary process

    (B)   highlight alternative budgetary systems

    (C)   show why incrementalism is used

    (D)   examine the shortcomings of Zero Base Budgeting

    (E)   present the behavioral approach to budgeting

2. According to the author, stable organizations which continue their opera-tions from year to year

    (A)   are more likely to use incrementalism

    (B)   are not involved in problem solving

    (C)   are more likely to have consistent sets of goals

    (D)   are more likely to examine their entire budget on a yearly basis

    (E)   avoid most budgetary problems

3. From the passage, programs receiving the most attention

    (A)   are part of incremental systems

    (B)   are usually newer programs

    (C)   generally fail to gain support

    (D)   have established support groups

    (E)   are the larger programs

4. According to the author, incrementalism can be explained in part by

    (A)   its comprehensiveness

    (B)   its thorough examination of all expenditures

(C) dependence on the previous year's budget

(D) a lack of alternative procedures

(E) a desire to minimize information and complexity

5. The author's reference to looking in one's own backyard (lines 35-36) first means

(A) the previous year's budget must be used as the base

(B) continuous organizations more often use incrementalism

(C) reexamining old programs before new ones are accepted

(D) searching for solutions similar to past strategies

(E) keeping costs down

6. From the passage, Zero Base Budgeting is

(A) another form of incrementalism

(B) a problem-solving strategy

(C) a strategy used to reduce the enormous problems of decision-making and calculations

(D) an unacceptable way of budgeting when compared with incrementalism.

(E) a method for examining existing programs

7. The author feels incrementalism is politically acceptable because it

(A) is more comprehensive

(B) does not raise settled issues

(C) avoids new alternatives

(D) keeps budgetary information at manageable levels

(E) is run on a yearly basis

8. The author would most likely agree that

(A) Zero Base Budgeting is preferred to incrementalism

(B) under incrementalism both old and new programs receive careful scrutiny

(C) extensive problem searches are more economical

(D) incrementalism may not be perfect but it is understandable

(E) the use of a zero base is an important part of incrementalism

Henry V came to the throne at the age of 25. He had demonstrated his military capacity but his ability in politics was less certain and his character was indeed dubious. The power-hungry Beauforts had easily used him in their shrewd political maneuvers and his unsteady and adolescent nature did not console those (5) who desired stability and sobriety in their king. In body, mind, and personality the gods had smiled upon Henry. He had an abundance of physical stamina and excelled in sports; according to a chronicler, he could run faster than a buck. He was ambitious, hotheaded, and loyal to his companions, with whom he caroused and wasted much of his time. In the words of a contemporary writer "he was the (10) fervent soldier of Venus as well as of Mars: and repeatedly became involved in unsavory adventures pursued in taverns and along dark London alleys." But like many men upon whom responsibility has fallen, Henry was transformed and became every inch the king. He immediately vowed a new life and resolved to do his duty. Everyone marveled at his sober and grave bearing, at his newfound (15) piety, at his deep sense of responsibility. He was glorified by subsequent historians and Shakespeare as the model king. Unfortunately for England, however, a model king who worked for glory and military conquest was not what she required. Rather, she needed a long reign by one such as Henry IV. The legacy left by Henry V to later ages may have been the heroic epic of great feats of arms (20) but the immediate legacy was 60 years of national bankruptcy and civil anarchy.

From the outset of his reign Henry's chief concern and only preoccupation was the conquest of France. Despite the still weak hold of the Lancastrian dynasty, the aristocratic plots, and the disorder in England, Henry thought only of imperialist ventures in France and of winning military prestige for his family. (25) Although he made a show of negotiating with the disunited French and was offered generous concessions, his claims were exorbitant. Henry was bent upon war and probably sincerely believed in his claims and in God's favor. While negotiating with the French, he secured parliamentary grants, forged an army, and looked to his transport and supplies; by the summer of 1415 he was prepared (30) to strike.

France proved to be a bottomless hole into which English men and money were poured. Henry, however, immediately pushed southward and spent most of 1421 and part of 1422 reducing more French strongholds. After a six months' siege of Meaux, worn out by his exertions and dysentery, he died in August 1422 (35) at the age of 35. He died amidst military renown and success but at the price of misery for France and economic and political shipwreck for England.

9. The primary purpose of the passage is to

    (A)   extol the virtues of the boy king

    (B)   chronicle English animosity toward the French

    (C)   explain how Henry contributed to England's problems

    (D)   describe the relationship between Henry IV and Henry V

    (E)   suggest how England could have avoided financial ruin

10. According to the passage, Henry's abilities were

    (A) untested in the political arena

    (B) beyond reproach

    (C) concentrated in his strength of character

    (D) most developed in the area of diplomacy

    (E) totally lacking

11. The author feels Henry V was probably considered a model king because

    (A) he led England to a position of prominence on the world stage

    (B) he led England to decisive victory over France

    (C) of his administrative abilities

    (D) of his gift for diplomacy

    (E) of his sense of duty and responsibility

12. By calling France a bottomless hole in line 31, the author is

    (A) referring to its numerous deep valleys

    (B) suggesting resources were expended without result

    (C) referring to the vacuous nature of French diplomats

    (D) suggesting France was not worth conquering

    (E) referring to France's topographical features

13. The mention of Venus and Mars in line 10 refers to

    (A) the Roman gods of love and war

    (B) the method of navigation used while crossing the English Channel

    (C) Henry's deep belief in astrology

    (D) a military tactic employed by Henry in the French campaign

    (E) Henry's religious beliefs

14. According to the author, in negotiating with France, Henry probably

    (A) did not have experienced advisors

    (B) was faced with French leaders unwilling to settle their differences

    (C) had forsaken his goal of conquest

    (D)   preferred conquest to compromise

    (E)   achieved his greatest success

15.   The author argues the effect of Henry's exploits on England was

    (A)   to bring disrepute to English diplomacy

    (B)   an increase in its status as a world power

    (C)   severe financial and governmental problems

    (D)   a long and successful rule by his successor

    (E)   his glorification as a model king

    The Reverend Jerry Falwell, founder of the Moral Majority, said in a television interview: "Homosexuality is immoral. The so-called 'gay rights' are not rights at all, because immorality is not right. God hates homosexuality, and so do we. But we do not hate the homosexual; we want to help him by helping him
(5) overcome his sin."
    Falwell speaks for a large number of Americans who feel that there is something deeply objectionable about homosexuality. In other societies, of course, people have other views. The rulers of present-day Iran agree with Falwell and take his view to an extreme: there, homosexuals may be castrated or
(10) killed or both. In England, on the other hand, a more tolerant attitude is taken, and all legal penalties were removed three decades ago. What attitude are we to take? One possibility is that we might agree with Falwell and say that homosexuality is in fact immoral. Or we might disagree and say that in fact homosexuality is *not* immoral. But there is a third alternative. We might say something like this:
(15) Falwell is expressing his own personal opinion, and many may agree with him. But others may have different opinions. Where morality is concerned, there are no "facts," and no one is "right." He has his opinion; others have their opinions; and that's the end of it.
    This is the basic thought behind *Ethical Subjectivism*. Ethical Subjectivism is
(20) the idea that our moral opinions are based on our feelings, and nothing more. On this view, there is no such thing as "objective" right or wrong. It is a fact that some people are homosexual and some are heterosexual; but it is not a fact that one is good and the other bad. So when someone such as Falwell says that homosexuality is wrong, he is not stating a fact about homosexuality. Instead, he
(25) is merely saying something about his feelings toward it.
    Of course, Ethical Subjectivism is not simply an idea about the evaluation of homosexuality. Exactly the same applies to any moral judgment whatever.
    We should be clear about what *kind* of theory this is. Ethical Subjectivism is not a theory about what things are good and what things are bad. It does not try to
(30) tell us how we should live or what moral opinions we should accept. It is not that sort of theory. Instead, it is a theory about *the nature of moral judgments*. It says that no matter what moral judgments we make, we are only expressing our

personal feelings, and nothing more. People who accept this theory will still have moral opinions, of course — they might be in favor of gay rights or opposed to
(35) them. But whichever stance they choose, they will not believe their choice represents the "truth." They will recognize that their opinions merely represent their own personal feelings.

16. The primary purpose of the passage is to

   (A) explain the theory of Ethical Subjectivism

   (B) offer an explanation for homosexuality

   (C) criticize Falwell's views

   (D) defend objective determinations of right and wrong

   (E) compare the moral views of different countries

17. From the passage, according to Falwell

   (A) there is no objective right and wrong

   (B) absolute moral rules cannot be maintained

   (C) homosexuality breeds intolerance

   (D) it is the act not the actor which must be corrected

   (E) Ethical Subjectivism only holds outside the realm of sexual conduct

18. According to the author, the central idea behind Ethical Subjectivism is

   (A) sexual tolerance

   (B) sexual promiscuity

   (C) that there is no absolute right and wrong

   (D) that moral judgments can only be objective

   (E) an acceptance of puritanical mores

19. Based on the passage, according to Ethical Subjectivism

   (A) Falwell's statement is wrong

   (B) moral judgments cannot be right or wrong

   (C) personal feelings should not lead to moral judgments

   (D) morality must be based on factual assertions

   (E) homosexuality should be banned

20. According to the passage, which of the following most closely adheres to Ethical Subjectivism on the issue of homosexuality?

    (A) Iran   (D) Falwell

    (B) England   (E) United States

    (C) France

21. From the author's discussion, moral absolutes

    (A) are an integral part of Ethical Subjectivism

    (B) can only be based on community mores

    (C) may exist under Ethical Subjectivism

    (D) must rest on objective factual determinations

    (E) come from divine intervention

22. As presented in the passage, under Ethical Subjectivism homosexuality would be

    (A) banned

    (B) not banned but not tolerated either

    (C) not banned but considered morally wrong

    (D) officially accepted

    (E) not officially right or wrong

It is generally assumed that human beings cannot carry out unconsciously the same kinds of intellectual activities they perform consciously, such as making plans and assessing risks. Yet our studies of patients in psychotherapy indicate that, in fact, people can unconsciously think, anticipate consequences and make
(5) and carry out decisions and plans. What is more, patients enlist these abilities in the service of working to become well — in the service of gaining control over their irrational beliefs, feelings and behaviors.

Most ideas about unconscious mental functioning and the therapeutic process have been developed by psychotherapists on the basis of clinical impressions,
(10) recorded as notes or recalled from memory. This approach has been fruitful for producing new ideas, but it cannot assess their relative value. Hence, the Mount Zion Psychotherapy Research Group has gone beyond the clinical method, choosing instead to depend on reliable data and to carry out rigorous, quantitative investigations that are planned in advance to test specific hypotheses.
(15) Our studies have focused on comparing the merits of two distinct psychoanalytic (Freudian) hypotheses about the nature of unconscious mental functioning. The two hypotheses can be evaluated empirically because they make distinct,

testable predictions about how patients will behave during therapy.

(20) Psychoanalytic theory assumes that, beginning in early childhood, powerful "mental contents" (thoughts and feelings) that are not tolerable to the conscious self become buried beneath what may be called a repression barrier, which consists of forces that prevent repressed material from reaching awareness. Nevertheless, the buried contents — which Sigmund Freud initially thought consisted mainly of sexual and aggressive impulses and later concluded also

(25) included beliefs, judgments and such emotions as shame and guilt — continue to influence mood and behavior. They thereby contribute to the symptoms that can propel people into therapy, such as inexplicable depression, unfocused anxiety and maladaptive behaviors that seem to be resistant to conscious control.

(30) Because the repression barrier limits people's conscious knowledge of why they act and feel as they do, thus limiting their control over parts of their personality, a major focus of psychoanalytic therapy is to help patients weaken their repressions and confront repressed material. The therapist asks patients to free-associate: to put into words any thoughts, images, memories and feelings that enter the mind. Such associations provide clues to the patients' unconscious

(35) motivations and concerns. The therapist may then interpret the patients' statements, pointing out what appear to be the underlying wishes, fears, beliefs, guilts or the like. Presumably the therapist's interpretations help patients to gain insight into the effects of the unconscious mind on their conscious thoughts, feelings and behaviors.

(40) Our studies suggest that the cognitive capacities of the unconscious mind have been underappreciated and that human beings can unconsciously carry out many intellectual tasks, including developing and executing plans for reaching certain goals. The implications for therapy are obvious: good therapists will carefully infer their patients' unconscious goals and strive to offer interpretations

(45) designed to advance movement toward these goals.

23. The primary purpose of the passage is to

   (A) describe Freudian theory

   (B) explain the research conducted by the Mount Zion Research Group

   (C) attack the notion of repression barriers

   (D) suggest that the unconscious mind affects behavior

   (E) warn against the use of psychotherapy

24. The author feels current ideas about unconscious mental functioning are

   (A) contrary to Freud's theories

   (B) not testable

   (C) based on inadequate data

(D)   repressions of psychoanalytic theory

(E)   anticipated consequences of repressed feelings

25.   According to the passage, psychoanalytic theory

(A)   is associated with Freud

(B)   relies on empirical testing

(C)   rejects the notion of repression barriers

(D)   suggests the unconscious mind consciously affects behavior

(E)   is wrong

26.   From the passage, empirical evaluation is most likely

(A)   derived from case studies

(B)   is closely associated with psychoanalytic theory

(C)   a way of measuring unconscious responses

(D)   a systematic method of scientific inquiry

(E)   how the unconscious mind evaluates feelings

27.   From the author's discussion, the effect of the repression barrier is to

(A)   release pent-up feelings and emotions

(B)   allow free association to begin

(C)   provide insight into unconscious mental functioning

(D)   minimize the importance of psychoanalytic theory

(E)   prevent people from understanding their actions

STOP

If time still remains, you may review work only in this section.
When the time allotted is up, you may go on to the next section.

Section III

Time—35 minutes
25 Questions

(Answer sheets appear in the back of this book.)

DIRECTIONS: The questions in this section are based on the reasoning contained in brief statements or passages. For some questions, more than one of the choices could conceivably answer the question. However, you are to choose the **best** answer; that is, the response that most accurately and completely answers the question. You should not make assumptions that are by common-sense standards implausible, superfluous, or incompatible with the passage. After you have chosen the best answer, blacken the corresponding space on your answer sheet.

1. According to Aristotle, one could, through abstract thought, discover all of the laws which govern the universe. Nor would it be necessary to check the results of one's reasoning by observation. Because of this tradition, no one until Galileo bothered to confirm the Aristotelian notion that bodies of different weights fall to the ground at different speeds. Galileo dropped balls of different weights, and found that they hit the ground at the same time. Experimentation has been the core of the modern scientific method ever since.

   Which of the following is an inference that can be drawn from the passage?

   (A) Experimentation was not stressed in pre-Galilean physics.

   (B) Since Aristotle's notions of physics were wrong, we cannot trust his works on logic either.

   (C) Abstract thought is of no use for reasoning about the physical universe.

   (D) Skepticism was at the core of ancient physics.

   (E) Galileo was a much better thinker than Aristotle was.

2. During the 1980s, studies were done to test the hypothesis that participation in intramural athletics helps freshmen students adapt more quickly to life in college. These studies determined that when friendships are formed among intramural team members, the students on those teams do in fact adapt more quickly to college life. However, when the team members do not develop friendships, intramural participation can actually retard the students' adaptation. The study further determined that students who do not

like athletics are much less likely to make friends with intramural team members than are students who like athletics.

Which of the following is a reasonable inference that can be drawn from the information given in the passage above?

(A) If the same studies were repeated for high school freshmen, the results would be the same.

(B) Participation in intramural athletics should be required for most college freshmen.

(C) Students who like athletics are healthier psychologically than students who do not.

(D) Students who do not like athletics make poorer students than those who do.

(E) Students who like athletics are more likely to benefit from intramural athletics than are students who don't.

3. All the teachers at Weston Academy will leave their mark on the future, through their students. Some of those teachers are true scientists, who bring the results of their research into the classroom. Others are artists who inculcate in their students a love of beauty. Still others are intolerable egotists, who lecture to hear themselves talk, rather to impart knowledge.

If the statements above are true, which one of the following must also be true?

(A) All true scientists will leave their mark on the future.

(B) Everyone who will leave a mark on the future is a teacher.

(C) The teachers will all leave a beneficial mark on the future.

(D) The future will be influenced both by true scientists and egotists.

(E) Students should have a wide range of teachers, to get a well-rounded education.

QUESTIONS 4–5

The Sheriff's crime prevention program uses the questionable method of inviting reformed criminals into area schools to warn students about the consequences of illegal behavior. What the students quickly realize is that the speaker has become a celebrity precisely because of those actions which he is warning them against. A better method of crime prevention would be to have citizens who have consistently avoided vice to speak in the schools about the rewards of a law-abiding life. These positive role models would convince more students to avoid illegal activities.

4. Which one of the following is an inference which can be drawn from the passage?

  (A) Some students can be persuaded not to engage in criminal activities.

  (B) Former criminals are never truly reformed.

  (C) The Sheriff's department is sympathetic to former criminals.

  (D) No one can persuade students not to engage in criminal activities.

  (E) Former criminals should never be allowed in schools.

5. Which one of the following, if true, most seriously weakens the author's argument?

  (A) Reformed criminals often find ways to profit from their past mistakes.

  (B) Students are likely to take the advice of someone who has been punished for past transgressions.

  (C) Many who have consistently avoided vice are often too busy to take time to speak in schools.

  (D) Students are unimpressed by those who got caught trying to get ahead the easy way.

  (E) The Sheriff's department has been sponsoring these events for years, and they have always been well received by educators.

QUESTIONS 6–7

Understanding the dynamics of policy making in any Communist government has always been problematic, but Castro's Cuba presents a particularly difficult case. Because we know so little of the major actors in the Cuban government, we cannot say with any certainty who, other than Castro himself, has the power to influence major policy decisions. However, it appears on the surface that the Cuban government is a duplicate of the Soviet government of the 1960s, and that officials with the same titles have or had the same functions in both systems. Therefore, we may conclude that by applying what we know of the Soviet system of the 1960s to the present-day Cuban system, we can develop an accurate description of Cuban policy making.

6. Taken separately, which of the following, if true, would undermine the author's conclusion that the Soviet example may be used to explain the Cuban system?

  (A) External political characteristics do not reflect internal political realities for Communist governments.

  (B) There are no differences among Communist political systems which cannot be observed from the outside.

(C) The Soviet political system underwent substantial changes in the 1980s.

(D) Cuba did not become Communist until after the Soviets.

(E) Castro based his political structure on that of the Soviets in the 1960s.

7. Which of the following, if true, would confirm the author's conclusion that the Soviet example can be used to describe the Cuban system?

(A) Policy making in the Chinese government closely resembles that of the Cuban system of today, and that of the Soviet system of the 1960s.

(B) Nikita Khrushchev, the Soviet leader from 1955-1964, was a close friend and advisor to Castro.

(C) The Cuban economy is presently experiencing the same types of difficulties that the Soviet economy experienced in the 1960s.

(D) Castro has on many occasions expressed his admiration for the pre-1970 Soviet system.

(E) After the revolution in Cuba in 1959, the new Communist government was expressly modeled on the Soviet political system.

8. Personal income tax rates for state X are expected to rise this year. One can predict that revenue from sales taxes will continue to decline in the next several months, as the economy continues to experience a downturn. Also, severance tax receipts have declined as the coal and gas industries have cut back on production. Since the state government is predicting a deficit for the present fiscal year, and since the state constitution disallows the carrying of a deficit over to the next fiscal year, lawmakers are bound to increase income taxes to cover the revenue shortfall.

Taken separately, which of the following, if true, would most seriously undermine the conclusion of the passage above?

(A) The needed revenue could be raised by eliminating waste in current programs.

(B) Income taxes in state X are already high, compared to the surrounding states.

(C) The revenue shortfall is likely to be very small without income tax increases.

(D) The economy will likely improve in the next fiscal year.

(E) Severance taxes account for only a small percentage of state X's income.

9.   The road crew includes both men and boys. All men are hateful and all boys are insubordinate. Every insubordinate person is hateful, so every person on the crew is hateful.

Which of the following is an assumption that would make the conclusion in the argument above logically correct?

(A)   There are no women or girls on the road crew.

(B)   Being hateful is the same as being insubordinate.

(C)   No member of the road crew is insubordinate.

(D)   No member of the road crew is hateful.

(E)   Men and boys do not work together on the road crew.

10.   Interviewer: Mayor Robinson, during your campaign you said that city governments should not take it upon themselves to provide public assistance to the needy. What do you think of Baltimore's plan to set up a city office to provide public health assistance?

Mayor Robinson: Well, when a city has a high percentage of needy citizens in poor health, then obviously something has to be done. I think that Baltimore's plan is right on target, and if it is well organized it can accomplish its purpose.

Which one of the following expresses the inconsistency in Mayor Robinson's views?

(A)   Big cities cannot go strictly by the book in dealing with social problems.

(B)   He now speaks favorably of a plan which is incompatible with his campaign statement.

(C)   He obviously thinks that public health assistance is more important than other types of public assistance.

(D)   Busy mayors do not have the time to cope with minor inconsistencies in their statements.

(E)   He thinks that one city should solve its problems in one way, while another takes its own approach.

11.   During the 1970s, Hart and Jaffa conducted experiments to test the hypothesis that there is no basic difference in the way men and women give directions. These studies showed that men, in giving directions, nearly

always rely on distance, as for example "Go three blocks and turn right."
Women, on the other hand, tend to give directions based on landmarks, as
in "Go to the big red building and turn right."

Which one of the following statements is a reasonable conclusion that can
be drawn from the information given in the passage?

(A) If the same studies that were conducted in the 1970s were repeated
     today, the results would.be different.

(B) Men should never seek directions from women, nor women from
     men.

(C) The researchers who conducted the experiment were probably men.

(D) Men are better at giving directions than women are.

(E) There is a difference in the way men and women perceive geographi-
     cal relationships.

12. The support program for unwed mothers is currently funded through chari-
     table donations and annual grants from the city. Private donations account
     for 60% of the program's budget, with the grants providing the other 40%.
     However, the city is experiencing its third year of budget deficits, so city
     grants for the program are sure to dry up. It appears that the program for
     unwed mothers will have to reduce its operations substantially in the near
     future.

     Which one of the following is an assumption necessary to the author's
     argument?

     (A) The program can provide the same level of support on much less
          money.

     (B) Charitable contributions will not increase enough to compensate for
          decreases in city grants.

     (C) The program is a low priority budget item to the city.

     (D) Private contributions will decrease when city grants decrease.

     (E) Unwed mothers need less support now than they did in the past three
          years.

13. If gasoline evaporates, it has been left in an open container. I have left this
     gasoline in an open container; therefore, it will evaporate.

     The pattern of reasoning in the above passage is the same as the pattern of
     reasoning in which of the following?

(A)   If Sam Smith is contented, he has had eight hours' sleep. Sam Smith has had eight hours' sleep; therefore, he is contented.

(B)   All golfers are boors; therefore, Jack, who is a boor, must be a golfer.

(C)   Anyone singing in public is a nuisance. If I only hum in public, I will not be a nuisance.

(D)   All musicians are talented; therefore, all talented men must be musicians.

(E)   Pointing is not polite. If I merely gesture, I am being polite.

QUESTIONS 14–15

Let a man be ever so successful in business, or his income ever so large; yet if he has no dedication to ethical behavior in all cases, whether it profits him or hurts his pocketbook, I would be the first to tell him that he was debased and selfish and had no claim to the title gentleman. In fact, it is almost always the case that those who make all decisions by their pocketbooks give back nothing to the society of which they are a part; the tapeworm infests the bowels of its host, eating away its sustenance until the host is dead from malnutrition.

14.   Which of the following is the main point of the passage above?

(A)   Unethical behavior is to be expected from the financially successful.

(B)   Greed is the result of unethical behavior.

(C)   Those who place money ahead of all other concerns deserve our sympathy.

(D)   A man can be a benefit to society and a gentleman only if he puts ethics ahead of profit.

(E)   Those who make decisions by their pocketbooks are generally shallow people.

15.   Which of the following is the point of the author's analogy about the tapeworm?

(A)   He who puts profit above all else is like a parasite on society.

(B)   Greed acts like a tapeworm within the souls of the wealthy.

(C)   Making decisions based on the profit motive is not good for business.

(D)   Profit alone can keep a businessman healthy.

(E)   One's acting ethically often goes unnoticed by society.

16. Modern life, while it has many advantages over the past, has its own set of difficulties. Most Americans nowadays are very mobile, moving from one area to another with great frequency. Most also live in urban areas, where a person does not even know his neighbors. These factors lead to a breakdown of the sense of community, and to feelings of alienation. This is the tragedy peculiar to our age. In times past most people lived their complete lives in small communities, where one person knew the other, and knew about the other's family and history. Now, that is impossible. Everything is so fast paced now that most of us are doomed to remain strangers to those around us.

Which of the following can be validly inferred from facts or premises expressed in the passage above?

(A) Modern life is characterized by a special form of alienation.

(B) Life is worse now than it used to be.

(C) Increased mobility of people is a bad thing.

(D) We do not need a sense of community.

(E) Urban areas are better than small communities.

17. Brand Y dog food sells for $8.00 a 25-pound bag, while brand X sells for $7.00 a 25-pound bag. Therefore, brand X is a better buy than brand Y.

Which one of the following, if true, would make the conclusion in the passage above a logical conclusion?

(A) A bag of brand X will last just as long as a bag of brand Y.

(B) A cup of brand X has the same nutritional value as a cup of brand Y.

(C) Brand X is more popular with dog owners than brand Y is.

(D) Dogs like the taste of both brands equally.

(E) Brand X is more attractively packaged than brand Y.

18. Since real estate prices are down in the city, this house would probably be a good buy.

Which of the following arguments most closely resembles the one above?

(A) Chicago had a record high 101 degrees today, so all of Illinois must be hot.

(B) Since only 67% of its graduates found employment last year, a degree from that school is not worth very much.

(C) Since Conners won last week's tournament, he is likely to win again this week.

(D) Since dogs are loyal, old Blue should be also.

(E) Since I hate picnics I'll just eat at home alone.

19. Computer manuals frequently need to be revised. The reasons for this are clear: constant improvements in microprocessing technology, the introduction of new computer software, and the discovery of new applications for computers in areas as diverse as animation and zoology, all may render current manuals inadequate. Any of these considerations may require a slightly new approach to the use of computers, in order that the user may stay abreast of the latest developments in his field.

Which of the following can be inferred from the argument in the above passage?

(A) Computer manuals are outdated as soon as they are written.

(B) New software has been developed specifically for use in the field of zoology.

(C) Mistakes in computer manuals are due to the authors' lack of knowledge about new applications.

(D) The discovery of new applications for computers necessitates the writing of new manuals.

(E) Improvements in microprocessing technology allows new applications for computers.

20. Robert: Striking by employees is counterproductive; while the strike goes on, the plant is effectively shut down, and the corporation loses money. This means that the employees themselves lose in the long run.

Leah: I disagree. Sometimes striking is necessary to get the attention of management. If the plant loses a little money, the management will be forced into making concessions they otherwise wouldn't.

The misunderstanding between Robert and Leah is based on

(A) different definitions of the word "strike."

(B) differing evaluations of the interests of the management.

(C) a disagreement over what is in the employees' long-term interest.

(D) different social agendas.

(E) different views on the need for negotiation.

QUESTIONS 21–22

At a professional development seminar, a speaker said: "Take every opportunity for advancement in your company. You may be comfortable and competent in your present job, but if you are offered a higher paying position for which you have no experience, take it anyway. The best way to develop the skills for a job is by doing the job itself. You may feel uncomfortable for a while, but most employers expect you to take a few weeks to grow into a new position. There comes a time when the little bird must leave the safety of the nest, spread its wings, and venture out into the larger world. It's a scary feeling the first time out, but before long the little bird is an accomplished flyer. Likewise, if you are willing to stretch yourself and accept a new challenge, you will be a more complete person in the long run."

21.   Which of the following statements best identifies a major weakness with the analogy used in the passage?

(A)   While learning to fly is natural for birds, not every employee has the natural ability to perform every job.

(B)   Birds are not able to weigh the pros and cons of their decisions, while people are.

(C)   The risk taken by the bird on its first flight is much more significant than the one taken by an employee moving up the job ladder.

(D)   Many times the bird cannot get back into the nest: likewise, the employee might not be able to get her old job back if she fails at the new one.

(E)   Many birds would not leave the nest if given the choice.

22.   In the author's analogy, which of the following would most closely parallel the little bird's nest?

(A)   the employee's skills

(B)   the new job the employee will take

(C)   the job the employee currently has

(D)   the employee's present level of skills

(E)   the company the employee presently works for

23.   The rate of inflation has risen with increased rapidity in the last few years. During the same period the cost of labor has fallen slightly, and worker productivity has remained constant. The cause of the increase in inflation must, therefore, be the rise in the cost of oil.

Which of the following statements, if true, would strengthen the conclusion above?

(A)   Oil prices have dropped 50% in the past three years.

(B)   Oil prices, along with labor costs and worker productivity, are major factors affecting the rate of inflation.

(C)   The price of domestic oil was regulated by the government during the period in question.

(D)   None of the above.

(E)   All of the above.

24.   A low level of capital accumulation in the form of personal savings is the major cause of unemployment, and ultimately of recessions. A low level of personal savings is unavoidable unless government provides incentives for saving, such as keeping a lid on inflation. Otherwise, many potential savers, rather than saving, will decide to spend their money now before its purchasing power declines.

Which of the following presuppositions is (are) necessary to the argument above?

(A)   The savings rate declines when the inflation rate goes up.

(B)   Unemployment leads to recession.

(C)   Recessions are avoidable if government keeps a lid on inflation.

(D)   Personal savings are unimportant.

(E)   Government should let the economy take care of itself.

25. Liz: A recent study showed that the U.S. population is now 52% female. As a result, a majority of the life insurance settlements now made go to the beneficiaries of female policyholders. Therefore, annual insurance rates should be higher for women than for men, to compensate for the greater number of claims.

Joe: I disagree. The same study also showed that women live an average of six years longer than men, so they pay premiums for a longer period of time. When you consider the difference the six years makes in the total amount paid in by the policyholder, it is clear that women's annual life insurance rates should be lower than men's.

In this conversation, Joe does which of the following?

(A)   He disagrees with each of the premises which Liz offers.

(B)   He proves that Liz didn't read the entire report that was cited.

(C)   He disagrees with Liz over how insurance rates for men and women are to be determined.

(D)   He accuses Liz of using inaccurate statistics.

(E)   He cites additional evidence which proves that men's rates should be lower.

STOP

If time still remains, you may review work only in this section.
When the time allotted is up, you may go on to the next section.

Section IV

Time—35 minutes
23 Questions

(Answer sheets appear in the back of this book.)

DIRECTIONS: Each group of questions in this section is based on a set of conditions. In answering some of the questions, it may be useful to draw a rough diagram. Choose the response that most accurately and completely answers the question and blacken the corresponding space on your answer sheet.

QUESTIONS 1–7

Julia is arranging 7 books — Biology, Economics, French, Mathematics, History, Philosophy and Sociology — on a bookshelf. The books will be arranged from left to right according to the following rules.

French is to the left of History

Philosophy is to the right of French

Biology is to the left of Mathematics

Sociology is to the right of Philosophy

Mathematics is to the left of Philosophy

Economics is to the left of French

1. Which book must be on the extreme right member of the shelf?

    (A) either Philosophy or Sociology

    (B) either Sociology or History

    (C) Philosophy

    (D) Sociology

    (E) History

2. If Economics is not on the extreme left, which book must be?

    (A) Biology   (D) History

    (B) French   (E) Sociology

    (C) Mathematics

3. Which of the following is impossible?

    (A) Sociology is on the extreme right

    (B) Biology is on the extreme left

    (C) Philosophy is on the extreme right

    (D) History is on the extreme right

    (E) Economics is on the extreme left

4. If the three books on the left side of the shelf are Biology, Economics and Mathematics, which book must be in the exact middle of the group?

    (A) Philosophy

    (B) French

    (C) History

    (D) either French or History

    (E) either History or Philosophy

5. If Mathematics is in the exact middle of the shelf, which of the following is impossible?

    (A) French is to the right of Biology

    (B) History is to the right of Sociology

    (C) Sociology is to the left of Philosophy

    (D) Biology is on the extreme left

    (E) Economics is on the extreme left

6. Which of the following arrangements, going from left to right, is impossible?

    (A) Biology, Economics, Mathematics, French, Philosophy, History, Sociology

    (B) Biology, Economics, French, Mathematics, Sociology, Philosophy, History

    (C) Biology, Economics, French, Mathematics, Philosophy, History, Sociology

    (D) Economics, French, Biology, Mathematics, Philosophy, Sociology, History

    (E) Biology, Mathematics, Economics, French, History, Philosophy, Sociology

7.   If there are two books to the left of Biology, which book is next to the book on the extreme left?

(A)   Mathematics   (D)   French

(B)   History   (E)   Philosophy

(C)   Economics

QUESTIONS 8–13

The 11 members of the Central High School Debate Team — 2 Freshmen, 2 Sophomores, 3 Juniors and 4 Seniors — are going to have a Team photograph taken. The members of the team will be arranged in a line on spaces numbered 1 through 11.

The Sophomores will not stand next to one another.

The Juniors always stand on consecutively numbered spaces.

Neither of the Freshmen will stand at the either end of the line.

A Junior is always at one end of the line.

No Senior will stand next to a Junior.

8.   If a Junior is standing in space 3, and a Sophomore in space 10, which of the following must be the case?

(A)   There is a Senior in space 8

(B)   There is a Senior in space 11

(C)   There is a Sophomore in space 4

(D)   There is a Freshman in space 4

(E)   There is a Sophomore in space 6

9.   If the Seniors are standing in spaces 2, 3, 6 and 7, which of the following is impossible?

(A)   The Freshmen are in spaces 1 and 8

(B)   The Sophomores are in spaces 1 and 4

(C)   There is a Junior in space 10

(D)   There is a Freshman in space 8

(E)   The Sophomores are in spaces 1 and 8

10.   Which of the following cannot be the case?

(A)   The Sophomores are in spaces 1 and 8

(B)   There are Juniors in spaces 9 and 11

(C)   The Seniors are standing on even-numbered spaces

(D)   The Freshmen are standing on odd-numbered spaces

(E)   The Sophomores are standing on odd-numbered spaces

11.   If the Seniors are standing together, and one of them is at one end of the line, which of the following is possible?

I.   The Freshmen are standing together

II.   The Freshmen are standing together and next to the Seniors

III. The Freshmen are not standing together

(A)   I only   (D)   Both I and II

(B)   II only   (E)   Both I and III

(C)   III only

12.   Which of the following is possible?

(A)   None of the odd numbered spaces are occupied by Juniors and Seniors

(B)   The Freshmen and Sophomores are on even-numbered spaces

(C)   No Freshman or Sophomore is on an even-numbered space

(D)   A Sophomore is on space 9 and a Sophomore is on space 10.

(E)   A Junior is on space 1 and a Freshman is on space 11.

13.   Which of the following must be the case?

(A)   A Senior is standing on space 8

(B)   A Junior is standing on space 3

(C)   One of the Freshmen must be standing on an even-numbered space

(D)   One of the Sophomores must be standing on an even-numbered space

(E)   Either a Freshman or a Sophomore must be standing on an even-numbered space

QUESTIONS 14–19

Three couples — the Ables, the Bakers, and the Carrs — have dinner together every Thursday night at Maxwell's Restaurant. To facilitate discussion, they always sat at a round table. The following rules always apply to the seating arrangements:

Mrs. Able always sits immediately to the left of Mr. Baker.

Mr. Able never sits next to Mr. Carr.

Mrs. Baker always sits directly across the table from Mr. Carr.

14. Which of the following CANNOT be true?

    (A) Mrs. Able is seated directly across from Mr. Able.

    (B) Mr. Able is seated next to Mrs. Able.

    (C) Mr. Able is seated directly across from Mr. Baker.

    (D) Mr. Carr is seated immediately to the right of Mr. Baker.

    (E) Mrs. Carr is seated directly across the table from Mrs. Able.

15. If Mrs. Able is seated next to Mr. Carr, which of the following COULD be true?

    (A) Mr. Able is seated directly across from Mr. Baker.

    (B) Mrs. Carr is seated next to Mrs. Baker.

    (C) Mrs. Able is seated directly across from Mr. Able.

    (D) Mrs. Carr is seated directly across from Mrs. Able.

    (E) Mr. Able is seated immediately to the left of Mrs. Able.

16. If Mr. Carr is seated immediately to the right of Mr. Baker, which of the following CANNOT be true?

    (A) Mrs. Carr is seated immediately to the right of Mr. Carr.

    (B) Mrs. Baker is seated immediately to the left of Mrs. Able.

    (C) Mr. Able is seated directly across from Mr. Baker.

    (D) Mr. Able is seated directly across from Mrs. Able.

    (E) Mr. Able is seated next to Mrs. Baker.

17. If Mrs. Baker is seated next to Mrs. Able, which of the following COULD be true?

    (A) Mr. Able is seated directly across from Mr. Baker.

    (B) Mrs. Carr is seated next to Mrs. Baker.

    (C) Mrs. Able is seated directly across from Mr. Able.

    (D) Mrs. Carr is seated directly across from Mr. Baker.

    (E) There is exactly one seat between Mr. Able and Mrs. Baker.

18. Which of the following must be the case?

    (A) The Able's always sit next to one another

    (B) Mr. Able never sits next to Mrs. Carr

    (C) The Carr's always sit next to one another

    (D) Mrs. Able sits to the right of Mr. Baker

    (E) Mr. Carr sits next to Mrs. Baker

19. If Mr. Able is seated directly across the table from Mrs. Able, which of the following COULD be true?

    (A) Mr. Carr is seated immediately to the right of Mr. Baker.

    (B) Mrs. Carr is seated next to Mrs. Baker.

    (C) Mrs. Carr is seated immediately to the left of Mr. Able.

    (D) Mrs. Baker is seated next to Mrs. Able.

    (E) Mr. Carr is seated immediately to the left of Mrs. Able.

QUESTIONS 20–23

Carlos is currently planning his schedule of classes for the fall semester. He is pursuing a double major in Biology and Philosophy and he needs to choose 5 classes from the following offerings — Biochemistry, Environmental Biology, Genetics, Physiology (all offered by the Biology Department), and Ancient Philosophy, Epistemology, Logic, Modern Philosophy and a Seminar on Kant (all offered by the Philosophy Department). Of these 9 courses, however, 4 — Biochemistry, Logic, Ancient Philosophy and Modern Philosophy — are required for graduation, and Carlos wants to take at least three of these courses during the fall semester. Carlos plans to take at least 2 courses from each department. Predictably, schedule conflicts have made his planning rather difficult.

Environmental Biology and Ancient Philosophy are offered at the same time.

Epistemology and Modern Philosophy are offered at the same time.

Logic and Genetics are offered at the same time.

20. If Carlos takes all four of the courses required for graduation, which of the following courses MUST he take?

    (A) Environmental Biology   (D) Seminar on Kant

    (B) Physiology   (E) Epistemology

    (C) Genetics

21. If Carlos takes three Philosophy courses, but Logic is not one of them, which of the following must be true?

    (A) He takes the Seminar in Kant.

    (B) He takes Epistemology.

    (C) He takes both Genetics and Physiology.

    (D) He takes Logic and Genetics.

    (E) He takes Epistemology and Modern Philosophy.

22. Which of the following courses must Carlos take?

    (A) Physiology   (D) Logic

    (B) Biochemistry   (E) Modern Philosophy

    (C) Seminar on Kant

23. Which of the following pairs of courses is it impossible for Carlos to take?

    (A) Environmental Biology and Seminar on Kant

    (B) Physiology and Ancient Philosophy

    (C) Ancient Philosophy and Genetics

    (D) Genetics and Environmental Biology

    (E) Biochemistry and Physiology

STOP

If time still remains, you may review work only in this section.
When the time allotted is up, you may go on to the next section.

LSAT Writing Sample

(Answer sheets appear in the back of this book.)

General Directions

You will have 35 minutes in which to plan and write an essay on the topic below. Read the topic and the accompanying directions carefully. You will probably find it best to spend a few minutes considering the topic and organizing your thoughts before you begin writing. In your essay, be sure to develop your ideas fully, leaving time, if possible, to review what you have written. **Do not write on a topic other than the one specified. Writing on a topic of your own choice is not acceptable.**

No special knowledge is required or expected for this writing exercise. Law schools are interested in the reasoning, clarity, organization, language usage, and writing mechanics displayed in your essay. How well you write is more important than how much you write.

Confine your essay to the blocked, lined areas on the front and back of the separate writing sample response sheet. Only that area will be reproduced for law schools. Be sure that your writing is legible.

Sample Topic

Directions: The scenario presented below describes two choices, either one of which can be supported on the basis of the information given. Your essay should consider both choices and argue for one and against the other, based on the two specified criteria and the facts provided. There is no "right" or "wrong" choice: a reasonable argument can be made for either.

Present an argument in favor of one of the two sides in the following case about the right of a private club to bar females from membership. Your argument should be based on the following two criteria:

- The U.S. Constitution guarantees the right to free association, which prohibits government from forcing citizens to associate with anyone at any time or place.

- The U.S. Constitution guarantees the right of equal protection under the law, forbidding discrimination on the basis of race, religion, sex, age, national origin, handicap, etc., especially in public institutions and private institutions receiving public financial assistance.

At a well-known school, a tradition of dining clubs for undergraduates has flourished for more than 240 years. These privately owned clubs border the campus and admit about 20 new student members yearly, who take three meals a day at the club. In 1970, when the all-male school went coed, all but one of the dining clubs, the CPU Club, began admitting females. In 1976, a female student, Ms. Lisa Radin, was denied membership because she was not a male. Radin filed suit in federal court, alleging that her Fourteenth Amendment civil rights had been violated and demanding that the CPU Club be forced to admit women. Radin argued that the school receives significant public aid for its students. She also argued that all-male institutions like the CPU Club deny women networking opportunities and vital contacts in the professions. Dave Mora, the CPU Club president, argued that the club is private, is separate from the school, and receives no public funding. He added that forcing the club to admit women would violate its members' constitutional right of free association.

STOP
If time still remains, you may review work only in this section.

TEST VI

ANSWER KEY

Section I — Logical Reasoning

1.	(B)	8.	(D)	15.	(E)	22.	(E)
2.	(E)	9.	(D)	16.	(E)	23.	(B)
3.	(B)	10.	(B)	17.	(A)	24.	(C)
4.	(B)	11.	(D)	18.	(E)	25.	(B)
5.	(E)	12.	(B)	19.	(A)	26.	(D)
6.	(A)	13.	(B)	20.	(C)		
7.	(A)	14.	(E)	21.	(B)		

Section II — Reading Comprehension

1.	(C)	8.	(D)	15.	(C)	22.	(E)
2.	(A)	9.	(C)	16.	(A)	23.	(B)
3.	(B)	10.	(A)	17.	(D)	24.	(C)
4.	(E)	11.	(E)	18.	(C)	25.	(A)
5.	(D)	12.	(B)	19.	(B)	26.	(D)
6.	(A)	13.	(A)	20.	(B)	27.	(E)
7.	(B)	14.	(D)	21.	(C)		

Section III — Logical Reasoning

1.	(A)	8.	(A)	15.	(A)	22.	(C)
2.	(E)	9.	(A)	16.	(A)	23.	(B)
3.	(D)	10.	(B)	17.	(B)	24.	(A)
4.	(A)	11.	(E)	18.	(D)	25.	(C)
5.	(B)	12.	(B)	19.	(D)		
6.	(A)	13.	(A)	20.	(C)		
7.	(A)	14.	(D)	21.	(A)		

Section IV — Analytical Reasoning

1.	(B)	7.	(D)	13.	(E)	19.	(E)
2.	(A)	8.	(B)	14.	(B)	20.	(B)
3.	(C)	9.	(A)	15.	(C)	21.	(A)
4.	(B)	10.	(C)	16.	(D)	22.	(B)
5.	(C)	11.	(E)	17.	(A)	23.	(D)
6.	(B)	12.	(B)	18.	(C)		

DETAILED EXPLANATIONS OF ANSWERS

Section I — Logical Reasoning

1. **(B)**   The legislator's argument jumps from "Men with long hair do not look like citizens" to "Men with long hair should not be allowed to vote." He wants then to exclude from those who can vote those who do not look like citizens, or — what amounts to the same thing — he wants to restrict the list of those who may vote to those who do look like citizens. This is what (B) says. (C) says something similar but stronger, that people who are allowed to vote do — not merely should — look like citizens. That is the state of affairs which the new law will bring about, but can hardly be the justification for favoring the law. (D) and (A) are related in the same way as (B) and (C), what should be and what is, but they take the opposite position, that anyone who looks like a citizen is or should be allowed to vote. This is clearly not in the legislator's mind, since clean-cut citizen-looking boys under age 19, for example, are not being offered voting rights. Claim (E) may well lie behind the legislator's position on the bill but does not play any role in the argument he gives.

2. **(E)**   The argument starts with one inverse correlation, less vitamin E with more rapid aging and concludes the opposite inverse correlation as well. (E) has the same pattern: less pressure gives more speed, so more pressure gives less speed. (C) and (D) both extend straight correlations: more coffee gives more heart speed, so less gives less, and less sleep gives less alertness, so more gives more. Both of these contain the one feature of the original argument which (E) lacks, that all the measurements are taken in terms of deviation from a norm — less E, more coffee, less sleep than normal, and so on. There is no normal pressure on a brake. (A) is also a form of straight correlation — more works faster — but it does not follow the form of starting from a correlation in one direction and inferring it in the other. Nor does (B), which is just a case of arguing that if you remove the cause of something, you prevent that something from occurring — not a correlation of variation at all.

3. **(B)**   The loaded question is recommended because it can be used to get a person to admit to an actionable offense quickly, as both examples show. (A) is clearly not correct, since the question of the truth of the admission forced out by the loaded question is irrelevant to the recommendation. Similarly, (C) does not apply, again because the truth of the confession — and thus the justice of the case — is not relevant to the recommendation. Neither (D) nor (E) fits, since both logical and ethical considerations do play a role in the recommendation — on the

one hand the virtue of speedily getting a confession, on the other the logical force of these question formats.

4.   **(B)**   If the speaker was a Truve he would have to say so, since Truves always tell the truth. So he must be a Falls. But Falls always lie, so his statement must somehow be false. His statement was that both natives were Falls. Since he is a Falls, the statement is false only if his companion is a Truve. The answer cannot be (A), since if both were Falls, the speaker, who as a Fall must lie, would have had to say they were both Truves. Neither (C) nor (D) can be the answer, because if the speaker was a Truve he should have had to tell the truth. But his answer contradicts both (C) and (D). (E) is not the correct answer, since it is logically possible to determine the tribes of the two natives from the statement.

5.   **(E)**   The pattern of argument here is from the claims that A (here good nutrition) is a worthwhile goal and that B (eating PerFooD Plus) is a means to A, to the conclusion that we ought to do B. But what we should do in such cases is always to use the best means to that goal, not just any one that comes along. Answer (A) points out that in this case we can reach the goal by at least one other means than the one the argument proposes, so the proposed means is not the best simply because it is the only means. Answers (B) and (C) each point to a way in which some other means is better than the one proposed, again attacking the claim that it is the best means over all. Finally, (D) points to a way in which the means might be dangerous, thus again arguing that it cannot be the best means. Only answer (E) does not point to any way in which the means proposed is not the best available. It is, then, the one case which is not an objection to the argument presented.

6.   **(A)**   The speaker backs up his claim that the label "Personal Banker" is a misrepresentation by pointing out that he never sees the same one twice and that those he sees do not know him or his situation. These claims make the point only if the label suggests both an on-going relationship and familiarity and it must be the "personal" part that carries this weight. The speaker apparently does believe that his bank is trying to mislead him, but he concludes this from the evidence, rather than assuming it, so (E) is not correct. While he is apparently unhappy about getting the service of people new to banking, he does not say that he either needs or deserves more, as (B) or (C) would require. Indeed, he does not complain about his service at all, except that it is not what the name leads him to expect, so (D) does not obviously fit into his complaint either.

7.   **(A)**   The rebuttal here takes the form of repeating the original argument only substituting the word "water" for the word "marijuana." The resulting argument must have the same form as the original, but has an absurd conclusion from obviously true premises. Thus, the reasoning of the original argument is shown to be defective. The reasoning of the original argument is, indeed, defective in the way that answer (B) suggests, but the rebuttal does not point this out explicitly. The version of the original argument is cited correctly, so (C) does not apply to

this case (the refuting argument is not an inaccurate version of the original but a different argument of the same form). It may be that the original argument is a sketch of a good argument (that, for example, the percentage of hard-drug users among former marijuana smokers is sufficiently higher than that among people who never used marijuana as to make a causal claim plausible), but, as in (B), the refutation given makes no mention of this (D). Finally, (E) is wrong because the original argument does not make a general claim nor does the refutation mention an exception.

8.   **(D)**   Although the speaker mentions a number of cases where a person is considered an adult at different ages for different purposes, the main complaint is about the price of movie tickets and the fact that, even after paying full price, the teenager cannot see adult movies. So, the action the complaint suggests could be either (D) or lowering the age at which people could see adult movies. But the latter option is not offered here. (E), raising the price of tickets for younger people, might relieve some of the sense of unfairness but would not really offer any relief to the teenager. The other three choices all speak to issues which are raised at most as evidence of the unfair or inconsistent position of society on the issue of when a teenager becomes an adult. This is, however, only background to the central complaint and so, actions to relieve this would not necessarily meet the complaint.

9.   **(D)**   The most reliable argument goes with the statistics that most closely apply to the particular case. Clearly the statistics for 80-year-old patients apply more closely to an 80-year-old patient than do statistics about patients in general, which include those for younger — and presumably sturdier — patients. So, (D) is to be preferred over (B). (C) is not based on any evidence at all, whether it is meant to average the two different items presented or is intended as an expression that the chances are undetermined. The two claims do not apply equally, so an average is inappropriate and Yvonne's claim is quite determinate. (E) appears to come from multiplying the two figures, which is not an appropriate calculation in this case, though that operation sometimes applies in probability. Adding two probabilities is also sometimes appropriate and that seems to be what was done to get (A). It is not, however, appropriate in this case.

10.   **(B)**   The argument is about who has the obligation to solve a problem and concludes that the obligation rests on those who created the problem in the first place. It is entirely reasonable in this question to assume that "the factory" is where the car was built. A car is typically built in only one factory and by one manufacturer who owns the factory. It is conceivable that the factory may not be responsible for everything the manufacturer does; it is sensible to presume that the manufacturer is responsible for its own factories. "Factory" and "manufacturer" in this text are synonymous. (B) is, therefore, the correct answer. (A) does not talk about obligation at all. (A) only talks about causes: What causes the problem will also cause the cure of the problem. With choice (C) the reader has no idea which car is being washed or who is responsible for cleaning it or why. It seems that a young child could not adequately wash a car. (C) is not the best

answer. (D) does not require the creator of the problem to solve it; (D) only compensates those involved for the harm done them. (E) does not place responsibility on anyone; it does say that the situation ought to be returned to a previous state.

11. **(D)**   The testing was inadequate, for it allowed that the apparent conversations might not be conversations at all. But the fact that the apes might have been responding to cues rather than conversing does not show that they were not in fact conversing; they might have been using American Sign Language after all. Failing to prove that apes use language is not the same as proving that apes fail to use language. Thus (A), (B), (C), all of which claim that no ape or at least no tested ape has learned a language, go too far in one direction. (E) may go too far in the other, since it seems to say that there are language using apes but they were not tested. But there is no evidence given that any apes do use language either.

12. **(B)**   The problem is to explain an effect, ketone in urine, and the explanation is found first in another case of ketone in urine. This arose from eating meat, so we expect that is what is happening in the new case. But, the rabbits have not eaten anything, so the meat is not what they have eaten. We are left then with the meat being themselves. (A) has the situation reversed, looking for an effect when the cause is known. (C) also seems to be about inferring effects from causes. If both eating meat and starving are deviant situations for rabbits, we should not be surprised, under this principle, to find ketone in the urine or, at least, some similarity between the two cases. (D) and (E) may both be about explaining an effect, but neither obviously applies here, for the case presented does not indicate whether Bernard's conclusion was simpler than any of its competitors (that eating vegetables surpasses ketone production for example) or that it was at all surprising (the ketone in the urine may have merely confirmed a view of hunger pangs that had long been suspected).

13. **(B)**   If he has unexcusedly late work, then, by the second rule, his regular work is not completed. So, by the first rule, he will not be permitted to do extra credit work. And, without that, he can get no better than a C. However, even if he did all his regular work on time or with permission to hand it in late, there is no guarantee that he will be permitted to do extra credit work (only that without the regular work done he cannot do extra credit), so (C) is not guaranteed. And, if (C) is not guaranteed, neither is (D), for the extra credit work is the only path to a B. But even if he did do the extra credit work, that only opens the possibility of a B, it does not guarantee it. Thus, (A) fails; the B is not guaranteed. And (E) fails as well, since he could do the extra credit work and still get a C.

14. **(E)**   Bob's argument seems to be that, since it is unlikely that Joe win four cuts in a row but has already won three in a row, it is highly unlikely that Joe will win the fourth as well. Trusting in this, he wagers an extra amount against Joe's winning the fourth cut. His probability argument is, then, that of (E). This argument is unreliable since the probability of winning a cut is the same at each cut, regardless of the outcome of the previous cut or cuts. Thus, while it is

unlikely (about one chance in 16) that Joe would win four cuts in a row, once Joe has won three, his chances of winning the next one are the same as of his winning the first one, about even. His reasoning is different from that in (C) because he focuses on the final event as being especially unlikely, not just any of the four cuts. Presumably, Bob would not argue that since Joe is not likely to win four cuts in a row, he is unlikely to win the first cut, as (C) would require him to do. Nor does Bob probably believe that winning any particular cut is unlikely, considered by itself, so he would not have reasoned from that premise as in (B) or (D). Finally, he clearly does not use the argument in (A), since he does not refer to the unlikelihood of Joe's having already won three cuts in a row, but only to the unlikelihood of his winning four.

15. **(E)** The writer argues that positive emotions may affect exercise beneficially. One of his premises is that heart rates during relaxation are lower than the heart rates during normal exercise. Thus if the reverse is true — that heart rates during normal exercise are half that of heart rates during relaxation (E) — the argument is weaker. If negative emotions such as anger raise the heart rate even higher than originally stated — from 33 to 66 beats per minute (B) — this would *strengthen* the argument. If, as the writer claims, exercise done in anger more than doubles the increase in heart rate done during normal exercise, then it must be true that the normal rate is one-half the angry rate (C). Finally, the argument is unaffected by the possibility that some people do not have positive emotions when they exercise (A).

16. **(E)** The passage argues that Paxamar can survive only by having a qualitative edge in weaponry. It implies that the loss of that edge erodes Paxamar's power to deter conflict. It states that the eroding of deterrence will be destabilizing to the region. The premise here is (A), that deterrence is stabilizing to the region. The passage asserts as a premise that Paxamar once had a qualitative edge (B) (which it has lost), that Paxamar is surrounded by its enemies (C), and that secret weapons would allow Shelbyville to surprise its enemies (D). The only statement that is not a premise is (E), that Paxamar has less sophisticated weapons than its enemies. True, the passage asserts that Paxamar has lost its onetime superiority; however, the passage does not make clear whether Paxamar and the other nations are now on a par in weaponry, or if the other nations have, in fact, surpassed Paxamar.

17. **(A)** We may *conclude* that housing demand will grow more slowly than before (A), on the *premise* that a smaller generation than before is now in its house-buying years (B). The argument asserts, but does not try to prove, that real estate boomed in the 1970s (C). It claims as a premise that demand for housing declines after 40, not 30 (D). And it denies that baby boomers are entering their house-buying years (E).

18. **(E)** We see from the opening sentence of the passage that Fresno has been changing as fast as any city in the Central Valley. The author admits that the city was once an undesirable place to live, and had the ambience of a bus station,

but had the fastest-growing population in the nation during the 1990s. Obviously, the changes have been for the better. Therefore, the conclusion must be (E), that the city is one of the fastest improving in the Central Valley. We can eliminate (A) since the information cited is a premise which supports the conclusion. (B) and (C) provide information on how the city used to be, before it began to improve. The passage suggests, but not as a conclusion, that Fresno is a big city (D).

19.   **(A)**   Among the signs of Freemasonry, the passage cites a Masonic square and compass on a new automobile (C) and the Boumi temple at Wyndhurst (A), not all new automobiles. While the passage suggests that the Masons are in the Towson Fourth of July parade, it does not necessarily imply that the entire parade consists of Freemasons (B), and answers (D) and (E) cannot be inferred from this passage.

20.   **(C)**   The groups claim that, because of leftover poisonous gases and residue ash, incinerated garbage doesn't disappear. If the gases and ashes themselves disappear, then the groups' argument would be weakened (C). One premise is that *many* plants have operational problems, but if some have no such problems (E), this fact would neither weaken nor strengthen the argument. Since the groups cite the Office of Technology Assessment as an authority, their argument would be stronger if the Office makes accurate estimations (D). And since the groups cite problems at the plants as support for their conclusion, the argument would be strengthened if more plants than previously thought had trouble processing the garbage (A) and if the trash-to-energy facilities generated even less energy than the 0.2 percent originally noted (B).

21.   **(B)**   The author argues that he knows a great deal about the world around him because of the confirmation of his senses. If his senses could deceive him (B), his argument would be weakened. He never implies that *all* appearances can be deduced from or explained by others, so answers (A) and (E) would neither hurt nor strengthen his argument. He *does* imply that he trusts only his senses (C), so this proposition adds nothing to nor takes anything away from the argument. And if the author has experienced the whole world (D) while verifying his experiences, then his argument would be strengthened.

22.   **(E)**   The feminist argues in part on biological evidence about which mammals bear responsibility for survival of individuals other than themselves. Even if this is all the evidence that is available (E), the argument would not be weakened. The argument would be weakened if, contrary to the cited evidence, males among a majority of mammals shared the responsibility for survival (B); the current systems were run by women (A), not men; female behavior could be as aggressive as male behavior in most species (C); and a more human world would be greedier and more unjust (D).

23.   **(B)**   The author argues that the phenomena of hypnosis and dreams ne-

cessitate the view that some psychological phenomena are not conscious (B). Thus he disagrees with the proposition that there is nothing psychical which is not also conscious ((A) and (D)), that the problems of dreams and hypnosis cannot be solved (C), and that his proposition (some psychical phenomena are not conscious) is refutable by logic (E).

24. **(C)** The passage claims that labor unions, employers, and older workers are not interested in reversing the trend toward early retirement. This does not support the proposition that they favor early retirement (C); they may take no position on it at all. The passage supports the claims that many gerontologists are against early retirement (A), and that, therefore, they differ with employers (D), who either favor it or take no position on it. It also claims that work effort has declined among the elderly since World War II (B) and that earnings among the elderly have declined as earlier retirement has increased (E).

25. **(B)** The writer's conclusion is that Vico scholars should devote more attention to Vico's views of his own time (B), on the premises that Vico was an original thinker (C) and that he discovered his own originality only slowly and tortuously (E). The writer acknowledges that others have said that Vico was ahead of his time (A) and that he anticipated nearly everything in our time (D), but the writer does nothing to support or to attack these views.

26. **(D)** On the premise that the pre-eighteenth century church couldn't exercise real power (D), the passage argues that the medieval church could only exercise episodic control over marriage and divorce. The passage denies that the church lacked the will to exercise its authority over marriages (A), that it could translate its formal authority into real power (C), and that it had a bureaucratic infrastructure (E). It states that the church held a virtual monopoly over marriage and divorce in medieval Russia, but not that it held a virtual monopoly of *power* over marriage and divorce (B).

Section II – Reading Comprehension

1. **(C)** (C) is correct because the author begins with an explanation of incrementalism, provides a test for incrementalism, then explains why it is used. (A) is incorrect primarily because it is overbroad. Although incrementalism is a part of the federal budgetary process, it is only one aspect of it, and this passage in no way describes, or even outlines, the entire budgetary process. Similarly, (B) is incorrect because the author is not concerned with alternative budgetary systems. Zero Base Budgeting is mentioned only in the first paragraph and only as a means of defining incrementalism. Thus, (D) is also incorrect. (E) is also overbroad. The author mentions only two parts of the behavioral approach which apply to incrementalism. There is no indication, and it cannot be assumed, that these items constitute the entire behavioral approach to budgeting.

2.   **(A)**   The purpose of the second paragraph is to present a test of incrementalism. The test involves the stability of the organization. Given the definition of incrementalism in the first paragraph, the reader can conclude stable organizations are more likely to use incrementalism. This conclusion also makes (D) incorrect. The third paragraph's discussion of how stable organizations consider new alternatives (problem solving) makes (B) incorrect. The author does not make a connection between stable organizations and the consistency of organizational goals (C). These two topics are considered separately and, given the information contained in the passage, the reader should not link the two. The third paragraph describes how stable organizations handle problem solving. The fourth and fifth paragraphs discuss additional problems faced by organizations. Thus, stable organizations certainly face *some* budgetary problems. Whether they are able to avoid *most* budgetary problems is not mentioned and should not be assumed (E).

3.   **(B)**   (B) is specifically indicated in the second sentence of the third paragraph. (A) is incorrect because, according to the first and third paragraphs, the vast majority of programs in incremental systems do not receive much attention. (C), (D), and (E) are incorrect because the author makes no connection between either how much support there is for a program or how large it is with whether it receives attention.

4.   **(E)**   It is true that the previous year's budget is an important factor in incrementalism (C), but this does not *explain* incrementalism, rather, it is a description of it. The final three paragraphs all discuss problems faced during the budgetary process and how incrementalism avoids or minimizes those problems. The common theme is the minimization of information and complexity (E). (A) and (B) are both wrong because they do not describe characteristics of incrementalism. The point of incrementalism is that it is not comprehensive and focuses most attention on new items in the budget (see previous question). (D) is incorrect because there is no indication in the passage of a lack of alternatives. The reverse is implied by the author in the fifth paragraph when he speaks of a desire to minimize the costs of problem solving.

5.   **(D)**   This is defined in lines 35–41. (A) is incorrect because the phrase has nothing specifically to do with the base. (It is also incorrect regarding incrementalism because the previous year's budget is *usually* used as the base, but does not have to be.) Even if the reader assumes continuous means the same as stable (it does not), (B) is incorrect because the phrase in question pertains to a problem solving strategy, not the continuousness of an organization. (C) is wrong because incrementalism specifically does not reexamine old programs. As noted in the third paragraph, new programs are the ones which receive the most attention. Keeping costs down (E) is one *reason* for looking in one's backyard first, but it does not tell us what the phrase *means*.

6. **(A)** (A) is the best answer. If one asked the author if zero could be the base in incrementalism, he would respond, "In a broad sense this can be zero, as in Zero Base Budgeting. Please read the first paragraph of my passage." (B) is incorrect because from the first paragraph we can conclude ZBB is a budgetary system — not a method of problem-solving. (C) is an incorrect answer because it is actually a definition of incrementalism. (D) is not the best answer because a zero base does not necessarily mean that that ZBB is more comprehensive than incrementalism. (E) is incorrect. Although existing programs are examined under ZBB, ZBB itself does not prescribe how the programs will be examined. There is no direct indication in the passage whether ZBB is accepted. We are only told it exists. The last sentence of the third paragraph seems to indicate that the author, at least, does not accept ZBB as a budgetary system.

7. **(B)** In the third paragraph the author notes how incrementalism does not raise settled issues. Given the political nature of the budgetary process, we can infer that not raising settled issues, which may have been difficult to decide, will foster political harmony. (A) is wrong because incrementalism is not considered comprehensive. The author describes in paragraph three how new alternatives are dealt with. Thus, incrementalism does not avoid new alternatives, making (C) incorrect. Although (D) is a goal and an explanation of incrementalism, it does not suggest *why* incrementalism is politically acceptable. There is no indication in the passage that the time frame of incrementalism makes it politically acceptable. There is also no indication that other, less politically acceptable budgetary systems do not run on a yearly basis. Thus, (E) is incorrect.

8. **(D)** (A) is incorrect because of the author's statement at the end of the third paragraph and his generally favorable description of incrementalism throughout the passage. Given the author's definition of incrementalism in the first paragraph, (B) is also incorrect. (C) is incorrect because the point of the fifth paragraph is to describe how to keep costs down by looking at the problem incrementally. (E) is wrong given how the author differentiates in the first paragraph between using last year's budget and zero as the base. (D) is correct because the author devotes a good portion of the passage to describing why incrementalism is used. Although the author does not specifically indicate any problems with incrementalism, the tone of the passage is resigned. The author seems to suggest incrementalism is forced on the budgetary process. There are some good points to it, but its shortcomings are not mentioned.

9. **(C)** In the first paragraph the author describes Henry's virtues and why he was hailed as the model king, and also how he was not the type of king England needed at the time. In the following paragraphs the author tells us that despite England's woes, Henry embarked on an imperialist campaign against France, which only exacerbated England's problems. (A) is incorrect because the author does not concentrate solely on Henry's virtues. In addition, it is suggested that these virtues contributed to England's problems. Although the passage does

mention Henry's desire to conquer France, this cannot be considered a *chronicle* of the animosity between the two countries (B). (D) is incorrect because Henry IV is only mentioned as the type of king England needed at the time. There is no mention of the relationship between Henry IV and Henry V. The author suggests that what England needed was a king such as Henry IV. He also argues that Henry V contributed to England's financial problems. Nevertheless, we cannot conclude that by having a king such as Henry IV England would have *avoided* financial ruin. We are not told the state of England's finances prior to the reign of Henry V so we do not know if they were already in trouble. In addition, the passage concentrates more on the actions of Henry than the financial status of the country. Thus, (E) is incorrect.

10.   **(A)**   The author makes this clear in the second sentence of the first paragraph. In this same sentence the author notes that Henry's character was also questioned, making (C) incorrect as well as (B). In the third sentence of the first paragraph the author suggests Henry was politically unsophisticated. In the second paragraph we are told of his unwillingness to reach a diplomatic resolution to his conflict with France. Thus, (D) is incorrect. (E) is incorrect because we are told in the first paragraph of Henry's demonstrated military capacity. In the final sentence the author again acknowledges Henry's military successes.

11.   **(E)**   In the middle of the first paragraph the author notes how everyone was surprised at the change in Henry upon assuming the throne, in particular, on his newfound piety and sense of responsibility. (A) is incorrect because the passage does not tell us about England's status as a world power during this period. In addition, given the author's repeated mention of England's problems, we can surmise that Henry was not responsible for leading his country to world prominence despite his military victories. The final two paragraphs make it clear that Henry did not lead England to a decisive victory over France (B), nor did he have a gift for diplomacy (D). (C) is incorrect because the author makes no mention of Henry's administrative abilities.

12.   **(B)**   The reference to a bottomless hole in line 31 is meant to suggest a problem which cannot be solved; in this case, conquering France. Despite allocating more and more resources to the problem, the solution is no closer. The passage makes no mention of France's geographical qualities, making both (A) and (E) incorrect. (C) is incorrect because the author does not discuss the quality of France's diplomats. We might infer, however, that they were willing to negotiate given their "generous concessions." The author makes it clear he thinks Henry should not have attacked France. Nevertheless, his reasons as stated in the second sentence of the second paragraph have to do with English problems, not the worthlessness of France. Thus, (D) is incorrect.

13.   **(A)**   Venus is the Roman goddess of love, and Mars the god of war. In the first paragraph the author tells us of Henry's military exploits and his carousing with his friends. The reference to Venus and Mars in line 10 follows these

remarks. (B), (C), and (D) are all incorrect because we are given no information regarding methods of navigation, Henry's astrological beliefs, or military tactics. We are also not told specifically about Henry's religious beliefs. The author does mention Henry's "newfound piety" upon assuming the throne, but the mention of Venus and Mars refers to Henry's activities *prior* to becoming king. Thus, (E) is also incorrect.

14.   **(D)**   The author states this directly in the second paragraph when he says, "Henry was bent upon war... ." This statement also makes (C) incorrect. (A) is incorrect because there is no suggestion in the passage that Henry was improperly or inadequately advised. We are told in the second paragraph that France offered "generous concessions," making (B) incorrect. Since Henry's negotiations with France failed and he also failed to conquer France, it cannot be said the negotiations were a success, let alone his greatest (E).

15.   **(C)**   This conclusion is made by the author in the last sentence of the passage. (A) is incorrect because it is overbroad and we are not given information regarding subsequent diplomatic efforts. We can reasonably conclude that Henry's diplomatic efforts were not well received by the French, but we cannot expand this conclusion to include either other nations or other English monarchs. As noted in the explanation to question 11, we are not told what England's status as a world power was during this time. In addition, given the author's mention that "60 years of national bankruptcy and civil anarchy" followed Henry's reign, we can infer that England was not a world power during this period. Thus, (B) is incorrect. (D) is incorrect because we are not given any information about Henry's successor. In addition, since the author notes 60 years of problems followed Henry's reign, we can conclude Henry's successor did not have a successful reign. Certainly Henry's exploits caused him to be glorified as the model king. The author says as much in the last sentence of the first paragraph. Nevertheless, this is the effect of Henry's exploits on the historians of later ages. The author states in that same sentence that the immediate effect Henry had on England was an extended period of financial and political turmoil. Thus, (E) is incorrect.

16.   **(A)**   The author uses attitudes toward homosexuality to illustrate and present the theory of Ethical Subjectivism. In the fifth paragraph the author specifically states that Ethical Subjectivism is not just about evaluations of homosexuality, but applies to any moral judgment. Although used as an example, the author makes no attempt to *explain* homosexuality (B). Similarly, the author is not *criticizing* Falwell's views. To do so would be contrary to Ethical Subjectivism. The author may object to Falwell's statements to the extent they suggest homosexuality is objectively immoral, but the statements are used only as an example, and are not the primary purpose of the passage (C). Similarly, mention of the views of homosexuality in Iran and England serve only as examples and

are not the major point of the discussion. Thus, (E) is also incorrect. (D) is wrong because the focus of the passage is Ethical Subjectivism which holds that moral judgments are only expressions of personal feelings and not objective determinations of right and wrong. In addition, the author does not imply that Ethical Subjectivism is any better or worse than any other moral philosophy. (To do so, of course, would be contrary to Ethical Subjectivism.)

17. **(D)** This is made clear from the last sentence of the first paragraph where he says he does not hate the homosexual, but rather the act of homosexuality. Given Falwell's statements and the author's use of them as an example of a person holding a moral judgment out as an objective determination of something that is wrong, it should be clear Falwell *does* believe in objective right and wrong, making (A) incorrect. For the same reasons, (B) is incorrect because Falwell *does* believe homosexuality to be absolutely immoral. Along the same lines, we might assume that since Falwell believes there to be objective rights and wrongs in sexual conduct, he does so in other areas as well. Nevertheless, we need not make this assumption to show (E) is incorrect. (E) is incorrect simply because there is no mention in the passage of Falwell's attitudes toward either Ethical Subjectivism or behavior outside the realm of sexual conduct. (C) is incorrect because the author does not suggest a connection between homosexuality and intolerance. In addition, the author notes England's tolerant attitude toward homosexuality.

18. **(C)** This is made clear in the last paragraph of the passage. (A) and (B) are incorrect because, as the author states in the fifth paragraph, Ethical Subjectivism is not just about homosexuality, but applies to *any* moral judgment. (D) is incorrect because it is just the opposite of what the author is arguing: moral judgments are *subjective*. This view is summed up in the last paragraph. (E) is incorrect because puritanical mores, such as those of Falwell, assume an absolute right and wrong, which is contrary to Ethical Subjectivism.

19. **(B)** This is what the author argues in the fourth paragraph. Individuals may agree or disagree with some behavior, but that behavior cannot be said to be objectively right or wrong. Falwell's statement is certainly an expression of his beliefs. To the extent his statement suggests homosexuality is objectively wrong it is contrary to Ethical Subjectivism. Nevertheless, to say that his statement was *wrong* would also be contrary to Ethical Subjectivism. Thus, (A) is incorrect. In the sixth paragraph the author specifically notes that adherents of Ethical Subjectivism can and do form moral judgments based on their personal feelings, making (C) incorrect. It is just that they do not consider these judgments to be objective. Continuing along these lines, it is clear the author recognizes that moral judgments will not be based solely on factual assertions, making (D) incorrect. (E) is incorrect because to ban homosexuality would require an objective determination that it is wrong which is contrary to ethical subjectivism.

20. **(B)** The author does not specifically tell us which of the choices does or does not follow Ethical Subjectivism. Nevertheless, we can infer from the discussion that Ethical Subjectivism requires a more tolerant attitude of the behavior of others, even if one disagrees with it. The author seems to use Iran and Falwell as examples of intolerant attitudes, making (A) and (D) incorrect. The author notes the tolerant attitude of the English government toward homosexuality (B). We are not given any information about either France or the United States (other than Falwell's attitudes), making both (C) and (E) incorrect.

21. **(C)** Ethical Subjectivism holds that there are no *objective* rights or wrongs. To the extent a moral absolute is objectively applied, it is contrary to Ethical Subjectivism. Nevertheless, in the sixth paragraph the author tells us that adherents of Ethical Subjectivism will have moral beliefs, but recognize that their beliefs only represent their personal feelings. If the strength of those beliefs reaches the point of being a moral absolute for that person it is still consistent with Ethical Subjectivism provided the person continues to recognize the subjective nature of the beliefs. (A) is incorrect because it cannot be said that moral absolutes are an *integral* part of Ethical Subjectivism. Some moral absolutes may be consistent with Ethical Subjectivism, and others not. (B) is incorrect because the thrust of the author's argument is that moral judgments are based on *personal* feelings, not group or community mores or norms. (D) is incorrect because the passage makes no direct connection between moral absolutes and objective factual determinations. Indirectly, since moral absolutes are moral judgments and since the author recognizes that under Ethical Subjectivism people will make moral judgments based on their personal feelings, it cannot be said that moral absolutes *must* be based on objective factual determinations. There is no mention in the passage of divine intervention, making (E) incorrect.

22. **(E)** The implication of making something officially right or wrong is that it is *objectively* right or wrong. According to the author, the attitude of Ethical Subjectivism is that individually people may make moral judgments, but should not do so in an objective sense. (A), (B), (C), and (D), in varying degrees, all suggest some form of objective determination of the appropriateness of homosexual behavior, and are, thus, all incorrect. Note with regard to (D) the difference between merely *tolerating* something and *accepting* it.

23. **(B)** Because the passage opens and concludes with the research, the main thrust of the passage is thus the research that the Mount Zion Research Group conducted. (A) is not the main topic because the writer only briefly described Freudian theory. (C) is not the best choice because the author seems to accept the Freudian concept of repression barriers. In fact, the author's research reports how feelings trapped by these barriers continue to influence behavior. The idea that the unconscious mind affects behavior is not a main topic in the six paragraphs; for that reason (D) is not the best answer. (E) is also incorrect. The

author does note that the clinical method of psychotherapy cannot evaluate the relative merits of new therapeutic ideas (second paragraph), but this is not a warning against using psychotherapy. In the fifth paragraph, the author suggests that once the ideas have been evaluated empirically, they can be applied by psychotherapists.

24.　**(C)**　This point is made in the second paragraph. The author suggests the clinical method, based on notes and impressions, is incomplete and unreliable for rigorously evaluating competing theories. The author argues that by empirically testing scientifically gathered data the relative values of these theories can be properly evaluated. Thus, the author also believes these theories to be testable, making (B) incorrect. (A) is also incorrect. The author agrees with Freud's theories, but not the way they have been tested in the past. (D) makes no sense. It appears to confuse the concept of repressions with the repressed feelings. Similarly, (E) confuses the possible substance of current ideas with the author's feelings about those ideas, and is, thus, incorrect.

25.　**(A)**　This is made clear in the third paragraph, where the author puts Freud's name in parentheses following the word *psychoanalytic*. (B) is incorrect because the author argues not enough empirical testing of psychoanalytic hypotheses has been done. In addition, psychoanalytic theory, *per se*, is independent of empirical testing. It is only the assessment of the relative value of the hypotheses that has suffered from a lack of empirical testing. (C) is incorrect because, as noted in the fourth paragraph, repression barriers are an important part of psychoanalytic theory as developed by Freud. (D) makes no sense. The point of discussing unconscious feelings and repression barriers is that these feelings are hidden from the conscious mind. These hidden feelings, argues the author, do affect behavior, but the patient is unaware of how or why. (E) is incorrect because the author's research confirms the general concepts of the theory. It is only the assumptions that the unconscious mind cannot carry out intellectual activities that are contradicted by the author's research.

26.　**(D)**　This is made clear in the last sentence of the second paragraph. It is also in this paragraph where the author rejects the case study or clinical method as being too impressionistic. Thus, (A) is incorrect. (B) is incorrect because the author argues in the second paragraph that past evaluations of psychoanalytic hypotheses followed the clinical method and must now be empirically tested. The author suggests reliable data must be subjected to rigorous quantitative examination. Specific methods of obtaining reliable data (e.g., how unconscious responses are measured) are not mentioned in the passage, making (C) incorrect. Similarly, the author does not discuss how the unconscious mind evaluates feelings. He only argues that unconscious feelings affect behavior. Thus, (E) is incorrect.

27. **(E)** The author discusses the repression barrier in the fourth paragraph. In the first sentence of the fifth paragraph the author states that the repression barrier prevents people from consciously understanding why they act and feel the way they do. (A) is incorrect because the effect of the repression barrier is just the opposite. According to the fifth paragraph, the therapeutic value of free association is in providing clues to what is hidden behind the repression barrier. Arguably, in a twisted bit of logic, if a person has no repression barrier, i.e., no repressed thoughts or feelings, there will be no need to free-associate. Nevertheless, (B) is incorrect because free association is not dependent on the existence of a repression barrier. It is simply a method which can be used whether or not a repression barrier exists. (C) is incorrect because the repression barrier *hides* thoughts and feelings from conscious awareness (fourth and fifth paragraphs). It is methods like the author's empirical testing and free association which provide insights into unconscious mental functioning. (D) is incorrect because the repression barrier is a part of psychoanalytic theory and does not directly affect it. Indirectly, as an important part of psychoanalytic theory, if the repression barrier exists, its effect would be to validate the theory.

Section III – Logical Reasoning

1. **(A)** This is a fairly easy question. The second sentence tells us that Aristotle did not believe that observation was necessary to confirm one's conclusions about the physical universe. The third sentence says that because of this belief, no one until Galileo bothered to test one of the tenets of Aristotelian physics. One can infer from this that before Galileo, physicists did little experimentation. The answer, then, is (A). (B) could not be correct. Just because Aristotle's physics was wrong does not mean his logic is also. Logic deals with the validity of arguments. No experimentation is necessary to confirm logical rules; they are known by abstract reasoning. (C) is wrong, because one cannot develop experiments to test hypotheses until one has a hypothesis to test. Abstract reasoning can supply that hypothesis. (D) may or may not be correct, but the passage does not supply enough information for us to make a judgment on it. If anything, it lends support to the opposite inference, that physicists since Galileo are more skeptical than were the ancient ones, since Galileo showed that hypotheses should not be accepted without proof. (E) is plausible, but not correct. Just because Aristotle made one mistake does not mean Galileo is the better thinker. Science was much less developed in Aristotle's time, and it is possible that he broke more new ground than Galileo did.

2. **(E)** Answer (A) is not correct. The situation of college freshmen is much different than that of high school freshmen. The latter do not, in most cases, have to move away from home to attend school. Nor do most high schools have intramural athletics. Answer (B) is plausible, but not the best of the answers. It asks the reader to make a judgment on the basis of limited information.

The passage does not tell us whether most freshmen have time to spare for athletics. If not, we might decide not to make intramural athletics a requirement, because negative factors, such a lower grades, outweigh the benefits to be derived. Answer (C) states a fact that is not supported by the passage. Just because these students adapt faster does not mean that some or most of them do not have other, very serious, psychological problems. Answer (D) would be true only if liking athletics is the major criterion for being a better student. (E) is the best answer. The passage states that students who like intramural athletics make friends with teammates, and thus adapt faster than they would otherwise. Students who don't like athletics don't make friends, and thus are not benefited by the athletics. Therefore, the former are more likely to benefit than the latter.

3. **(D)** The passage states that all teachers at the academy will leave their mark on the future. Some are egotists, some are true scientists. The answer, therefore, is (D). Eliminate (A) because a statement about all scientists everywhere is beyond the scope of the passage. Eliminate (B) because it is not established by the passage. Eliminate (C) because the mark left by the egotists may not be a good one. Eliminate (E) because the passage makes no statement to support it.

4. **(A)** The last sentence of the passage implies that at least some students can be convinced to avoid crime, so the best answer is (A). (B) is not supported by the passage: even though the former criminals are cashing in on their previous crimes, they are not now doing anything illegal. Eliminate (C) because it implies that the reason the department uses former criminals in the program is for their benefit, when it is really for the benefit of the students. (D) is clearly contradicted by the last sentence of the passage. (E) is beyond the scope of the argument. To say that former criminals should not be allowed to speak to students about their experiences is not the same as saying they should never be allowed on school grounds.

5. **(B)** The passage argues that the program fails because the students see the reformed criminals as hypocrites who are profiting from past mistakes, and are thus unwilling to heed their advice. Only (B) directly contradicts this point. (A), (C), and (E) avoid the main point of the passage, while (D) lends it support.

6. **(A)** The argument of the passage is that, *on the surface*, the Cuban system is an exact duplicate of the Soviet system of the 1960s. The phrase "on the surface" refers to the external characteristics of the system. Therefore, statement (A) would undermine the conclusion of the passage. If what we see on the surface of Communist governments is misleading, using the Soviet system for comparison would be highly questionable. (B) is simply a restatement of (A), so it too would undermine the conclusion if it was not negative. (C) is beside the point, because the passage concerns the 1960 Soviet government, and any changes since then are irrelevant to the argument. (D) would not undermine the author's conclusion. (E) is true, according to the passage, and would not undermine the author's conclusion.

7.   **(A)**   (A) is the best answer. It may be put in the form of a syllogism: If Ch = Cu; and Ch = So; then Cu = So. (Ch is China, Cu is Cuba, and So is the Soviet Union.) In other words, if China's policy making is identical to that of the 1960s Soviet system, and also to that of the present Cuban system; then the Cuban and 1960s Soviet systems must be identical. Eliminate (B) because the fact that Castro and Khrushchev were friends would not prove that Castro copied the Soviet system. That both systems experienced the same economic problems would not alone establish that the systems were identical (C). Eliminate (D) since expressing admiration for something and copying it are not synonymous. (E) is more plausible than any alternative except (A). The passage does not tell us whether changes have been made in the Cuban system since 1959, so we cannot assume that the system is unchanged. Perhaps wholesale changes have been made. Therefore, eliminate (E).

8.   **(A)**   Answers (C), (D), and (E) can be eliminated fairly easily. (C) is nixed by the fact that state X cannot constitutionally run a deficit, no matter how small, so that something will have to be done to balance the books. An income tax increase may well be the solution. (D) is beside the point, because the problem is in the current fiscal year, and increased revenues next year will not help at the present. (E) is also beside the point, which is that a budget deficit is imminent, and must be eliminated. That leaves (A) and (B). (B) is plausible, but not the best answer. Income taxes may be high already, but since other tax revenues are declining, the state may have no choice but to raise them further to balance the budget. (A) is the best answer. If the state could balance the budget by eliminating wasteful programs, no tax increase would be necessary.

9.   **(A)**   Assumption (A) is necessary to make the conclusion correct, since one cannot assume on the basis of the first sentence that the road crew contains ONLY men and boys. Assumption (B) is not necessary to the conclusion, since the passage establishes that everyone on the crew who is insubordinate is also hateful, but not everyone who is hateful is necessarily insubordinate. It is not necessary, then, for the purposes of the conclusion, that insubordination and hatefulness be synonymous. Assumptions (C) and (D) contradict one of the premises of the argument, so they are not possibilities. The correct answer, then, is (A). (E) would not make it logically correct.

10.   **(B)**   Mayor Robinson said during the campaign that cities should not give public assistance to the needy. In answer to the interviewer he speaks favorably of a plan which does just that, so the answer is (B). Answer (A) is not supported by the passage. Answer (C) is plausible, but not the best, because the mayor's answer gives it indirect support at most. (D) receives no support from the passage. (E) is eliminated by the fact that the campaign statement was phrased in general terms, and therefore was meant to include all cities.

11.   **(E)**   One might conclude from this study that men perceive topography (geographical relationships) in terms of distance, while women perceive topography

in terms of notable landmarks. There is no reason, based on the passage, for us to conclude that (A) the same studies would produce different results today. Nor is it clear that (B) men should not seek directions from women, and vice versa. A man could easily find a place with directions based on landmarks, while women could do the same based on distance. It is impossible to tell from the passage whether (C) the researchers are men or women. One type of directions is as good as another in terms of helping someone find a place, so eliminate (D). This leaves (E), which one might validly conclude from the study.

12. **(B)**   The last sentence of the passage makes answer (A) very unlikely. Answer (B) is a necessary conclusion. If it is true that the program will be cut because of the decrease in city grants, then it is obvious that overall funding will not remain the same. This means that charitable contributions will not increase enough to maintain current funding levels. We cannot tell from the passage how much emphasis the city puts on the program (C). Perhaps the city is going to cut back on funding even for high priority items. (D) is not a necessary conclusion, because even if private contributions remain the same, the overall budget will be smaller. The unwed mothers might need more support now than before, but if funds are cut they will get less anyway (E).

13. **(A)**   The reader should note that the question asks which pattern of reasoning is parallel to that in the passage; it does not ask if a pattern is valid or invalid. (A) is closest to that pattern. Answer (B) cannot be correct; it starts with the generalization. Answers (C) and (E) start with a generalization; the writer then gives an "if-then" statement. The patterns of (C) and (E) are not the same as that in the passage. Answer (D) goes from the sentence to a deduction. Again, the pattern is not the same and (D) is an incorrect answer.

14. **(D)**   (D) is clearly the best answer to this question. The passage says that those who put profit ahead of ethics are not gentlemen; and that they are usually of no benefit to society. Eliminate (A) because the passage says nothing about how common or likely unethical behavior is from the wealthy. Eliminate (B) because it appears that unethical behavior is the result of greed. Sympathy is not mentioned or alluded to in the passage, so the answer is not (C). The passage says nothing about the intellects of unethical or greedy people, so eliminate (E).

15. **(A)**   The author says that those who make decisions as dictated by their pocketbooks give nothing back to society. The analogy about the tapeworm carries the argument a step further, to make the point that not only do they give nothing back, but they also act as parasites on society, sapping its vitality. The answer, then, is (A). Eliminate (B) because the author's concern is for the welfare of society, not of the greedy. (C) is beyond the scope of the passage. (D) and (E) receive no support from the passage.

16. **(A)** The passage says that the alienation caused by loss of sense of community is the tragedy peculiar to our age. Therefore, (A) may be inferred from the passage. The passage says that modern life has many advantages over the past, so (B) may not be inferred. (C) could possibly be inferred but it is not the best answer. (D) seems to contradict the author's feelings and (E) cannot be validly inferred.

17. **(B)** Eliminate (A) because one would expect one 25 lb. bag to last as long as another 25 lb. bag. Eliminate (E), since the packaging is of minor consideration. The reader must now decide which of the three remaining answers is the best. The owners might like one brand better than another (C), but they may be basing their opinion on inconsequential factors, such as advertising or packaging. Dogs might like the taste of both equally (D), but one might have little nutritional value. Nutritional value, of course, is the most important consideration in buying food for dogs or people. If brand X is equal to brand Y in this respect, but costs less, it is obviously the better buy. The best answer is (B).

18. **(D)** The passage reasons from the general to the particular. One class of things, real estate in this city, is down in price; therefore, a member of this class, this particular house, must be a good buy (down in price). Eliminate (A) because it reasons from the particular to the general: from Chicago to the state where it is located. (B) uses a fact about graduates of a school to form a judgment about that school. The graduates are not the general class of things of which this school is a member. (C) argues that something is likely to happen because it has happened before. One might choose (E) thinking that picnics is a class of things, and the speaker is making the following argument: since I hate all picnics, I would hate the one today. However, one cannot tell if the speaker means that he will stay home from: today's picnic (one member of the class) or from all future picnics (the entire class). (D) is exactly like the passage. Dogs is the class, old Blue the particular member of the class.

19. **(D)** It is not clear from the passage how quickly improvements are being made, so the manuals may be up-to-date for a short while after they are written. This eliminates (A). Eliminate (B) because the passage says *new applications* have been found for Zoology, not that new software had been written for it. Perhaps only software has been found useful in that field. Eliminate (C) because the passage does not imply that the authors made mistakes, only that when the manuals were written the new applications had not yet been discovered. Eliminate (E) because it is not clear from the passage that new technology is responsible for the new applications. Perhaps the new applications were possible with the old technology, but had not yet been discovered. This leaves (D), which is one of three factors listed by the passage as necessitating the writing of new manuals.

20. **(C)** Both speakers agree that the word "strike" means a work stoppage, so eliminate (A). The interests of management are not discussed, so eliminate (B). While the speakers may have different social agendas (D), this is not clear from the passage, since they both appear to be concerned with the long-term interests of the workers. Eliminate (E) since negotiation is not discussed. The argument obviously centers on what is in the long-term interests of the workers; more specifically whether they will benefit in the long run from a strike. The answer, then, is (C).

21. **(A)** The problem with the analogy is that some employees do not have the potential to take on tougher jobs, while birds potentially have the ability to fly (A). Eliminate (B) and (E) because decision making is not central to the passage, since the employee should always say yes to a promotion. Eliminate (C) because, as the speaker says, the bird must learn to fly. It would face risks every bit as great if it did not. Nor are events in the life of a bird as significant as those in the life of a human. Eliminate (D) because it carries the analogy in a different direction instead of showing that the situations of the bird and employee are not analogous.

22. **(C)** The closest parallel to the nest is (C), the employee's present job. The nest is safe, the present position comfortable. Eliminate (A) because the employee's skills are parallel to the bird's learning to fly. Eliminate (B) because the job the employee will take is parallel to the bird's having to leave the nest. (D) is not the answer because skills are possessed by the employee, they are not a station or position to be occupied. Eliminate (E) because the employee is never encouraged to seek employment with another company, whereas the bird is said to leave the nest.

23. **(B)** The conclusion would be strengthened by statement (A) if it was phrased positively. Note that the statement would not PROVE the conclusion, but it would strengthen it. Statement (B) also strengthens the conclusion. If it is true the author has addressed all of the major factors and eliminated those which could not be at fault. That leaves only the one to which he attributes the rise in inflation. We cannot tell from the loose phrasing in (C) whether it would strengthen or weaken the argument. That the government regulated the price of domestic oil could mean that the price was held constant or reduced, neither of which would strengthen the argument. Because (B) is correct, and the only correct answer, (D) and (E) cannot be correct.

24. **(A)** The statement "A low level of personal savings is unavoidable unless government ... keeps a lid on inflation" implies that there is an inverse relation between inflation and the savings rate. When the first goes up, the second goes down. Thus, statement (A) is a necessary presupposition to the argu-

ment. That unemployment leads to recession is not necessarily presupposed by the passage (B). Sentence one says that low savings leads to unemployment and to recession. However, the relationship between unemployment and recession is not established. Statement (C) is not presupposed by the argument that low levels of savings is the major cause of recession does not mean that it is the only cause. There may be other causes which are not listed, (D) and (E) are not among them. The answer, then, is (A).

25. **(C)** Joe does not (A) disagree with each of her premises. One of her premises is that insurance rates should be commensurate with the amount recovered (settlements); in other words, those who get greater benefits (more settlements) should pay more. Joe must agree, because he uses the same premise to show that women's premiums should be lowered. They pay longer, therefore the total amount they pay becomes disproportionate to the amount recovered unless their annual rates are lower. He does not prove (B), since she could have read it and misunderstood it; or she may have simply ignored the parts that she disagreed with. (C) is the best answer. Liz thinks that the gender that receives the most settlements should pay the highest rates. Joe thinks that the gender that pays in for a longer time should have annual rates reduced to compensate. He does not (D) challenge Liz's statistics. He merely quotes others to support his position. His evidence proves not that men's rates should be lower (E), but that women's rates should be lower.

Section IV – Analytical Reasoning

QUESTIONS 1–7

This is a set of linear operation problems. Begin by collecting all the data at your disposal. The relations "is to the left of" and "is to the right of" are transitive relations — if x is to the left of y and y is to the left of z, then x must be on the left of z. In these problems, certain features of the ordering are guaranteed. The following *sequences* cannot be violated, although there can be additional letters between the members of these sequences:

E – F – H
B – M – P
E – F – P – S
left   right

All correct answers *must* satisfy those sequences. Draw 7 spaces and, from left to right, fill in the blanks as needed.

1. **(B)** Which book must be on the extreme right? The initial data provides

three options, H, P and S, but P is always to the right of S, so either H or S must be on the extreme right. Thus (B) is the correct answer.

2. **(A)** The initial data provide only 2 options for the left-most member of the set, B and E. Thus, if it is not E it must be B, and (A) is the correct answer. (B), (C), (D) and (E) each violate one of the restrictions on ordering given above.

3. **(C)** (A) and (D) are not impossible since either S or H is on the extreme left. (B) and (E) are not impossible since either B or E is on the extreme left. Thus, (C) is impossible, S is to the right of P and the correct answer.

4. **(B)** If the three left-most books are B, E and M, F must be in the exact middle of the group and (B) is the correct answer. (A) is incorrect because P is to the right of F. (C) is incorrect since H is to the right of F. (D) and (E) include answers that are known to be wrong as options, and should be rejected. Always reject an answer that lists a known error as an option.

5. **(C)** (C) is the correct answer because it violates the condition that S is to the right of P. A quick scan of the initial data should reveal this. If it does not, then construct orderings that satisfy the other options. Though time consuming, a "brute force" approach to this problem will reveal that B – E – F – M – P – S – H and E – B – F – M – P – H – S satisfy each of (A), (B), (D) and (E).

6. **(B)** Here you need to examine each of the given orderings for conformity to the rules. (B) alone fails the test.

7. **(D)** If B is the third from the left, then only E and F can be to the left of B, and, since E is to the left of F, F has to be next to the extreme left. Thus, (D) is the correct answer.

QUESTIONS 8–13

This is another set of linear ordering problems. One potentially tricky aspect of this problem set is that since both Sophomores and Seniors are used in the ordering, you cannot use the letter S for both groups. Use care in the choice of letters that stand for members of the discrete groups. Note that since the Juniors always stand together and one of them is on an end of the line, there are only 2 base options upon which to build:

```
Option 1    J  J  J
            1  2  3  4  5  6  7  8  9  10  11


Option 2                         J  J   J
            1  2  3  4  5  6  7  8  9  10  11
```

For option 1 there must be either a Freshman or a Sophomore in space 4 and a Sophomore or a Senior in space 11. For option 2 there must be either a Sophomore or a Senior in space 1 and either a Freshman or a Sophomore in space 8.

8. **(B)**   This problem uses option 1 and, placing a Sophomore in space 10 requires placing a Senior in space 11 (Freshmen won't stand on the end and the Sophomores won't stand together). Thus, (B) is the correct answer. Each of (A), (C), (D) and (E) could be, but need not be, the case.

9. **(A)**   This problem requires option 2. (A) is correct for it places a Freshman on one end of the line. (C) is not impossible, it must be the case. (B), (D) and (E) could be, but need not be, the case.

10. **(C)**   For this problem you need to examine both options, since the stem does not specify one of them. (A) is incorrect, this is possible under option 1. (B) clearly is not impossible. (C) is impossible, and the correct answer, for, under either option, it places a Senior next to a Junior. (D) and (E) are both possible under either option.

11. **(E)**   In this problem 4 spaces exist between the Seniors and the Juniors and they need to be filled within the rules. I is possible, So – F – F – So is acceptable. II is not acceptable. Placing the Freshmen together next to the Senior would require placing the Sophomores next to one another. III is possible, F – So – F – So is acceptable. Thus, (E) is the correct answer.

12. **(B)**   (A) is not possible. Under option 1 place the Seniors on spaces 5, 7, 9 and 11. (B) is possible. Under option 1 place the Freshmen and Sophomores on spaces 4, 6, 8 and 10. (C) is impossible. Either a Freshman or a Sophomore must be on an even space next to a Junior. (D) and (E) are not possible because they violate conditions of the problem.

13. **(E)**   This question can be answered immediately by recalling that either a Freshman or a Sophomore must stand next to a Junior. But the only open space next to a Junior is an even numbered space. Thus, (E) is the correct answer. Each of (A), (B), (C) and (D) could be, but need not be, the case.

QUESTIONS 14–19

This is another set of linear ordering problems. As with the previous group, there is a problem with notation here since there are 2 A's, 2 B's and 2 C's. Develop a scheme for keeping track of who's who. You might underline the letter standing for the female member of the pair or circle the letter standing for the male member. The scheme you choose is irrelevant, but some scheme is needed. In these examples, I have circled the letter standing for the female member of the pair. The initial conditions allow for only two possible seating arrangements:

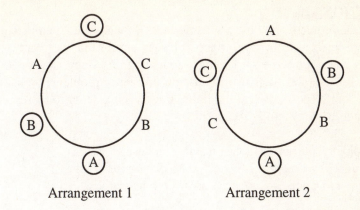

Arrangement 1   Arrangement 2

14. **(B)**   (A) is allowed under arrangement 2. (B) is the correct answer be-cause neither arrangement allows the Ables to sit together. (C) is allowed under arrangement 1. (D) is allowed under arrangement 1. (E) is allowed under arrange-ment 1.

15. **(C)**   This problem requires arrangement 2. (A) is impossible as under arrangement 2, the Ables are seated across from one another. **Note**: since reject-ing answer (A) *because* of information given as answer (C), and the question is which is possible, you can stop. (C) is the correct answer. (B) is wrong, Mrs. Carr is between Mr. Carr and Mr. Able. (D) is wrong, Mrs. Carr is seated across from Mr. Baker. (E) is wrong, the Ables are seated directly across from one another.

16. **(D)**   This problem requires arrangement 1. (A), (B), (C) and (E) are all incorrect as these arrangements must be the case under arrangement 1. (D) is the correct answer, under arrangement 1 the Ables cannot sit across from one an-other.

17. **(A)**   This problem requires arrangement 1, but here you are looking for an acceptable arrangement (in the previous 2 questions you were looking for impossible arrangements). Only (A) satisfies all of the conditions, and it is the correct answer.

18. **(C)**   Here you need to examine both arrangements, since none is speci-fied, and see which features remain constant regardless of the specific arrange-ment. (A) is never the case. (B) occurs in Arrangement 1, but not in Arrangement 2. (C) is always the case. (D) and (E) violate conditions of the argument.

19. **(E)**   For this problem arrangement 2 is needed. (A) is impossible, Mr. Carr is seated between Mrs. Able and Mrs. Carr. (B) is impossible, Mrs. Carr is seated between Mr. Carr and Mr. Able. (C) is impossible, Mrs. Carr is seated to the right of Mr. Able. (D) is impossible, Mrs. Baker is seated between Mr. Able and Mr. Baker. Thus, only (E) is possible and the correct answer.

QUESTIONS 20–23

These problems involve a selection task in which the members of one group are to be selected from several pools. It may appear that there are two pools, but actually there are three — Biology Courses, Philosophy Courses and Required Courses — and the pools overlap. Begin this set of problems by listing all of the data at your disposal. Be careful not to use the same letter to represent both Environmental Biology and Epistemology.

Biology Courses — B, G, En and P (choose at least 2)
Philosophy Courses — Ep, L, A, M, S (choose at least 2)
Required Courses — B, L, A and M (choose at least 3)

The following pairs are excluded since the members of each pair are offered at the same time — En and A, Ep and M, and L and G.

20. **(B)** Since 3 of the 4 required courses are Philosophy courses, he must choose a Biology course as his fifth course, so (D) and (E) are incorrect. But A excludes En, and L excludes G, so (A) and (C) are incorrect. Thus he must take P and (B) is the correct answer.

21. **(A)** (A) must be true. In order to take 3 required courses, excluding L requires him to take A and M, excludes Ep, so he must take S. (B) is false because M and Ep are offered at the same time and he must take M. (C) is false because he takes B and *either* G *or* P, but not both. (D) violates the conditions of this question. (E) violates a condition of the problem.

22. **(B)** He must take B, and here is why. Assume that he does not take B, then he must take L, A, and M. But A excludes En and L excludes G, so it becomes impossible for him to take the necessary 2 Biology courses. (B) is the correct answer. If this is not readily apparent, the best strategy is to construct acceptable schedules that omit the course given in the answer. Such a brute force approach is time consuming, but it works.

23. **(D)** For this problem either a brute force or a deductive solution is possible. By brute force the acceptable sets B – L – M – En – S; B – A – M – P – G account for answers (A), (B), (C) and (E). So (D) is impossible and the correct answer. By deduction, the pair G and En (answer (D)), excludes both A and L, but then the requirement of taking 3 required courses is violated.

LSAT Writing Sample – Demonstration Essay

The CPU Club should not be forced to admit women, because as a private institution, it is made up of members who enjoy the constitutional right of free association. Its all-male status is supported by some 240 years of tradition, and

a majority of its members are not students at the publicly supported college (because they are alumni of that institution).

As CPU Club president Dave Mora points out, this dining club is a private association, with constitutionally guaranteed rights to include and exclude whomever its members choose. The club building is privately owned and sits on privately owned land that borders, but is not a part of, the college campus. The membership fee that the students pay to the CPU Club is private money and not derived from public grants or loans for their higher education. Therefore, while most of the active members are students of a private college that receives public funds, their association with the CPU Club is socially and financially separate from that institution of higher learning.

The more-than-240-year-old tradition of the CPU Club as a private all-male institution confirms its status as deserving the constitutional protection of the right to free association. To force gender integration upon the club violates a long tradition of autonomy and self-governance. While the college bordering the dining clubs went coed in 1970, this should not automatically change every institution surrounding the campus. Indeed, it may be argued that because male and female students are able to associate with one another in other settings (classroom, laboratory, college dorms, pubs, etc.) this one exclusive club should be preserved in the name of diversity. To force the CPU members to accept a group of people into its private club would be like the government requiring families to accept strangers into their living rooms. Moreover, such compulsion may breed more resentment against women, which the policy intends to overcome.

Finally, the charge made by Ms. Radin that all of the CPU Club members are students of an institution receiving federal financial support ignores the large number of alumni members who are no longer formally associated with the college. These graduate members retain their ties with the club (periodically taking meals there and paying an annual fee) even though they are now in business, are in the professions, or even are retired.

An argument underlying Ms. Radin's assertion of the need for gender integration is indeed this alumni membership in the club, which she claims gives the student members unfair advantage in "networking" in their future careers. If every private association that might have some career advantage were required to be opened to all groups equally, no advantages or even personal relations could exist. Besides, the market economy works better if individuals are left free to make decisions about associations, rather than having the state dictate relations and policies.

So, because the CPU Club is a private institution separate from the college, because it has a 240-year tradition of all-male membership, and because many of its members are currently not students at the college that receives federal aid, it should be protected by the constitutional guarantee of freedom of association and not be forced to admit women.

Demonstration Essay Explanation

This is a good essay because it presents arguments in a clear, calm manner on a highly controversial issue. It acknowledges the strengths of the opposing argument (that public institutions legally cannot discriminate on the basis of race, sex, etc.) and frames the argument around the "private" nature of the club and the individual right to freedom of association. It should be noted that the opposing argument could easily be employed in answering this sample topic. The essay uses every fact available in the topic to support the argument, brings in outside information to bolster those facts, and uses analogies effectively to support this decision. It varies sentence length and breaks the paragraphs up into a logical sequence.

The first paragraph states the case and summarizes the three reasons supporting that case. The second paragraph elaborates on the primary rationale for not forcing gender integration of the club on the grounds that it is private and enlists facts from the sample (the dollar amount of the dues) and outside information (that this money does not derive from federally funded student financial aid). The third paragraph, emphasizing the club's traditional ties to the college, acknowledges the precarious position all-male clubs were placed in after 1970, when the college went coed, but tries to get around this difficulty by repeating the "autonomous" nature of the clubs, as well as appealing to the opposition's goal of "diversity" (because men and women will mix together in other places on and around the campus). Finally, this paragraph effectively employs an analogy (the government forcing people into your living room) to bolster its claim of individual rights of free association. The fourth paragraph develops the third argument that the presence of non-student club members proves CPU's separation from the college and again employs an analogy concerning governmental control over all personal relationships that might constitute "networking." The fifth paragraph concludes by repeating (in different form) the three arguments for choosing the case for the club.

LSAT

Law School Admission Test

ANSWER SHEETS

LSAT TEST I – ANSWER SHEET

Section I

1. Ⓐ Ⓑ Ⓒ Ⓓ Ⓔ
2. Ⓐ Ⓑ Ⓒ Ⓓ Ⓔ
3. Ⓐ Ⓑ Ⓒ Ⓓ Ⓔ
4. Ⓐ Ⓑ Ⓒ Ⓓ Ⓔ
5. Ⓐ Ⓑ Ⓒ Ⓓ Ⓔ
6. Ⓐ Ⓑ Ⓒ Ⓓ Ⓔ
7. Ⓐ Ⓑ Ⓒ Ⓓ Ⓔ
8. Ⓐ Ⓑ Ⓒ Ⓓ Ⓔ
9. Ⓐ Ⓑ Ⓒ Ⓓ Ⓔ
10. Ⓐ Ⓑ Ⓒ Ⓓ Ⓔ
11. Ⓐ Ⓑ Ⓒ Ⓓ Ⓔ
12. Ⓐ Ⓑ Ⓒ Ⓓ Ⓔ
13. Ⓐ Ⓑ Ⓒ Ⓓ Ⓔ
14. Ⓐ Ⓑ Ⓒ Ⓓ Ⓔ
15. Ⓐ Ⓑ Ⓒ Ⓓ Ⓔ
16. Ⓐ Ⓑ Ⓒ Ⓓ Ⓔ
17. Ⓐ Ⓑ Ⓒ Ⓓ Ⓔ
18. Ⓐ Ⓑ Ⓒ Ⓓ Ⓔ
19. Ⓐ Ⓑ Ⓒ Ⓓ Ⓔ
20. Ⓐ Ⓑ Ⓒ Ⓓ Ⓔ
21. Ⓐ Ⓑ Ⓒ Ⓓ Ⓔ
22. Ⓐ Ⓑ Ⓒ Ⓓ Ⓔ
23. Ⓐ Ⓑ Ⓒ Ⓓ Ⓔ
24. Ⓐ Ⓑ Ⓒ Ⓓ Ⓔ
25. Ⓐ Ⓑ Ⓒ Ⓓ Ⓔ
26. Ⓐ Ⓑ Ⓒ Ⓓ Ⓔ
27. Ⓐ Ⓑ Ⓒ Ⓓ Ⓔ
28. Ⓐ Ⓑ Ⓒ Ⓓ Ⓔ
29. Ⓐ Ⓑ Ⓒ Ⓓ Ⓔ
30. Ⓐ Ⓑ Ⓒ Ⓓ Ⓔ

Section II

1. Ⓐ Ⓑ Ⓒ Ⓓ Ⓔ
2. Ⓐ Ⓑ Ⓒ Ⓓ Ⓔ
3. Ⓐ Ⓑ Ⓒ Ⓓ Ⓔ
4. Ⓐ Ⓑ Ⓒ Ⓓ Ⓔ
5. Ⓐ Ⓑ Ⓒ Ⓓ Ⓔ
6. Ⓐ Ⓑ Ⓒ Ⓓ Ⓔ
7. Ⓐ Ⓑ Ⓒ Ⓓ Ⓔ
8. Ⓐ Ⓑ Ⓒ Ⓓ Ⓔ
9. Ⓐ Ⓑ Ⓒ Ⓓ Ⓔ

10. Ⓐ Ⓑ Ⓒ Ⓓ Ⓔ
11. Ⓐ Ⓑ Ⓒ Ⓓ Ⓔ
12. Ⓐ Ⓑ Ⓒ Ⓓ Ⓔ
13. Ⓐ Ⓑ Ⓒ Ⓓ Ⓔ
14. Ⓐ Ⓑ Ⓒ Ⓓ Ⓔ
15. Ⓐ Ⓑ Ⓒ Ⓓ Ⓔ
16. Ⓐ Ⓑ Ⓒ Ⓓ Ⓔ
17. Ⓐ Ⓑ Ⓒ Ⓓ Ⓔ
18. Ⓐ Ⓑ Ⓒ Ⓓ Ⓔ
19. Ⓐ Ⓑ Ⓒ Ⓓ Ⓔ
20. Ⓐ Ⓑ Ⓒ Ⓓ Ⓔ
21. Ⓐ Ⓑ Ⓒ Ⓓ Ⓔ
22. Ⓐ Ⓑ Ⓒ Ⓓ Ⓔ
23. Ⓐ Ⓑ Ⓒ Ⓓ Ⓔ
24. Ⓐ Ⓑ Ⓒ Ⓓ Ⓔ
25. Ⓐ Ⓑ Ⓒ Ⓓ Ⓔ
26. Ⓐ Ⓑ Ⓒ Ⓓ Ⓔ
27. Ⓐ Ⓑ Ⓒ Ⓓ Ⓔ
28. Ⓐ Ⓑ Ⓒ Ⓓ Ⓔ
29. Ⓐ Ⓑ Ⓒ Ⓓ Ⓔ
30. Ⓐ Ⓑ Ⓒ Ⓓ Ⓔ

Section III

1. Ⓐ Ⓑ Ⓒ Ⓓ Ⓔ
2. Ⓐ Ⓑ Ⓒ Ⓓ Ⓔ
3. Ⓐ Ⓑ Ⓒ Ⓓ Ⓔ
4. Ⓐ Ⓑ Ⓒ Ⓓ Ⓔ
5. Ⓐ Ⓑ Ⓒ Ⓓ Ⓔ
6. Ⓐ Ⓑ Ⓒ Ⓓ Ⓔ
7. Ⓐ Ⓑ Ⓒ Ⓓ Ⓔ
8. Ⓐ Ⓑ Ⓒ Ⓓ Ⓔ
9. Ⓐ Ⓑ Ⓒ Ⓓ Ⓔ
10. Ⓐ Ⓑ Ⓒ Ⓓ Ⓔ
11. Ⓐ Ⓑ Ⓒ Ⓓ Ⓔ
12. Ⓐ Ⓑ Ⓒ Ⓓ Ⓔ
13. Ⓐ Ⓑ Ⓒ Ⓓ Ⓔ
14. Ⓐ Ⓑ Ⓒ Ⓓ Ⓔ
15. Ⓐ Ⓑ Ⓒ Ⓓ Ⓔ
16. Ⓐ Ⓑ Ⓒ Ⓓ Ⓔ
17. Ⓐ Ⓑ Ⓒ Ⓓ Ⓔ
18. Ⓐ Ⓑ Ⓒ Ⓓ Ⓔ
19. Ⓐ Ⓑ Ⓒ Ⓓ Ⓔ
20. Ⓐ Ⓑ Ⓒ Ⓓ Ⓔ

Section IV

1. Ⓐ Ⓑ Ⓒ Ⓓ Ⓔ
2. Ⓐ Ⓑ Ⓒ Ⓓ Ⓔ
3. Ⓐ Ⓑ Ⓒ Ⓓ Ⓔ
4. Ⓐ Ⓑ Ⓒ Ⓓ Ⓔ
5. Ⓐ Ⓑ Ⓒ Ⓓ Ⓔ
6. Ⓐ Ⓑ Ⓒ Ⓓ Ⓔ
7. Ⓐ Ⓑ Ⓒ Ⓓ Ⓔ
8. Ⓐ Ⓑ Ⓒ Ⓓ Ⓔ
9. Ⓐ Ⓑ Ⓒ Ⓓ Ⓔ
10. Ⓐ Ⓑ Ⓒ Ⓓ Ⓔ
11. Ⓐ Ⓑ Ⓒ Ⓓ Ⓔ
12. Ⓐ Ⓑ Ⓒ Ⓓ Ⓔ
13. Ⓐ Ⓑ Ⓒ Ⓓ Ⓔ
14. Ⓐ Ⓑ Ⓒ Ⓓ Ⓔ
15. Ⓐ Ⓑ Ⓒ Ⓓ Ⓔ
16. Ⓐ Ⓑ Ⓒ Ⓓ Ⓔ
17. Ⓐ Ⓑ Ⓒ Ⓓ Ⓔ
18. Ⓐ Ⓑ Ⓒ Ⓓ Ⓔ
19. Ⓐ Ⓑ Ⓒ Ⓓ Ⓔ
20. Ⓐ Ⓑ Ⓒ Ⓓ Ⓔ
21. Ⓐ Ⓑ Ⓒ Ⓓ Ⓔ
22. Ⓐ Ⓑ Ⓒ Ⓓ Ⓔ
23. Ⓐ Ⓑ Ⓒ Ⓓ Ⓔ
24. Ⓐ Ⓑ Ⓒ Ⓓ Ⓔ
25. Ⓐ Ⓑ Ⓒ Ⓓ Ⓔ
26. Ⓐ Ⓑ Ⓒ Ⓓ Ⓔ
27. Ⓐ Ⓑ Ⓒ Ⓓ Ⓔ
28. Ⓐ Ⓑ Ⓒ Ⓓ Ⓔ
29. Ⓐ Ⓑ Ⓒ Ⓓ Ⓔ
30. Ⓐ Ⓑ Ⓒ Ⓓ Ⓔ

LSAT TEST I – WRITING SAMPLE TOPIC

STOP

If time still remains, you may review work only in this section.
When the time alloted is up, you may go on to the next section.

LSAT TEST II – ANSWER SHEET

Section I

1. Ⓐ Ⓑ Ⓒ Ⓓ Ⓔ
2. Ⓐ Ⓑ Ⓒ Ⓓ Ⓔ
3. Ⓐ Ⓑ Ⓒ Ⓓ Ⓔ
4. Ⓐ Ⓑ Ⓒ Ⓓ Ⓔ
5. Ⓐ Ⓑ Ⓒ Ⓓ Ⓔ
6. Ⓐ Ⓑ Ⓒ Ⓓ Ⓔ
7. Ⓐ Ⓑ Ⓒ Ⓓ Ⓔ
8. Ⓐ Ⓑ Ⓒ Ⓓ Ⓔ
9. Ⓐ Ⓑ Ⓒ Ⓓ Ⓔ
10. Ⓐ Ⓑ Ⓒ Ⓓ Ⓔ
11. Ⓐ Ⓑ Ⓒ Ⓓ Ⓔ
12. Ⓐ Ⓑ Ⓒ Ⓓ Ⓔ
13. Ⓐ Ⓑ Ⓒ Ⓓ Ⓔ
14. Ⓐ Ⓑ Ⓒ Ⓓ Ⓔ
15. Ⓐ Ⓑ Ⓒ Ⓓ Ⓔ
16. Ⓐ Ⓑ Ⓒ Ⓓ Ⓔ
17. Ⓐ Ⓑ Ⓒ Ⓓ Ⓔ
18. Ⓐ Ⓑ Ⓒ Ⓓ Ⓔ
19. Ⓐ Ⓑ Ⓒ Ⓓ Ⓔ
20. Ⓐ Ⓑ Ⓒ Ⓓ Ⓔ
21. Ⓐ Ⓑ Ⓒ Ⓓ Ⓔ
22. Ⓐ Ⓑ Ⓒ Ⓓ Ⓔ
23. Ⓐ Ⓑ Ⓒ Ⓓ Ⓔ
24. Ⓐ Ⓑ Ⓒ Ⓓ Ⓔ
25. Ⓐ Ⓑ Ⓒ Ⓓ Ⓔ
26. Ⓐ Ⓑ Ⓒ Ⓓ Ⓔ
27. Ⓐ Ⓑ Ⓒ Ⓓ Ⓔ
28. Ⓐ Ⓑ Ⓒ Ⓓ Ⓔ
29. Ⓐ Ⓑ Ⓒ Ⓓ Ⓔ
30. Ⓐ Ⓑ Ⓒ Ⓓ Ⓔ

Section II

1. Ⓐ Ⓑ Ⓒ Ⓓ Ⓔ
2. Ⓐ Ⓑ Ⓒ Ⓓ Ⓔ
3. Ⓐ Ⓑ Ⓒ Ⓓ Ⓔ
4. Ⓐ Ⓑ Ⓒ Ⓓ Ⓔ
5. Ⓐ Ⓑ Ⓒ Ⓓ Ⓔ
6. Ⓐ Ⓑ Ⓒ Ⓓ Ⓔ
7. Ⓐ Ⓑ Ⓒ Ⓓ Ⓔ
8. Ⓐ Ⓑ Ⓒ Ⓓ Ⓔ
9. Ⓐ Ⓑ Ⓒ Ⓓ Ⓔ

10. Ⓐ Ⓑ Ⓒ Ⓓ Ⓔ
11. Ⓐ Ⓑ Ⓒ Ⓓ Ⓔ
12. Ⓐ Ⓑ Ⓒ Ⓓ Ⓔ
13. Ⓐ Ⓑ Ⓒ Ⓓ Ⓔ
14. Ⓐ Ⓑ Ⓒ Ⓓ Ⓔ
15. Ⓐ Ⓑ Ⓒ Ⓓ Ⓔ
16. Ⓐ Ⓑ Ⓒ Ⓓ Ⓔ
17. Ⓐ Ⓑ Ⓒ Ⓓ Ⓔ
18. Ⓐ Ⓑ Ⓒ Ⓓ Ⓔ
19. Ⓐ Ⓑ Ⓒ Ⓓ Ⓔ
20. Ⓐ Ⓑ Ⓒ Ⓓ Ⓔ
21. Ⓐ Ⓑ Ⓒ Ⓓ Ⓔ
22. Ⓐ Ⓑ Ⓒ Ⓓ Ⓔ
23. Ⓐ Ⓑ Ⓒ Ⓓ Ⓔ
24. Ⓐ Ⓑ Ⓒ Ⓓ Ⓔ
25. Ⓐ Ⓑ Ⓒ Ⓓ Ⓔ
26. Ⓐ Ⓑ Ⓒ Ⓓ Ⓔ
27. Ⓐ Ⓑ Ⓒ Ⓓ Ⓔ
28. Ⓐ Ⓑ Ⓒ Ⓓ Ⓔ
29. Ⓐ Ⓑ Ⓒ Ⓓ Ⓔ
30. Ⓐ Ⓑ Ⓒ Ⓓ Ⓔ

Section III

1. Ⓐ Ⓑ Ⓒ Ⓓ Ⓔ
2. Ⓐ Ⓑ Ⓒ Ⓓ Ⓔ
3. Ⓐ Ⓑ Ⓒ Ⓓ Ⓔ
4. Ⓐ Ⓑ Ⓒ Ⓓ Ⓔ
5. Ⓐ Ⓑ Ⓒ Ⓓ Ⓔ
6. Ⓐ Ⓑ Ⓒ Ⓓ Ⓔ
7. Ⓐ Ⓑ Ⓒ Ⓓ Ⓔ
8. Ⓐ Ⓑ Ⓒ Ⓓ Ⓔ
9. Ⓐ Ⓑ Ⓒ Ⓓ Ⓔ
10. Ⓐ Ⓑ Ⓒ Ⓓ Ⓔ
11. Ⓐ Ⓑ Ⓒ Ⓓ Ⓔ
12. Ⓐ Ⓑ Ⓒ Ⓓ Ⓔ
13. Ⓐ Ⓑ Ⓒ Ⓓ Ⓔ
14. Ⓐ Ⓑ Ⓒ Ⓓ Ⓔ
15. Ⓐ Ⓑ Ⓒ Ⓓ Ⓔ
16. Ⓐ Ⓑ Ⓒ Ⓓ Ⓔ
17. Ⓐ Ⓑ Ⓒ Ⓓ Ⓔ
18. Ⓐ Ⓑ Ⓒ Ⓓ Ⓔ
19. Ⓐ Ⓑ Ⓒ Ⓓ Ⓔ
20. Ⓐ Ⓑ Ⓒ Ⓓ Ⓔ

Section IV

1. Ⓐ Ⓑ Ⓒ Ⓓ Ⓔ
2. Ⓐ Ⓑ Ⓒ Ⓓ Ⓔ
3. Ⓐ Ⓑ Ⓒ Ⓓ Ⓔ
4. Ⓐ Ⓑ Ⓒ Ⓓ Ⓔ
5. Ⓐ Ⓑ Ⓒ Ⓓ Ⓔ
6. Ⓐ Ⓑ Ⓒ Ⓓ Ⓔ
7. Ⓐ Ⓑ Ⓒ Ⓓ Ⓔ
8. Ⓐ Ⓑ Ⓒ Ⓓ Ⓔ
9. Ⓐ Ⓑ Ⓒ Ⓓ Ⓔ
10. Ⓐ Ⓑ Ⓒ Ⓓ Ⓔ
11. Ⓐ Ⓑ Ⓒ Ⓓ Ⓔ
12. Ⓐ Ⓑ Ⓒ Ⓓ Ⓔ
13. Ⓐ Ⓑ Ⓒ Ⓓ Ⓔ
14. Ⓐ Ⓑ Ⓒ Ⓓ Ⓔ
15. Ⓐ Ⓑ Ⓒ Ⓓ Ⓔ
16. Ⓐ Ⓑ Ⓒ Ⓓ Ⓔ
17. Ⓐ Ⓑ Ⓒ Ⓓ Ⓔ
18. Ⓐ Ⓑ Ⓒ Ⓓ Ⓔ
19. Ⓐ Ⓑ Ⓒ Ⓓ Ⓔ
20. Ⓐ Ⓑ Ⓒ Ⓓ Ⓔ
21. Ⓐ Ⓑ Ⓒ Ⓓ Ⓔ
22. Ⓐ Ⓑ Ⓒ Ⓓ Ⓔ
23. Ⓐ Ⓑ Ⓒ Ⓓ Ⓔ
24. Ⓐ Ⓑ Ⓒ Ⓓ Ⓔ
25. Ⓐ Ⓑ Ⓒ Ⓓ Ⓔ
26. Ⓐ Ⓑ Ⓒ Ⓓ Ⓔ
27. Ⓐ Ⓑ Ⓒ Ⓓ Ⓔ
28. Ⓐ Ⓑ Ⓒ Ⓓ Ⓔ
29. Ⓐ Ⓑ Ⓒ Ⓓ Ⓔ
30. Ⓐ Ⓑ Ⓒ Ⓓ Ⓔ

LSAT TEST II – WRITING SAMPLE TOPIC

STOP

If time still remains, you may review work only in this section.
When the time alloted is up, you may go on to the next section.

LSAT TEST III – ANSWER SHEET

Section I

1. Ⓐ Ⓑ Ⓒ Ⓓ Ⓔ
2. Ⓐ Ⓑ Ⓒ Ⓓ Ⓔ
3. Ⓐ Ⓑ Ⓒ Ⓓ Ⓔ
4. Ⓐ Ⓑ Ⓒ Ⓓ Ⓔ
5. Ⓐ Ⓑ Ⓒ Ⓓ Ⓔ
6. Ⓐ Ⓑ Ⓒ Ⓓ Ⓔ
7. Ⓐ Ⓑ Ⓒ Ⓓ Ⓔ
8. Ⓐ Ⓑ Ⓒ Ⓓ Ⓔ
9. Ⓐ Ⓑ Ⓒ Ⓓ Ⓔ
10. Ⓐ Ⓑ Ⓒ Ⓓ Ⓔ
11. Ⓐ Ⓑ Ⓒ Ⓓ Ⓔ
12. Ⓐ Ⓑ Ⓒ Ⓓ Ⓔ
13. Ⓐ Ⓑ Ⓒ Ⓓ Ⓔ
14. Ⓐ Ⓑ Ⓒ Ⓓ Ⓔ
15. Ⓐ Ⓑ Ⓒ Ⓓ Ⓔ
16. Ⓐ Ⓑ Ⓒ Ⓓ Ⓔ
17. Ⓐ Ⓑ Ⓒ Ⓓ Ⓔ
18. Ⓐ Ⓑ Ⓒ Ⓓ Ⓔ
19. Ⓐ Ⓑ Ⓒ Ⓓ Ⓔ
20. Ⓐ Ⓑ Ⓒ Ⓓ Ⓔ
21. Ⓐ Ⓑ Ⓒ Ⓓ Ⓔ
22. Ⓐ Ⓑ Ⓒ Ⓓ Ⓔ
23. Ⓐ Ⓑ Ⓒ Ⓓ Ⓔ
24. Ⓐ Ⓑ Ⓒ Ⓓ Ⓔ
25. Ⓐ Ⓑ Ⓒ Ⓓ Ⓔ
26. Ⓐ Ⓑ Ⓒ Ⓓ Ⓔ
27. Ⓐ Ⓑ Ⓒ Ⓓ Ⓔ
28. Ⓐ Ⓑ Ⓒ Ⓓ Ⓔ
29. Ⓐ Ⓑ Ⓒ Ⓓ Ⓔ
30. Ⓐ Ⓑ Ⓒ Ⓓ Ⓔ

Section II

1. Ⓐ Ⓑ Ⓒ Ⓓ Ⓔ
2. Ⓐ Ⓑ Ⓒ Ⓓ Ⓔ
3. Ⓐ Ⓑ Ⓒ Ⓓ Ⓔ
4. Ⓐ Ⓑ Ⓒ Ⓓ Ⓔ
5. Ⓐ Ⓑ Ⓒ Ⓓ Ⓔ
6. Ⓐ Ⓑ Ⓒ Ⓓ Ⓔ
7. Ⓐ Ⓑ Ⓒ Ⓓ Ⓔ
8. Ⓐ Ⓑ Ⓒ Ⓓ Ⓔ
9. Ⓐ Ⓑ Ⓒ Ⓓ Ⓔ

10. Ⓐ Ⓑ Ⓒ Ⓓ Ⓔ
11. Ⓐ Ⓑ Ⓒ Ⓓ Ⓔ
12. Ⓐ Ⓑ Ⓒ Ⓓ Ⓔ
13. Ⓐ Ⓑ Ⓒ Ⓓ Ⓔ
14. Ⓐ Ⓑ Ⓒ Ⓓ Ⓔ
15. Ⓐ Ⓑ Ⓒ Ⓓ Ⓔ
16. Ⓐ Ⓑ Ⓒ Ⓓ Ⓔ
17. Ⓐ Ⓑ Ⓒ Ⓓ Ⓔ
18. Ⓐ Ⓑ Ⓒ Ⓓ Ⓔ
19. Ⓐ Ⓑ Ⓒ Ⓓ Ⓔ
20. Ⓐ Ⓑ Ⓒ Ⓓ Ⓔ
21. Ⓐ Ⓑ Ⓒ Ⓓ Ⓔ
22. Ⓐ Ⓑ Ⓒ Ⓓ Ⓔ
23. Ⓐ Ⓑ Ⓒ Ⓓ Ⓔ
24. Ⓐ Ⓑ Ⓒ Ⓓ Ⓔ
25. Ⓐ Ⓑ Ⓒ Ⓓ Ⓔ
26. Ⓐ Ⓑ Ⓒ Ⓓ Ⓔ
27. Ⓐ Ⓑ Ⓒ Ⓓ Ⓔ
28. Ⓐ Ⓑ Ⓒ Ⓓ Ⓔ
29. Ⓐ Ⓑ Ⓒ Ⓓ Ⓔ
30. Ⓐ Ⓑ Ⓒ Ⓓ Ⓔ

Section III

1. Ⓐ Ⓑ Ⓒ Ⓓ Ⓔ
2. Ⓐ Ⓑ Ⓒ Ⓓ Ⓔ
3. Ⓐ Ⓑ Ⓒ Ⓓ Ⓔ
4. Ⓐ Ⓑ Ⓒ Ⓓ Ⓔ
5. Ⓐ Ⓑ Ⓒ Ⓓ Ⓔ
6. Ⓐ Ⓑ Ⓒ Ⓓ Ⓔ
7. Ⓐ Ⓑ Ⓒ Ⓓ Ⓔ
8. Ⓐ Ⓑ Ⓒ Ⓓ Ⓔ
9. Ⓐ Ⓑ Ⓒ Ⓓ Ⓔ
10. Ⓐ Ⓑ Ⓒ Ⓓ Ⓔ
11. Ⓐ Ⓑ Ⓒ Ⓓ Ⓔ
12. Ⓐ Ⓑ Ⓒ Ⓓ Ⓔ
13. Ⓐ Ⓑ Ⓒ Ⓓ Ⓔ
14. Ⓐ Ⓑ Ⓒ Ⓓ Ⓔ
15. Ⓐ Ⓑ Ⓒ Ⓓ Ⓔ
16. Ⓐ Ⓑ Ⓒ Ⓓ Ⓔ
17. Ⓐ Ⓑ Ⓒ Ⓓ Ⓔ
18. Ⓐ Ⓑ Ⓒ Ⓓ Ⓔ
19. Ⓐ Ⓑ Ⓒ Ⓓ Ⓔ
20. Ⓐ Ⓑ Ⓒ Ⓓ Ⓔ

Section IV

1. Ⓐ Ⓑ Ⓒ Ⓓ Ⓔ
2. Ⓐ Ⓑ Ⓒ Ⓓ Ⓔ
3. Ⓐ Ⓑ Ⓒ Ⓓ Ⓔ
4. Ⓐ Ⓑ Ⓒ Ⓓ Ⓔ
5. Ⓐ Ⓑ Ⓒ Ⓓ Ⓔ
6. Ⓐ Ⓑ Ⓒ Ⓓ Ⓔ
7. Ⓐ Ⓑ Ⓒ Ⓓ Ⓔ
8. Ⓐ Ⓑ Ⓒ Ⓓ Ⓔ
9. Ⓐ Ⓑ Ⓒ Ⓓ Ⓔ
10. Ⓐ Ⓑ Ⓒ Ⓓ Ⓔ
11. Ⓐ Ⓑ Ⓒ Ⓓ Ⓔ
12. Ⓐ Ⓑ Ⓒ Ⓓ Ⓔ
13. Ⓐ Ⓑ Ⓒ Ⓓ Ⓔ
14. Ⓐ Ⓑ Ⓒ Ⓓ Ⓔ
15. Ⓐ Ⓑ Ⓒ Ⓓ Ⓔ
16. Ⓐ Ⓑ Ⓒ Ⓓ Ⓔ
17. Ⓐ Ⓑ Ⓒ Ⓓ Ⓔ
18. Ⓐ Ⓑ Ⓒ Ⓓ Ⓔ
19. Ⓐ Ⓑ Ⓒ Ⓓ Ⓔ
20. Ⓐ Ⓑ Ⓒ Ⓓ Ⓔ
21. Ⓐ Ⓑ Ⓒ Ⓓ Ⓔ
22. Ⓐ Ⓑ Ⓒ Ⓓ Ⓔ
23. Ⓐ Ⓑ Ⓒ Ⓓ Ⓔ
24. Ⓐ Ⓑ Ⓒ Ⓓ Ⓔ
25. Ⓐ Ⓑ Ⓒ Ⓓ Ⓔ
26. Ⓐ Ⓑ Ⓒ Ⓓ Ⓔ
27. Ⓐ Ⓑ Ⓒ Ⓓ Ⓔ
28. Ⓐ Ⓑ Ⓒ Ⓓ Ⓔ
29. Ⓐ Ⓑ Ⓒ Ⓓ Ⓔ
30. Ⓐ Ⓑ Ⓒ Ⓓ Ⓔ

LSAT TEST III – WRITING SAMPLE TOPIC

STOP

If time still remains, you may review work only in this section.
When the time alloted is up, you may go on to the next section.

LSAT TEST IV – ANSWER SHEET

Section I

1. Ⓐ Ⓑ Ⓒ Ⓓ Ⓔ
2. Ⓐ Ⓑ Ⓒ Ⓓ Ⓔ
3. Ⓐ Ⓑ Ⓒ Ⓓ Ⓔ
4. Ⓐ Ⓑ Ⓒ Ⓓ Ⓔ
5. Ⓐ Ⓑ Ⓒ Ⓓ Ⓔ
6. Ⓐ Ⓑ Ⓒ Ⓓ Ⓔ
7. Ⓐ Ⓑ Ⓒ Ⓓ Ⓔ
8. Ⓐ Ⓑ Ⓒ Ⓓ Ⓔ
9. Ⓐ Ⓑ Ⓒ Ⓓ Ⓔ
10. Ⓐ Ⓑ Ⓒ Ⓓ Ⓔ
11. Ⓐ Ⓑ Ⓒ Ⓓ Ⓔ
12. Ⓐ Ⓑ Ⓒ Ⓓ Ⓔ
13. Ⓐ Ⓑ Ⓒ Ⓓ Ⓔ
14. Ⓐ Ⓑ Ⓒ Ⓓ Ⓔ
15. Ⓐ Ⓑ Ⓒ Ⓓ Ⓔ
16. Ⓐ Ⓑ Ⓒ Ⓓ Ⓔ
17. Ⓐ Ⓑ Ⓒ Ⓓ Ⓔ
18. Ⓐ Ⓑ Ⓒ Ⓓ Ⓔ
19. Ⓐ Ⓑ Ⓒ Ⓓ Ⓔ
20. Ⓐ Ⓑ Ⓒ Ⓓ Ⓔ
21. Ⓐ Ⓑ Ⓒ Ⓓ Ⓔ
22. Ⓐ Ⓑ Ⓒ Ⓓ Ⓔ
23. Ⓐ Ⓑ Ⓒ Ⓓ Ⓔ
24. Ⓐ Ⓑ Ⓒ Ⓓ Ⓔ
25. Ⓐ Ⓑ Ⓒ Ⓓ Ⓔ
26. Ⓐ Ⓑ Ⓒ Ⓓ Ⓔ
27. Ⓐ Ⓑ Ⓒ Ⓓ Ⓔ
28. Ⓐ Ⓑ Ⓒ Ⓓ Ⓔ
29. Ⓐ Ⓑ Ⓒ Ⓓ Ⓔ
30. Ⓐ Ⓑ Ⓒ Ⓓ Ⓔ

Section II

1. Ⓐ Ⓑ Ⓒ Ⓓ Ⓔ
2. Ⓐ Ⓑ Ⓒ Ⓓ Ⓔ
3. Ⓐ Ⓑ Ⓒ Ⓓ Ⓔ
4. Ⓐ Ⓑ Ⓒ Ⓓ Ⓔ
5. Ⓐ Ⓑ Ⓒ Ⓓ Ⓔ
6. Ⓐ Ⓑ Ⓒ Ⓓ Ⓔ
7. Ⓐ Ⓑ Ⓒ Ⓓ Ⓔ
8. Ⓐ Ⓑ Ⓒ Ⓓ Ⓔ
9. Ⓐ Ⓑ Ⓒ Ⓓ Ⓔ

10. Ⓐ Ⓑ Ⓒ Ⓓ Ⓔ
11. Ⓐ Ⓑ Ⓒ Ⓓ Ⓔ
12. Ⓐ Ⓑ Ⓒ Ⓓ Ⓔ
13. Ⓐ Ⓑ Ⓒ Ⓓ Ⓔ
14. Ⓐ Ⓑ Ⓒ Ⓓ Ⓔ
15. Ⓐ Ⓑ Ⓒ Ⓓ Ⓔ
16. Ⓐ Ⓑ Ⓒ Ⓓ Ⓔ
17. Ⓐ Ⓑ Ⓒ Ⓓ Ⓔ
18. Ⓐ Ⓑ Ⓒ Ⓓ Ⓔ
19. Ⓐ Ⓑ Ⓒ Ⓓ Ⓔ
20. Ⓐ Ⓑ Ⓒ Ⓓ Ⓔ
21. Ⓐ Ⓑ Ⓒ Ⓓ Ⓔ
22. Ⓐ Ⓑ Ⓒ Ⓓ Ⓔ
23. Ⓐ Ⓑ Ⓒ Ⓓ Ⓔ
24. Ⓐ Ⓑ Ⓒ Ⓓ Ⓔ
25. Ⓐ Ⓑ Ⓒ Ⓓ Ⓔ
26. Ⓐ Ⓑ Ⓒ Ⓓ Ⓔ
27. Ⓐ Ⓑ Ⓒ Ⓓ Ⓔ
28. Ⓐ Ⓑ Ⓒ Ⓓ Ⓔ
29. Ⓐ Ⓑ Ⓒ Ⓓ Ⓔ
30. Ⓐ Ⓑ Ⓒ Ⓓ Ⓔ

Section III

1. Ⓐ Ⓑ Ⓒ Ⓓ Ⓔ
2. Ⓐ Ⓑ Ⓒ Ⓓ Ⓔ
3. Ⓐ Ⓑ Ⓒ Ⓓ Ⓔ
4. Ⓐ Ⓑ Ⓒ Ⓓ Ⓔ
5. Ⓐ Ⓑ Ⓒ Ⓓ Ⓔ
6. Ⓐ Ⓑ Ⓒ Ⓓ Ⓔ
7. Ⓐ Ⓑ Ⓒ Ⓓ Ⓔ
8. Ⓐ Ⓑ Ⓒ Ⓓ Ⓔ
9. Ⓐ Ⓑ Ⓒ Ⓓ Ⓔ
10. Ⓐ Ⓑ Ⓒ Ⓓ Ⓔ
11. Ⓐ Ⓑ Ⓒ Ⓓ Ⓔ
12. Ⓐ Ⓑ Ⓒ Ⓓ Ⓔ
13. Ⓐ Ⓑ Ⓒ Ⓓ Ⓔ
14. Ⓐ Ⓑ Ⓒ Ⓓ Ⓔ
15. Ⓐ Ⓑ Ⓒ Ⓓ Ⓔ
16. Ⓐ Ⓑ Ⓒ Ⓓ Ⓔ
17. Ⓐ Ⓑ Ⓒ Ⓓ Ⓔ
18. Ⓐ Ⓑ Ⓒ Ⓓ Ⓔ
19. Ⓐ Ⓑ Ⓒ Ⓓ Ⓔ
20. Ⓐ Ⓑ Ⓒ Ⓓ Ⓔ

Section IV

1. Ⓐ Ⓑ Ⓒ Ⓓ Ⓔ
2. Ⓐ Ⓑ Ⓒ Ⓓ Ⓔ
3. Ⓐ Ⓑ Ⓒ Ⓓ Ⓔ
4. Ⓐ Ⓑ Ⓒ Ⓓ Ⓔ
5. Ⓐ Ⓑ Ⓒ Ⓓ Ⓔ
6. Ⓐ Ⓑ Ⓒ Ⓓ Ⓔ
7. Ⓐ Ⓑ Ⓒ Ⓓ Ⓔ
8. Ⓐ Ⓑ Ⓒ Ⓓ Ⓔ
9. Ⓐ Ⓑ Ⓒ Ⓓ Ⓔ
10. Ⓐ Ⓑ Ⓒ Ⓓ Ⓔ
11. Ⓐ Ⓑ Ⓒ Ⓓ Ⓔ
12. Ⓐ Ⓑ Ⓒ Ⓓ Ⓔ
13. Ⓐ Ⓑ Ⓒ Ⓓ Ⓔ
14. Ⓐ Ⓑ Ⓒ Ⓓ Ⓔ
15. Ⓐ Ⓑ Ⓒ Ⓓ Ⓔ
16. Ⓐ Ⓑ Ⓒ Ⓓ Ⓔ
17. Ⓐ Ⓑ Ⓒ Ⓓ Ⓔ
18. Ⓐ Ⓑ Ⓒ Ⓓ Ⓔ
19. Ⓐ Ⓑ Ⓒ Ⓓ Ⓔ
20. Ⓐ Ⓑ Ⓒ Ⓓ Ⓔ
21. Ⓐ Ⓑ Ⓒ Ⓓ Ⓔ
22. Ⓐ Ⓑ Ⓒ Ⓓ Ⓔ
23. Ⓐ Ⓑ Ⓒ Ⓓ Ⓔ
24. Ⓐ Ⓑ Ⓒ Ⓓ Ⓔ
25. Ⓐ Ⓑ Ⓒ Ⓓ Ⓔ
26. Ⓐ Ⓑ Ⓒ Ⓓ Ⓔ
27. Ⓐ Ⓑ Ⓒ Ⓓ Ⓔ
28. Ⓐ Ⓑ Ⓒ Ⓓ Ⓔ
29. Ⓐ Ⓑ Ⓒ Ⓓ Ⓔ
30. Ⓐ Ⓑ Ⓒ Ⓓ Ⓔ

(Section I, continued)

10. Ⓐ Ⓑ Ⓒ Ⓓ Ⓔ
11. Ⓐ Ⓑ Ⓒ Ⓓ Ⓔ
12. Ⓐ Ⓑ Ⓒ Ⓓ Ⓔ
13. Ⓐ Ⓑ Ⓒ Ⓓ Ⓔ
14. Ⓐ Ⓑ Ⓒ Ⓓ Ⓔ
15. Ⓐ Ⓑ Ⓒ Ⓓ Ⓔ
16. Ⓐ Ⓑ Ⓒ Ⓓ Ⓔ
17. Ⓐ Ⓑ Ⓒ Ⓓ Ⓔ
18. Ⓐ Ⓑ Ⓒ Ⓓ Ⓔ
19. Ⓐ Ⓑ Ⓒ Ⓓ Ⓔ
20. Ⓐ Ⓑ Ⓒ Ⓓ Ⓔ
21. Ⓐ Ⓑ Ⓒ Ⓓ Ⓔ
22. Ⓐ Ⓑ Ⓒ Ⓓ Ⓔ
23. Ⓐ Ⓑ Ⓒ Ⓓ Ⓔ
24. Ⓐ Ⓑ Ⓒ Ⓓ Ⓔ
25. Ⓐ Ⓑ Ⓒ Ⓓ Ⓔ
26. Ⓐ Ⓑ Ⓒ Ⓓ Ⓔ
27. Ⓐ Ⓑ Ⓒ Ⓓ Ⓔ
28. Ⓐ Ⓑ Ⓒ Ⓓ Ⓔ
29. Ⓐ Ⓑ Ⓒ Ⓓ Ⓔ
30. Ⓐ Ⓑ Ⓒ Ⓓ Ⓔ

LSAT TEST IV – WRITING SAMPLE TOPIC

STOP

If time still remains, you may review work only in this section.
When the time alloted is up, you may go on to the next section.

LSAT TEST V – ANSWER SHEET

Section I

1. Ⓐ Ⓑ Ⓒ Ⓓ Ⓔ
2. Ⓐ Ⓑ Ⓒ Ⓓ Ⓔ
3. Ⓐ Ⓑ Ⓒ Ⓓ Ⓔ
4. Ⓐ Ⓑ Ⓒ Ⓓ Ⓔ
5. Ⓐ Ⓑ Ⓒ Ⓓ Ⓔ
6. Ⓐ Ⓑ Ⓒ Ⓓ Ⓔ
7. Ⓐ Ⓑ Ⓒ Ⓓ Ⓔ
8. Ⓐ Ⓑ Ⓒ Ⓓ Ⓔ
9. Ⓐ Ⓑ Ⓒ Ⓓ Ⓔ
10. Ⓐ Ⓑ Ⓒ Ⓓ Ⓔ
11. Ⓐ Ⓑ Ⓒ Ⓓ Ⓔ
12. Ⓐ Ⓑ Ⓒ Ⓓ Ⓔ
13. Ⓐ Ⓑ Ⓒ Ⓓ Ⓔ
14. Ⓐ Ⓑ Ⓒ Ⓓ Ⓔ
15. Ⓐ Ⓑ Ⓒ Ⓓ Ⓔ
16. Ⓐ Ⓑ Ⓒ Ⓓ Ⓔ
17. Ⓐ Ⓑ Ⓒ Ⓓ Ⓔ
18. Ⓐ Ⓑ Ⓒ Ⓓ Ⓔ
19. Ⓐ Ⓑ Ⓒ Ⓓ Ⓔ
20. Ⓐ Ⓑ Ⓒ Ⓓ Ⓔ
21. Ⓐ Ⓑ Ⓒ Ⓓ Ⓔ
22. Ⓐ Ⓑ Ⓒ Ⓓ Ⓔ
23. Ⓐ Ⓑ Ⓒ Ⓓ Ⓔ
24. Ⓐ Ⓑ Ⓒ Ⓓ Ⓔ
25. Ⓐ Ⓑ Ⓒ Ⓓ Ⓔ
26. Ⓐ Ⓑ Ⓒ Ⓓ Ⓔ
27. Ⓐ Ⓑ Ⓒ Ⓓ Ⓔ
28. Ⓐ Ⓑ Ⓒ Ⓓ Ⓔ
29. Ⓐ Ⓑ Ⓒ Ⓓ Ⓔ
30. Ⓐ Ⓑ Ⓒ Ⓓ Ⓔ

Section II

1. Ⓐ Ⓑ Ⓒ Ⓓ Ⓔ
2. Ⓐ Ⓑ Ⓒ Ⓓ Ⓔ
3. Ⓐ Ⓑ Ⓒ Ⓓ Ⓔ
4. Ⓐ Ⓑ Ⓒ Ⓓ Ⓔ
5. Ⓐ Ⓑ Ⓒ Ⓓ Ⓔ
6. Ⓐ Ⓑ Ⓒ Ⓓ Ⓔ
7. Ⓐ Ⓑ Ⓒ Ⓓ Ⓔ
8. Ⓐ Ⓑ Ⓒ Ⓓ Ⓔ
9. Ⓐ Ⓑ Ⓒ Ⓓ Ⓔ

10. Ⓐ Ⓑ Ⓒ Ⓓ Ⓔ
11. Ⓐ Ⓑ Ⓒ Ⓓ Ⓔ
12. Ⓐ Ⓑ Ⓒ Ⓓ Ⓔ
13. Ⓐ Ⓑ Ⓒ Ⓓ Ⓔ
14. Ⓐ Ⓑ Ⓒ Ⓓ Ⓔ
15. Ⓐ Ⓑ Ⓒ Ⓓ Ⓔ
16. Ⓐ Ⓑ Ⓒ Ⓓ Ⓔ
17. Ⓐ Ⓑ Ⓒ Ⓓ Ⓔ
18. Ⓐ Ⓑ Ⓒ Ⓓ Ⓔ
19. Ⓐ Ⓑ Ⓒ Ⓓ Ⓔ
20. Ⓐ Ⓑ Ⓒ Ⓓ Ⓔ
21. Ⓐ Ⓑ Ⓒ Ⓓ Ⓔ
22. Ⓐ Ⓑ Ⓒ Ⓓ Ⓔ
23. Ⓐ Ⓑ Ⓒ Ⓓ Ⓔ
24. Ⓐ Ⓑ Ⓒ Ⓓ Ⓔ
25. Ⓐ Ⓑ Ⓒ Ⓓ Ⓔ
26. Ⓐ Ⓑ Ⓒ Ⓓ Ⓔ
27. Ⓐ Ⓑ Ⓒ Ⓓ Ⓔ
28. Ⓐ Ⓑ Ⓒ Ⓓ Ⓔ
29. Ⓐ Ⓑ Ⓒ Ⓓ Ⓔ
30. Ⓐ Ⓑ Ⓒ Ⓓ Ⓔ

Section III

1. Ⓐ Ⓑ Ⓒ Ⓓ Ⓔ
2. Ⓐ Ⓑ Ⓒ Ⓓ Ⓔ
3. Ⓐ Ⓑ Ⓒ Ⓓ Ⓔ
4. Ⓐ Ⓑ Ⓒ Ⓓ Ⓔ
5. Ⓐ Ⓑ Ⓒ Ⓓ Ⓔ
6. Ⓐ Ⓑ Ⓒ Ⓓ Ⓔ
7. Ⓐ Ⓑ Ⓒ Ⓓ Ⓔ
8. Ⓐ Ⓑ Ⓒ Ⓓ Ⓔ
9. Ⓐ Ⓑ Ⓒ Ⓓ Ⓔ
10. Ⓐ Ⓑ Ⓒ Ⓓ Ⓔ
11. Ⓐ Ⓑ Ⓒ Ⓓ Ⓔ
12. Ⓐ Ⓑ Ⓒ Ⓓ Ⓔ
13. Ⓐ Ⓑ Ⓒ Ⓓ Ⓔ
14. Ⓐ Ⓑ Ⓒ Ⓓ Ⓔ
15. Ⓐ Ⓑ Ⓒ Ⓓ Ⓔ
16. Ⓐ Ⓑ Ⓒ Ⓓ Ⓔ
17. Ⓐ Ⓑ Ⓒ Ⓓ Ⓔ
18. Ⓐ Ⓑ Ⓒ Ⓓ Ⓔ
19. Ⓐ Ⓑ Ⓒ Ⓓ Ⓔ
20. Ⓐ Ⓑ Ⓒ Ⓓ Ⓔ

Section IV

1. Ⓐ Ⓑ Ⓒ Ⓓ Ⓔ
2. Ⓐ Ⓑ Ⓒ Ⓓ Ⓔ
3. Ⓐ Ⓑ Ⓒ Ⓓ Ⓔ
4. Ⓐ Ⓑ Ⓒ Ⓓ Ⓔ
5. Ⓐ Ⓑ Ⓒ Ⓓ Ⓔ
6. Ⓐ Ⓑ Ⓒ Ⓓ Ⓔ
7. Ⓐ Ⓑ Ⓒ Ⓓ Ⓔ
8. Ⓐ Ⓑ Ⓒ Ⓓ Ⓔ
9. Ⓐ Ⓑ Ⓒ Ⓓ Ⓔ
10. Ⓐ Ⓑ Ⓒ Ⓓ Ⓔ
11. Ⓐ Ⓑ Ⓒ Ⓓ Ⓔ
12. Ⓐ Ⓑ Ⓒ Ⓓ Ⓔ
13. Ⓐ Ⓑ Ⓒ Ⓓ Ⓔ
14. Ⓐ Ⓑ Ⓒ Ⓓ Ⓔ
15. Ⓐ Ⓑ Ⓒ Ⓓ Ⓔ
16. Ⓐ Ⓑ Ⓒ Ⓓ Ⓔ
17. Ⓐ Ⓑ Ⓒ Ⓓ Ⓔ
18. Ⓐ Ⓑ Ⓒ Ⓓ Ⓔ
19. Ⓐ Ⓑ Ⓒ Ⓓ Ⓔ
20. Ⓐ Ⓑ Ⓒ Ⓓ Ⓔ
21. Ⓐ Ⓑ Ⓒ Ⓓ Ⓔ
22. Ⓐ Ⓑ Ⓒ Ⓓ Ⓔ
23. Ⓐ Ⓑ Ⓒ Ⓓ Ⓔ
24. Ⓐ Ⓑ Ⓒ Ⓓ Ⓔ
25. Ⓐ Ⓑ Ⓒ Ⓓ Ⓔ
26. Ⓐ Ⓑ Ⓒ Ⓓ Ⓔ
27. Ⓐ Ⓑ Ⓒ Ⓓ Ⓔ
28. Ⓐ Ⓑ Ⓒ Ⓓ Ⓔ
29. Ⓐ Ⓑ Ⓒ Ⓓ Ⓔ
30. Ⓐ Ⓑ Ⓒ Ⓓ Ⓔ

LSAT TEST V – WRITING SAMPLE TOPIC

STOP

If time still remains, you may review work only in this section.
When the time alloted is up, you may go on to the next section.

LSAT TEST VI – ANSWER SHEET

Section I

1. Ⓐ Ⓑ Ⓒ Ⓓ Ⓔ
2. Ⓐ Ⓑ Ⓒ Ⓓ Ⓔ
3. Ⓐ Ⓑ Ⓒ Ⓓ Ⓔ
4. Ⓐ Ⓑ Ⓒ Ⓓ Ⓔ
5. Ⓐ Ⓑ Ⓒ Ⓓ Ⓔ
6. Ⓐ Ⓑ Ⓒ Ⓓ Ⓔ
7. Ⓐ Ⓑ Ⓒ Ⓓ Ⓔ
8. Ⓐ Ⓑ Ⓒ Ⓓ Ⓔ
9. Ⓐ Ⓑ Ⓒ Ⓓ Ⓔ
10. Ⓐ Ⓑ Ⓒ Ⓓ Ⓔ
11. Ⓐ Ⓑ Ⓒ Ⓓ Ⓔ
12. Ⓐ Ⓑ Ⓒ Ⓓ Ⓔ
13. Ⓐ Ⓑ Ⓒ Ⓓ Ⓔ
14. Ⓐ Ⓑ Ⓒ Ⓓ Ⓔ
15. Ⓐ Ⓑ Ⓒ Ⓓ Ⓔ
16. Ⓐ Ⓑ Ⓒ Ⓓ Ⓔ
17. Ⓐ Ⓑ Ⓒ Ⓓ Ⓔ
18. Ⓐ Ⓑ Ⓒ Ⓓ Ⓔ
19. Ⓐ Ⓑ Ⓒ Ⓓ Ⓔ
20. Ⓐ Ⓑ Ⓒ Ⓓ Ⓔ
21. Ⓐ Ⓑ Ⓒ Ⓓ Ⓔ
22. Ⓐ Ⓑ Ⓒ Ⓓ Ⓔ
23. Ⓐ Ⓑ Ⓒ Ⓓ Ⓔ
24. Ⓐ Ⓑ Ⓒ Ⓓ Ⓔ
25. Ⓐ Ⓑ Ⓒ Ⓓ Ⓔ
26. Ⓐ Ⓑ Ⓒ Ⓓ Ⓔ
27. Ⓐ Ⓑ Ⓒ Ⓓ Ⓔ
28. Ⓐ Ⓑ Ⓒ Ⓓ Ⓔ
29. Ⓐ Ⓑ Ⓒ Ⓓ Ⓔ
30. Ⓐ Ⓑ Ⓒ Ⓓ Ⓔ

Section II

1. Ⓐ Ⓑ Ⓒ Ⓓ Ⓔ
2. Ⓐ Ⓑ Ⓒ Ⓓ Ⓔ
3. Ⓐ Ⓑ Ⓒ Ⓓ Ⓔ
4. Ⓐ Ⓑ Ⓒ Ⓓ Ⓔ
5. Ⓐ Ⓑ Ⓒ Ⓓ Ⓔ
6. Ⓐ Ⓑ Ⓒ Ⓓ Ⓔ
7. Ⓐ Ⓑ Ⓒ Ⓓ Ⓔ
8. Ⓐ Ⓑ Ⓒ Ⓓ Ⓔ
9. Ⓐ Ⓑ Ⓒ Ⓓ Ⓔ

10. Ⓐ Ⓑ Ⓒ Ⓓ Ⓔ
11. Ⓐ Ⓑ Ⓒ Ⓓ Ⓔ
12. Ⓐ Ⓑ Ⓒ Ⓓ Ⓔ
13. Ⓐ Ⓑ Ⓒ Ⓓ Ⓔ
14. Ⓐ Ⓑ Ⓒ Ⓓ Ⓔ
15. Ⓐ Ⓑ Ⓒ Ⓓ Ⓔ
16. Ⓐ Ⓑ Ⓒ Ⓓ Ⓔ
17. Ⓐ Ⓑ Ⓒ Ⓓ Ⓔ
18. Ⓐ Ⓑ Ⓒ Ⓓ Ⓔ
19. Ⓐ Ⓑ Ⓒ Ⓓ Ⓔ
20. Ⓐ Ⓑ Ⓒ Ⓓ Ⓔ
21. Ⓐ Ⓑ Ⓒ Ⓓ Ⓔ
22. Ⓐ Ⓑ Ⓒ Ⓓ Ⓔ
23. Ⓐ Ⓑ Ⓒ Ⓓ Ⓔ
24. Ⓐ Ⓑ Ⓒ Ⓓ Ⓔ
25. Ⓐ Ⓑ Ⓒ Ⓓ Ⓔ
26. Ⓐ Ⓑ Ⓒ Ⓓ Ⓔ
27. Ⓐ Ⓑ Ⓒ Ⓓ Ⓔ
28. Ⓐ Ⓑ Ⓒ Ⓓ Ⓔ
29. Ⓐ Ⓑ Ⓒ Ⓓ Ⓔ
30. Ⓐ Ⓑ Ⓒ Ⓓ Ⓔ

Section III

1. Ⓐ Ⓑ Ⓒ Ⓓ Ⓔ
2. Ⓐ Ⓑ Ⓒ Ⓓ Ⓔ
3. Ⓐ Ⓑ Ⓒ Ⓓ Ⓔ
4. Ⓐ Ⓑ Ⓒ Ⓓ Ⓔ
5. Ⓐ Ⓑ Ⓒ Ⓓ Ⓔ
6. Ⓐ Ⓑ Ⓒ Ⓓ Ⓔ
7. Ⓐ Ⓑ Ⓒ Ⓓ Ⓔ
8. Ⓐ Ⓑ Ⓒ Ⓓ Ⓔ
9. Ⓐ Ⓑ Ⓒ Ⓓ Ⓔ
10. Ⓐ Ⓑ Ⓒ Ⓓ Ⓔ
11. Ⓐ Ⓑ Ⓒ Ⓓ Ⓔ
12. Ⓐ Ⓑ Ⓒ Ⓓ Ⓔ
13. Ⓐ Ⓑ Ⓒ Ⓓ Ⓔ
14. Ⓐ Ⓑ Ⓒ Ⓓ Ⓔ
15. Ⓐ Ⓑ Ⓒ Ⓓ Ⓔ
16. Ⓐ Ⓑ Ⓒ Ⓓ Ⓔ
17. Ⓐ Ⓑ Ⓒ Ⓓ Ⓔ
18. Ⓐ Ⓑ Ⓒ Ⓓ Ⓔ
19. Ⓐ Ⓑ Ⓒ Ⓓ Ⓔ
20. Ⓐ Ⓑ Ⓒ Ⓓ Ⓔ

Section IV

1. Ⓐ Ⓑ Ⓒ Ⓓ Ⓔ
2. Ⓐ Ⓑ Ⓒ Ⓓ Ⓔ
3. Ⓐ Ⓑ Ⓒ Ⓓ Ⓔ
4. Ⓐ Ⓑ Ⓒ Ⓓ Ⓔ
5. Ⓐ Ⓑ Ⓒ Ⓓ Ⓔ
6. Ⓐ Ⓑ Ⓒ Ⓓ Ⓔ
7. Ⓐ Ⓑ Ⓒ Ⓓ Ⓔ
8. Ⓐ Ⓑ Ⓒ Ⓓ Ⓔ
9. Ⓐ Ⓑ Ⓒ Ⓓ Ⓔ
10. Ⓐ Ⓑ Ⓒ Ⓓ Ⓔ
11. Ⓐ Ⓑ Ⓒ Ⓓ Ⓔ
12. Ⓐ Ⓑ Ⓒ Ⓓ Ⓔ
13. Ⓐ Ⓑ Ⓒ Ⓓ Ⓔ
14. Ⓐ Ⓑ Ⓒ Ⓓ Ⓔ
15. Ⓐ Ⓑ Ⓒ Ⓓ Ⓔ
16. Ⓐ Ⓑ Ⓒ Ⓓ Ⓔ
17. Ⓐ Ⓑ Ⓒ Ⓓ Ⓔ
18. Ⓐ Ⓑ Ⓒ Ⓓ Ⓔ
19. Ⓐ Ⓑ Ⓒ Ⓓ Ⓔ
20. Ⓐ Ⓑ Ⓒ Ⓓ Ⓔ
21. Ⓐ Ⓑ Ⓒ Ⓓ Ⓔ
22. Ⓐ Ⓑ Ⓒ Ⓓ Ⓔ
23. Ⓐ Ⓑ Ⓒ Ⓓ Ⓔ
24. Ⓐ Ⓑ Ⓒ Ⓓ Ⓔ
25. Ⓐ Ⓑ Ⓒ Ⓓ Ⓔ
26. Ⓐ Ⓑ Ⓒ Ⓓ Ⓔ
27. Ⓐ Ⓑ Ⓒ Ⓓ Ⓔ
28. Ⓐ Ⓑ Ⓒ Ⓓ Ⓔ
29. Ⓐ Ⓑ Ⓒ Ⓓ Ⓔ
30. Ⓐ Ⓑ Ⓒ Ⓓ Ⓔ

LSAT TEST VI – WRITING SAMPLE TOPIC

STOP

If time still remains, you may review work only in this section.
When the time alloted is up, you may go on to the next section.

11 AM / OCS / 2·9·07 FRI

Took 2nd test this AM + got rhmy [rhythm] but too ½ concuse. Derek Boerger is probably carry the [...] I must slow myself down. Larry Teich says strategy is superb - like Skin consume 1st then read passage thghly [thoroughly] then read answers, eliminate wrong rest choose.

Things are going better than 2 weeks ago + at this point I'm somewhere between confident + self-doubting.

Important thing seems to be to see slumps + well-rested/ relaxed + up a good attitude from now. In some ways, I have nothing to lose by shoring up the process of barging bottles [LSAT] + just taking has reminded me of the harsh practices of my late father in the 60s + 70's.

Photos Stone after 6·10·'92 he was not the same -- strictened out on his third time to type II diabetes. Mom stuck by him + all of us no matter what he did.

The LSAT is one objective proof put of a person's ability to treat read, think, + write ... Probably there is some correlation + success in law school.

It's been an odd start to the New Year... I think I am wise + give Mom much space. The pressure to succeed in enormous. Will look at sample [...] 2 st came at 11:30 + get food at Brooks [...]

Additional Answer Sheet – LSAT TEST __

Section I

1. (A) (B) (C) (D) (E)
2. (A) (B) (C) (D) (E)
3. (A) (B) (C) (D) (E)
4. (A) (B) (C) (D) (E)
5. (A) (B) (C) (D) (E)
6. (A) (B) (C) (D) (E)
7. (A) (B) (C) (D) (E)
8. (A) (B) (C) (D) (E)
9. (A) (B) (C) (D) (E)
10. (A) (B) (C) (D) (E)
11. (A) (B) (C) (D) (E)
12. (A) (B) (C) (D) (E)
13. (A) (B) (C) (D) (E)
14. (A) (B) (C) (D) (E)
15. (A) (B) (C) (D) (E)
16. (A) (B) (C) (D) (E)
17. (A) (B) (C) (D) (E)
18. (A) (B) (C) (D) (E)
19. (A) (B) (C) (D) (E)
20. (A) (B) (C) (D) (E)
21. (A) (B) (C) (D) (E)
22. (A) (B) (C) (D) (E)
23. (A) (B) (C) (D) (E)
24. (A) (B) (C) (D) (E)
25. (A) (B) (C) (D) (E)
26. (A) (B) (C) (D) (E)
27. (A) (B) (C) (D) (E)
28. (A) (B) (C) (D) (E)
29. (A) (B) (C) (D) (E)
30. (A) (B) (C) (D) (E)

Section II

1. (A) (B) (C) (D) (E)
2. (A) (B) (C) (D) (E)
3. (A) (B) (C) (D) (E)
4. (A) (B) (C) (D) (E)
5. (A) (B) (C) (D) (E)
6. (A) (B) (C) (D) (E)
7. (A) (B) (C) (D) (E)
8. (A) (B) (C) (D) (E)
9. (A) (B) (C) (D) (E)
10. (A) (B) (C) (D) (E)
11. (A) (B) (C) (D) (E)
12. (A) (B) (C) (D) (E)
13. (A) (B) (C) (D) (E)
14. (A) (B) (C) (D) (E)
15. (A) (B) (C) (D) (E)
16. (A) (B) (C) (D) (E)
17. (A) (B) (C) (D) (E)
18. (A) (B) (C) (D) (E)
19. (A) (B) (C) (D) (E)
20. (A) (B) (C) (D) (E)
21. (A) (B) (C) (D) (E)
22. (A) (B) (C) (D) (E)
23. (A) (B) (C) (D) (E)
24. (A) (B) (C) (D) (E)
25. (A) (B) (C) (D) (E)
26. (A) (B) (C) (D) (E)
27. (A) (B) (C) (D) (E)
28. (A) (B) (C) (D) (E)
29. (A) (B) (C) (D) (E)
30. (A) (B) (C) (D) (E)

Section III

1. (A) (B) (C) (D) (E)
2. (A) (B) (C) (D) (E)
3. (A) (B) (C) (D) (E)
4. (A) (B) (C) (D) (E)
5. (A) (B) (C) (D) (E)
6. (A) (B) (C) (D) (E)
7. (A) (B) (C) (D) (E)
8. (A) (B) (C) (D) (E)
9. (A) (B) (C) (D) (E)
10. (A) (B) (C) (D) (E)
11. (A) (B) (C) (D) (E)
12. (A) (B) (C) (D) (E)
13. (A) (B) (C) (D) (E)
14. (A) (B) (C) (D) (E)
15. (A) (B) (C) (D) (E)
16. (A) (B) (C) (D) (E)
17. (A) (B) (C) (D) (E)
18. (A) (B) (C) (D) (E)
19. (A) (B) (C) (D) (E)
20. (A) (B) (C) (D) (E)
21. (A) (B) (C) (D) (E)
22. (A) (B) (C) (D) (E)
23. (A) (B) (C) (D) (E)
24. (A) (B) (C) (D) (E)
25. (A) (B) (C) (D) (E)
26. (A) (B) (C) (D) (E)
27. (A) (B) (C) (D) (E)
28. (A) (B) (C) (D) (E)
29. (A) (B) (C) (D) (E)
30. (A) (B) (C) (D) (E)

Section IV

1. (A) (B) (C) (D) (E)
2. (A) (B) (C) (D) (E)
3. (A) (B) (C) (D) (E)
4. (A) (B) (C) (D) (E)
5. (A) (B) (C) (D) (E)
6. (A) (B) (C) (D) (E)
7. (A) (B) (C) (D) (E)
8. (A) (B) (C) (D) (E)
9. (A) (B) (C) (D) (E)
10. (A) (B) (C) (D) (E)
11. (A) (B) (C) (D) (E)
12. (A) (B) (C) (D) (E)
13. (A) (B) (C) (D) (E)
14. (A) (B) (C) (D) (E)
15. (A) (B) (C) (D) (E)
16. (A) (B) (C) (D) (E)
17. (A) (B) (C) (D) (E)
18. (A) (B) (C) (D) (E)
19. (A) (B) (C) (D) (E)
20. (A) (B) (C) (D) (E)
21. (A) (B) (C) (D) (E)
22. (A) (B) (C) (D) (E)
23. (A) (B) (C) (D) (E)
24. (A) (B) (C) (D) (E)
25. (A) (B) (C) (D) (E)
26. (A) (B) (C) (D) (E)
27. (A) (B) (C) (D) (E)
28. (A) (B) (C) (D) (E)
29. (A) (B) (C) (D) (E)
30. (A) (B) (C) (D) (E)

Additional Answer Sheet
LSAT TEST __ – WRITING SAMPLE TOPIC

STOP
If time still remains, you may review work only in this section.
When the time alloted is up, you may go on to the next section.

10:15 AM FRI 2·9·07/OCS

Still getting less than ½ of fee ?'S right. the study in process + actually that fee$ is meant to throw you off mentally --- Probably should take me more 35 min. but + then relax for rest of the day + do what I want. Perhaps a check from CASCAPS will arrive today or tomorrow but do not want to ask Derek alone or Mom for more & still next week.

Yesterday, Wed, + Tues then were all positive progressions + a good day today will help me be at peace w/ myself in the AM + confident I had good judgement like the thing in Aug + Sept (meds + fees) for the 9·17·06 marathon walk.

Progresses did not miss-spend the $160-4⁰⁰ over the past week — getting excellent book bargains + eating foods which help readjust my brain + my more Changy + well/even-tempered self self.,,

The cover I get fee too 21 + Tues 24 the better I feel about myself ... 6 days til 2·15·07 30 day anniversary of seight, Jim Ellison,

Will be relieved to talk fee 4 hr fee + just leave fee rest + Capt. Will not think of cancelling seuse tue Mon. or so,— 7 weeks since against w/ Harold, true relax, calm + someone cares

REA's Test Preps
The Best in Test Preparation

- REA "Test Preps" are **far more** comprehensive than any other test preparation series
- Each book contains up to **eight** full-length practice tests based on the most recent exams
- **Every** type of question likely to be given on the exams is included
- Answers are accompanied by **full** and **detailed** explanations

REA publishes over 70 Test Preparation volumes in several series. They include:

Advanced Placement Exams (APs)
Biology
Calculus AB & Calculus BC
Chemistry
Economics
English Language & Composition
English Literature & Composition
European History
French
Government & Politics
Physics B & C
Psychology
Spanish Language
Statistics
United States History
World History

College-Level Examination Program (CLEP)
Analyzing and Interpreting Literature
College Algebra
Freshman College Composition
General Examinations
General Examinations Review
History of the United States I
History of the United States II
Human Growth and Development
Introductory Sociology
Principles of Marketing
Spanish

SAT Subject Tests
Biology E/M
Chemistry
English Language Proficiency Test
French
German

SAT Subject Tests (cont'd)
Literature
Mathematics Level 1, 2
Physics
Spanish
United States History

Graduate Record Exams (GREs)
Biology
Chemistry
Computer Science
General
Literature in English
Mathematics
Physics
Psychology

ACT - ACT Assessment

ASVAB - Armed Services Vocational Aptitude Battery

CBEST - California Basic Educational Skills Test

CDL - Commercial Driver License Exam

CLAST - College Level Academic Skills Test

COOP & HSPT - Catholic High School Admission Tests

ELM - California State University Entry Level Mathematics Exam

FE (EIT) - Fundamentals of Engineering Exams - For both AM & PM Exams

FTCE - Florida Teacher Certification Exam

GED - High School Equivalency Diploma Exam (U.S. & Canadian editions)

GMAT - Graduate Management Admission Test

LSAT - Law School Admission Test

MAT - Miller Analogies Test

MCAT - Medical College Admission Test

MTEL - Massachusetts Tests for Educator Licensure

NJ HSPA - New Jersey High School Proficiency Assessment

NYSTCE: LAST & ATS-W - New York State Teacher Certification

PLT - Principles of Learning & Teaching Tests

PPST - Pre-Professional Skills Tests

PSAT / NMSQT

SAT

TExES - Texas Examinations of Educator Standards

THEA - Texas Higher Education Assessment

TOEFL - Test of English as a Foreign Language

TOEIC - Test of English for International Communication

USMLE Steps 1,2,3 - U.S. Medical Licensing Exams

U.S. Postal Exams 460 & 470

Research & Education Association
61 Ethel Road W., Piscataway, NJ 08854
Phone: (732) 819-8880   **website: www.rea.com**

Please send me more information about your Test Prep books.

Name _____

Address _____

City _____ State _____ Zip _____

REA's Test Prep Books Are The Best!

(a sample of the <u>hundreds of letters</u> REA receives each year)

" I am writing to congratulate you on preparing an exceptional study guide. In five years of teaching this course I have never encountered a more thorough, comprehensive, concise and realistic preparation for this examination. "
Teacher, Davie, FL

" I have found your publications, *The Best Test Preparation...*, to be exactly that. "
Teacher, Aptos, CA

" I used your *CLEP Introductory Sociology* book and rank it 99% – thank you! "
Student, Jerusalem, Israel

" Your GMAT book greatly helped me on the test. Thank you. "
Student, Oxford, OH

" I recently got the French SAT II Exam book from REA. I congratulate you on first-rate French practice tests."
Instructor, Los Angeles, CA

" Your AP English Literature and Composition book is most impressive."
Student, Montgomery, AL

" The REA LSAT Test Preparation guide is a winner! "
Instructor, Spartanburg, SC

(more on front page)